WALK A LONELY STREET

WALK A LONELY STREET

ELVIS PRESLEY, COUNTRY MUSIC *&*
THE TRUE STORY *of* HEARTBREAK HOTEL

by TONY PLEWS

GEORGE SMITH
PUBLICATIONS

This book should be played at 45rpm.

First published December 2020.
George Smith Publications
172 Boston Road, London W7 2HP
www.georgesmithpublications.com

ISBN 978-1-9997218-2-4

Third edition, May 2021

Designed and typeset by Tony Plews in
Adobe Garamond Pro 10/12 & **Chatype**,
the official font of the city of Chattanooga.

The characters in this book are all real. To the best of my knowledge, the events took place as written but, due to the nature of this story, there are several incidents that have required dramatic licence, and some conversations have been re-imagined.

For Mark,
who played a good tune

Note to the reader

THIS IS A BOOK OF STORIES; a collection of tales to be told, central among which is the long-hidden saga of "Heartbreak Hotel", Elvis Presley's era-defining breakthrough record. It is also a book of connections, circles and echoes; hundreds of related shorter stories presented chronologically to tell a much bigger tale.

It is not a book that adheres to the usual rules of notes and citations, being more of a novel than a work of academic reference. But at the foot of many pages, should you wish to pursue the topics further, you will find a nod to the relevant main source material.

There are perhaps a dozen key characters within this volume, and their adventures are told in episodic fashion, crossing over with minor players and events in real time, so to better establish context for the main story.

Also told are the tales that set the scene: the birth and growth of country music; the narrow distance between inspiration and plagiarism in songwriting; the struggle for women to be recognised in the hillbilly music business; and scores of other themes that rise and fall as the pages turn and the weeks and years go by.

As in life, characters arrive, play their parts, and then disappear. Their influence may not always be immediately apparent but the story would not be the same without their fleeting contribution. Strange, isn't it? Each man's life touches so many other lives.

Doubtless, there are simpler and shorter ways to tell this tale, but none that are so intriguing, thorough and involving. The narrative unfolds as it actually happened, and the myriad disparate threads eventually come together, weaving a saga of music, ambition, crime, love and death.

And at the heart of this book is the story of a bright, talented, good-looking boy from Memphis who saw no difference between black and white — neither in music nor in people.

Websites that have proven invaluable to this book:

countrydiscography.blogspot.com
elvis-collectors.com
elvisechoesofthepast.com
elvisrecords.com
keithflynn.com
nowdigthismagazine.co.uk
scottymoore.net
theelvisforum-phoenix.com

Thank you

THANK YOU seems such an inadequate phrase, but I hope the following will accept my sincere gratitude for their much-valued contributions to this book:

Debbie May (Nashville Public Library), John Shipley (Miami-Dade Public Library System), and the George A. Smathers Libraries, University of Florida; Robert Lay (University of Oklahoma); John Rumble (Country Music Hall of Fame and Museum); Kate Convissor, for sharing her photographs of the San Solana Mission;

Janet Newbury (author *Sing Your Heart, Wilburn Boys*), Ronny Weiser (Rolling Rock Records), Richard Weize (Bear Family Records), Dominique Anglares and David Dennard, for sharing their knowledge of the early days of rockabilly and country music;

Kathleen Loveridge (proof reader) and Gordon Minto (editor), for keen eyes, clear minds and encouraging words; Paul Combs and Anthony Stuchbury, for the disk scans; Kevan Budd and Ernst Mikael Jørgensen, for their advice; Colin B, for the gift of the BBC video;

Lisa Dodson, Michael Kilbourne and Wink Gilbert, for sharing their memories of Tommy Durden and the Gilbert family; Frances Pinney Erickson, Mitchell Pomper and Art Kenney for sharing photographs and memories of their late father, mother and father-in-law respectively; the Axton family and the estate of Mae Boren Axton for their photographs and assistance.

I also offer grateful thanks to my friends and family, who have done everything in their power to uplift me in this endeavour, all of them knowing how important the very idea of writing a book is to me.

This project began on 25th April 2011 as an online conversation on the Elvis Collectors' forum, a wonderful place to investigate Presley's creative legacy. This book is indebted to the thousands of well-researched topics on display there. Many members have supported my work, but none more so than Robin, John and "the fool". I suspect you will see your contributions on every page.

But mainly, I'd like to thank my wife, Maria, for confirming there was a book to be written in the first place. At the beginning of my research, she indulged me by listening to a two-minute precis of the central plot.

"I thought it might be dull," she replied, "but that sounds really rather good."

When I was a boy

WEDNESDAY 25TH DECEMBER 1974
SOUTH SHIELDS, NORTH-EAST *of* ENGLAND

I CAN'T REMEMBER a time when I didn't know the music of Elvis Presley. It wasn't possible to grow up during the 1960s and 1970s without hearing his records and, certainly in England where I lived, he was almost worshipped among the working classes. There was a mythical quality about his very existence: his vibrant music seemed so much bigger than everything else on the radio, the unique voice lending a widescreen setting to a seemingly endless run of hits.

By the summer of 1977, the myth had turned to Greek tragedy as Presley fell from grace in spectacular fashion, and he died at the absurdly early age of forty-two. The world was shocked to learn of how this charismatic young man had struggled to cope with unprecedented fame, eventually taking refuge in the prescription medication that hastened his death.

For over twenty years, Presley had presented himself immaculately, keeping his private life hidden. When the press was eventually given a glimpse of his human failings they went for the jugular. His reputation and achievements were besmirched by inaccuracies and slander. False biographers and lazy journalists stripped him bare, and his glorious records were ignored.

My own first Elvis LP had arrived three years earlier in 1974 — I was nine and had requested it as a Christmas gift from my grandmother; my father then contributed Presley's marvellous 45rpm cover of Chuck Berry's "Promised Land"; my mother supplied the all-important Dansette-style record player.

The media interest in Presley's passing stirred my curiosity further and I began to learn more about his career — gathering books, records and videotapes along the way. His reputation was at an all-time low, and it was a tough time to be an Elvis fan. When you're twelve it can be frustrating trying to discuss the sheer emotional excitement of his best records, his contribution to the civil rights movement, the nature of the human condition, the spiritual value of music, and the transformative power of art.

In the early 1990s, the slow process of re-building Presley's reputation began, and it continues to this day. Thanks to the efforts of Peter Guralnick (biographer), Roger Semon (artistic director) and Ernst Mikael Jørgensen (producer), we were afforded a view of Elvis the musical visionary. The mythology that still surrounded him was again stripped away, but this time with care and diligence, and listeners were able to sympathise with, and revel in, the intelligent artist at the heart of this unique recorded legacy.

The removal of the myths was central to the destruction of Presley's reputation but was also an essential part of rescuing Elvis, and it's been fascinating and refreshing to spend the past two decades looking honestly at the man rather than the legend.

But part of me (the nine year-old boy) misses the mythical Elvis: he always seemed very comfortable in that setting, and his talent made him appear more than mortal. His history contains many extraordinary adventures and, within this work, I happily reclaim Presley's mythical status. I have tried to hold fast to the facts as they are now understood, but where dramatic licence was required, I embraced it.

This is very likely the book I wanted to write when I was twelve. In all humility, I hope by now I have found the prose to do the music justice.

TP · LONDON · 2020

Country music
— sometimes called hillbilly
or country *&* western —
is just like the blues,
in that it is *folk* music.

That is to say,
it is the music of the people.

RCA Victor 47-6420 (45rpm)
"Heartbreak Hotel" / "I Was The One"
Elvis Presley
Released 27th January 1956

Image courtesy of Paul Combs at www.elvisrecords.com

The legend of "Heartbreak Hotel"

By the summer of 1956, Elvis Presley and his hit record "Heartbreak Hotel" were the talk of the entertainment business. The explosive singer had risen from obscurity to worldwide fame in less than two years, and his remarkable debut release for RCA Victor Records sold millions of copies around the world, ushering in the modern cultural era.

Journalists and listeners wondered what had inspired the writing of such an unusual and evocative song. The record label credited the composition to Mae Boren Axton (a music business publicity agent), Tommy Durden (a professional musician) and Elvis himself. Axton in particular was always happy in the years that followed to re-tell the tale of how they came to write their signature hit. A precis of that oft-told story might read thus:

> In the autumn of 1955, Tommy Durden was moved by a short article in the *Miami Herald* newspaper which told of a mysterious and anonymous suicide. The unknown man had destroyed all evidence of his identity but had left a hand-written note which said, "I walk a lonely street", and local police were asking for help to identify the victim.
>
> Durden felt sure there was the germ of a song in that stark phrase and he brought the idea to friend and fellow composer Mae Boren Axton. She was also touched by the story and suggested they should put a Heartbreak Hotel at the end of that lonely street.
>
> Axton, who knew the young hillbilly singer Elvis Presley, proposed they might write the song for the emerging star (she had already promised Elvis she would write his first hit record). Durden agreed but their efforts were interrupted by a visit from mutual friend Glenn Reeves (a deejay, songwriter and performer). Reeves, who thought the song title absurd, politely rejected an invitation to join the composing team, saying he had to run an errand but offered to drop in on his way back from town.
>
> By the time he returned, the song was written — it took Mae and Tommy just twenty-two minutes — and Durden had already laid

down a basic demo tape. Axton asked Reeves to record a better version in a style similar to Presley's own, and she again offered the deejay a share in the rights. Reeves did tape a Presleyesque demo but he still demurred regarding a composing credit.

To make the song financially attractive to Presley, it was decided to offer him a one-third writer's credit (a common industry practice), if he would make it his first single when, as planned, his recording contract was purchased from Sun Records by RCA Victor. Axton played the new demo for the fast-rising star in November 1955, and he was delighted with the song, agreeing immediately to Mae's terms.

Significantly though, and despite overtures from other companies, Axton gave the all-important lucrative publishing contract to her friend Buddy Killen at Tree, at that time a small and relatively ill-starred Nashville publishing house.

Presley recorded the song for RCA in January 1956 — re-inventing Reeves' demo in a dramatic and striking fashion — and within four months it was the best-selling record in the country, eventually moving over five million copies.

Subsequently, Tree became one of the most eminent music publishers of all time, Durden took an extended holiday funded by his first royalty cheque, and Axton tried to replicate their success with "Welcome to the Club", a solo composition, but the song sounded like a pale repeat of "Heartbreak Hotel" and it sank without trace.

Despite the enormous success of his first RCA single, Presley never recorded another offering from Tree, nor another by Axton or Durden, and neither writer achieved notable success with any other song or singer.

Over the years, as Presley's fame grew, the legend of "Heartbreak Hotel" became the most famous story-behind-the-song in pop music. After the singer's death, almost every Presley biography made mention of it, and Axton would always oblige for each new interviewer, sometimes adding a little extra fact to paint a more detailed picture.

But curiously, at no time did anyone come forward with a copy of the original and elusive newspaper report. Nor was any subsequent evidence as to the identity of the anonymous suicide victim discovered.

In 1993, the British Broadcasting Corporation produced its own "Heartbreak Hotel" TV documentary. Axton and Durden were interviewed and, at long last, a copy of the original *Miami Herald* newspaper article was apparently revealed for the first time. The front page of the 1st October 1955 edition was displayed and it seemed to show the article, just as the writers had always said. Closer examination, however, suggested the BBC's front page had been doctored and the actual 1st October edition of the *Miami Herald* contained no reference to a suicide story at all.

Other anomalies began to surface: Buddy Killen remembered discussing the song with Axton as early as July 1955 rather than in the autumn; publisher Murray Nash insisted he had also been offered the rights to the hit; popular singing duo The Wilburn Brothers claimed they had been shown the song before Elvis.

In more recent years, rumours have spread to the effect that Axton played no part in the creative writing process and acted more as a facilitator, making sure the song reached the right people (Presley and/or his manager-elect, Tom Parker) in return for her own co-writing credit. There was further talk of Tommy Durden resenting the attention lavished on Mae Boren Axton and wishing to clarify his position as the primary songwriter. When interviewed, however, Axton and Durden always re-affirmed the accepted story, right up until their respective deaths in 1997 and 1999.

But what lingered on was a suspicion that the whole story had not been revealed: the many random pieces of the jigsaw puzzle did not always fit comfortably together. The missing newspaper and the anonymous victim were not the only unsolved mysteries.

This is what has gone before. What follows is perhaps somewhat closer to the truth.

There is a tale to be told.

WALK A LONELY STREET

ELVIS PRESLEY, COUNTRY MUSIC *&*
THE TRUE STORY *of* HEARTBREAK HOTEL

Part 1: Dixie

If you would understand anything,
observe its beginning and
its development.
Aristotle

Lincoln: "Dixie"

MONDAY 10TH APRIL 1865
WASHINGTON D.C.

COLONEL PARKER was known for his excellence with words. His penmanship made him the obvious choice to transcribe the documents of surrender on Palm Sunday, 9th April 1865. A native American, Colonel Ely Parker had served as General Grant's adjutant since the Chattanooga Campaign. As the signatures were affixed at the Appomattox Court House, the defeated General Lee remarked, "I am glad to see one real American here."

Parker responded, "We are all Americans, sir." The War Between the States was over, although news spread slowly and emancipation came to Texas as late as 19th June.

The following day, Monday 10th April, two hundred miles away, a jubilant crowd gathered outside the White House and called for the victorious President to make an appearance. Lincoln eventually emerged and cautiously addressed the throng. He was happy, but not boastful: he knew, more than anyone, the cost to the country of four years of civil war. Over half a million Americans lay dead at the hands of their countrymen. The South was decimated; its people were hungry, just barely alive.

Lincoln's thoughts had already turned to the future. His task was to re-build the nation, to mend the wounds, and remove the divisions. Noticing a band within the crowd, he asked if they would play the popular tune, "Dixie". Although written as a minstrel song by a Northerner, Daniel Emmett, "Dixie" had been appropriated by the South as it prepared for war. Recognising the great power of music — and having a personal liking for the tune — Lincoln joked that the song could be considered fair booty.

The band struck up the march and the folk cheered. Lincoln, a dreamer of dreams, was encouraged. Perhaps the nation could be healed. Perhaps the South could be reconciled with the North. Perhaps the American people would be as one: North and South, black and white, rich and poor.

By Good Friday, Lincoln would be fatally wounded, felled by a single bullet from John Booth, a Confederate sympathiser, who fled, according to some, shouting, "The South is avenged!"

Abraham Lincoln, James M. McPherson

Julia Howe: war and peace

SUNDAY 9TH JUNE 1872
BOSTON, MASSACHUSETTS

FAME CAME LATE TO JULIA HOWE. Aged forty-two, the daughter of a wealthy Wall Street stockbroker had come to public attention when she was challenged to write new words to the popular tune, "John Brown's Body". Using scripture as her inspiration, she composed "The Battle Hymn of the Republic", which opened with the stirring lines,

"Mine eyes have seen the glory
of the coming of the Lord.
He is trampling out the wine press,
where the grapes of wrath are stored.
He hath loosed the fateful lightning
of His terrible swift sword:
His truth is marching on."

The song was published in the February 1862 edition of the *Atlantic Monthly* and soon became the unofficial anthem of the Union Army in the war between North and South. Having lived her life in the shadows, Howe was suddenly propelled into the spotlight and decided to use her new-found celebrity to promote the struggle for women's rights.

One of her key proposals was for a national day to recognise the value of motherhood. She requested the second Sunday in June 1872 be marked as America's first Mothers' Peace Day Observance in Boston. Initially, the concept was not popular or successful but in later years it would evolve into Mother's Day, one of the most beloved and honoured of U.S. celebrations.

Howe died in 1910, aged ninety-one. She was survived by five of her six children and also by her two great creations, a song for battle and a day for peace.

The Battle Hymn of the Republic: A Biography of the Song That Marches On,
John Stauffer & Benjamin Soskis

The west Texas town of El Paso, 1

MONDAY 19TH AUGUST 1895
ALAMEDA AVENUE, EL PASO, TEXAS

JUST AFTER 11:00 PM, Constable John Sellman pushed open the door of the Acme Saloon on Alameda Avenue in El Paso and looked for the notorious gunfighter who had threatened his son. John Wesley Hardin stood at the bar playing dice with friends. Hardin had moved into town insisting he was a reformed character, but the long-suffering citizens of El Paso knew better.

Hardin whirled around and went to draw one of the two guns he always carried, but the constable was too fast. In an instant, Sellman put a bullet from his .44 into the outlaw's brain, and shot him twice more as he fell. He then calmly walked out onto Alameda Avenue and surrendered himself.

Hardin, aged forty-two, was buried the following day in Concordia Cemetery, a short walk from the saloon. Police later found an unfinished autobiography among his possessions.

Sellman had been an officer in the border town for several years and had already put an end to six other villains. He had fought for the Confederacy during the civil war and had since developed something of a reputation.

Less than twelve months later, Sellman was killed in a gunfight with a U.S. Marshall and was laid to rest in an unmarked grave near Hardin.

Davenport Daily Republican, Iowa, 3rd October 1895
Galveston Daily News, Texas, 20th August 1895

John Sousa: always faithful

JUNE 1906
LIBRARY OF CONGRESS, WASHINGTON D.C.

PERSPIRING UNDER THE INTENSE SUNSHINE, fifty-one year-old John Sousa climbed the steps to the Library of Congress. One of America's most popular composers, he had been invited to testify to the Committee on Patents regarding U.S. copyright law, a subject close to his heart, and even closer to his wallet. Sousa was greatly concerned about the emerging new technologies and wanted to ensure his compositions were properly protected.

Sousa, a musical prodigy, had enjoyed a long and successful career. His father, a trombonist in the U.S. Marines, was convinced his son would run off and join a circus band, and so he had him enlisted from the age of thirteen. The boy grew up to be a fine conductor and composer, and his great marches were admired the world over. As a tribute to the Marines, he wrote a piece named for their motto, "Semper Fidelis", which was adopted as their official theme.

At the committe hearing, Sousa was questioned by Frank Currier, a New Hampshire Republican, who was playing devil's advocate. Currier suggested that Sousa intended to tax or ban all forms of public singing. Sousa's response was direct and witty: "I have never known that it was unlawful to get together and sing," he said, and indeed, eventually, common sense and reason carried the day.

The new copyright act became law on 1st July 1909 and it allowed a work to be protected for twenty-eight years, after which it could be copyrighted again for another twenty-eight year period.

Sousa, of course, just wanted to protect his creations, and had not believed that the simple act of getting together and singing should be regulated. He recognised the value of amateur culture; the importance of people making music for their own pleasure.

Remix: Making Art and Commerce Thrive in the Hybrid Economy, Lawrence Lessig

Pity the poor immigrant, I

PERHAPS LATE 1906
WINNIPEG, CANADA

Though born in Russia, Harry Krolik had no memories of his homeland. Baby Harry and his parents, Joseph and Annie, were driven from Mogilev in the summer of 1906 by the rash of pogroms that plagued Jewish communities in the early twentieth century. As with so many of their countrymen and women, they made the arduous journey across the Atlantic towards peace and safety. But rather than head for entry via the obvious Ellis Island immigration station, they docked in Canada, establishing roots firstly in Montreal, and then more permanently in Winnipeg.

Joseph, twenty-six, was a barber by profession. His wife, four years his junior, was pregnant on arrival, and gave birth to their daughter, Rebecca, in February 1907, just before Harry's first birthday. Joseph feared that life for his family would be hard, but he consoled himself with one simple thought: people would always need haircuts.

The Kroliks were just one family among countless thousands arriving on the North American continent every month, and most did indeed find themselves sailing in the shadow of Lady Liberty as they disembarked at Ellis Island. Always crowded to capacity, the New York station had become a symbolic door for those who wished to enter in and claim their part of the American dream.

As the decades passed, the island gained several vivid soubriquets: some who were refused entry called it Deportation Dock; others joyfully referred to it as the Gateway of Hope; and some, whose dreams were dashed, dubbed it Heartbreak Hotel.

Fergus Falls Daily Journal, Minnesota, 16th November 1954

Jimmie Rodgers: when I was a boy

PERHAPS 1910
ON THE ROAD

THE BOY CAME FROM Meridian, Mississippi, near the state border with Alabama. Not yet thirteen, he'd run away from home and joined a travelling medicine show. Entertaining was pretty much all he cared about.

Just the previous year he'd organised his own tent show, taking it on the road locally. He sang, played mandolin, banjo and guitar, and had fallen in love with the life of an itinerant musician. He'd already entered and won amateur singing contests and had an ear for all types of music.

He knew his widowed father would soon catch up and drag him back home again. But when he was old enough, he'd head out on his own, following the railway lines and singing to the folks who would surely come and listen to him.

Jimmie Rodgers tuned his mandolin, coughed, and then, as the snake-oil salesman finished his spiel, he stepped up in front of the crowd ready to perform. The boy had no message; he wasn't trying to preach or teach: he was just an entertainer.

Meeting Jimmie Rodgers, Barry Mazor

Abe Lastfogel: just walkin' in the rain

SUMMER 1912
TIMES SQUARE, NEW YORK CITY, NEW YORK

ABE LASTFOGEL looked at the piece of paper in his hand. He was fourteen and had quit school believing it was time he earned a wage. The note contained details of two businesses looking for an office boy. He slipped out of his tenement home at Third Avenue and Forty-Ninth Street and, while he walked, he pondered which position to take: the tailor shop on Thirty-Sixth Street, or the talent agency on Times Square?

His head told him the tailor shop would be the better long-term bet. But it was raining, and Times Square was closer. He duly presented himself, damp and nervous, at the up-and-coming William Morris Agency, which had been born the exact same year as its prospective new office boy.

The short-sighted scrappy-looking kid with just ten cents in his pocket was hired on the spot.

The Agency: William Morris and the Hidden History of Show Business, Frank Rose

Irving Berlin: taking care of business

THURSDAY 13TH FEBRUARY 1913
HOTEL CLARIDGE, NEW YORK CITY, NEW YORK

IRVING BERLIN looked across the table at celebrated Irish-American composer Victor Herbert. In years to come they would sit at a piano together and, using only the black notes, Irving would audition his latest song for Herbert on the upright.

At the conclusion of the tune, Herbert would smile and pronounce it a smash hit. Irving would glance nervously and ask, "Do you think I should study composition?"

"You have a natural gift for words and music," Herbert would reply. "Learning theory might help you a little, but it could cramp your style."

Sitting now in the Hotel Claridge, Irving focused fully on the matter in hand: the formation of the American Society for Composers, Authors and Publishers (ASCAP). Also gathered at the table were great men like Jerome Kern and John Sousa. They were all determined to found an organisation that would, in light of the new copyright act, ensure creative people were properly paid for their work via royalties.

Irving had been catapulted to fame in 1911 with the release of his debut hit, "Alexander's Ragtime Band". There had been some uncomfortable industry talk of Berlin having appropriated black music by recording a ragtime song, a musical form associated with Negro artists like Scott Joplin.

Irving didn't know too much about that, but he did know there was big money to be made. Sheet music, live performances, the new medium of radio, and even perhaps the tentative steps into recording would all generate considerable revenue. Indeed, different versions of that very song had occupied the top four spots in the fledgling hit parade, the most popular being Collins and Harlan on the Victor label. Performers and singers would be paid too, of course, but the real rewards were in composing and publishing — and ASCAP would administer the funds.

This was show *business*, after all, and if there was one thing that Irving Berlin knew about, it was taking care of business.

As Thousands Cheer: The Life of Irving Berlin, Laurence Bergreen
The New York Times, 23rd September 1989

The Colonel: the great Showman

WEDNESDAY 19TH FEBRUARY 1913
SARATOGA HOTEL, CHICAGO, ILLINOIS

WILD-WEST LEGEND and showman, Colonel William "Buffalo Bill" Cody grinned and acknowledged the applause. Now aged sixty-seven, his glory days were behind him, but his charisma and the magic of his name still lingered.

He had met with a small group of like-minded "out-of-doors showmen" and agreed that the time had come for an international organisation that would cater to the needs and wishes of carnival people everywhere, through good times and bad. Thus, the Showmen's League of America was born, and the Colonel was elected its first president.

They chose the elephant as the symbol of the League, describing their choice vividly: *The elephant in rampant, with uplifted trunk, exemplifying in every particular the characteristics of the showman, not only alert and sagacious, but victorious as well.*

Four years later, determined to care for its members in life and in death, the League purchased a large plot in Woodlawn Cemetery, Chicago, bordered by five white statues of elephants with lowered trunks, which was dubbed the Graveyard of the Clowns, or, more formally, Showmen's Rest.

showmensleague.org

The shoe shine boy's last cigarette

SATURDAY 13TH FEBRUARY 1915
EL PASO, TEXAS

DELTA RICHARD PINNEY, a seventeen year-old shoe shine boy, was working in the El Paso police station on Stanton Street when word came: officer down on South Florence Street.

The patrolmen responded quickly and Pinney, fascinated, followed them as they ran the short distance to the alley west of Florence Street, between Third and Fourth Streets. Mounted Patrolman Gus Chitwood had been sent there earlier with other officers to investigate reports of a man firing a pistol.

The suspect had emerged from a doorway and shot Chitwood in the chest with a .41 calibre handgun while he was searching the alley. He died within a few minutes, a week short of his forty-first birthday. After being fired upon by other officers, the gunman escaped, but was captured within the hour.

The suspect, Dave Jones, alias Robert Grayson, was taken to the police station and, under interrogation, he confessed to Chitwood's murder and also to the killing of another El Paso policeman the previous December.

According to the police report, Jones then attempted to grab an officer's handgun and was shot and killed by the other patrolmen in the office of the Chief of Detectives.

Chitwood, who had been due home that evening to celebrate the eighth birthday of his daughter, Rosebud, was the fourth El Paso patrolman to be killed in the line of duty.

When the shoe shine boy had arrived at the crime scene, Gus was already dead, lying on his back with a cigarette still in his mouth. Pinney took and saved the cigarette until it fell apart from age.

Delta Richard Pinney, or D.R. as people called him, was no stranger to danger: since the age of fifteen he had been acting as a messenger boy, running information across the Mexican border to Pancho Villa in Juarez. Tall, slim and blue-eyed, Pinney had already learned that the world was a hard place and there were men who would take your possessions and your life if you'd let them. He vowed he would protect himself and everything he held dear by all means necessary.

Texas Lawmen, 1900-1940: More of the Good and the Bad, Clifford Caldwell & Ronald DeLord
El Paso Herald-Post, Texas, 18th February 1915 & 15th December 1958
Officer Down Memorial Page: Gus Chitwood (online)

A.P. and Sara get married

FRIDAY 18TH JUNE 1915
MACES SPRING, VIRGINIA

ALVIN PLEASANT CARTER, twenty-three years-old and known to all as A.P., trembled as he stood before the preacher and took Sara Dougherty, who was not yet seventeen, as his wife. Actually, A.P. trembled all the time: his mother said it was because she was almost struck by lightning while she was still carrying him. Whatever the reason, it added to the general sense of oddness about the tall, awkward young man.

Sara, though, was a handsome girl and her beautiful singing voice had attracted A.P. from the first. A.P. was obsessed with music and Sara's talent marked her as special. But Sara was not the only gifted member of her family: cousin Maybelle (who would marry one of A.P.'s younger brothers, Eck) also sang, and she played the best guitar you ever heard.

And when the three of them — A.P., Sara and Maybelle — took to singing together, well, that was really something to hear.

Will You Miss Me When I'm Gone? The Carter Family & Their Legacy in American Music, Mark Zwonitzer with Charles Hirshberg

Thomas Bishop: from beyond the grave

AT SOME POINT IN 1916
NEW YORK

THOMAS BISHOP had been dead for over a decade when his name was thrust in front of the masses. Way back in 1864 he'd launched a minstrel troupe in Chattanooga which folded after Lincoln's assassination. Bishop then took to attaching his name to popular compositions, such as "When Johnny Comes Marching Home Again", and also the civil war ballad, "Kitty Wells", which became famous anew when recorded by several acts in the late 1920s.

Whether he actually had anything to do with the writing of these songs is anybody's guess, but in 1916, ten years after his death, Bishop's friend, John MacIntyre published a work entitled *The Composer of The Battle Hymn of the Republic* in which he claimed at least part-ownership of the anthem on behalf of the deceased, a claim he repeated in 1935 on the centenary of Bishop's birth.

Let's assume for a moment that Bishop's assertions were false. Why would anyone claim authorship of a song they didn't write? For fun? For recognition? Maybe. But the answer is probably quite straightforward.

For money.

The Composer of The Battle Hymn of the Republic, John MacIntyre

Pinney in uniform: over here

AT SOME POINT IN 1917
EL PASO, TEXAS

PINNEY JOINED THE EL PASO POLICE FORCE as soon as he was able. He volunteered for the newest and most innovative department: the motorcycle squad. The city barely had any proper roads and the motorcycles were primitive and uncomfortable, but Pinney knew he'd made the right decision. He had a natural skill with mechanical devices and it was a sure bet that, in his spare time, if he wasn't fishing he'd have his hands inside an engine.

A photographer from the *El Paso Times* lined up the 1917 team with their bikes outside the police station, and snapped their picture for posterity. Pinney, at nineteen the youngest recruit, was placed at the end of the row, furthest from the camera.

He worked hard at being a policeman, training long hours and learning to handle all forms of firearms safely and efficiently. Indeed he became an expert shot with pistol and rifle: he was damn sure that what had happened to Officer Chitwood wasn't going to happen to him.

However, D.R.'s service with the police department was cut short when his country responded to the war in Europe and young Americans were called up. And as they prepared to join the struggle overseas, they were serenaded by rousing patriotic tunes. Several composers came up with new songs, while some singers and record labels plundered the archives.

Inevitably, "The Battle Hymn of the Republic" was dusted off and recorded onto the new-fangled fragile 10 inch 78rpm disks, the most notable version being by Reinald Werrenrath on the Victor label (Victor 45121). Catching the public's imagination, it reached number four in the pop chart. Bullets were flying and people were dying. And records were selling.

El Paso Times website, Trish Long

When Mae met Ernest

PERHAPS LATE 1917
ELLIS COUNTY, TEXAS

NANNIE MAE BOREN sat in in her father's car as he drove to one of the two ranches they owned in Ellis County. They chatted as they journeyed. Mae (as she was known) just loved to talk, but when her father managed to squeeze in a word or two, he described the people who lived in the neighbouring houses they passed. One family's name stuck in Mae's mind, simply because she thought it was kinda funny: Tubb. How silly was that? It reminded her of the big tin baths they used for washing.

Soon after this, Mae actually met the Tubb family. She was particularly struck by Ernest who, at the grand age of three, was six months her senior. He had the bluest eyes and the cutest smile.

The childhood memory of Ernest, his amusing name, and his bright blue eyes stayed with Mae throughout her whole life. Of course, Mae was quite comfortable around boys. She had seven older brothers and one younger. Her family, the Borens, were well respected in Ellis County, and were aspirational, to say the least. They were not a demonstrative family as far as affection was concerned, but they loved each other.

Nannie Mae — named precisely and exactly after her mother — was very happy living in Texas. Little did she know that her adored father, Mark, had already made plans to relocate the whole clan to Oklahoma.

It would be over twenty years before she heard from blue-eyed Ernest Tubb again.

Country Singers As I Know 'Em, Mae Boren Axton

Pinney in uniform: over there

THURSDAY 12TH SEPTEMBER 1918
EL PASO, TEXAS

THE THIRD DRAFT of compulsory conscription came into effect on 12th September 1918, and D.R. Pinney was summoned. There was talk of the enemy being on the ropes, but Pinney knew there was no guarantee of his own safety: a cornered rat is a dangerous rat.

He joined the 315th Motor Unit — he couldn't resist the opportunity to continue working with engines — and was seasick for the entire thirty-day journey to France. He served as a motorcycle despatch rider, dodging bullets and bombs, hour by hour, day by day. Of all the recruits who landed with Pinney and joined the despatch team, he was the only one left alive come the armistice.

He was then shipped back to Fort Bliss in El Paso to serve as a regimental sergeant major in charge of testing military equipment. As he vomited his way through the month-long return journey, he may have taken to pondering his position. Aged twenty, he'd already seen more than enough action for one lifetime. Maybe he daydreamed a little about settling down somewhere quiet, perhaps taking himself a wife, maybe opening his own motorcycle repair shop.

El Paso Times website, Trish Long

Abraham Lincoln's younger brother

MONDAY 15TH DECEMBER 1919
MORGAN COUNTY, GEORGIA

STANDING ON HIS TIP-TOES, Abraham Lincoln Durden peered into his old hand-me-down crib. There lay his new-born younger brother, Thomas Russell, the latest and last of the ten Durden children born to Alonzo and Carrie. Over a period of twenty-one years, Carrie had delivered nine sons and one daughter, and share-cropper Alonzo did his utmost to ensure they were all fed, clothed and educated.

The Durdens were poor and prayerful, but also literate, which was unusual in their part of Morgan County, located between Walker's Farm and Madison Pond.

Several visitors stopped by to offer their sincere congratulations on young Tommy's safe arrival, and Alonzo and Carrie were grateful for their kindness. All of the well-wishers were black: the Durdens were the only white family in the neighbourhood.

Census 1920

Sam Phillips: born different

FRIDAY 5TH JANUARY 1923
NEAR FLORENCE, ALABAMA

HIS FIRST BREATHS on Friday 5th January 1923 could easily have been his last, but Samuel Cornelius Phillips proved himself a natural survivor. He was the youngest of seven. He and his immediate brother, Jud, had been something of an afterthought, and more or less grew up in each other's pockets.

They were poor, naturally, living on a farm their daddy rented and, like so many of their class, they clung to the notion of moral correctness. But the family's sense of "right" came not just from religious belief, but from a burning inner sense of justice and equality.

Sam's father worked hard in the fields all year round. His mother raised the children and tended to the home, rarely finding time to sit and rest. But once in a while she'd pick up the guitar from the corner and sing old folk songs like "Aura Lee", the civil war ballad. They shared their frugal home with Sam's Aunt Emma, a deaf mute, with whom Sam learned to communicate at a young age. He was always her favourite.

The young brothers were both remarkable in their own ways: Jud, for example, possessed a charisma and a gift with words that suggested a career in the pulpit, or maybe even politics. But there was about Sam a sense of "differentness". It was difficult to sum up what it was that separated Sam from everyone else. Perhaps it could be called a spirit of intensity or conviction.

He looked at the world around him and could see that people born with black skin were treated unfairly. But not by Sam's family and not by Sam. Black and white worked together in the fields. He heard the sound of their tools striking the ground, mixed with the birdsong and the wind. He heard the labourers singing. To Sam it all came together in harmony in his head, like one beautiful symphony.

Sam Phillips: The Man who Invented Rock 'n' Roll, Peter Guralnick

Jimmie Davis goes to college

THE MID-1920S
LOUISIANA

JIMMIE DAVIS never really knew when his birthday was. As one of eleven children raised in abject poverty in Beech Springs, Louisiana, his parents had no means of keeping track of dates and anniversaries. Jimmie figured he was born about the turn of the century.

He was a good boy who listened carefully when his daddy told him that education was the only sure way to escape. So Jimmie studied hard and, against all the odds, booked himself a place at Louisiana College and then went on to earn a master's degree from the state university.

During his years of studying, he also sang occasionally with quartet groups and soon worked out that their audiences would much rather hear popular tunes and hymns than classical pieces. When he left university in the mid-1920s, he put in a couple of years as a teacher, and by the end of the decade, he'd signed on as a court clerk in Shreveport, but had also lined up part-time work as a singer on radio KWKH.

Throughout the next decade, Jimmie Davis slowly made his way up the ladder as a public servant and as a popular singer. And as he pushed for higher office, he had no hesitation in strapping on his guitar and using his talent to pull in the crowds before laying his political pitch on 'em.

By 1938, Jimmie Davis had been elected Shreveport's Commissioner of Public Safety, the top job in the city's fire and police departments. He had educated himself and had escaped the poverty of his childhood; but he was still learning.

You Are My Sunshine: The Jimmie Davis Story, Gus Weill
The New York Times, 6th November 2000

Pinney: love and marriage, I & II

MONDAY 25TH FEBRUARY 1924
LAS CRUCES, NEW MEXICO

UPON HIS RELEASE FROM THE ARMY, D.R. Pinney did indeed set up his own motorcycle repair shop in El Paso. And in the summer of 1920, he took himself a wife, a lady named Ruth Hockett. They married in Las Cruces, New Mexico, an hour's drive north.

But the marriage was short-lived and, on 25th February 1924, he hitched up on a more permanent basis with Iva Sanders, who was six years his senior. They moved to nearby Hudspeth County in Texas, where Pinney continued working in his own motor mechanic business.

There was some talk in town of his having made a pile of money trading and dealing, but if this was true then he was staying tight-lipped about it.

Life on the border was tough, and a man needed a good woman by his side. Pinney felt sure Iva was that woman.

Monkey business

EARLY SUMMER 1925
DAYTON, TENNESSEE

CELEBRATED LAWYER Clarence Darrow pushed through the crowd as he made his way into the Dayton courthouse. The Tennessee summer heat was oppressive and the tension among the people was almost a physical thing.

Dayton, a small town located midway between Knoxville and Chattanooga, had become a point of national focus. Darrow was defending the right of John Scopes and teachers in general to instruct their pupils in the theory of evolution. The trial would become popularly known as the Scopes Monkey Trial.

As he climbed the steps, the lawyer couldn't help but notice a man busily selling Columbia gramophone records outside the courthouse. Frank Walker, the salesman and the man behind the record, was in his element: he had a talent for knowing what would sell and a great understanding of folk music. He recognised the tradition of "singing the news" and decided to exploit it to its fullest extent. If there was a big event or a disaster — man-made or natural, it didn't matter — someone somewhere would always write a song about it. The sinking of the *Titanic*, for example, was a record producer's dream.

Walker, a Columbia executive in his mid-thirties, had decided to give tradition a helping hand and commissioned Carlos B. McAfee to write a song about the trial while it was still in session. He then recorded Vernon Dalhart singing the tune with minimal accompaniment, and had the record pressed as soon as humanly possible ("The John T. Scopes Trial", 15037-D). By the end of the trial, he'd sold sixty thousand copies on those steps.

Standing just outside the courthouse and watching events closely was a fiery young preacher with a piercing stare who carried sheet music of a song he had written on the self-same topic named "Darwin's Monkey Trot". He lacked Walker's business contacts and the compostion had no commercial impact at all. But J.D. Boren, one of Mae's seven older brothers, had written more for love of his Lord and not necessarily for manna.

Mike Seeger's interview with Frank Walker, 19th June 1962

The Garden and *An American Tragedy*

DECEMBER 1925
MADISON SQUARE GARDEN, NEW YORK CITY, NEW YORK

LOADING HIS HEAVY WHEELBARROW with wet cement, John Ernst Steinbeck gingerly pushed it up a wooden ramp to the masons waiting high above on the rickety scaffolding. The new Madison Square Garden, the third building to bear the name, was almost complete but the labourers were still turning in muscle-tearing eighteen-hour days to meet the pre-Christmas deadline.

Steinbeck, named precisely and exactly after his father, was twenty-three years-old and harboured a not-so-secret ambition to be a writer. He'd left Stanford University without graduating, and had spent the intervening period learning at the University of Life. Part of him relished the opportunity to work in such a physical way, believing it to be an essential part of his education as a writer.

But he'd already grown to hate New York and he detested his poor living conditions in Brooklyn. Most of all, he hated that he was so exhausted when he arrived home each night that he had no energy for writing, or even reading. The year 1925 had been a landmark period for American literature: amongst others, Fitzgerald had published *The Great Gatsby*, Hemingway released *In Our Time*, and Dresier's *An American Tragedy* had captured the country's imagination.

Steinbeck, a tough, physically commanding man, longed to wrestle with words and characters, as he did with tools and wheelbarrows. His mother's brother, a man of some influence, made a few phone calls and the aspiring author landed a job as a cub reporter on the *American* magazine. The pay wasn't much but Steinbeck was finally putting ink on paper. He was a step closer to realising his dream.

John Steinbeck: A Biography, Jay Parini

The things we do for love

PERHAPS SUMMER 1926
DETROIT, MICHIGAN

Harry Krolik had grown up a bright, hardworking young man. Not for him the life of a barber like his father; Harry was studying to be a pharmacist. But during the summer break of 1926, he got the urge to go travelling and on 6th August he crossed over the Canadian border into the United States for what was perhaps intended to be a short visit. He remained for seventeen months. And the reason for his extended stay can be summed up in two words: Edith Borin.

Edith, a year younger than Harry, was also Russian-born, and her family had settled in Detroit shortly before her third birthday: the Borins had fled their motherland for the same reason as the Kroliks.

In the summer of 1926, aged twenty, Edith saw Harry Krolik for the first time, and romance blossomed. They met, fell in love, married, and moved from Detroit to Chicago.

By Christmas 1927, Edith realised she was pregnant, but whatever joy she may have felt was short-lived. In January 1928, her husband was obliged to return to Canada. It's possible the authorities demanded his return, or maybe he had family business to attend to. He applied for a return visit to Chicago in February, but permission was denied.

Ralph Peer: a dollar a year

LATE 1926
THE VICTOR TALKING MACHINE COMPANY, CAMDEN, NEW JERSEY

IN THE TWENTY-FIVE YEARS since its formation, the Victor Talking Machine Company had received all sorts of oddball business propositions, but Ralph Peer's suggestion was unlike any other. Victor not only manufactured gramophones, but it also recorded music for its own label. The key was, of course, to find songs the public wanted to hear and buy.

Peer, an enterprising man in his mid-thirties, was offering to act as Victor's roving scout, touring the South searching for untapped blues and hillbilly talent. He would cover hundreds of miles in a quest to find new artists. He offered to sign the new acts to Victor; he would act as producer and A&R (artist and repertoire) man; he would personally supervise the sessions and deliver the final masters, ready for release. And he would do all this for the princely salary of one dollar a year.

What he actually wanted, and what he indeed received, was permission to act as manager to the talent he discovered, and to take control of the copyrights for all new songs he recorded. To handle the publishing, he established Southern Music, which he signed with ASCAP (although they were very picky about which types of song they would register), and he became the most important and influential figure in folk music.

And all for a dollar a year.

countrymusichalloffame.org
peermusic.com

Jimmie Rodgers: looking for the sunshine

EARLY 1927
FLORIDA

LIKE HIS FATHER BEFORE HIM, Jimmie Rodgers took a job on the railway. Or at least he tried to. Life was not easy for the rail-workers and Jimmie grabbed any position he could find, usually serving as a brakeman, and often travelling all over the country,

He'd generally take his guitar along with him and would sing for anyone who'd care to listen because he still dreamed of being an entertainer. Whenever possible he'd hit out for warmer climates like Florida — which proved much too humid — and soon he moved on to Asheville, North Carolina. And then he moved on again. And again.

It wasn't that Jimmie was looking for a sun tan: he'd been diagnosed with tuberculosis which was as good as receiving a death sentence. Sunny weather was medically recommended to ease his symptoms. The only possible hope of a cure was rest, and this was not something that life as a brakeman, nor as an entertainer, offered.

For Jimmie Rodgers, every song he sang stood a chance of being his last.

Meeting Jimmie Rodgers, Barry Mazor

Presley on the radio, I

SATURDAY 18TH JUNE 1927
RADIO WSM, NASHVILLE, TENNESSEE

PRESLEY'S NERVES WERE SHOWING as he waited for his call to the microphone. His friends and family were listening at home; the powerful transmitter sent the signal loud and clear across the South. The radio station WSM was twenty months old. It had been established as a promotional tool by the National Life and Accident Insurance Company, and was named for their slogan ("We Shield Millions").

On 28th November 1926, in a break from their usual programming, WSM had broadcast a live performance by traditional folk musician "Uncle" Jimmy Thompson. The audience response was overwhelmingly positive. So much so that within a month the station had scheduled a regular Saturday night old-time music show and called it *Barn Dance*.

None of that mattered to the anxious musician waiting in the fifth-floor studio who wiped the sweat from his palms. He watched the Pickard Family as they stood centre stage singing their hit record, "Kitty Wells", and momentarily allowed himself to dream of emulating their success.

The song ended, the applause began, and the stage manager gave him a thumbs-up. Frank Presley grabbed his fiddle and stepped out for his one and only appearance on *Barn Dance*. Ten minutes later, his moment of fame and glory over, he packed up his instrument and disappeared into the night.

A Good-Natured Riot, Charles K. Wolfe
The Grand Ole Opry: The Making of an American Icon, Colin Escott

The birth of country music, I

MONDAY 25TH JULY 1927
STATE STREET, BRISTOL, TENNESSEE

On a hot July day, Ralph Peer set up his recording gear in a hat warehouse in Bristol. He'd placed advertisements in local newspapers, inviting musicians and singers to come and audition. This was the second of his field recordings, the first being held in the spring focusing on black performers singing blues, or what Peer dubbed "race" music. His aim this time was to capture "hillbilly" acts, as he called them: white artists singing old-time songs. The market for folk music was small, and the records rarely troubled the pop chart so, to keep track of who was hot and who was not, separate weekly listings were published using the epithets suggested by Peer. Still, a disk might top the hillbilly chart yet not sell enough to even enter the pop chart at all.

But Peer remained positive. He had anticipated fourteen days of sessions, but it became clear during the first week he did not have enough applicants. Therefore, a further set of advertisements were printed, this time drawing attention to the financial success of previous "Ralph Peer discoveries". This seemed to do the trick, and altogether Peer recorded nineteen performers and seventy-six songs, justifying his optimism.

On Monday 1st August, The Carter Family arrived for an audition and, three days later, Jimmie Rodgers also made an appearance. Peer recorded both artists at the promised rate of $50 per song and was impressed, but gave no signal to them that anything special would come of the sessions. The artists returned home and Peer made release plans for some of the music.

These were not the first folk songs professionally recorded. But, if it was ever possible to establish an official starting point for what we now call country music, then this was it.

Classic Country: Legends of Country Music, Charles K. Wolfe
Will You Miss Me When I'm Gone? The Carter Family & Their Legacy in American Music, Mark Zwonitzer with Charles Hirshberg
countrymusichalloffame.org
peermusic.com

The Chattanooga Boys' second session

FRIDAY 4TH NOVEMBER 1927
ATLANTA, GEORGIA

FRANK WALKER GREETED THE ALLEN BROTHERS, Austin and Lee, as they arrived for their second Columbia recording session. They made pleasant small talk, but there was tension in the air. Walker had already approved their song choices for the day, and they decided to start with the track "Chattanooga Blues". The song subsequently became so popular that the brothers were nicknamed The Chattanooga Boys.

But those present at the session were aware of the legal case hanging over their heads. The Allen Brothers' first session for Columbia seven months prior had produced their single, "Salty Dog Blues". All had been well until Columbia, confused by the word "Blues" in the title, advertised the song in their list of forthcoming "race" records — a selection made up of Negro artists.

The Allen Brothers, who were both white, sued Columbia for $250,000 to compensate them for the perceived racial slur. Black performers sang black songs and white performers sang white; and never the twain shall meet.

Before the case came to court, Austin and Lee had jumped ship and moved to Victor Records. Not long afterwards, Walker followed suit and was appointed head of Victor's budget label, Bluebird Records.

The Encyclopaedia of Country Music (Second Edition),
Edited by Paul Kingsbury, Michael McCall & John W. Rumble
Mike Seeger's interview with Frank Walker, 19th June 1962

The Carter Family for sale

EARLY NOVEMBER 1927
STATE STREET, MACES SPRING, VIRGINIA

MAYBELLE CARTER and her husband, Eck, could hardly believe their ears. It had been over three months since Maybelle, A.P., and Sara had recorded for Mr Peer and they'd not heard a word from him. Now, here the pair stood outside Mr McLister's store and he had a phonograph playing music out of his shop onto the street. And what was he playing but a Carter Family record on the Victor label: "Poor Orphan Child", coupled with "Wandering Boy" (Bluebird 20877), both recorded in Bristol. They purchased several copies and rushed back home to play them for A.P. and Sara, who were also amazed.

Royalty cheques from Mr Peer soon followed, as did a request for a second session of original songs, this time in New Jersey. A.P. broke into a panic and decided the only way to assemble sufficient new material for the recordings was to roam the countryside gathering the words and tunes of old-time songs from the common folk, which he did. Sometimes he was gone for weeks at a time.

Upon his return, he would re-write and edit with Sara and Maybelle to ensure Mr Peer could copyright the "new" songs. In this way, The Carter Family assembled a vital collection of variations upon ancient ballads and strains, preserving them for future generations.

Maybelle took to expanding her already astonishing skill as a guitarist, learning new techniques with a fierce determination. Her talent was remarkable, and although she didn't brag about it, she considered herself a professional and took great pride in her abilities.

Sara, meanwhile, resigned herself to their new career. She had little interest in show business and, apart from the financial rewards, resented the way in which her life was being taken away from her, one song at a time.

Classic Country: Legends of Country Music, Charles K. Wolfe
Will You Miss Me When I'm Gone? The Carter Family & Their Legacy in American Music, Mark Zwonitzer with Charles Hirshberg

The secret song, 1

WEDNESDAY 30TH NOVEMBER 1927
VICTOR STUDIO, CAMDEN, NEW JERSEY

He was surprised and disappointed that Ralph Peer hadn't yet been in touch, because Jimmie Rodgers had just naturally assumed that the Victor man would have been knocked out by his singing, playing and songwriting.

Except ... well, Jimmie had gambled during the Bristol session: there was a great song he'd had up his sleeve but hadn't wanted to play it for Mr Peer because it was ... different. It was a song Jimmie called "T for Texas" and it was all about a gal named Thelma, but he was worried Mr Peer might consider it unsuitable. He figured he'd bring it along to the second session when Mr Peer invited him back. Only, Jimmie hadn't been invited back.

So, Rodgers and his wife travelled to New York and checked themselves into a fine hotel. Jimmie turned up on Mr Peer's doorstep and announced he was ready for his next session. Peer was impressed with Jimmie's bold approach and arranged for studio time on the Wednesday.

Just as Jimmie had hoped, Mr Peer loved the song, particularly the yodels thrown in to punctuate the verses. Peer retitled it "Blue Yodel" and the record, when released in early 1928 (Victor 21142), became a big seller in the hillbilly market and Jimmie Rodgers became Peer's golden goose

The Carters would sing the songs of righteous love and morality: Jimmie, meanwhile, would sing everything else, and together they would make Ralph Peer rich.

Meeting Jimmie Rodgers, Barry Mazor

Jim and Harry join the *Opry*

WEDNESDAY 1ST FEBRUARY 1928
RADIO WSM, NASHVILLE, TENNESSEE

JIM DENNY, almost seventeen, had once again snuck in to watch the evening's performance. He had signed on as a mailroom clerk for National Life but he was drawn to its successful WSM *Barn Dance* radio show and had already offered his services as a bouncer to remove unruly audience members.

He loved the music and, although he wasn't musical himself, knew he wanted to be involved in some fashion. He watched the stage manager. He learned. He watched the director. He learned.

He also watched the new announcer, Harry Stone, making his first appearance that evening. Harry was a difficult man, but he was a professional and Jim respected that. Heck, Jim knew that he himself was not an easy person to get along with all the time.

Jim Denny had ambitions for his own future at radio WSM and he figured Harry Stone might be a man to carry some influence on *Barn Dance* … Damn, he kept doing that. He had to start calling the show by its new name … the *Grand Ole Opry*.

A Good-Natured Riot, Charles K. Wolfe
The Grand Ole Opry: The Making of an American Icon, Colin Escott

A.P. meets Esley

A SUNDAY MORNING, PERHAPS EARLY 1928
KINGSPORT, TENNESSEE

HIS RELENTLESS SEARCH for new old songs had taken A.P. Carter to some strange places. Driving in a royalty-bought shiny red Chevrolet, he found himself in the black section of Kingsport. While scouting around, he was introduced to Lesley "Esley" Riddle, a twenty-three year-old guitarist who had had plenty of time to focus on his music following an industrial accident in which he'd lost a leg.

Esley was encouraged by his friends to play a few tunes for Mr Carter and the recording star was impressed. A.P. offered Esley a job on the spot. For the next four years he would function as A.P.'s musical dictaphone. They would scour the byways together, and he would learn the tunes, while A.P. noted down the words.

When they returned home every few weeks, Esley would play the songs for Maybelle, and she would interpret the tracks into the Carter style. Once A.P. had polished and worked out the harmonies, Sara would add her beautiful lead vocal, and another Carter Family hit was born.

A.P. and Esley, white man and black man touring the South together in the big red Chevy, had some high-old adventures hunting songs. And maybe without anyone even realising it, the guitarist added more than a touch of the blues to the Carter Family sound.

Will You Miss Me When I'm Gone? The Carter Family & Their Legacy in American Music, Mark Zwonitzer with Charles Hirshberg

What's in a name?

WEDNESDAY 27TH JUNE 1928
MOUNT SINAI HOSPITAL, COOK COUNTY, CHICAGO

HARRY KROLIK managed to make a fleeting visit to see his heavily pregnant wife in April 1928. She was living at 1421 South Millard Avenue, a mile away from Mount Sinai Hospital, which had been built in 1912 to cater for poor immigrants from Eastern Europe, specifically those of Jewish heritage. Edith was comforted to know the hospital was nearby, because her husband wouldn't be. Harry reassured her that all would be well with the baby and he would work out a way for the family to be together permanently.

But when Edith's time came, Harry's words and Harry himself were far away. Their son was born at 4 o'clock in the morning on 27th June 1928. He was named Alvin Bert, but the administrator of births wasn't paying attention when Edith registered the new arrival. The surname on the certificate was recorded as "Krolick" and Edith's maiden name was listed as "Boran".

Harry wouldn't see his son until November, when he would then stay with his young family for just over a year, before being again drawn back over the border to his father's house in Winnipeg. Whatever it was that was causing Harry to be apart from his wife and son — perhaps education, or parental illness, maybe legal problems — must have been serious, because it was surely agony for him to be apart from his loved ones.

The Carter Family's third session

THURSDAY 14TH FEBRUARY 1929
VICTOR STUDIO, CAMDEN, NEW JERSEY

THE CARTERS WERE BOOKED IN for two days of recording with Mr Peer in New Jersey, beginning on Valentine's Day. They captured a beautiful song entitled "I'm Thinking Tonight of My Blue Eyes" which drew from several sources lyrically. Musically, however, Maybelle remembered she'd known the tune all her life.

When released as a single four months later (Victor 40089), it became a signature song for the Carters. It captured the essence of their sound: that sense of loss, that feeling of tragic, unrequited or separated love.

As more sessions and live performances followed, A.P. spent months on the road with Esley, collecting songs, and Sara raised their children and tended single-handedly to the farm. Slowly, she drifted away from her husband, unable to compete with the charms of his new mistress: fame.

Will You Miss Me When I'm Gone? The Carter Family & Their Legacy in American Music,
Mark Zwonitzer with Charles Hirshberg

Eddy Arnold: when I was a boy

WEDNESDAY 15TH MAY 1929
HENDERSON, CHESTER COUNTY, TENNESSEE

IT WAS EDDY ARNOLD'S ELEVENTH BIRTHDAY and he'd spent much of the day playing with his friends in the fields. Eddy was a polite boy, the youngest in his family. His father, a respected giant of a man, ran his own farm, but life had been unkind of late and he found himself in debt and his health was fast fading. Recently, he'd been confined to his bed.

Eddy kept out of the way, often singing to himself and strumming the guitar he had on permanent loan from a cousin. He loved listening to the *Opry* each Saturday, as his whole family gathered around the radio. Eddy delighted in the ballads that told a story — songs like "Casey Jones", which recounted the tragic tale of the brave engineer. Jones' widow lived up the road apiece in Jackson, and that just made the story all the more real.

Eddy and his companions played together throughout the afternoon, enjoying the late-spring sunshine. At 5 o'clock he heard the dinner bell ringing far off in the distance. It normally tolled at noon but Eddy instantly understood its message. He prepared to run the mile and a half back home, telling his friends, "I got to go now. My daddy's dead."

Eddy Arnold: Pioneer of the Nashville Sound, Michael Streissguth

The death of Anna van den Enden

FRIDAY 17TH MAY 1929
BREDA, THE NETHERLANDS

NEWLY-WED ANNA VAN DEN ENDEN lay on the kitchen floor in the living quarters behind her husband's shop. She was twenty-three years-old and had recently married Willem the greengrocer, who was out on his usual morning delivery round. She had been struck with a hard object several times about the head from behind, and now lay in a pool of her own blood, life ebbing from her body.

Her assailant ransacked the apartment in a futile search for money. Then, apparently being familiar with the ways of animals, he shook pepper all around to deter police dogs from tracking him down. He slipped out of the door and disappeared through the backstreets.

The police were soon alerted and they investigated the death, but no charge was ever made. The murderer escaped and was never brought to justice. To this day, the death of Anna van den Enden remains unsolved.

The Colonel: The Extraordinary Story of Colonel Tom Parker and Elvis Presley, Alanna Nash

Steinbeck's Depression

PERHAPS LATE AUGUST 1929
SAN FRANCISCO, CALIFORNIA

JOHN STEINBECK at last published his first novel in the summer of 1929. *Cup of Gold* was a flimsy pirate story but the author was happy to receive a $250 advance from his publisher. He'd been living in San Francisco off his father's favour for almost a year, sharing a small apartment with his lover.

They lived hand-to-mouth for much of the time, borrowing when possible, stealing when necessary. If Steinbeck saw the publication of his first novel as some form of potentially life-changing moment, he was swiftly disabused. Sales were slow and all hope of progress was wiped out a couple of months later when the stock market crashed, heralding the beginning of the Great Depression. Suddenly, hard-working Americans were made destitute and thrust into unimaginable poverty and indignity.

For himself, Steinbeck was philosophical: he had no money to lose. But the suffering and distress he witnessed among his fellow citizens struck a chord deep within him, and gave birth to an artist who had something to write about.

John Steinbeck: A Biography, Jay Parini

Steve Sholes' first day at RCA

AUTUMN 1929
RCA VICTOR, CAMDEN, NEW JERSEY

IF THERE WAS A PLACE below the bottom rung of the Depression-hit corporate ladder, then Steven H. Sholes was surely occupying it. The plump eighteen year-old had arrived for his first day as a messenger boy at the newly-merged RCA Victor. The Radio Corporation of America, an electronics giant, had purchased the Victor Talking Machine Company at almost exactly the same time that Sholes had polished his shoes and presented his polite self at the back door.

Steve was planning to work part time while he studied for his degree at Rutgers. He loved music — he played saxophone and clarinet — and the thought of being part of the music business in any capacity genuinely excited him. And so he decided that when he was through with college he'd apply for a full-time position at RCA Victor.

Steve was an educated, well-spoken young man who absolutely knew the value of preparation and hard work. But he was also streetwise enough to understand the ways of the world. His father, George, was a traffic officer at the Victor factory office. The conversation had been played out countless times in businesses and offices all over the country: *My boy is leaving school soon … do you think we can find him a job here?*

Eddy Arnold: Pioneer of the Nashville Sound, Michael Streissguth
The Encyclopaedia of Country Music (Second Edition),
Edited by Paul Kingsbury, Michael McCall & John W. Rumble
Billboard, 20th March 1961

Pity the poor immigrant, II

SATURDAY 19TH OCTOBER 1929
WAIKIKI, HAWAII

As darkness fell on a June evening, the tall, ungainly nineteen year-old boy stepped off the gangplank in Mobile, Alabama, trying his best to look inconspicuous. Keeping his head down and his pace steady, he slipped through the waterside gates and disappeared into America. Having visited the country briefly only once before, his command of the English language was poor and his every word was heavily coated with his native Dutch accent.

Just a few weeks earlier, Andreas van Kuijk had hastily packed a small bag and jumped aboard a ship leaving Breda. His siblings and his widowed mother knew nothing of his departure until he was well out to sea. He had left behind all of his possessions and had vanished overnight.

When he reached the city limits, Andreas picked up speed and started running. He hitched lifts, journeying deeper and deeper inland, taking himself further and further away from the coast. He finally stopped in Huntingdon, West Virginia, and took refuge in a travelling carnival where his fractured English was not a hindrance. Almost everyone there had a secret to hide and they were unlikely to ask questions.

Over the next two weeks, Andreas fell in love with his new home — the country and the carnival — and revealed a natural empathy for the elephants and, indeed, creatures of all types. It was as if he could communicate with the animals; words were not a barrier.

But, much though the idea appealed to him, hiding within a carnival was not the answer to his problems: he needed a job, a place to live and regular food. Desperate times called for desperate measures. On 20th June, when the carnival passed near Fort McPherson, southwest of Atlanta, Georgia, the rebellious and ill-disciplined Andreas joined the U.S. Army and signed up for a three-year stint starting in Hawaii, the most remote and out-of-the-way posting he could find.

When he arrived in Waikiki on 19th October 1929, Andreas met a man who would have a significant influence on his life: Captain Thomas Parker aged forty-two, from Nebraska.

"Nice name," thought Andreas, "nice anonymous name."

The Colonel: The Extraordinary Story of Colonel Tom Parker and Elvis Presley, Alanna Nash

Tommy Durden: when I was a boy

SUNDAY 15TH DECEMBER 1929
NINETEENTH PRECINCT, PUTNAM, FLORIDA

THE DURDENS UP AND LEFT GEORGIA and settled in rural Florida, near Gainesville. The years went by and the children began to fly the nest. By the time Tommy celebrated his tenth birthday, shortly before Christmas 1929, half of his siblings had moved on.

Tommy was growing into a tall, gangly boy with a love of music. An older brother fooled some with a Hawaiian guitar and Tommy couldn't resist picking it up and trying his hand when no one was looking.

Best of all, he relished sneaking down to one of the local black churches on a Sunday night and sitting outside to listen to the glorious spirituals coming through the open doors. Tommy adored the sound, and became aware of how close secular black music was to the wonderful gospel tunes he heard every Sunday.

One didn't talk about these things, naturally, but Tommy was yet another white boy who fell in love with the blues.

Elvis Presley, Writing for the King: The Stories of the Songwriters, Ken Sharp
Census 1930

The missing movie, I

SEPTEMBER 1930
HOLLYWOOD, CALIFORNIA

JOAN CRAWFORD was several films into what would prove to be a long and glorious acting career when she was cast in the movie version of a flop Broadway production entitled *Great Day*. The musical play had closed after twenty-nine performances which coincided with the stock market crash, but it was clear to anyone with ears why MGM had bought the rights: the score was simply wonderful.

Composers Vincent Youmans, Billy Rose and Edward Eliscu had supplied an impeccable collection of songs: the title track and "More Than You Know" became standards, but it was the anthemic "Without a Song" that established itself as the keeper.

The movie was set along the Mississippi, and Crawford was cast as a roadhouse entertainer. It was anticpated that MGM would produce a popular and profitable feature — except they didn't.

After eight weeks of shooting, they pulled the plug. No one explained why and no one saw one second of filmed material.

Show Tunes: The Songs, Shows, and Careers of Broadway's Major Composers, Steven Suskin
www.joancrawfordbest.com/filmsgreatday.htm
www.legendaryjoancrawford.com/greatday.html

The Carters meet Jimmie Rodgers

WEDNESDAY 10TH JUNE 1931
LOUISVILLE, KENTUCKY

RALPH PEER NEEDED A GIMMICK: disk sales had been affected by the Depression and even Jimmie Rodgers was looking for a boost. It was Peer's idea to have his two greatest discoveries record together in the hope of lifting sales figures, and so a three-day summit with the Carters was convened in Louisville beginning on 10th June.

The sessions were reasonably successful, but no great music was recorded. Jimmie himself was so wasted with tuberculosis that Maybelle had to fill in his guitar parts. But even while he struggled for breath, there was life in the old dog yet. In between songs, Jimmie raised his eyebrows at Maybelle and made sure she knew that he would if she would.

She wouldn't and she didn't.

Will You Miss Me When I'm Gone? The Carter Family & Their Legacy in American Music,
Mark Zwonitzer with Charles Hirshberg

The arrival of Bing Crosby

WEDNESDAY 2ND SEPTEMBER 1931
ON THE AIR

AT THE AGE OF SEVEN, Harry Crosby, living in Spokane, Washington, had a life-changing moment. His neighbour was reading her favourite Sunday newspaper which featured a comic section called the *Bingville Bugle*. It took the form of a mock-hillbilly publication and humorously reinforced the Southern stereotypes, which some could easily have found offensive. The young Harry found it innocently amusing and laughed along with his neighbour when they read it together. She dubbed him "Bingo from Bingville", in reference to his enthusiasm for the newspaper and, over time, his accepted name simply became Bing.

Bing had a rare talent for singing and, when he grew up, he followed a career in show business, his reputation progressing as the industry made important technical developments. When modern microphones emphasised the role of the singer, Crosby perfected the technique of crooning intimately, and he spent the 1920s moving up from one band to another. Eventually, he emerged as the consummate singer of the popular song.

On Wednesday 2nd September 1931, aged twenty-eight, he launched his own solo career with a radio broadcast, and became the most famous singer on the planet. Records, radio shows, live performances, movies, and, in years to come, television, all fell within his remit. He appealed to listeners of every genre, and recorded songs that registered with every type of customer.

There had never been an entertainer like him and, it was widely agreed, there never would be again.

The Rise of the Crooners: Gene Austin, Russ Columbo, Bing Crosby, Nick Lucas, Johnny Marvin and Rudy Vallee, Nick Lucas, Michael Pitts, Frank Hoffmann, Dick Carty & Jim Bedoian

Tex Ritter, live at the Garden

FRIDAY 14TH OCTOBER 1932
MADISON SQUARE GARDEN, NEW YORK CITY, NEW YORK

MOUNTING HIS FAITHFUL four-legged companion, Woodward "Tex" Ritter adjusted the brim of his ten-gallon hat and cantered out into the dark. When he started singing, the Yankee audience at the seventh annual World Series Rodeo at Madison Square Garden greeted him warmly. He looked like the genuine article and he sounded like the genuine article. He *was* the genuine article.

Ritter was twenty-seven years-old and a long way from his home state. A decade previously, he'd studied Law at the University of Texas, but he'd fallen in love with authentic cowboy and folk songs, under the guidance of celebrated musicologist, John Lomax. Tex had a pleasant voice and could play the part of the western heroes that featured in the songs he studied and adored. It was a natural step for him to move into show business as one of the new breed of singing cowboys.

By 1929 he was starring on radio KPRC in Houston and then set out with a musical troupe touring the South and Mid-West, ending up on Broadway in the New York production of *Green Grow the Lilacs*, in which he was required to sing four traditional folk songs.

Though successful, the play was long forgotten until Rodgers and Hammerstein took it as the plot for their revolutionary stage musical, *Oklahoma!*, ten years hence.

Tex played no part in that later triumph, but on this Friday night at Madison Square Garden, he stood there at the end, his arms stretched out in the spotlight, the audience applauding rapturously.

He was a true son of the South who had conquered the North.

Country Music, U.S.A. (Second Revised Edition), Bill C. Malone

The Carters: a family affair

EARLY FEBRUARY 1933
MACES SPRING, VIRGINIA

COY BAYS was the direct opposite of A.P. Carter. He was openly affectionate, he was amusing and he enjoyed spending time with Sara Carter. He was also A.P.'s cousin. The Bays lived nearby and the families had always been close.

During A.P.'s song-hunting forays, Coy had taken to visiting Sara and the pair had fallen hopelessly and deeply in love. When A.P. caught wind of this, he was furious but, as this was family, he didn't want to make a public show of it. He spoke with Coy's folks and it was decided the whole Bays family would sell up and move out west.

By early February, the property was sold and the deal was done. When the truck was loaded and the passengers were on board, the extended family came to bid them goodbye. As the Bays started their long journey, Maybelle and her children, Helen and June, wept uncontrollably. Maybelle was carrying her third daughter, Anita, who would be born the following month.

Sara was not there to watch the leaving: she remained at home, her heart and her spirit finally crushed by the weight of fame and success. A few weeks later, she packed her bags and moved away from her husband and children to live on the other side of the mountain.

Will You Miss Me When I'm Gone? The Carter Family & Their Legacy in American Music, Mark Zwonitzer with Charles Hirshberg

Tom Parker's lost weekend

FRIDAY 17TH FEBRUARY 1933
FORT BARRANCAS, NEAR PENSACOLA, FLORIDA

IN HIS INFREQUENT LETTERS HOME, Andreas van Kuijk had now taken to signing with the name "Tom Parker". His family knew he was serving in America, but they didn't know exactly where. And, for that matter, neither did the U.S. Army.

He had been on the run for one hundred and forty days when he finally surrendered himself on 17th February 1933 and returned to Fort Barrancas near Pensacola. No one could figure out what had made him go AWOL.

When his tour of duty on Waikiki had ended, he had transferred to Florida, which was one of the easiest postings in the whole U.S. Army, and then re-enlisted for a second term on 19th June 1932. He had looked at the America of the Great Depression and didn't like it, so he decided to stay with the devil he knew. As a reward, he was promoted to Private First Class, a rank that seemed to please him beyond all sensible perspective.

But something changed within his demeanour. The oppressive burden of conformity and obedience had eventually proven too heavy. Three years of obeying rules and yes-sirring had taken their toll on his rebellious nature and, quite without warning, he'd upped and disappeared.

Upon his eventual return in February, he was locked up in solitary confinement for two months. Deprived of human contact, his mind collapsed and he was transferred to the Walter Reed Army Medical Center in Washington on 19th June, shortly before his twenty-fourth birthday.

But still no one could work out what he'd been doing with his one hundred and forty missing days which began on 27th September 1932.

Coincidentally, on that very day, the Ringling Brothers circus had arrived in Pensacola for a twenty-four-hour stopover. On 28th September they were gone. And so was Tom Parker.

The Colonel: The Extraordinary Story of Colonel Tom Parker and Elvis Presley, Alanna Nash

Oliver Hood: "Sunshine"

AT SOME POINT IN THE MID-1930S
LAGRANGE, TROUP COUNTY, GEORGIA

OLIVER HOOD WAS VIEWED BY MANY in the city of LaGrange as a renaissance man. The mill-worker and part-time music teacher was handsome, intelligent and gifted. His neighbours came to him for advice and also just to spend time and shoot the breeze with this remarkable fellow.

On Sunday afternoons, locals would gather outside his house to hear him sing and play the mandolin. He composed his own songs, scribbling the lyrics on random pieces of paper, or on off-cuts of fabric or sackcloth. Hood gave no thought to copyrighting his creations or registering himself as the writer. He wrote purely to sing and share with the townsfolk. He sometimes took old tunes and made them new. You couldn't *own* a song. Songs and music belonged to everyone. In this way, Hood was carrying on the folk music tradition that had existed for centuries. It was only in recent times that people had taken on the fancy notion of songs as property.

His neighbours loved to hear him sing his own compositions, and they would request their favourite tune on a weekly basis, crying, "Sing for us, Oliver; sing 'You Are My Sunshine'."

And he did. And his audience were sure to tell their friends, not just of this amazing man, but also of the wonderful songs he wrote and sang. News slowly spread, often by word-of-mouth, sometimes travelling as far abroad as South Carolina.

From original research by Toru Mitsui, originally printed in the November 1990 issue of *Chronicles: A Magazine of American Culture*, a publication of The Rockford Institute

Daddy's home, I

TUESDAY 14TH MARCH 1933
ALBANY PARK, CHICAGO, ILLINOIS

SOME BIRTHDAYS ARE MEMORABLE. For Harry Krolik his twenty-seventh would remain imprinted in his mind for the rest of his life. On that day, 14th March 1933, he was granted permanent residency in the United States, and could at last join his wife, Edith, and their son, Alvin, who were by now living at 4934 Monticello Avenue in Albany Park, Chicago. It was a three-storey detached building near the Chicago River, and it was the family's third address in as many years.

Twelve months previously, Edith had arranged for the misspellings on Alvin's birth certificate to be corrected. He was now almost five years-old and his father had been absent for three very important formative years. There is no way of knowing the impact a missing father has on a child. Some become particularly attached to their mother; others carry on seemingly as normal.

And some rebel.

"The Death of Jimmie Rodgers"

FRIDAY 26TH MAY 1933
TAFT HOTEL, NEW YORK CITY, NEW YORK

JIMMIE RODGERS breathed his last on 26th May 1933 at the Taft Hotel in New York. He was thirty-five years-old. Two days earlier, he'd recorded what would be his final four sides for RCA Victor, and had been so weak he'd needed to lie down on a makeshift cot between takes.

Appropriately, of the four songs, two looked back to the old days, and the others extolled the joys of life in the South. The performances were good and gave little indication that Rodgers was on the verge of succumbing to tuberculosis.

Within a month of his passing, tribute records began to appear, the first of which was by up-and-coming yodeller Gene Autry, and was bluntly entitled "The Death of Jimmie Rodgers". Some may have considered this exploitation to be in bad taste, but Autry and his ilk were simply adhering to the folk tradition of singing the news. The trick was to get the timing right and judge the mood of the people.

Many genuinely loved Rodgers and his music, but of all those who mourned the singer, no one shed more tears than the finance department at RCA Victor.

Meeting Jimmie Rodgers, Barry Mazor

Young love

SATURDAY 17TH JUNE 1933
PONTOTOC, MISSISSIPPI

LYING ON YOUR WEDDING CERTIFICATE isn't necessarily the best way to start married life. Thankfully, true love conquers all, and it's for sure that when Vernon Elvis Presley and Gladys Love Smith married on 17th June 1933, it was for love and not money. Gladys, twenty-two, reduced her age by two years for the ceremony in nearby Pontotoc, and Vernon, seventeen, added five to his. They'd first met in church in their home town of East Tupelo, and they were smitten. Both were dirt poor with little chance of improving their social position.

Vernon had no trade and was regarded as a very private person by his neighbours. Some called him lazy but, to be fair, there was little work to be had. Gladys was a lively, upbeat woman, with a love of dancing and music — Jimmie Rodgers was a favourite.

The Depression had hit the residents of East Tupelo hard, and Vernon and Gladys were somewhere near the bottom of the pile. They spoke to land-owner Orville Bean, and he loaned them the substantial figure of $180, so they might build their own small home near their families.

The two-room house was of a type known as a shotgun shack: you could fire a shotgun through the front door and it would exit through the back door without hitting anything in between.

The Presleys lived in harmony with their neighbours, both white and also the nearby black community. They worked when work was available; they listened to the *Grand Ole Opry* on Saturday; they worshipped on Sunday.

Last Train to Memphis: The Rise of Elvis Presley, Peter Guralnick

Tom Parker: I ain't got no home

SATURDAY 19TH AUGUST 1933
WALTER REED ARMY HOSPITAL, WASHINGTON D.C.

STEPPING OUT OF THE military hospital into the August sunshine, Tom Parker at last breathed the fresh air of freedom. Because of his mental and emotional problems, he'd been granted an honorable discharge from the U.S. Army.

He still wrote infrequent letters to his long-suffering family. Soon though, the letters would dry up altogether and his kin would assume the worst. His family was correct: Andreas van Kuijk was indeed dead, and he had been completely replaced by Thomas Andrew Parker.

His grasp of the English language was now much better but a careful listener could still pick out a slight lisp and a Dutch accent whenever he spoke. And Tom did like to talk. Indeed, he talked himself into a job at the Johnny J. Jones Exposition where, to his delight, he was made responsible for the pony rides.

He embraced everything about the carnival world and ingratiated himself with each employee in a determined effort to learn the ropes. He studied hard, figuring out how to deal with the authorities, how to sell, how to make money, how to advertise, how to smooth over difficult situations, and which palms to grease at the right time.

He came up with several money-spinning promotions, one of which involved staging a marriage ceremony on top of the Ferris wheel every time they pitched at a new location. It was faked, of course, and usually involved two carny kids, but Tom knew how to draw in the punters, and weddings always made for an easy headline.

Once he'd absorbed all he could, he packed his bags and moved up to the greatest of the carnivals: the Royal American. Throughout the summer he toured the country and in the winter he took refuge in Tampa, Florida — the traditional shelter for carnivals — which, for want of a better word, became his home.

The Colonel: The Extraordinary Story of Colonel Tom Parker and Elvis Presley, Alanna Nash

Ottis Whitman, Jr: just like Jimmie

PERHAPS 1934
GRANT PARK, TAMPA, FLORIDA

Ottis Whitman, Jr, aged eleven, was a quiet boy. He tried to avoid speaking in public because he suffered from a stutter which restricted his every word. But he was a happy child and idolised his father. They went fishing and played sports together, especially baseball, Ottis' favourite game.

On Saturday evenings the family sat around the radio and listened to the *Grand Ole Opry* and other music shows. Little Ottis had no particular dreams of being a musician, but he'd noticed how everyone had lit up when a yodeller like Jimmie Rodgers came over the airwaves.

"Heck," thought Ottis, "that's no big deal. I can do that."

And he did. And to the astonishment of his whole family, when Ottis sang and yodelled, there was not the slightest trace of a stutter.

Mr Songman: The Slim Whitman Story, Kenneth L. Gibble

Hiram Williams: when I was a boy

LATE SUMMER 1934
GEORGIANA, ALABAMA

HIRAM WILLIAMS LOVED MUSIC. Just eleven years-old, he had already learned the basics of guitar playing. He'd also learned the basics of hard drinking. He loved the old-time music he heard from his neighbours and on the *Grand Ole Opry* radio show, but nothing prepared him for the sounds he experienced one summer's morning as he set up his shoe shine gear near the train depot.

A fifty year-old black man named Rufus "Tee-Tot" Payne sat beside him on the sidewalk and uncased his guitar. He winked at Hiram, cleared his throat and started to play a type of music the boy had never heard before. He was transfixed. After the performance, the boy gave his name and attached himself to the minstrel for the rest of the summer.

So it was that Hiram "Hank" Williams first met the blues.

Hank Williams: The Biography, Colin Escott with George Merritt & William MacEwen
Lovesick Blues: The Life of Hank Williams, Paul Hemphill

My brother he is in Elysium

TUESDAY 8TH JANUARY 1935
EAST TUPELO, MISSISSIPPI

LESS THAN A YEAR into their marriage, Gladys Presley conceived. Her pregnancy was not easy, and the news that she was expecting twins added to her anxiety. When her time came, she was attended by Dr William Hunt, an experienced and respected practitioner within the poverty-stricken neighbourhood.

Early one frosty morning in January, she gave birth to a still-born son, named Jesse Garon. It's difficult to imagine the pain and heartache that swamped the small dark room. Those present knew the other twin was waiting to be delivered, and the tension must have been unbearable. Thirty-five minutes later, just after 4:30 AM, full of life, Elvis Aron arrived, and grateful prayers were offered up.

The boy had been named for Vernon and his best friend, Aaron Kennedy, although the "a" sound had been shortened to chime with Garon. The family couldn't afford the doctor's bill and it was covered by welfare.

Jesse was buried the next day, in an unmarked grave in nearby Priceville Cemetery. Gladys never forgot her first-born son, and reminded the growing Elvis of him often in conversation. Elvis visited the cemetery frequently, and for the rest of his life his lost brother remained a presence and an enigma.

Last Train to Memphis: The Rise of Elvis Presley, Peter Guralnick

"The Fate of Dewey Lee"

WEDNESDAY 8TH MAY 1935
ARC RECORDING STUDIO, NEW YORK CITY, NEW YORK

Ralph Peer had been very concerned when he'd heard of the split within The Carter Family; he feared it would be bad for business. However, even though A.P. and Sara were proceeding with a divorce, he persuaded them to continue as a family recording unit. Sara agreed because she had no other means of support. She remained cold but professional in her relations with A.P., and many good songs were recorded and released to a public who knew nothing of the separation.

But A.P. was struggling without his soon-to-be ex-wife. He hadn't realised quite how much she had contributed to the writing and re-writing sessions over the years. A.P. was now forced to work with almost any material he could find to meet his obligations to Mr Peer and to the Decca label, where Peer and the Carters now resided.

In 1935 he wrote "The Fate of Dewey Lee", a narrative song based on the true story of a 1931 murder victim, and the Carters recorded it in May in New York. After the single's release (M13430), A.P. came to regret the disk, fearing it was in bad taste, and feeling he was exploiting too recent a tragedy.

"He's still got people living," said A.P., "I shouldn't have done that."

Will You Miss Me When I'm Gone? The Carter Family & Their Legacy in American Music, Mark Zwonitzer with Charles Hirshberg

Red Foley: "Old Shep"

MONDAY 9TH DECEMBER 1935
FURNITURE MART BUILDING, CHICAGO, ILLINOIS

IT WAS NO SECRET why Clyde Foley was nicknamed "Red". His ginger hair marked him out in a crowd. So did his vocal talent. But he'd been plugging away for five years without any progress. This was his fifth recording session since 1933, and none of the singles released so far on the small Melotone label had made any impact. Today's session was a little different though: usually he recorded with a small band, but here he was with just his voice and his guitar.

He'd brought a tune he'd written himself with a very personal lyric about a dog, and entitled it "Old Shep", though it was really about his own boyhood pet named Hoover, a German shepherd.

Melotone released the single in 1936 (M6-03-53) but it died — just like the dog in the song. So Foley put it to one side and carried on playing and travelling, hoping to hit the big time one day.

Finally, in 1941, a decade after he'd started in the music business, the mighty Decca label signed him up and Foley re-recorded "Old Shep" at his debut session. The single was released in May 1941 (5944) and it was instantly hailed as a hillbilly classic. Indeed, for the next ten years it stood as Foley's signature tune.

Radio listeners loved to hear Red crooning the song. For many, it reminded them of their own dear departed pet. Learning the words by heart, they would sing along with Red, tears rolling down their cheeks.

http://countrydiscography.blogspot.co.uk/2010/01/red-foley.html
http://countrymusichalloffame.org/full-list-of-inductees/view/red-foley

Mae: my words are my weapons

SATURDAY 25TH JANUARY 1936
TAHLEQUAH, OKLAHOMA

MAE BOREN AXTON sat down with complete confidence. She and her East Central College team-mate had just delivered a glorious argument in the semi-final of the district debating tournament. They had sailed through the first rounds and she fully expected her carefully chosen and beautifully spoken words to provide a ticket to the final. The opposing team from Oklahoma City University looked uneasy.

Mae loved words. She loved gently coaxing them into the right order so the listener heard and understood her point of view. She would hold fast to the facts as far as was possible, but there were ways of using language which allowed one to project certain parts of the truth while leaving the less desirable elements in the shadows.

She was a good writer and a good speaker, and she was much in demand. Last autumn she had played in the Little Theater group; now she was booked at two churches for Mother's Day in May, and a week later she'd be speaking at the end of term banquet.

It seemed everyone was telling her how good she was. Her high school friend, Nellie Whitaker, was a fervent supporter of her talents. But the praise she most sought was that of her father, Mark Boren. The family name meant something in Oklahoma, just as it had meant something in Texas. That's why Mae had insisted on using the double-barrelled styling after her marriage to college football star, John Axton, in August 1934. Mae considered herself neither beautiful nor brilliant, but her husband did not share her opinion and adored her.

Her eight brothers were all forging ahead in their chosen careers. Brother Lyle, just a couple of years older than Mae, was already making steps towards Congress, re-inforcing her feeling of being "extraneous" within the family. A trophy in the debating tournament would be small compared to her siblings' achievements but, just for once, it would mean that she would be the golden child; she would be number one.

The adjudicators stood and faced the teams; the head judge smiled, turned away from Mae's table and congratulated the girls from Oklahoma City on their victory.

Country Singers As I Know 'Em, Mae Boren Axton
Ada Evening News, Oklahoma, 30th January, 10th May & 14th May 1936
Personal correspondence between Lyle Boren & Mae Boren Axton

Hank Snow: my boy

THURSDAY 6TH FEBRUARY 1936
HALIFAX, NOVA SCOTIA, CANADA

CLARENCE "HANK" SNOW lay asleep and exhausted on the bed. He'd watched the ambulance speed away in the early hours of the morning, taking his pregnant wife off to hospital to try and overcome the serious complications that had arisen as she went into labour.

Hank, aged twenty-one, was attempting to make his way as a hillbilly singer, trying desperately to gain a foothold in the Canadian market. He'd endured a difficult childhood, and had emerged as a short and feisty adult, lacking in humour but full of determination. He had his heart set not just on national success, but stardom throughout the whole continent. Within the year, he'd sign for the Canadian branch of RCA Victor and would begin his slow ascent up the ladder of fame; but what a long climb it would be.

A knock at the door woke him at noon and a neighbour told him he was wanted on the phone. He was relieved to hear from the hospital that all was well with mother and baby. Hank would name his newborn son for his musical hero, and he mapped out his boy's future in one fell swoop. Jimmie Rodgers Snow would follow in his father's footsteps and become a country singer. Whether he wanted to or not.

The Hank Snow Story, Hank Snow with Jack Ownbey & Bob Burris

Bobby Ross: Marie's boy

TUESDAY 18TH MARCH 1936
TAMPA, FLORIDA

Bobby Ross didn't know it, but today, just after his eleventh birthday, his mother was divorced for the second time. Marie Mott ditched William Sayre, as she had ditched Bobby's father, Robert Ross senior, eight years earlier. What Bobby *did* know was that his mom was seeing a new guy named Tom and he was kinda fun.

Tom worked on the carnival, just like his mom, and for the past year he'd been sorta hanging around. Sometimes he let Bobby ride on the ponies for free and he showed him lots of tricks. Tom talked in a different language when he got mad, but he was real nice to his mom; he never hit the bottle and he never laid a hand on Bobby.

Bobby liked him and figured he wanted to be just like Tom when he grew up. In a few years' time, Bobby would understand that Tom and his mom were married but the weird thing is that Bobby couldn't even remember going to the wedding.

Funny guy, that Tom Parker, funny guy.

The Colonel: The Extraordinary Story of Colonel Tom Parker and Elvis Presley, Alanna Nash

"Crescent City Blues"

FRIDAY 16TH OCTOBER 1936
ST CHARLES HOTEL, NEW ORLEANS, LOUISIANA

HE SANG THE SWEETEST BLUES you'd ever want to hear. His high trembling voice lent an air of sophistication to the numbers he performed throughout the Mississippi juke joints, sawmills and dancehalls, not too far from New Orleans, or the "Crescent City", as it was sometimes called. But as good as his voice was, it paled beside his talent as a pianist.

Eurreal "Little Brother" Montgomery came from a musical family and had hit the road at the age of eleven, playing and singing his way around the South, slowly building a reputation for himself.

He had recorded some fine sides for RCA Bluebird in the early 1930s, but it was during the company's last serious field recordings in October 1936 that Montgomery recorded the mother lode of his legacy. In the St Charles Hotel he laid down almost two dozen tracks, some vocal, some instrumental, and all beautiful.

"Crescent City Blues", in particular was a triumph of piano playing, and his singing on the self-composed "Something Keeps A-Worrying Me" was a joy ... "Now, mama, that's all right, most any old way that you do," he crooned.

Great artists such as Willie Dixon, Otis Spann, Little Johnnie Jones, Skip James and Sunnyland Slim came to admire his performances. But no one was listening as intently as Arthur Crudup and Gordon Jenkins, two young men from very different sides of the tracks.

Mississippi Blues Commission
http://sundayblues.org
http://www.msbluestrail.org
http://www.wirz.de/music/montgfrm.htm

Tex Ritter: movie star

THURSDAY 22ND NOVEMBER 1936
HOLLYWOOD, CALIFORNIA

GRAND NATIONAL PICTURES INC. hadn't promised Tex Ritter the earth. They were a new company, eager to tap into the growing market for singing-cowboy movies, and Tex seemed the right man for the job.

Grand National produced low budget B-grade films, in which Tex was required to look the part and sing his way through several pleasant songs at somewhat improbable moments. His first feature, *Song of the Gringo*, a forgettable romp set in the old west, was released in November 1936.

Tex was happy to see his name in lights and take the money. And for the next decade that's what he did, working his way through dozens of pictures for Grand National and other studios, too. He wore different hats and costumes, but the movies were essentially the same. And they all made a profit. They didn't need a title; they could've just had a number and they still would've sold. Customers all over the country happily paid a dime to watch Tex sing to the bad guys he'd just beaten up.

For a man like Ritter, who understood the genius and beauty of music, it must have hurt to sell even just a little of his soul in this way. His acting career had started promisingly, but any dreams of art had been drowned in the river of commerce.

Country Music, U.S.A. (Second Revised Edition), Bill C. Malone
The Internet Movie Database

Joe and Pee Wee: the professionals

EASTER WEEKEND, LATE MARCH 1937
RYMAN AUDITORIUM, NASHVILLE, TENNESSEE

JULIUS "PEE WEE KING" KUCZYNSKI was an unlikely hillbilly performer. For one thing he came from Milwaukee; for another he played the accordion. But, most importantly, he was a consummate professional. He and his band, The Golden West Cowboys, wore matching western outfits and played with absolute precision, wasting no time while on stage, or at the microphone.

And in Joe L. Frank, Pee Wee's father-in-law, they had their ideal manager, because he shared their vision. Music was their living and they took great pride in their craft.

So when they pulled up at the *Opry* for their audition on a snowy Easter weekend, they had every confidence they'd be accepted on radio's fastest-growing hillbilly music show. Harry Stone didn't take much convincing and the Cowboys were set up as *Opry* regulars from June.

The *Opry* itself had undergone some recent changes. As a reflection of its expanding popularity it had taken over the Ryman Auditorium, a large former church, and now broadcast from there every Saturday. The venue was run-down, the seats were uncomfortable and there was absolutely no air conditioning, but the acoustics were to die for.

Pee Wee joined the Musicians' Union, the first *Opry* act so to do, and encouraged his band members to take their careers very seriously, including lead singer, Jack Skaggs.

Many current WSM acts were part-timers, or semi-professionals. Joe Frank and Pee Wee King brought a sense of discipline and flash to the industry. Not everyone appreciated this, but King did very well for himself and, for the first time, hillbilly show people understood that a smart, well-organised manager like J.L. Frank could make a real difference to an artist's career.

The Grand Ole Opry: The Making of an American Icon, Colin Escott

Fred Ritchie's last request

SATURDAY 7TH AUGUST 1937
STATE PRISON, NASHVILLE, TENNESSEE

FRED RITCHIE had three days left to live. He was on Death Row in Nashville State Prison, sentenced to the chair for murdering his wife. He sat with his ear glued to the radio, hoping Warden Joe Pope had managed to phone WSM and grant his last request. The familiar theme music of the *Grand Ole Opry* struck up and listeners all over the South moved in a little closer so as not to miss one moment of the show.

Soon enough, the announcer intoned they were going to perform a special number following a particular request from Tennessee. Ritchie sat, with tears filling his eyes, as the strains of "When I Take My Vacation in Heaven" filled his cell.

On Tuesday 10th August, sentence was served and thirty-two year-old Fred Ritchie breathed his last. Perhaps he died happy. Such was the power of the *Opry*.

The Grand Ole Opry: The Making of an American Icon, Colin Escott
www.tn.gov/correction/media/tnexecutions.html

The photograph, I

TUESDAY 16TH NOVEMBER 1937
EAST TUPELO, MISSISSIPPI

ORVILLE BEAN WAS A HARD MAN AND Vernon Presley felt sure the land-owner had treated him unfairly regarding the sale of a hog. Vernon knew it was worth much more than the meagre $4 cheque he'd received, so he and two accomplices — one of whom was Gladys' brother — altered the written amount to ensure they received appropriate recompense.

Obviously, the bank recognised their clumsy attempt at forgery, and the authorities were notified. Vernon was secured in the county jail in November 1937, awaiting trial. Gladys was distraught and when, six months later, Vernon was sentenced to three years in the dreaded Parchman Penitentiary, she was beside herself with worry.

The Presleys had overcome difficulties before — a 1936 tornado had killed over two hundred people in Tupelo — but now they were faced with one of their own being taken away. Gladys, thinking on her feet, arranged for a family photograph to be taken before Vernon was transferred.

When the picture was developed and printed, it revealed a portrait of three unsmiling figures: Vernon and Gladys, tense and fearful, looking to their left; central was the two year-old Elvis, dressed in dungarees and a dapper hat. The background was a dull, mottled, prison grey. Gladys' left hand reached round the back of the group to clutch her handsome husband's shoulder, in a forlorn attempt to hold the shattered family together.

Elvis & Gladys, Elaine Dundy
Last Train to Memphis: The Rise of Elvis Presley, Peter Guralnick

Roy Acuff: scared of the sunshine

SATURDAY 5TH FEBRUARY 1938
RYMAN AUDITORIUM, NASHVILLE, TENNESSEE

ROY ACUFF SAW THE WORLD SPINNING around him again, his knees gave way and he collapsed to the ground. It had happened twice before and, when he eventually came to, the young man knew his career in sport was over before it had begun.

Acuff had lived for baseball but a severe case of sunstroke — picked up while trying out for the Knoxville Smokies in 1929 — left him with a permanent fear of sunshine. Hiding in the shadows and emerging only after sunset, Roy honed his fiddle skills and launched a career in hillbilly music. He became an entertainer extraordinaire.

He started at the bottom of the bill, playing medicine shows in the early 1930s, alongside small-time acts like Pappy Gilbert and The Gilbert Sisters. Eventually, Roy and his band, The Smoky Mountain Boys, auditioned for the *Opry* in October 1937, but it did not go well.

On 5th February 1938, however, they were hanging around backstage at the Ryman Auditorium when an unexpected space arose in the *Opry* playing order. Acuff and his boys were quickly thrust on stage and they launched into an impromptu version of "The Great Speckled Bird", a curious religious composition Acuff had picked up on his travels. The melody sounded just like The Carter Family song, "I'm Thinking Tonight of My Blue Eyes", but no one paid too much mind because Roy sang with such tearful conviction.

Within days, Acuff and his song were the talk of Nashville. His personal integrity and sincerity made him into one of the most highly regarded and admired hillbilly talents of his generation. He became the standard bearer for the *Opry*, a firm link to the old-time music that had originally inspired the programme.

But as Roy gained more popularity and success, he became concerned about his finances. He had written some of his own songs and it seemed so unfair that he should give his publishing rights to someone else's company. He would look into this problem and find a solution.

Detroit Country Music: Mountaineers, Cowboys and Rockabillies, Craig Maki with Keith Cady
The Grand Ole Opry: The Making of an American Icon, Colin Escott

Blood is thicker than water

FRIDAY 25TH MARCH 1938
COMANCHE, OKLAHOMA

JOHN AXTON HAD FINISHED HIS FOURTH YEAR at East Central in the summer of 1936. He was popular and respected, and, as captain of the Tigers football team, had received the prestigious player of the year award. His loving wife Mae was so proud of him, and rejoiced when he took a post as football coach at a school in Comanche, where she too soon secured a teaching job.

On 25th March 1938, their first son, Hoyt Wayne, arrived and they restructured their lives around him, and also around his younger brother, Johnny, born two years later — by chance, the choice of names echoed those of Mae's favourite Texan movie star, the emerging John Wayne.

As with so many young families, they found the going tough, and money was always in short supply. Mae and John continued improving themselves, picking up extra qualifications whenever possible, and moved from town to town and from school to school if it meant a step up the career ladder. Mae would also sometimes pen articles for newspapers and magazines — a skill which came very naturally to her — and this helped balance the family budget a little.

They would often communicate with Mae's brother, Lyle, who had been elected to Congress in November 1936. Occasionally, they'd ask for his help in small financial matters, but would always make a point of repaying the loans. More interestingly, they would also request assistance in finding new positions, including much discussion regarding a possible vacancy for John in the postal service.

Mae adored her brother, and she had little restraint in asking him to use his authority for her benefit. She was young and idealistic, but she was under no illusions about how to get ahead in the real world.

Country Singers As I Know 'Em, Mae Boren Axton
Ada Evening News, Oklahoma, 4th January *&* 5th November 1936
Personal correspondence between Lyle Boren *&* Mae Boren Axton

The Shelton Brothers

JUNE 1938
RECORD RELEASE

THERE WAS NO TELLING what would catch on with the record-buying public; and singers, publishers and producers were willing to try anything to achieve success. The Shelton Brothers (Joe and Bob) weren't the first to resort to using old civil war songs, but they were the first to record and have a hit with the 1861 ballad "Aura Lee". It proved a popular tune for the Texan siblings when released on Decca in June 1938 (5533), but nothing could replace their self-composed signature song "Just Because" in the hearts of their listeners.

That particular track, however, provided a perfect view of the complex and sometimes litigious world of songwriting and music publishing. The Sheltons originally recorded "Just Because" at their first session in August 1933, and it was released on RCA Bluebird (B-6052) under the pseudonym of The Lone Star Cowboys. Composer credit went to the Attlesley brothers (the Sheltons' real family name) and a Leon Chappelear.

Two years later, they re-recorded the song and released it for Decca (5100), this time using their stage names, The Shelton Brothers. The writing credit now belonged to Joe and Bob Shelton, and a fellow composer named Sid Robin. At some point in this twenty-four-month process, the song became the property of Leeds Music, an ASCAP company founded in 1935.

Over a decade later, in the summer of 1948, Peer Publishing launched a lawsuit against Leeds claiming that *they* actually held the copyright on "Just Because". What's more, Peer insisted the song had been written, not by the Sheltons, but by Hubert Nelson and James Touchstone. And in conclusion, they demonstrated that it had been recorded and released by Nelstone's Hawaiians in 1929 (V-40273).

Leeds countered that the tune was ancient and in the public domain anyway. Peer, however, was adamant and pushed ahead with legal proceedings. All in all, it seemed like an awful lot of trouble to go to for a song that hadn't sold many records, nor much in the way of sheet music. But in the eyes of the publishing houses, every composition was an asset and a potential hit.

And you never knew who might record a song one day.

Billboard, 19th June, 7th & 14th August 1948

Pinney: love and marriage, III

MONDAY 27TH JUNE 1938
ALAMOGORDO, NEW MEXICO

PINNEY'S MARRIAGE TO IVA SANDERS ended in divorce. By this time, he was living in Sierra Blanca, Texas, on the highway, southeast of El Paso. Marrying an older woman hadn't worked out so, in the summer of 1938, Pinney reversed field and hitched up with Edna Winston. She was twenty-seven to his forty.

The wedding took place in Alamogordo, New Mexico, to the north, but they settled in El Paso and spent most of the next decade making a living in the lively border town.

Some remember Pinney rejoining the police department for a time. This being the case, doubtless he'd have impressed the new recruits with his skills as a mechanic and as a marksman. They'd have listened spellbound as he explained his credo for life: "I am a gentle person, as my friends know, and if a man needs and wants something I have, I will often give it to him. But don't let him try to take it away from me."

Tom hits the road

AT SOME POINT IN 1938
ON THE ROAD

FAME IS A FICKLE MISTRESS, as Gene Austin could testify. A decade earlier, he'd been perhaps the hottest singer in show business, helping to pioneer a new gentler form of singing that perfectly exploited modern recording techniques. Many, including Bing Crosby, followed in his footsteps, always acknowledging a stylistic debt to their predecessor.

Austin's 1928 Victor recording of "My Blue Heaven" (20964) was an industry phenomenon, selling an unmatched five million copies. But by the time he bumped into Tom Parker in 1938, the glory days were long gone and, rumour had it, so too was the money. His standing was much reduced and he had been usurped by his disciples.

Parker himself was branching out into assorted promotions and general hustling, and the chance to work with a star of Austin's former stature was irresistible. He hit the road, advertising the singer's forthcoming live appearances and built him up as if he was still a chart-topping act.

Parker's advertising methods were simple and direct: say it loud and then say it again. Essentially, he applied all he had learned about publicity from the carnival into this new venture. Classy and creative it was not, but it worked, and people flocked to see Gene Austin perform his biggest hits.

Their association lasted about a year, although Parker held onto his star's name for a while thereafter, knowing full well the suckers in the real world were often awed by that sort of thing.

The Colonel: The Extraordinary Story of Colonel Tom Parker and Elvis Presley, Alanna Nash

And now, a few words from Sara Carter

FEBRUARY 1939
RADIO XERA, VILLA ACUNA, MEXICO

SARA CARTER leaned into the radio mike late one night between songs, and did something completely out of character: she spoke. It had been almost six months since the Carters had moved to Texas to accept a contract on the powerful radio XERA, situated just over the Mexican border. Because the radio station was outside of U.S. jurisdiction, it could broadcast how and when it wanted, and the signal would penetrate for hundreds of miles across the continent. Consequently, the Carters' fame spread to a new level — and a bigger audience.

The Carters were still contracted to Mr Peer and to Decca Records, but performing daily on XERA guaranteed them a substantial listenership and a catch-free regular income: they didn't have to wait for the accountants to work out their royalties months after the fact. They also suspected that for every ten dollars they earned, Mr Peer picked up ten thousand.

Family relationships remained frosty, but polite. Six years had passed since Sara and her lover, Coy, were separated. They had tried to establish contact during that time but their letters were often intercepted. Sara needed to know if the torch she still carried was held in vain.

"I'd like to dedicate this next song to Coy Bays in California," she said, and then launched into the Carters' most popular and beautiful song of separation, "I'm Thinking Tonight of My Blue Eyes".

Over one thousand miles away, Coy Bays was tuned in and received the message loud and clear. He packed his bags and headed for the border. The couple married before the end of the month.

It is said that A.P. attended the ceremony, hidden at the back of the church, staring blankly ahead, like a dead man still standing.

Classic Country: Legends of Country Music, Charles K. Wolfe
Will You Miss Me When I'm Gone? The Carter Family & Their Legacy in American Music, Mark Zwonitzer with Charles Hirshberg

Daddy's home, II

MONDAY 6TH FEBRUARY 1939
EAST TUPELO, MISSISSIPPI

GLADYS PRESLEY LOST THE HOUSE. With Vernon locked up, she was unable to afford the repayments to Mr Bean and he demanded the key, so she and her son packed their sparse belongings and moved in with nearby family. Her husband's absence was the catalyst for a change in fun-loving Gladys. She became less open and more guarded. She smiled less and worried more.

In particular, she worried about Elvis, and became mildly (but understandably) obsessive about his wellbeing. She'd already lost a son, a husband and a home, so she watched over Elvis like a hawk. He became the centre of her life. As a result, they bonded very closely. To some extent, his adoration replaced the love of a husband, and she became his lost twin.

Vernon was released in early February 1939, having served less than a year. It had been difficult enough finding work before his misdemeanour, but it was almost impossible now he had a criminal record. On a practical level, the family had very few resources, so Gladys turned to the church. There would often be shared meals after the services, and she humbly took advantage of the Lord's bounty.

They also regularly took part in the lively and emotionally-charged worship. Vernon and Gladys found comfort in the inspiring sermons that promised better days to come and, having strong voices, they were happy to lose themselves in the congregational singing.

From his earliest days, Elvis would squirm off his mother's lap, and stumble his way to the front of the church, near the choir. He would clap along, and try to sing, noting how the adults smiled at his cute antics. He always associated the harmonious sound with happiness, love, and safety.

Gospel music became a sanctuary for Elvis — and he immersed himself in it at every opportunity.

Elvis & Gladys, Elaine Dundy
Last Train to Memphis: The Rise of Elvis Presley, Peter Guralnick

The Grapes of Wrath

EARLY APRIL 1939
SAN FRANCISCO, CALIFORNIA

SUCCESS CAME AT LAST TO John Steinbeck in 1937 with the publication of his novella *Of Mice and Men*. For the author, it was a double-edged sword: he loved the adulation, but hated the intrusion. All of this was amplified in April 1939 when he released his masterpiece, *The Grapes of Wrath*, a further study of the downtrodden underclass.

Both works were recognised as worthy and important, but Steinbeck faced considerable abuse from those who insisted he had a personal, un-American agenda, be it communist, Zionist, or socialist.

Chief among his detractors was the Congressman from Oklahoma, Lyle Boren, Mae's brother and confidant. He objected vehemently to Steinbeck's portrayal of Oklahomans, declaring, "The painting Steinbeck made is a lie, a black, infernal creation of a twisted, distorted mind," and the novel was banned by school boards in several states, including New York and California.

The book's title was chosen by Steinbeck's wife, Carol, and the author was so taken by it, he insisted the full text of "The Battle Hymn of the Republic" be printed in the endpapers.

And buried deep within the novel was Steinbeck's simple but heartfelt tribute to the beauty of those who could sing and play guitar, bringing comfort and inspiration to the common folk around them, culminating in this poignant thought —

And each wished he could pick a guitar, because it is a gracious thing.

John Steinbeck: A Biography, Jay Parini

Sam Phillips on Beale Street

AT SOME POINT IN 1939
BEALE STREET, MEMPHIS, TENNESSEE

HE HAD GROWN UP A SICKLY CHILD, but Sam Phillips retained a great belief in his own individuality, and realised he saw the world differently to most folks. White people around him were not necessarily "evil" but they seemed to recognise no particular problem in the way the Negro community was being subjugated. For Sam, however, personally and privately, it was a curiosity and a crime.

For several years, the Phillipses had shared their home with a blind black man down on his luck named "Uncle" Silas. He was a fellow of some wit and intelligence, with a gift for storytelling that Sam found irresistible. From Silas, Sam found confirmation that the soul of the black man was every bit as rich and precious as his own.

Therefore, when presented with the opportunity at the age of sixteen to go on a road trip to hear a noted preacher in Dallas with brother Jud and a carful of friends, he immediately accepted, knowing the journey would require a stopover in Memphis, and Sam would at last be able to see Beale Street with his own eyes. The city was already developing a reputation as a vibrant cultural centre and Beale Street was considered by many as the home of the blues and a focal point for black music. Silas had woven tales of Africa into stories of Beale Street, and Memphis had become a sort of Mecca for the teenager.

Upon arrival, Sam felt he had glimpsed heaven. His senses were joyously assaulted, not just by the occasionally outrageous sights and beautiful sounds, but more importantly by the taste of freedom itself that threatened to overwhelm him.

He made a decision that day: Memphis would be his city.

Sam Phillips: The Man who Invented Rock 'n' Roll, Peter Guralnick

The Pine Ridge Boys: "Sunshine"

TUESDAY 22ND AUGUST 1939
KIMBALL HOUSE HOTEL, ATLANTA, GEORGIA

FRANK WALKER'S REPUTATION within the music business continued to grow. Since moving from Columbia Records to RCA Victor, he'd re-doubled his efforts to source the best hillbilly acts and the best folk songs to record.

And so it was he found himself producing The Pine Ridge Boys' first recording session in a temporary studio on a hot summer's day in Atlanta. The duo, Marvin Taylor and Doug Spivey, had built a name for themselves with live performances and radio shows, and now they had a chance to endorse their fame by making records.

The first song they laid down was a new one to Walker, called "You Are My Sunshine".

"Nice tune," said Frank. "Did you write it yourselves?"

"No," came the response. "We picked it up from a red-headed girl from South Carolina. It wasn't her song either, but she said if we were going to record it we should get it copyrighted. Maybe we'll do that."

The single was released the following month (Bluebird-8263), listing the composer as "Traditional", and The Pine Ridge Boys never did get around to registering the copyright.

Pickin' on Peachtree: A History of Country Music in Atlanta, Georgia, Wayne W. Daniel

The Rice Brothers Gang: "Sunshine"

WEDNESDAY 13TH SEPTEMBER 1939
DECCA STUDIO, NEW YORK CITY, NEW YORK

PAUL RICE and his older brother Hoke fronted a five-piece band, and they made a reasonable living playing various radio shows and small gigs around the South. They'd been signed by Decca in 1938 and had recorded a couple of sessions. Though they were clearly a hillbilly group, they also dabbled in light classics and considered themselves a cut above the usual corny image, and the inclusion of a saxophone player within their line-up confirmed their ambition.

They'd spent some time in Shreveport, Louisiana, playing on station KWKH, and while there they made the acquaintance of newly-appointed Commissioner of Public Safety, Jimmie Davis, who was doing very nicely for himself on stage and off.

The disks released from the first Rice Brothers sessions hadn't sold well, but Decca invited them back to make some new recordings in September 1939. They captured eighteen songs that day, most of which were issued over the next couple of years and, according to The Rice Brothers, all bar one were cover versions.

Right in the middle of the session, Paul Rice brought out a song he insisted he'd written in 1937 entitled, "You Are My Sunshine", having apparently been inspired by a seventeen-page fan letter from a girl in South Carolina. The single was released in March of 1940 (Decca 5763), and it's likely the Rices used it as part of their live repertoire from this point on to ensure it received as much publicity as possible.

Sure enough, people began to hear the song, and it soon came to the attention of the Commissioner of Public Safety.

Pickin' on Peachtree: A History of Country Music in Atlanta, Georgia, Wayne W. Daniel
www.hillbilly-music.com

The Carters: the next generation

LATE SEPTEMBER 1939
RADIO XERA, SAN ANTONIO, TEXAS

ECK CARTER had all the nervous energy of his older brother, A.P., but it was welded to a sharp business brain. He could see The Carter Family musical unit was beginning to fail. Sara's re-marriage was putting a strain on the group. And maybe not this year, maybe not even next year, but soon, the original Carter Family would collapse.

So when he received an enquiry from recently relocated radio XERA about his and Maybelle's three daughters, he became very interested. The programmers wanted to know if Helen (12), June (10), and Anita (6) shared in the family talent and would they be interested in a performing contract? Eck assured them they *did* share in the family talent — and they *would* be very interested in a contract.

Helen played guitar and had a reasonable voice; Anita sang beautifully; but June ... well, June was something of a problem. She was a tomboy who had a gift for comedy, but the Carters didn't do comedy. They bought her an autoharp and, en route to Texas, she learned to accompany her sisters on a dozen songs.

They played with Maybelle, Sara and A.P., and also with Sara and A.P.'s children, becoming a popular radio attraction. A new generation of Carters had arrived.

Classic Country: Legends of Country Music, Charles K. Wolfe
Will You Miss Me When I'm Gone? The Carter Family & Their Legacy in American Music, Mark Zwonitzer with Charles Hirshberg

The birth of BMI

SATURDAY 14TH OCTOBER 1939
NEW YORK CITY, NEW YORK

ASCAP CONTINUED as a very successful company, but it conducted itself with all the quirks and foibles of a private gentlemen's club. Royalties were not distributed in a fashion that was always considered fair. New publishing houses joining ASCAP, for example, were often dismayed to discover they were on a much lower royalty rate than those who had joined when the company was originally founded in 1913. ASCAP was also sniffy about the type of songs it would accept: show tunes, light classical and popular numbers were approved, but many hillbilly, folk, blues, and R&B (rhythm & blues) songs were denied.

Broadcasters and radio stations were also frustrated by the somewhat arbitrary way in which fees were set for use of copyrighted songs. And when, in 1939, ASCAP announced they would double the charge, many within the industry felt a change was required.

Following a tense discussion at the National Association of Broadcasters' annual convention in September 1939, a rival organisation, Broadcast Music Inc. (BMI), was established in New York on 14th October, to represent the neglected niche musical genres. Thus encouraged, radio stations rejected ASCAP's demands and played only songs from non-ASCAP sources. As a consequence, BMI — and its members — reaped the rewards. And the general public were exposed to a much wider variety of folk music via the radio.

Progress was slow, but heads were turned when influential publishing giant Ralph Peer registered his vast catalogue with the new company. The conflict was resolved in May 1941 when a settlement was reached and ASCAP-managed songs returned to the airwaves, now played alongside tunes from the upstart BMI.

But, as the outside world slid into war, so too the music business seemed determined to do battle with itself: the conflict was not yet over.

Restless Giant: The Life and Times of Jean Aberbach & Hill and Range Songs, Bar Biszick-Lockwood

The gospel of Sam Phillips

OCTOBER 1939
NEAR FLORENCE, ALABAMA

HANDSOME WAS A WORD many would have applied to the young Sam Phillips. Charismatic was another. Precocious might also have made the list. He had a definite sense of style. His hair was combed just so, his clothes were smart and well pressed, and he was possessed of a remarkable self-confidence. He approached the local superintendent of schools and demanded to know why his school marching band — Sam was a competent if unspectacular drummer — was so poorly equipped.

Not only did Sam have a series of questions and complaints for the stone-faced official, he also had a number of solutions, one of which was that he would personally learn to play the sousaphone in order to improve the sound of the band. Sam adored the marches of Sousa and indeed loved music in general: that feeling of being wrapped up in sound was inspiring and comforting to him.

His mother's family were musically gifted and Sam felt himself pulled towards music of all types. The Phillipses' frugal income had allowed for the purchase of a record player and one 78rpm disk — a Jimmie Rodgers single — and although Sam knew his future was not that of a musician, he felt sure that music's ability to communicate across all barriers (age, race, sex, class) was a beautiful, perhaps almost a sacred thing.

It was brother Jud who had the fire and the brimstone in his voice, but if Sam could somehow harness the equality, the passion and the grace of music, then that surely would be a gospel worth preaching.

Sam Phillips: The Man who Invented Rock 'n' Roll, Peter Guralnick

On the way to Henderson

LATE 1939
CHESTER COUNTY, TENNESSEE

IN THE DECADE since the death of his father, Eddy Arnold had himself grown into a rugged and impressive figure of a man. After a one-off amateur appearance on a local radio station, he'd made the decision in his early teens to pursue the path of a guitar-playing singer, and had spent much of the past five years living hand-to-mouth in a bid to make his mark. Gene Autry (singer of "The Death of Jimmie Rodgers") was Eddy's idol, and he aimed to emulate the crooner's style.

Eddy had teamed up with a young fiddler named "Speedy" McNatt, and they'd played every imaginable sort of gig in a whole bunch of towns, but their big break wouldn't come. And while they remained friends, they drifted apart career-wise. Speedy then partnered Gabe Tucker, a Kentucky musician, and Eddy did accompany them every now and then, but it just wasn't working out.

So Eddy packed his bags and headed back to Henderson to take stock of his life. On the way home, he tuned in to station WSM and heard Pee Wee King and The Golden West Cowboys coming over loud and clear with their neat disciplined sound. Listening more closely, Eddy realised the group was missing the voice of its lead singer, Jack Skaggs. Putting two and two together, Arnold figured they'd parted company, and quickly composed a letter addressed to King and his manager, J.L. Frank, offering his services.

By early 1940, Eddy Arnold was employed as a vocalist and guitarist in the slickest hillbilly band in America, and was performing on the *Opry* most Saturday nights.

Eddy Arnold: Pioneer of the Nashville Sound, Michael Streissguth

Jimmie Davis: "Sunshine"

MONDAY 5TH FEBRUARY 1940
DECCA STUDIO, NEW YORK CITY, NEW YORK

JIMMIE DAVIS had been working part time in the music business for almost ten years. He'd recorded dozens of records — occasionally backed by The Shelton Brothers — and had registered a few hits. His career as a public servant had certainly benefited from his singing and playing. He'd also featured in a series of westerns with the likes of Jimmy Wakely and Tex Ritter. But in early 1940, Jimmie made a move that cemented his place in musical and political history.

He saw The Rice Brothers singing "You Are My Sunshine" at KWKH and felt sure he heard a potential hit record. So, after the show, Davis offered Paul Rice $35 for the copyright. Rice, who maybe hadn't even written the song anyway, was happy to see the dollar bills in his hand rather than wait months for the publishing company to send him a thin cheque.

The Rice Brothers' single had just been released so it still carried the Paul Rice composer credit, but on 30th January 1940, Davis and his bandleader Charles Mitchell registered the song with Southern Music Publishing, owned by Ralph Peer, and then recorded their own version six days later on 5th February 1940.

It was issued the following month (Decca 5813) and, with Davis' higher profile and wider contacts, it effortlessly outsold the previous two recordings, and became one of the most popular songs of all time across all genres. Jimmie Davis reaped the benefit in more ways than one: his bank account swelled; his popularity as a performer mushroomed; and four years later he was elected Governor of Louisiana.

You Are My Sunshine: The Jimmie Davis Story, Gus Weill
The New York Times, 6th November 2000

Tommy Durden: all at sea

TUESDAY 7TH MAY 1940
JACKSONVILLE, DUVAL, FLORIDA

TOMMY DURDEN MOVED OUT of the family home like his brothers and sisters before him. He roomed with a Mr H.W. Desportes, Jr, a bachelor and attorney-at-law who owned his own house on East First Street in Jacksonville.

The tall, gangly boy had grown into a tall, gangly man with a gentle nature and a deep voice. He was a friendly guy whose love of music had never left him. But a man needs to make a living and Tommy's father was dead set against him attempting any kind of career as an entertainer. So, Tommy signed up as a deck hand on a tug boat.

Thirty months later, when the world was in a yet darker place, he enlisted in the U.S. Navy, and through all of his time on ship, Tommy would sing for his crewmates; his gentle voice caressing pop, country and the occasional blues-type number.

Census 1940

The Pine Ridge Boys meet Steve Sholes

FRIDAY 11TH OCTOBER 1940
KIMBALL HOUSE HOTEL, ATLANTA, GEORGIA

STEVE SHOLES HAD FINALLY received the call he'd been waiting for. His boss, Frank Walker, had invited him down to Atlanta to supervise his first hillbilly session, a follow-up set of recordings for The Pine Ridge Boys.

Steve was still feeling a little fragile following his mother's death in the summer, but he was keen to show Walker he could handle this job. For the last four years he'd been moving up at RCA Victor. He was a quiet, urbane young man who didn't believe in making a scene or blowing his own trumpet. He felt that hard work would bring its own reward. Sometimes he even took a drop in salary to ensure he was moving in the right direction.

Hillbilly — and blues music, which also fell under Walker's remit — remained the poor cousin of pop for the major record labels. There was little attention paid to it from a marketing point of view, thus when Sholes or Walker pitched their recordings at the weekly label meetings, many of the executives left the room or fell asleep.

But Sholes was determined. He prepared for this session meticulously, booking a suitable room at the Kimball House Hotel, arranging for equipment and an engineer, and talking to Marvin and Doug about their suggested repertoire for the day.

Together they drew up a list of twelve songs — Steve wanted the session to be as productive as possible — and the one that caught Steve's eye and stayed in his memory for years to come was the fourth number, "Old Shep", as released by Red Foley on the Melotone label a few years prior.

It was a good day for Sholes, and his steady rise through the ranks, working in hillbilly and R&B, picked up pace from here on in.

Eddy Arnold: Pioneer of the Nashville Sound, Michael Streissguth
The Encyclopaedia of Country Music (Second Edition),
Edited by Paul Kingsbury, Michael McCall & John W. Rumble
Hank Williams: The Biography, Colin Escott with George Merritt & William MacEwen
Billboard, 20th March 1961

The dog catcher

WEDNESDAY 16TH OCTOBER 1940
HILLSBOROUGH COUNTY HUMANE SOCIETY, TAMPA, FLORIDA

EUROPE HAD BEEN AT WAR for over a year and America readied itself in case it too was dragged into the conflict. Eligible men were obliged to declare their status and, in October 1940, Tom Parker completed his registration card, still listing veteran pop singer Gene Austin as his official employer, and making no reference at all to his own previous military adventures.

Actually, Austin no longer played any part in the former carnival worker's life. Parker had since accepted a position well suited to his talents, having taken over at the Hillsborough County Humane Society. He was, as many have subsequently pointed out, the neighbourhood dog catcher.

But Parker embraced the job and, as with every situation in his life, approached it as if playing a game. He received free accommodation for himself and his family, free transport, and he came up with so many astonishing fund-raising ideas that the society actually began to turn a profit. This was unheard of, and he delighted in his own ingenuity, although several of the procedures were of a dubious moral nature. Regardless, he fed human interest stories about the animals to the local press who lapped it up.

For years to come, Parker would regale acquaintances with tales of the various wheezes he pulled in this role. The best one of all was the cemetery he opened in the back yard where, for a not insubstantial fee, bereaved owners could bury their beloved pets, complete with a hand-built casket, an overpriced headstone, and second-hand flowers.

All supplied by Tom Parker, of course.

The Colonel: The Extraordinary Story of Colonel Tom Parker and Elvis Presley, Alanna Nash

Roy Acuff's tears

PERHAPS 1941
MONTGOMERY, ALABAMA

EVERY ASPIRING MUSICIAN NEEDS A HERO. For seventeen year-old Hank Williams it was Roy Acuff. He loved the emotion that Roy poured into a song and tried to copy the sound that had become Acuff's trademark.

Hank's family had moved to Montgomery in 1937, and whenever Roy played locally Hank was sure to buy a ticket and hang around backstage with his guitar, just hoping for a chance to talk to the great man and maybe pick a little. Acuff was aware of the persistent skinny teenager, but paid him little mind.

Hank had already decided that music would be his career, and if he could follow in the footsteps of his idol he'd be happy. Acuff was the biggest hillbilly star on the circuit. You just booked a hall for him and the people came in their droves. Acuff stood in the spotlight, singing his heart out with tears rolling down his cheeks, and the audience in the palm of his hand.

Hank Williams: The Biography, Colin Escott with George Merritt & William MacEwen

Alvin's first day at Lake Geneva

SEPTEMBER 1941
LINN, WISCONSIN

ALVIN KROLIK REALLY WANTED to do well in class, but something would always distract him and then he was in trouble again. Everyone agreed he was bright; he just seemed to live in his own fantasy world most of the time.

In a loving attempt to straighten the boy out, his parents, Harry and Edith, secured a place for him at the military high school on the south shore of Lake Geneva in Wisconsin, eighty miles from their home in Chicago. The school catered for grades 9 to 12 and its key intention was to mould young men into outstanding citizens, using strict military structure and religious principles.

On his first day, as thirteen year-old Alvin familiarised himself with the building, he was struck by two enormous murals that took pride of place in the east and west wings. Donated by the classes of 1939 and 1940, and painted by noted Chicago artist, Louis Grell, the paintings depicted the 1841 meeting of fur trader John Kinzie with the Native American Potawatomi.

Alvin adored the murals and, in fact, fancied himself as an artist. Whether his creative inclinations could survive a four-year stint in a military academy remained to be seen.

Chicago Daily Tribune, Illinois, 22nd June 1952

"Howdee!"

PERHAPS LATE 1941
TAMPA, FLORIDA

TOM PARKER KNEW NOTHING at all about hillbilly music. What he did know, however, was when the big stars like Roy Acuff and Pee Wee King played in Florida, they did so to capacity crowds. As *Billboard* itself later pointed out, "There was gold in them thar hillbillies."

So Parker began to dabble in folk-based fund-raising concerts for the Humane Society, and he surprised himself with his determination and attention to detail. The performers were also pleased, and Roy Acuff even offered him a job, but Parker had no inclination to leave Tampa for Nashville at that time.

Other promoters put up posters: Parker papered the town. Other promoters took out clever radio spots: Parker kept the words simple and shouted loudly. He looked at the bigger picture and tied in local shops and businesses to offer discounts and vouchers for his customers, increasing his audience numbers and cutting down on advertising costs. Again, everything he'd learned about promotions from the Royal American, he applied to hillbilly music.

One of his regular performers was truly impressed by his ability to think outside of the box. Her name was Sarah Colley, an intelligent and well-read woman in her late twenties, who appeared under the stage name of Minnie Pearl, the eternally-frustrated hick spinster. She'd recently signed with the *Opry* and was on her way to becoming the South's premier comedienne. Her signature opening line, "Howdee!", would guarantee a raucous audience response.

She liked Tom, and would always happily join one of his concert parties. In an age when many *Opry* stars didn't even have bank accounts and carried their life savings in a suitcase, she recognised he was a forward thinker.

Actually, what he was thinking at that time was, going forward let's not raise funds for the Humane Society, let's just raise funds for me.

The Colonel: The Extraordinary Story of Colonel Tom Parker and Elvis Presley, Alanna Nash

"That's All Right"

LATE 1941
EAST TUPELO, MISSISSIPPI

Arthur "Big Boy" Crudup, Mississippi-born, was thirty-six years-old when he signed to RCA Bluebird to make some blues. He'd worked on the fringes for many years, but now he had his chance to strike it big. He was required to record four original songs in Chicago in November 1941. Never having written his own material before, he sought the counsel of fellow blues singer, Tampa Red. His advice was simple and direct: find an old blues; take a couple of lines; throw in some words of your own; and assemble a brand new song.

So, Crudup borrowed from his musical hero, Little Brother Montgomery, and also from blues giant, Blind Lemon Jefferson, and he wrote "If I Get Lucky". The single was released in late 1941 (RCA Bluebird 064876-1), and proved successful. Crudup loved the lyrics he'd part-assembled and part-written, particularly the opening words, "That's all right, mama." Indeed, he recycled these words over several songs, before finally going the whole hog and titling a 1946 release with that actual line. By that time, Steve Sholes, had achieved some influence in the R&B department of RCA and it's likely the record landed on his desk for approval before release.

Elvis Presley, meanwhile, perhaps as early as his seventh birthday, became familiar with the works of Arthur Crudup. There was a curious paradox within the boy's life. Although his mother, Gladys, was fanatical about his safety, she had every confidence she had raised him right — and his manners were impeccable. She knew that even if he was out of her sight, he would not be endangering himself or embarrassing the family name. Hence, he was at liberty to wander with considerable freedom.

Every now and then, he'd plant himself outside the local black church, and soak up the glorious gospel sounds. Other times, he'd wander down to the town's black quarter, named Shakerag, and hear the records of Arthur Crudup and many others, coming through the windows and doors.

There was the *Opry*, gospel, and blues. To Elvis it all came together in harmony in his head, like one beautiful symphony.

Last Train to Memphis: The Rise of Elvis Presley, Peter Guralnick
http://www.scottymoore.net/thatsallright.html

The Carter Family: *Life*

LATE NOVEMBER 1941
MACES SPRING, VIRGINIA

A.P. GREETED THE NEW YORK PHOTOGRAPHER graciously when he arrived for the shoot. Lord knows, the Carter house was not an easy place to get to, and the visitor looked tired and thirsty. *Life* magazine had taken note of the family and had decided to run a big feature on the Carters in the early December issue.

Whenever The Carter Family appeared in public, or visited a recording studio, they considered it a simple matter of pride to dress in their best going-to-meeting clothes. Not for them the hillbilly bibs and overalls. A.P. wore a suit and tie, and the Carter women dressed as fine as they could afford. Their fans and listeners loved them all the more for the way in which they presented themselves, avoiding the country hick clichés.

And so, hundreds of pictures were taken in and around the house, as A.P. and Sara once again put aside their personal differences for the sake of the family business. The photographer skilfully captured the somewhat incongruous images of the beautifully dressed Carters and their children in the rural setting. Young June in particular took great delight in posing for the camera, although she was convinced the New Yorker couldn't actually understand a word of her thick Virginia accent.

A.P. knew that a feature in *Life* magazine might be the key to a new level of national success. Hillbilly music still appealed to a mainly Southern market: this could be the beginning of something much bigger.

The photographer filled a whole basket with used flashbulbs, packed up his gear and started the long trek back to New York. The Carters waited patiently for the next issue of *Life* to hit the newsstand.

Just a few days later, on Sunday 7th December, Pearl Harbor was attacked and the press shifted their attention completely to the hostilities. The Carter Family story was shelved and it never did run.

Classic Country: Legends of Country Music, Charles K. Wolfe
Will You Miss Me When I'm Gone? The Carter Family & Their Legacy in American Music, Mark Zwonitzer with Charles Hirshberg

Sam Phillips for the defence

EARLY JANUARY 1942
NEAR FLORENCE, ALABAMA

ALMOST BY CHANCE, Sam Phillips had fallen into the world of radio broadcasting. Although his life was already busy — he still worked every day after school — in the summer of 1941 he decided that the cream of the school marching band should form a small dance orchestra too, playing popular tunes and swing numbers. Only the most committed players could sign up, and he drove them hard. With Sam at the helm, what they lacked in accuracy they made up for in enthusiasm.

As they arrived for a gig one night, Sam was surprised to discover the show would be broadcast on local radio. He was even more surprised when the producer suggested that, as band leader, Sam should do the on air announcements. He did it. He liked it. Word spread that here was a young man — he was still only nineteen — who knew how to communicate.

Soon, he was working every afternoon at station WLAY, but still Sam did not think of radio as a career. He believed he had already found his calling. He would study Law and become a Clarence Darrow, a champion of the underdog, a righter of wrongs. The drama of it appealed to him but, more importantly, this was how he would make a difference in the world.

Then, suddenly, life dealt three crushing blows, changing his destiny forever: Pearl Harbor was attacked, plunging America into the war; a month later in early January, Sam's father died; then, without consultation, Jud, Sam's older brother, joined the Marines, leaving Sam at home to fend for three dependents.

He painfully withdrew from school, and was obliged to speak to the draft board about taking his name off the list due to family hardship, which caused him no little shame. Sam kept his shattered dreams to himself, and carried on with his radio work.

For consolation he would turn to a book he'd received as a school prize several years earlier, named *I Dare You!*, a popular tome of inspirational thoughts. Among the many pages and messages, perhaps this is one that leapt out during Sam's darkest hour: *I dare you, young man, you who come from a home of poverty — I dare you to have the qualities of a Lincoln.*

Sam Phillips: The Man who Invented Rock 'n' Roll, Peter Guralnick

Mae tunes in

APRIL 1942
FREDERICK, OKLAHOMA

THE ATTACK ON PEARL HARBOR forced many American men to examine their own conscience, and John Axton was no exception. He and Mae were working at a school in Frederick — he coaching football, she teaching English, journalism and music — near the Oklahoma-Texas border, but John could hear the call of his country.

Mae, of course, was worried. Hoyt had just turned four and Johnny was only eighteen months. She would support her husband in whatever decision he made, but these were difficult times.

To keep her mind distracted, she listened to the radio while tending to their children, and in between the ominous news bulletins she kept hearing a bouncy mid-tempo song called "I'm Walking the Floor Over You". It was a hillbilly number, not a genre with which Mae was familiar, and it had been a hit on the folk chart for several months. But now it was being played on pop stations too — indeed, Bing Crosby would soon record a cover version — becoming what the music business called a "crossover hit".

It had broken through as an honest-to-goodness *pop* song. And this was one of those rare occurences when folk songwriters and publishers made serious money, as the song sold all over the nation and, indeed, all over the world. For a hillbilly artist to also be a pop(ular) singer or to record a pop(ular) hit was a sign they had truly made the big time.

Having grown so attached to the song, Mae listened to the announcer to see who was singing. And to her absolute astonishment she discovered it was none other than Mr Ernest Tubb — her little blue-eyed friend from the great state of Texas.

Country Singers As I Know 'Em, Mae Boren Axton
Ernest Tubb: The Texas Troubadour, Ronnie Pugh

Roy, Fred and Jenny

AT SOME POINT IN 1942
ACUFF-ROSE MUSIC PUBLISHERS, NASHVILLE, TENNESSEE

FRED ROSE HAD BEEN just what Roy Acuff was looking for: an honest songwriter with an eye for business. In 1942, they formed Acuff-Rose, the first Nashville-based song publishing company, to look after their own songs and attract other hillbilly writers too.

Actually, some were now referring to the genre as country & western (c&w), in an attempt to elevate its status. But whatever it was called, the talent soon came rolling in, and dozens of aspiring composers stepped through the front door of Acuff-Rose.

And Fred had a useful gift for improving songs. Wishful tunesmiths came to him with their drafts and he'd re-arrange the words or change a note and presto! — the song became a commercial juggernaut. Sometimes Fred took a writer's credit for his work, other times he was happy just to get the copyright. Acuff-Rose soon became *the* place in Nashville to publish your new hillbilly song.

Fred Rose was a recovering alcoholic who stayed on the straight and narrow as far as booze was concerned, but when pretty brunette Jenny Lou Carson stepped into his office he knew he was facing a different sort of temptation.

Carson, sister of Red Foley's second wife, had come to see Rose about the possibility of having some of her songs published. She had talent and Rose recognised it straight away, even if the idea of a female songwriter in Nashville seemed a little … weird.

Fred took good care of Jenny Lou. And her songs.

Christmas is banned (almost)

FRIDAY 29TH MAY 1942
LOS ANGELES, CALIFORNIA

POPULAR SINGERS CAME AND WENT, but still Bing Crosby remained untouchable. To have Bing record your song was a guarantee of success, and that's why Irving Berlin had sought him out to capture his latest composition, "White Christmas". The composer was convinced the song was a potential monster hit and had written a movie, *Holiday Inn*, around it. In May 1942, Bing recorded the soundtrack, laying down the central song in just two takes, accompanied by The Ken Darby Singers.

Crosby's session was quickly squeezed in, along with dozens of others for top artists, to avoid the latest trouble to hit the music business. James Petrillo, president of the American Federation of Musicians, had called for a recording ban from 1st August 1942 as a protest against the lack of royalty payments to musicians. They could still play live concerts and also record patriotic V-disks, but all other sessions were prohibited.

For the most part the strike held firm, and when stockpiled recordings began to run out the big record companies eventually started talking to the unions. The ban officially ended on 11th November 1944, RCA Victor being one of the last to capitulate.

"White Christmas", meanwhile, released in 1942 (Decca 18429), became the biggest-selling record of all time, soon overtaking the previous title holder, "My Blue Heaven", confirming Crosby's reputation as a hit-maker without equal.

Billboard, 1st November 1947

Technical Advisor, I

AUGUST 1942
TAMPA, FLORIDA

TOM PARKER could not have been more excited. In his official role as manager of the Humane Society, he'd been invited by a Warner Brothers film crew to supply dogs on a local movie set for a specific scene. So he assembled his cast, and drove down to Drew Field where the production of *Air Force* was being filmed.

The top man was Hal Wallis, one of the most successful producers in Hollywood — he was currently also working on *Casablanca*, directed by Michael Curtiz — and Parker was starstruck when he wandered around the set.

Now, come along with me on a little diversion here: let's say it's likely Tom got talking to some of the bigwigs loitering behind the camera. That's possible, yes? Maybe he asked them if, as official provider of the dogs, perhaps his name might be featured in the credits. That's also possible, agreed?

What if, to fob him off, one of those guys told Parker, "Sure, your name will be credited on screen. We'll call you the … the Technical Advisor." So Parker might have gone home that day, pleased as punch. Imagine how he'd have felt when he watched the finished movie several months later, and his name was not mentioned at all. Imagine what he might have cooked up in his head by way of revenge. Of course, he had no influence, no power at the moment, but one day …

The Colonel: The Extraordinary Story of Colonel Tom Parker and Elvis Presley, Alanna Nash

The Carter Sisters and Mother Maybelle

MARCH 1943
RADIO WBT, CHARLOTTE, NORTH CAROLINA

THE ORIGINAL CARTER FAMILY disbanded as quietly as it had formed. When their last radio contract expired in Charlotte in March 1943, they went their separate ways without announcement or fanfare.

But Eck and Maybelle had made their own plans. In June, they hit the road as "The Carter Sisters and Mother Maybelle". The Carter name still carried some weight but it would be no easy ride. Maybelle led the troupe as singer and guitarist; Eck was the full-time manager; Helen sang and played accordion; and Anita was singing and working on bass fiddle.

June carried on being June. Maybelle had introduced her to Minnie Pearl, who had encouraged her comedy ambitions. She gave June some old scripts and advised, "Read these but don't imitate me. Create your own character."

June took the advice to heart and invented a different approach. One time, she walked across the stage dragging a long wooden plank.

"Hey, where you going?" asked Maybelle, playing the stooge from the microphone.

"I'm looking for a room," she deadpanned. "I've got my board."

Will You Miss Me When I'm Gone? The Carter Family & Their Legacy in American Music, Mark Zwonitzer with Charles Hirshberg

Johnny Bragg: in the jailhouse now

THURSDAY 6TH MAY 1943
STATE PRISON, NASHVILLE, TENNESSEE

JOHNNY BRAGG STARTED SERVING HIS 594-year prison sentence on 6th May 1943, his seventeenth birthday. As a Southern black boy, unjustly framed for several crimes, he knew he had little chance of ever seeing the outside world again. Behind bars, he quickly learned to keep himself to himself and stay out of trouble. Difficult inmates had been known to simply disappear overnight.

For several years, Bragg just drifted through prison life: he had nothing to aim for, and no hope of escape or release. Eventually, he noticed acapella vocal groups harmonising in the courtyard and lunchroom. Bragg had a musical ear and could spot the strengths and weaknesses of individual singers. He also had a wide musical palette, and a liking for white pop music — and not just stereotypical R&B and gospel.

Most importantly, he was intelligent enough to understand that the imprisoned singers found a personal freedom in their performances. Before long, he lent his strong tenor to one amateurish group and took on a position of leadership within the quintet.

Under his guidance, they dubbed themselves The Prisonaires, and Bragg became fascinated with all aspects of the group's work, from repertoire to harmony and, though illiterate, he began writing original songs.

The group sang at Sunday prison services and the chaplain would also request a special recital before each execution. Johnny and the boys would sing a tearful spiritual while the prisoner was strapped to the chair. When the deed was done, Bragg volunteered to remain behind and help remove the body, aware that one day it could be him being serenaded.

Just Walkin' in the Rain, Jay Warner

Eddy Arnold: on my own

MAY 1943
MONTGOMERY, ALABAMA

THERE WAS AN open agreement within The Golden West Cowboys: anyone who felt they could better themselves was free to move on at any time. Eddy Arnold had married Sally Grayhart in November 1941 and she'd been a constant source of support, encouraging him to aim higher. He'd also spoken to station manager Harry Stone at WSM, and he had offered a solo radio show if and when Eddy moved out on his own.

That day came in May 1943 when the Cowboys were playing the City Auditorium in Montgomery. The parting was amicable and Eddy took with him two valuable lessons: firstly, the importance of assembling a trusted band around you; secondly, it was essential to have good management.

So Eddy hired Speedy McNatt and Gabe Tucker and added Leroy Wiggins on steel guitar, calling themselves Eddy Arnold and his Tennessee Plowboys. Soon they would be small-time regulars on the *Opry* roster.

And on 5th October 1943, Eddy signed a management contract with Dean Upson, newly-appointed head of the Artists Service Bureau at the *Opry*. It was his job to find bookings for *Opry* performers, and he ensured WSM took the customary fifteen percent fee for all gigs that mentioned the radio show by name. This was not at all popular with the artists, who felt it was unfair exploitation.

Dean Upson was a hardworking man but he was no J.L. Frank. He had requested a five-year contract, but cautious Eddy signed for twelve months with an additional one-year option. One of Upson's first official acts was to negotiate and complete a recording deal for Eddy with RCA Victor.

Imagine Eddy's joy when he received this news. But then imagine his frustration when he remembered his contract was effectively nullified by the nationwide recording ban.

Eddy Arnold: Pioneer of the Nashville Sound, Michael Streissguth

Sam Phillips: wired for sound

MONDAY 13TH DECEMBER 1943
NEAR FLORENCE, ALABAMA

ON THE DAY SHE FIRST SAW SAM PHILLIPS, Becky Burns knew she'd met the man she would marry. Their courtship lasted a little over two years, and they wed quietly in the weeks leading up to Christmas 1943. Sam was drawn to her not just for her looks and intelligence, but because she had one of the best damn radio voices he'd ever heard. She'd considered a career as a singer or a station announcer, but so devoted was she to her new husband she put her ambitions aside and concentrated on supporting him in his work.

Sam was now completely obsessed by the world of sound. He continued working in radio and took his passion to an extreme level: he studied electrical engineering; he catalogued all the records in the station library; he went through every individual song and worked out the precise settings required for them to be played over the air with maximum fidelity (78rpm disks usually sounded awful on the radio, but not on Sam's shows).

He worked long hours with feverish determination and, in the late spring of 1944, he suffered what amounted to a nervous breakdown, checking himself into a sanatorium for several weeks. Upon his release, he was relieved of his job so went looking further afield, in particular Nashville, the city that was becoming a serious player in hillbilly music.

He auditioned at WSM, knowing full well he had neither the experience nor the timbre to claim a spot as an *Opry* announcer. Sam was interviewed by a fellow named Jim Bulleit, with whom he'd had previous commercial dealings. Bulleit himself had a fine speaking voice and an extensive vocabulary. He wore many different hats in the music business, being much too perky and enthusiastic for just one job. He liked Sam, but he turned him down, as anticipated.

Sam was nothing if not determined and he landed a spot on radio WLAC in Nashville. Geographically, it was a step in the opposite direction to Memphis, his dream location. But Sam knew it was the right move.

Sam Phillips: The Man who Invented Rock 'n' Roll, Peter Guralnick

Mississippi Slim

AT SOME POINT IN THE EARLY 1940S
NETTLETON, MISSISSIPPI

As per his contract, Tex Ritter was obliged to tour the country with his latest western movie. Between film shows, Tex would take to the stage and entertain the crowd. It was a good promotional tool for the studios, but it meant Tex (and many other B-movie stars) was required to play in every backwater theatre known to man. Glamorous it was not.

And so it was that Tex came to Nettleton, Mississippi, and as he signed autographs and showed off his six-guns, he noticed a familiar face in the audience. Carvel Ausborn, who sang country songs under the name of Mississippi Slim, was smiling up at the star, and standing beside him was his excited kid brother, James.

Historically speaking, Mississippi Slim was a nobody. He played small gigs and sang on local radio stations, and just about scratched a living. He idolised Jimmie Rodgers and Ernest Tubb. He had distant family connections to people who worked with the likes of Minnie Pearl, but Slim knew he had already reached his own personal career peak.

Almost every professional country musician that passed through these parts had played with Slim at some point, and they all respected him. He sang pleasantly, and looked the part with his cowboy shirt and neckerchief. But there were hundreds — maybe thousands — of players like Slim all over the South. They'd all harboured dreams of great success and fame when they started out, but those hopes had long since faded.

But today was a red letter day for Mississippi Slim: he had been singled out by Tex Ritter, and the movie star had invited him to come up on the stage and sing a song or two for the people. It was moments like this that made it all worthwhile.

Last Train to Memphis: The Rise of Elvis Presley, Peter Guralnick

Whither thou goest, I will go

LATE SEPTEMBER 1944
NEW YORK

JOHN AXTON VOLUNTEERED for naval service and was posted to New York for training. For Mae, there was no question that she and the boys would accompany him: that's how important the concept of Family was to her. So they packed their belongings and rented a new place as near as possible to the military base.

In late September 1944, Lt John Axton received his posting: he would serve in the South Pacific, a theatre of war fraught with danger. Mae, thinking on her feet, arranged for a family photograph to be taken before John was transferred. With their husband and father gone, Mae, Hoyt and Johnny had little option but to return to Ada, Oklahoma.

For the next eighteen months, Mae did her considerable best to give her sons a normal life — visits to grandparents, football games, birthday parties — and she continued her occasional forays into journalism to pick up a few extra dollars whenever possible.

Of course, not all of her writing was for financial gain. She loved to immerse herself in poetry, and sometimes wrote a stanza or two, revealing a touch of the melodramatic — "And left me to suffocate and die amidst a murky, musty gloom, until a single tear appeared to rescue me."

Every telegram or phone call could bring the worst kind of news, and Mae found great comfort in her beloved words.

Country Singers As I Know 'Em, Mae Boren Axton
Ada Evening News, Oklahoma, 26th September 1944
Personal correspondence between Lyle Boren & Mae Boren Axton

The death of Bozo the Wonder Dog

MONDAY 13TH NOVEMBER 1944
MIAMI, FLORIDA

THE SHOWMEN'S LEAGUE OF AMERICA continued to open new offices across the nation and, in early 1944, the Miami chapter was established. On 13th November, Tom Parker was welcomed into this branch, having been nominated by (future league president) Ben Weiss. To all intents and purposes, this marked Tom Parker's official entry into show business. And his arrival coincided with a decision to leave the Humane Society and move full time into music promotion.

Parker finished his stint at the Society with a flourish. Bozo the Wonder Dog had died at the end of October, having allegedly entertained forty-million paying customers and earned $100,000 for his owner, Captain Lower. Parker organised a purpose-built silk-lined casket, and ordered a monument with the dog's picture in glass.

The owner collected a $10,000 insurance policy on Bozo, his four-legged star, who throughout his extensive career had demonstrated remarkable feats of mind-reading. But it didn't take a mind-reader to figure out that Parker would have extracted every possible cent from the grieving Captain Lower.

Billboard, 25th November 1944 & 5th February 1954
Ironwood Daily Globe, Michigan, 5th November 1943

Eddy Arnold records in Nashville

MONDAY 4TH DECEMBER 1944
WSM STUDIO, NASHVILLE, TENNESSEE

LESS THAN A MONTH after the long-running recording dispute was settled, Eddy Arnold was booked in for his first session. And RCA Victor, hoping to secure as much music as possible, was happy to allow Eddy to sing in the radio WSM studio, Nashville, rather than delay the procedure by transporting him and his band to its Chicago set-up. Accordingly, Eddy became the first ever folk artist to hold a significant recording session in Nashville.

He laid down four songs on 4th December 1944, which resulted in a couple of modest placings on the *Billboard* C&W chart, but sales were far too small to trouble the magazine's pop listing (and Eddy's music was the wrong colour to feature on the R&B chart). Subsequent sessions produced further minor hits but Eddy began to slowly make his mark.

Shortly before Eddy's debut RCA session, he had renewed his rolling one-year contract with manager Dean Upson, and it was at this time that he first bumped into Tom Parker, the man who would change his life. Parker was working in advance promotions and he found himself backstage at the *Opry*. He struck up a brief and innocent conversation with Eddy at the Ryman Auditorium, and made a definite impression on the Tennessee Plowboy, as Eddy was now nicknamed.

A brief time later, Parker was doing some work in Tampa for Jim Bulleit (who was wearing his promoter hat on that day), and the Plowboy just happened to be on the bill. Tom and Eddy picked up their previous conversation and Eddy was mighty impressed with Tom's big-talking vision of Eddy's future career. In fact, for the next few months, it seemed every time Eddy turned around, Tom Parker was just a-walking by.

Eddy Arnold: Pioneer of the Nashville Sound, Michael Streissguth

The rise of Hill & Range, I

SATURDAY 9TH DECEMBER 1944
NEW YORK CITY, NEW YORK

JULIAN AND JEAN ABERBACH, Austrian brothers who had fled Europe to avoid the Nazis, registered their own BMI music publishing company, Hill & Range Songs, on 9th December 1944. They had a history in publishing, focusing mainly on show tunes, but since arriving in America they'd spotted a potentially lucrative hole in the market: country & western music (hence the obvious pun in the company name).

They were quick-witted, suave, and hard-working, and were always looking for a new angle. Their intention was to target influential people within the industry, and top of their list was recently-demobbed Steve Sholes at RCA Victor, particularly when he signed popular group The Sons of the Pioneers just after Christmas. Sholes steered the Pioneers away from the hillbilly market and moved them towards the pop chart. It was a financially sound policy, and the Aberbachs were keen to supply good quality, appropriate material — to the Pioneers and to Sholes.

Steve would soon be appointed Studio and Custom Manager of RCA Records, as well as Manager of Country & Western and Rhythm & Blues Repertoire. He was a big fish in a small pond. Hillbilly and race records, as some still called them, provided useful extra revenue for the major labels, but were only a very small part of their general income. Steve Sholes was determined to see his portion of the market increase, and put plans in place to help realise this. Finding the right artists and the best songs was key to his strategy.

Jean Aberbach had an ace-in-the-hole with regard to Sholes: they'd met in the early 1940s when Steve was serving in the army's V-disk project. Sholes had been one of a six-man team responsible for selecting all of the morale-boosting music. He was instantly impressed with Jean's cultured approach to life, and recognised his own spirit of politeness and diligence within the Austrian.

The two became friends, often relying upon the other's taste and judgement during business negotiations. It was a mutually satisfying relationship; and one that bode well for the future.

Restless Giant: The Life and Times of Jean Aberbach & Hill and Range Songs, Bar Biszick-Lockwood
Billboard, 4th May 1968

Colonel Fred Rose

EARLY APRIL 1945
BATON ROUGE, LOUISIANA

As governor of Louisiana, Jimmie Davis carried all sorts of unusual powers, including the right to confer the rank of honorary Colonel upon the great and the good. The title itself carried no authority, but for those who chose to actually use it — and not everybody did — it suggested a certain air of gravitas.

Fred Rose was appointed Colonel by Governor Davis in the early spring of 1945. Fred and Jimmie had been friends for several years and their paths had crossed many times backstage. For Fred Rose, whose music publishing concern, Acuff-Rose, was going from strength to strength, this simply reinforced his unassailable position at the top of the ladder.

Billboard, 7th April 1945

Tex Ritter, Capitol recording artist

TUESDAY 1ST MAY 1945
RADIO RECORDERS STUDIO, LOS ANGELES, CALIFORNIA

When Tex Ritter's movie career petered out, a new door opened. In the early summer of 1942, Tex had been one of the first artists to sign for the fledgling Capitol Records company. He'd had precious few hits during the previous decade with Columbia and Decca, but now he felt things were looking up.

Slowly but surely, he started making progress as a recording star, and by 1944 he'd registered his first hillbilly number one record with "I'm Wasting my Tears on You" (Capitol 174), which also reached number eleven on the pop chart, a rare and notable occurrence.

Success breeds success: Ritter was now a big man in the music business and better songs began to come his way. On 1st May 1945, he arrived at the RCA-owned Radio Recorders Studio in Los Angeles and laid down a new song for Capitol written by Jenny Lou Carson that he hoped would also hit the top spot. Carson had composed "You Two-Timed Me One Time Too Often" and published it — naturally — through Acuff-Rose.

Ritter's instincts were right. The song became the biggest hillbilly disk of the late summer (Capitol 206) and confirmed his place at the top table. But Tex was always gracious. When younger artists came to him for advice and guidance, he didn't hesitate to offer help. For example, when up-and-coming fellow Texan, Henry "Hank" Thompson, caught Ritter's eye, he gladly recommended him to Capitol and they wisely snapped him up.

Tex himself was, of course, pleased with this new chapter in his life. His second hillbilly number one hit brought with it a sense of having arrived. It was a good song. Quite remarkably, it also marked the first time a female songwriter had hit the top spot in the country chart. Clearly, the times they were a-changing.

Country Music, U.S.A. (Second Revised Edition), Bill C. Malone

Hula Boogie, I

MONDAY 21ST MAY 1945
COLD BAY, ALASKA

ALMOST TWO YEARS into his navy service, Tommy Durden was transferred to the newly-built minesweeper U.S.S. *Mirth* and sailed for duty in Bermuda, operating from St George's Bay, sweeping the channels and conducting anti-submarine patrols. By Valentine's Day 1945 the ship was en route to the Panama Canal.

It was at this point, however, that Tommy and his fellow crewmates began to wonder what the hell was going on. Without warning, they turned north and headed for Alaska, and on 3rd May they anchored in Cold Bay along with two hundred and fifty other American craft.

The *Mirth* had been selected to take part in a top secret mission codenamed Project Hula. Joseph Stalin, the Russian leader, was apparently very keen to participate in the allied naval push against Japan and he had plenty of sailors. But what he lacked were ships. Following confidential negotiations, the Americans agreed to lend part of their fleet to the Russians and they converged in Alaska in the spring for the handover.

For several days, the U.S. sailors talked their Soviet counterparts through the ins and outs of their new vessels and on 21st May, mission accomplished, Tommy Durden boarded a ship bound for Washington. From there he journeyed home to Florida. Tommy's war was over.

Some time later, the American government made polite enquires about the return of their craft, but by then the Cold War had begun and the Russians were no longer dancing to Project Hula.

Project Hula: Secret Soviet-American Cooperation in the War against Japan, Richard A. Russell
U.S. World War II Navy Muster Rolls 1938-1948 for the period ending 21st May 1945

Sam Phillips reaches heaven

TUESDAY 26TH JUNE 1945
MEMPHIS, TENNESSEE

SAM PHILLIPS HAD NEVER BEEN LATE FOR WORK. But on 26th June 1945, his very first day of radio employment in Memphis, he overslept. He was twenty-two years-old, a husband and a father, and he'd secured a job at station WREC, where his reputation and duties rapidly expanded as the owners recognised his talent and expertise. This was what he'd dreamed of for years. He was working in the music business in his favourite city in the whole wide world.

One of his roles was that of engineer and producer for the live broadcasts of the big swing bands, like Tommy Dorsey and Freddy Miller. There were no appearances from the great black band leaders: no Count Basie, no Duke Ellington. That's just how Memphis was, and it burned Sam, not just the absurd inequality of the situation, but that white Memphis was missing out on such fabulous music.

Sam became the in-demand engineer for the big band sessions. He developed great precision in microphone placement and even followed the sheet music to ensure the relevant soloists would be properly highlighted. He also insisted on pushing the rhythm section way up front contrary to popular practice. It all required some skill and a lot of nerve, qualities that Sam held in spades.

But as happy and comfortable as he was in his job, he still felt the pull of his old calling. Was he making a difference? He was living in Memphis and he was working with white bands for a white radio station and all around him, on Beale and beyond, black artists were making astonishing music with little opportunity for it to be properly heard. The pressure for Sam to do something about it became more and more insistent.

Sam Phillips: The Man who Invented Rock 'n' Roll, Peter Guralnick

The Bad Nauheim tapes, I

JULY 1945
BAD NAUHEIM, GERMANY

THE GERMAN ARMY COLLAPSED and the allied troops swept across Europe, eventually moving into Germany itself. Jack Mullin, U.S. soldier and army electronics expert, rolled into Bad Nauheim near Frankfurt looking for something he'd never seen but had heard nightly on German radio: a medium for recording and playing back near-perfect sound. Back home in the States, music was recorded directly to disk which allowed no editing and was limited in terms of clarity. Pre-war records, generally speaking, were of too poor a quality to be played over the radio, hence the requirement for live broadcast performance.

But Mullin had heard the Berlin Philharmonic apparently playing through the night on German stations, and the sound was much too good to have been disk-recorded. Had Hitler really ordered the musicians to play live from dusk until dawn, or was there a secret recording method waiting to be liberated along with the rest of Europe?

Mullin found his answer in a castle in Bad Nauheim: reels of magnetic tape and a recording device named the Magnetophon. Mullin filed his official report and, as the war came to its end, he disassembled the tape-recording machine and, to conform with regulations, shipped it back to his home address in thirty-five separate packages.

The following year, he demonstrated the new recording technique to Bing Crosby who immediately understood its implications and invested $50,000 of his own personal fortune into the small electronics firm, Ampex, who were interested in working with Mullin. Crosby had grown tired of performing live on various radio shows and would have preferred to pre-record his contributions. The invention of magnetic tape machines made this a viable option because of the superior sound quality on offer.

The music industry quickly cottoned on to the potential of this new recording method, which would also allow for editing and overdubbing. Thus, Ampex machines became an essential product for all serious radio and recording operations, and Bing Crosby's investment became one of the smartest moves in entertainment history.

Bing Crosby and Magnetic Recording, John Vardalas, Ph.D.
Pavek Museum of Broadcasting: http://www.pavekmuseum.org/jmullin.html

Elvis Presley: when I was a boy

WEDNESDAY 3RD OCTOBER 1945
FAIR AND DAIRY SHOW, TUPELO, MISSISSIPPI

ELVIS PRESLEY WAS A SHY, well-mannered ten year-old boy. He wore glasses; his blond hair was unruly, no matter how much his mother attempted to smooth it down; and he struggled with a stutter. In school photographs, he was the only child in dungarees, but no one noticed because so often he just blended into the background.

It was a matter of some surprise then, that he found himself on stage in front of hundreds of people at the annual Mississippi-Alabama Fair and Dairy Show, preparing to sing in a children's talent contest. The competitors were all white, though one boy was done up as a blackface minstrel. Several wore costumes, and some had extensive experience of performing. But not Elvis. He didn't even have accompanying music — he'd be singing on his own.

His choice of repertoire was unusual; Red Foley's "Old Shep" was the tune. But this was a song that haunted the youngster, because he could relate to it all too well. His own faithful dog, Tex, had succumbed to mange and had been destroyed. And, perhaps for the first time outside of his beloved gospel music, the young Elvis Presley related emotionally to a song and also — crucially — found he could affect others by his singing: grown women became teary when he'd crooned the number in school assembly.

The emcee lowered the microphone and Elvis sang his heart out for three minutes. He took fifth place, and was very happy with that, walking on air for the rest of the day. Or at least until he stepped out of line, and his mother slapped his behind, puncturing his ego completely.

His family were proud of him, but no one was happier than Mrs Oleta Grimes, the school teacher who had put his name forward for the contest, having been so moved by his school assembly performance. Mrs Grimes was, as all in Tupelo knew, the daughter of wealthy land-owner — and the Presleys' nemesis — Orville Bean.

Life's funny that way, sometimes, isn't it.

Elvis & Gladys, Elaine Dundy
Last Train to Memphis: The Rise of Elvis Presley, Peter Guralnick

Eddy signs with Tom

OCTOBER 1945
TAMPA, FLORIDA

IN OCTOBER 1945, when his contract with Dean Upson expired, Eddy Arnold signed with Tom Parker, giving twenty-five percent to guarantee his new manager's exclusive services. As a regular on the *Opry* and holding an RCA Victor contract, he was well placed to go forward with the right representation. And Eddy, now aged twenty-seven, was convinced that Parker was the man to lead the way.

Upson was not pleased, but he had bigger fish to fry at that time. On a separate point of principle, he resigned his position at the *Opry* and moved on to Shreveport where he joined radio station KWKH which was looking to set up its own rival show entitled the *Louisiana Hayride*.

Tom Parker, meanwhile mapped out his plan for Eddy Arnold, and it was one which would take a hillbilly singer much further than anyone had before dared hope. Steve Sholes at RCA Victor had also taken notice of his company's new recording artist, and was now personally supervising the sessions, helping to pick out the best songs.

Eddy was not a prolific songwriter but his name did occasionally appear as a co-writer on his records. This was often due to a common industry practice whereby the singer would be given a writer's credit as an extra incentive to record the song. Although this may seem unfair or perhaps even dishonest, a mediocre song would often achieve success because of a singer's reputation or talent, which did justify the situation morally.

At this point, Eddy had the ideal manager and a top producer on board. All he now needed was a regular supply of good tunes.

Eddy Arnold: Pioneer of the Nashville Sound, Michael Streissguth
Louisiana Hayride: Radio and Roots Music along the Red River, Tracey E.W. Laird

When Tommy met Boots

PERHAPS AUTUMN 1945
TALLAHASSEE, FLORIDA

BACK ON DRY LAND and released from service on 24th October, Tommy Durden, civilian, moved in with his parents in Welaka, Florida, and decided to pursue his dream of working in the music business. His father was still sceptical, but Tommy insisted he'd be so successful he'd drive up one day in a pea-green Cadillac.

Before the end of the year he'd joined a travelling tent troupe out of Kentucky and was working a show called the *All-American Barn Dance* as a steel guitar player. It was when they hit Tallahassee that Tommy first ran into Betty Lee "Boots" Gilbert of The Gilbert Sisters backstage. Boots' siblings, Wink and Dot, were married to two other cast members, and Tommy just took to them all right away. He loved to sit in with the extended family as they played, and it seemed obvious to all concerned that the six of them should get together and perform as a unit. And that's exactly what they did — and as they often found themselves accompanying singing cowboys, they dubbed themselves The Westernaires.

It was also obvious that Tommy was smitten with Boots, and he wooed her with his usual mixture of modesty, good humour and gentleness. In turn, Boots was taken with Tommy's polite ways and she really liked him — heck, everybody liked Tommy — and eventually he won her over.

On Tuesday 8th April 1947 they tied the knot in Harrison County, Mississippi, and Tommy was sure he'd found the love of his life.

Detroit Country Music: Mountaineers, Cowboys and Rockabillies, Craig Maki with Keith Cady
Author's correspondence with Boots Gilbert's family
Department of Veterans Affairs BIRLS Death File, 1850-2010
Florida State Population Census 1945

Jack Stapp comes home

NOVEMBER 1945
RYMAN AUDITORIUM, NASHVILLE, TENNESSEE

IT HAD TAKEN JIM DENNY almost twenty years to climb to the top of the *Opry* tree but he'd done it. His early days as a bouncer and mail-room clerk were far behind him. As the House Manager and soon-to-be Head of the *Opry* Artists Service Bureau (replacing Dean Upson), he was one of the three most powerful men in country music. One of the others, Harry Stone, Station Manager, was standing beside him and together they greeted the third as he walked through the door.

"Welcome home, Jack," said Denny. Jack Stapp smiled at his colleagues and affirmed it was good to be back and he was looking forward to resuming the job he'd started in 1939. Stapp had spent the previous twenty-two months on active service in London broadcasting Allied propaganda.

As WSM Programme Director and Head of Recruiting New Talent, his influence and importance was every bit as far-reaching as his colleagues. They were all astute businessmen with a clear understanding of how to make the *Opry* grow even bigger. They needed stars, great show people who made great hit records. They decided to seek out only the best country *&* western performers and they resolved that the *Opry* touring shows would play only the most prestigious venues.

Thus, Stone, Denny and Stapp dragged the quaint and antiquated *Opry* into the modern post-war world. The results were astonishing.

Billboard, 1st December 1945
http://countrymusichalloffame.org/full-list-of-inductees/view/jack-stapp
http://countrymusichalloffame.org/full-list-of-inductees/view/jim-denny

Presley on the radio, II

TUESDAY 8TH JANUARY 1946
EAST TUPELO, MISSISSIPPI

WITH MONEY SO HARD TO COME BY, there was a limit to what the Presleys could afford for Elvis' eleventh birthday. Some remember he'd requested a bike, but it was too expensive. Others recall he'd asked for a small rifle, but his mother would have quashed that idea. Eventually, and perhaps with some encouragement, he settled on a guitar — nothing special you understand, just a basic child's instrument. The purchase was made from the Tupelo Hardware Store, and the boy set to learning how to play.

He received instruction from various friends and family, especially Pastor Frank Smith, who showed him how to make simple bass runs, which Elvis loved. And after several months, Elvis — this shy, stuttering boy — felt able to test his abilities.

Every Saturday afternoon, radio WELO held a talent show at the Tupelo courthouse — presumably the same building where Vernon had been tried — and the performances were broadcast to a local audience. Most weeks, Elvis would travel over there with his pal, James Ausborn, to take his turn singing on air, and to hang around with the host of the show, James' older brother, Mississippi Slim.

Elvis' repertoire was very limited, his guitar playing was rudimentary, and his young voice was thin and uncertain. But this was something he just had to do. He rarely talked about his time at WELO, then or later in life. But it was important to him to be around musicians, to hear Slim tell his tales of meeting Tex Ritter, and of being on the same bill as the stars Elvis had heard performing on the *Opry*. And as he sang, he felt a calmness in his soul, and there was not a trace of a stutter in his words.

In the autumn, he began high school. He told no one about his guitar playing or singing. Few classmates remembered him. One or two recollected him having a liking for music, but all agreed there was nothing special at all about this anonymous boy.

Last Train to Memphis: The Rise of Elvis Presley, Peter Guralnick

The rise of Hill & Range, II

MONDAY 28TH JANUARY 1946
LOS ANGELES, CALIFORNIA

"TUMBLING TUMBLEWEEDS" was one of the most prized and lucrative copyrights in the world of hillbilly music. Originally recorded in 1935 by The Sons of the Pioneers, it had turned into a perennial hit and a serious money maker. The Aberbach brothers, lacking cash, but blessed with energy and ingenuity, combed through the existing contracts for this song and found a tiny loophole in the legalese — which allowed them to capture just the smallest part of the copyright. Moneywise, it was no big deal, but they had put down a marker.

Meanwhile, they continued to woo Steve Sholes at RCA Victor. They presented good quality songs for The Sons of the Pioneers' recording sessions — songs that continued to move the group into the middle of the road, exactly where Sholes wanted them to be.

Then they began to make a play for the attention of several hillbilly singers, including rising star, Eddy Arnold, who was also now under the direction of Sholes, and who had made it known he was always looking for strong material. Encouraging though this was, the brothers knew they had neither the reputation nor the financial muscle to capture the signatures of the big stars and songwriters. Therefore, they applied their considerable intelligence to this thorny problem, knowing that their future depended upon finding a solution.

Restless Giant: The Life and Times of Jean Aberbach & Hill and Range Songs, Bar Biszick-Lockwood

Johnnie, Jack and Chester

EARLY 1946
KNOXVILLE, TENNESSEE

JOHNNIE WRIGHT FELL IN LOVE with Ellen Deason, the girl next door, and they married in 1937. A few years later he teamed up with Jack Anglin and they formed a singing duo simply named Johnnie and Jack. Both partnerships were for life as far as Johnnie was concerned. Ellen also came along for the musical ride: she had a sweet voice — and she wasn't painful to look at either.

They first made their mark on WPTF North Carolina. Ellen sang well, but the station boss convinced the group she needed a stage name, something catchier than Ellen Wright. Eventually, they settled on Kitty Wells, drawing on the civil war ballad for inspiration. Women singers were seen as an added attraction in country music; they didn't headline, and shy "Kitty" was happy with that.

It was while they were working in Knoxville in early 1946 that they first met a quiet young fiddler named Chester "Chet" Atkins, a Tennessean with a love of guitars. They welcomed Chet into their band and he soon gravitated to a solo spot. Before he moved on to another outfit, Chet received some sound advice from Johnnie: "You play a good fiddle, son, but if I was you I'd concentrate on the guitar."

Chet Atkins: Me and My Guitars, Chet Atkins, Russ Cochran & Michael Cochran
In The Country of Country, Nicholas Dawidoff
http://countrymusichalloffame.org/full-list-of-inductees/view/chet-atkins

"The Last Train for Memphis"

EARLY 1946
ADA, OKLAHOMA

Having safely returned from his naval duties in early 1946, John Axton took on the position of Head of History at Ada High School in February. His family were relieved to welcome him back, and they soon settled into a familiar routine.

Mae also filled in as a teacher, but she was spending more and more of her spare time writing for pleasure and occasional profit. In the late spring, she took her hobby one step further and tried her hand at composing a couple of pop songs. The manuscripts would be mislaid over the years but both titles were copyrighted for posterity.

It's likely the songs consisted of words without music because, although she played piano a little, Mae would never reckon herself a musician.

The first, "I Can Prove it by My Heart", was surely a formulaic love song, of the sort that smothered the pop chart during the 1930s and 1940s, and was perhaps inspired by her husband's homecoming.

But the second composition carried an altogether more mysterious and prescient title, and would be of much more significance in years to come.

Its name: "The Last Train for Memphis".

Ada Evening News, 24th February 1946

"Steel Guitar Boogie"

JUNE 1946
RECORD RELEASE

In the summer of 1946, Bernie Kaii Lewis and His Hawaiians released a new single, "Drums of Samoa" coupled with "Steel Guitar Boogie" (Majestic 1065), and, although it sold poorly, the instrumental B-side caught the ear of many a steel guitar player. *Billboard*, though, didn't care for it at all, reviewing it as "a muddy facsimile of the eight-beat stuff."

The track carried an untypical song title: Lewis' many compositions usually bore a Polynesian name, as per the A-side. But Tommy Durden, out on the road with The Westernaires, heard and loved the number and began experimenting with words to see if he could write lyrics to Bernie's tune with the intention of performing it with his own group.

Billboard, 19th October 1946
Inside The Blue Hawaii Recording Sessions, David English, 2010, www.elvis-collectors.com

Agnes Sampson's main squeeze, I

SUNDAY 4TH AUGUST 1946
CHICAGO, ILLINOIS

AGNES SAMPSON DIDN'T DO NERVOUS. A delightful if somewhat precocious fourteen year-old, she looked the audience and the judges straight in the eye, placed her fingers on the keys and launched into her chosen accordion number.

She was one of the first northwest side musicians to enter the Chicago Music Festival competition, now in its seventeenth year, at the Lyon and Healy recital hall. She was a pretty and popular girl and her talent and occasionally ribald wit made her a natural at parties.

This wasn't to be her year. She came second in the contest, but she'd win for the next three years in a row. Agnes was a good Jewish girl who respected her parents but knew her own mind. She would go on to attend the renowned Von Steuben High School and had already decided on a career as a performer. She had her eye on semi-professional radio appearances too.

Chicago television was also waking up to the potential of aspiring entertainers, and local media entrepreneur Russ Davis would soon launch his very lucrative talent show *The Knickerbocker Hours*, drawing from the never-ending queue of starstruck novices.

So, Agnes continued studying, practising and playing. Her parents wished nothing more for her than to find a good husband and settle down. But even if Mr Right happened to come along, she could still follow her ambition to be a professional accordionist and singer. Mr Right would have to play second fiddle.

Chicago Daily Tribune, Illinois, 14th July & 5th August 1946, 2nd April 1950
Chicago Film Archives

Fred Rose: it takes one to know one

SATURDAY 14TH SEPTEMBER 1946
ACUFF-ROSE, NASHVILLE, TENNESSEE

As a recovering alcoholic, Fred Rose recognised the type straight away, but as a talented songwriter, he also recognised a kindred spirit: Hank Williams was genuinely gifted. Sure, some of his stuff needed polishing, but that's what Fred did best. Dozens of would-be composers had stepped through the front door but the tall, thin fellow from Montgomery was something special.

Not only was Williams a creative poet, he also had a charismatic performing style. With Acuff's industry contacts and Rose's ability to refine and choose hits, the boy could go far.

On that day, 14th September 1946, Hank Williams signed a publishing contract with Acuff-Rose. One of Fred's associates, Murray Nash, sat quietly in the corner throughout the meeting, as did Fred's son, Wesley, who held open the door as Hank left the offices.

The elder Rose smiled broadly. He had a good feeling about this and asked Murray to look after the Williams catalogue from now on. It would take some time, but, if they could keep Hank off the bottle, there was magic and money to be made.

Hank Williams: The Biography, Colin Escott with George Merritt & William MacEwen
Lovesick Blues: The Life of Hank Williams, Paul Hemphill
Murray Nash: Rock 'n' Roll Pioneer, an essay by Bo Berglind

The rise of Hill & Range, III

SEPTEMBER 1946
CBS STUDIO, HOLLYWOOD, CALIFORNIA

BOB WILLS HAD BEEN IN THE BUSINESS since the late 1920s and, with hits like "Ida Red", had built himself up to be one of the biggest stars in hillbilly music, certainly of those based on the west coast. He came from a musical clan — his father was a fiddle champion and younger brother Johnny Lee also had a band. Borrowing a little from the blues, Bob had invented a popular style of music known as western swing, and by the end of the war he was grossing $340,000 a year, which made him a very desirable target for Jean and Julian Aberbach.

Capturing Wills' signature on a publishing contract would be a major coup for Hill & Range. But the issue was: how to do it? Wills was rich and successful and the Aberbachs had no financial resources with which to tempt the star.

It was then that the brothers hit upon their magic idea and decided to employ a device they'd previously used only on a small scale: shared ownership. Unable to offer a large cash advance to coax Wills away from his current publisher, they would appeal to his ego. They suggested opening a new company, Bob Wills Music, Inc., in which Hill & Range would hold only fifty percent of the stock and Bob would hold the balance. This was in stark contrast to the usual deals whereby the publishing companies owned almost all of the rights to their songs.

The benefits for the singer were threefold: firstly, because he owned half the company, he would receive a much greater return (composers usually received only a tiny percentage of their own publishing revenue); secondly, he had the added vanity factor of having his own named publishing company; and thirdly, he had the two smartest, hardest-working young men in the business pushing his material.

For the Aberbachs, it meant they would take a much lower cut than all the other publishing houses, but it gave them a foot in the door and they were confident of their own ability to make it work.

Wills looked at the proposal from every angle and knew it was a good deal. All of his future self-composed songs would be placed in his new company. And if another writer offered Bob a song to record then he would insist the copyright be given to Bob Wills Music too. The composer would, in effect, lose all of his publishing rights, but he'd be well compensated by substantial sales figures and writer's royalties if the singing star was popular enough, which Bob certainly was. This became the Aberbachs' template deal for all future negotiations.

Bob Wills signed on 17th May 1946, and when he next visited the recording studio in September, it was as co-director of his own publishing house.

One of the songs he taped at this session was named "Brain Cloudy Blues" (credited to Wills and lead vocalist, Tommy Duncan) which borrowed heavily from "Milk Cow Blues", a 1934 blues single by Kokomo Arnold, which had also been recorded by Bob's brother in 1941.

In this way, Wills was attempting to merge the two distinct threads of American folk music, blues and hillbilly, within western swing. He wasn't alone in this: several artists were experimenting, but no one as yet had achieved a true breakthrough, commercially or artistically.

The Aberbachs, of course, were more than aware of the potential monetary rewards of finding a crossover artist, be it from the black or white side of the fence.

Country: The Twisted Roots of Rock 'n' Roll, Nick Tosches
Restless Giant: The Life and Times of Jean Aberbach & Hill and Range Songs, Bar Biszick-Lockwood

The rise of Hill & Range, IV

WEDNESDAY 11TH DECEMBER 1946
NASHVILLE, TENNESSEE

On the back of his mega-hit, "Walking the Floor Over You", Ernest Tubb had risen to the highest level of c&w fame, and he'd also become a cornerstone of the *Opry*. Yet all who met him agreed that he remained the most honest, likeable and humble man in show business.

His publishing was being handled by American Music in a typically one-sided and unadventurous fashion. The Aberbach brothers had made great strides in Hollywood once they'd secured Bob Wills' signature, and they now viewed Tubb as their potential entry point for the rapidly-growing Nashville publishing scene.

Knowing that Tubb had real influence in the hillbilly music community, they wooed him with the same deal that had so impressed Bob Wills. Ernest duly signed on 11th December 1946, and when fellow performers asked about the Ernest Tubb Music Inc. tag that soon appeared on all of his records and sheet music, he was only too happy to tell them about those nice boys from Hill & Range. Tubb was such a respected man that, just as Jean and Julian had planned, the other singers and songwriters paid close attention to what he said.

Very quickly and very quietly, before the major publishing houses even realised what was happening, Nashville started beating a path to the Aberbachs' door. The brothers pursued Eddy Arnold yet more intently and continued to cast their net to all corners of the hillbilly music scene. Within six months, the notoriously volatile but very successful bluegrass star, Bill Monroe, had also signed, too late for the Aberbachs to capture his signature tune, the Peer-published "Blue Moon of Kentucky", but Nashville certainly noticed this development, and many publishers began to take against these upstart Austrians.

Their percentage may have been low but the Aberbachs' income was rising, and their plans were working out exactly as they'd hoped.

Restless Giant: The Life and Times of Jean Aberbach & Hill and Range Songs, Bar Biszick-Lockwood

Nickels and dimes

SUNDAY 13TH APRIL 1947
AKRON, OHIO

STANDING IN THE WINGS of the Armory in Akron, Eddy Arnold was ready to begin his most prestigious concert since signing with Tom Parker. The manager had made a number of significant changes over the past few months, not all of which were appreciated by those in Eddy's band.

It seemed that they were constantly on the road, heading for somewhere new, spreading the word about Eddy Arnold. Parker lived and breathed for his client and there was no doubting his dedication and application. But he had a tendency to be blunt with those who surrounded Eddy, and this created tension. As well as increasing their workload, he'd taken the band members off their percentage-based wage and put them on a flat salary.

He'd also removed the little financial perks they'd enjoyed, like selling Eddy Arnold songbooks before concerts. Tom, who often seemed to care more about the nickels and dimes than the dollars, loved the sweet little side deals afforded by songbooks and the like. Sometimes, he'd even prowl the aisles and hawk them himself, much to the band's annoyance. But Parker didn't care about being unpopular with the band. He was employed to make money for Eddy — and for himself — and that was the end of the matter.

The Akron gig was a step up in prestige within the hillbilly market. For the first time, it took an artist out of the hayseed arenas and placed him on a higher plain. *Billboard* magazine was impressed — and Parker continued to regularly place advertisements within that publication, always drawing attention to the fact that this was a double act: EDDY ARNOLD, managed by TOM PARKER.

The concert was a great success and created quite a buzz within the industry. Eddy was also now talking to the Aberbach brothers about a publishing contract. The commercial breakthrough was surely coming and Tom Parker could almost smell the money already.

Eddy Arnold: Pioneer of the Nashville Sound, Michael Streissguth

Art for art's sake

MONDAY 21ST APRIL 1947
CASTLE STUDIO, NASHVILLE, TENNESSEE

Frank walker sat in his RCA Victor office in August 1945 and took the call from MGM who made him an offer he couldn't refuse. They intended to open their own record division and wanted Walker to head the company. They would give him plenty of time to set up the label, and he could hand pick his own artists.

MGM Records was officially launched in spring 1947 and it attracted a wide range of singing stars, big and small. Bob Wills was one of the first to join, for example, and, with Fred Rose's intervention, Hank Williams also signed to the label and made his first recordings on 21st April, accompanied by Red Foley's band.

He taped the customary four songs in three hours, including his first single, "Move It On Over" (MGM 10033). Also recorded was a stirring gospel track, "I Saw the Light", which Williams composed, leaning heavily on other religious songs. Walker recognised the obvious fact that Hank had talent, both as a songwriter and a singer, and could be a big hillbilly seller for his new company.

In the studio, Williams kept admonishing the band if they played too black or too fancy, "Keep it vanilla, boys," but it was Hank's delivery that made the difference. He'd listened very carefully to Tee-Tot all those years ago and now the white soul just poured into the grooves.

Hank Williams: The Biography, Colin Escott with George Merritt & William MacEwen

Tailor-made advice

AT SOME POINT IN THE LATE 1940S
126 BEALE STREET, MEMPHIS, TENNESSEE

SAMUEL LANSKY was a good and caring father who wanted nothing but the best for his sons, Bernard and Guy. During the late 1940s, he set them up in business at 126 Beale Street in a clothes shop, and left them to their own devices. Originally, the brothers sold army surplus, but Bernard quickly saw that Beale Street — and the wider neighbourhood — was full of characters who demanded a more creative and distinctive style of clothing.

So he invested in a selection of gloriously coloured outfits and sharp-cut suits and accessories, and the customers beat a path to the Lanskys' door. The majority of the clientele was black, and ranged from entertainers to ordinary folk who just wanted to say something special about themselves in the way they dressed.

By the turn of the decade, the two white boys were selling clothes of every conceivable style and colour to black customers in the home of the blues. And always, Samuel Lansky's advice, given on Bernard's eighteenth birthday, resonated: "You can conquer anything as long as you work hard."

http://www.lanskybros.com/Lansky-Bros-History.aspx

Start spreading the news

SPRING 1947
KILGORE, TEXAS

RECORDING CONTRACT IN POCKET, Hank Williams couldn't wait to tell his show business buddies about his deal with MGM. And one of his first visits was to Jim Reeves, a twenty-three year-old sharecropper's son living in Kilgore, Texas. Jim was, of course, happy for his friend. He was also probably more than a little envious.

A serious injury had put paid to Jim's long-term plans of being a professional baseball player so, with the support and encouragement of his wife, Mary, he was trying to make it as a singer.

James Travis "Jim" Reeves had always loved singing — he worshipped Jimmie Rodgers — but progress was frustratingly slow as he struggled to make ends meet playing bars and honky tonks, which was where he'd first met Hank. Reeves had eventually landed a job on radio KGRI, but was employed more as a deejay and station announcer than as a performer.

Sometimes he'd sit in the studio and pick up his guitar and croon along to the great pop and country hits he was broadcasting. Almost no one could hear him, of course, because the microphone was switched off when the disks were spinning. For the most part, Jim Reeves was singing for an audience of one: the station engineer on the other side of the glass.

Jim Reeves: His Untold Story, Larry Jordan

When Tom and Eddy met Jean and Julian

SUNDAY 18TH MAY 1947
RCA VICTOR STUDIO, CHICAGO, ILLINOIS

CALM AND COMPOSED AS ALWAYS, Eddy Arnold arrived at the RCA studio in Chicago, ready for what would prove to be a life-changing recording session. The Aberbach siblings had been wooing Eddy about opening his own music publishing firm, and producer Steve Sholes certainly agreed it could be a wise move, ensuring a steady flow of good songs and providing an extra source of income for Eddy.

But Eddy would not be moved. Yes, he liked the brothers and liked some of the demos they'd presented to him, but he was dedicated to his trade. He did not want to be swayed by financial considerations: if he liked a song then he would record a song, and he didn't want publishing concerns to cloud his judgement, although he did willingly indulge in a deal whereby the singer would sometimes be given a share of the writer's credit as an extra incentive.

Tom Parker stood on the sidelines and observed. Publishing was an area that he, as yet, did not fully understand. But he knew the Aberbachs were masters of their craft, so he watched — and he learned.

Meanwhile, the Austrians continued to charm Eddy, and the singer finally relented and agreed to accept a yearly retainer, ensuring that if he came across an unpublished song he liked he would push it towards Hill & Range. In return, they would double their efforts to find suitable material for him to record.

But, in a noble attempt to keep himself focused on the songs, he still refused the usual fifty percent. Sensing the importance of keeping Tom Parker onside, the Aberbachs offered the cut directly to Parker who, with Eddy's blessing, gladly accepted the royalties. Parker and the Aberbachs then settled into a very cosy relationship.

And on 18th May 1947, working with Steve Sholes and Hill & Range, Eddy began the recording sessions that would place him at the top of the hillbilly chart for almost every week of the next eighteen months.

Eddy Arnold had arrived. Parker, Sholes and the Aberbachs could not have been happier.

Restless Giant: The Life and Times of Jean Aberbach & Hill and Range Songs, Bar Biszick-Lockwood

Big Al out of Chicago

SUMMER 1947
54 WEST RANDOLPH STREET, CHICAGO, ILLINOIS

ALBERT DVORIN, a likeable deep-voiced bear of a man, finished his time in the army, and then followed his childhood dream, opening his own talent agency, booking and promoting local acts. The early days were rough, so he was doubly pleased to receive a friendly phone call from Tom Diskin, an old college buddy. Tom was managing his singing sisters, Patty, Nancy and Marge, as The Dickens Sisters, and wondered if Al had any openings for them.

Al soon lined up paying gigs for the girls with the likes of Victor Borge, and it was a pleasure to have his pal Tom hanging around again. In fact, Tom more or less became part of the agency, answering the phone and helping Al, who was impressed with the efficiency and organisational skills of his wiry, smooth-talking buddy.

Sometimes bookings were a little thin for the sisters, but as all acknowledged, it was better than working for a living.

Billboard, 21st June & 20th December 1947, 10th November 1951
http://aldvorin.com/Home.htm

Red Foley joins Hill & Range

MID-JULY 1947
NASHVILLE, TENNESSEE

HAVING SECURED Ernest Tubb's signature and endorsement, and with Eddy Arnold racing up the hillbilly chart, the Aberbach brothers swept through Nashville like a new broom. Their main competitor, Acuff-Rose, suddenly found itself in a vulnerable place. Supremely confident of his position, Roy Acuff had left Nashville and the *Opry* the previous year to advance his career in Hollywood.

Meanwhile, Fred Rose, great songwriter though he was, was no salesman, and he was so absorbed by the promising talent of Hank Williams he had no time for the day-to-day business of publishing. Added to which, Rose had a reputation as a song-tinkerer (for which he would often take a paid credit) and not all songwriters appreciated that.

Not surprisingly, Hill & Range moved into the vacuum created by Acuff's absence, and in July announced they'd given a $10,000 advance from their swelling coffers to Red Foley, one of C&W music's biggest stars and a singer with potential for a lucrative pop crossover hit. Indeed, by September, their joint firm, Home Folks Music, was established and ready to make money — money for Foley, and for the Aberbachs, too.

Moreover, songwriters who were not performers themselves noted that the Hill & Range stable was growing at a remarkable rate, and the company already had a selection of top notch stars on its books. If a composer gave his song to the Aberbachs it greatly increased the chances of it being recorded by Red Foley, Bob Wills, Ernest Tubb, Eddy Arnold, or any of the other Hill & Range superstars.

Jean and Julian had risked it all on the idea of being as generous as possible with their clients, and that gamble was now paying off. Big time.

Restless Giant: The Life and Times of Jean Aberbach & Hill and Range Songs, Bar Biszick-Lockwood
Billboard, 19th July 1947

The lucky red shirt, I

SATURDAY 26TH JULY 1947
FROM OKLAHOMA TO FLORIDA

SHE WAS A WOMAN WELL-VERSED in the art of presentation, and had a talent for keeping her own business private. Whenever she spoke about family life or her marriage she painted a rosy picture, as indeed many couples try to do. Who wants to display their dirty laundry?

But it is to Mae Boren Axton's credit as a professional that she managed to keep her divorce from husband John out of the public eye. On 26th July 1947, John started the one thousand-mile journey to his new home in St Petersburg, Florida, the Sunshine State. He travelled alone.

John had been accepted as the new Head Basketball and Track Coach at St Petersburg Senior High, along with the position of Assistant Football Mentor. Facts are uncertain and details are sketchy, but it's possible that Mae objected to his suggested uprooting of their family and offered an ultimatum: if you take the job, you lose us. For whatever reason, John took the job.

Coach Axton made an immediate impact with the sports teams in his remit and his success was impressive. A grateful student gave him a gift, a lucky red shirt, and he wore it faithfully to every game. Soon enough, his fabled "Green Devil" basketball team had taken the Big Ten Conference title and, inevitably, other schools, teams and colleges began to pitch offers for the charismatic teacher.

Meanwhile, Mae accepted a teaching job in Seymour, Texas, taking the boys with her. But by late 1948, a rapprochement had occured and Mae consented to move to Florida in time for John to begin a new coaching position in Jacksonville beginning the following summer.

The couple were officially remarried in St Petersburg, on 12th February 1949. Maybe John wore his lucky red shirt under his tuxedo this time.

Country Singers As I Know 'Em, Mae Boren Axton
Ada Weekly News, Oklahoma, 31st July 1947

Chet Atkins joins RCA Victor

MONDAY 11TH AUGUST 1947
CHICAGO, ILLINOIS

SOMETIMES TALENT CAN BE A CURSE as well as a blessing. Chet Atkins had played with various performers since leaving Johnnie and Jack and had been fired from several positions all over the South. He played well — too well. His finger-picking style mixed together all forms of music, including jazz and pop, which didn't always sit easily with the country listeners.

In the spring of 1947 he'd sent a demo disk to Steve Sholes, and the RCA man was impressed. But he was not willing to take a chance on a young unknown guitarist without some kind of support.

So he spoke to Jean Aberbach of Hill & Range and explained he'd be willing to sign the artist if he knew the Aberbachs were handling the publishing. Grateful for the tip, Jean pursued the twenty-three year-old player, and Atkins was signed to RCA Victor and Hill & Range almost simultaneously.

His first recording session was held on 11th August 1947 and, although the hits would be a while in coming, Sholes recognised Atkins' abilities, not just as a guitarist, but as a man who was very comfortable and useful in a studio, whether playing for himself or supporting others as they recorded.

As the months went by, Sholes, Atkins, and Jean Aberbach developed a very close professional relationship. Jean would supply the songs, Chet would oversee the sessions, and Steve would liaise between the two, striking a precise balance between gentle courtesy and productive discipline.

Restless Giant: The Life and Times of Jean Aberbach & Hill and Range Songs, Bar Biszick-Lockwood
http://jukebox.au.nu/instromania/instro_monsters/chet_atkins/1.html

Tommy Dorsey: the million dollar deal

MONDAY 8TH SEPTEMBER 1947
NEW YORK CITY, NEW YORK

IN THE WIDER WORLD outside of hillbilly and blues music, the majority of the country was buying big band and swing records. Tommy Dorsey's orchestra was one of the most successful, and had fostered such talent as singer Frank Sinatra and drummer Gene Krupa. Not surprisingly, the forty-one year-old band leader was much in demand.

So much so, that he opened a syndicated disk jockey coast-to-coast radio show on 8th September, which was likely to guarantee him a cool $1,000,000 a year. Things were looking good for Dorsey, who had recently settled a long-running feud with his older brother, Jimmy, who also ran his own band.

The producer behind the radio show was Lou Cowan, an enterprising man who believed in giving the public good quality programmes. During the war he'd been appointed director of *Voice of America*, and he knew there was a need for intelligent and honest broadcasting.

He also knew there was serious money to be made in media. He was keeping one careful eye on the early days of television, and was sure there were also great financial prospects in popular music. He kept meaning to talk to his old army buddy, Jack Stapp, about that, especially as he kept hearing from colleagues of how the *Grand Ole Opry* was making such great strides forward.

Billboard, 13th September 1947

How do you get to Carnegie Hall?

THURSDAY 18TH SEPTEMBER 1947
CARNEGIE HALL, NEW YORK

A SURE SIGN OF THE *Opry*'s ambitious intentions came in the autumn of 1947, when Jim Denny booked two nights at New York's prestigious Carnegie Hall. Ernest Tubb and Minnie Pearl topped the bill, and there was much jollity and sarcastic talk of hayseeds and country hicks among the city-slicker journalists. They were sure hill-billy music wouldn't travel well to the North.

But their laughing stopped when six thousand people were turned away from the full house on Thursday 18th September, and it was the same story for the second show on the Friday. Jim Denny took home a hefty slice of the $12,000 gross for WSM, and country music moved up a significant notch in the eyes of the general music business.

The *Opry* itself was doing its best to keep up to date, and also tried to allow its stars as much leeway as possible. Roy Acuff, for example, still climbing the ladder in Hollywood and unable to return to Nashville, was permitted to phone in a performance one Saturday, which was played live to the actual audience over the speakers at the Ryman Auditorium, and then broadcast over the air.

An elderly lady, who had paid for her ticket and just taken her seat, looked around the Ryman hoping to discover where Acuff's disembodied voice was coming from. Confused, she approached the doorman and asked, "How much extra does it cost to see 'em?"

The Grand Ole Opry: The Making of an American Icon, Colin Escott

The western heroes

SEPTEMBER 1947
TUPELO, MISSISSIPPI

THE PRESLEYS MOVED to a designated "white" house in a "colored" area of Tupelo, just as Elvis started seventh grade. At this time, he felt comfortable enough to start taking his guitar to his (white-only) school each day, playing ballads and country songs for his uninterested classmates at lunch time.

Two other important developments quickly followed the move: firstly, he joined the public library, sparking a life-long love of reading; and secondly, he became acquainted with Sam Bell, a black neighbour of his own age.

The boys spent much of their after-school time together, having fun and ignoring racial conventions, with other playmates, black and white. They entered the local cinema through colour-separated doors, but once inside, Elvis would leap over the barrier and sit beside his friend, watching the movie, carefully noting how the cowboys stood and walked, then trying his best to adopt that macho stance when the film ended. Afterwards, he and Sam would shoot each other down with imaginary pistols, and ride invisible horses into the sunset, dreaming of being western heroes.

Sam's folks were none too pleased to hear their son had befriended a white boy — these situations often developed unpleasantly for the black half of the relationship — so Sam brought Elvis home to meet his parents and grandparents, hoping he could change their minds.

As they talked, Elvis drew upon his immaculate manners, and impressed the sceptical and wary Bells. When the young Presley went back home that night, Sam's daddy said, much to Sam's astonishment, that it would be okay for the boys to carry on playing together.

The reason? "No white boy ever called me 'Sir' before."

Last Train to Memphis: The Rise of Elvis Presley, Peter Guralnick
Televised interviews with Sam Bell

The Westernaires

OCTOBER 1947
THE SOUTH

LIFE ON THE ROAD was rarely as glittering as the public imagined. Tommy Durden and his five compadres had spent much of 1947 supporting western movie star and musician, Dub "Cannonball" Taylor, and then playing under a selection of touring headliners such as Webb Pierce and a new fellow who was coming through named Hank Williams. Dub Taylor moved on to appear in several films with successful singing cowboy Jimmy Wakely (his 1943 hit "I'll Never Let You Go" was still very popular).

In November, The Westernaires signed with Bob Steele, a veteran western star, and played up to four shows a day for nine months touring the South, ending up in Galveston. Tommy Durden would feature as lead vocalist in the show, and every sweet love song he sang was directed at his wife.

Now, Boots was a good woman and she genuinely liked Tommy, but had begun to wonder if he was the man with whom she wanted to spend the rest of her life.

Billboard, 18th October 1947 & 1st May 1948
The Robesonian, North Carolina, 3rd November 1947

"My Happiness"

WEDNESDAY 10TH DECEMBER 1947
DAMON RECORDING STUDIO, KANSAS CITY, MISSOURI

POPULAR PIANO AND VOCAL DUO, Jon and Sondra Steele, were ushered into the studio on 10th December, just in time to beat the latest controversy to hit the music business. Union boss James Petrillo had called for another recording ban, starting from 1st January 1948, in response to radio's growing preference for playing records rather than featuring live musicians on air.

The Steeles laid down two tracks in December. The first was a forgettable topical novelty number entitled "They All Recorded to Beat the Ban", but the second was a keeper — a simple ballad entitled "My Happiness", which rushed up the pop chart in early 1948, eventually becoming *Cashbox* magazine's record of the year.

But one of the big problems facing the record companies, during what turned out to be a year-long ban, was their inability to produce instant cover versions. Usually, if a song became popular for one label, or in one genre of music, a handful of different versions on various labels would appear in record shops within just a few weeks, hoping to cash in on the original.

With "My Happiness" proving such a hit, producers were desperate to get around the ban, and so some resorted to using a trick initiated during the previous dispute: vocal-only recordings. One such acapella cover version was recorded on Friday 30th April 1948 in New York for Decca, by jazz queen Ella Fitzgerald, with a typically seductive and sensual performance, and it also enjoyed considerable chart success, before the union then demanded a ban on choral sessions too.

Ella Fitzgerald: An Annotated Discography, J. Wilfred Johnson
Billboard, 8th May 1948 & 5th February 1949

Hank Snow joins Hill & Range

PERHAPS MARCH 1948
HOLLYWOOD BOULEVARD, LOS ANGELES, CALIFORNIA

LEAVING HIS WIFE AND SON behind in Canada, Hank Snow headed for Texas, hoping to make the step forward that had eluded him at home for almost a decade. But life for the hillbilly singer proved even tougher in America, and he soon found himself with dwindling resources and no sign of success.

He took on a singing job in a small Dallas nightclub called the Silver Spur, but the owner — a shady fellow named Jack Ruby — tended to rub people the wrong way, and when Hank opened his mouth once too often, he was shown the door. So Hank kept moving on and ended up in Hollywood.

He befriended Ernest Tubb, who shared his love of Jimmie Rodgers. Tubb gave him encouragement and a few good leads, but bookings were in short supply and Snow's cash ran out. His final throw of the dice was to sell his abilities as a songwriter. He met up with representatives from Ralph Peer's Southern Music, who were connected with Snow's Canadian publisher, but they had little time for his hard luck story and he left empty-handed.

During their conversations, Ernest Tubb had mentioned Hill & Range to Snow and the Canadian walked the few blocks to the publisher's L.A. office and was greeted by Julian Aberbach himself. He listened intently as Snow talked about his recordings for RCA Canada and his hopes for the future. Snow then suggested he would sign to Hill & Range in exchange for $300.

Aberbach shrugged and wrote out a cheque for $1,000 and passed it to the flabbergasted musician. No contract was signed that day, but an understanding had been reached. A few weeks later, the paperwork was completed and Aberbach set about obtaining all of Snow's old copyrights from his Canadian publisher. Hill & Range had great faith in Snow's potential.

It should come as no surprise then to learn that Steve Sholes soon offered Hank a contract with RCA Victor too, and promised to book studio time when the latest industry recording dispute was settled.

Classic Country: Legends of Country Music, Charles K. Wolfe
The Hank Snow Story, Hank Snow with Jack Ownbey & Bob Burris
Restless Giant: The Life and Times of Jean Aberbach & Hill and Range Songs, Bar Biszick-Lockwood
Mary Ferrell Foundation, Commission Document 1254, Random Notes of Jack Ruby
Billboard, 13th March 1954

Elmer Laird: "Poison Love"

FRIDAY 7TH MAY 1948
LAIRD AUTO DEALERS, HARRIS, TEXAS

ARKANSAS-BORN AND SHREVEPORT-RAISED, Tillman Franks played bass semi-professionally, and joined with some musician buddies when they appeared on new radio show, the *Louisiana Hayride* — Shreveport's answer to the *Opry* — on station KWKH. The producers were hoping to emulate the success of the WSM broadcast but intentionally gave their programme a fresher twist, appealing more to the youngsters.

But a musician's life was hard and money was scarce, so Franks put his bass aside and took a job in Harris, Texas, working under a used-car auto-dealer, Elmer Laird, who had an interest in hillbilly music. A successful businessman, he sponsored bands and local radio shows.

Together with Franks, Laird wrote a song named "Poison Love". Tillman organised a demo version, and Elmer hoped to get the track to a big-name singer, maybe even someone like Eddy Arnold.

But on 7th May, everything changed. An argument developed in Laird's office. An aggressive customer raised his voice, pushed past Laird and stepped outside. Laird went to follow but the young man turned around and produced a knife, stabbing Laird through the heart on the steps of his own dealership.

The ambulance came quickly but Laird succumbed on his way to hospital. "Don't let me die 'til I talk to my wife," Laird had said as he was being placed on the stretcher. But it was too late. Right there, in his own place of business, a Texas retailer had been mortally wounded.

Franks handed in his notice shortly after. Mrs Laird gave him the demo disk of "Poison Love" and put him on a bus bound for Nashville. She made Franks promise to give the record to Eddy Arnold to see if he would record it when the current industry dispute ended.

Franks kept his promise, but Eddy, riding high on the charts, politely turned it down.

Hank Williams: The Biography, Colin Escott with George Merritt & William MacEwen
Voices of the Country: Interviews with Classic Country Performers, Michael Streissguth
Nu Country website, Dave's diary obituary of Tilman Franks

Pinney: The Busy Bee

AT SOME POINT IN THE LATE 1940S
BUSY BEE LIQUOR STORE, 3728 ALAMEDA AVENUE, EL PASO, TEXAS

DELTA PINNEY AND HIS WIFE, Edna, invested in a small storefront property on the crossroads of Alameda Avenue and North Latta Street. It was south of the railway lines and near Concordia Cemetery, where John Wesley Hardin lay, and on the same road where he'd been felled — a reminder that El Paso remained a dangerous city.

The shop was an unremarkable rectangular construction: one storey, double windows at the front, with living accommodation at the rear. They would sell liquor, with a sideline of fishing equipment. Inside, Pinney had the shelves and cabinets arranged in precise military style. There was little fancy about the premises — it was tidy and practical. The bottles stood to attention within the square display cupboards. A stag's head or two adorned the whitewashed walls. A selection of plain framed pictures added colour.

Behind the counter stood a long tall shelving unit and behind that was the door through to the living quarters. Pinney optimistically dubbed the store "The Busy Bee" and had the name set outside above the windows in a simple, classic style. A small electric sign hung above the building advertising "LIQUOR".

Pinney knew there was good money to be made in this line of work. He also knew that, apart from gas stations, it was the place most likely to be robbed by opportunist amateur thieves. Texas could be a lethal place for retailers. So he took precautions. At various points around the shop he hid an assortment of firearms, loaded and ready. Should anyone burst in, waving a gun and threatening his livelihood, his family or his life, Pinney would be ready to defend himself wherever he might be on the floor.

His credo held firm.

A gift for Tom Parker

PERHAPS MID-1948
BATON ROUGE, LOUISIANA

CRISS-CROSSING THE COUNTRY, setting up deals and contracts, Tom Parker would often make it his business to visit with former carnival colleagues and acquaintances — old times were most definitely not forgotten as far as Parker was concerned.

In 1948, while travelling through Baton Rouge with Gabe Tucker — one of Eddy's musicians who was now playing a bigger part behind the scenes — Tom decided to drop in on Bob Greer, a friend from way back, currently working for Governor Jimmie Davis.

Bob was pleased to see Tom and Gabe, and they talked and laughed about the old days. And at the punchline of one of Parker's best tales, Gabe declared that anyone who could snow folks with almost military precision like Parker surely deserved a proper title like a "Colonel" or something. This provoked another burst of raucous laughter, but when the hilarity finally faded, Bob saw the other two guys were looking at him with suddenly serious faces.

Realising that the spontaneous gag had now become one hell of a good idea, Bob took the cue and rang his boss, Governor Davis. Jimmie was almost at the end of his one-term residency, and probably didn't care either way by this time. He despatched the official "Honorary Colonel" certificate to Bob, post haste.

Parker received the paperwork and smiled broadly. Unlike more modest recipients, he decided to make full use of his title.

"In future, Mr Tucker," he barked, "you will make sure everyone addresses me as *Colonel*."

The Colonel: The Extraordinary Story of Colonel Tom Parker and Elvis Presley, Alanna Nash

Bobby Ross: Tom's boy, 1

EARLY AUGUST 1948
NASHVILLE, TENNESSEE

SLUMPED IN HIS CHAIR, Steve Sholes took the call from *Colonel* Tom Parker ("Where the hell did the 'Colonel' bit come from?" wondered Steve). He had always found Parker a difficult man to deal with. Eddy Arnold was a big-seller — they both knew it — and Tom was forever on the phone making new demands, but this call was the best one yet. Tom's stepson, Bob Ross, was working for the Parker organisation, but at the age of twenty-three he was looking to spread his wings.

"I figured you might find a position for him up at RCA, Steve. How about taking him on as your assistant?"

Steve, of course, agreed, and appointed Ross — who was certainly bright and capable — as the RCA Victor Southern Representative. Actually, he didn't have a choice, but there wasn't much for the personable young man to do at RCA anyway as there was no recording going on.

Still, he pondered, how long would the boy last?

Billboard, 14th & 28th August 1948, 2nd July 1949

Eddy Arnold leaves the *Opry*

SATURDAY 11TH SEPTEMBER 1948
RYMAN AUDITORIUM, NASHVILLE, TENNESSEE

SATURDAY NIGHTS would never be the same. Eddy Arnold had been a regular feature on the *Grand Ole Opry* since 1940, and they'd both done well by one another. Of late, however, when touring, Eddy had dropped any reference to the *Opry* in his advertising. This was done at Tom Parker's instigation to save the fifteen percent fee, and also to demonstrate to Eddy that he was now able to promote himself without relying on his WSM position.

Eddy's astonishing record sales and chart dominance put him above all other hillbilly stars, and his hits were beginning to cross over into the lucrative pop chart too.

The *Opry*, of course, remained very beneficial to its artists, but the pay was low and it did tie-up the performers almost every Saturday night during the year. Wherever they might be touring, they had to rush back to Nashville for the broadcast.

Thus, after much persuasion from Parker, Eddy agreed not to renew his *Opry* contract and strike out on his own. He gave his last performance on 11th September 1948, an emotional occasion for star and audience. At the end of the show he came off stage and sobbed in the arms of Minnie Pearl.

Behind the Grand Ole Opry Curtain, Robert K. Okemann
Eddy Arnold: Pioneer of the Nashville Sound, Michael Streissguth

Tommy and Tex: "Crossroads"

FRIDAY 17TH SEPTEMBER 1948
ON THE ROAD

TEX RITTER poured yet another whiskey for himself and Tommy Durden. The bottle was almost empty, but they both knew there was a good supply of further bottles, if required.

"Here's to my boy; here's to Jonathan," announced Tex, raising his glass and toasting his new-born son. One of the hazards of life on the road was missing family events, and the birth of his second son had passed him by. Career-wise though, Tex was flying high, and he'd recently hooked up with The Westernaires for a long-running tour.

Tex had made a good friend in Tommy Durden and they would let off steam most nights by draining a glass or two and shooting the breeze. The tour would run for about a year and the crowds would come to see the famous star with his band and his horse.

Tommy was also feeling the detrimental effect of life on the road: he and Boots were together almost twenty-four hours a day, but already the cracks were beginning to show in their young marriage. They were both good people, but it just wasn't working out. And as with so many musicians before and after, he took his pain and fashioned a song. Blues fan Tommy named it "Crossroads", but it was a country ballad, and the simple words of sadness and honest confusion spoke volumes:

I'm standing at the crossroads, I'll go the way the wind blows:
What you say will show the way to me.
I'm asking for the last time for you to say you'll be mine:
Your answer, dear, will make it clear to see.
And if you say we're through then I'll stop loving you,
For I know I can find someone who'll bring me peace of mind,
So please say Yes or No, dear, that's all I want to know, dear,
I'm standing at the crossroads, which way do I go?

Joplin Globe, Missouri, 16th October 1949

Bright lights, big city

SATURDAY 6TH NOVEMBER 1948
MEMPHIS, TENNESSEE

With little fanfare and even less notice, the Presleys packed their belongings into an old 1937 Plymouth, and drove the one hundred miles to Memphis on Saturday 6th November 1948. One can speculate about the whys and wherefores, but Vernon and Gladys were simply trying to improve their lot by moving to a big bustling city, which would give them — and their son — better options.

On the Monday, thirteen year-old Elvis enrolled in Humes High School — a vast all-white establishment whose population was greater than that of East Tupelo itself. According to family legend, Vernon dropped his son at the school gates, but Elvis was so nervous he ran back to their tiny new apartment, arriving there even before his daddy.

Soon though, the family settled in the city, and Elvis, for whom music was becoming a quiet obsession, joyously discovered — as Sam Phillips had before him — the vast cornucopia that Memphis had to offer: in church, on Beale Street, in live performances — and also on the radio.

Last Train to Memphis: The Rise of Elvis Presley, Peter Guralnick

Radio WDIA

LATE 1948
MEMPHIS, TENNESSEE

BLACK MUSIC was absolutely under-represented on Memphis radio: in fact, it was barely there at all, though that situation began to improve in late 1948. It would be reassuring to learn that some civic-minded citizen started a crusade for equality in the arts, but the truth is that finance was at the heart of the change.

The main purpose of radio was to make money by selling advertising, and entrepreneurs John Pepper and Bert Ferguson knew the city was full of a potential black audience to whom products could be promoted.

They opened station WDIA in 1947 as an all-white channel; but then from October 1948 onwards, slowly moved over to all-black as the ratings for black deejays and black music went through the roof. The station hired broadcasters like Professor Nat D. Williams and Riley King, who very promptly made a name for themselves.

Of course, although the station aimed itself at black audiences, the airwaves themselves knew no such discrimination. Listeners of all races and backgrounds were intrigued and often excited by the WDIA programming. And no one, but no one, was happier than Elvis Presley and Sam Phillips.

Sam Phillips: The Man who Invented Rock 'n' Roll, Peter Guralnick

Chester meets the Carters

PERHAPS LATE 1948
RADIO WNOX, KNOXVILLE, TENNESSEE

FINGERS COLLECTIVELY CROSSED, the Carters arrived at the small WNOX studio hoping this radio gig would be a step nearer the big time. They'd paid their dues over the past five years. The youngest, Anita, was now fifteen and beginning to blossom into a beauty. They were known and respected, but they hadn't yet stepped out of the shadow of the original Carter Family. They needed a little touch of magic, something to lift them as musicians, and as a performing unit. At WNOX studio they found that little touch of magic sitting in a corner tuning his guitar.

Chet Atkins was now over a year into his RCA Victor recording contract, but the big hit record would not come and he was still picking and playing regular small-time gigs in order to pay the rent.

But Maybelle adored his talent and, once the girls saw through his quiet, almost backward manner, they realised what he could bring to their sound. They all raised themselves several notches higher when Chet played with them.

There were a thousand reasons why Chet's style shouldn't have fitted in with the Carters', but it did. He joined the group and they were on their way.

Will You Miss Me When I'm Gone? The Carter Family & Their Legacy in American Music, Mark Zwonitzer with Charles Hirshberg

The rise of the independents

JANUARY 1949
MANHATTAN, NEW YORK

THE LATEST RECORDING BAN came to an end in January 1949. During the hiatus, record companies had made the most of their free time and came up with two new disk formats, launched in summer 1948 and January 1949 respectively: the 12 inch 33⅓rpm long-playing album and the 7 inch 45rpm single. Both offered higher fidelity for the listener — the former giving the customers a longer uninterrupted listening experience, and the latter making life easier for the vital jukebox industry — as well as cutting down on transportation costs.

More changes were afoot during this difficult time. Small businessmen began to open their own independent record labels, hoping either to make a quick buck or, in a few notable cases, record some exciting music. One such entrepreneur was blues- and jazz-loving Turkish immigrant, Ahmet Ertegun, who founded Atlantic Records (and also Progressive Music, a publishing company), just before the ban. Soon, independent labels began to spring up all over the country, covering almost all genres of music.

The simple truth was that the recording business that emerged from the strike in January 1949 was not the same one that had closed its doors in December 1947.

Music Man: Ahmet Ertegun, Atlantic Records and the Triumph of Rock 'n' Roll,
Dorothy Wade & Justine Picardie

A helping hand from Colonel Tom

THURSDAY 3RD FEBRUARY 1949
FOX THEATRE BUILDING, ATLANTA, GEORGIA

OTTIS "SLIM" WHITMAN had to keep pinching himself to make sure he wasn't dreaming. Here he was, just a few days after his twenty-fifth birthday, only a month after the Petrillo dispute had ended, making a record for RCA Victor. A year earlier he'd taken up singing semi-professionally in Tampa, Florida, and in the autumn he'd received a visit from "Colonel" Tom Parker. Tom had heard Slim singing on WFLA radio and wanted to tell him he had a big future in the music business. Furthermore, he was recommending him to Steve Sholes at RCA.

"Ideally," joked Tom, "I'd like to manage you myself, but I'm a bit tied up with my boy, Eddy. However, I have a young man, name of Bob Ross; he's about your age. He's done some work for Mr Sholes up at RCA, but he's going to step down from that position because I think he'd make a fine manager for you."

Tom was right. Bob was a heck of a nice guy, and here he was on Slim's first session, filling in on piano. Mr Sholes himself was behind the control desk, and there was Chet Atkins on guitar and Jerry Byrd on steel guitar.

One of the numbers lined up for Slim to sing was called "Paint a Rose on the Garden Wall" and Bob was also going to do the narration section. The Hill & Range song was about a boy's love for his mother. Bob figured his mom, Marie, would love it, whether the song was a hit or not. She did, and it wasn't.

But Slim would always be grateful to the Colonel, insisting it was Tom who'd first given him a break. There were those, however, who whispered that Parker saw a potential threat to his boy, Eddy, and he pulled several strings to keep Whitman just where he wanted him, acting as a shadowy "special advisor" to his stepson.

As if Tom Parker would do such a thing …

Mr Songman: The Slim Whitman Story, Kenneth L. Gibble

Hank Snow's first American recordings

TUESDAY 8TH MARCH 1949
RCA VICTOR STUDIO, CHICAGO, ILLINOIS

CLARENCE "HANK" SNOW, had to keep pinching himself to make sure he wasn't dreaming. Here he was, just a few weeks before his thirty-fifth birthday, only two months after the Petrillo dispute had ended, making a record for RCA Victor. Hank had been struggling to gain a foothold in America but now, with a Hill & Range publishing contract in his back pocket, he felt sure his fortunes were about to improve. His wife and son, recently transplanted to America, were depending on him.

Hank had been making records in Canada since 1936, but he was still lacking a bona fide hit south of the border. He and Mr Sholes had spent the previous day running through songs they intended to record, and Snow pushed forward a track he'd written called "I'm Movin' On". Sholes listened intently, but shook his head, asking if the singer had anything more suitable.

In all, they recorded eight songs on that Tuesday, and RCA chose a ballad called "Marriage Vow" as the first single release. It was a Jenny Lou Carson composition, published by Hill & Range, but Snow wasn't overly fond of it. And when issued, the record scraped into the C&W top ten but didn't sell in the way Hank had hoped.

All the while, though, Snow's mind kept drifting back to the song Mr Sholes had rejected … he felt sure it could be a hit, but how to convince his sceptical producer?

The Hank Snow Story, Hank Snow with Jack Ownbey & Bob Burris
Restless Giant: The Life and Times of Jean Aberbach & Hill and Range Songs, Bar Biszick-Lockwood

Oscar Davis: "Don't you dare miss it!"

APRIL 1949
SOMEWHERE ON THE ROAD

OSCAR DAVIS was a genius and a fool. A dapper, erudite man with a gift for promotion, he was a well-respected laughing stock in show business. There was nothing he couldn't sell. He could spot a rising talent blindfolded during a blackout. He could get more money for an act than any other promoter living. But he never had a dollar to his name. Oscar lived for today — and he lived well.

During the 1930s and early 1940s, Oscar learned his trade promoting carnivals, jamborees and hillbilly acts, and he developed a gift for devising brilliant and irresistible slogans. An acquaintance of Tom Parker, he was the complete antithesis of the miserly ex-carny, but they had the utmost admiration for each other's craft.

Davis had several irons in the fire during the late 1940s, but he took one look at Hank Williams and dropped them all. The drunkard and the prodigal signed a management contract in April 1949. Davis immediately started spreading the news: "Hank Williams is coming to town: don't you dare miss it!"

Billboard, 3rd September 1949
http://leeharrisonline.tripod.com/hankwilliams/
http://www.scottymoore.net/oscardavis.html

The Parkers move in

PERHAPS APRIL 1949
EDDY ARNOLD'S HOUSE, MADISON, TENNESSEE

Although he was always happy to acknowledge his manager's absolute commitment to the cause, there were times when even Eddy Arnold questioned Tom Parker's sanity. For instance, in 1949, Parker decided he could no longer do his job properly if he continued living in Tampa, Florida, while his only client lived in Madison, Tennessee.

Tom's solution was brilliant, but bizarre. He would simply move into Eddy's house and live with Eddy's family. In fact, he'd also bring his own wife and stepson, too. Of course, Tom didn't expect to pay anything for this. Heck, he was just trying to do his job to the best of his ability.

And so, for weeks at a time, the Parkers would board with Eddy and Sally Arnold. Mrs Arnold, tired of playing housemaid, soon made it clear to her husband that this was a situation that had to be resolved.

Eddy had another property locally and, so rumour has it, he literally gave the keys to the Parker family and that is where they lived for many happy years to come. This was but one example of Parker's great talent for living rent-free, certainly when it came to office space.

Eddy, concerned about Parker's obsessive style, took him to one side and suggested he should take some time off, or maybe choose a hobby like golf.

But Parker looked him straight in the eye and replied, "You're my hobby."

Eddy Arnold: Pioneer of the Nashville Sound, Michael Streissguth

Hank Thompson's big gamble

PERHAPS SPRING 1949
ST PETERSBURG, FLORIDA

MAE BOREN AXTON re-read the letter confirming that husband John had been accepted on next year's teaching staff at Robert E. Lee High School, Jacksonville, Florida. It guaranteed a higher standard of living, and Mae was determined her family would finally put down solid roots and establish a permanent home after the upheaval of the past two years.

Perhaps it was in May, as the Axtons started packing to leave St Petersburg, that Mae first became acquainted with a fellow Texan named Hank Thompson. He told her how he had spent the last three years trying to make a name for himself as a country singer, just like the Carters to whom he'd listened on border radio while growing up. Touring western star, Tex Ritter, had helped get him signed to Capitol in 1947, which resulted in a handful of modest records.

He accepted a spot on the *Grand Ole Opry*, but saw how poorly paid (and sometimes how poorly treated) the performers were, and he soon walked away leaving a big Hank-shaped hole in the roster.

Without a regular radio show, Hank had to rely on record sales and concert takings. His style of western swing was reasonably popular in Texas, but the folks in Oklahoma just plain adored him, so he decided to relocate there. But what he now needed was a big hit to support his bold move.

Mae didn't know much about country music but wished him well. Sure enough, late in 1951, Hank's wife, Dorothy, brought to her husband's attention a song she'd heard called "The Wild Side of Life". The lyric was a little risqué, telling the story of a honky tonk angel (a prostitute) and initially Hank didn't care too much for it.

Credited to William Warren and one Arlie A. Carter, the tune was pretty much identical to Acuff's "Great Speckled Bird", and Thompson taped it in Dallas in November 1951. Amazingly, it spent fifteen weeks at number one on the *Billboard* country chart the following summer (Capitol F1942). Thompson had his hit and his signature song. Now his future was assured — with or without the *Opry*.

Country Singers As I Know 'Em, Mae Boren Axton
St Petersburg Evening Independent, Florida, 16th April 1959
St Petersburg Times, Florida, 24th June 1949
Unknown Newspaper, 9th September 1987

"Blues Stay Away From Me", I

FRIDAY 6TH MAY 1949
KING RECORDING STUDIO, CINCINNATI, OHIO

NOT ALL PERFORMERS who left the *Opry* were as fortunate as Hank Thompson. The Delmore Brothers, Alton and Rabon, were among the most popular *Opry* stars of the 1930s (they'd helped Roy Acuff get his start) but since leaving the show in 1939 they'd found the going tough, despite writing many excellent songs. Also, ignorant of the ways of the music business, they'd been unable to capitalise on their talent in any meaningful fashion.

They'd started at Columbia, moved to RCA Bluebird, then onto Decca, and they were now working for King Records, a company they'd opened themselves. Little did they know it, but they were already being ripped-off by their own label.

Financially, they were a disaster area. Creatively, they were excellent. Since moving to Memphis in 1947, they'd been inspired by the thriving music scene, and had laid down some wonderful recordings for King (in Cincinnati), such as "Freight Train Boogie" and "Hillbilly Boogie", which established a template of sorts for a new type of country music. They were blurring the strict borders between black and white traditions.

At King they worked with black producer, Henry Glover, who made a crucial contribution to their recording session on 6th May 1949. Rabon had written a song called "Blues Stay Away From Me" and played it to Glover, who suggested using a riff he'd written for the soundtrack of the all-black 1948 movie, *Boarding House Blues*. Session guitarist, Zeke Turner, did a little work on it and the finished take was superb, but would the notoriously fickle hillbilly audience accept such a blending of musical styles?

The track was released in September 1949 on King 803 and was a c&w number one, going on to become The Delmore Brothers' biggest hit.

http://en.delmore-brothers.com/page02bio_en.html
http://en.wikipedia.org/wiki/The_Delmore_Brothers
http://www.nativeground.com/articles/99-the-delmore-brothers-by-john-lilly.html

George Morgan: "Candy Kisses"

SUMMER 1949
NASHVILLE, TENNESSEE

GEORGE MORGAN was in a unique but unfortunate situation. He held the number one spot in the hillbilly chart with a debut self-composed smash hit, and yet he'd just been dumped by his manager, Oscar Davis, in favour of Hank Williams.

George had signed on at the *Grand Ole Opry* in September 1948 as a replacement for the smooth crooning sound of Eddy Arnold. Unusually, George had arrived at the *Opry* without a hit record, because the Petrillo ban had postponed his recording career. As soon as the dispute was resolved, Morgan was booked into the studio. His first single, "Candy Kisses", was released in February 1949 (Columbia 20547) and it sped to the top of the c&w listing.

So George sat atop the folk music world without any professional guidance. But he was not alone for long. Perhaps at Oscar Davis' suggestion, he met with Tom Parker's stepson, Bob Ross, who promptly cancelled his management contract with Slim Whitman — although he continued as Whitman's advisor and agent — and hitched up with George Morgan.

Tom Parker was pleased his stepson was moving up the ladder so speedily ... and you could bet he was only too happy to offer advice when required. Just as long as it didn't interfere with his boy, Eddy.

Tom and Bob and Eddy and George became one big happy family. Indeed, not by chance, Morgan was also soon signed to RCA Victor and Hill & Range.

Nice guy, that Tom Parker; always looking out for the other fellow.

Billboard, 24th September 1949

Buddy Killen gets backstage

SOMETIME IN 1949
BIRMINGHAM, ALABAMA

ENVY IS A TERRIBLE THING; especially between friends. But there was no denying William "Buddy" Killen was jealous of his friend Autry Inman. Autry was living the life that sixteen year-old Buddy could only dream of: he was a professional musician.

Buddy, who still attended school in Florence, looked forward to those vacation days when Autry would travel through Alabama playing on a package tour and he would trail after him, watching the great hillbilly stars and applauding his friend playing in the band.

Buddy managed to get out as far as Birmingham on one occasion. George Morgan was headlining and Buddy was impressed. He sang his hit, "Candy Kisses", and the audience loved him.

Between shows, Autry took Buddy backstage to meet the cast and Buddy was starstruck when he met George. But he was intrigued by a tall, quiet-spoken, almost skeletal performer, who had won over the crowd playing an old song from way back when.

Buddy briefly introduced himself to the thin man who tipped his hat and offered his name with a slow drawl: "Hank Williams, glad t' know ya, Buddy."

By the Seat of my Pants, Buddy Killen with Tom Carter

Hank Williams: "Lovesick Blues"

SATURDAY 11TH JUNE 1949
RYMAN AUDITORIUM, NASHVILLE, TENNESSEE

FRED ROSE didn't even like the damn song, but Hank insisted it would be a hit. He'd been singing the old hillbilly tune on the road for years and it always went down a storm. Rose pointed out all of the musical reasons why the song was unsuitable, but Hank recorded it anyway, just before Christmas 1948. The session musicians sided with Fred Rose. Steel guitarist Jerry Byrd thought the song was a mess and out of metre.

Fred had been publishing Hank Williams' songs for three years. He'd edited Hank's rougher compositions before release, and helped him pick the best cover material, too. He prided himself that he knew a hit when he heard one. "Lovesick Blues" was not going to be a hit, and if there was one thing Hank Williams needed right now it was a hit.

Hank's star had been rising for a while, but he was hampered by an all too accurate reputation for drinking and hell-raising. His songwriting and performing style were better than just about anyone else in the hillbilly field, but promoters were reluctant to take a chance on a no-show.

Publisher Fred Rose and manager Oscar Davis had been trying to move their boy on from the *Hayride* and get him a spot on the *Grand Ole Opry*, knowing full well it would catapult him to stardom. But the *Opry* wanted a hit record and a guarantee of sobriety. Hank was insistent he could stay off the liquor, and he was also convinced that "Lovesick Blues" was a number one hit.

Rose struggled to track down the publishing information on the old song — the trail was a fractured nightmare — but he managed to get the record released. Within two weeks it had sold an astonishing 48,000 copies, dislodging George Morgan's "Candy Kisses" from the top spot in the hillbilly chart on 7th May 1949.

This was good news for Fred Rose who was determined to re-establish his pole position, both from a personal and a professional viewpoint. His "friend", Jenny Lou Carson, had recently jumped from his bed and from Acuff-Rose, and she now resided as an exclusive songwriter with Hill & Range.

Desperate to push Williams forwards, Rose spoke personally to Jack Stapp and Harry Stone at the *Opry*, but still they refused. As a final sweetener, he offered them the writers' credit on a song he had on his desk, a sure-fire hit called "Chattanoogie Shoe Shine Boy". This clinched the deal and Williams left the *Louisiana Hayride* and strolled onto the *Opry* stage on 11th June to claim his place in hillbilly history.

Hank stole the show with "Lovesick Blues". He took three, four, five encores — maybe more — but the Ryman audience wouldn't let him go. The era of Hank Williams had arrived.

Oscar Davis took careful note: under the right circumstances, Jack Stapp was a man with whom one could do business.

Lovesick Blues: The Life of Hank Williams, Paul Hemphill
Restless Giant: The Life and Times of Jean Aberbach & Hill and Range Songs, Bar Biszick-Lockwood

In my room

TUESDAY 20TH SEPTEMBER 1949
MEMPHIS, TENNESSEE

THE PRESLEYS were finally given decent public housing in the autumn, a year after they had arrived in Memphis. They moved into Lauderdale Courts, a modest, bustling, ambitious complex of buildings and families, all of whom had great hopes for the future.

And it was here the soon-to-turn-fifteen Elvis Presley first encountered a group of like-minded people, at least with regard to playing the guitar. He befriended three or four guys who hung around together on the communal lawn, and picked and sang a little. There was also a fellow named Johnny Black who was learning to play bass, like his older brother Bill.

Elvis never put himself forward and didn't solo, but he strummed along in the background and joined in with the rough harmonies. If anyone stumbled over a lyric, Elvis might be the one to pipe up with the correct words — it was as if he'd memorised every song he'd ever heard.

The repertoire was exclusively white: pop, gospel and hillbilly. The songs were mainly ballads (slower and therefore easier to play), with the occasional novelty number thrown in for good measure. Through his own inquisitive searching — from Beale Street, from church, from listening to radio WDIA — the teenage Presley had built up a solid knowledge of black music, but (as Sam Phillips himself had already realised) he knew that publicising this among his white friends might not necessarily be a sensible move. So he opted, understandably, for caution.

At home, in the privacy of his own bedroom, he'd listen to music of every conceivable tempo and hue, and then lose himself in his meticulously stored and filed comic book collection. He imagined himself as Captain Marvel, Jr, his favourite superhero, with immaculately quiffed black hair, a lightning bolt on his chest, and a short cape draped around his shoulders.

He would smile at this thought, and then reach over and cue up one of his precious Arthur Crudup singles on RCA Bluebird, bought with the nickels and dimes he'd earned doing odd jobs in his spare time.

Elvis & Gladys, Elaine Dundy
Last Train to Memphis: The Rise of Elvis Presley, Peter Guralnick

When Slim Whitman met Eddy Arnold

PERHAPS LATE 1949
MUTUAL NETWORK, NASHVILLE, TENNESSEE

HIS RCA VICTOR RECORDS weren't selling and Slim Whitman had been pestering his part-time agent, Bob Ross, for weeks. So Bob, keen to keep his client happy, chatted with his esteemed stepfather and managed to line up a thrice-weekly slot on Mutual Network radio. This required Slim and his wife to move from their cosy Tampa home to a cramped, mouse-ridden Nashville apartment. But they went, and Slim made his small-time broadcasts on Mondays, Wednesdays and Fridays.

Slim knew he was working near the bottom of the pile but, ironically, and not entirely by chance, each time he walked into the radio studio, he bumped into Eddy Arnold, the biggest hillbilly star in the country — managed by Tom Parker — who was recording his own very popular network show in the same building.

And that's how close Slim Whitman was to success: it passed him by three times a week.

Mr Songman: The Slim Whitman Story, Kenneth L. Gibble

"Blues Stay Away From Me", II

PERHAPS LATE 1949
DALLAS, TEXAS

JOE POOVEY, just eight years-old, was transfixed by the music coming out of the drugstore jukebox. "Blues Stay Away From Me" by The Delmore Brothers had become Joe's raison d'être. He couldn't get enough of it and kept hanging around the store, hoping a patron would invest another nickel and request Joe's favourite song.

Was it the harmonica, the brothers' harmonies, or the insistent guitar figure that drew Joe? He didn't know for sure, but his imagination was captured completely. His parents, Aligene and Bernice, rather than pour cold water on his passion, encouraged him to sing and learn an instrument.

He started on the six-string lap string and sang along with some songs by that new fellow on the radio, Slim Whitman. Soon, however, he picked up an acoustic guitar and realised he was destined to be not a sideman, but a singing frontman. Joe applied himself with missionary zeal and, by the age of twelve, he'd formed his first band, The Hillbilly Boys.

What Joe needed was exposure. He set his sights on the *Big D Jamboree*, a weekly radio show broadcast out of Dallas, intended to rival the *Hayride* and the *Opry*. Opened in 1947, it had become a focal point for musicians all over the Texas area, with songwriters, performers and producers flocking to the Dallas Sportatorium each Saturday. Joe was auditioned and signed up before his thirteenth birthday, and developed quickly from an adolescent novelty into a seasoned and talented *Jamboree* regular.

Poovey wasn't the only pre-teen star-in-the-making: the *Hayride* was currently launching its own entertaining twelve year-old out of Chicago named Tommy Sands, who'd been in the business since the age of eight.

Both were country boys and both played straight hillbilly, but there was something else going on that Joe Poovey in particular couldn't quite put his finger on … something about the bluesy feel of that Delmore Brothers record that stayed in the back of his mind …

Restless Giant: The Life and Times of Jean Aberbach & Hill and Range Songs, Bar Biszick-Lockwood
Groovey Joe Poovey Greatest Grooves CD Sleeve Notes, David Dennard with Ian Wallis
http://www.rockabillyhall.com/JoePoovey1.html

Charline Arthur: twenty with a Bulleit

LATE 1949
JIM BECK STUDIO, DALLAS, TEXAS

IT WAS INEVITABLE that Jim Bulleit would eventually get around to opening his own record label, simply because he'd tried pretty much every other available music business avenue in his quest for success.

Bullet Records was launched in 1946, and it should be noted that the opening of an independent label was a bold and novel move — but Jim was not short of self-confidence. He scored at the end of 1947 with "Near You" by Francis Craig, but other hits were slow in coming.

Also at that time, in Nashville, he recorded The Five Bars, a black vocal group led by the beautiful voice of Jimmy Sweeney and, although Bullet Records did have a "race" subsidiary label, he released "I'm All Dressed Up With a Broken Heart" (Bullet 1009) as a "popular" record to see if it made any impact. It didn't, and Sweeney moved on to MGM where he continued to slide between genres with little progress.

Every now and then, Bulleit took a chance with a wild card in the hope of hitting the jackpot and, in late 1949, he authorised a session with a twenty year-old lady by the name of Charline Arthur.

The daughter of a Pentecostal preacher, she'd bought her first guitar at the age of seven, using money saved by collecting empty beer bottles. She'd written her first song, "I've Got the Boogie Blues", at the age of twelve, and was performing on Texas radio a year later.

She recorded that very song for Bullet Records but the single was unsuccessful. Bulleit used the Jim Beck studio, recognising the owner — an entrepreneur in his mid-thirties — as a man of some talent.

Ignoring the setback, Charline concentrated on her live appearances, building a reputation as a fearless and exciting performer. In an age when women were expected to know their place, Charline Arthur carved out a space for herself, wearing sparkly costumes far removed from the twee gingham dresses of her contemporaries.

She kept on plugging away hoping someone, somewhere, would notice and give her the break she knew she deserved.

A Shot in the Dark: Making Records in Nashville, 1945-1955, Martin Hawkins
The King's Singer, *Mojo*, October 2017, Christopher Kennedy

A helping hand for Hank Snow

PERHAPS NOVEMBER 1949
RYMAN AUDITORIUM, NASHVILLE, TENNESSEE

THE DOUBTS THAT Hank Snow had expressed about his first RCA single had proven well-founded. The single did reasonable business, but it wasn't the smash hit he'd been hoping for, and he remained anxious about the future.

During the summer, he'd bumped into Oscar Davis, and made a bid for his services as manager. Davis was a big player in country music and it would have been a great step forward for Snow if he were to have signed with him. Oscar was flattered, but felt the timing wasn't good. Besides, he had his hands full holding on to Hank Williams.

As 1949 moved towards its close, a depressed Snow eventually reached out again to his friend Ernest Tubb for solace and advice. Tubb, a true friend indeed, offered to recommend Hank to the *Opry*. It was almost unheard of for the *Opry* to sign a singer without a big hit record, but Tubb's word was good at WSM and Hank was signed by Jim Denny to a modest contract, starting 7th January 1950.

Convinced that good times were just around the corner, Hank started looking for a place to put down roots and, on the advice of Eddy Arnold, took a place in nearby Madison, Tennessee, by chance just a few minutes' drive from Eddy's manager, Tom Parker.

The Hank Snow Story, Hank Snow with Jack Ownbey & Bob Burris

Silent night

SATURDAY 24TH DECEMBER 1949
BUSY BEE LIQUOR STORE, 3728 ALAMEDA AVENUE, EL PASO, TEXAS

THE LIGHT WAS FADING as Pinney stood inside the store, looking out at the last-minute festive shoppers bustling by. It had been a profitable day. Liquor sales always went through the roof in the weeks leading up to Christmas. He wondered what time he should close up.

At 8:00 PM the shop door opened and in walked two men, Louis Adams and Jim Turner, both aged thirty-one. Adams, originally from Dallas, was on parole from a California prison, and they had arrived on a freight train that day.

Pinney instantly registered that all was not well. His police and military experience warned him these men were trouble. Adams produced a pistol and declared, needlessly, "This is a hold up." The shopkeeper slowly stepped towards the counter when instructed. As he moved nearer the till, he suddenly reached below and pulled out two pistols, shooting at both bandits, who immediately returned fire. Adams shot five times, shattering bottles, but missing Pinney.

Pinney, however, did not miss and both men hit the ground, wounded but not dead. Police were called and the suspects were taken to El Paso General Hospital, and from there to the court for sentencing in the New Year.

Pinney had known this day would come. Such a shame it had to happen on Christmas Eve.

El Paso Herald-Post, Texas, 26th December 1949 & 6th January 1950

The death of Nannie Mae Boren

SUNDAY 1ST JANUARY 1950
WEWOKA, OKLAHOMA

THE DEATH OF A PARENT is not something for which one can ever adequately prepare. Mae's mother and namesake unexpectedly fell ill on Christmas Day 1949, and passed away one week later on the first day of the new decade. She was seventy-seven.

Such was the local standing of the Boren family that the news made the front page of the *Ada Evening News*. Mae, her father, and her brothers were devastated at this loss.

But sometimes the death of a loved one can be seen as the beginning of a new chapter in the lives of those who remain behind. Mae, a woman of strong Christian conviction, would have been familiar with the notion that when God closes one door he opens another.

Country Singers As I Know 'Em, Mae Boren Axton
Ada Evening News, Oklahoma, 2nd January 1950

The Memphis Recording Service

MONDAY 2ND JANUARY 1950
706 UNION AVENUE, MEMPHIS, TENNESSEE

THE SUCCESS OF all-black Memphis radio station WDIA had been the catalyst for Sam Phillips to finally heed the call to do something important with his life. And his choice of action was gloriously obtuse and eccentric. He would open an independent professional recording studio. It would not be exclusively black in its intended clientele, but that would be the main thrust of its purpose. Sam would allow the downtrodden an opportunity to raise their voices, and maybe make a record.

He'd recently fallen in with a lady named Marion Keisker, a very popular radio presenter. And, although Sam remained happily married with two young sons, he and Marion started a private affair which would last for almost seven years. She took on the position of Sam's Girl Friday, and devoted herself to his cause, giving him love, encouragement, money and absolute commitment.

During the autumn, they located a small but ideal building at 706 Union Avenue, on the corner of Marshall, beside a cheap, welcoming restaurant called Taylor's. Sam and Marion spent every waking moment scrubbing, scraping, painting and wiring to ensure the new business would be ready to launch on the first working day of the second half of the twentieth century.

Sam dubbed the company the Memphis Recording Service, and installed an impressive neon sign in each of the two storefront windows. He was very clear in his mind though: this was a recording studio and not a record label. Record labels caused no end of problems and complications. It was Sam's job to encourage artists — rough-hewn unique talents — to come through the door and make history on tape.

It would be a challenge. Most black singers and musicians would incorrectly assume that the white guy at the desk was looking to steal from them or take advantage in some clever way. But the thought of the music he could potentially record would make every second of the struggle worthwhile in Sam's eyes.

Sam Phillips: The Man who Invented Rock 'n' Roll, Peter Guralnick

Luke the Drifter

TUESDAY 10TH JANUARY 1950
CASTLE STUDIO, NASHVILLE, TENNESSEE

HANK WILLIAMS was climbing the hillbilly chart yet again with his latest single, the beautiful lament, "I'm So Lonesome I Could Cry", but was still itching to develop in other areas, and had been hassling Fred Rose about this for some time. The nation's new C&W star wanted to record a series of recitations that gave a strong moral message to the listener. However, wily old Fred Rose knew that if a customer punched up a Hank Williams single on a jukebox and a sermon came out of the speaker then it would sink his career.

And so, a compromise was reached: Williams would record under a pseudonym, Luke the Drifter, an identity which soon became the worst kept secret in show business. Hank would even perform some of the narratives on stage, saying, "Here's a song by my half-brother, Luke ..."

For Luke's first session in January 1950, he recorded four songs, one of which was "Beyond the Sunset", with words taken from the popular anthology, *Poems That Touch the Heart*, and another was "The Funeral", the heartbreaking story of a black child's burial to the sombre accompaniment of an organ playing one of Fred Rose's old tunes.

Most of Luke's songs contained an ethical point: stay on the straight and narrow and treat your brother fairly. And when Fred Rose submitted publishing information to MGM for "The Funeral" he noted there should be no writer or publisher credit on the label ... though he himself was still to receive half of the composer's royalty.

Hank Williams: The Biography, Colin Escott with George Merritt & William MacEwen

Bobby Ross: Tom's boy, II

JANUARY 1950
NASHVILLE, TENNESSEE

THERE'S NO QUESTION that Bob Ross relied upon his famous stepfather during the early days of his own career. But Bob was a good-looking, personable young man, who had many skills and attributes at his disposal.

Still, it didn't hurt to have the manager of the country's most popular hillbilly crooner as part of your intimate circle. And when Tom found out his boy and beloved daughter-in-law were expecting their first baby — a daughter to be partially named after Parker's wife, Marie — he did his darndest to make sure the family was well set up financially.

By the end of January 1950, Ross, as well as advising Slim Whitman and managing George Morgan (Bob had handed in his notice at RCA), was also appointed travelling field representative for Hill & Range Music Publishers.

It's not always *what* you know ... sometimes it's *who* you know.

Billboard, 28th January 1950

"Chattanoogie Shoe Shine Boy"

SATURDAY 25TH FEBRUARY 1950
THE COVER OF *BILLBOARD* MAGAZINE

RED FOLEY, Jack Stapp and Harry Stone were thrilled to find themselves not just at number one on the country chart, but also pictured on the front cover of *Billboard* magazine.

Foley's recording of Stapp and Stones' composition "Chattanoogie Shoe Shine Boy" had caught on like wildfire since its release the previous month. Foley was delighted; the song even looked like it would replace "Old Shep" as his signature tune. Sadly, it wasn't published by his own personal Hill & Range company, but Roy Acuff and Fred Rose seemed to have this one all sewn up.

The weird thing was that Red had no idea the guys from the *Opry* wrote songs at all, but you couldn't argue with success. And it was a great success, not just for Foley, but also for the other six versions which had been released since January, some by country stars and some by pop singers like Bing Crosby. This was a true and overwhelming crossover pop song.

The real winners, of course, were Acuff-Rose (as publishers), and Stapp and Stone (as composers). And when the royalties started rolling in they'd be swimming in gravy.

Billboard, 21st January, 25th February & 11th March 1950
http://countrydiscography.blogspot.co.uk/2010/01/red-foley.html

The Carters: stand by your man

EARLY 1950
RYMAN AUDITORIUM, NASHVILLE, TENNESSEE

THIS NIGHT had been a long time coming. The *Opry* brass had contacted Eck Carter several months ago offering his family a small but regular spot on the show. During negotiations, however, they'd made it clear the contract was just for the Carters — there was no place for the Atkins boy and his fancy picking. Eck turned them down. Few people ever turned down the *Opry*, but Eck Carter did.

They came back a few weeks later with the same contract, but a higher price. Eck's answer was the same: "Chet is family now, where we go, he goes."

They came back a third time with an even higher price, but still no spot for Chet. When Eck turned them down again they began to get the message.

Finally, the *Opry* signed the Carters — and Chet Atkins. They took to the stage and blew the audience away at precisely the moment when the show, and hillbilly music generally, exploded into unprecedented popularity. A combination of crossover hits like "Chattanoogie Shoe Shine Boy", clever public relations, and the strict policy of hiring only the biggest hillbilly stars, began to pay off.

Country music at last hit the big time.

Will You Miss Me When I'm Gone? The Carter Family & Their Legacy in American Music,
Mark Zwonitzer with Charles Hirshberg

The birth of country music, II

EARLY 1950
JACKSONVILLE, FLORIDA

For several months, if not years, Mae Boren Axton had been pushing her own name among editors and publishers, picking up the occasional commission, and earning an extra dollar or two as her articles and essays were printed in newspapers and magazines.

Shortly after the death of her mother, Mae accepted a task from *Life Today*, a national magazine, inviting her to explore the fast-rising profile of country music. Mae knew next-to-nothing about hillbilly tunes, but she threw herself into the project with her customary enthusiasm. She travelled to Dallas and spoke to the stars of the *Big D Jamboree*, and did likewise in Shreveport with the *Louisiana Hayride*, making friends and networking, using all of her considerable communication skills.

But it was in Nashville that she struck gold, for it was while researching the *Opry* that she made the acquaintance of Fred Rose and Minnie Pearl, who became not only trusted friends, but also passports into all avenues at WSM and beyond.

Mae's subsequent article was a success, so much so that her talents were requested by other publications who also wished to exploit the world of c&w music. Much to Mae's surprise, she developed a love not only for the singers, songwriters and performers, but also for the music itself.

This passion, combined with her literary talent, ensured Mae became one of the go-to people in hillbilly circles. If you needed a write-up for a magazine, a tour programme or promotional literature, then Mae Boren Axton was your woman. It was not a position to which she had necessarily aspired, but she welcomed it with open arms.

Country Singers As I Know 'Em, Mae Boren Axton

Eddy Arnold on the silver screen

AT SOME POINT IN 1950
CINEMA SCREENS NATIONWIDE

ONWARDS AND UPWARDS, that was the phrase that summed up Tom Parker's approach to managing Eddy Arnold. They'd moved on from the *Opry*; they'd expanded their concert base; and Steve Sholes was overjoyed with Eddy's record sales. Parker promoted his client during every waking moment, generally capitalising on his down-home, good-ole-country-boy appeal.

For Tom Parker, the next obvious step was to thrust his client into the world of TV and cinema, but for this he required specialist advice. The best place to go was, without question, the William Morris Agency, long-established as the number one talent broker in the country, and certainly the first choice of anyone seriously looking to break into Hollywood. But professional help of this calibre didn't come cheap, and the agency took a straight ten percent off the top.

Parker generally dealt with Harry Kalcheim at William Morris, but the real power now lay with Abe Lastfogel who, since his lowly beginnings as an office boy, had risen to be manager of the Los Angeles branch. Parker and Lastfogel hit it off straight away. Both were dedicated, hard-working, and street smart. Between them they lined up numerous Eddy Arnold TV appearances and arranged for two movies to be made by Columbia, *Feudin' Rhythm* and *Hoedown*, exploiting Eddy's hillbilly persona.

The movies were released in 1950 and 1951 respectively. Both were profitable, but neither set box-office records. The singer toured with the films and pushed the name of Eddy Arnold to new corners of the country.

Yet Eddy was beginning to wonder if he could ever escape his plowboy image. He also began to wonder if Tom Parker's brash approach to marketing was what he himself wanted. At RCA Victor, Steve Sholes was gently easing Eddy more into the middle-of-the-road musically, and Eddy had a liking for that.

Even in his own eyes, Eddy was no movie star. He was a singer, not even specifically a country singer … just a singer.

Eddy Arnold: Pioneer of the Nashville Sound, Michael Streissguth

Red, Jack and Harry in Chattanooga

SATURDAY 4TH MARCH 1950
CHATTANOOGA, TENNESSEE

JACK AND HARRY left it to Red to make the speeches. The mayor of Chattanooga had invited them all to a fete and presented them with the keys to the city. Foley's hit song had created such good publicity that the mayor figured it was the least he could do. Jack and Harry were getting used to the idea of being celebrities, although the thought of the cash that would soon be rolling in was nice, too.

Meanwhile, back in Nashville, a Mrs Minnie Lee Biggs filed a complaint against the WSM men, claiming "Chattanoogie Shoe Shine Boy" had, in fact, been written by her late husband in August 1947, a year before he died. At stake was about $100,000 worth of royalties.

The case dragged on for two years, until Mrs Biggs agreed to settle out of court and received $7,500 in exchange for acknowledgement of Stapp and Stone as the writers of the song. By this time, Stone had left WSM to pursue a career as a radio consultant.

For Jack Stapp, however, the case had been a revelation. Claiming authorship of a song was a risky business. Clearly, the best way to make real money in country music came from publishing.

Billboard, 11th March, 1st April & 29th July 1950 & 8th March 1952

Johnnie and Jack: "Poison Love"

MONDAY 27TH MARCH 1950
BROWN RADIO PRODUCTIONS, NASHVILLE, TENNESSEE

THE LATE ELMER LAIRD'S "Poison Love" had done the rounds and had ended up in the fast-growing Hill & Range catalogue. Thus, when Steve Sholes was looking for suitable material for an upcoming Johnnie and Jack session, the Aberbachs were only too happy to add it to the list.

The session on 27th March 1950 (with Kitty Wells on backing vocals) was the duo's second RCA Victor date — the first had not produced anything of note. Sholes guided the recordings with his usual efficiency and grace. Amidst seven other numbers, mainly a selection of gospel-influenced tracks, Laird's song was recorded and chosen as the first single. Issued later that year (21-0377), it reached number four on the *Billboard* country chart: Johnnie and Jack finally had a bona fide hillbilly top ten record.

Notably, the record label carried the writer's credit, "Mrs Elmer Laird". The deceased hadn't managed to speak to his wife before breathing his last, but he'd bequeathed her a genuine hit.

Hank Williams: The Biography, Colin Escott with George Merritt & William MacEwen
Voices of the Country: Interviews with Classic Country Performers, Michael Streissguth
Nu Country website, Dave's diary obituary of Tilman Franks

Hank Snow: "I'm Movin' On"

TUESDAY 28TH MARCH 1950
BROWN RADIO PRODUCTIONS, NASHVILLE, TENNESSEE

HANK SNOW was a man living on the very edge of his frayed nerves. He'd been playing the *Opry* each week of the New Year, receiving minimal polite applause from the audience who didn't know who the heck he was. And why would they? He was still without the smash hit almost all *Opry* stars were required to supply.

Mr Sholes called him back to the recording studio for his second session, a year after the first, hoping to produce something a little more fruitful. Still, in the back of his mind, Snow carried his special song, the one Mr Sholes had turned down in March 1949.

So, Hank took a gamble as they ran through potential material for the new session and threw in his song again, hoping Sholes might forget he'd heard and rejected it before. And amazingly, that's exactly what happened. The producer picked "I'm Movin' On" as the first release from the session (RCA 48-0328, May 1950) and it hit the number one spot in the c&w chart for what seemed like the rest of the year.

The *Opry* crowd then received him ecstatically, and Hank Snow could finally relax a little and enjoy his long-awaited success.

The Hank Snow Story, Hank Snow with Jack Ownbey & Bob Burris

"Do you want to die?"

WEDNESDAY 29TH MARCH 1950
BUSY BEE LIQUOR STORE, 3728 ALAMEDA AVENUE, EL PASO, TEXAS

THE SUITED MAN, staring out from under the brim of his hat, pointed his black automatic pistol directly at Pinney, and waited for a response to his lethal question. It was dark outside the shop. Pinney remained calm, and looked into the robber's eyes, as if weighing up the man and his intentions.

The shopkeeper replied, "Let's get it over with," and pulled a pistol from under the counter, firing off six rounds at the bandit who stood less than a yard away. The would-be robber also emptied his gun of bullets, sending glass and liquor flying all over the store. Pinney took one in the left hand.

The villain turned and staggered into a waiting car, then sped off east on Alameda. Police were called, and they retrieved all twelve bullets from the woodwork, doors and walls. The chief of detectives suggested the man therefore had escaped untouched, or perhaps a bullet may have passed completely through his body.

Pinney, however, was in no doubt: "I was only two feet from him, across the counter, when we started firing. I don't see how I could have missed him at that distance."

El Paso Herald-Post, Texas, 30th March 1950

Alvin Krolik's lost weekend

SUNDAY 16TH APRIL 1950
U.S. NAVAL HOSPITAL, QUEENS, NEW YORK

ALVIN KROLIK had been on the run for eleven days when he finally surrendered himself at the U.S. Naval Hospital St Albans in Queens, New York, on Sunday 16th April 1950. He'd last been seen leaving the Marine Barracks Base in Philadelphia at noon on 5th April.

Alvin had joined the Marines aged seventeen, four years prior to this incident, and his service record was far from exemplary. In October 1946 he'd been punished for direct disobedience of an order. Just three months later, he was sentenced to five days bread and water for another infringement. He twice went AWOL in April 1949; and he'd spent time in the sick bay since the autumn of that year.

And now, having handed himself in, the military authorities decided he should remain at the naval hospital to receive medical care: the boy was obviously sick.

Less than three months later, on Sunday 25th June, the Korean People's Army crossed the 38th parallel and America decided it was once again at war.

The U.S. Marines prepared themselves for battle. They needed every able-bodied man … but did they need Alvin Krolik?

Red Hot and Blue

AT SOME POINT IN 1950
MEMPHIS, TENNESSEE

DURING THE EARLY DAYS of the Memphis Recording Service, Sam Phillips handed out business cards which declared he'd record literally anything. Although Sam had set up the studio as a focal point for black artists, he still had to pay the bills. And so, members of the public were encouraged to step inside, lay down a few dollars, and make a personal double-sided acetate disk, whether they were singers, guitarists, accordion players or trombonists. Sam also used his mobile unit to tape weddings, funerals, conventions and graduations, as and when required.

Business was regrettably slow, but it was all so exciting to Sam and Marion. They felt they were part of something very special that was beginning to happen in Memphis itself. This feeling intensified when Sam encountered a new local radio deejay named, coincidentally, Dewey Phillips. Dewey, an eccentric, unpredictable and loud figure, was a white man who played almost every style and colour of music on his perfectly titled late-night show, *Red Hot and Blue*, on station WHBQ.

Phillips and Phillips met, talked, and both recognised a kindred spirit. They encouraged each other to keep pushing forward, focusing on the exciting black music that they knew was growing more popular with — and more acceptable to — all audiences.

And almost every night, in his small room, Elvis Presley tuned his radio to WHBQ; and for two hours he absorbed every record Dewey played, incorprating each one into the vast library he already had catalogued in his head.

Sam Phillips: The Man who Invented Rock 'n' Roll, Peter Guralnick

Slim Whitman goes south

MAY 1950
RADIO KWKH, SHREVEPORT, LOUISIANA

THERE WAS SOME DEBATE in Bob's mind as to whether Slim would go for the idea. The pay, $18 a week, was lousy, and it would mean moving yet again, this time from Nashville to Shreveport. The *Louisiana Hayride* had been looking for a new star since Hank Williams had transferred to the *Opry*. Slim Whitman wasn't that star, but everyone else on the show had moved one step up the ladder — which left a vacancy on the bottom rung.

Coincidentally, Slim bumped into Hank Williams himself at this time and he gave the struggling singer some sound advice about appearing on the *Hayride*: "You're a yodeller, right? Well, you go down there, rear back, and let 'em have it."

So that's what Slim did, and he was signed to start appearing from May 1950. However, he wasn't an instant triumph; his lack of between-song patter proved a difficulty for the audience. He toured with a number of the *Hayride* stars like Faron Young, "Little" Tommy Sands, The Wilburn Brothers, and Kitty Wells, but seemed unable to make any headway.

After a year of living hand-to-mouth in Shreveport, Slim decided enough was enough. One Saturday night on air, he made a quiet, stuttering speech announcing his intention to retire from the entertainment business. Ironically and wonderfully, at that moment, the audience took him to their hearts and applauded the shy yodeller.

Slim quickly changed his mind about quitting and, from this point onwards, his career started a rapid climb. "Shoot," he thought, "I might be able to quit my day job with the Post Office and take up singing full time."

Mr Songman: The Slim Whitman Story, Kenneth L. Gibble

When Bobby met Hank

SATURDAY 3RD JUNE 1950
THE COVER OF *BILLBOARD* MAGAZINE

THE SMILING FACE OF Hank Snow beamed out from the cover of *Billboard* magazine. He'd actually made the front page, yet more evidence of his change in fortunes. In the picture, Hank was flanked by Harry Stone and Steve Sholes, while the blurb noted Hank's personal management was being handled by none other than Bob Ross.

Ross had been on board with Snow since early April and was doing some fancy juggling, looking after George Morgan and Slim Whitman, pitching for the Aberbachs, and now booking the Canadian, who was just shifting into the big time with "I'm Movin' On".

But he was soon to discover that Snow was no easy ride: he had a temper to match his height. The professional relationship lasted all of three months. It was a tough period in general for managers of guys named Hank, as Williams and Oscar Davis had parted company too, during the spring.

By September, with his record topping the charts, Snow signed to a new man, A.V. Bamford, a colourful Cuban who had considerable experience of show business.

Billboard, 8th April, 3rd June, 1st July & 3rd September 1950

When Mae met Glenn

PERHAPS AT SOME POINT IN 1950
CHILDRESS, TEXAS

NOW THAT SHE HAD CAUGHT the country music bug, Mae Boren Axton was steeping herself in all things hillbilly. Sometimes when driving around in Texas, Oklahoma or Tennessee, she would hear talented young local deejays over the car radio, and would actively seek out the station and introduce herself, knowing that these people could prove useful and influential in years to come. That may be how she came to meet twenty year-old Glenn Reeves in Childress, Texas, near the Oklahoma border.

Reeves was tall and good looking, with an engaging personality. He also had a strong singing voice and, when not spinning platters for KCTX, he performed with a young hillbilly band from nearby Shamrock. Mae had written a couple of C&W songs for herself — just to see if she could — and was interested to know how they would sound if played by a proper band.

She arranged with Glenn to bring his group into the radio station and record her personal demos. Among the players was a young rascal on fiddle, not yet out of school, named Roger Miller. Roger couldn't play that well and Mae noted his part on both songs sounded pretty much the same.

But Mae was pleased with the demos — although she knew nothing would come of the primitive compositions — and she probably slipped the boys a few dollars for their trouble. She also thanked Glenn for his efforts, knowing she'd made a good friend, and suggested if she could ever return the favour, then he shouldn't hesitate to give her a call.

Country Singers As I Know 'Em, Mae Boren Axton
Glenn Reeves / *Johnny on the Spot* CD Sleeve Notes, Martin Hawkins & Richard Weize

Pinney: love and marriage, IV

FRIDAY 13TH OCTOBER 1950
BUSY BEE LIQUOR STORE, 3728 ALAMEDA AVENUE, EL PASO, TEXAS

CAREFUL READERS OF THE *El Paso Herald-Post* would have seen a small notification buried deep within their newspaper on Friday 13th October 1950. It declared that Edna Pinney was no longer associated with The Busy Bee Liquor and Tackle Company, and ownership had now passed solely to D.R. Pinney.

This notice made no reference to the simple fact that Pinney's third marriage had ended in divorce. He'd come to the conclusion that Edna (and her mother) were simply in it for the money and, when confronted with this opinion, she physically attacked him. Pinney pulled a gun and escorted both women from the premises.

Were he the type of man given to deep introspection, Pinney might have become morose, but he had an admirably straightforward approach to life. By the end of February 1951, the shopkeeper had married Francisca Parra Frias, aged nineteen, to his fifty-three, whom he had met across the border, through his aquaintance with Pancho Villa.

And it seemed he had finally found true love, for not only did they marry, but they started a family together: their first child, Frances, was born on 20th December 1951, Francisca's twentieth birthday.

El Paso Herald-Post, Texas, 13th October 1950

Hank Snow: come fly with me

SUNDAY 5TH NOVEMBER 1950
BALTIMORE, MARYLAND

WITH HIS SIGNATURE SONG "I'm Movin' On" riding high on the hillbilly chart, Hank Snow was going places, and his price per gig was rising all the time. But Hank had already parted company with his manager A.V. Bamford and would soon sign with a fellow Canadian, named Norm Riley.

Jim Denny, meanwhile, booked him for a six-night stay with the Carters and Chet Atkins at the Hippodrome in Baltimore, beginning on 28th October, and Hank's share of the gate was $900, once the *Opry* had taken its cut. He hung around for a few days after the last concert, then, with his pay in his wallet, he boarded a plane bound for Nashville, feeling flush with money — and flushed with success.

Adding to his triumph, he found himself sitting near to none other than Eddy Arnold and also Colonel Tom Parker, the stepfather of his previous manager but one. Throughout the flight, there was much good-natured show business chat and lots of backslapping, and when the plane landed, the parties went their separate ways.

Hank arrived home in a jubilant mood. He dropped his guitar case and luggage in the front room, then reached for his wallet in his jacket pocket. It was gone. And the $900 was gone too. He immediately phoned his Baltimore hotel but they hadn't found anything. Becoming increasingly fraught, he made further enquires with the airline and the cab company but to no avail.

Hank Snow never did find that wallet.

The Hank Snow Story, Hank Snow with Jack Ownbey & Bob Burris
Billboard, 4th & 25th November 1950

Tommy Sands: "Love Pains"

PERHAPS LATE 1950
FREEDOM RECORDING COMPANY, HOUSTON, TEXAS

NOW AGED THIRTEEN, Tommy Sands of the *Louisiana Hayride* was lined up for his first recording session at Freedom Records in Texas, where his family had recently relocated. He'd been in the business for half of his life and he was the son of two musicians, so the whole idea of performing came naturally to him.

In his sweet and unbroken voice, he taped two uptempo hillbilly numbers, "Love Pains" and "Syrup Soppin' Blues", and they were released early in the New Year (Freedom 5022), but sold almost nothing. The truth was that Tommy, like Joe Poovey from the *Big D Jamboree*, was stuck in no-man's land: too young to be sexy, and too old to be cute.

Tommy returned to his long list of Texas one-nighters, hoping some big-time manager would recognise his talent and send him on his way to fame and fortune.

Billboard, 26th July 1952

Hula Boogie, II

PERHAPS LATE 1950
FREEDOM RECORDING COMPANY, HOUSTON, TEXAS

THERE IS NO SET PATTERN for how a marriage breaks up. Tommy Durden and Boots Gilbert just drifted apart, even though they were on stage together almost every day. There was sadness; but no acrimony. They liked each other too much to let bitterness spoil their friendship, so they dried their tears and decided the show must go on.

Meanwhile, The Westernaires were pushing to make records and, in the autumn of 1950, they recorded a single for the Texas-based Four-Star label, which featured a Tommy and Boots duet, entitled "That's Where You Dropped Your Candy" (Four-Star 1500). The record flopped, and when Tommy presented a couple of new songs for the next session, the label declared them too "poppy" and decided against extending the contract.

And so it was, in late 1950, just as Tommy Sands vacated the studio, The Westernaires changed labels and found themselves at the Freedom Recording Company, laying down Tommy Durden's "Crossroads", and his lyricised version of Bernie Kaii Lewis' "Steel Guitar Boogie", now named "Hula Boogie". The former was played as a slightly maudlin ballad with a funereal organ backing, but the latter fairly jumped out of the grooves with a fine mandolin solo from the former Mrs Durden and a sparkling steel guitar accompaniment by guest player, Herb Remington. Tommy's lyrics displayed a great confidence, along with a sense of clarity and order. The rhymes were clean and strong, and scanned beautifully.

The single was credited to Tommy Durden and The Westernaires and was released in January 1951 (Freedom 5025). Listed as sole composer on both sides, Tommy waited for the dollars to start coming in.

Hank and Anita, I

FRIDAY 26TH JANUARY 1951
BROWN STUDIOS, NASHVILLE, TENNESSEE

MAYBELLE CARTER and Hank Snow's wife, Minnie, had become fast friends. Both were new in Nashville; they shared a love of family and also of card playing, and they spent much of their free time together. Inevitably, Hank Snow met young Anita Carter and invited her to duet on his new RCA Victor material.

They gathered at Brown Studios in January but, before the session, Steve Sholes took Anita to one side. He warned her Hank had a notorious temper — and an inflated ego — and she should tread carefully around the superstar. Anita, just seventeen, nodded and took her place at the microphone as Hank arrived.

The first song began and they weren't but two verses in when Anita called a halt to the proceedings and fixed Hank with a hard stare: "Hush, Hank," she said. "You're singing on my part." The studio fell deathly silent, and Sholes held his breath.

Snow stared at the girl, threw back his head and roared with laughter.

The single from this session, "Bluebird Island", was issued two months later (RCA Victor 48-0441) and reached number four in the c&w chart, providing yet another hit record for Hank Snow.

Will You Miss Me When I'm Gone? The Carter Family & Their Legacy in American Music,
Mark Zwonitzer with Charles Hirshberg

Truth or Consequences

SATURDAY 3RD FEBRUARY 1951
BUSY BEE LIQUOR STORE, 3728 ALAMEDA AVENUE, EL PASO, TEXAS

BARELY OUT THEIR TEENS, Perkins, Wells and Wright had stolen the pistol from a pawn shop in Albuquerque. The bullets had been purchased in the aptly named town of Truth or Consequences in New Mexico. Next stop: El Paso.

They'd planned the robbery for five days, knowing the Saturday night takings in liquor stores were high. The trio were on leave from the air force, and this was their second robbery. They'd botched a previous attempt in the autumn, but this time there would be no mistake. They'd already picked out their target at the crossroads of Alameda and North Latta.

The Busy Bee had been held up twenty-six times since opening: but only those occasions that involved gunfire had made the local press. Not one attempt had yet proven successful.

At 9 o'clock, the three men pulled up outside the store. Perkins remained at the wheel with the motor running. Wells and Wright entered and waited quietly until the customers left. They asked Pinney for a bottle of whiskey from the shelf behind the counter and, as he turned, Wells shoved a .38-calibre Colt revolver against his stomach. Wright kept watch by the door.

Pinney suggested they help themselves to the till, but they'd better be quick because he was sure he could hear a customer's car coming. Both men grabbed handfuls of notes, forgetting the thin, middle-aged shopkeeper, who pulled out one of his secreted weapons and shot Wells where he stood.

Wright was making his escape, but Pinney hit him hard with his next shot as he ran out of the door, sending dollar bills cascading into the street. Wells struggled to his feet pointing the Colt at Pinney, who finished the airman with two more bullets. Wright, wounded but not dead, and Perkins, the intended getaway driver, were arrested to stand trial in June.

The twenty-seventh assault on The Busy Bee had ended like all those before them.

Corpus Christi Times, Texas, 5th February 1951
El Paso Herald-Post, Texas, 5th February 1951

Conflict resolution, Texas style

AT SOME POINT IN 1951
DALLAS, TEXAS

NO ONE WAS EXACTLY SURE how the fight had started, but few doubted it was Jack Ruby who had thrown the first punch. The Silver Spur had developed a reputation as perhaps the most notorious night spot in Dallas, but customers still turned up for the music and the atmosphere.

Playing that night was Willis "Dub" Dickerson, guitarist, hillbilly singer, and songwriter, who had already recorded a few sides at the Jim Beck studio, and was beginning to make a name for himself. Within a couple of years he'd sign for the Capitol label and achieve a measured level of success.

But on the night of the fight, he was just a guy in the band who happened to disagree with the club owner, Jack Ruby, a man quite accustomed to resolving conflict with either words — as Hank Snow knew only too well — or with his fists, as Dub Dickerson soon discovered.

Tables, bottles, chairs and instruments flew all over the Silver Spur as the two men clashed in a no-holds-barred exchange of views. When Ruby moved his attack below the belt, Dickerson knew the gloves were off and bit through Ruby's left index finger, bringing the struggle to a bloody conclusion.

Dub handed in his notice and headed on to pastures new, eventually landing in Nashville. For Ruby, this sort of thing was part and parcel of his daily routine. He had the top half of his finger surgically removed and carried on as before. This was no big deal.

At least it wasn't his trigger finger.

Dub Dickerson / *Boppin' in the Dark* CD Sleeve Notes, Kevin Coffey et al

"Rocket 88"

MARCH 1951
706 UNION AVENUE, MEMPHIS, TENNESSEE

Business began to improve a little at the Memphis Recording Service. Sam Phillips had set up a couple of loose connections with independent labels, one of them being Chess Records in Chicago, so that if, by chance, he did manage to record someone with commercial potential, he would at least have some way of getting the song out there.

He taped Riley King, the young deejay from WDIA, singing under the name "B.B. King"; he also recorded Joe Hill Louis, a fabulous one-man band; and several other black artists, all of whom received Sam's undivided attention in the studio. He had extraordinary patience behind the console. The clock meant nothing. A lifelong student of human behaviour, he would humour, cajole and encourage, looking to preserve on tape something unique, something special, something of the very soul of the singer.

The abuse he received from acquaintances was remarkable but not unexpected. He'd generally kept his feelings on equality to himself, but there was no disguising his position now he was openly recording and promoting black musicians. But progress just seemed so slow.

And then it happened.

B.B. King recommended a band called The Kings of Rhythm, led by a hyperactive pianist called Ike Turner. They turned up for the session full of enthusiasm and carrying a busted guitar speaker, and Sam loved the distorted sound it produced. They had brought a bouncy uptempo number called "Rocket 88", named for the current dream car from General Motors.

Sam recognised it was lifted from a 1948 hit, "Cadillac Boogie" by Jimmy Liggins, but he didn't care. The feel of the new song was wonderful. He had sax player Jackie Brenston take over the vocals (much to Turner's chagrin), and then leased the finished song to Chess Records. In early June it hit the top spot in the R&B chart (Chess 1458). It was like nothing else that had been recorded before. It was rhythm & blues but with a more insistent beat, and Sam loved every second of it.

Local newspaper *The Commercial Appeal* ran a feature on the record on 28th March 1951, declaring: "Sam's direct search is for musician-composers in the hillbilly or race field who can record their own songs. If anybody wants to bring him a song, he'll be glad to look it over."

Elvis Presley, as keen a student of R&B as anyone else in the city, bought the single, read the article, noted Mr Phillips' comments, and marvelled that this amazing song had been recorded in a studio in his own home town.

Sam Phillips: The Man who Invented Rock 'n' Roll, Peter Guralnick
The Commercial Appeal, Memphis, 28th March 1951

Hula Boogie, III

SATURDAY 14TH APRIL 1951
DECCA RECORDING STUDIO, NEW YORK CITY, NEW YORK

When Tommy Durden's single hit the streets, two hillbilly singers rushed to cover "Crossroads" — Johnny Hicks in Houston (Columbia 20826), and Johnny Nelms in New York (Decca 9-46318). Neither sold well — nor did Tommy's original.

To make matters worse, when Tommy attempted to register his copyright on "Hula Boogie", Bernie Kaii Lewis' lawyer raised a strong objection to Tommy's borrowing of "Steel Guitar Boogie", and he lost all rights to the song — lyrics and all. "Hula Boogie" was henceforth credited solely to Lewis, who added yet another Polynesian title to his canon. It was a further blow for the likeable singer.

Over the next few months, Tommy drifted away from The Westernaires, while Boots fell head-over-heels in love and married steel guitarist, Chuck Hatfield. Nevertheless, Tommy always kept in touch and was always respectful. He rarely voiced his sadness, keeping his feelings hidden deep within. But he never got over the pain of losing Boots, and carried a torch for her for years to come.

Hank Snow takes advice

JUNE 1951
HOLLYWOOD, CALIFORNIA

A DIVORCEE IN HER EARLY THIRTIES, Lola Bernice "Bea" Terry was smart, industrious and determined. Working in the PR business in Hollywood demanded all of these characteristics — and she had them in spades. Bea was one of the top names in the hillbilly field: if you had a song, a show, or a singer that needed pushing, then Bea was the woman to call.

There were relatively few females in positions of authority within country music, but Hank Snow, whose career was thriving, recognised her abilities and hired her to advise on his next steps forward. Also, believing himself to be something of a ladies' man, he would certainly have enjoyed the novelty of having a woman on his team. But Bea was a tough cookie and stood for no nonsense. Business and pleasure rarely mixed in her world.

During that summer, Hank also finally realised a dream: introducing his fifteen year-old son, Jimmie Rodgers Snow, as part of his touring show. Jimmie was a shy lad with a pleasant singing voice who had no desire to take to the stage. But to disappoint his father meant incurring his wrath, and that was something Jimmie had already learned not to do.

Jim Reeves: His Untold Story, Larry Jordan
Billboard, 2nd & 23rd June 1951, 2nd August 1952

At home in Jacksonville

AT SOME POINT IN 1951
JACKSONVILLE, FLORIDA

THE AXTON FAMILY finally found themselves a permanent home. Their address became 3239 Dellwood Avenue, running parallel to and just south of Route 90 as it passed east to west through Jacksonville. John's great run of coaching success continued at Robert E. Lee, and Mae was now well established in the English department at Landon School, also working in the drama office, and directing the establishment's periodical, *The Lion's Roar*.

With both sons growing up fast, Mae found herself with a little more time on her hands, allowing her to devote attention to writing and other profitable activities — for as any parent will tell you, money is always in short supply.

Mae branched out further into promotions for hillbilly shows that passed through Florida, never risking her own money, just advising and advertising, as required by the promoters who were looking for someone with good local knowledge and a way with words.

Country Singers As I Know 'Em, Mae Boren Axton
Glenn Reeves / *Johnny on the Spot* CD Sleeve Notes, Martin Hawkins & Richard Weize

Love and mercy

WEDNESDAY 13TH JUNE 1951
EL PASO, TEXAS

THE TRIAL OF THE two surviving airmen who had attempted to rob The Busy Bee in February had become something of a cause celebre in El Paso. It seems the boys came from good stock, and their parents were able to produce solid character references from respected community figures. It was a complex case — they were still minors in the eyes of the court — but, essentially, they were each given seven-year suspended sentences.

Pinney himself, now married to his new love, Francisca, was barely mentioned in the newspaper reports and that's how he liked it. His self-defence of property and person was entirely correct within Texas law. It brought him no pleasure to kill, but every man who came into The Busy Bee carrying a gun had made a decision. Pinney had made his own decision years ago when he saw the body of Officer Chitwood lying dead.

The father of Albert Wright spoke to the press about his wounded son: "His trouble came from emotional difficulties. His girl refused to marry him until she finished school. His officers then told him he was going to Korea, and ninety percent of the men sent there don't return. I stayed at his bedside for ten days after he was shot in attempting the robbery. The doctors didn't give him much chance to live. When he regained consciousness he told me, 'Dad, I'm glad they caught me. Now I won't lead a life of crime. I'm sorry.'"

After the trial, strangers congratulated him because his son was given a second chance to be a good citizen. People visited at the Gateway Hotel, where he was staying, to present best wishes.

"I've never seen another town like El Paso," said Mr Wright. "It has a most understanding attitude."

El Paso Herald-Post, Texas, 8th, 11th, 12th *&* 13th June 1951

Hank Williams goes home

SUNDAY 15TH JULY 1951
MONTGOMERY, ALABAMA

RETURNING HERO Hank Williams was scheduled to perform on 15th July 1951 in his home town of Montgomery. The shows were sponsored by the Jaycees (United States Junior Chamber), a nationwide, philanthropic, community organisation. Hank was in two minds about his visit. Although he had some fond memories of Montgomery, he recalled the occasions he'd been disowned as an unreliable drunk.

Also on the bill that day were Chet Atkins, the Carters and Hank Snow, but it was Williams the crowd had come to see: he was the superstar; he was the man with the songs that everyone knew.

Before the performance, Williams took his band to a barbecue stand he favoured, and treated everyone to lunch. As they were fixing to leave, the black owner came rushing towards Williams holding his bill-clip which she'd found on the floor. He took the money from the clip and put the wad of notes in her hand saying, "Thank you."

Just then, Hank realised he hadn't brought his guitar for the shows, so his cousin ran down to the local music store. He returned with a new model, saying the owners would be honoured if the great Hank Williams would accept it as a gift. The star smiled bitterly. He remembered a time when the store wouldn't extend him a dime's worth of credit and today they were giving him a guitar.

It would have been easy for Hank to see the bright side of this situation, but by now he was edging too far over into the shadows.

Hank Williams: The Biography, Colin Escott with George Merritt & William MacEwen

Big Tom, little Tom

JULY 1951
54 WEST RANDOLPH STREET, CHICAGO, ILLINOIS

THE EDDY ARNOLD RADIO SHOW needed a little freshening up, so the singing Dickens Sisters were brought in for their moment in the spotlight. They went over well with the singer and the audience, and from the summer of 1951 they became part of the Eddy Arnold troupe.

Tom Parker was happy enough because they were not expensive, but what really impressed the Colonel was the sisters' brother and manager, Tom Diskin, who operated out of a small talent office in Chicago, owned by Al Dvorin.

Parker was wise enough to know his arrogant blustering approach to business didn't sit comfortably with everyone. It might be useful to have a man like Tom Diskin around — a smooth-talker, someone with charm and a little more class.

As was his way, Tom Parker slowly moved in on Tom Diskin. There was no rush, no need to upset the apple cart. Parker hadn't formulated a plan yet, but the diminutive Diskin was too good to waste.

Billboard, 11th August 1951 & 23rd February 1952

Jack and Lou plant a Tree

AT SOME POINT IN 1951
NASHVILLE, TENNESSEE

THE LEGAL DEBACLE OVER "Chattanoogie Shoe Shine Boy" had embarrassed Jack Stapp, but had also taught him a valuable lesson: the big money in music came from publishing. He talked over the situation with his good friend, radio and TV producer, Lou Cowan, whom he'd first met during the war and who was always looking for the next big thing. They decided to open their own publishing company.

But Stapp did have a potential problem: the president of WSM radio, Mr John DeWitt, was growing increasingly concerned at the conflicts of interest that existed within his organisation. The ongoing legal nonsense with the song was a perfect example: DeWitt felt his company was being compromised. If executives at the *Opry* started up their own publishing houses the relationships would be wide open to corruption.

Therefore, Stapp and Cowan decided to found their company in a very quiet fashion. There wasn't an office, nor was there a telephone number. It was almost a covert operation, so it was hardly surprising that their one and only employee — musician and song-plugger Jerry Byrd — made no headway at all attracting songwriters.

Cowan's wife, Polly, dubbed the invisible company "Tree Publishing" and, had Stapp and Cowan seen fit to invest any of their personal wealth in the firm, it would probably have been operating at a loss. As it was, assuming Byrd was paid on a commission-only basis, there were virtually no expenses and no income.

Not surprisingly, Tree did not grow at all.

By the Seat of my Pants, Buddy Killen with Tom Carter

Odd man out

SEPTEMBER 1951
MEMPHIS, TENNESSEE

ENTERING HIS JUNIOR YEAR at high school, sixteen year-old Elvis Presley began to re-invent himself. Perhaps he already entertained the idea of being a professional singer and knew he needed an image to go with the music dancing around in his head. The obvious step would have been to assemble a hick cowboy look, like every hillbilly singer before him, but Presley's awakening creativity demanded something more eclectic and noticeable.

The first step was the hair. His long dirty-blond locks were impossible to control, so he applied tonic and Vaseline, constantly sweeping the strands up into what he called the "Tony Curtis style". Presley had seen the young actor in the exciting 1950 movie, *Winchester '73*, and wanted to cultivate that sensitive-but-manly look.

Next, he took to growing his sideburns long, much longer than his peers. He always maintained he was aping the truck drivers who constantly passed through Memphis. They were dangerous-looking guys, and Elvis loved that air of rebellion and potential violence.

Finally, he took himself down to Beale and stood outside Lansky's clothing store. He walked by a hundred times, sometimes pressing his nose up against the glass, all the better to see the vivid and beautifully-cut garments therein. Bernard Lansky, noticing the boy, stepped outside one time and invited him inside to browse. Presley politely declined. Growing hair and sideburns was cheap. Buying top-of-the-range clothes was expensive.

But he worked after school, earned a few dollars and eventually picked out a selection of items — perhaps a pink jacket, a pair of black trousers with a white stripe down the seam, a block green shirt — and completed the look he had been aiming for. He wanted to copy the extravagant and devil-may-care characters he'd admired walking around Beale Street, and Lansky's became his tailor-of-choice for the rest of his life.

Having assembled a distinctive — perhaps unique? — look, he presented himself this way every single day, be it at school, at church or at his part-time jobs, regardless of the abuse. If he was intending to be noticed, then he had certainly succeeded.

Last Train to Memphis: The Rise of Elvis Presley, Peter Guralnick

Buddy Killen bids goodbye to Florence

SATURDAY 8TH SEPTEMBER 1951
FLORENCE, ALABAMA

AGED EIGHTEEN YEARS, a nervous Buddy Killen stood at the door of the air force recruiting office in Florence just before noon on a Saturday. The Korean conflict loomed large for his generation, and several of his school friends had already joined up. Some had come home in a pine box.

Buddy had considered the possibility of becoming a professional bass player, but on this day he made an impulsive decision and walked smartly up to the recruiting sergeant.

"Hi, I'm Buddy Killen. I'd like to join the air force, sir."

"Buddy, we'd love to have you, but I'm getting ready to close up for today. Do you think you could come back Monday?"

So Buddy returned home, saying nothing to his parents. On the Sunday afternoon, however, he received a surprise call from his musician friend Autry Inman in Nashville, offering him a job playing bass. Buddy packed his case and his instrument, and had his father drive him to Nashville — one hundred and twenty miles away from Florence, and seven thousand miles from Korea.

By the Seat of my Pants, Buddy Killen with Tom Carter

Tommy Durden: on my own

SATURDAY 6TH OCTOBER 1951
WALKER HOTEL, ODESSA, TEXAS

SINCE LEAVING THE WESTERNAIRES, Tommy Durden had picked up small-time gigs in Texas, and had advertised for musicians to play with him. He was soon visiting Odessa, Galveston and other popular nightspots in the state, eventually gaining a fifteen-minute TV programme on KTXL San Angela, called *Tommy Durden Sings*. He played a mixture of songs but "Crossroads" always featured in his repertoire.

His life became that of a wandering troubadour. His home, such as it was, was in Gainesville, Florida, but the road — particularly the Sunshine State itself and Texas — was where he found comfort.

The Abiline Reporter News, Texas, 21st October & 4th November 1953
Billboard, 6th October 1951
The Galveston News, Texas, 13th June 1952

The Sunshine Sisters

MONDAY 5TH NOVEMBER 1951
CASTLE STUDIO, NASHVILLE, TENNESSEE

JEAN CHAPEL watched her sister, Martha Carson, standing at the studio microphone as the tape rolled and the band kicked in. This was Martha's big chance and Jean couldn't have been happier for her.

Martha had been working in the music business for over ten years: first with her two siblings as The Sunshine Sisters and, more recently, on radio WNOX with her husband, James, as The Barn Dance Sweethearts.

Unfortunately, James' philandering had since put an end to their marriage and to their professional relationship, but what had shocked Martha was the reaction of their fans. Many accused *her* of doing wrong and, after one particularly bitter exchange, Martha retreated to a car and sobbed.

In the midst of her frustration and tears, the genesis of a song popped into her head. She reached down on the floor of the car and picked up an old blank cheque, and on the back she scribbled the words of what would soon become her signature song, "Satisfied", while hot tears rolled down her cheeks.

Shortly afterwards, in July 1951, she was in Nashville and chanced to meet publisher Fred Rose. She sang the song for him and he was impressed, arranging a November session for Martha to tape her inspired composition, accompanied by a small group, including sister Jean on backing vocals, and Chet Atkins on guitar.

The record was promptly issued on the Capitol label (F1900) before Christmas and its enormous and lucrative hillbilly success marked the beginning of Martha Carson's stardom.

Guess who got the publishing rights?

Classic Country: Legends of Country Music, Charles K. Wolfe

Buddy's big break

NOVEMBER 1951
RYMAN AUDITORIUM, NASHVILLE, TENNESSEE

After seven weeks on the road, Buddy Killen was just getting to grips with his first bass-playing job and with the life of a professional musician. Then he was sacked. It seems the band had decided they needed a player who could also tell jokes. Killen, who had no experience of comedy, was out.

He spent the next week desperately searching for work and then, as luck would have it, George Morgan's bassman pulled out of a gig and Buddy took the spot behind Morgan on the *Opry* the following Saturday. Within months, he was given the place on a permanent basis.

He became great friends with George and, by natural extension, with Bob Ross, George's manager — and also with Marie and Tom Parker, Bob's mother and stepfather. Buddy almost came to think of Marie as a surrogate parent, hugging when they met up: it was as if they were one happy family.

By the Seat of my Pants, Buddy Killen with Tom Carter

Hank's revolving management door

NOVEMBER 1951
NASHVILLE, TENNESSEE

DURING THE SUMMER OF 1951, Hank Snow and his then current manager, Norm Riley, having been together for all of six months, signed a new three-year contract and decided to branch out in a different direction as a partnership. They opened their own publishing venture, Riley-Snow Music, and then launched a promotions company handling various acts in the c&w field.

Yes, sir, things were looking good. Hank had finally found a manager who measured up to his exacting standards. This was the beginning of something special.

But by Christmas, Riley was out the door and went off to manage a recently-founded vocal gospel group, The Jordanaires, and Hank was looking for a new man yet again.

Billboard, 14th July, 10th November & 8th December 1951

The blue Cadillac

AT SOME POINT IN 1952
NASHVILLE, TENNESSEE

BARELY ABLE TO BELIEVE HIS EYES, Buddy Killen stared long and hard at the brand new, powder-blue Cadillac convertible that pulled up alongside him as he was walking on Woodmont Boulevard. At the wheel was Hank Williams.

"Hey, Killen, want to go for a ride?"

Buddy climbed into the passenger seat, joking that he would only come if he was allowed to drive. They headed on out towards Hillsboro Road and Hank suggested the bass player should join his next tour. Buddy was flattered, but confessed he was now signed up with George Morgan, and even though he was still able to freelance, he was booked solid for the next few weeks.

"Hell, I'm hotter than Morgan. You can make more money with me," Williams laughed.

He pulled over beside a drug store and left Buddy in the car. Hank went in through the front door and disappeared into the back office with the chemist. Buddy flicked through one of the many comic books strewn over the back seat — Hank adored comic books.

A few minutes later, a man looking just like Hank and wearing the exact same clothes came back out and sat at the wheel of the Cadillac. Buddy looked carefully at the driver. It was Hank, all right, but somehow he was a different man.

Buddy wondered just what kind of medicine Hank was taking.

By the Seat of my Pants, Buddy Killen with Tom Carter

Sunrise

JANUARY 1952
706 UNION AVENUE, MEMPHIS, TENNESSEE

THE LOSS OF HIS MOTHER at the beginning of 1952, was a severe emotional blow to Sam Phillips. Having buried her, he buried himself yet deeper in his work.

A towering blues singer named Chester "Howlin' Wolf" Burnett was his latest discovery. The Wolf was so profound and so charismatic it was like working with an Old Testament prophet. But Sam was destined to lose the Wolf, and King, and Turner. Record labels were able to offer a better overall deal than the Memphis Recording Service. Also, although Sam was very careful with his money, he wasn't yet up-to-speed on the intricacies of music business finance.

A case in point would be the copyright to "Rocket 88". A more worldly-wise producer would have speedily snapped up the song for his own company. Sam gave it no thought: in fact, he didn't even *have* a publishing company. Chess took the song and donated it to their lawyer in exchange for services rendered, who sold it on to, of all people, Hill & Range.

So, in the early spring, Sam followed the path he'd insisted he would always avoid. He opened his own record label, dubbing it "Sun", to act as the outlet for the acts he was taping at the Memphis Recording Service.

There was still just Sam and Marion: he working furiously in all aspects of the two businesses; she seated in the reception area, fastidiously taking care of administration, and looking after all the budding stars who drifted in off the street to make a two-sided acetate disk, hoping Mr Phillips would do for them what he'd already done for others.

Sam Phillips: The Man who Invented Rock 'n' Roll, Peter Guralnick

Hank and Anita, II

WEDNESDAY 23RD APRIL 1952
NBC-TV STUDIOS, NEW YORK CITY, NEW YORK

TO HIS ADORING PUBLIC it seemed as though he was on top of the world; but Hank Williams was struggling. Between his back pain, the pills, the alcohol, the personal problems with his soon-to-be ex-wife, and his domineering mother, there was little comfort he could take. Yes, he remained the biggest star on the c&w circuit, but it was tougher than anyone knew for Hank to cope with the pressures in his life.

Yet every now and then, when he absolutely had to be at his best, he could reach inside and pull the rabbit out of the hat with a grace that looked effortless. In late April 1952, Hank and his fellow *Opry* stars were booked on the *Kate Smith Evening Hour*, the NBC-TV show that went up against the successful *Arthur Godfrey Talent Scouts* programme over on CBS.

Hank positively radiated confidence as he sang "Cold, Cold Heart"; and when he duetted with Anita Carter — Maybelle and the sisters were also featured — on "I Can't Help It", it seemed as if time stood still, so riveting was the performance.

In July, Hank taped four songs for record release and the refrain from one of them told the bitterest truth: "The good Lord only knows what I go through."

Hank Williams: The Biography, Colin Escott with George Merritt & William MacEwen

Kitty Wells answers back

SATURDAY 3RD MAY 1952
CASTLE STUDIO, NASHVILLE, TENNESSEE

THE COUNTRY MUSIC BUSINESS had thrown up all sorts of unusual characters over the years. Jay Miller was a segregationist record producer who loved the blues and played Cajun. He heard Hank Thompson's mega-hit, "The Wild Side of Life", and felt inspired to compose a reply entitled "It Wasn't God Who Made Honky Tonk Angels". He simply used the same tune, the one which had also featured on Roy Acuff's "Great Speckled Bird", and the Carters' "I'm Thinking Tonight of My Blue Eyes" — virtually the same melody Maybelle remembered from her childhood.

Lyrically, however, the song was a revelation. For the first time in hillbilly music, a writer — and a male writer at that — dared to put across the female perspective on failed relationships. Not that this seemed to matter much at the time because no one got to hear the song. Miller had recorded it with Al Montgomery, a pump attendant, and it went nowhere.

But on 3rd May 1952, Kitty Wells covered the number (Decca 9-28232), with husband Johnnie Wright on bass, and her career as the Queen of Country Music began.

Three interesting developments grew out of this release: people bought the record by the bucket-load; Wells topped the country charts for weeks, redefining women's role in country music; and Ralph Peer — the very man who had taken possession of hundreds of ancient ballads and folk tunes — in a moment of unparalleled irony, sued for breach of copyright.

In The Country of Country, Nicholas Dawidoff
Record Makers and Breakers: Voices of the Independent Rock 'n' Roll Pioneers, John Broven

Hank Williams: it's all dark

MAY 1952
EL PASO, TEXAS

MINNIE PEARL cradled Hank's head as he vomited again. He'd been booed offstage at the matinee performance and was clearly in no fit state to be performing, but the promoter insisted he be ready for the evening show.

The drink and the pills were taking their toll on this troubled, gifted man, and Minnie feared for the life of her friend. In a forlorn attempt to lift his spirits, she sang the words of Hank's 1948 single, "I Saw the Light".

He tried to join in. His voice cracked and suddenly he stopped. With empty eyes, he looked straight at the commediene.

"That's just it, Minnie. There ain't no light. It's all dark."

Hank Williams: the Biography, Colin Escott with George Merritt & William MacEwen
Lovesick Blues: The Life of Hank Williams, Paul Hemphill
Minnie Pearl: An Autobiography, Minnie Pearl with Joan Dew

The Snowmen's League

AT SOME POINT IN THE EARLY 1950S
TENNESSEE

FOR TOM PARKER, the biggest buzz of show business came from playing the game. Making money was nice, but controlling the players was the absolute highlight of his endeavours.

At some point, maybe in the early 1950s, he came up with his greatest prank of all: his very own fraternal organisation, called the *Snowmen's* League of America. Parker took its jolly punning name from the real-life Showmen's League, and declared himself Chief Potentate.

In common parlance, to snow someone meant to pull a clever trick without the victim realising, or to bamboozle a person with words — and it often involved a one-sided financial deal.

Membership was strictly by Parker's invitation only, and he welcomed show business cronies — and also those for whom he had a professional respect — to his club. The league had no actual power, of course, but as Parker's influence grew within the industry, so too did the imagined prestige of being a Snowman.

In years to come, when Parker enrolled politicians and statesmen, he would print up membership cards, stationery and rule books, expanding the jape yet further. But for now, he contented himself with a nudge, a knowing wink and firm handshake.

The Colonel: The Extraordinary Story of Colonel Tom Parker and Elvis Presley, Alanna Nash

Slim Whitman finally hits the big time

MAY 1952
KWKH STUDIO, SHREVEPORT, LOUISIANA

RCA VICTOR lost interest in Slim Whitman when it became clear his sales were not going to improve. However, the yodeller refused to be discouraged and was approached by Imperial Records about something he'd been singing on the *Hayride*, entitled "Love Song of the Waterfall". Slim had picked up on the song in 1951, and his subsequent recording for Imperial (45-8134) hit top ten in the hillbilly chart.

Greatly encouraged by this, Slim chose the most unlikely follow-up, but one which allowed him to display his vocal prowess from the off: "Indian Love Call". In May 1952, he and his band squeezed into the small KWKH studio and taped this dramatic, almost operatic number. It was released in July (45-8156) and proved to be the record that finally launched Slim into the big league. Within a year, it had sold a million copies.

Slim decided that the time had come for him to take on a full-time manager, so he parted company amicably with agent Bob Ross. And, at long last, he handed in his notice at the Post Office.

Mr Songman: The Slim Whitman Story, Kenneth L. Gibble
Billboard, 20th June 1953

In memory of Jimmie Rodgers

26TH MAY 1952
ARLINGTON, VIRGINIA

HANK SNOW was on tour in Canada when he heard of a memorial concert happening in Virginia on the nineteenth anniversary of Jimmie Rodgers' premature passing. But he wasn't going to let a little thing like distance stop him from paying tribute to his idol.

So he talked logistics with his latest managerial acquisition, Hubert Long, and sure enough he performed at the event in honour of Rodgers. This set his mind to thinking. Perhaps next year, he himself could organise a bigger and better tribute concert in Jimmie's home town of Meridian to mark the twentieth anniversary.

There was only one man he knew who would be willing to help him in this venture, and he resolved to speak to fellow Rodgers devotee, Ernest Tubb, as soon as possible.

Billboard, 2nd February, 5th & 12th July 1952

Agnes Sampson's main squeeze, II

SUNDAY 22ND JUNE 1952
CHICAGO, ILLINOIS

AGNES SAMPSON never looked prettier than on her wedding day. The studio portrait printed in the *Chicago Daily Tribune* was beautiful. She had grown from a confident teenager into a kind, good-humoured woman, and had realised her dream of becoming a professional entertainer. She played the accordion and sang, sometimes alone, sometimes as part of a trio. They performed at nightclubs, cocktail parties, and anywhere else they could wangle a booking.

Up until today, she'd lived with her parents on Kedzie Avenue, a stone's throw from her fiancé's family on Eastwood Avenue, framed on the north and the east by the river. Nobody was entirely sure what either set of parents actually thought about the wedding. The bride and groom were well-matched: they were both blessed with a strong profile; they were bright; and each had a rebellious streak a mile wide.

Agnes' intended husband was tall, dark and handsome and a few days short of his twenty-fourth birthday. His hair was carefully combed and slicked back from his striking features. Most of his spare time was filled with artistic pursuits, especially painting in oils. He'd served in the military — he told folks he'd been a judo instructor in the Marines — but no one could quite figure out whether he'd served in Korea or not. Agnes probably knew, but neither of them gave much away in terms of detail.

Before dusk on Sunday 22nd June, the deed was done and troths were pledged. They began their new life together as Mr and Mrs Alvin Krolik.

Chicago Daily Tribune, Illinois, 22nd June 1952 & 25th August 1955

Mae's invitation

SUMMER 1952
NASHVILLE, TENNESSEE

Radio WSM valued the *Grand Ole Opry* so highly that each November they would organise an anniversary weekend to celebrate their main money-spinner. There'd be presentations and special performances, and it acted as a splendid advertisement for the number one C&W radio show, bolstering its position at the top.

In 1952, in recognition of the fact that radio stations were playing more records than ever — the disks had better fidelity and it was cheaper than using live musicians — the organisers of the twenty-seventh anniversary celebrations announced they would also hold a small convention on the side, honouring the deejays who were spinning those hillbilly disks.

During the summer, when the dates for the anniversary weekend were announced, Minnie Pearl invited her friend Mae Boren Axton to come along for an all-expenses-paid jaunt. Mae was only too happy to accept, noting the details in her diary at once.

Out in Hollywood, Bea Terry also marked the dates on her calendar. The WSM anniversary weekend was a major event for those in the C&W PR profession. She then sat at her typewriter and tapped out a polite note to Hank Snow informing him she'd decided to move on to pastures new, and wouldn't be advising him from this point onwards.

What she didn't tell Hank was that she'd been introduced to a promising singer named Jim Reeves — who bore an uncanny resemblance to her ex-husband — and had decided to focus her considerable energies on building up his career.

Country Singers As I Know 'Em, Mae Boren Axton
Jim Reeves: His Untold Story, Larry Jordan

"I just liked music."

A SHORT DIVERSION ON
THE NATURE OF MUSICALITY

IF ANYONE SHOULD THINK of the young Elvis Presley listening to music during his teenage Memphis years, chances are they imagine a skinny blond boy playing through a pile of hot R&B records, sneaking into blues clubs, or sitting with his ear glued to the radio, checking out the latest grooves on WHBQ. And whilst there is an element of truth to this picture, it by no means captures anything like the full story. Elvis was much too open-minded to restrict himself to one genre of music.

Music coursed through every fibre of his being: it moved and fascinated him. His hands drummed a non-stop tattoo. His leg trembled and bounced, as if he had a soundtrack only he could hear in his head. He played guitar and could already accompany himself on self-taught piano. In years to come he would also teach himself electric bass, and he had a natural talent for percussion.

His small but growing record collection revealed a fascinating range of styles: there was pop, country, blues, and gospel, alongside disks by Mario Lanza, and the Metropolitan Opera. There was no particular sign of jazz, and he would only listen to show tunes if sung by his favourite singers (like Roy Hamilton), but everything else seemed to be fair game.

Several years hence, a Broadway arranger would be amazed to walk in on Elvis sitting alone in a rehearsal studio, playing his way through Beethoven's *Moonlight Sonata*. He, like so many, had fallen for Presley's persistent modesty about his ambition and his talent.

In truth, in his early years, Elvis was a sponge. He soaked up influences and styles and incorporated all he heard in everything he sang. He worked hard and he studied his craft. Obviously, he knew the difference between the various genres, and he was very aware of the colour split, but he just didn't care about this. He would listen to and draw from everything that caught his ear — be it opera or the *Opry*.

He just liked music. Music, period.

Since my baby left me

LATE JULY 1952
CHICAGO, ILLINOIS

HOW SOON AFTER MEETING SOMEONE do you realise you want to marry them and spend the rest of your lives together? How soon after marrying someone do you realise you've made a dreadful mistake and you need to separate?

For Agnes Sampson it took five weeks to understand that her marriage to Alvin Krolik should never have happened. At the end of July, she packed her bags and her accordion, and moved back in with her parents, beginning divorce proceedings soon after.

The legal paperwork cited cruelty but that was likely legalese to cover the simple fact that Agnes felt she'd made a huge error.

What went wrong? That will forever remain a mystery between husband and wife. But Alvin took it hard. Some men of a sensitive nature might have looked back on their life at this point and seen nothing but sadness: a troubled childhood; an absent father; a difficult military career; and now a failed marriage.

Alvin Krolik, an artistic and frustrated soul, henceforth took refuge in the shadows, and sought comfort in the night.

"Hound Dog": Big Mama Thornton

WEDNESDAY 13TH AUGUST 1952
RADIO RECORDERS STUDIO, LOS ANGELES, CALIFORNIA

TWO SMART white Jewish boys from Los Angeles, Jerry Leiber and Mike Stoller, had met up in 1950 at the age of seventeen. In each other they found a kindred spirit of rebelliousness and a love of blues music and black culture. It was only a short time before they started writing their own songs and pitching them to local singers.

Stoller had a great ear for blues tunes and Leiber could string together the wittiest, sexiest narrative lyrics you ever heard. By 1952, they'd gained enough credibility to be invited to write for noted and fearsome blues diva, Willie Mae "Big Mama" Thornton. The boys composed "Hound Dog", a clever, double-entendre, mid-tempo blues, expressly for her in about ten minutes flat. They arrived at Radio Recorders studio for the session on 13th August 1952 and, much to their surprise, the teenagers discovered that they'd also be producing the track.

Seated at the sound desk, to encourage and aid them in their mission, was the big-boned figure of thirty year-old chief engineer, Thorne Nogar. An affable and well-organised man, he'd worked as a cinema projectionist before serving with the Marines, and then established a solid reputation as one of California's finest audio men. Leiber and Stoller wisely leaned on his talents, and the resultant recording was a thing of rare beauty.

The single was issued in early 1953 (Peacock 1612) and, during the spring, it caught on like a house on fire, hitting the number one R&B spot for seven weeks. Being just the singer, Thornton made little serious money from her new signature song but, as composers, Mike and Jerry did very nicely, thank you. Or at least they should have, if only Peacock had not been ripping them off.

A whole host of cover versions sprang up (black and white) but none that challenged Big Mama's for quality or popularity. This adventure greatly boosted Leiber and Stoller's confidence — to the point where it could easily be confused with arrogance: they were the hippest, most talented dudes on the block and they knew it.

Restless Giant: The Life and Times of Jean Aberbach & Hill and Range Songs, Bar Biszick-Lockwood
Big Spring Daily Herald, Texas, 22nd August 1943

Hank Williams: wedding bells

SUNDAY 19TH OCTOBER 1952
MUNICIPAL AUDITORIUM, NEW ORLEANS, LOUISIANA

IT WAS A WARM AFTERNOON and Hank Williams gazed into the eyes of his new young bride, Billy Jean Jones. She smiled back at him. They had secretly tied the knot the previous day, in case Hank's former wife decided to show up at the service and make a scene but, to all intents and purposes, this ceremony on Sunday 19th October was the real wedding.

Billy Jean was hillbilly singer Faron Young's ex-girlfriend, but it was clear the bride and groom were smitten with one another. Oscar Davis — now back in Williams' team as a consultant — had organised the ceremony, and several *Opry* stars were in attendance. The couple exchanged vows in the New Orleans Municipal Auditorium.

It was a simple, small wedding. There were seven thousand paying customers in the congregation. Just a few hours later, they'd do the whole thing over again for a new crowd at the evening show.

Oscar Davis: publicity genius.

Lovesick Blues: The Life of Hank Williams, Paul Hemphill
Billboard, 15th November 1952

Jim Reeves' big chance

OCTOBER 1952
SHREVEPORT, LOUISIANA

After months of persuasion, persistence and failed auditions, Jim Reeves was finally signed by the *Louisiana Hayride* in the late summer of 1952— not as a singer though, but as one of the team of emcees and announcers.

An unexpected benefit for Jim was that he was once again sharing stage time with Hank Williams. The *Opry* had grown tired of Hank's drunken antics and cancellations, and had shown him the door. The *Hayride* welcomed him back with open arms, but he remained unpredictable and, despite PR work to the contrary, was slipping further down the ladder in terms of health and sobriety.

Inevitably, he began to miss shows at the *Hayride* too, and the producers were often left looking for last minute replacements. And that's how Jim Reeves first came to sing on the show in October 1952.

It was a notable time all round for Reeves — now under the guidance of Bea Terry — as he also met up with Fabor Robison, a controversial country music entrepreneur, who subsequently signed the singer to his own label, Abbot Records.

Over the course of the next year, Jim Reeves enjoyed two substantial hillbilly hits with novelty songs — "Mexican Joe" (Abbot 116) and "Bimbo" (Abbot 148) — both of which were high-register uptempo tracks. It wasn't exactly what Jim wanted to sing, but Robison cajoled him into the sessions, ignoring the singer's requests for slower and lower-pitched songs.

But Jim's records sold well and, as Robison surely pointed out, you can't argue with success.

Jim Reeves: His Untold Story, Larry Jordan

The c&w deejay convention, I

FRIDAY 21ST NOVEMBER 1952
NASHVILLE, TENNESSEE

THE WSM ANNIVERSARY WEEKEND began on the Friday, and the debut deejay convention proved surprisingly successful. So much so, that the organisers decided to make this a regular part of the annual celebrations.

It was a small affair, and was certainly dwarfed by the main show, but deejay representatives from twenty states came and mixed with the many celebrities who were in town for the anniversary.

Mae Boren Axton was in attendance as the invited guest of Minnie Pearl, and was in her element, pressing the flesh and mingling from dawn 'til dusk. It's likely she bumped into Buddy Killen for the first time, and she took an instant liking to the polite and personable young bass player who found himself in demand with various touring bands, including those of George Morgan and Hank Williams.

She also made the acquaintance of a lovely man from Memphis named Bob Neal. The deejay and promoter was super-smart: he covered it beautifully with his down-home accent and perfectly modulated on-air voice, but Mae certainly recognised his talent.

Also in attendance was Bea Terry, PR guru, who was on hand to present Hank Williams with an award. Hank was there too, but only just.

Country Singers As I Know 'Em, Mae Boren Axton
Elvis in the Words of Those Who Knew Him Best, Rose Clayton & Dick Heard
Hank Williams: The Biography, Colin Escott with George Merritt & William MacEwen
Jim Reeves: His Untold Story, Larry Jordan
Billboard, 22nd November 1952

The birth of Jamboree Attractions

NOVEMBER 1952
5050 FLETCHER STREET, CHICAGO, ILLINOIS

MANAGER AND CLIENT, Tom Parker and Eddy Arnold had come a long way together, and no one could deny that the Colonel had given his all for the singer. But as he was charging twenty-five percent for his exclusive services, neither could anyone deny he'd been well recompensed for his efforts.

Parker liked the money, and he liked the prestige of being the manager of a big-time country star, but he knew there was only so far he could take Eddy Arnold. He had led him to a successful publishing house, to TV shows, to Hollywood movies, and now he'd even booked him for a second season in Las Vegas for May 1953.

But the Colonel was bored, and he figured it would do no harm if he played around a little behind Eddy's back. So he spoke to his new pal, Tom Diskin, who had recently joined Team Arnold, helping Parker on the road, and decided to set him up in the bookings business. Parker put in most of the money and they founded a company called Jamboree Attractions, based in Chicago. Diskin would act as managing director and Parker, the majority shareholder, would keep his own name out of it.

So Tom Diskin opened for business and started looking for new talent to manage, promote and exploit, ably and quietly advised by his silent boss, in a fashion not entirely dissimilar to that of Jerry Byrd and Jack Stapp over at Tree Publishing.

Billboard, 11th August 1951, 23rd February & 20th September 1952

Mae and Glenn: friendship

LATE 1952
PERHAPS CHILDRESS, TEXAS

Of all the people Mae had met in country music, the one she held most dear was Glenn Reeves. And their friendship was indeed just that: Mae was too much in love with her husband to ever consider straying, and Glenn himself was now also happily married.

But whenever Mae passed near Childress, you could bet she'd visit Glenn, sometimes to talk about the business, or sometimes just to shoot the breeze. Towards the end of 1952, however, they took their friendship a step further, professionally speaking, and started messing with the idea of composing songs together.

They wrote and copyrighted four numbers around the turn of the year: "Just the Dreaming Kind"; "What a Fool I Am to Cry"; "I Just Didn't Know What to Do"; and "Memory of an Old Love". None of these came to anything, but the last song was particularly interesting because, although registered to Mae and Glenn, the small print made it clear it was a solo Reeves composition.

As per many other creative collaborations, they had decided to split the credits equally, regardless of contribution. It was, of course, a move intended to protect and preserve their most important asset: their friendship.

Country Singers As I Know 'Em, Mae Boren Axton

Hill & Range joins ASCAP

DECEMBER 1952
NEW YORK CITY, NEW YORK

MUSIC BUSINESS REGULATIONS forbade songwriters from holding both ASCAP and BMI memberships. It was a case of one or the other. Of course, some then invented pseudonyms to try and capture as much revenue as possible, but it was not an easy process.

The Aberbachs wanted to broaden their horizons and decided to found an ASCAP-based subsidiary, allowing them to open their doors to ASCAP-registered writers. They tried to facilitate a deal, but the ancient and inflexible rules of ASCAP were stacked against them. If they opened this new company, then they would instantly be placed on a very low royalty rate, no matter how many records they sold. Only original, or very old, ASCAP houses received premium rates.

Jean Aberbach developed a friendship with music business attorney, Lee Eastman, who had, over the years, acquired several old ASCAP publishing companies, one of which was named Ross Jungnickel.

The Jungnickel catalogue contained very little of value, but Jean wasn't interested in the songs — he was interested in the company. Eastman, who was also frustrated by ASCAP's policies and was hoping to teach them a lesson, agreed to transfer all of his Jungnickel copyrights into another of his old ASCAP companies, and then sell the empty shell to the Aberbachs for a sizeable sum.

The Aberbachs then began filling the old established company with their newly-copyrighted ASCAP songs, guaranteeing themselves a much higher royalty rate.

The Aberbach brothers: businessmen extraordinaire.

Restless Giant: The Life and Times of Jean Aberbach & Hill and Range Songs, Bar Biszick-Lockwood

Lunch in Chattanooga

WEDNESDAY 31ST DECEMBER 1952
CHATTANOOGA, TENNESSEE

TOMMY DURDEN gathered his small group around him at noon in the Alibi Club, Galveston. They had a big show planned for the New Year's Eve crowd and he wanted to make sure they were well rehearsed and polished.

At about the same time, eight hundred miles away in Chattanooga, Hank Williams punched up crooner Tony Bennett on the jukebox and the strains of "Cold, Cold Heart" filled the diner. It was Hank's most lucrative cover song, and a big crossover pop hit for Bennett, even though he had to be persuaded into recording a hillbilly number.

Williams was on his way to Charleston, West Virginia, for his own New Year's Eve gig; he was being chauffeured by student Charles Carr. They'd stopped for lunch at a roadside diner because the snow was beginning to whip up. Carr felt sure that they wouldn't get to Charleston in time for the 7:00 PM show that night, and was trying to ease Hank into the powder-blue Cadillac and get back on the road.

But Hank was in no hurry at all. At their previous stop in Fort Payne he'd ordered a shave, a shoe shine and a pint of whiskey. The respectful waiter at Chattanooga served sandwiches and referred to the lanky star as "Mr Williams". Carr made enquiries about chartering a private plane because the blizzard seemed to be thickening.

Hank fumbled in his jacket pocket and pushed the half-eaten sandwich away from him. He summoned the student driver and then bid goodbye to the customers and staff.

The polite waiter watched as Hank ducked into the snow flurries while Carr held open the door. He then picked up the plate and noticed to his absolute astonishment that Williams had left a $50 tip.

Lovesick Blues: The Life of Hank Williams, Paul Hemphill
The Galveston News, Texas, 31st December 1952

Buddy Killen: the show must go on

THURSDAY 1ST JANUARY 1953
MEMORIAL AUDITORIUM, CANTON, OHIO

IT WAS THE COLDEST DAMN NEW YEAR that Buddy Killen could remember. He was supposed to have played bass in Charleston, West Virginia, on New Year's Eve as part of the Hank Williams package, but the show had been cancelled at the last minute because of the blizzard.

The performers decided to leave for the next gig in Canton straight away, in the hope of getting there on time. As far as anyone knew, Hank was still travelling through the snow.

But when Buddy arrived in Canton late morning for the 2:00 PM show there was no sign of Hank. The band and co-stars milled about backstage until the promoter gathered them all together and broke the news that Hank Williams had died in the back of his car en route to Ohio. No one doubted the cause of death would have involved alcohol or pills.

The musicians were stunned, but in their common grief decided to play the show regardless.

At 2 o'clock the hushed Canton audience was informed of the circumstances. Darkness fell in the theatre and a single spotlight focused on the empty microphone. The band struck up "I Saw the Light" and Buddy Killen played bass for Hank Williams one last time.

By the Seat of my Pants, Buddy Killen with Tom Carter

"What about Frank Clement?"

JANUARY 1953
STATE PRISON, NASHVILLE, TENNESSEE

Aged thirty-two, Frank Clement, a dedicated Christian, became the youngest serving governor in the country, and he came to office with a radical agenda. At the top of his list was penal reform.

Nashville State Prison, for example, had for years received occasional morale-boosting shows from hillbilly and blues singers, but under Clement these concerts became much more frequent. Ernest Tubb, Red Foley, Roy Acuff and George Morgan were among those who now played.

Johnny Bragg, still leading The Prisonaires, had gained a position of trust within the institution, maintaining the performance auditorium and taking care of the visiting stars. He sometimes chatted with the singers backstage and they were interested to hear he had written some songs of his own. In later years, Bragg would recall talking with Hank Williams about a lyric concerning a cheating heart, and the *Opry* star passed over a $5 bill in exchange for Johnny's time.

Governor Clement realised the good PR value of the group and regularly brought The Prisonaires to his mansion to sing for his political guests, demonstrating the way in which these fallen men had been helped to rebuild their lives.

Clement and Bragg developed a friendship based on mutual respect, and both men were aware that Clement's list of reforms was closely linked to the public perception of The Prisonaires. The group was invited to perform on radio stations and their fame — or notoriety — soon began to spread.

Clement was rewarded for his forward thinking by being appointed one of the Jaycee's Ten Outstanding Young Men of 1953. Not everyone approved of the governor's plans, however, and the laid back way in which he dealt with these "boys" did not sit easy with all Southerners. But many liberated listeners were tuned in and some were very interested in this group, and not just for the novelty value.

Just Walkin' in the Rain, Jay Warner

Sam bites the Bulleit

JANUARY 1953
706 UNION AVENUE, MEMPHIS, TENNESSEE

JIM BULLEIT noted that Sam Phillips had opened his own record label. Bulleit had been impressed with Sam's approach when they'd met for the WSM interview in Nashville a decade earlier, so he contacted him with a view to working together as partners in Sam's new venture. Sam could see the pitfalls — Bulleit was an unpredictable man — but he also embraced the fact that his potential partner was a significant name in the business, and he did have a certain charm about him.

Besides, due to slow business, the Sun label had more or less gone into hibernation during the autumn of 1952, so Jim's suggestion came at a good time. In January 1953, Jim Bulleit hit the road promoting Sun, while Sam stayed in the studio and made magic.

It soon proved obvious that Jim was a man who didn't understand the word "budget" and he was certainly no judge of character when it came to establishing industry connections. However, Sam had little choice but to play along. He was bleeding money from his business concerns and had just put down a $2,000 deposit on a $10,000 family home at 1028 McEvers Circle in Memphis.

But in the spring, Jim Bulleit came through with a tantalising lead. He had received word from a small-time Nashville publisher, Red Wortham, about a vocal group named The Prisonaires. So Jim brought this to Sam's attention — and he was excited at the possibilities. After weeks of official debate, it was decided Johnny Bragg's group could make a record for Sun, with the ultimate aim being to further demonstrate the success of Governor Clement's prison reforms.

Bragg had co-written an ideal song entitled "Just Walkin' in The Rain", and it was agreed the group would be escorted to Mr Phillips' studio on 1st June. There was little risk of the boys absconding. They knew they'd be shot dead before they'd even reached Beale Street.

Sam Phillips: The Man who Invented Rock 'n' Roll, Peter Guralnick

Tom Parker's second strike

MONDAY 9TH FEBRUARY 1953
RADIO WFAA, DALLAS, TEXAS

THE SINGER HAD THE AUDIENCE by the scruff of the neck. The song was a little risqué, certainly in terms of the way in which it was being put across, but the paying customers weren't objecting. Some might have considered it vulgar and overly physical, but Tom Parker knew talent when he saw it.

And what made this entertainer even more unusual was that she was a woman; a woman seemingly without a care as to how she was perceived. Charline Arthur sang and performed in a decidedly provocative fashion.

Being tied up with Eddy Arnold as he was, Parker felt unable to do anything directly for her. He also shied away from signing such a firebrand to his shadow company, Jamboree Attractions, but he did recommend Charline to Steve Sholes at RCA Victor. Sholes was still somewhat bemused by Parker's bum steer regarding Slim Whitman, but decided to take a chance.

At her first session on 9th February 1953, Sholes supervised the recording of four songs. The singles released were not profitable so Steve booked a new date in September and brought in Chet Atkins (who was moving away from the Carters) to sprinkle a little magic dust — not just on guitar, but also as co-producer.

At the autumn session, Charline recorded four good songs, including one named "He Fiddled While I Burned", supplied by a fellow named Buck Ram, who had previously composed hits and arrangements for The Ink Spots and had co-written Bing Crosby's "I'll Be Home For Christmas".

But the sessions did not proceed smoothly. Sholes had reckoned without the obvious culture clash between the conservative Atkins and the flamboyant Arthur. Charline continued to make great music, but the public wasn't buying. Even after Kitty Wells' hit record, maybe the world wasn't quite ready yet for such a liberated female.

Sholes was again unimpressed by Parker's talent-scouting.

The Texas State Historical Association

"Hound Dog": Rufus Thomas

SUNDAY 8TH MARCH 1953
706 UNION AVENUE, MEMPHIS, TENNESSEE

BIG MAMA THORNTON'S "Hound Dog" had been in the shops for two weeks, and already it was recognised as a classic of the genre. So much so that people within the industry paid it the ultimate compliment: they rushed to tape their own cover version (which, as composers, made Leiber and Stoller very happy), or they ripped off the tune, lyrics and style and made their own record (which did not make Leiber and Stoller happy at all).

Sam Phillips recognised an opportunity to make a quick buck for his struggling label. He re-wrote the number as an answer song from a male perspective, and called it "Bear Cat". He drafted in celebrity deejay Rufus Thomas, from station WDIA, to record the single in early March, and released it within a fortnight (Sun 181). Being very similar to Thornton's hit, the single did well and brought in much-needed revenue and publicity.

Technically speaking, it was Sun's first hit record, and Sam himself was credited as the composer. Unfortunately, its success was also its downfall because it attracted attention, and Leiber and Stoller's publishers decided to sue. The judge found against Phillips, and Sun sustained a serious financial blow.

Restless Giant: The Life and Times of Jean Aberbach & Hill and Range Songs, Bar Biszick-Lockwood
Sam Phillips: The Man who Invented Rock 'n' Roll, Peter Guralnick
www.americanbluesscene.com

The lucky red shirt, II

FRIDAY 27TH MARCH 1953
HUMES HIGH SCHOOL, MEMPHIS, TENNESSEE

He was listed twelfth in the printed programme as "Guitar Solo: Elvis Presley". The annual talent show at Humes High School was a much-anticipated attraction, and eighteen year-old Elvis had decided to participate.

On Thursday 26th March, the day before the show, he had registered for vocational work with the Tennessee State Employment Security Office ahead of his graduation on 3rd June (the first in his family to achieve that distinction), but he'd known for some time that this was not where his heart lay.

So, shortly after his birthday in January, he had begun to put his carefully worked plans into operation, agreeing to play guitar and sing in front of his peers on a class entertainment day. This toe-in-the-water effort was met with some enthusiasm, and when his teacher suggested trying out for the talent show, he sheepishly agreed.

He wasn't particularly well known at school and the risk of humiliation ran high in his active imagination. First prize was an encore — and the kudos of winning, naturally. He borrowed a solid red shirt for the occasion, hoping it would bring him luck, and strolled out centre stage clutching his guitar. Unable to afford a guitar strap, he rested his foot on a wooden chair and sang, once again, "Old Shep".

It was clear to everyone in the auditorium — except the singer himself — that he'd won the coveted encore. Students he didn't even know came up afterwards and offered congratulations. The girls stood a little closer, transfixed by his handsome features. For the rest of his life, Elvis Presley remembered this performance, and remained genuinely surprised at how popular he suddenly became at school.

Emboldened, he added his name to the list of performers for Humes' variety concert in April ("Elvis Prestly, guitarist" (*sic*) read the programme), and sang a couple of songs, one by Pee Wee King, and also Teresa Brewer's pop hit, the cute and catchy "Til I Waltz With You Again". He followed the record's arrangement closely, enjoying the occasional stops and starts in the song's structure, maybe flashing a smile to the front row, and received yet more encouragement.

His mind was then made up. He knew his daddy wouldn't approve — "I never saw a guitar player worth a damn" — but his attention focused more and more on the little recording studio on Union owned by that remarkable Mr Phillips.

The new Sun release "Bear Cat" was simply wonderful in Elvis' opinion, and maybe Mr Phillips would be someone who could help him make sense of the melange of tunes and styles running through his head. He'd already walked past the door a dozen times, always noticing the pretty blonde lady behind the desk, sometimes even catching a glimpse of Mr Phillips himself.

He would scrape together the $4 required to make a personal demo at the Memphis Recording Service, borrowing the money from a supportive friend if necessary. Perhaps Mr Phillips would recognise his talent, and maybe — just maybe — they'd make some music together.

Last Train to Memphis: The Rise of Elvis Presley, Peter Guralnick
Original research by Johnny Saulovich

Jim Denny branches out

APRIL 1953
NASHVILLE, TENNESSEE

JIM DENNY had laughed himself silly watching Jack Stapp pussy-footing his way through the music publishing business. Jim knew that without publicity, Tree would get nowhere. It seemed crazy to Denny that Stapp was unwilling to lean on his own celebrity status and exploit his position for his own gain.

Denny was not afraid of WSM President John DeWitt's disapproval and, to draw a line in the sand, in April 1953 he opened his own BMI publishing house with *Opry* star, Webb Pierce. Using his industry contacts he requested Hill & Range to act as the selling agents. He named the company Cedarwood. Whether or not this was some sort of private joke — you can't see-der-wood for the Tree(s) — no one knew.

Within days, he'd leaked the news to *Billboard* who followed this up to see if any other *Opry* executives were involved in this dubious practice. They phoned WSM and spoke to Stapp's secretary, Millie Kirkham. She transferred the call to her boss, and *Billboard* asked Mr Stapp if he himself was in any way connected with the world of music publishing. Stapp bit his tongue and declined to comment.

Denny welcomed songs from all-comers and, by December, *Billboard* would chart his company among the most bankable hillbilly publishers of 1953. Tree was not listed.

By the Seat of my Pants, Buddy Killen with Tom Carter
Billboard, 25th May 1953

Goodbye, Eddy: hello, Tommy

TUESDAY 5TH MAY 1953
LAS VEGAS, NEVADA

IN RETROSPECT, Tom Parker would remember it as one hell of a week. In early May 1953, he and Tom Diskin had signed sixteen year-old singer Tommy Sands to Jamboree Attractions, and Diskin had broadcast it — using only his own name — via *Billboard* magazine.

At the same time, Eddy Arnold was opening a very successful season with The Dickens Sisters at the Hotel Sahara in Las Vegas, and his themed album, *To Mother*, would be played on air non-stop this coming Sunday, which just happened to be Mother's Day

Grateful though Eddy was for his success, he'd grown increasingly tired of his manager's shameless and relentless sales pitch. Eddy was a conservative man and Tom Parker was not. When they had been gathered in an elevator recently with some business associates, Tom turned to Eddy and loudly asked, "Which one of our planes did you fly in on today?" knowing full well his client did not own a fleet of aircraft.

For Parker, it was always about the money and the game. Since opening Jamboree Attractions, he'd remembered what fun it had been working at grass roots level. But Arnold was bound to discover that his exclusive contract was exclusive no more.

Sure enough, in Las Vegas, Eddy intercepted a telephone call that gave the game away. He confronted Tom and demanded an end to their partnership. The Colonel reluctantly conceded, but they remained friends, Eddy even insisting Parker continue as his bookings agent, because he was, after all, the best in the business.

When it was publicly announced several weeks later, the separation was big news in hillbilly circles. Henceforth, Eddy acted as his own manager. Parker went back to basics, starting over, and declared he was now with Jamboree Attractions and working with Tommy Sands.

The first order of business was to get the Sands boy a recording contract and Parker knew exactly who to talk to about that. He also knew that building up Tommy Sands was going to take time and money, and the first big pay cheque was some way off.

The Colonel: The Extraordinary Story of Colonel Tom Parker and Elvis Presley, Alanna Nash
Billboard, 18th April, 9th, 16th & 23rd May 1953

The Jimmie Rodgers Memorial, I

TUESDAY 26TH MAY 1953
MERIDIAN, MISSISSIPPI

DEVOTED RODGERS FANS, Hank Snow and Ernest Tubb had invested serious amounts of time organising the Jimmie Rodgers Memorial Concert to be held on 26th May 1953, the twentieth anniversary of the singer's death. Hank had also released a tribute album to coincide with the event (RCA Victor LPM-3131 *Hank Snow Salutes Jimmie Rodgers*), and his boy, Jimmie Snow, had duetted on two of the LP tracks.

There were reports that hotels were sold out within a fifty-mile radius of the celebration and, although not everything ran smoothly, the event was considered a great success, especially as the original Carter Family reunited for a one-off appearance in honour of their late friend and label-mate. Post performance, Hank immediately started making plans for a follow-up concert for 1954.

The highlight of the day for Hank was the presentation of an original Jimmie Rodgers guitar to his son. Snow Jr smiled when he received the instrument but it probably mattered little to him: aged seventeen, he was already beginning to tire of the life bequeathed to him by his father.

Billboard, 4th April & 9th May 1953

Daylight robbery

MONDAY 1ST JUNE 1953 (MORNING)
EL PASO, TEXAS

PINNEY'S WIFE, Francisca, put the takings from the shop in her purse, placed the purse in her handbag, and began the short, regular morning journey to the bank on the corner of Texas Avenue and Stanton Street. She was carrying $341.

Their eighteen month-old daughter, Frances, and new-born Dickie, accompanied her, while daddy minded the store.

It was when Francisca neared the bank that she first realised something was awry. A red-haired man wearing jeans and a blue shirt was following them. As she reached the corner of North Stanton Street, he made his move, running past her and grabbing the handbag. He fled down an alley and escaped without trace.

Francisca Pinney and her children were, thankfully, unharmed, but heaven only knows how D.R. reacted to the thought of his young family being robbed in broad daylight.

El Paso Herald-Post, Texas, 1st June 1953

According to Johnny Bragg ...

MONDAY 1ST JUNE 1953 (AFTERNOON)
706 UNION AVENUE, MEMPHIS, TENNESSEE

A YOUNG MAN IS STANDING OUTSIDE 706 Union Avenue, peering through the window, early afternoon at the beginning of June 1953. He has squeezed out of school just a couple of days before the graduation ceremony because there is something he's just gotta do.

Battered amateur guitar in hand, he quietly opens the door, four dollar bills burning a hole in his pocket. The reception is empty. The desk where the pretty lady usually sits is unoccupied. But inside the studio is Mr Phillips, talking to a group of black men, rehearsing them, running over the same song, time and again. The young man places his guitar carefully up against the wall, secretes himself just out of view, and listens.

After each take, Mr Phillips gently draws attention to the lead singer's inadequate diction. He might possibly get away with that on stage, and even on the radio, but here in a commercial recording studio, notes Mr Phillips, it just isn't good enough. But he says it in a way that is uplifting and not at all discouraging.

An hour or two earlier, the trusty and the guard who had escorted the group from Nashville State Prison, knowing there was no security risk, went next door to Taylor's for a coffee, while Phillips continued to rehearse the group, inspiring them to find the right sound, pushing Johnny Bragg to sing more clearly. He never loses his temper, but the atmosphere in the studio has become a little weary.

At this point, the tall white teenager with long hair and a solid green coat steps in from the waiting room, where he's been silently observing the session. Mr Phillips raises his eyebrows as if to say, "This is all I need." The boy stutters an apology and politely insists he can help the singer improve his enunciation. Bragg, not wanting to blow his big moment, grabs hold of this unlikely lifeline and pleads with Mr Phillips to give the boy (and him) a chance.

Bemused, Phillips suggests he'll take a one-hour lunch break and when he returns he hopes Bragg will have made some progress. He's planned and negotiated this session for weeks, and he's desperate for it to succeed.

He exits the studio, leaving the convicts and the teenager to stumble through an hour of intense practice on "Just Walkin' in The Rain".

Bragg has a wide knowledge of white music styles, and the boy has a remarkable and innate understanding of black music: somehow it all comes together, and in sixty minutes, man, the song is sorted.

When Sam returns, the tape machine rolls and he recognises instantly there is a significant improvement. The boy stands forgotten to one side in the studio through hours' more work. He's missed his afternoon lessons and there'll be hell to pay tomorrow morning. Sam works the group until dusk, eventually confident he's recorded a hit.

As the sun sets and the guard and the trusty return from Taylor's, the boy suddenly feels surplus to requirements. He turns up the collar of his jacket, collects his guitar and, hidden by the lively chat and numerous bodies, leaves the studio. Too late, Sam turns towards the closing door: "Hey, what's your name, son?"

Just Walkin' in the Rain, Jay Warner
Sam Phillips: The Man who Invented Rock 'n' Roll, Peter Guralnick

Sam Phillips' impossible dream

WEDNESDAY 15TH JULY 1953
706 UNION AVENUE, MEMPHIS, TENNESSEE

LIFE WAS BECOMING very complicated for Sam Phillips: the partnership with Jim Bulleit was proving absurdly stressful. Consequently, Sam had taken on his own brother, Jud, to supervise Jim, but he had a bad feeling about how that would work out; and the legal nonsense over "Bear Cat" was now coming to a head. All of these situations were a drain on his finances — and money was something Sam didn't have.

He was thrilled, though, about the release of The Prisonaires' first single in mid-July (Sun 186), and it received a glowing review in the *Memphis Press-Scimitar* on the day of issue. The article certainly brought attention to the fact that Sam Phillips was a man to be taken seriously in the world of blues music.

But this very thought had begun to trouble Sam. He saw his mission as being quite simple: he was to give a voice to the unheard Negro talent in the South, and also to publicise blues music and black culture, in an attempt to promote equality between the races. But what if the racism was so ingrained in the Southern white listeners that they wouldn't — or couldn't — hear this great music, simply because the singer just happened to be black.

Perhaps what he needed to do was to surprise and confuse his more elusive audience. He often joked with Marion, "If I could find a white man who had the Negro sound and the Negro feel, I could make a billion dollars." And then they'd both laugh, partly because they knew Sun Records was not about getting rich, but also because the very thought of finding such a singer was a pipe dream.

Elvis, Jerry Hopkins
Last Train to Memphis: The Rise of Elvis Presley, Peter Guralnick
Sam Phillips: The Man Who Invented Rock 'n' Roll, Peter Guralnick

Gordon Jenkins' second dream

SUMMER 1953
THE DECCA OFFICES, NEW YORK

GORDON JENKINS was not what he seemed. He'd spent most of the previous two decades acting as a composer, arranger and conductor for some of the biggest names in show business. He'd clocked up hours with Benny Goodman, Billie Holliday, Ella Fitzgerald and Louis Armstrong, to name but a few.

In doing so, he had developed a unique string-laden style of orchestration. Every note reeked of a classical background, and singers and bands flocked to him to be embraced in his cultured technique.

But Jenkins' musical tastes went beyond the works of the great classical composers. The son of a respected church organist, he'd abandoned high school to play in a St Louis speakeasy and had spent much of his youth gathering an enviable collection of jazz and blues 78s.

During the summer of 1953, Jenkins fine-tuned his latest recording opus, a gorgeous suite of classical and pop music entitled *Seven Dreams*. The LP didn't contain songs, as such, it was more of an early concept album, following the general theme of a journey, intended for release on Decca in the autumn (DL-79011).

And for those who had ears to hear, Jenkins' influences were coming through loud and clear. Hidden within the "Second Dream", was a vocal track, "Crescent City Blues", sung by his second wife, Beverley Mahr, which borrowed its title and part of its tune from one of Jenkins' favourite blues artists: Little Brother Montgomery.

His head and his reputation were in the concert hall, but his heart and his dreams were still in the speakeasy.

Goodbye: In Search of Gordon Jenkins, Bruce Jenkins
Billboard, 31st October 1953

"I sing all kinds."

SUMMER 1953
706 UNION AVENUE, MEMPHIS, TENNESSEE

On a hot saturday in the summer of 1953, Sam Phillips was out of the office, leaving Marion Keisker to manage the studio. She wasn't running professional sessions, you understand, but if anyone came in to make a personal acetate she would oblige. As it happened, it was a busy day, and Marion was rushing between reception and control booth, keeping customers satisfied, while also answering the phone, filing paperwork, and generally taking care of business.

Elvis Presley stood outside the distinctive neon-lit windows and took a deep breath. He'd parked his truck nearby — he was a driver for local company Crown Electric now — and intended to record two songs, hoping Mr Phillips would notice him. He entered, guitar in hand, and joined the queue of nervous performers.

Each time Marion re-appeared in the reception to usher a new customer into the studio, she smiled and dabbed the sweat from her brow, apologising to everyone in her perfect radio voice for the unseemly delay. Elvis couldn't be sure, but he thought her gaze seemed to linger on him a little longer with each visit, which was quite likely bearing in mind the unusual length of his hair and sideburns. This being a working day, he was dressed in overalls, and not his usual spectacular attire.

As the queue shortened, Elvis became acutely aware that Mr Phillips himself was not in the studio that day, and a wave of disappointment washed over him. At that moment, the door opened and in came a young sailor, accompanied by an older woman (his mother), who embraced Marion enthusiastically. A less competent person would have grown agitated by this unexpected intrusion on an already hectic day, but Marion was the original multi-tasker. She calmly led her newly-arrived friends into the control booth, because it seemed probable she'd be spending most of the afternoon there, and they could chat while Marion worked the machines.

At last it was Elvis' turn to perform and, sensing his fear (his leg never stopped trembling), Marion made small talk while she prepared herself. He told her he was making a record for his mother, and she smiled warmly which seemed to settle his anxiety.

"What kind of singer are you?" she enquired.

"I sing all kinds."

"Who do you sound like?"

"I don't sound like nobody."

"Do you sing hillbilly?"

"Yeah, I sing hillbilly."

"Who do you sound like in hillbilly?"

He paused a beat, as if considering.

"I don't sound like nobody."

At this, she smiled again, and he felt very at ease at the microphone. The singer and the secretary developed an instant bond. She would play the part of enthusiastic audience and he would sing just for her.

He recorded two songs directly to acetate disk: the first was a simple take on Ella Fitzgerald's hit version of "My Happiness", and the second was a cover of The Inkspots' weepy ballad, "That's When Your Heartaches Begin". And it was while he was singing the first song that Marion heard something special in his untrained voice. She looked at her friend standing beside her in the console, who nodded and agreed that the boy's singing gave her goose-bumps. Marion quickly threaded an old tape through the machine, and made a copy of the remainder of the first song and all of the second. The performances were slow, and perhaps a little fragile, but Marion wanted Sam to hear this voice.

Using the reverse of some spare labels for The Prisonaires' recently recorded follow-up single, she typed Elvis' name and the song titles and then pasted them to either side of the disk. Job done, she took a note of his name, address, and a contact telephone number. Marion also wrote "Good ballad singer: hold" on the tape lest it should be wiped before Sam had a chance to listen. The boy took this as a very encouraging sign and, acetate in hand, left the studio and went back to work. It would surely now just be a matter of time until Mr Phillips called him.

Elvis, Jerry Hopkins
Last Train to Memphis: The Rise of Elvis Presley, Peter Guralnick

Byrd leaves Tree

PERHAPS SUMMER 1953
NASHVILLE, TENNESSEE

JACK STAPP was, to say the least, not amused. Jim Denny's well-publicised Cedarwood Music was a sensation, and his own company was an unknown failure. Clearly, if Tree was going to succeed then a change of approach was required. The first step was to let song-plugger, Jerry Byrd, go. It wasn't entirely Jerry's fault that he'd brought in precious little business, but the time had come for Stapp to admit his mistakes and make a fresh start with a new man.

Now, it just so happened that Buddy Killen had recorded several demos for Jack Stapp at no charge over the previous few months: he had an upbeat personality, he was building a name for himself, and he was desperate to get ahead. The life of a freelance bass player did not pay well, and Jack was looking for an ambitious musical man who needed to get ahead.

Jack called Buddy to his office and offered him $35 a week to moonlight as a song-plugger.

"How would you like to work for Tree?" asked Jack.

"Gee," replied Buddy, "I don't know anything about publishing."

"I don't either, I wouldn't know a hit song if it jumped up and bit me," sighed the *Opry* man. "We'll learn together."

By the Seat of my Pants, Buddy Killen with Tom Carter
Billboard, 25th May 1953

Johnny Cash: on the radio

MONDAY 3RD AUGUST 1953
U.S. AIR FORCE BASE, LANDSBERG, GERMANY

RETURNING TO BARRACKS on a hot summer evening, John R. Cash opened the carefully wrapped, fragile package he'd received through the post. Inside were 78rpm records by his favourite hillbilly singers: "Kwaliga" by Hank Williams, "Going Steady" by Faron Young, "Rub-A-Dub-Dub" by Hank Thompson, "How's the World Treating You?" by Eddy Arnold, and "That's Me Without You" by Webb Pierce.

He'd been stationed in Germany for almost two years and had regularly written to his best girl, Vivian Liberto, back in San Antonio, Texas. They had first met only weeks before his posting and, although they had spent little time together, their letters were already full of talk of their wedding.

Cash, born in Arkansas in 1932, was raised in typical Southern poverty. His older brother, Jack, had been killed in a horrific sawmill accident in 1944, and this tragedy shadowed John throughout his life. He was similar to many other boys of his age: he loved cowboy films, he sang hymns in church, and he balanced working with schooling. He joined the air force for no specific reason, but it turned out he had a singular gift for Morse code, and he became a specialist in picking up Soviet radio signals.

While in Germany he also discovered a talent for singing. It was nothing particularly special, but his deep, deep voice made an impression on his uniformed peers. When off duty, he tuned in to the *Opry* and taught himself to play rudimentary guitar.

At some point, he took the obvious step of trying to compose an original number. Mixing words, tunes and themes from Jimmie Rodgers' "Blue Yodel" and Gordon Jenkins' "Crescent City Blues", he added some lyrics of his own, and eventually fashioned a song he called "Folsom Prison Blues".

But Cash was just fooling around really. He had no thoughts of being a musician. He was gonna see out his time in the air force and go back and marry his girl.

I Walked the Line: My Life with Johnny, Vivian Cash with Ann Sharpsteen
Johnny Cash: The Biography, Michael Streissguth

Tommy Sands at RCA Victor

TUESDAY 4TH AUGUST 1953
RCA VICTOR STUDIO, CHICAGO, ILLINOIS

NO ONE KNEW just how long it took Tom Parker to persuade Steve Sholes to sign Tommy Sands to an RCA recording contract. Parker's previous recommendations, Slim Whitman and Charline Arthur, had proven to be expensive failures, and now the Colonel was trying to foist this young boy upon the reluctant producer.

The one thing in Sands' favour was that on this occasion, Parker himself had a commitment to the artist and, although Sholes may not have cared much for Parker personally, he had to acknowledge he was a very effective and dedicated manager.

On 4th August — and then again in September and December — Tommy sang his heart out for Sholes and recorded his first three RCA singles. Some of the songs were published by Jamboree Music, Parker's latest wheeze. He figured if the Aberbachs could make a go of it then he could do it better. His attempt was short-lived: all three singles flopped.

Parker kept the boy moving, doing show after show in the hope of a breakthrough. He also brought in other performers, like comedienne Minnie Pearl, as part of his general stable of artists, touring throughout the South, hoping Tommy Sands would start selling records.

Meanwhile, Parker's bank balance moved down, just as Steve Sholes' level of frustration moved up.

Billboard, 5th September & 21st November 1953

Glenn Reeves calls in a favour

SUMMER 1953
RADIO KCTX, CHILDRESS, TEXAS

GLENN REEVES had married Viola Joyce Clark in Shamrock in 1951 and their daughter, Glenna Joyce, was born just before Christmas that same year. Twelve months later, Viola fell pregnant again, and Glenn became uneasy about his future.

The songwriting venture with Mae Boren Axton had come to nothing. He was still stuck playing records on KCTX in a two-bit town and his band had drifted apart: young fiddler Roger Miller had gotten himself arrested and, faced with the choice of prison or the army, he'd quickly signed up and was shipped out to Korea.

In the early summer of 1953, Glenn contacted his friend Mae, and asked if she could help find a job with better prospects in Florida. Eager to assist, she landed him a spot at station WPDQ in Jacksonville, and Glenn travelled out there by himself at the end of July.

For the next seven weeks he roomed with the Axtons while he established himself and located some suitable accommodation for his expanding family. His second daughter, Patricia, was born on the last day of August, and two weeks later they all made the thirteen-hundred mile journey east to Florida. They settled at 6256 Gloucester Road, just a fifteen-minute drive from the Axtons. Glenn's parents trailed after them the following year so they could be near their granddaughters.

As far as Glenn was concerned, things just had to get better.

Country Singers As I Know 'Em, Mae Boren Axton
Glenn Reeves / *Johnny on the Spot* CD Sleeve Notes, Martin Hawkins & Richard Weize
http://www.rogermiller.com/bio1.html

The Aberbachs get religion

WEDNESDAY 14TH OCTOBER 1953
NEW YORK CITY, NEW YORK

THE ABERBACH BROTHERS were always looking for a new angle, always planning ahead; and throughout the early 1950s they'd kept a careful eye on the growing market for gospel music, particularly as Eddy Arnold had racked up a number of promising religious records.

In June 1952, they came to an arrangement with Stamps-Baxter, the world's biggest gospel music publishers. The company was honest but disorganised, and so Hill & Range taught them the art of collecting royalties and pushing copyrights. The deal was formally recognised on 14th October 1953, when their new umbrella company, Affiliated Music Enterprises, opened. By the end of 1956, Jean and Julian had become the leaders in this field, working with great writers like Thomas A. Dorsey, whose popular song "Peace in the Valley" eventually passed into their hands.

Having broken into gospel music, it seemed logical to also look further into R&B. Hill & Range had already shown foresight by purchasing half of Progressive Music in 1950, the publishing arm of Atlantic Records, and they followed this by establishing their own company — St Louis Music — as a repository for all acquired songs that didn't fit comfortably into the hillbilly category. This wasn't some pie-in-the-sky long shot, however. The brothers were hip enough to recognise that blues music was on the up — and it wasn't just the black audience who were listening and buying.

Restless Giant: The Life and Times of Jean Aberbach & Hill and Range Songs, Bar Biszick-Lockwood

The c&w deejay convention, II

PERHAPS OCTOBER 1953
NASHVILLE, TENNESSEE

THE SECOND C&W deejay convention was coming up fast. The WSM anniversary weekend would be held in a month's time, and excitement was already rising. The first gathering had proven surprisingly popular and things had stepped up a gear since then. Bigger numbers and yet bigger stars were expected to participate.

Once again, Mae Boren Axton received an advance call from Minnie Pearl. Mae had decided that she'd be attending the weekend, but not as Minnie's guest. She wouldn't and couldn't impose again. But Minnie was calling because she was in a bit of a fix. She was about to publish her very own book, *Minnie Pearl's Diary*, and the deejay convention would be the ideal spot to set up a launch table, and sell copies. There would be good money to be made and good publicity to be garnered.

The problem was that Minnie had just broken her arm and this made life very difficult. Mae did not hesitate for one second, and instantly offered her services as helper and gofer for the entire weekend. It could possibly restrict her personal networking opportunities, of course. But then again, if you're standing under a big sign with the name of the most famous hillbilly comedienne writ large it could be argued you'd meet more people than ever.

Mae was more than happy to come to the aid of her stricken friend. Metaphorically and physically, she would lend a hand.

Country Singers As I Know 'Em, Mae Boren Axton
Billboard, 22nd October 1953

The darkness in my soul

SUNDAY 18TH OCTOBER 1953
CHICAGO, ILLINOIS

SLIPPING AWAY from a more genteel society, Alvin Krolik kept company with villains, lowlifes and streetwalkers. Newly separated from his wife of five weeks, he took solace in oil painting, producing canvas after canvas. Through his art he sought not only comfort but also recognition. Agnes was gone from his life but he intended to demand her attention through his works. If he could attain fame as an artist, she'd be obliged to acknowledge him. But his paintings rarely sold, and a new and more desperate plan was forged.

He fell in with a Chicagoan truck driver named Eugene Cosco, and together they plotted a life of petty but daring crime. Using Alvin's car, Cosco would act as the getaway driver, while Krolik affected burglary or robbery upon assorted liquor stores, restaurants, Western Union offices and hotels in the west and north sides. Seven, eight, nine times, their scheme bore fruit.

Sometimes the victims resisted and Krolik used his combat training to complete the crime. He probably wielded a pistol; certainly Cosco, waiting in the purring vehicle, kept a firearm ready just in case. Alvin never had cause to use the gun. The threat was enough to encourage his victims to part with the cash.

The authorities were at a loss to understand how the recurrent criminals managed to avoid detection. Eventually, in October, a witness took note of the car registration plate and Krolik was hauled in. The police placed him in a suspect line-up, that the victims might pick him out. For several minutes, they walked up and down, slowing each time they passed Krolik.

"This looks a little like the robber," they'd say, "but he's much too young. The guy who took my money was older, maybe in his mid-sixties." And so, Krolik was released, absolved of blame.

Jubilant, he returned to his apartment, pleased with his own ingenuity and resourcefulness. The police were so stupid they'd never catch him, and part of him was disappointed in this. If he could not be caught, how would he achieve recognition?

He phoned Cosco and told him to prepare for yet another sortie that night. Then he sat in front of his mirror and took out his oils and palette. Picking up a brush, he again carefully mixed the colours and began to apply the paints to his face. With great skill and patience, he aged himself by forty years, and then stepped out into the night.

Bedford Gazette, Pennsylvania, 3rd November 1953
Chicago Daily Tribune, Illinois, 3rd November 1953
Dixon Evening Telegraph, Illinois 3rd November 1953
Miami News, Florida, 3rd November 1953
Vidette Messenger, Indiana, 3rd November 1953

A person who walks on a lonely street

MONDAY 2ND NOVEMBER 1953
ALBANY PARK POLICE STATION, CHICAGO, ILLINOIS

THE DESK SERGEANT looked up from his never-ending paperwork. The handsome young man standing in front of him smiled and spoke confidently.

"My name is Alvin Krolik. You're investigating ten robberies. I'm your man."

Several of the officers recognised him from last month's failed line-up, but he looked thinner now, almost like he hadn't eaten since then.

The story came tumbling out: the failed marriage; the oil paintings; the ingenious disguise. The sergeant demanded the name of his accomplice but Alvin remained silent. This was *his* problem and he didn't want his friend implicated. But now that they had Krolik, the police soon identified Cosco and picked him up at his home in Ainslie Street, where they also found two guns and several bottles of whiskey.

The story was too good to keep quiet, and details were leaked to the press. Photographs were taken (with the officers in the picture, naturally) showing Alvin applying paint to Cosco's rugged features. Alvin briefly became a celebrity and the reporters encouraged him to speak about the line-up fiasco. He did not disappoint them.

"Don't blame the witnesses; they could never have picked me. But since that day, I've lost twenty pounds because of fear and worry. I'm an artist, and the pictures I've painted bring $50 to $150. I taught myself to paint; I received no instruction. Several of my painted canvases are now on exhibit in a north side cocktail lounge.

On top of that, I'm a writer — I've written an autobiographical account of a crime spree. My manuscript is in the hands of a New York publisher, and I expect to hear from them next week. Let me quote the preface of the book:

If you stand on the corner with a pack of cigarettes or a bottle and
have nothing to do in life, I suggest you sit down and think.
This is the story of a person who walks on a lonely street.
I hope this will help someone in the future.

My troubles started a year ago when my wife, Agnes, divorced me. After that, I kept slipping and meeting the wrong sort of people. Finally, I went completely haywire on the stickups. I still love Agnes madly. I surrendered to the police because I have to get this thing off my mind. I'm tired of the panderers and streetwalkers I've been living with."

He talked a little about wanting to join the police. The officers pointed out this was now unlikely owing to his criminal activities, but indicated they'd be requesting leniency from the judge owing to Krolik's decision to confess.

Most importantly of all for Alvin, the reporters secured a quote from Agnes: "He's just a neglected boy who never really matured and needs help. I wish him the best."

Bedford Gazette, Pennsylvania, 3rd November 1953
Chicago Daily Tribune, Illinois, 3rd November 1953
Dixon Evening Telegraph, Illinois, 3rd November 1953
Miami News, Florida, 3rd November 1953
Vidette Messenger, Indiana, 3rd November 1953

Telephones that don't ring

PERHAPS DECEMBER 1953
706 UNION AVENUE, MEMPHIS, TENNESSEE

SIX MONTHS was a long time to wait for a phone call that never came. Elvis Presley's self-confidence probably took quite a beating as he waited in vain for a reply following his summer visit to the studio. Had the lady even played the tape to Mr Phillips? Had she written down the right telephone number?

The Memphis Recording Service carried on making recordings and Sun Records carried on releasing singles. One of their latest, a blues called "Tiger Man", sung by Rufus Thomas, just blew the young Elvis away. He bought a copy at once, although its lack of chart placement would suggest no one else did. The song was co-written by Sam, who'd finally sorted himself out with a publishing company of his own, named Hi-Lo.

Elvis walked past the studio occasionally, catching Marion's eye and smiling. Once in a while, he'd put his head in the door, and politely enquire if she knew of a band that needed a singer. She didn't.

Marion had indeed played the tape of Elvis' singing for Sam, but he just didn't get it, mumbling, "He needs a lot of work," or something of that nature. She brought his name up in conversation now and again — indentifying him as "the kid with the sideburns" — but there was just too much going on in Sam's life at that time. He even had ambitions to launch his own radio station, on top of everything else.

So Elvis made an early New Year's resolution: if he hadn't heard from Mr Phillips by 1st January, he'd somehow find another $4 and summon the courage to go and make another personal disk.

Last Train to Memphis: The Rise of Elvis Presley, Peter Guralnick

Tom Parker joins the caravan

PERHAPS DECEMBER 1953
NEW YORK CITY, NEW YORK

HEAD OF RCA C&W SALES, Bob McCluskey came up with a brainwave in late 1953: a short tour featuring a host of popular RCA country stars. Starting in late February 1954, it would visit ten cities in fifteen days, and was grandly titled the RCA Victor Country & Western Caravan. Chet Atkins was scheduled to appear and Eddy Arnold was mentioned as the headliner.

Tom Parker, now on the outside at RCA since his split with Arnold, recognised this as an opportunity to maintain a presence while he waited for Tommy Sands to break big, so he threw his name into the hat for promoter of the tour.

McCluskey wasn't happy at the notion of having Parker on board, and made his feelings known that if Parker was given the job he should be kept far away from the $50,000 allocated for promotions. But the Colonel knew the right people at RCA, and not only was Tom put in charge of the tour over McCluskey, he was given the entire kitty in advance and told to keep whatever he didn't spend.

McCluskey, shaking his head in disbelief, packed his bags and set off down south looking for appropriate venues for the tour.

The Colonel: The Extraordinary Story of Colonel Tom Parker and Elvis Presley, Alanna Nash
Billboard, 16th January & 23rd January 1954

The make-up bandits

DECEMBER 1953
CHICAGO, ILLINOIS

KROLIK AND COSCO had their day in court in December 1953. The press had already grown tired of the story and had moved on to new items of interest. The "make-up bandits", as they were dubbed, had each been held to the grand jury in $30,000 bond.

They came before Charles S. Dougherty, the colourful chief justice of the criminal court. He'd read the police reports and agreed that Alvin's was a case that required leniency, saying, "This is the first man to appear before me who apparently showed sincere contrition." He freed Krolik, placing him on probation for five years.

Eugene Cosco's fate was not reported in the newspapers. What little curiosity the press had in this case was confined to Alvin. He'd achieved his brief brush with fame, and Agnes had acknowledged him in print.

He was still obliged by court order to repay the $774 he had stolen, but that was a price worth paying.

Anniston Star, Alabama, 25th August 1955
Chicago Daily Tribune, Illinois, 5th November 1953 & 25th August 1955

When Sam met Elvis

MONDAY 4TH JANUARY 1954
706 UNION AVENUE, MEMPHIS, TENNESSEE

IT WAS LIKELY VERY QUIET in the Memphis Recording Service when Elvis once again placed his four dollar bills on the desk. Marion said how nice it was to see him, perhaps wishing him good luck for the New Year. He felt the warmth of her greeting wash over him as she ushered him through into the studio.

And there was Mr Phillips. He nodded at the boy quizzically, feeling they may have met before somewhere. Marion tried to catch Sam's attention, silently mouthing, "This is the kid with the sideburns!", but Elvis remained blithely unaware. He just kept looking at Mr Phillips.

Sam cued up the direct-to-acetate machine. Elvis may have had a prepared speech — six months is a long time to write your script — but no words came. He cleared his throat and nodded that he was ready to begin.

His choice of songs was perhaps intended to demonstrate his versatility to Mr Phillips. In the summer, he'd crooned a couple of ballads by black singers. Now, he brought out two country pop numbers: "I'll Never Stand in Your Way", by Joni James, and "It Wouldn't be the Same Without You", by Lily Ann Carol, both of which had been co-composed by the esteemed Fred Rose. Again, Elvis closely followed the recorded versions, his guitar trying — and failing — to fill in for the accompanying orchestras.

His nerves got the better of him in Mr Phillips' presence, and the performances were listenable but not remarkable. If Elvis was waiting for Sam to rush out of the booth, declaring that he was a real talent, then he was to be disappointed. And yet, Sam did fleetingly recognise something in the voice: a sense of proud humility — and a desperate need to communicate — he'd previously known only among his black clientele.

But Sam let it go and passed the disk to Elvis to take to Marion, so she could type up the labels. Elvis readied himself to say a thousand things to Mr Phillips: he wanted to tell him how much he loved "Tiger Man"; how he thought "Rocket 88" was just the greatest; how he felt Johnny Bragg was a beautiful singer; how he admired Mr Phillips for what he was doing.

In his head, he said all of those things. In reality, he smiled back at Sam and stuttered, "Thank you, sir. Thank you very much."

Last Train to Memphis: The Rise of Elvis Presley, Peter Guralnick

Royalties and loyalties

THURSDAY 7TH JANUARY 1954
CASTLE STUDIO, NASHVILLE, TENNESSEE

THERE HAD BEEN some small progress but Buddy Killen was already feeling the frustration of working for an invisible publishing company. He had persuaded Jack Stapp to buy him a $50 RCA portable tape machine so he could play and record new songs when required. And Buddy now had a tiny office in Old Hill Building on Church Street, which contained a desk, a chair, a filing cabinet and a phone. Stapp had also convinced the president of BMI to advance Tree $2,000 a month against future royalties. But the royalties weren't coming, and Buddy's faith in Tree was dwindling.

So much so that he decided to publish his own compositions through Cedarwood. On 7th January, George Morgan recorded four songs at Castle, one of which, "I Think I'm Gonna Cry", was written by Buddy and was assigned to Jim Denny's company. The title of Buddy's song, which was issued as a B-side and went nowhere chart-wise, summed up his mood.

This wasn't so much a question of loyalty. For Buddy it was about survival — money was tight and he needed to place his songs with the publishers most likely to guarantee him a revenue. Unfortunately, that's what other songwriters thought too when considering Tree.

Hank Snow, meanwhile, selling big and making serious money, had just appointed yet another manager, Dub Albritton, his fifth in four years. Snow had little patience with these characters: he expected a greater sense of commitment from them, but they had all proven a let-down.

Did no one understand the concept of loyalty anymore, the Canadian wondered? Would he ever find a man of vision and integrity?

By the Seat of my Pants, Buddy Killen with Tom Carter
Billboard, 8th April, 3rd September & 25th November 1950, 8th December 1951, 5th January 1952 & 19th December 1953

Harmony in Hollywood, I

SUNDAY 21ST FEBRUARY 1954
HARMONY RECORDERS, 1479 VINE STREET, HOLLYWOOD, CALIFORNIA

BOB ROSS HAD many fingers in many pies, and one of his most successful ventures was the small recording studio he set up just opposite the RCA and NBC studios near Sunset Boulevard. Named Harmony Recorders, it was a popular spot for singers and songwriters to visit and demo their latest songs, or to copy tapes to disk.

On 21st February, Jim Reeves popped in with just his guitar for accompaniment and laid down a ten-track demo tape, focusing on a softer and mellower style of singing.

He felt he wasn't receiving proper financial recompense (Robison was a notoriously stingy manager), so his choice of Harmony as a demo studio was not necessarily a coincidence. It could be most useful to let Bob Ross hear his work, especially as he had strong connections to RCA Victor, Hill & Range and Colonel Tom Parker, all of whom moved in the circles to which Jim aspired

The notion of impressing Ross came not from manager Fabor Robison, but from Jim's PR advisor, Bea Terry. They'd met two years previously and formed an instant professional attraction which had blossomed — so it was rumoured — into a full blown love affair. Reeves kept this from his wife, and it was to Bea he turned when looking for advice on how to break away from Robison and Abbot Records.

The day after his Harmony session, Bea threw a Hollywood party in Jim's honour, inviting a selection of country & western celebrities. She was determined to move her man up a level, perhaps getting him a permanent place on the *Opry* and maybe signing with a major record label.

And when Bea set her mind on something ...

Jim Reeves: His Untold Story, Larry Jordan

The Wilburn Brothers

TUESDAY 23RD FEBRUARY 1954
CASTLE STUDIO, NASHVILLE, TENNESSEE

SIBLINGS TEDDY AND DOYLE WILBURN had been in show business since before they could shave, and on Roy Acuff's recommendation they and their two older brothers had been signed up to the *Opry* during the Second World War, but had been restricted in their performances due to child labour laws.

They both served in Korea during the early 1950s, then relaunched their careers as a duo upon their return. In 1954, they signed with the Decca label and on 23rd February, working with hillbilly star Webb Pierce, they recorded a mid-tempo waltz called "Sparkling Brown Eyes", which sailed into the C&W top five during the summer (Decca 9-29107).

The Wilburn Brothers established themselves in the hillbilly world and were renowned for their harmonies as well as for their astute business sense, moving into publishing and promotion.

The day after they signed the Decca contract, they were introduced to PR specialist Mae Boren Axton, and a lifelong and trusted three-way friendship was born. Teddy, Doyle and Mae — and their extended families too — formed a strong bond, visiting each other's homes, sharing time, and sharing burdens.

That's what friends are for.

Country Singers As I Know 'Em, Mae Boren Axton
Billboard, 25th November 2003

Dixie

TUESDAY 23RD FEBRUARY 1954
ELLIS AUDITORIUM, MEMPHIS, TENNESSEE

Sixteen-year old Dixie Locke was Elvis' new girl. They fell head over heels in early February, and saw each other almost every day from that point on. She knew Elvis loved music, and he sang to her occasionally. He did talk about a couple of records he'd made, but never played them for her.

On Tuesday 23rd February, they attended the monthly All Night Gospel Singing at Ellis Auditorium. Elvis adored the gospel quartets — for him, there were no finer voices — and he made a point of trying to get to know the singers when they hit Memphis. The deep-voiced J.D. Sumner of The Sunshine Boys, for example, always looked out for Elvis when they played locally. But Elvis' favourite groups were The Statesmen and The Blackwood Brothers, the latter hailing from Memphis itself.

Sometimes, Elvis and Dixie would also sit in the audience for popular deejay Bob Neal's show at radio WMPS, enjoying the hillbilly and gospel performers. They'd often visit Charlie's Record Shop, and Elvis would play 78s by some of his favourite R&B performers for his best girl.

But he didn't speak to Dixie about Mr Phillips, nor did he speak about how dejected he'd felt when there'd again been no call back. He'd given the matter some thought and his mind kept drifting back to that "Rocket 88" article in *The Commercial Appeal*: "Sam's direct search is for musician-composers in the hillbilly or race field who can record *their own songs.* If anybody wants to bring him a song, he'll be glad to look it over."

Elvis felt sure he had a listenable voice, but what he didn't have was a song. He'd tried a little songwriting — everyone who could play guitar tried to write at some point — but it didn't come to him. All he knew about song-writing was the way Arthur Crudup did it: take a little bit from this track, and a little bit from that track, and throw in a few words of your own.

So, in the privacy of his own bedroom, he pulled out his Crudup singles, picked up his guitar, and started making notes.

Last Train to Memphis: The Rise of Elvis Presley, Peter Guralnick

The Colonel is the boss

EARLY MARCH 1954
FLORIDA

SOMETIMES, IT'S IMPOSSIBLE to remember when or where you first met someone — it just seems as if you've always known that person. And so it was with Mae Boren Axton and Tom Parker. In all the years to come, in all the dozens of times she spoke so fondly of the Colonel, Mae rarely, if ever, spoke of how and when they first bumped into each other.

Theoretically, it could have happened at any time from early 1950, when Mae caught the hillbilly bug, or maybe she met him through her friendship with Minnie Pearl. But perhaps it's more likely to have happened when Tom went back to his roots and split from Eddy Arnold in the summer of 1953. He'd have more often been in contact with the lower levels of C&W promotion from that point onwards, and needy of the talents of someone like Mae Boren Axton.

So let's say, for the sake of argument, that when Tom visited Florida in March 1954 he made the acquaintance of Jacksonville's queen of country music promotion. He was on an extended trip, hitting Miami and Orlando, organising dates for Eddy Arnold, and spending time with comedian Andy Griffith, singer Webb Pierce, and (curiously) Hank Snow's ex-manager, Hubert Long, among others.

Mae was a dedicated networker and she'd have made it her business to meet this notorious big wheel as he passed through her home state, and Parker would certainly have recognised a kindred spin-minded spirit. And, in the same way that Parker needed Tom Diskin, he saw that Mae too could have a part to play in his plans for Jamboree Attractions. She was slick with words and she knew people. He tested her, requiring some simple tasks, perhaps writing good PR for his Jamboree acts, placing useful names in local newspapers, taking care of one or two show dates in his absence.

She passed with flying colours but, so legend has it, early in their dealings, they disagreed on a point of principle. Parker got on his high horse and overruled her, declaring, "The Colonel is the boss."

"That's fine," she replied. "You be the boss, but don't ever ask me to do anything for you again."

Parker, shocked by her response, apparently mumbled an instant apology, realising her potential value to his organisation. Mae smiled, and the incident was forgotten.

It was quite a group of lieutenants Parker was gathering: there was Diskin always by his side; Oscar Davis — redundant since Hank Williams' death — acting as advance man on the road; and now Mae bringing up the rear. It was the best qualified management and PR team in country music.

All they needed was the right artist.

Billboard, 6th March *&* 6th May 1954

A favour for Red

EARLY 1954
BRADLEY STUDIO, NASHVILLE, TENNESSEE

JIMMY SWEENEY had moved from Bullet to MGM and now found himself at Hickory Records, an off-shoot of Acuff-Rose, in the hope that he'd finally make some progress: he was a black singer recording for a C&W company in Nashville, but wasn't selling much of anything to anyone.

In early 1954, Jimmy taped three new Hickory tracks at Bradley Studio and, as the session ended, he (and talented session guitarist, Harold Bradley) picked up a few extra bucks by doing a favour for publisher Red Wortham. They laid down a simple demo of a plaintive Latin-flavoured ballad that Red was planning to pass on to Sam Phillips, hoping it might prove suitable for The Prisonaires.

It was no special song, really, and Red just scribbled the title across the disk in red wax pencil: "Without You".

The King's Singer, Mojo, October 2017, *Christopher Kennedy*

Slapback

EARLY 1954
706 UNION AVENUE, MEMPHIS, TENNESSEE

When it came to upgrading the recording equipment at 706 Union, Sam Phillips was ruthless. Only the best would do, and he often flew in the face of financial logic. At the beginning of 1954, he purchased an Ampex 350 tape recorder, which represented a serious investment for his struggling company.

He experimented, trying to achieve a fuller sound for his records. He'd played around with echo effects for some time, but when he started looking more carefully at his new purchase, it suddenly occurred to him that if he had two Ampex machines he could link them and achieve a clever tape-delay effect, giving the bigger and more exciting sound he was looking for. So, throwing caution to the wind, he bought a *second* Ampex.

He called his new tape effect "slapback", and it allowed him to centre the listeners' attention on the voice without detracting from the essential underlying rhythm.

He tried the process on a group he was recording; Doug Poindexter and The Starlite Wranglers. Unusually for Sam, they were a white hillbilly outfit. Vocalist Doug was no great singer — and the band as a whole was nothing special — but there were two members who registered strongly with Sam: Bill Black, a jolly, bear of a man, playing a mean upright bass; and Scotty Moore, a quiet, talented guitarist determined to beat Chet Atkins at his own game.

Neither musician was technically accomplished, but Sam connected with both, and he sensed a fascinating enthusiasm and an openness in their approach. When released in the spring, the Wranglers' record failed miserably, and Scotty and Bill — who both still had day jobs — put their dreams on hold. But Sam liked the guitarist and the bassman, and was confident of their abilities as good, solid backing musicians.

All they needed was the right artist.

Sam Phillips: The Man who Invented Rock 'n' Roll, Peter Guralnick

Mae Boren Axton: "Count Me In"

WEDNESDAY 17TH MARCH 1954
NASHVILLE, TENNESSEE

WHENEVER SHE stopped off in Nashville, Mae Boren Axton made a point of visiting Minnie Pearl. On St Patrick's Day 1954, Mae and Minnie were joined by Capitol recording artist, Dub Dickerson (Jack Ruby's sparring partner), who in turn was pursued by Wesley Rose of Acuff-Rose. Rose had come to remind Dickerson that he needed to find one more song for his recording session that evening.

"Not to worry," said Minnie with a sly wink to her friend, "Mae will write something for Dub this afternoon."

Wesley nodded and said he'd be back in a couple of hours to pick up the manuscript. When Mae had finished choking on her coffee, she pointed out she couldn't write a song in two hours — if at all!

"Sure you can," said Minnie. "You know, love stuff and all that kind of carrying on."

Dickerson had built a reputation as "the boy with a grin in his voice", and often inserted a giggle into his recordings, no matter how incongruous. So Mae picked up a notepad and wrote a simple humorous lyric on the spot and passed it to Dub, instructing him to come up with a tune.

The song — "Count Me In ('Cause I Like That Kind of Carrying On)" — was more of a novelty number than anything else, but Dub did indeed tape it that very day. The publishing went to Acuff-Rose. Dub also recorded a song for Cedarwood — and a song for Tree — during the same session.

The song was released as a B-side a couple of months later (Capitol F2821) and though sales weren't notably healthy — and the rushed lyrics carried an odd metre — Mae had been reminded of how much she enjoyed songwriting.

Country Singers As I Know 'Em, Mae Boren Axton

Back in the honky tonk

MONDAY 22ND MARCH 1954
CAPITOL RECORDING STUDIO, HOLLYWOOD, CALIFORNIA

LIFE HAD BEEN GOOD TO Hank Thompson since he'd scored his big number one hit, "The Wild Side of Life", back in 1952. He hadn't managed to reach the top spot again, but his records sold and his shows were well attended.

In fact, getting a song on a Hank Thompson recording session was such a good financial bet that many writers were prepared to be flexible. Therefore, Thompson was able to exercise a little bit of leverage when it came to songwriting credits.

Chuck Harding, for example, had been a Blue Bonnet Records label-mate with Hank back in the 1940s and he'd released a catchy self-composed number entitled "She's Just a Honky Tonk Girl" (Blue Bonnet 117), which sold badly. But now that Hank had a reputation as the man who sang hit songs about honky tonks, it found its way into his Capitol recording schedule at the beginning of spring 1954. The track did well when released as a Thompson single (Capitol F2823), hitting the *Billboard* C&W top ten.

But observant purchasers would have noted the writing credits had been expanded; the name of Hank Thompson now nestling beside Chuck Harding's on the label.

The B-side

MONDAY 12TH APRIL 1954
DECCA RECORDING STUDIO, NEW YORK CITY, NEW YORK

OFFICIALLY SPEAKING, Bill Haley had only been in show business since the turn of the decade, but he'd worked around the fringes for ten years prior to that. In the early fifties, he'd formed The Saddlemen, and they sang bouncy western swing with a definite beat. It was good music for dancing, and Haley had an ear for a commercial tune. He was experienced enough to know there was a potential market for R&B music played with a hillbilly feel. In June 1951, he had covered "Rocket 88" in a less intense, but very listenable, style, and registered some small success.

Renaming his group The Comets — using the obvious astronomical pun — Haley continued performing and recording, building up a name for himself and, in the spring of 1954, the outfit signed with Decca Records, and assembled on 12th April for their first session under the new contract.

They first laid down a solid version of a Haley composition "Thirteen Women", which borrowed a riff from The Drifters' "Such a Night". Apparently, the song was something of a nightmare to record, and by the time they'd achieved a finished master, they had just fifteen minutes left to tape a B-side.

So they launched into a one- or two-take recording of an uptempo track called "Rock Around the Clock". The song was an obvious re-write of Hank Williams' "Move It On Over", and the guitarist lifted his solo from a previous Haley single, but it had an infectious beat. Session over, the boys packed up their gear and headed for the next gig.

The single did quite well for itself in the summer (Decca 9-29124), and the B-side passed into obscurity because, well, that's what B-sides do, don't they?

The RCA Country & Western Caravan

SUNDAY 25TH APRIL 1954
ASHEVILLE, NORTH CAROLINA

THE RCA VICTOR Country & Western Caravan tour finally kicked-off on 25th April — the proposed February date had not proven practical — with Tom Parker at the reins, accompanied by Bob McCluskey and also Steve Sholes, who was to oversee live recordings for an intended LP release.

The cast included Parker-find Charline Arthur, emcee Eddie Hill, who had recently signed to Jamboree, and Minnie Pearl, another Jamboree associate. Intriguingly, the original headliner, Eddy Arnold, was off the bill and had been replaced by Hank Snow.

The tour was a triumph and the resultant album (RCA Victor LPM-3220) went down well too. Top-of-the-bill Hank Snow observed the way Parker ran the tour with such efficiency, and couldn't help but admire his professionalism. Snow made a mental note that this was a man to be taken seriously and, should his current manager prove unreliable, then he may have already found a suitable replacement. He returned home to make final preparations for what would turn out to be another excellent and popular Jimmie Rodgers Memorial Concert in May.

Parker, for his part, was well aware of Snow — he was perhaps the most popular hillbilly singer on the charts — but he kept his own counsel. He performed his duties diligently, as always, then went back to Madison when the Caravan tour ended in Little Rock. How much of the advance money he took home with him is anybody's guess.

The Colonel: The Extraordinary Story of Colonel Tom Parker and Elvis Presley, Alanna Nash
Billboard, 23rd January, 24th April & 8th May 1954

Johnny Bragg: Still in the jailhouse

SATURDAY 8TH MAY 1954
STATE PRISON, NASHVILLE, TENNESSEE

DELIGHTED THOUGH he'd been with the sales of The Prisonaires' first record, as Sam Phillips recorded their fourth single — in the prison itself on 8th May 1954 — he acknowledged he had grown increasingly frustrated with the rate of return on each new disk. He still loved their music, but the public wasn't buying. This latest track, "There is Love in You", released two months later (Sun 207), would continue the downward spiral.

Sam packed up his gear and headed home to Memphis with the new tapes, but also with a demo acetate disk given to him at the session by Jim Bulleit's publisher friend, Red Wortham. Whether it was intended for The Prisonaires, or if he just thought the song worthy of Sam's attention, wasn't entirely clear, but Sam took the disk anyway.

It was Wortham, as publisher, who had taken most of the profit from The Prisonaires' debut hit single. He had also previously co-written (ironically) "I Don't Want Your Money, I Want Your Time", the B-side of Kitty Wells' signature hit. By mid-1954, believing the joyride to be over, he sold the rights for "Just Walkin' in the Rain" to singing-cowboy Gene Autry.

Governor Frank Clement, meanwhile, was beginning to realise some level of progress with his rehabilitation programme. Using The Prisonaires as the spearhead of his slow revolution, he felt that attitudes were beginning to change. Indeed, as the months passed by, some group members were even nominated and accepted for parole.

Some. But not Johnny Bragg.

Just Walkin' in the Rain, Jay Warner
Sam Phillips: The Man Who Invented Rock 'n' Roll, Peter Guralnick

George 'n' Slim at the *Opry*

SATURDAY 15TH MAY 1954
RYMAN AUDITORIUM, NASHVILLE, TENNESSEE

SLIM WHITMAN WAS HOT. Since joining Imperial, it seemed he could do no wrong. His previous record, "Secret Love", had been a c&w smash, but it was bettered by his new release, "Rose Marie". The musicians around Slim had warned against recording the song, but Slim was adamant. He'd even bet one of his troupe $10 that it would enter the top five within six weeks. Slim won the bet.

So it came as no surprise that he was invited to play the *Opry* as the hit single climbed up the c&w chart in May. George Morgan was also booked to play that night, and Bob Ross must have been tickled to see them both performing on radio's biggest hillbilly show.

Soon, Slim Whitman would be invited to join the *Opry* as a regular member, for in the summer of 1954, he was at the top of his game and at the top of the tree.

Mr Songman: The Slim Whitman Story, Kenneth L. Gibble
Billboard, 15th May 1954

A rainy Saturday afternoon

SATURDAY 29TH MAY 1954
706 UNION AVENUE, MEMPHIS, TENNESSEE

IN MID-1954, Sam Phillips found himself in a curious state of inertia. He'd certainly recorded some fabulous music — he believed Sun 192 "Mystery Train"/"Love My Baby" by Little Junior Parker's Blue Flames to be the finest piece of vinyl on God's good earth — but his blazing sense of mission was fading. And on a thundery, wet Saturday afternoon in late May, he gazed out of the window and wondered what the future held.

Marion suggested, and he agreed, that the inclement weather would guarantee them a quiet day at the office, so he pulled out the substantial collection of acetate demos he'd collected from various publishers over the past few months. He hoped he might find a good song to use with one of his current artists. Maybe there'd be a track in there for Doug Poindexter, or perhaps something he could play to guitarist Scotty Moore, who was often popping into the studio these days.

He made his way through each disk, playing some for as long as a verse, some for two, and others to the very end. The door to the reception was open and Marion listened too while she typed and filed. But there was nothing that grabbed Sam's attention.

Eventually, he came upon the acetate he'd brought back from Nashville Prison earlier in the month. There was no artist name, nor a composer credit. It carried simply the title — "Without You".

Sam listened to the ballad, sung in a high register, probably a young black voice, he thought. He listened to it again. And then again, by which time Marion had noted his interest. It didn't sound like anything Sam might usually have wanted to record. And there was something about the voice that reminded Marion of … someone? But she couldn't put her finger on it.

Sam took the disk off the turntable and looked at it, as if it might contain instructions as to what he should do next.

"Ah, to hell with it," thought Sam. They turned off the lights, put on their coats, locked the door, and journeyed to their respective homes through the humid downpour.

Sam Phillips: The Man Who Invented Rock 'n' Roll, Peter Guralnick

Jim Shell: man in the shadows

FRIDAY 4TH JUNE 1954
DALLAS, TEXAS

THE NEWLY WED Mrs Mitzie Shell walked out of the church with the immaculately dressed groom, and also with an unusual problem. She still wasn't sure how to describe him to folks. Some women might say, "Here's my husband; he's a plumber," or "Here's my husband; he's a lawyer."

But twenty-four year-old Jim Shell did not fit comfortably into any box. He was … something to do with the music business. Did he sing? No, not really. Did he play an instrument? Well, a little guitar, perhaps. Was he a manager? No, he didn't have that position. How about a songwriter or a producer? Yes, sometimes. Any hit records so far? No, not at the moment.

Born in Shreveport, Louisiana, on 20th June 1930, and raised in Dallas, Texas, Jim Shell was a man with ambition — you might call him an entrepreneur. He knew there was money to be made in the music business, and he tried to cover as many bases as possible. He ingratiated himself with those in charge of the *Big D Jamboree* and sought out new artists and writers. He was planning to open his own recording studio (it would be on Nicholson Drive in Dallas) and publishing company (Rebel Publishing). He also acted as an occasional talent scout for various local labels (Imperial, Starday, Columbia, King).

He was the sort of man who seemed to know everyone. He was the sort of man who could get things done. He was friendly with performers, musicians, producers, label owners, deejays and managers. He was becoming one of the go-to guys in the Dallas area.

He'd already met with Joe Poovey — who was auditioning at the *Big D Jamboree* — and they'd talked about songs, talked about writing songs and talked about maybe trying to get Joe a contract on a big label. They both liked hillbilly music, but felt sure there was change in the air. If they were lucky, if they were in the right place at the right time, maybe they could be a part of that change.

Email conversations with Dave Dennard

Alvin Krolik: free at last

PROBABLY JUNE 1954
CHICAGO, ILLINOIS

IN THE EARLY SUMMER OF 1954, Alvin Krolik made the final payment on the $774 he owed on his ten robberies. He was subsequently released from his probation, and walked out of the courthouse a free man. The shadow of Agnes still hung over him, and he carried his grief heavily, but now had an obligation to no one.

At some point over the next few months, he made the acquaintance of Chicago media entrepreneur, Russ Davis. The mogul had produced and presented many radio and TV programmes — talent shows, Bible stories, documentaries, daytime magazines — but he was most famous for his wrestling extravaganzas, which he personally narrated in flamboyant style.

On the surface, all was going well for Davis, but underneath he was struggling with alcohol dependency, and his wife and business partner, Sylvia, had recently walked out on him. But he took a liking to Alvin — he was knocked out by his paintings — and decided to see if he could do something to help this gifted, but somewhat troubled young man.

Chicago Daily Tribune, Illinois, 25th August 1955
Chicago Film Archives

Buddy Killen: the last Boy Scout

SATURDAY 12TH JUNE 1954
CASTLE STUDIO, NASHVILLE, TENNESSEE

SITTING IN THE STUDIO, waiting for the boys to arrive, Buddy Killen looked long and hard at the blue record label on the 45rpm in his hands. There was his own name printed clearly below the hole. This was his first ever record release as a singer, two sides on the Republic label.

The A-side, "Big Jim", was written by Lonnie Coleman who had placed it with Tree. The record had just been released that week (7095-45) and Buddy was excited about it. He'd always been in the shadows of the music business — the bass player and the song plugger — but maybe this was his chance to step into the spotlight.

Working as Tree's sole employee was tough going. He'd had the occasional minor victory, but the breakthrough record remained out of reach. Buddy was very good at networking, but it seemed no one wanted to give him the right song for the right artist. On this release, he figured as he was also the singer, maybe he could push even harder for success.

The studio doors opened and The Jordanaires walked in, greeting him with smiles and handshakes. The four-man gospel vocal group had, through various incarnations, been in show business for almost five years. Gordon Stoker (tenor), Neal Matthews (second tenor), Hoyt Hawkins (baritone) and Culley Holt (bass) brought some of the fervour associated with black gospel music into their slick white c&w sound. They were superb singers and good performers — and had been on the *Grand Ole Opry* since the turn of the decade.

But their biggest contribution to the world of popular music was the invention of the Nashville Numbers System. Instead of working in chords, the group broke everything down into a series of simple numbers. That way, if a band or producer wanted to try a change of key then The Jordanaires had no trouble at all adapting. This approach caught on among the rapidly-growing group of local session players. Soon, the Nashville musicians would be known as the most flexible and versatile in the business, and artists would flock to Tennessee to sample that magic.

Buddy had brought a new Tree song for The Jordanaires, entitled

"Be Prepared", and they chose to make it their first recording at the session. In their usual efficient manner, they had it completed and in the can right on schedule. Buddy went back to his tiny office with a good feeling about The Jordanaires' latest recording and also about his own new single.

Neither release had any chart impact whatsoever.

How Nashville Became Music City U.S.A.: 50 Years of Music Row, Michael Kosser

Tommy Sands at RCA (but only just)

WEDNESDAY 16TH JUNE 1954
RADIO WFAA, DALLAS, TEXAS

STEVE SHOLES recorded Tommy Sands' fifth RCA single on 16th June 1954 and, when released in the summer, it followed all the others into the dusty corners of the lowest reaches of the chart. But Tommy was a super-nice guy and Sholes was struggling to blame him for the failures.

Tom Parker was still working hard: he'd opened up opportunities on the road, on the radio, even on TV, and now he was also trying to figure out some deal for Tommy Sands to try his hand at acting.

To demonstrate the level of commitment required to be an actor, Parker drove Sands into the desert. He advised the boy to walk several miles to the nearest diner — by which time he'd be covered in sweat, dust and dirt — and he should stand at the window and act pitiful. If a customer offered to buy him a meal he had passed Parker's test and had a future as an actor.

But somewhere deep down, Sholes and the Colonel already knew that the time of Sands was running out.

The Colonel: The Extraordinary Story of Colonel Tom Parker and Elvis Presley, Alanna Nash
Billboard, 24th July 1954

"What else do you sing?"

SATURDAY 26TH JUNE 1954
706 UNION AVENUE, MEMPHIS, TENNESSEE

PERHAPS MARION was out on an early lunch break when she ran into her friend again. They'd not seen each other for almost a year but the conversation came easily, as it always did with Marion.

"How's your son, the sailor?" she enquired.

Apparently, he was fine, and was hoping to come home on leave soon. They chatted for several more minutes, before Marion's friend dropped a glorious gift in her lap.

"Whatever became of that boy who sang so well in the studio when we were there — the one with the sideburns?"

A light went on in Marion's head and, bidding a swift goodbye, she scurried back to the studio. She knew Sam would be tinkering in the booth, and she knew he'd be humming that darn "Without You" tune. It had fascinated — Marion would say obsessed — him for a month, and finally Marion knew who it was she was reminded of when she heard the demo.

"Elvis who?" said Sam, when she passed on the information.

"The kid with the sideburns!"

"Oh. Him. Well. Do you have his number?"

Marion pulled out her year-old note, and picked up the phone. It was about noon. Marion asked Elvis if he could be there by three. In later years, he liked to joke that he arrived before she'd even hung up.

And so, heart thumping through his vivid pink shirt, he sat in the studio with Mr Phillips, listening to the demo. He listened once, maybe twice, and certainly by the third time, he had it memorised. Sam switched on the Ampex, and Elvis played and sang the number all the way through. Sam nodded, and asked for another take. Then another. And another. The performances were at best, like his previous recordings, amateurishly interesting.

Sam quickly sussed that the boy saw himself as a ballad singer, but he didn't have the voice nor the experience for it just yet. He looked more closely at the tall figure standing in the studio, and silently considered the hair, the sideburns, the clothes, and the rakishly handsome face. By God, he looked different! He was an individual who point-blank refused to conform.

And Sam respected that. And he saw more than a little of himself in this nerve-wracked, stuttering kid who took such pride in his appearance.

He switched off the tape recorder and forgot about the demo. Stepping down onto the studio floor, he reassured Elvis that he was doing just fine.

"What else do you sing, son? Play me something that really means something to you."

And for three hours, Elvis played song after song after song. There was pop, country, gospel, some Dean Martin, a little Bing Crosby, maybe some Mario Lanza, and occasionally he strayed close to R&B with a popular ballad, like Lonnie Johnson's "Tomorrow Night", but that's as far as he dared go. Elvis hadn't quite worked Mr Phillips out just yet. He wasn't sure how he would react if he reached into that vast hidden part of his repository. In Memphis, one had to be careful about everything connected with race.

As dusk fell — Marion had drawn the blinds and was long gone — Elvis made his way home, exhausted and elated. He'd received no promises from Mr Phillips, other than "We'll be in touch."

And Sam? Well, he didn't know what the hell to think. The boy had something special, but he just couldn't figure out what it was. He was a paradox. He seemed terrified, but wanted to put himself forward as a singer. He looked like a rebel, but spoke of little other than making some money to help his parents. He dressed black, but sang hillbilly and white pop. He came from nothing, but carried himself like he owned the world.

He'd sleep on it, but Sam wasn't at all sure where this was heading.

Last Train to Memphis: The Rise of Elvis Presley, Peter Guralnick
Sam Phillips: The Man Who Invented Rock 'n' Roll, Peter Guralnick

Coffee at Taylor's

SATURDAY 3RD JULY 1954
706 UNION AVENUE, MEMPHIS, TENNESSEE

THE MOST IRONIC ELEMENT of any story involving Sun Records concerns Taylor's, the restaurant next door, which almost became an extension of Sam's office over the years. Sam Phillips built his business on the recording of Afro-American talent, but not one of these performers was permitted to eat at the neighbouring restaurant due to the colour segregation rules.

On the first Saturday in July, Sam and Marion took a booth together to grab an afternoon coffee. All week, she'd been pestering him about Elvis. How was the audition? Did he make a recording? What are you going to do next? And Sam had been unable to answer her questions, because he still didn't know what to make of the boy.

As such, he was very happy to see guitarist Scotty Moore, who got off work at 2:00, slip unexpectedly into the seat beside Marion. Perhaps now there'd be a change of topic. Indeed, Scotty had come to ask how Doug Poindexter's single was selling — badly as it turned out — but he was much more interested in Marion's conversation, to Sam's annoyance.

Sam updated Scotty on the story so far, and Scotty remembered hearing Marion talking about "the kid with the sideburns" a few months back. Ever open to new ideas, Scotty asked if maybe he could invite the boy over to his house to play a little. Sam conceded it would be good to get a second opinion, and ordered the coffees while Marion went back to the office. She retrieved the telephone number for Scotty, who went home to phone Elvis, intending to introduce himself — not quite legitimately — as a representative of Sun Records, and suggest they meet on Sunday afternoon.

Elvis himself was now in a state of mourning. The previous day, along with several thousand other Memphians, he'd attended a funeral service at Ellis Auditorium. Two members of the city's favourite home-grown gospel group, The Blackwood Brothers, had perished in a plane crash on the Wednesday. He and Dixie were among the inconsolable congregation.

Governor Frank Clement had delivered a heartfelt eulogy. A distraught J.D. Sumner had already been drafted in to replace the group's late bass singer. The usually all-white galleries were filled with tearful mourners from the black community, and it seemed as if the whole city wept that day. Compounding Elvis' misery, a sobbing Dixie had been obliged to leave town on Saturday morning to take a pre-planned family vacation in Florida.

Elvis had given the whole matter a great deal of thought. Life was fleeting, and no one knew what tomorrow might bring. If opportunites presented themselves then they should be embraced without fear or hesitation.

He put the latest Blackwood Brothers' single, "His Hand in Mine" (RCA Victor 20-5709) on his player and lost himself over and again in the words and music, singing all the parts, high, mid and low, his eyes still red from the tears.

As he cued up the record for yet another round, his neighbour knocked to let him know there was a phone call from a Mr Moore of Sun Records.

Last Train to Memphis: The Rise of Elvis Presley, Peter Guralnick
Original research by Johnny Saulovich

Independence Day

SUNDAY 4TH JULY 1954
983 BELZ STREET, MEMPHIS, TENNESSEE

ARRIVING AT SCOTTY'S HOUSE shortly after noon on Independence Day 1954, Elvis was resplendent in white shirt, pink-and-black striped trousers, and white buck shoes. He knocked at the front door, and Scotty's wife almost left through the back door when she caught sight of the hair and the sideburns.

Elvis (19) and Scotty (22) introduced themselves and grabbed a Coke. They picked up their guitars and strummed a little. They spent some time finding songs they both knew all the way through. Again, Elvis stayed on the safe side of the colour fence, singing ballads and country numbers. He noticed a big stand-up bass in the corner of the room, and Scotty explained that he stored it between gigs for his bandmate and near-neighbour, Bill Black, who would be popping in soon, at Scotty's invitation. Elvis nodded, but didn't have much in the way of conversation.

By the time Bill arrived, the mood was convivial and laid back, but there was a definite sense of being examined as far as Elvis was concerned. But there was also laughter — Bill brought it with him wherever he went — and the trio played through a dozen tunes or more. Elvis went home, with a promise from the guitarist that he'd be in touch. Bill and Scotty shrugged at each other. Scotty (who had really wanted Elvis to be something special) phoned Sam to report that he and Bill thought Elvis had a pleasant voice, but they couldn't see anything particularly noteworthy about him — apart from his appearance.

Sam thanked them for their efforts; then made a decision.

"The studio's free tomorrow night. Why don't you and Bill stop by, and we'll see how he sounds on tape with a little back-up? There's no need to trouble Doug or the rest of the Wranglers. Give the boy a ring, will you. See if he can come about 7:00."

Elvis, of course, was thrilled to receive Scotty's call, and struggled to sleep that night, even more so than usual, so excited was he. It was a pity that Dixie wasn't in town so he could share his wonderful news with the love of his life. Although their courtship had been short, they'd already discussed marriage, and had spent many hours planning their future.

But, deep inside, Elvis must have known that if anything came of the audition then their relationship would change irrevocably. In retrospect, he realised she would be the last person he would ever meet whom he could be sure loved him just for himself, and not for what he would become.

Meanwhile, across the city, at West Memphis airport, Johnny Cash touched down on the last part of his journey home from Germany. His fiancée, Vivian, waited by the gate and, as he joyfully stepped out as a civilian, he swept her off her feet and into his arms, promising to marry her as soon as humanly possible. He was home at last. When he woke in the morning, there'd be no more uniforms, and no more duties, and no more separation from his beloved.

As from tomorrow, everything would be different.

I Walked the Line: My Life with Johnny, Vivian Cash with Ann Sharpsteen
Last Train to Memphis: The Rise of Elvis Presley, Peter Guralnick

ILLUSTRATIONS, I

El Paso's first police motorcycle squad in 1917. Pinney is far right. Photo by Jimmy North, courtesy of Frances Pinney Erickson.

A young Agnes Sampson with her brothers, courtesy of Mitchell Pomper.

Pinney behind the counter at The Busy Bee, in the early 1950s, courtesy of Frances Pinney Erickson.

The Busy Bee, 3728 Alameda Avenue, El Paso, Texas, in the early 1950s, courtesy of Frances Pinney Erickson.

The Boren family in Texas, circa 1916, courtesy of the estate of Mae Boren Axton.

The Boren family in Oklahoma, circa 1934, courtesy of the estate of Mae Boren Axton.

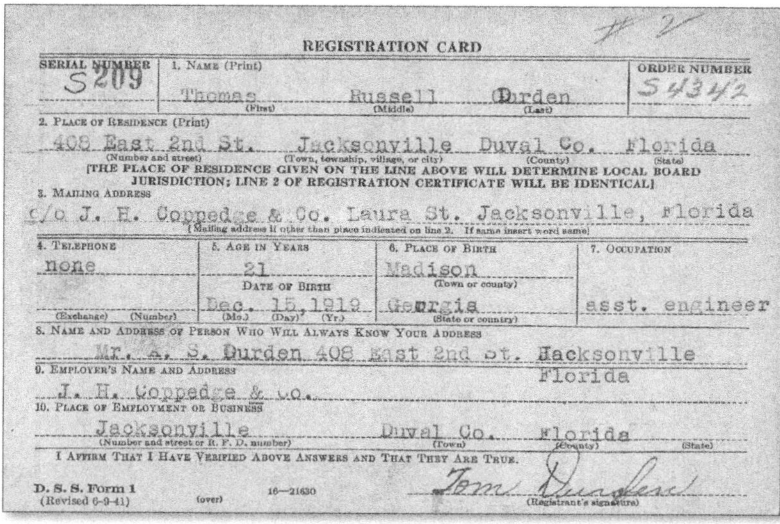

2

REGISTRATION CARD

SERIAL NUMBER S209

1. NAME (Print) Thomas Russell Durden (First) (Middle) (Last)

ORDER NUMBER S4342

2. PLACE OF RESIDENCE (Print)
408 East 2nd St. Jacksonville Duval Co. Florida
(Number and street) (Town, township, village, or city) (County) (State)
[THE PLACE OF RESIDENCE GIVEN ON THE LINE ABOVE WILL DETERMINE LOCAL BOARD JURISDICTION; LINE 2 OF REGISTRATION CERTIFICATE WILL BE IDENTICAL]

3. MAILING ADDRESS
c/o J. H. Coppedge & Co. Laura St. Jacksonville, Florida
[Mailing address if other than place indicated on line 2. If same insert word same]

4. TELEPHONE none (Exchange) (Number)

5. AGE IN YEARS 21
DATE OF BIRTH Dec. 15, 1919 (Mo.) (Day) (Yr.)

6. PLACE OF BIRTH Madison (Town or county) Georgia (State or country)

7. OCCUPATION asst. engineer

8. NAME AND ADDRESS OF PERSON WHO WILL ALWAYS KNOW YOUR ADDRESS
Mr. A. S. Durden 408 East 2nd St. Jacksonville Florida

9. EMPLOYER'S NAME AND ADDRESS
J. H. Coppedge & Co.

10. PLACE OF EMPLOYMENT OR BUSINESS
Jacksonville Duval Co. Florida
(Number and street or R. F. D. number) (Town) (County) (State)

I AFFIRM THAT I HAVE VERIFIED ABOVE ANSWERS AND THAT THEY ARE TRUE.

D. S. S. Form 1 (Revised 6-9-41) (over) 16—21630

Tom Durden
(Registrant's signature)

Tommy Durden's draft card which led to his involvement in Project Hula.

The Westernaires, Tommy singing and Boots on mandolin, courtesy of Art Kenney.

Agnes Sampson, professional entertainer, courtesy of Mitchell Pomper.

The picture of Alvin Krolik that Agnes Sampson always kept, courtesy of Mitchell Pomper.

PUTS IT IN BOOK

Artist-Writer Admits Chicago Crime Spree

International News Service

Chicago, Nov. 3 — Alvin Krolik, 25, walked into a Chicago police station and startled veteran officers with an unusual story.

"I'm an artist," he said, "and the pictures I've painted bring $50 to $150.

"On top of that, I'm a writer — I've written an autobiographical account of a crime spree.

"I want to tell you about that crime spree — 10 robberies — I'm your man."

Man of Disguises

Krolik, a former Marine Corps judo instructor, then told how he used his knowedge of painting to disguise his features and those of an accomplice — Eugene Cosco, 28, in his life of crime.

He also quoted the preface of his manuscript yesterday when he voluntarily surrendered. It read:

"If you stand on a corner with a pack of cigarettes or a bottle and have nothing to do in life, I suggest you sit down and think.

"This is the story of a person who walks on a lonely street. I hope this will help someone in the future."

He admitted 10 holdups on Chicago's West and Northwest Sides and said his victims were unable to identify him because he used oil paints on his face.

Cosco, arrested by police, admitted his part in the holdups of liquor stores, restaurants, Western Union offices and hotels. Cosco said he waited in a car while Krolik held up the victims.

Krolik said his troubles started a year ago after his former wife, Agnes Sampson, 21, an accordionist in a night club, divorced him. She said their five-week marriage was a mistake.

After the divorce, he said, "I kept slipping" and began associating with the "wrong kind of people." He continued:

"Finally, I went completely haywire on the stickups. I still love Agnes madly."

She commented:

"He's just a neglected boy who never really matured and needs help. I wish him the best."

Krolik said his manuscript, written before the crime spree, is in the hands of a New York publisher from whom he expects to hear next week.

Wanted To Be Cop

He stated that despite his crimes, his greatest ambition is to become a policeman. He has submitted an application to join the force and was to have taken his physical examination next January. Because of his record, he cannot join the police force.

Krolik said he used his knowledge of judo when he flattened a hotel manager who resisted during one of his earlier robberies.

The artist-writer-criminal explained that he surrendered to police because "I have to get this thing off my mind." He added:

"I'm tired of the panders and streetwalkers I've been living with."

Police said they would seek leniency for him in court because he surrendered voluntarily and they believe he can be rehabilitated.

Alvin Krolik's first brush with the law as reported in the Miami News, *3rd November 1953.*

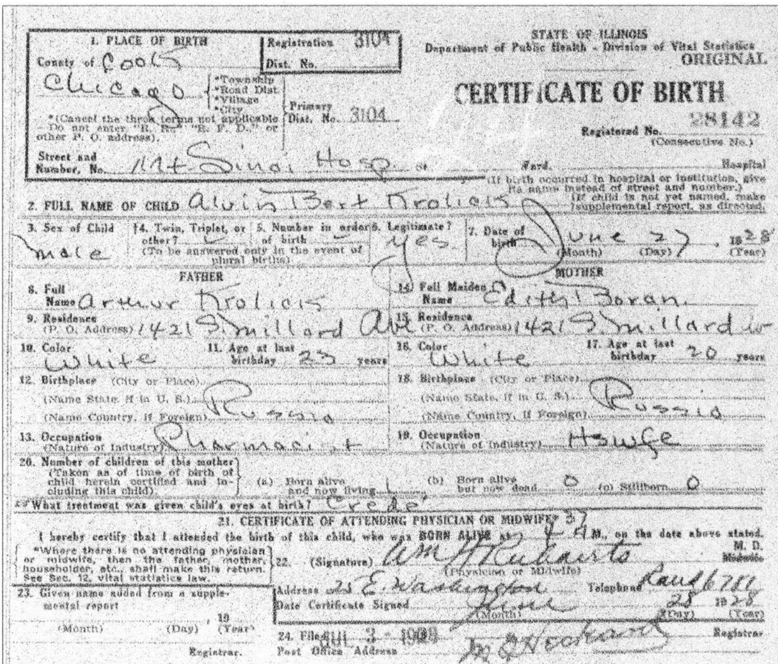

1. PLACE OF BIRTH
County of Cook
Chicago *Township *Road Dist. *Village *City
*(Cancel the three terms not applicable. Do not enter "R. R." "R. F. D." or other P. O. address).
Registration Dist. No. 3104
Primary Dist. No. 3104
Street and Number, No. Mt Sinai Hosp. ... Ward. ... Hospital
(If birth occurred in hospital or institution, give its name instead of street and number.)

STATE OF ILLINOIS
Department of Public Health - Division of Vital Statistics
ORIGINAL
CERTIFICATE OF BIRTH
Registered No. 28142 (Consecutive No.)

2. FULL NAME OF CHILD Alvin Bert Krolicis
(If child is not yet named, make supplemental report, as directed.)
3. Sex of Child: male
4. Twin, Triplet, or other? —
5. Number in order of birth (To be answered only in the event of plural births.)
6. Legitimate? yes
7. Date of birth: June 27, 1928 (Month) (Day) (Year)

FATHER
8. Full Name: Arthur Krolicis
9. Residence (P. O. Address): 1421 S. Millard Ave
10. Color: White
11. Age at last birthday: 23 years
12. Birthplace (City or Place) (Name State, if in U. S.) (Name Country, if Foreign): Russia
13. Occupation (Nature of Industry): Pharmacist

MOTHER
14. Full Maiden Name: Edith Boran
15. Residence (P. O. Address): 1421 S. Millard Av
16. Color: White
17. Age at last birthday: 20 years
18. Birthplace (City or Place) (Name State, if in U. S.) (Name Country, if Foreign): Russia
19. Occupation (Nature of Industry): Hswfe

20. Number of children of this mother (Taken as of time of birth of child herein certified and including this child): (a) Born alive and now living 1 (b) Born alive but now dead 0 (c) Stillborn 0
What treatment was given child's eyes at birth? Credé

21. CERTIFICATE OF ATTENDING PHYSICIAN OR MIDWIFE*
I hereby certify that I attended the birth of this child, who was BORN ALIVE at 7 4 M., on the date above stated.
*When there is no attending physician or midwife, then the father, mother, householder, etc., shall make this return. See Sec. 12, vital statistics law.
22. (Signature) Wm H Richarts M. D. (Physician or Midwife)
Address 25 E. Washington Telephone Rand 6781
Date Certificate Signed June 28 1928 (Month) (Day) (Year)
23. Given name added from a supplemental report ... 19 ... (Month) (Day) (Year) Registrar.
24. Filed Jul 3 - 1928 ... Registrar
Post Office Address

Alvin Krolik (central) demonstrates his disguise technique on Eugene Cosco, November 1953, as the police look on. From the author's collection, photographer unknown.

Alvin Krolik's erroneous birth certificate, note also his father's alias, one of several.

The Axton family, 1944,
courtesy of the estate of Mae Boren Axton.

Mae on Jacksonville Beach, 1958,
courtesy of the estate of Mae Boren Axton.

Smilin' Jack Herring & his Swingbillys,
Tommy far right, courtesy of Art Kenney.

Part 2: Glory

Works of art are of
an infinite loneliness
and nothing can reach them
so little as criticism.
Only love can grasp them
and keep hold of them
and be just to them.
Rainer Maria Rilke

Lincoln: Glory

EARLY SUMMER 1954
LINCOLN UNIVERSITY, CHESTER COUNTY, PENNSYLVANIA

AMERICANS WERE NOW LIVING IN A NEW ERA. The old ways had changed; another division between black and white had been dissolved. Horace Bond, as a figure of some importance in the black community, knew that the words he would speak at this moment would carry considerable weight.

He had come a long way from his home town of Nashville in his fifty-three years. His commitment to civil rights and equality in education had been spurred on by a Ku Klux Klan assault when he was just eight. He'd studied hard and had graduated with honours from Lincoln University, Pennsylvania, in 1923.

The university, founded in 1854 as the first institution anywhere in the world for the education of African Americans, was originally named after Jehudi Ashmun, a white minister and social reformer. It was retitled twelve years later following Lincoln's assassination.

In 1945, Bond was elected the first black president of the university, and he put his talents and position to good use when he worked with the National Association for the Advancement of Colored People in the U.S. Supreme Court case of *Brown vs Board of Education*. After three years of debate and legal argument, a decision was handed down on 17th May 1954 which established that American schools could not be segregated on the basis of colour.

It was a landmark occasion in the country's history and a leap forward for the civil rights movement. As a man of note, Horace Bond was required to comment on the victory and, realising the importance of the moment, he considered carefully.

He looked out at the assembled crowd and, just as Lincoln himself had done in the days following the civil war, he used a song to pull his people together. Taking a deep breath and steadying himself at the podium, he opened with these words: "Mine eyes have seen the glory of the coming of the Lord!"

The Battle Hymn of the Republic: A Biography of the Song That Marches On,
John Stauffer & Benjamin Soskis

The secret song, II

MONDAY 5TH JULY 1954
706 UNION AVENUE, MEMPHIS, TENNESSEE

MONDAY 5TH JULY 1954 was the longest working day of Elvis Presley's life. A thousand times he glanced at his watch, willing his shift to be over. When the whistle finally blew, he rushed home, took a shower, combed his hair twice, changed his clothes and, guitar in hand, left in time to arrive at 706 Union before 7:00 PM.

Marion had gone for the day, Scotty and Bill were already uncasing their instruments, and Sam was laughing at Bill's latest wisecrack. He looked up as the boy came in through the front door and then, five short paces later, nervously stepped down onto the studio floor itself. They all shook hands, and the first thing Elvis noticed was the heat. Lacking all but the most basic air conditioning, the Memphis Recording Service was an oven by this time of day, and the four men were soon dabbing sweat from their foreheads.

Sam reassured the boy that this evening was just going to be an informal session: Elvis would be putting a few songs on tape — this time with a couple of backing musicians — to see how it sounded. He positioned three microphones precisely, and gave each player instructions on where to stand. Sam placed Elvis nearest the control booth, but had him face away from the window, lest the producer's gaze un-nerve him further. Scotty and Bill formed the other two corners of the triangle, and all three looked in at one another, just six feet apart.

Elvis and Bill checked their instruments against Scotty's beautiful bronze-finished Gibson ES295, which was always perfectly tuned for studio work. The conversation inevitably turned to repertoire, and a handful of songs were suggested and discarded: the challenge was to find something that all three musicians knew well and could play all the way through.

Eventually, they settled on a most obscure selection: "Harbor Lights", a 1950 number one pop hit for The Sammy Kaye Orchestra. It was a mid-tempo ballad given a Hawaiian flavour by the use of steel guitar. As was the way of things, it had charted for several different artists, and the vocal line that Elvis had in his head was that of Bing Crosby's, no less. Elvis owned the Crosby single — he also loved the B-side, the similarly exotic "Beyond the Reef" — and it was a song he'd sung often in his room, maybe even to Dixie.

As they played a chord or two, Sam slipped into the control booth and cued up the Ampex. This being just a try-out session, he didn't bother setting the second machine, but decided to record the boys "dry", without echo. He started the tape rolling while they were still gently strumming, then silently caught their attention and nodded for them to begin.

The first two takes didn't get past the guitar introduction, but the third was complete. Scotty's opening notes rang clear and true, capturing the balmy and still studio atmosphere. Elvis self-consciously crooned his way through the tune, throwing in a whistling section for good measure. The song ended, and Sam praised the boys, calling for another take at a slightly faster tempo. It was a tactic he often used, trying to catch the musicians by surprise. They obliged: Elvis played around with the words a little; Scotty — probably to Sam's annoyance — added a stream of over-complex guitar fills; Bill plunked on the first beat of each bar.

They tried another two aborted takes, one of which fell apart because Scotty's accompaniment became so intricate that Elvis lost the rhythm. Hoping to shake things up again, Sam called for a key change. So the trio lowered the song, giving it more of a melancholy edge. Scotty continued over-filling, causing Sam to suggest maybe he should bring a bottle of bourbon next time to slow him down a little. They tried yet another take without directing the song anywhere new.

Elvis had been in the studio for maybe the best part of forty minutes. The heat was suffocatingly oppressive. He remained quiet between takes, unsure of exactly what was expected of him, but keenly aware that everything revolved around his performances. The next take sort of just dissolved, and all present knew the song had run out of steam.

Sam suggested they try something else. Elvis listened while titles were tossed about. Pop numbers, hillbilly hits and ballads were all floated, but no one, not even Mr Phillips, talked about the blues. And why would they? White musicians in a Memphis studio — even a studio usually dedicated to black performers — were unlikely to know about, much less sing anything from, the R&B chart.

Eventually, they chose Leon Payne's 1949 country hit "I Love You Because", a fiddle-led ballad, but Elvis' vocal line was inspired by Eddie Fisher's 1950 pop cover. As he had done with the first song of the evening, Elvis took his inspiration from the best singer. Sure, he knew the hillbilly version, but he matched himself against the smooth crooning of the pop artist rather than the pedestrian original.

Sam changed tapes and they spent much of the next hour running through take after take of their new selection. Again, Elvis played with the words; sometimes he whistled; sometimes he tried a dramatic narration. Scotty resisted overplaying, and when he got it right it was beautiful. Bill still plunked on the beat.

This pattern was repeated over and again with different songs as the minutes drifted slowly by. Sam grew impatient inwardly — although he would never allow his players to see any negative emotion — because he sensed the boy was holding back. There was something he wasn't revealing. Yes, he sang well, but Sam had already realised they didn't have the next Red Foley or Bing Crosby in the studio. Scotty, just three years older than Elvis but seeming decades more mature, was wondering why he was wasting a Monday night. Bill carried on plunking, knowing the session was heading nowhere.

They'd been playing and replaying for hours. Sam, sure that nothing of worth had been recorded, was beginning to use the same reels, taping over previous performances. The enthusiasm that had filled the studio at 7:00 PM was all but gone. The boys were tired, hot and sweaty. All three musicians had work the next morning. There was the occasional yawn and regular glances at watches. Maybe it was 10 o'clock. Maybe 11. Perhaps even later.

Sam came out onto the floor to call a short break. The guys picked up a Coke. Sam returned to the booth to sort through the tapes. Bill put down his bass and laid flat out beside it. Scotty slumped into a chair and fanned himself with a newspaper. Elvis remained standing at the mike, guitar still strapped, hair still perfectly combed, sweat-soaked shirt sticking to his back.

No one felt the sense of frustration more keenly than him. The studio was silent. All evening he'd been following the general suggestions of pop and hillbilly tunes (which he genuinely loved, of course) — songs they'd all known how to play. Heck, he'd nominated some of the choices himself. But the conversation had never turned to the other side of the musical fence. At no point had Mr Phillips followed Elvis' carefully imagined but unlikely script: "Do you know any blues, son?"

The hour was late. This was the session Elvis had been dreaming of for a year or even longer. And he knew that any minute now, Mr Phillips was going to call time and his big moment would be gone forever. Elvis had not wanted to expose himself or his musical tastes to people he barely knew. He hadn't wanted to risk potential ridicule. But, with the Blackwoods' tragedy in mind, he sensed he stood at a crossroads and, inspired, made a decision.

Seemingly out of the blue, Elvis started strumming his guitar rhythmically and loudly on an insistent A chord. Scotty and Bill looked up, surprised. Until now, Elvis had played slowly and quietly all evening. After a bar or two, Elvis sang the words, "Well, that's all right, now mama". Bill laughed and leapt to his feet, amused by the catchy beat and, although he didn't recognise the song, grabbed his bass and started not plunking but *slapping*. Scotty — also unfamiliar with the tune — picked up his guitar, figured out the key and started filling in where he could.

Sam, still in the booth and facing away from the band, stopped dead: chills ran down his spine. This was his "Marion" moment. The point at which he realised the boy had something special; something that connected emotionally with the listener. He, of course, *did* recognise the song, and the sense of swing and rhythm coming from the three untrained musicians was simply irresistible. He put down the tape box and turned around. Elvis still faced away from the glass, but Sam could see him physically involved in the performance, bouncing on his toes. Scotty and Bill, both beaming, were focused more on Elvis' left hand, looking for the chord changes.

Sam stepped down onto the studio floor and asked, "What are you boys doing?" The song abruptly stopped — although Bill, ever the clown, insisted on hitting a couple of extra notes — and the trio looked sheepishly at the producer, like children caught messing about by their father after lights out. "Ah, we're just fooling around, Mr Phillips," Elvis suggested, barely suppressing his stutter.

Now, what Sam wanted to do was grab Elvis by the shoulders and shout, "Why have you been holding out on me? You should have told me you knew Crudup's stuff! What other blues do you know?" But what he actually did was to say, "Well, it sounds pretty good. Let's back up, see if we can find a place to start over, and get it on tape."

The boys looked at one another and shrugged. Elvis clarified he was playing A, D and E chords, then suggested it might be nice to have a guitar solo after the second verse. Sam meanwhile was furiously cueing up the Ampex, partly terrified that they'd be unable to recreate the magic in a formal take. Maybe he should have just recorded the jam. There was no time to set up the slapback: he needed to get this on tape *now*.

Sam gave the okay and Elvis accidentally brushed against one guitar string. There was no count in, no take number announcement. He started strumming and Bill jumped right in on the second beat, and then both men stopped. It wasn't quite right. They tried again, this time getting as far as the end of the first line, with Scotty following the vocal melody, before coming to a halt. Sam held his breath.

They started yet again. Two bars of introduction, then Elvis started singing, Scotty once more following the tune. The guitarist quickly realised he should be filling in between the lines, so he changed tack, looking for a less cluttered approach. Bill was still slapping, and the physicality of his playing created a percussive clicking sound, making the band seem much bigger than it was. Scotty's solo spot came and he wandered around the strings, finding some good notes, but he sounded too stiff. The take finished. It didn't quite have the looseness of what he'd heard when the boys were jamming but, damn it, Sam knew they were almost there.

"Sounds good! Now, Bill, you let Elvis have a little more space in the intro; don't jump in too fast. Scotty, I swear, if I'd wanted Chet Atkins on this session I would have flown him in from Nashville — keep it simple, son. Elvis, you're doing just fine. Maybe we can ease back a little on the tempo. Okay, let's try it again, just one more time for Sam."

After hours of tension, there was suddenly a sense of grace and freedom in the cramped sweatbox of a studio. The boys were ready; Elvis was a ball of energy; Bill was chewing gum and smiling; Scotty was attentive and serious. Elvis hit the opening riff, clear and strong, with just the slightest drop in tempo, allowing the song to breathe. Bill jumped in perfectly, a beat later than previously — Sam was right; it worked much better this way. Scotty watched Elvis as the second bar of introduction came to an end, waiting for the vocal to kick in, so he could feed off his lines. But Elvis didn't come in as scheduled and Sam's heart skipped a beat. The riff kept going for an extra half a bar before Elvis, now absolutely in command of the song and teasing the band, started in with the lyric. And Sam loved this — it was different! It would catch the listener by surprise.

The performance swung beautifully, but Sam stood quite motionless throughout the take. He didn't want anything to interrupt the moment. Scotty found the ideal balance between complexity and simplicity, and his guitar solo perfectly complemented Elvis' singing. Bill drove the song along, giving it the essential bounce and lightness of touch. But it was Elvis who was the catalyst. His acoustic guitar playing had, up until now, been a handicap. But suddenly, it was the glue that held everything together. And his vocals were a revelation. This was an adult song about a failing relationship, and Elvis sang it like a bird. He brought together the lust of Jimmie Rodgers and the piety of the Carters, all in a single performance.

Just two minutes after the song had begun, Elvis rang the final note and stood absolutely still, waiting for the all clear from Mr Phillips. When it came, the players laughed and relaxed. Sam was exhilarated. For the first time, he'd captured the spirit of his black artists through a white band. But Elvis wasn't simply a white boy singing the blues: he was a poor young Southerner singing in a way that made barriers and divisions irrelevant.

They listened to the playback and self-consciously mocked their own performances. It began to occur to Scotty and Bill that they'd actually played on a blues. When the tape ended, the boys stopped laughing and a tense silence filled the small room. One voice wondered whether it'd be allowed to be played on radio. After another short silence, the answer came back, "Good God, they'll run us out of town."

Sam sent the boys home, although none of them would be able to sleep that night. Elvis walked on air all the way. Scotty drove Bill and their instruments back to Belz. Sam stayed in the booth and played the song again. It was black, white, country, blues, gospel and pop all mixed together. But overall, and most importantly, it was the sound of *youth*. American popular music of all genres was dominated by singers who were in their late twenties and beyond. Why? Because it took so damn long to make a breakthrough, to get a record contract, to get on the radio, to achieve recognition.

He wondered to himself again why the boy hadn't told him he knew blues songs. But, in truth, Sam entirely understood Elvis' need for discretion. One tended not to talk about these things — hell, even with Dewey he skirted around the obvious conversation — but he felt sure he'd found a white boy who was not only non-prejudiced, but who also adored black culture as much as he did. He knew they'd achieved something truly special, but wasn't at all sure what was going to happen next.

He put the tape in a Scotch box and left it on his desk in the booth. He locked up, then made his own way home, thinking to himself, "Imagine a kid like that knowing Crudup." The following morning, Sam, Scotty and Bill would all tell the same tale to their wives over breakfast "… and then, out of nowhere, this crazy boy just started singing this song."

And that's the story everyone, including Elvis, told from that point on.

Crudup's After Hours

TUESDAY 6TH JULY 1954 (EARLY HOURS)
706 UNION AVENUE, MEMPHIS, TENNESSEE

But let's pause for a moment and hang around outside 706 Union as the clock ticks past midnight and Sam closes the door. Let's quietly sneak back into the now empty studio, turn on a single light in the booth, switch on the Ampex, thread the tape back onto the reel, and listen again to what was recorded that night.

Sam Phillips was a man who knew and loved the blues, and when he heard Elvis singing the lyrics of a Crudup number he naturally assumed the song was "That's All Right", because, well, those were the literal words he heard coming out of Elvis' mouth at the beginning of the song.

But as a true Crudup devotee might tell you — a devotee like Elvis perhaps — Crudup used and re-used lyrics on a regular basis. In theory, when Sam heard the first four lines of Elvis' song, he really could have been listening to "If I Get Lucky", "Dirt Road Blues", "I Want My Loving" or, indeed, "That's All Right", because they all open with the same words.

And if we listen very closely to the whole of Elvis' version, what we hear is something which is lyrically very different indeed to Arthur Crudup's "That's All Right". In fact, what we hear is a medley of words taken from all the above listed songs, and also a line or two from Crudup's "Mean Old 'Frisco Blues", not to mention various phrases that Elvis himself seems to have invented (the "sure/door" couplet has no known Crudup reference, for example).

Elvis' song is not really a cover of "That's All Right" — it is a compilation of at least three, but maybe as many as five, separate Crudup recordings. In fact, one could easily go a step further and assert that Elvis Presley had composed his own Arthur Crudup song, almost as an homage to Crudup's style of writing.

Therefore, we can say with all certainty that Elvis was not merely parroting Crudup's original disk. Elvis' song has a much wider scope than that. But, the assumption has always been that Elvis launched into this song off-the-cuff, so it's no real surprise that he was just grabbing lyrics out of the air from various songs as he half-remembered them: that is the nature of inspired improvised composition.

But, as we sit here at Sam's desk in the early hours of Tuesday 6th July 1954, let's wind the tape back to the rough take just before the finished master; the take where Scotty hadn't quite got his act together and Bill came in a little too early. Let's listen again to Elvis, and make a careful note of the words he has apparently improvised (and we now know he's definitely not simply copying a favourite single he's learned off-by-heart).

As we list the precise words that Elvis sings on this earlier take, we notice something very odd, and surprising: the lyrics on the rough take are *exactly the same* as those on the finished master. There is not a syllable, not a conjunction, not an inflection, that changes. The assumption has always been that Elvis leapt into the Crudup song on a whim, without any forethought whatsoever. But we now understand that he wasn't copying Crudup's original version of "That's All Right" at all. This was Elvis' own personal version of a Crudup-type song: if he'd improvised it on the spot, pulling in lyrics randomly from perhaps five songs, how on earth would he be able to reproduce the exact same improvisation a few minutes later without changing a single letter of his supposedly unplanned interpretation?

The answer to this question is obvious: he couldn't have done this. *No one* could have done this. And the conclusion that must be drawn is simple: Elvis Presley arrived at 706 Union Avenue on Monday 5th July 1954 with a song he'd already written for himself in the style of his adored blues hero Arthur Crudup, because Mr Phillips had made it very clear in the newspaper article that he was looking for singers who had a song to bring to the table.

And rather than write a song conventionally, Elvis assembled a Crudup montage — a medley of Crudup lyrics and new Crudupesque phrases — in the hope that Mr Phillips would invite him to sing it ("Do you have anything you've written yourself?" or even "Do you know any blues, son?"). When the opportunity did not present itself, and when Elvis felt his time with Sam was running out, he revealed his secret song — and revealed also his own love of the blues — in a seemingly improvised fashion.

Elvis told nobody about this ever. He was content to go along with the notion that it was a spontaneous event for the simple reason that it was way cooler to give that impression. Read carefully through every interview Elvis went on to give throughout his entire career: he always attributed his success to luck. But as the old stage-mother gag had it, the harder my son worked the luckier he got.

And so, the turning point of American popular culture, the fateful meeting of black and white music, was forever cast as a happy accident, because no one noticed that Elvis Presley's song was so very different to Arthur Crudup's original. And no one gave a moment's credence to the thought that a shy Southern boy could possibly have known precisely what needed to happen to American popular music, and assembled and wrote his own blues song.

But that's exactly what he did.

The interview, I

TUESDAY 6TH JULY 1954
RADIO WHBQ, MEMPHIS, TENNESSEE

DEWEY PHILLIPS DIDN'T KNOW what to make of the acetate that Sam played for him. And that pleased Sam. Dewey never lied to his buddy. If he didn't like a Sun record then he wouldn't play it on air, and Sam valued that level of honesty. He'd cut the acetate first thing that morning with the express intention of bringing it to Dewey. The deejay listened to the song again. He listened carefully. He knew Crudup's stuff, obviously, and certainly recognised where the song was coming from.

At some point in the conversation, Dewey had discovered that the singer — heck, the whole band — was white. Sam and Dewey could both see the issue. Hillbilly stations wouldn't touch it because it was blues. Black stations would ignore it because Elvis was white. Who was going to play the damn record on the radio? And then Dewey made a decision. *He* would play it.

After work, when Elvis heard his song was to be debuted on Dewey's show, he nearly fainted with excitement. Unable to deal with the situation, he headed to the cinema and hid in the dark, watching his heroes on the screen, wondering what sort of public humiliation he'd have to deal with tomorrow. Half way through the movie, he felt a hand on his shoulder. Turning, he recognised his father's face. Vernon had tracked him down to tell him that Dewey had played the record and all hell had broken loose — in a good way. The station switchboard had lit up and they were playing the acetate over and again. The deejay was demanding Elvis come in for an on-air interview at once.

So Elvis was more or less dragged to the station, and he sat opposite Dewey while his own record was broadcast all over Memphis and beyond. He sat there, facing the most outrageous white deejay in the South, and he didn't have a thing to say. Sensing his crippling nerves, Dewey cracked a joke and shot the boy a smile. "Sir, I don't know nothing about being interviewed," said Elvis. "Just be polite and don't say nothing dirty, son," came the reply. "I'll let you know when you're on."

It seemed to Elvis that the interview would never start. Meanwhile, Dewey was asking him all sorts of questions, and it was all he could do to stutter his way through the simple answers — Lord knew how he'd cope when Dewey actually switched on the mike. Dewey casually asked where he'd gone to school, and Elvis responded, "Humes High, sir." He couldn't imagine why Dewey wanted to know this, but was happy to play the game.

"Well, that's about it," said the deejay. "Thanks for coming in, Elvis."

"Huh? Aren't you going to interview me, sir?"

"I just did, son. The mike's been open the whole time."

Elvis broke into a cold sweat. But thousands of excited listeners were now party to the truth. Humes High was a segregated school.

This cat was white.

Last Train to Memphis: The Rise of Elvis Presley, Peter Guralnick
Sam Phillips: The Man Who Invented Rock 'n' Roll, Peter Guralnick

The pop song

WEDNESDAY 7TH JULY 1954
706 UNION AVENUE, MEMPHIS, TENNESSEE

SAM PHILLIPS HAD A PROBLEM: he had half of a potential hit record. The Memphis reaction to Dewey's playing of "That's All Right" had been sensational. But how was Sam going to recreate that inspired moment and come up with a B-side that matched what they'd already committed to tape? He called the boys back into the studio after work on the Wednesday, and they gathered in the small room feeling proud of what they'd already done, but also fearful they wouldn't be able to do it again.

So they followed the pattern. They threw titles around and worked on this song for an hour, then that song for an hour, and the mood this time stayed upbeat. Elvis felt able to suggest R&B songs that Scotty and Bill didn't know (although Sam did), and they stayed loose while they played and failed, repeatedly.

It was Bill who provided the breakthrough. Maybe they were daring each other to suggest the least likely song to record, and the bassman started mimicking Bill Monroe's hallowed waltz, "Blue Moon of Kentucky". Aping Monroe's distinctive falsetto, there were many who would have considered Bill Black's clowning sacrilegious. But at 706 Union, nothing was now off limits, and Elvis took up the challenge, ignoring the ¾ time signature and riding the tune as an easy four-in-the-bar mid-tempo shuffle number.

Sam knew they were on to something and he goaded the boys to see if they couldn't re-invent the song. They toiled for hours, but it didn't seem like work at all. Each new take increased the tempo and took the song a step further away from its original form. A key moment came when Elvis created a brand new opening on the spot. Setting up a Crudup-like rhythm, he wrote a whole section that owed nothing at all to Monroe's hit. It seemed to free up a completely different part of his voice and the words came tumbling out in a deep slurry fashion.

It was glorious, and became better still when Sam added slapback to the vocals. If anything, it was even more daring than "That's All Right", and the participants were drenched in sweat and exhausted when they called it day.

And Sam understood exactly what they'd achieved. He knew that the two songs removed all barriers, racial and otherwise. Elvis, Scotty and Bill had redefined what constituted a modern mainstream record. Although some would say Elvis was simply singing the blues on a country number, Sam hit it on the head early in the session while the boys were still playing around with the format. As a rough take stumbled to an end, Sam guffawed and pronounced loudly:

"Hell, that's different. That's a *pop song* now, nearly 'bout!"

Last Train to Memphis: The Rise of Elvis Presley, Peter Guralnick
Sam Phillips: The Man Who Invented Rock 'n' Roll, Peter Guralnick

In quick succession

MONDAY 19TH JULY 1954
MEMPHIS, TENNESSEE

A WHOLE BUNCH OF STUFF then happened very quickly in the nascent career of Elvis Presley. The day after they recorded the B-side, Marion wrote to ASCAP enquiring after the copyright owners for the two songs (Wabash Music and Peer, both BMI). On the following Monday, at Sam's suggestion, Scotty signed on as Elvis' manager, agreeing to split any profits 50/25/25 across the trio. Sam then arranged for them to play a low key gig on Saturday 12th at the Bon Air club, a small local venue, full of patrons who didn't always take kindly to guys dressed like Elvis — but the brief performance went down well.

And on Monday 19th, the single was released (Sun 209), and sold an astonishing four thousand copies in its first week. Elvis was not known and Sun's distribution system was limited, but he was certainly a hit in Memphis.

Dixie returned from holiday and stepped into the whirlwind whipping around her boyfriend and she couldn't have been prouder, but she already noticed the world was changing for him. As indeed it was for Scotty and Bill. The Starlite Wranglers were not impressed by their defection to this punk kid's cause, and the hillbilly dance band imploded.

Elvis, Scotty and Bill were still holding down day jobs — they hadn't made a cent between them so far — and progress in country music was a slow business: they could expect a long, hard slog, assuming they made any headway at all.

But Sam was determined. The night after the Bon Air gig, he called popular Memphis deejay, Bob Neal, who was organising his big annual country music concert at the Overton Shell (an open air amphitheatre), scheduled for Friday 30th July. Sam sweet-talked his way through the conversation and, sure enough, Bob — the nicest of guys — offered the boy a spot on the show, as long as he joined the Musicians' Union first.

Top of the bill for the gig would the most popular and hottest singing star in country music: none other than Slim Whitman.

A Boy from Tupelo, Ernst Mikael Jørgensen
Last Train to Memphis: The Rise of Elvis Presley, Peter Guralnick
Sam Phillips: The Man Who Invented Rock 'n' Roll, Peter Guralnick

When Elvis met Slim

FRIDAY 30TH JULY 1954
THE OVERTON SHELL, MEMPHIS, TENNESSEE

SLIM WHITMAN ARRIVED in plenty of time for the 8:00 PM Overton Shell show in Memphis, and noted a new name had been added at the bottom of the bill ("Ellis Presley", another notable success for the printing industry), but gave it little thought.

It was a sticky night, and even bearing in mind they were playing outdoors, the heat was overwhelming. Slim liked to watch the other performers, so he hung around in the wings to check out the competition.

By some odd stroke of scheduling, Elvis, Scotty and Bill would be on just before Slim himself. And Slim must have raised his eyebrows at the sight of this handsome rake dressed in a pastel suit with a fancy two-tone tie, frantically pacing up and down backstage. One thing he certainly would have recognised was that the boy was terrified and, had he stood closer, he'd have heard and sympathised as the teenager stuttered and mumbled his way through a confidence-boosting conversation with Sam Phillips.

At last, it was showtime and the trio ran on stage for their first gig in front of a serious audience. To some extent — and compared to Elvis — Scotty and Bill were seasoned veterans, but they'd never played this big a show. They hit into "That's All Right" and Elvis, as a natural reaction to the music and also due to his nerves, started to shake his legs in tempo. And, unknown though he was, the audience — particularly the young female part of it — responded enthusiastically, which confused him no end.

As the song finished to loud applause, Elvis turned and conferred with his band, requiring to know what all the fuss was about. Scotty and Bill laughed, telling him it was his "shaky leg" that was getting the girls so riled up. Elvis considered this for a moment and turned back towards the applauding crowd. He launched into "Blue Moon of Kentucky" and, like a scientist, decided to test his band's theory. Sure enough, the more he moved, the louder the reaction.

Sam Phillips was beside himself with joy. The kid looked like a movie star; he sang like a dream; he dressed with attitude; he seemed to know every blues and hillbilly song Sam had ever heard; and he was able to perform in such a way that the crowd surrendered at his feet. All at once, Sam Phillips saw the future — and he grinned from ear to ear.

Slim Whitman, however, had to follow the hometown boy on stage. Ever the gentleman, he joined in the applause and sincerely declared to the crowd that he'd enjoyed the performance just as much as they had.

When Slim returned to Shreveport, he made sure to tell the producers of the *Hayride* about the exciting young talent he'd seen in Memphis, maybe even mentioning it to his old friend Bob Ross when next they met.

A week later, Slim Whitman would release his new single. It would be the last top ten hit of his entire career. The winds of change were blowing.

A Boy from Tupelo, Ernst Mikael Jørgensen
Last Train to Memphis: The Rise of Elvis Presley, Peter Guralnick
Mr Songman: The Slim Whitman Story, Kenneth L. Gibble
Sam Phillips: The Man Who Invented Rock 'n' Roll, Peter Guralnick

Bobby Ross: on the radio

AUGUST 1954
TAMPA, FLORIDA

DURING THE SUMMER OF 1954, Bob Ross came to a decision: he was now a father, and the time had come to put his family first. He couldn't go travelling all over the country on a moment's notice promoting this artist or that song.

He'd already invested in Harmony, his own Hollywood recording studio, and so, when his contracts with Hill & Range and George Morgan ended, he took a much less demanding job as a disk jockey on station WFLA in his home town of Tampa, Florida.

His family would be happier, and Bob probably figured he'd live a lot longer without all the stress and hassle that management entailed.

Billboard, 4th September & 13th November 1954

All the news that's fit to print

SATURDAY 7TH AUGUST 1954
BILLBOARD MAGAZINE, PAGE 39

ONE OF THE GREAT UNSUNG HEROES of American popular music was a fellow named Paul Ackerman. As editor of the weekly *Billboard* magazine, a trade publication for all areas of show business, he had considerable influence regarding what was and what wasn't printed. He held a high regard for folk music, black and white, and ensured at least one full page per issue was devoted to each genre.

His job was not made any easier by the regular threatening messages he received — and this was a scenario with which Sam Phillips was also well acquainted — warning him to stay away from "that nigger music". Ackerman, like Sam (and Elvis too for that matter), tried to ignore the abuse and carried on about his business.

A clever manager or publicist would use the hillbilly and blues pages for free advertising and, without question, Colonel Tom Parker was an avid fan of the "Country & Western Records" section, as it was titled, often planting stories about his artists and, indeed, himself.

The column featured charts, record reviews, concert news and a healthy smattering of general gossip. And page 39 of the 7th August 1954 edition was, in many ways, a typical page, in a typical issue of the periodical.

It covered all the usual bases and the ardent reader would have noted the following: Hank Snow was top of the hillbilly chart with a Hill & Range song; other big-sellers included Slim Whitman, Eddy Arnold, Johnnie and Jack, Hank Thompson, Kitty Wells and Red Foley dueting, and a singer named Terry Fell who was being wooed by RCA; there were news items regarding Tommy Sands, Minnie Pearl, Fabor Robison, Jim Reeves, Tex Ritter, Charline Arthur, The Wilburn Brothers, and, not surprisingly, Tom Parker; and it was announced that one of The Dickens Sisters had become a mother (they'd never again perform as a trio).

And in the Talent section of that particular page, Elvis Presley — who on 7th August was playing a small gig in Memphis with Scotty and Bill — was given a glowing record review, the canny writer pointing out that his disk (Sun 209) had potential in hillbilly and blues markets.

And so, for anyone who ever wondered about the first time Tom Parker would have become aware of the name "Elvis Presley", here is your answer.

Billboard, 7th August 1954

Bill Monroe hears the news

MID-AUGUST 1954
MEMPHIS, TENNESSEE

IN THE MONTH SINCE Elvis, Scotty and Bill's first session, Sam Phillips had been almost constantly on the road, trying to expand Sun's market, attempting to convince every deejay and distributor of the vital importance of this new sound. Some listened and some didn't. There was more resistance than even Sam would have expected.

Still, the record climbed the local chart, with "Blue Moon of Kentucky" proving even more popular than the A-side. Whenever possible, Sam ushered the trio back into the studio because he knew a second release would be needed to maintain momentum.

At 706 Union, they followed the now established formula: they played through anything and everything, looking for a groove to follow. They tried ballads, including a haunting take on the pop standard "Blue Moon", which Elvis and the boys transformed into a glorious "lost cowboy" number, using a Slim Whitman-style yodel. But Sam knew he couldn't use it as a single. Songs were tried, taped, and then taped over, time and again.

Elvis probably ran through some R&B numbers, hoping to replicate the magic of the first single, but nothing came easy. He tried "Tiger Man", Sun's earlier hit record, and maybe Sam initially enthused about it — perhaps even cutting a trial acetate or two, to Elvis' delight. But the producer was desperately anxious to ensure the follow-up record was as distinctive as the debut release and, much to Elvis' disappointment, everything was rejected. Sam seemed obsessed and it was vital that every single was, to his ears at least, a killer.

Most of these day-to-day happenings blended into one blurry memory for the immediate participants — "We weren't making history," said Scotty later, "we were making a living." — but Elvis seemed to memorise every event, so keenly was he experiencing these adventures.

And it was true that some within the industry were beginning to take notice. Bill Monroe, of all people, heard what the boy had done with "Blue Moon of Kentucky", and looked forward to receiving the royalties. More importantly, on 4th September, Monroe re-recorded his signature tune with a souped-up second half, as a gentle nod to the revolutionary performance that was catching on wherever Sun Records could find a willing distributor.

And if Bill Monroe — guardian of all that was pure and proper in bluegrass music — was willing to listen with an open mind, then there was surely hope for the rest of the world, too.

A Boy from Tupelo, Ernst Mikael Jørgensen
Last Train to Memphis: The Rise of Elvis Presley, Peter Guralnick
Sam Phillips: The Man Who Invented Rock 'n' Roll, Peter Guralnick

Mae, Hank and Wanda

PERHAPS LATE SUMMER 1954
OKLAHOMA

MAE BOREN AXTON had settled in Florida but much of her heart and many of her family still resided in Oklahoma, and she visited as often as she could, but not as often as she would have liked. In particular, she missed spending time with her father, who still lived alone since the death of his wife.

During one visit, Mae sat down to watch television after dinner with her relatives and, gosh, on came the *Hank Thompson Show*. Didn't Hank look grand in his outfit — and wasn't his singing just wonderful? Mae well remembered the nervous young man she'd met back in 1949. He'd done well for himself, and his latest hit, "Honky Tonk Girl", was a great tune.

Hank had a guest on the show this evening, a pretty young thing name of Wanda Jackson. Well, Mae nearly fell off the sofa when she appeared. Damned if it wasn't the daughter of her old school friend, Nellie Whitaker. Here she was, almost seventeen, and singing up a storm. Hank Thompson recognised talent when he saw it — and young Wanda was the real thing.

Country Singers As I Know 'Em, Mae Boren Axton

"Good Rockin' Tonight"

MID-SEPTEMBER 1954
706 UNION AVENUE, MEMPHIS, TENNESSEE

IT SHOULD BE CLEARLY UNDERSTOOD that even though Sun 209 was selling well locally and in one or two other markets such as Texas, it was nowhere near troubling the hillbilly chart, let alone the pop hit parade. Sun, which was primarily known as a blues label, was struggling to find people willing to stock and sell a new record by an unknown white boy.

Also, Jim Bulleit had done some damage to Sun's reputation, which made Sam's job harder still. Added to which was the eternal problem of cashflow in relation to a small hit record. Sam had to pay to have the records pressed; he'd give them out to shops and dealers; but then he wouldn't receive payment for those records until weeks or even months later.

And Sam understood that a new release would soon become essential, and so the boys continued to work in the studio at every opportunity. Again, they taped song after song, from a variety of sources: they tried Lonnie Johnson's R&B ballad "Tomorrow Night" and Jimmy Wakely's 1943 hit "I'll Never Let You Go". They cut a fine version of The Shelton Brothers' "Just Because" (now owned by Leeds Music, if you're still following that particular thread), and perhaps dozens more. They jammed on Martha Carson's "Satisfied", but Sam pushed on, demanding something different, something better.

Finally, the trio hit upon a Dean Martin ditty, "I Don't Care if the Sun Don't Shine", that Elvis knew from a 1953 movie (and Elvis just *loved* Dean Martin). While they worked it up in the studio, it became clear the song was somewhat short, so Marion wrote an extra verse for which publishers Famous Music — owned by Paramount Pictures — insisted she receive no official credit. Elvis turned in a delightful and bubbly performance. He used the back of his guitar as a percussion instrument, and Scotty and Bill gelled perfectly behind. The finished track was infectious and irresistible, and Elvis effortlessly beat Dub Dickerson at his own game, singing with a playful grin in his voice.

The flip side was slower in coming. Sam was looking for an R&B song to balance the single, as per the first record. Eventually, Elvis came up with Roy Brown's "Good Rockin' Tonight", a brass-led stomper from 1947 on De Luxe Records (1093) which owned the publishing too via its in-house company, Blue Ridge. Wynonie Harris also hit with it the following year, but it was Brown that Elvis had in mind when he launched his own attack on the song.

Lacking a horn section, Elvis roared into the number with what would soon become a Presley trademark, hollering a long acapella "Weeeellllll!" The band kicked in tough and hard, and on the finished record it's clear that everything the boys had learned from two months of playing in front of small audiences had been poured into this performance. It was breathtaking, sexy and dramatic. And it wasn't just a fabulous record (Sun 210) — more importantly, it added to the arsenal of songs they could feature on stage, and Elvis knew that both sides, but especially "Good Rockin' Tonight", could be used to thrilling effect.

And it was important their stage repertoire be at its very best in the weeks to come because Sam Phillips had been hard at work behind the scenes, and he'd managed to book a trial performance on the *Louisiana Hayride* for mid-October. But the truly astonishing news was that, having cashed in almost every favour he was owed, on 2nd October, less than three months after their first recording session, the boys would be at the Ryman Auditorium playing a guest spot on the *Grand Ole Opry*.

A Boy from Tupelo, Ernst Mikael Jørgensen
Last Train to Memphis: The Rise of Elvis Presley, Peter Guralnick
Sam Phillips: The Man Who Invented Rock 'n' Roll, Peter Guralnick

The fall of Hank Snow

PERHAPS LATE SEPTEMBER 1954
GALLATIN ROAD, MADISON, TENNESSEE

TOM PARKER KNEW that Hank Snow would ring. Actually, he thought he'd ring earlier, but the call itself was not a surprise. Snow needed a manager and Parker was available. Tom had been at his most impressive during the Caravan in the spring, hoping the Canadian would notice him, and indeed he had.

There were other things that Parker knew: he knew he preferred managing younger singers who were less set in their ways; he knew he liked to look after all of his artists' finances and then pass on their share after he'd taken his own, and there was no way a tightwad like Snow would allow that to happen; he knew Snow discarded managers like other men changed shirts, so this would likely be a short appointment; but he knew most of all that he needed a big star to put him back on top, and Hank Snow — owner of the prime ego in country music — fitted the bill perfectly.

After the phone call, Snow, who was virtually Parker's next-door neighbour, drove to his would-be manager's garage-located makeshift office. On entering, he extended his hand and thanked "Tom" for making time to see him. Parker wasn't having any of this familiarity nonsense and informed Snow in no uncertain terms he was always to be addressed as "the Colonel" from this point onwards.

Snow then sat while Parker paced back and forth speaking at great length about how he would build the singer into one of the principal stars in the nation. Snow, who felt he already *was* one of the principal stars in the nation, remained silent, but had to admire the Colonel's vision and drive. Parker spoke about his promotions company, Jamboree Attractions (and its sister organisation, Jamboree Music), which looked after great performers like Minnie Pearl and Tommy Sands.

Despite himself, Snow was impressed, and, over the course of two or three subsequent meetings, agreed to all of the Colonel's management terms, which presumably included the usual twenty-five percent cut. To keep things neat and tidy, Parker decided their arrangement should officially start on 1st January 1955, but in the interim he would act as Snow's ad hoc manager for a one-off payment of $2,500. Payable immediately. Snow pulled out his cheque book and handed over the suggested amount. He then drove home and prepared songs for his forthcoming *Opry* broadcast on the first Saturday of October. Tom, meanwhile, returned to his desk, finalising details for a ten-day Eddy Arnold tour of the South, a month hence.

Many years later, when Hank got around to writing his memoirs, he was unable to put an exact date to this first meeting with Parker. He simply described the season as "the fall", which, in retrospect, seems very appropriate.

The Hank Snow Story, Hank Snow with Jack Ownbey *&* Bob Burris

Presley on the radio, III

SATURDAY 2ND OCTOBER 1954
RYMAN AUDITORIUM, NASHVILLE, TENNESSEE

PRESLEY'S NERVES WERE SHOWING as he waited for his call to the microphone. His friends and family were listening at home. The powerful WSM transmitter sent the radio signal loud and clear across the South. Then a young man walked up to him.

"Hi," he said, "I'm Buddy Killen. I play bass on the *Opry*."

"Hi," the singer replied. "I'm Elvis Presley."

"What's the matter with you?" asked Buddy.

"I'm scared. If Mr Phillips would let me leave, I'd get out of here. These people are going to hate me."

"No, they won't, you'll do fine," Buddy optimistically responded.

Elvis fidgeted some more; Buddy kept up the support. Elvis had already met (and apologised to) Bill Monroe backstage. With Bill you didn't know if you would get a handshake or a sock to the jaw — the former, thankfully.

At last, his time came. Chet Atkins had just vacated the stage and Scotty got a real kick about plugging into the same socket that his idol had used. Hank Snow was the host for this part of the show. It has been suggested that he forgot Presley's name during his introduction. Elvis and his boys played "Blue Moon of Kentucky". There was polite applause. The audience did not know Elvis or his record. Hank Snow remembered his own less than enthusiastic debut. Elvis thanked the crowd and left the stage on cue.

Elvis, Scotty and Bill picked up their gear and strolled across the street to visit Ernest Tubb's cramped record store from where the *Midnite Jamboree* radio show was broadcast each week after the *Opry*. Elvis was honoured to meet the esteemed singer, and performed his song for a second time.

Thus, Elvis' first visit to Nashville came to a close. The earth had not moved. The *Opry* still stood. Elvis had no hit record and the *Opry* didn't want or need him. Elvis' performance was always intended to be a one-off — Sam had been clear on that with Jim Denny. Some viewed the evening as a setback. Sam Phillips considered it a complete triumph.

By the Seat of my Pants, Buddy Killen with Tom Carter
The Hank Snow Story, Hank Snow with Jack Ownbey & Bob Burris

Local knowledge

AUTUMN 1954
KNOXVILLE, TENNESSEE

THE MAJOR RECORD LABELS had representatives posted all over the country looking for the next big act or money-spinning musical trend. RCA had appointed under Steve Sholes a bright fellow named Chick Crumpacker as their man in charge of c&w promotion, and he in turn had a thirty-three year-old New Yorker called Brad McCuen keeping an observant eye on the Tennessee area.

While visiting a record shop in Knoxville, McCuen started a conversation with the owner who played for him "That's All Right". McCuen gave no indication as to what he thought of the song, he just raised his eyebrows.

"I'm selling a box of this a day," said the owner.

McCuen expressed surprise: "It's just a normal rhythm & blues record, isn't it?"

"No, it isn't. It's selling to a country audience."

McCuen purchased two copies and sent one to Steve Sholes.

Last Train to Memphis: The Rise of Elvis Presley, Peter Guralnick

Mae's predicament

PERHAPS EARLY OCTOBER 1954
JACKSONVILLE, FLORIDA

There are times in the life of a family that are so sensitive that the secrets they keep are impenetrable. So it was with the Borens and the Axtons in the late summer of 1954. As she turned forty, a crisis arose in Mae's life that she hid from almost everyone.

It's possible she had been running to and from Oklahoma during this period, so let's speculate and suggest that the predicament may have concerned her remaining family in that state. Let's say, for example, that her beloved widowed father had become very ill. In later years, Mae would write in very disparaging terms about "the dread cancer" as she put it, so let's speculate further and suggest that Mark Boren had been diagnosed with a serious cancer, and it required a costly operation and very expensive follow-up nursing care.

This may be accurate, or it may be far-fetched, but it's for sure that Mae needed money. Indeed, she needed a large amount of money by about the first day of November, and she'd need much more in the months thereafter. Yes, she had siblings, some of whom were better off than she was, but it would have been unthinkable for Mae not to contribute if it was indeed her father's life on the line.

And so, in desperation, she likely spoke to Tom Parker, the most powerful person within her network, who was, of course, now manager-designate for Hank Snow. She wasn't asking for charity, and she wouldn't accept a handout. Tom liked Mae and felt she could be a useful person in years to come. He offered her a position as Snow's well-paid PR advisor — in the style of Bea Terry, one might say. Hank would bitch about the expense, but Tom was sure he could square it.

Mae accepted gratefully, despite knowing the first pay cheque wouldn't arrive in time. In return, she declared her undying devotion to the Colonel (who hadn't personally parted with a penny), and then packed her bags, and started the nine-hour drive to Nashville for a music business conference beginning on Sunday 10th October, to start promoting her new employer — the one and only Hank Snow.

Country Singers As I Know 'Em, Mae Boren Axton
Billboard, 23rd & 30th October 1954

Presley on the radio, IV

SATURDAY 16TH OCTOBER 1954
MUNICIPAL AUDITORIUM, SHREVEPORT, LOUISIANA

THE SECOND SINGLE — "Good Rockin' Tonight"/"I Don't Care if the Sun Don't Shine" — was already available in Memphis shops and would go on general release in November. Encouraged by the rapid progress they were making, Sam and the boys drove to Shreveport, on Saturday 16th October, ready for their debut performance on the *Louisiana Hayride*. Unlike their night at the *Opry*, which had been organised as a one-off visit, this was intended as a live audition. If the trio went down well, it could result in a year-long contract and the opportunity to broadcast their songs far beyond Sun's usual distribution radar.

Elvis was, as usual, anxious, and Sam positioned himself in the audience, in case he might be needed to cue the applause. There were various stars wandering around backstage (Tillman Franks, composer of "Poison Love", was playing bass in the house band that night) and many took notice of Presley's outrageous wardrobe.

The boys bounced out and gave convincing performances of both sides of their first single. The audience reaction was polite, just as it had been at the *Opry*, but there was a feeling that Elvis hadn't truly connected as well as he might. They were scheduled to perform again later in the show, and by that time Elvis was less tense and he bowled the audience over — those present in the auditorium and also those listening at home. The *Hayride* signed him up without hesitation.

In less than fifteen weeks, Elvis had recorded and released two singles, signed a contract with Sun Records, played two-dozen gigs, performed at the *Opry*, and signed up with the *Hayride*. His rate of ascent was unprecedented, but Sam knew they'd need all the help they could get to keep moving forward.

Scotty had been functioning as Elvis' manager since July, but Sam (much to Scotty's relief) offered Bob Neal an opportunity to get in on the act. Bob had a wide range of contacts in the business, and he agreed to set up several dates for the trio over the next few weeks. If it all worked out to everyone's satisfaction, maybe they'd look at a proper management deal running from the first day of the New Year. Elvis was happy with this proposal: Bob was an awfully nice guy, and Elvis loved his radio show. Indeed, when the two men were formally introduced, the deejay realised that this was the kid with sideburns who had often sat and watched his performances.

But the beautiful irony of Bob's appointment was not lost on those involved: he was employed by radio station WMPS, which had a very strict broadcast policy — and many of Bob's peers and superiors felt there was no place for the Presley boy's blues-inflected records on their station.

A Boy from Tupelo, Ernst Mikael Jørgensen
Last Train to Memphis: The Rise of Elvis Presley, Peter Guralnick
Sam Phillips: The Man Who Invented Rock 'n' Roll, Peter Guralnick

Radio WDVH

MONDAY 18TH OCTOBER 1954
KINCAID ROAD, GAINESVILLE, FLORIDA

TOBY DOWDY, Buster Vaughn and Tom Hanssen combined their cash and their surname initials and launched five thousand watts of daytime country music on radio station WDVH from Kincaid Road, Gainesville. Toby Dowdy, a local musician and entrepreneur, told the press they had invested $65,000 and expected the signal to broadcast to both Florida coasts. Dowdy, who also had a stake in WMBR-TV, declared the venture would be built on a foundation of music, news and sports.

Among the many new station deejays was Smilin' Jack Herring, a drummer who also led his own band, the Swingbillys, that featured Pee Wee Jenkins (saxophone), Bob Chisholm (guitar), and Tommy Durden (steel guitar). They played small clubs, dance halls and the occasional big show.

They had a good time; they played music; they made a living.

A phone call from New Orleans

WEDNESDAY 27TH OCTOBER 1954
CITY AUDITORIUM, NEW ORLEANS, LOUISIANA

THE TEN-DAY EDDY ARNOLD TOUR rolled out on 27th October with a forty-eight-hour visit to New Orleans. Oscar Davis had already been through the city a couple of days previously, acting as advance man for Jamboree Attractions which, under the direction of Tom Parker, still handled the Tennessee Plowboy's bookings. Oscar had visited local radio stations and smothered the town with advertising: there really was no finer promotions man working in hillbilly music.

Oscar moved on from venue to venue, and would soon be heading for Memphis to prepare for the Sunday gigs. Tom Diskin followed behind with the star, watching over the last minute details. Sometimes Oscar would double-back if he had time, to check with Tom Parker and report on any potential hitches. Parker himself would flit from place to place, overseeing the operation.

This was a tour which would present no problems as far as the Colonel could see. It would be business as usual. He'd been running Eddy Arnold tours for almost ten years and could do this in his sleep by now.

New Orleans had a large hillbilly audience, although it was primarily known, of course, for its R&B market. The number one local star was Fats Domino who, since the turn of the decade, had been producing a steady stream of excellent singles on the small Imperial label. His current hit, "Love Me"/"Don't You Hear Me Calling You" (Imperial X5313), had just been released, and music fans, black and white — Elvis included — couldn't help but warm to this talented artist.

During the two-day New Orleans stopover, the Colonel took time to ring *Billboard* and pass on some gossip: as from 1st January, he'd be managing Hank Snow and Hank Snow Enterprises — the umbrella organisation the Canadian used to cover all his business activities.

This wasn't deemed headline news, although it did top the gossip column of the C&W page. Hank was big. Parker was big. But if *Billboard* made a feature out of every new Hank Snow managerial appointment it would need to publish twice weekly.

Billboard, 6th November 1954

When Oscar met Elvis

FRIDAY 29TH OCTOBER 1954
RADIO WMPS, MEMPHIS, TENNESSEE

BUSINESS WAS THE ORDER OF THE DAY when Bob Neal welcomed Oscar Davis into the radio WMPS studio on the last Friday of October. The dapper promotions man had come to record local advertising spots for the Eddy Arnold tour, which also featured The Jordanaires and would hit Memphis on Sunday. Oscar had already received reports that the two nights in New Orleans had gone well, and tonight the star would play in Baton Rouge.

Oscar taped a couple of short but distinctive radio ads — "The Eddy Arnold Show is coming to Memphis: don't you dare miss it!" — and then sat down with Bob to shoot the breeze.

Oscar wanted to hear if Bob knew anything about a new kid everyone seemed to be raving about. Was his name Alvin? Or maybe it was Ellis? Bob chuckled and clarified the name of the young singer. He did know of him — indeed, he was even considering a management offer. Oscar indicated he'd really like to observe the boy in action, and Bob offered to drive him out to the Eagle's Nest club that night so he could see the singer for himself.

The club seated sixty patrons and was fast becoming one of Elvis' regular haunts. At 9:00 PM, Oscar, Bob and Bob's wife, Helen, found a table and waited for the main attraction. When he appeared they were not disappointed. There were cheers and occasional screams from the audience, as the boy worked himself into a sweaty frenzy on the stage, singing all of his records and a selection of other tunes.

"Amazing! Simply amazing. I've never seen anything like it," said Oscar as Bob brought Elvis to the table when the show was over. The promoter then produced a handful of tickets for the Sunday night Eddy Arnold show at the Ellis Auditorium, insisting they all come as his guests. Oscar would be in Nashville on Saturday to set up the next dates but he'd drive back to Memphis in time to meet them at the concert.

Elvis was ecstatic. Eddy Arnold was a big name but, far more importantly, The Jordanaires, one of his favourite gospel harmony groups, would be on the bill: they were the real stars as far as Elvis was concerned.

A Boy from Tupelo, Ernst Mikael Jørgensen
Last Train to Memphis: The Rise of Elvis Presley, Peter Guralnick

Mae Boren Axton: a friend in need

PERHAPS SATURDAY 30TH OCTOBER 1954
RYMAN AUDITORIUM, NASHVILLE, TENNESSEE

THE DEADLINE for Mae's first required payment for her father's care was imminent. She'd sort of fooled herself into thinking that now she was representing Hank Snow, the money would magically appear. But her pay cheque wouldn't arrive in time for the Monday cut off, and she was $1,000 short on the promised figure.

During the course of a telephone conversation with the Wilburns on the previous Wednesday from Nashville, she'd spilled the beans to the brothers about her lack of cash. Maybe they'd heard a rumour, or perhaps the pressure just proved too much and she'd blurted it out. Either way, they said they'd be in Nashville on Saturday for the *Opry* and they'd meet with her to sort it out.

Mae thanked them for their kindness, but she knew hillbilly performers just didn't have that kind of spare cash hanging around. She began to make tentative enquiries about taking a bank loan, while still trying to focus on her new full-time day job.

Saturday night backstage at the Ryman, sure enough, the Wilburns presented Mae with a brown paper bag containing exactly $1,000 in assorted bills and small change. They'd scraped together everything they owned, and missed their own mortgage payment to help Mae honour her obligation. She accepted the bag with tears streaming from her carefully mascaraed eyes.

Two weeks later, Mae's commission cheque cleared and she recompensed the brothers. But she knew her debt to them — and indeed her debt to Tom Parker — was much greater than a simple cash repayment.

Country Singers As I Know 'Em, Mae Boren Axton
Billboard, 23rd October 1954

Backstage at the Ellis

SUNDAY 31ST OCTOBER 1954
ELLIS AUDITORIUM, MEMPHIS, TENNESSEE

WHEN THE FIRST ACT ENDED, the cast mingled backstage, hoping to relax and cool down during the intermission. Hoyt Hawkins wondered if he might have time to grab a bite to eat and was about to consult his fellow Jordanaires when Oscar Davis appeared and took his arm and steered him towards an odd-looking boy with long sideburns wearing a white jacket and a pink shirt who almost seemed to be hyperventilating as the promoter introduced them.

"Hoyt, this is Elvis Presley, a singer from right here in Memphis and he's just starting out."

Hawkins extended his hand and Elvis grabbed it with both of his and started a long stuttering speech about how much he'd enjoyed the show and how he loved gospel music and for sure The Jordanaires were one of his favourite groups and he'd seen them a hundred times at the All-Night Singings and if he ever made a name for himself in this business he was going to ask Hoyt and the group to sing with him —

Hoyt interjected a "Thank you" in order to stop the never-ending sentence, and finally managed to prise his right hand free, calling over his buddies so they could share in the adulation. Eddy Arnold joined the conversation too, and Elvis was overjoyed to be in such exalted company.

Oscar eventually escorted the boy, who couldn't stop smiling, to the stage door and bid him good night. Elvis, Scotty and Bill had been discussing whether or not they should quit their day jobs and go after show business fame full time. After a night like tonight, Elvis resolved he would hand in his notice this very week and encourage the boys to do the same, which they duly did.

Oscar closed the door behind Elvis, and shrugged his shoulders. He'd been weighing up his loyalty to his employer against his loyalty to his own wallet and had finally made his reluctant decision: tomorrow, when they met up in Madison, he would tell Tom Parker about the remarkable new talent he'd discovered.

A Boy from Tupelo, Ernst Mikael Jørgensen
The Colonel: The Extraordinary Story of Colonel Tom Parker and Elvis Presley, Alanna Nash
Last Train to Memphis: The Rise of Elvis Presley, Peter Guralnick

The last messenger

MONDAY 1ST NOVEMBER 1954
GALLATIN ROAD, MADISON, TENNESSEE

THE SIXTH AND SEVENTH GIGS of Eddy Arnold's tour were scheduled for Nashville and, because Tom Parker lived nearby in Madison, his home became the base of operations for two days.

Oscar arrived at the house on Gallatin Road where Tom was lunching in the yard with a business acquaintance. He needed to tell Tom at once about this boy. It was just like when he'd first seen Hank Williams: Oscar knew he'd found a star.

The advance man tried to play it cool but he started rambling, and Parker picked random words out of the jumbled phrases — "Amazing act"; "Wild performance"; "Excited kids"; "Screaming girls"; "Elvis Presley" — until Oscar eventually ran out of breath and sat down as Tom Parker himself stood up. The Colonel then left the table without a word and was not seen again by Oscar, nor by his lunch companion, for the rest of the tour. Tom Parker disappeared. But Oscar had done his duty, and subsequently went down in history as the man who first told Tom Parker about Elvis Presley.

Of course, it should be pointed out that Oscar Davis was not the only man through the years who laid claim to this dubious honour: at least two or three other candidates have stepped forward. And one would assume that all but one of these men are lying. Presumably, the others are imposters who are seeking a claim to fame as they spin their tales. But to fall in with this idea is to miss the point entirely — and to underestimate Tom Parker.

All of these alleged messengers believe they are telling the truth because they did indeed all tell Tom Parker about this rousing young singer from Memphis. Which of them was the first is inconsequential. The point is that Parker had contacts all over the South who had instructions to keep him informed of any emerging talent, and they certainly did their master's bidding.

In fact, Oscar Davis was likely the last of them to give Parker the word, but when a man of that calibre splutters out stuttering praise — and one combines that praise with previous reports of interest — then it is time to take action.

So where did Tom go?

The Colonel: The Extraordinary Story of Colonel Tom Parker and Elvis Presley, Alanna Nash

Bobby Ross: Tom's boy, III

EARLY NOVEMBER 1954
TAMPA, FLORIDA

As she quickly packed her suitcase, Marie Parker mused again that her husband was the most considerate and romantic of men. She'd had nothing planned at all on this Monday — she was just washing the dishes after lunch — and then Tom strode into the kitchen (leaving his guests in the yard) and suggested they take a few days vacation.

He said they should visit Bobby down in Tampa to see how his new deejay job was working out. And she could also spend time spoiling their four year-old granddaughter, Sharon Marie, which was the best part of the deal.

Tom was keen to hit the road: if they left now, they'd arrive just after midnight. There was no rush to hurry back, said Tom. If it was okay with their hosts they could stay a few days, maybe even until the weekend.

The Rosses were, of course, delighted to see the Parkers, and greeted them with genuine Southern hospitality. Marie took Sharon to the park every day; they enjoyed big family meals together; Tom took some time to catch up with old Floridian friends; and each evening, after dinner, the ladies listened to the radio while Bobby and Tom sat out on the porch and talked a little shop.

Of course, no one really knows what they discussed out there. But there was a reason Tom Parker wanted to consult with his stepson — who was not only a deejay with his finger on the pulse, but also a former manager of a certain Canadian hillbilly singer.

I'd wager that Tom had two major topics of conversation: what do you know about this Elvis Presley kid, and just how gullible is Hank Snow?

Billboard, 13th November 1954

A busy Saturday

SATURDAY 6TH NOVEMBER 1954
VARIOUS POINTS SOUTH

AT THE MUNICIPAL AUDITORIUM, TAMPA, the Colonel and his good lady rounded off their short holiday by attending Bobby Ross' Saturday WFLA *Hoedown* show. Never one to let any situation go to waste, Tom rang *Billboard* to inform them of his visit, and the magazine mentioned this in the following week's gossip column, ensuring free publicity for the Colonel and Bobby.

In *Billboard* itself on that first Saturday in November, the two highlighted new C&W singles were Hank Snow's latest (both sides were Hill & Range tunes) and Elvis' second disk. Hank's record sold very heavily. Elvis' didn't.

Anyone following the progress of Sun Records at that time — and trust me, no one was — would have noted the catalogue number of Elvis' new record was Sun 210. This meant, in simple terms, Sam Phillips had done nothing but promote and record Elvis Presley since the release of Sun 209, Elvis' debut record, back in mid-July.

Also on that busy November Saturday, Elvis, Scotty and Bill — who were now full-time professional musicians — were making their first contracted regular performance on the *Louisiana Hayride* in Shreveport. Despite being lauded by the crowds, Elvis still suffered from crippling stage fright and had to have co-star Jim Reeves literally push him onstage when cued.

When the dust had settled from all this frenetic activity, Tom Parker sat at his desk in his garage-based office and ran through the plan once again in his head. The Presley boy clearly had potential, but if the Colonel was going to make a move for him then he would need money. Taking over and building up young stars did not come cheap. Parker, who was still leaking cash over Tommy Sands, knew this better than anyone.

As the clock neared midnight, he placed a pen and a sheet of paper very precisely on the desk, then positioned a chair for an anticipated visitor directly opposite his own. Tomorrow morning, he'd ring Hank Snow and invite him over to discuss a very important business proposition.

It was always a little worrying when Tom Parker smiled. But this night, as he retired, he was positively beaming.

A Boy from Tupelo, Ernst Mikael Jørgensen

A screenwriters' fantasia

NOVEMBER 1954
GALLATIN ROAD, MADISON, TENNESSEE

"HOW ABOUT A CIGAR, HANK?" said Parker as his client took a seat. Snow had rarely felt so overwhelmed with courtesy, especially during his brief dealings with the Colonel. As he leaned forward to accept Parker's lit match, the maestro began his pitch.

Tom spoke about a fantastic business opportunity for both of them, which was above and beyond the already-agreed management contract. He suggested they should also join forces in a talent and promotions company to be called "Hank Snow Enterprises-Jamboree Attractions" or, as it would be printed on the posters, "Hank Snow Attractions".

The idea in itself was sound and clever. Tom and Hank would sign up other performers and put shows out on the road. Potential entertainers (and indeed the public) would be drawn by the name of Hank Snow, and wherever the shows played they'd be billed as a Hank Snow production, whether he actually appeared or not. It would act as a guarantee of quality for the punters and would also offer extra publicity for the Canadian. The basic business plan would be for Snow to join the existing Jamboree set-up. It would make full use of Hank's fame and the Colonel's promotional talents.

"I want to make you a partner," enthused Parker.

"Why?" replied Snow.

"Well, why shouldn't you be a partner in a bookings agency? Look, I made a contract for us. We split everything right down the middle."

Snow picked up the paper and began to read aloud: "An agreement between the party of the first part and the party of the second part —"

"We hire a couple of other acts and we've got our own show. We play the circuit and we roll."

"I don't know anything about how to get any bookings."

"Let me worry about the business end. All you gotta do is sign this little piece of paper. And be sure to use your real name, Clarence."

It all sounded very straightforward and Hank could absolutely see the sense in what the Colonel was saying. He signed, resolving to have his lawyer look it over at some future date.

"I almost forgot: we need $1,775.00," Parker added, very matter-of-factly.
"$1,775.00 ?!"
"A cheque will do."
"Are you nuts? You had two and a half grand off me in September."
"I'll try to explain: Tom Diskin owns part of Jamboree and you'll need to pay off his share and then buy in to my share, too."
Snow looked him in the eye, and then pulled out his chequebook and completed the deal.
"I hope I'm not making a mistake," said the star.
"Now, now, partners shouldn't quarrel. You're making a smart move."
Snow stood and made ready to leave. Parker blew on the still-drying ink, saying he should think of it as if he'd just invested in something solid — like a new property.
"And this will take care of your share of the lease. See you later, partner."

The Hank Snow Story, Hank Snow with Jack Ownbey & Bob Burris

The Colonel's contract

A SHORT DIVERSION ON
THE NATURE OF CONTRACTS

STORIES WERE THE Colonel's stock in trade. Whenever he had an audience, he loved to drag out tales of his show business past. He adored talking about the scams and jokes he'd played. There was the story about painting sparrows yellow and selling them as canaries; there was also the one about twelve-inch hot dogs (regular hot dogs placed cleverly in one-foot rolls); or the time he put a hot plate under a cage of hens and charged to watch Tom Parker's Dancing Chickens.

People would chuckle, knowing they themselves were much too smart to be tricked into believing his anecdotes. But Parker was one step ahead, and he understood his stories would be viewed sceptically, adding to his air of mystery — the real gag was that the yarns were all true and he'd hoodwinked the listener yet again.

One of his favourite tales centred upon the nature of contracts, and he'd wheel it out anytime he was inviting someone to make a deal:

> *The first time I signed a contract, I went to collect my money. But the promoter turned me down and pointed to the section of the contract which stipulated why I wouldn't get paid. So I cut out that paragraph and stuck it on a separate piece of paper. The next time I got suckered in, I found the new paragraph that kept me apart from my money, and I cut and pasted that new section on the same sheet. And I kept on doing this until the page was full. And then I had my own contract for folks to sign. And that's the piece of paper you're holding now, son.*

And then Parker would laugh loudly. Maybe he was talking about his partnership contract with Hank Snow when he told this tale. Who knows? Parker never did clarify, not wishing to spoil a good story.

But, as Snow later discovered, Hank Snow Attractions was not incorporated as a company; there were no proper financial records, and no taxes were paid. It was a smooth machine that allowed Hank Snow to regularly deposit money for special events but not to withdraw any profits at all.

Ever.

The Hank Snow Story, Hank Snow with Jack Ownbey & Bob Burris

The first of the disciples

AUTUMN 1954
706 UNION AVENUE, MEMPHIS TENNESSEE

COUNTRY BOYS ALL OVER THE SOUTH were beginning to hear Elvis' records played on the radio and some began to wonder if maybe Mr Phillips could do for them what he'd done for Elvis.

A twenty-two year-old hopeful named Carl Perkins drove from Jackson to Memphis with his two bandmates in their 1941 Plymouth with the dream of securing an audition for Sun. When Carl approached Marion she gave him the official company line: We're just too busy promoting Elvis to consider working with anyone else. But, as luck would have it, Sam himself walked in the door and Carl more or less begged the producer for just a few minutes of his time. Sam didn't have the heart to refuse, so he listened to the trio and knew at once they had something special.

A short while later, Johnny Cash also turned up at 706 Union. Since his air force discharge and marriage, he'd tried his hand at door-to-door sales, but his lack of success and the clarion call of Elvis' music had convinced him to try his hand at being a professional singer instead.

The best story relating to his audition is probably apocryphal but it's too good not to repeat. Sam recognised that the deep-voiced Cash was a genuine talent but his repertoire leaned a little too heavily on hymns and religious songs. So he told him, "Son, I like what you're doing but I need something I can sell. Why don't you go out and sin a little and then come back and see me again."

Sam Phillips: The Man Who Invented Rock 'n' Roll, Peter Guralnick

Something old, something new

MONDAY 15TH NOVEMBER 1954
706 UNION AVENUE, MEMPHIS, TENNESSEE

ALTHOUGH ELVIS' SECOND SINGLE was bursting with quality and originality it was not selling well compared to "That's All Right"/ "Blue Moon of Kentucky". Indeed one of Sam's biggest problems was that the first single, although it never neared the charts, remained a steady seller by Sun's standards throughout the South, and customers were overlooking the new disk. Elvis needed to progress, he needed to break into new territories, and Sam needed to be one step ahead of the game.

So, in mid-November, the boys were called back to the studio to try and capture a third single to release by the end of the year. And this time Sam definitely *was* ahead of the game because he'd brought in an original song for Elvis — "You're a Heartbreaker", composed by a Tennessee theatre manager called Jack Sallee.

Sam had done some promotional recordings for Sallee and mentioned he was always looking for material for his new star. Jack went home, wrote the song (his first) and came back to 706 Union and gave it to Sam. What made it even more appealing was that Sam was able to put the song into Hi-Lo, his own publishing company.

Judging by Elvis' finished record, it all seems to have been captured effortlessly, which means it probably took several hours (days?) of hard work, trial, error and effort. Taped with slapback, it was a deceptively happy number (the singer is criticising his previous lover, comparing her disparagingly to his new girl), and Elvis sang it in a high register. Scotty's guitar rang tastefully true and clear, and Bill drove the mid-tempo song forward with his clickety-clack slap bass sound. It was a direct continuation of the poppy radio-friendly sound they'd established on "I Don't Care if the Sun Don't Shine", and Sam had high hopes for it, especially as he'd be receiving double money — records and publishing — on this one.

For the flip side, they transformed Kokomo Arnold's R&B "Milk Cow Blues", mixing it with Bob Wills' version, and borrowing heavily from brother Johnny Lee Wills' take, too. Kokomo's and Johnny's singles had been re-issued in the mid-1940s, and that's when Elvis first heard them.

But he drove the song to a much darker place than any of the previous versions. After a cleverly-faked intro, the number kicked-off ("Weeeellllll!") at a hectic pace, and Elvis rode it like he was breaking in a wild stallion. He went low, then hit falsetto notes, pushed himself to the limit at times, then dropped back a little, throwing in asides to the band — "Ah, let's milk it" — and finished with a beautiful drawn out lowing sound as the record faded, the first of his Sun singles so to do. Scotty's guitar work was striking throughout — as he truly uncovered his own style of playing — and Bill slapped as if pursued by the devil himself.

Whatever Bob and Johnny Lee Wills had attempted to do in terms of blending white and black music was taken to a whole new level by the artistry of this recording. It was every bit as uncompromising and uncommercial as its flip side was listenable and catchy.

Recognising that they had re-invented the song, Sam renamed it "Milkcow Blues Boogie" and pencilled in a release date of late December, hoping it would be the c&w chart-hitting breakthrough record they needed.

A Boy from Tupelo, Ernst Mikael Jørgensen

"I Got a Woman"

THURSDAY 18TH NOVEMBER 1954
ATLANTA, GEORGIA

SINCE LOSING HIS SIGHT at the age of seven, Ray Charles had been pushed lovingly and relentlessly by his mother, and instructed to embrace life without fear. She knew the world would have little sympathy for a blind black boy from Georgia growing up during the Depression, and so she encouraged his independence at all times. Her lessons were timely because by the age of fifteen, Ray was orphaned.

Having lost his sight and his parents and also a younger brother, Ray Charles was no stranger to tragedy, but he refused to buckle. He had been enrolled in the Florida School for the Deaf and Blind, discovering in himself a talent for music, and decided to try for a career as a singer and pianist in the post-war years, travelling throughout the Sunshine State.

In 1952, aged twenty-one, he signed an Atlantic Records recording contract with Ahmet Ertegun and new co-owner (and ex-*Billboard* reporter) Jerry Wexler. His early records for Atlantic were good, solid R&B numbers and sold respectably. But on 18th November 1954, in Atlanta, Ray taped a song called "I Got a Woman". The tune, format and style were taken lock-stock-and-barrel from the recent gospel record "It Must Be Jesus" by The Southern Tones, a black quartet, released as Duke 205 in the spring.

There was a loose but calculated drive to Ray's recording, subtly different to all that had gone before. It was a new sound which took black music to a new place, just as "That's All Right" had done with hillbilly.

The record was released in December (Atlantic 45-1050) and was an instant hit on the R&B chart. Elvis added it to his live act at once, replacing the fade-out ending with a glorious burlesque-type climax.

Ertegun and Wexler (who were both white) were pleased at the single's progress and looked forward to more Ray Charles hit records. And over at Hill & Range, the Aberbachs — part-owners of Atlantic's publishing company, Progressive — also raised a glass to its success. The song wasn't a pop hit (although Jo Stafford covered it as "I Got a Sweetie"), and it never broke out of the niche blues market, but it was a step closer to the genre-smashing crossover that the Austrians felt sure was just around the corner.

The c&w deejay convention, III

FRIDAY 19TH NOVEMBER 1954
NASHVILLE, TENNESSEE

OVER EIGHT HUNDRED DEEJAYS squeezed into the third annual convention during the WSM anniversary weekend. This was up from the five hundred and fifty who'd made the 1953 meeting such a success. Stars were in attendance to receive awards and press the flesh.

Singer Webb Pierce, who co-owned Cedarwood Publishing with Jim Denny, was very much the focal point of the weekend having been voted most played artist of the year, and Eddy Arnold was selected as the number one popular vocalist. Hank Snow scored well in all polls too, and flew in from touring Montreal to ensure he was present. After just four months in the business, Elvis Presley was voted eighth most promising c&w act, but did not make the convention.

Webb Pierce had yet more reason to celebrate when Cedarwood appeared in *Billboard*'s list of 1954's most notable c&w publishing houses, which delighted Jim Denny. Indeed, the *Opry* man insisted on flagrantly advertising his notorious company by sponsoring the opening Friday event of the convention weekend, a cocktail party from 4:00 until 6:00 PM.

Everyone who was anyone attended, and the drinks flowed freely, the guests commenting on Denny's largesse. And perhaps, sitting alone in the shadows, Jack Stapp raised a bitter glass of champagne to his *Opry* colleague and publishing opponent. Tree, of course, had not made the list of top publishers. Tree songs rarely troubled the charts, and were generally of low quality sung by second-rate acts.

Jack Stapp was a peaceful man with patience aplenty. But he was going to do everything in his power to ensure this time next year he wasn't sitting at a Cedarwood party drinking Jim Denny's fucking cocktails.

Billboard, 30th October, 20th November & 4th December 1954

Money for nothing

PERHAPS DECEMBER 1954
3339 DELLWOOD AVENUE, JACKSONVILLE, FLORIDA

At some point before Christmas 1954, an envelope landed on Mae Boren Axton's doormat, containing a cheque from Acuff-Rose Music Publishers. This was to cover her royalty payments on Dub Dickerson's "Count Me In", the song she'd written in no time at all back in the spring.

And although the figure was small, it triggered a thought in Mae's mind: songwriting came easily to her, and maybe she could keep on writing and pushing her songs to bring in a little more of the cash she so definitely needed. She'd already worked out that the process was much easier when working with other people — Minnie Pearl had more or less given her the title and Dub had supplied the tune — so she resolved to speak again to "the boy with a grin in his voice" to see what else they could cook up.

Thus began a most intensive period of creativity and composition for Mae Boren Axton.

The bigger knife

PERHAPS 1954
BUSY BEE LIQUOR STORE, 3728 ALAMEDA AVENUE, EL PASO, TEXAS

YOUNG FRANCES PINNEY was most certainly a daddy's girl. She loved her father, and would always find time to sit in the doorway between the store and the rear apartment, just so she could be near him. She was accustomed to hearing the odd altercation between her father and would-be robbers. Most were seen off the premises without bloodshed or violence. Sometimes, Pinney's steely gaze was enough to cool the intentions of the desperate young men.

On one occasion, a youth entered the shop and produced a knife. Pinney, sensing his heart wasn't in it, reached below the counter and produced a machete, saying: "Son, that is not a knife — but this is."

The terrified bandit took flight, and Pinney chased him to the end of the block. He shrugged his shoulders at the curious glances given him by his wife and daughter as he walked past them back into the store.

When Marty met Tom

TUESDAY 7TH DECEMBER 1954
CASTLE STUDIO, NASHVILLE, TENNESSEE

MARTY ROBBINS was discharged from the navy in 1947. During his wartime service he'd learned to play guitar, and then set himself the task of earning a living through picking, singing and songwriting. By the time he'd landed a contract with Columbia in 1952, he'd mastered his craft. His second single, the self-composed "I'll Go on Alone" (Columbia 21022), was a hillbilly chart-topper and, having then joined the *Opry*, his future seemed assured.

At some point during his early hungry years, however, he'd foolishly signed a bad contract, and it was bleeding him dry. On his travels, he met and struck up a conversation with Tom Parker and confessed his costly error. Parker asked a simple question: Did he want to get out of the contract?

Robbins obviously replied in the affirmative and, amazingly, by the next time they met up, Tom had done the deed. Robbins was jubilant, but when the Colonel then offered his services as a manager (in the pre-Hank Snow years), Robbins refused. He'd just escaped from one contract — and didn't want to be shackled to another. But he made a sincere and welcome promise to Tom Parker: Any time you need me, just call and I'll come running.

Marty's subsequent Columbia singles all sold well, but failed to trouble the upper reaches of the chart so, at his December 1954 session in Nashville, He decided to cover the popular regional hit, "That's All Right", and laid down a countrified version of Presley's Sun single. It was released just before the end of the month (Columbia 4-21351), and became Robbins' biggest hit in almost two years, dwarfing sales of the poorly distributed Presley disk.

Consequently, for most Southern listeners in 1955, "That's All Right" was a Marty Robbins record. What's that you say? Elvis? Elvis who?

The letter

MONDAY 13TH DECEMBER 1954
MEMPHIS, TENNESSEE

UNDERSTANDABLY, all of the attention was on Elvis — and Scotty and Bill were sometimes overlooked. The trio was never a straightforward three-piece band. It was always ELVIS, Scotty and Bill (as per the record label credit). Or ELVIS and The Blue Moon Boys. Or often, just ELVIS. But there's no doubt the guitarist and the bassman played a significant part in the singer's initial and continued success.

Amidst the chaos of life on the road, Scotty was the calm, quiet voice of reason. He was the serious one, the person responsible for getting the band from A to B on time and in one piece. He wasn't the oldest member of the band but he was most certainly the designated adult.

Bill was good humour personified — "He never met a stranger," said Scotty — and he kept the band loose on stage and off. But more importantly, on those occasions when Elvis' stage antics backfired and the crowd took against him, it was Bill who dragged out all the old bass player comedy routines so beloved of hillbilly audiences, and saved the show.

They were a good team. Oh, they fell out from time to time — you couldn't drive hundreds of miles each night between gigs and not come to blows every now and then. But they were a band of brothers and they bonded in a way that only musicians can, and they were often joined by Elvis' schoolmate, Bobby "Red" West, acting as roadie and the first of what would eventually become Elvis' small personal entourage.

Scotty, of course, was also still acting as Elvis' temporary manager until the end of the year, and on 13th December, determined to do his job properly right up until his final managerial day, he was still trying to arrange new gigs further afield: he posted a letter to a bookings agency in Chicago, hoping they might fix up the band with dates in that city.

A month later, Scotty received a polite stock reply on headed stationery saying that, unfortunately, there was no local demand for hillbilly groups. The letter was signed by a Mr Tom Diskin of Jamboree Attractions.

Scotty Moore had that letter framed and displayed on his wall until his dying day.

A Boy from Tupelo, Ernst Mikael Jørgensen
That's All Right, Elvis, Scotty Moore

When Tommy Sands met Elvis

SATURDAY 1ST JANUARY 1955
EAGLES' HALL, HOUSTON, TEXAS

TEXAS WAS FAST BECOMING a home from home for Elvis, Scotty and Bill. Their records were well received in that state, and the boys toured extensively, playing small clubs, schoolhouses and just about anywhere they could find a stage with a microphone and juice for an amplifier. They had a new single to promote — "Milkcow Blues Boogie"/ "You're a Heartbreaker" (Sun 215) — and on New Year's Day they were booked in at the Eagles' Hall club in Houston. Sharing the bill with Elvis was, of all people, Tommy Sands, the Colonel's young protégé.

Parker had not signed an exclusivity pact with Hank Snow, so he was at liberty to watch over his other professional concerns, and he retained a great fondness for Sands. The feeling was entirely mutual: Tommy always spoke well of the Colonel. But with RCA about to release what would turn out to be his seventh and final flop single, manager and client both knew their time together was coming to an end.

It just hadn't worked out, even though Tommy had given his all as a performer and no one could accuse the Colonel of having scrimped a penny in his attempts to push the boy forward. Tommy was doing more deejay work these days anyway, and was still very keen to break into acting, but he was always happy to turn up for small gigs such as this one at Eagles' Hall.

So on this day of days — the beginning of Tom Parker's contract with Hank Snow, and Bob Neal's with Elvis — the question was begging: Who booked Tommy Sands on the same bill as Elvis Presley? Was it just a coincidence, or was someone looking for an inside report on a potential new client?

A Boy from Tupelo, Ernst Mikael Jørgensen

Helen Hall answers back

MONDAY 3RD JANUARY 1955
JIM BECK'S STUDIO, DALLAS, TEXAS

A WIFE AND MOTHER IN HER LATE TWENTIES, Helen Hall was not obvious star material. But, boy, could she write and sing. She'd signed to the *Big D Jamboree* in October 1954, and a few months later, found herself standing in Jim Beck's studio ready to make her first recordings for the small Coral label.

The microphone was lowered to match her diminutive frame — she stood just under five feet — but the talent that poured forth was substantial. One quick listen would tell you that this was an artist to be reckoned with. She recorded a quartet of her own compositions, all of which reinforced the novel idea that men were not always the innocent parties in relationship breakdowns.

The first two tracks chosen for single release (Coral 9-61359) were catchy and relentless in this approach. "Wasted Life" pulled no punches whatsoever, and "Honky Tonk Husband" was a scathing response to Hank Thompson's "Honky Tonk Girl". Hall had noticed — how could she not? — that Kitty Wells' answer record had put her on the map, and Helen hoped her own song would do likewise.

She knew her disk would need lots of promotion, which meant radio shows and concerts. Show business friend, Charline Arthur, and fan club president, Mrs Martha McCullars, offered their unconditional support. This was Helen's moment: she had the determination, and she had the songs.

Nothing was going to stop her: it was now or never.

Helen Hall: A Big D Jamboree's 5 Feet Gal, Dominique "Imperial" Anglares
Billboard, 12th March 1955

Jean and Tom: the agenda

TUESDAY 4TH JANUARY 1955
PERHAPS NASHVILLE, TENNESSEE

NOW THAT THE COLONEL was officially managing Hank Snow it was not surprising that he should meet up with his publisher, Hill & Range, just four days into the new arrangement. During their lunchtime meeting they discussed Snow's career, his music, and his publishing concerns. Tom Parker and Jean Aberbach had collaborated for almost ten years and had learned — and earned — much from one another.

But the get-together extended far beyond lunch and possibly as far as dinner, for it seemed Tom and Jean had much to talk about. And without question, they spent a good portion of that Tuesday discussing the upstart singer from Memphis.

Any doubts about this should be allayed by the knowledge that, within two weeks, Parker had engineered a meeting with the Presley camp; while on 25th January, Hill & Range opened negotiations with Wabash Music, a small blues-based company — which happened to own the rights to the compositions of one Arthur Crudup.

Restless Giant: The Life and Times of Jean Aberbach & Hill and Range Songs, Bar Biszick-Lockwood

When Mae met Blanche

PERHAPS JANUARY 1955
FLORIDA

A FLORIDA HOUSEWIFE who wrote songs in her spare time, Blanche Carter, had been mailing manuscripts to New York record companies for years, but they were always rejected and returned. At the beginning of 1955 she met up with Mae Boren Axton by chance, and Mae, who was still waiting for that call from Dub Dickerson, was interested to hear of Blanche's hobby and suggested they sit down and compose something together.

The song they wrote was called "Only a Fool (Would Believe)". Blanche slipped the finished sheet music into an envelope and posted it to New York, as she'd done a dozen times before. It was picked up by Progressive Music (owned by Atlantic Records) and copyrighted on 24th January. They had no particular artist in mind for the composition so they put it on file in case it might prove useful in the future.*

This was disappointing, but Blanche remained undeterred. And while Mae moved on, Blanche picked up her pen and started again on yet another new song. Maybe this one would be the big one.

Billboard, 2nd February 1957

---

*Atlantic recording star Lavern Baker taped the song on 14th June 1956 in New York City, but to this day it remains unheard and unissued.

Murray Nash Associates

JANUARY 1955
NASHVILLE, TENNESSEE

As far as Murray Nash was concerned, the dawn of 1955 marked a new beginning in his life. He'd parted company with Acuff-Rose the previous summer and, although the separation wasn't entirely amicable, he bore no ill will. Sadly, Fred Rose had unexpectedly passed away on 1st December. Nash had served as a pallbearer, and this added to the sense of his own previous life being laid to rest.

As the New Year opened, Murray took up three initiatives. Firstly, he signed on as editor of *Country & Western Jamboree*, a new magazine which greatly appealed to him. He sought talented writers to give his publication the best possible start, and this brought him into contact with Mae Boren Axton, and the two hit it off splendidly.

Secondly, with acquaintances Ray Scrivener and Charles Bingham, he bought out the small independent Republic Records label. The company had been in existence since 1952 and was notable for its lack of success (Buddy Killen's solo single from 1954 was one of its many flops). Murray inherited a struggling stable of talent, including a young fellow named Pat Boone — Red Foley's son-in-law — who seemed intent on being the new Frank Sinatra.

Murray's third venture was the founding of a new publishing company, again with Scrivener and Bingham. Murray Nash Associates opened in January and was located in the building next door to WSM, and had the declared intention of accepting only straight C&W material. Murray was intrigued to hear that Mae Boren Axton not only offered journalistic services, but also dabbled in songwriting, and he encouraged her to bring any and all compositions to him.

Ray Scrivener wasn't too keen on this idea. Maybe he didn't like the thought of female songwriters, or perhaps he didn't care for the way Murray announced his conviction that Mae was a real talent who should be nurtured. Either way, Scrivener kept his thoughts to himself but one day, perhaps when Murray wasn't around, he'd tell Mae a few home truths.

Murray Nash: Rock 'n' Roll Pioneer, an essay by Bo Berglind

Rendezvous in Shreveport

SATURDAY 15TH JANUARY 1955
MUNICIPAL AUDITORIUM, SHREVEPORT, LOUISIANA

STALKING WOULD HAVE BEEN too strong a word for it, but both Toms — Diskin and Parker — were certainly on Elvis' trail, figuratively and sometimes literally. And now that Bob Neal had taken over as manager, Elvis' status had upgraded from busy to hectic, playing at least one show almost every day, making him a difficult man to keep up with.

Frustratingly, the venues were often hundreds of miles apart because Neal was simply booking whatever he was offered in an effort to push Elvis' name forward. Elvis, Scotty and Bill would play a gig, drive for several hours (grabbing sleep en route), play another gig, drive for several more hours, and so on, for weeks at a time.

The Jamboree men just missed seeing the trio in New Boston, but spent some time talking to deejay Ernest "Uncle Dudley" Hackworth after the show, and he sang the group's praises, reinforcing the Colonel's interest.

Scotty was also convinced he'd seen Parker lurking in the back of the auditorium as early as November 1954, when they played Texarkana, but it wasn't until Saturday 15th January that Parker and Diskin officially made their presence known, having watched Elvis at the *Hayride* that night.

They spoke to Bob Neal, expressing their admiration for the boy's stagecraft. Maybe, Parker suggested, they could put the trio on a Jamboree package next month, perhaps trying to break him in new territories? By the close of the conversation, Parker had secured permission to start promoting Elvis as a guest artist on Jamboree tours.

Meeting over and mission accomplished, Parker and Diskin moved straight on to Hollywood, then to San Francisco, Portland and Houston. What business they had there was anyone's guess, but they spent all of their travelling time plotting the next moves for Presley.

Hank Snow, meanwhile, began a four-day stint in Florida on Tuesday without the presence of either of the Toms — but as Hank was playing the Sunshine State it's likely he was ably attended to by the very capable and very grateful Mrs Boren Axton.

A Boy from Tupelo, Ernst Mikael Jørgensen
Last Train to Memphis: The Rise of Elvis Presley, Peter Guralnick
Billboard, 15th & 22nd January 1955

Mae Boren Axton: let me try again

THURSDAY 27TH JANUARY 1955
CASTLE STUDIO, NASHVILLE, TENNESSEE

FRESH FROM HER MINI-TOUR with Hank Snow, Mae Boren Axton had persuaded Dub Dickerson to work with her on two more songs for his next session on 27th January 1955. The first number, "I Must've Drove My Mules Too Hard" was a none-too-subtle double-entendre hillbilly track, co-written with Dub and a fellow named Larry Stevens — which, in all likelihood, was a pseudonym for Murray Nash, who also took the publishing. It was, in fact, the first song ever to be registered to Murray Nash Associates, which gives an indication of how highly Mae was rated by Nash, if not necessarily by Ray Scrivener.

An Axton-Dickerson track was also recorded that day entitled "That's Not All", a simple song with an awkward metre that was rightly left on the shelf, something that wouldn't have pleased Cedarwood who had secured copyright.

A third song was taped, "Under the Heading of My Business" — a solo Dickerson composition — and this was chosen as the A-side single with "Mules" as the flip. Dub passed the publishing rights onto that nice Buddy Killen fellow from Tree who kept hanging around and asking for songs.

Dub managed to insert a giggle into every track — even if he wasn't laughing all the way to the bank. The single was released as Capitol F3099 in the spring but nothing came of it.

Dub Dickerson: *Boppin' in the Dark* CD Sleeve Notes, Kevin Coffey, et al
Billboard, 23rd April 1955

Making plans

LATE JANUARY 1955
MADISON, TENNESSEE

After a week of travelling, Parker and Diskin arrived back in Madison: they had made plans on their whistle-stop tour, and now began working in earnest. Tom Diskin, seated at the office typewriter, started corresponding to inform all interested parties that they had a new boy on the books who was "absolutely going to be one of the biggest things in the business in a very short time."

Parker, meanwhile, turned his attention to finalising Hank Snow's forthcoming mid-February tour of the South. He'd already made the decision to add Presley's name to the bill. It would be a short and simple test of the boy's potential: five shows over five days. If things went well, then they could look at more ambitious proposals.

What Hank thought about this isn't known, but Bob Neal was elated to hear his artist would be sharing the stage with Snow, and also with Charline Arthur, and popular *Opry* comedian Whitey "The Duke of Paducah" Ford, an old friend of Parker's.

Parker then wrote to Harry Kalcheim of William Morris, enclosing a couple of Elvis' Sun singles and a recently-taken publicity photograph. He indicated that he thought the boy showed promise, and invited the agency to offer thoughts on how to build up his profile.

The Colonel called Steve Sholes to talk about their now mutual interest in Hank Snow. Sholes knew about Parker's management takeover of the Canadian and wasn't thrilled about the news. Tom noted that Hank's RCA contract would soon be up for re-negotiation and the two men booked a date to meet. Sholes groaned inwardly, feeling sure Parker would petition a king's ransom for his client's future services.

Parker then turned the conversation to Elvis Presley ("I'm sure you've heard about him, Steve" — he had, via Crumpacker and McCuen), and suggested the young man might really be going places. He then further suggested he now had an inside line on this new act and he might sound out the possibility of bringing him over to RCA Victor.

The RCA man had little interest in this new artist, especially as he was being recommended by Tom Parker. Steve hadn't forgotten the bum steers about Slim Whitman, Charline Arthur and Tommy Sands. Nevertheless, ever the diplomat, Steve politely thanked Parker for the information and requested he be kept up-to-date on developments.

Parker replaced the telephone receiver and lit a new cigar. His intentions were simple. He wanted to manage Elvis Presley just like he'd handled Eddy. This meant involving Hill & Range, RCA Victor and William Morris, hence his communications with all three parties. It also meant taking Sam Phillips, Sun Records, and eventually Bob Neal, out of the picture.

And where did Hank Snow fit into these plans? Hank Snow was a means to an end.

A Boy from Tupelo, Ernst Mikael Jørgensen
Last Train to Memphis: The Rise of Elvis Presley, Peter Guralnick

The pink Cadillac

EARLY FEBRUARY 1955
706 UNION AVENUE, MEMPHIS TENNESSEE

THE SIMPLE TRUTH WAS that Elvis' third single — "Milkcow Blues Boogie"/"You're a Heartbreaker" — was not selling well, certainly when compared to his first. Yes, it was musically compelling — but it was not shifting units, and Sam was disappointed. He was disappointed for two reasons: firstly, deep in his soul he wanted people to hear this music and for it to change their attitude to life; secondly, he desperately needed the money.

He kept his financial concerns to himself, but the professional relationships with his brother Jud and with Bulleit had fallen through and both were demanding severance pay amounting to several hundred dollars. Added to which, Sun Records owed $8,000 in back taxes, and the cashflow situation between pressing plant and retailers was proving almost terminal.

Sam felt very strongly that Sun must not, and would not, become a one-artist company but Elvis definitely represented his best bet for making a breakthrough — artistically, racially and financially — so he kept squeezing in sessions between the seemingly endless run of small gigs and radio shows.

In early February, they worked long and late hours to get something on tape for the fourth single. The boys laid down their own version of "I Got a Woman", exactly as they'd been doing it on the road, where it was proving a showstopper. Then they tried a lovely mid-tempo song, "Tryin' to Get To You", which had been recently released by a black combo named The Eagles. They probably tried many other numbers too, but Sam was like a man possessed. Whatever it was he was looking for (a commercially-successful, radio-friendly, crowd-pleasing, culturally-satisfying piece of genius) was slow in coming, and he rejected them all.

Eventually, Elvis hit upon a self-composed R&B release from Arthur Gunter, titled, "Baby, Let's Play House" (Excello 2047). Issued in November 1954, the song had been well received but didn't trouble the chart at all, and Excello were already preparing Gunter's next single for early March.

Lyrically, the song was a daring choice. Apart from the blunt insinuation of the title itself, it also featured one of the hardest-hitting lines in blues history: "I'd rather see you dead, little girl, than to be with another man." Just as he'd done with one side of his first record, Elvis took a laid back original and transformed it into a barnstormer. He wrote a new opening, repeating the word "baby" in a bubbling, suggestive tone — also thinking of Arthur Crudup's similar song "Come Back Baby" — and drove the band forward relentlessly.

The church-going boy wittily amended a lyric from the staid "You may get religion" to the uber-cool "You may have a pink Cadillac", and one can almost hear his grin on the finished take. It was tough, macho, sexy and catchy. It was every bit as uncompromising as "Milkcow Blues Boogie", but with the added bonus of being commercial.

Best of all, as the song ran towards its end, Elvis — who was clearly pleased with his own performance — threw in a Dub-like chuckle, thus puncturing the over-the-top butch effect, and letting the listeners in on the joke. A lesser producer would have winced and demanded a re-take.

Sam Phillips stopped the session right there, knowing he'd found imperfect perfection.

Sam Phillips: The Man Who Invented Rock 'n' Roll, Peter Guralnick

Sowing seeds, I

SUNDAY 6TH FEBRUARY 1955
ELLIS AUDITORIUM, MEMPHIS, TENNESSEE

THE ELLIS AUDITORIUM, one of the most prestigious concert halls in Memphis, seated twelve thousand paying customers, and the joint was buzzing on the first Sunday in February 1955. There were two hillbilly shows lined up that day, both featuring the same impressive cast list, including Martha Carson and also The Wilburn Brothers. Somewhere near the bottom of the bill was Memphis' own Elvis Presley.

Just seven months into his professional career, Elvis remained endearingly starstruck in the presence of his musical heroes, and gushed to Carson about how much he loved her song, "Satisfied", and then listed all of her other records, many of which he seemed to know by heart.

The matinee performance went well, and between shows, in anticipation of the imminent tour with Hank Snow, Bob Neal had arranged a summit meeting with all interested parties to iron out any last minute details, and also to pool thoughts about future plans. The gathering took place in Palumbo's restaurant, and when Elvis and Scotty rushed over from the nearby auditorium they were greeted by Bob Neal, Sam Phillips, Tom Diskin, Oscar Davis and, chomping on a cigar, Colonel Tom Parker.

Bob called the meeting to order and thanked everyone for taking the time to attend. Firstly, he wondered, did anyone have any concerns about how things currently stood?

"Well," said Parker abruptly, "the boy will get nowhere on a label like Sun Records."

The table fell silent. Parker had certainly captured everyone's attention with the most aggressive opening line imaginable. However, no matter how crude he may have been, there was an element of truth in what he'd said, and the financially-pressed Sam Phillips knew it.

Nonetheless, the meeting suddenly exploded into a loud argument, with Sam almost having to be physically restrained, while Diskin tried to clarify what Parker had meant to say, and Bob desperately attempted to calm the waters. Oscar Davis was shocked by Parker's obnoxious tactics and just glared at his employer who simply sat and observed the chaos he'd created. Elvis and Scotty glanced at each other wondering what the hell was going on.

When peace was finally restored, Bob suggested they confine their conversation to plans about the tour itself. A little while later, the two musicians took their leave to prepare for the second show, while the businessmen remained and discussed the possibility of further tours together. Eventually, when the coffee pot was empty and all was settled, they uneasily shook hands and returned from whence they'd come.

Parker's plan had gone almost exactly as scheduled. He'd carelessly reckoned without Sam Phillips — who was a much tougher character than anyone he'd ever met before — but the most important point was that Elvis had heard what he'd said about getting nowhere on Sun Records, and, despite the angry reactions, no one at the table had disputed this prediction.

The first seeds of dissent had been sown.

Last Train to Memphis: The Rise of Elvis Presley, Peter Guralnick

Glenn Reeves makes a record

PERHAPS FEBRUARY 1955
PERHAPS JACKSONVILLE, FLORIDA

ALTHOUGH LIFE FOR Glenn Reeves was better in Florida than it had been in Texas, the job of a local radio deejay was still relatively low paid. Outside of his contracted hours, therefore, Glenn took on extra work as a singer and guitarist. Mae Boren Axton had assembled a small multi-purpose band that she booked whenever she had an opening or if a touring artist needed a pick-up group, and Glenn acted as leader and musical director.

During a casual conversation between Mae and Glenn, it was suggested that the deejay should try his hand at recording a single. Mae knew of a fellow in Texas named Bob Tanner who was looking for new product for his TNT (Texas 'n' Tanner) label. Glenn was excited by the idea, even more so when Mae suggested they write the two required sides together. Bob Tanner would receive the publishing rights, so he was satisfied with the deal.

For the first song, a slow hillbilly weeper called "The Blues are out Tonight", they called in Dub Dickerson to help, and borrowed heavily from Hank Williams' "I'm So Lonesome I Could Cry".

The second track was an uptempo, fiddle-led number, "I'm Johnny on the Spot", and Mae invited friend Ted Carpenter to assist with the tune. When the song was copyrighted, therefore, the credits read "Axton-Carpenter-Reeves", but what few realised (other than Bill Tanner and a BMI administrator) was that the Axton in question was Mae's husband, John, who was listed with BMI as the official composer. Why did Mae give the composition credit to John? Tax reasons perhaps? Or was he the "Johnny" in the song title? Who knows?

It mattered little ultimately, because neither song scored any airtime or chart action when released as TNT 120 in March 1955.

Country Singers As I Know 'Em, Mae Boren Axton
Glenn Reeves / *Johnny on the Spot* CD Sleeve Notes, Martin Hawkins & Richard Weize

"How Do You Think I Feel?"

SUNDAY 13TH FEBRUARY 1955
LUBBOCK, TEXAS

Having been raised as an obedient clone of his own father and his father's musical hero, nineteen year-old Jimmie Snow was blown away when he shook hands with Elvis Presley, a six-feet tall vision of rebellion and freedom.

Elvis, Scotty and Bill were due to join the Hank Snow package on Monday 14th, but a warm up gig (without Hank but with Jimmie) had been arranged in Lubbock on the Sunday, and it was here that the two young men first met, appearing on the same bill.

Jimmie was now recording for RCA (naturally). His previous single — "How Do You Think I Feel?" — had made little impact, nor had his new release, "Love Me" (a Leiber and Stoller c&w song). The resentment Jimmie felt towards his father intensified when he met Elvis, who seemed to be living life on his own terms, and Jimmie idolised him from the start.

But young Snow was just one of many who changed direction when they encountered Presley. At the bottom of the bill in Lubbock that day, for example, was an eighteen year-old local called Buddy Holly, who watched Elvis and instantly understood where popular music was going to go. A teen named Roy Orbison attended a Presley show and was so profoundly affected he struggled to comprehend what he'd seen.

Unlike Buddy and Roy, Jimmie was, of course, forbidden to change his own personal style of dress or music, but he was sure to hang out with his new best pal whenever possible — because the Colonel had already insisted on him doing so, reporting back regularly on everything Elvis Presley was thinking, doing and saying.

Jimmie genuinely liked Elvis, which added to his growing sense of discomfort. It was bad enough to spy on a colleague. But spying on a friend was tantamount to betrayal. In private, Jimmie opened another bottle of liquor and popped a few more pills to deaden the pain.

Hank Snow felt sure he was raising his son to follow in the footsteps of the giants of country music, and indeed he was. But it wasn't Jimmie Rodgers the boy was emulating. It was Hank Williams.

Last Train to Memphis: The Rise of Elvis Presley, Peter Guralnick

A promising start

MONDAY 14TH FEBRUARY 1955
ROSWELL, NEW MEXICO

VALENTINE'S DAY marked the official beginning of Elvis' contract with Hank Snow Attractions, and they started the five-day tour in New Mexico. Snow headlined, and also on the bill were Charline Arthur, the Duke of Paducah and Jimmie Snow.

The tour was well received and profitable. Hank was the star, of course, but he observed that the boy seemed to grow in confidence and popularity with every show. Elvis occasionally added a Snow tune to his repertoire in tribute to the Canadian, and Hank noted it was always some obscure B-side that he chose, demonstrating his considerable knowledge of hillbilly music.

Elvis' performances were wild — he delivered every song as if his life depended on it — and Hank wasn't entirely sure if this fitted comfortably into his own family-friendly image. He and the Colonel had spoken about this, but Tom had convinced Hank that the boy was going to be a big star, and they should encourage Elvis to attach himself to their new company on a permanent basis as soon as possible. Thus, regardless of his personal distaste for Elvis' music, Hank continued to build him up backstage, and Tom sometimes dropped a bonus payment in Elvis' pocket whenever he played a Hank Snow Attractions gig.

It had been a promising start, and a second tour was scheduled for the following week, this time without Hank, but with Mother Maybelle and The Carter Sisters. In fact, the only fly currently in Parker's ointment was Sam Phillips. Tom had not allowed for the producer's steely nature, and now understood that separating Elvis from Sun would be difficult.

So, Parker wrote to Steve Sholes and temporarily downplayed the possibility of bringing Presley to RCA. Perhaps, he wrote, Steve might like to hear some new demo tapes Tommy Sands had recently recorded instead? Sholes replied negatively but politely. It was in his best interests to keep Parker sweet: Hank Snow's contract renewal negotiations were fast approaching and it was for sure that Parker would be demanding the earth.

Last Train to Memphis: The Rise of Elvis Presley, Peter Guralnick

The power of the deejay

SATURDAY 19TH FEBRUARY 1955
NEW YORK CITY, NEW YORK

Deejays were exerting more and more influence over the listening and buying habits of teenagers. Alan Freed in New York, for example, was playing a selection of great R&B disks on radio WINS, and his expanding audience was becoming hip to the vast range of glorious music that was racially off limits.

Similarly, in Cleveland, Bill Randle — who, like Freed, looked more like a college professor than a deejay — had developed a reputation on station WERE as a man who could spot a potential hit record, and his listeners tuned in avidly.

Therefore, it was understandable that Jean Aberbach, just three days before securing the Wabash catalogue and a set of Arthur Crudup songs, should meet with the Cleveland deejay. Elvis needed support in the North and Aberbach was keen to get Randle onside regarding Presley's first Sun record. Perhaps Bill would consider playing "That's All Right", or indeed several of the other wonderful tunes that Jean had at his disposal.

Randle was a clever man, and was already very familiar with Presley's music, but Jean Aberbach was a smooth and persuasive talker. Both men knew Elvis was booked to appear in Cleveland the following Saturday, for his first gig outside the South. And a little push from Bill Randle could go a long way.

Quite what Bill Randle hoped to gain out of this remains a mystery; unless that is Aberbach (or indeed Tom Parker) had suggested he would have a greater involvement somewhere down the line. If this was indeed the situation then it was a classic Parker tactic and one that paid dividends for the Colonel time and again.

Restless Giant: The Life and Times of Jean Aberbach & Hill and Range Songs, Bar Biszick-Lockwood

The royal family

SUNDAY 20TH FEBRUARY 1955
LITTLE ROCK, ARKANSAS

IT SEEMED THAT EVERY TIME Elvis turned around he was faced with yet another of his musical idols. But to be introduced to Maybelle Carter in Little Rock, as he started his second Tom Parker-organised tour, was like meeting royalty.

Mama Maybelle took to the boy at once — perhaps she was reminded of that other smooth-talking hillbilly cat, Jimmie Rodgers — but she was perceptive enough to realise her daughters would also be drawn to this polite, handsome-as-heck youngster, and she drew a very careful line in the sand regarding fraternisation backstage. But the charms of Anita Carter were irresistible and Elvis used every trick in his rapidly-expanding book to attract her attention.

The short tour with the Carters was not profitable and Parker took a small financial hit, but was convinced of the boy's long term potential. When the run ended on Thursday 24th February, Elvis, Scotty, Bill and Bob spent the next day driving to Cleveland for their first Northern gigs. Elvis was not known in Ohio, but his two performances at the Circle Theatre went down well.

Bill Randle was present at the concerts on Saturday 26th February and invited Elvis back to his radio studio for a broadcast interview, during which he played all three Sun singles. Randle, like Maybelle and so many others, was struck by the boy's charisma, and felt he could indeed be going places. The deejay was also impressed by Bob Neal's talents and agreed they could work together in the future to their mutual benefit. As a parting gift and a show of good faith, Randle gave Neal a contact telephone number for the prestigious *Arthur Godfrey Talent Show* in New York.

The boys piled into their exhausted automobile and began the long trek back to Memphis. It had been almost three weeks since they'd left home. Elvis looked forward to sleeping in his own bed and then seeing Dixie: they'd have a lot to talk about.

Last Train to Memphis: The Rise of Elvis Presley, Peter Guralnick
Restless Giant: The Life and Times of Jean Aberbach & Hill and Range Songs, Bar Biszick-Lockwood

"Blues Stay Away From Me", III

SUNDAY 6TH MARCH 1955
706 UNION AVENUE, MEMPHIS TENNESSEE

ACTUALLY, WHEN ELVIS MET UP AGAIN with Dixie it seemed they didn't really have that much to talk about at all. They were living in different worlds, and Elvis was not willing to share what was happening to him out on the road.

He found himself without a confidant, sometimes being unable to express himself honestly even to his mother. He was always surrounded by people, but there was a growing sense of loneliness: no one understood the excitement, the pressure, the exhaustion, or his desperation to succeed. And taking a day or two off just increased his feelings of isolation.

It was quite a relief then, when Sam invited the musicians back into the studio on the Sunday to search for a flip side to "Baby, Let's Play House" so they could issue a much-needed new single as soon as possible. And once again, Sam was ahead of the game. He'd picked up "I'm Left, You're Right, She's Gone", a solid, mid-tempo catchy country number by Stan Kesler and Bill Murray, two hillbilly songwriters. They'd based the tune on an advertising jingle for Campbell's soup and, sensing that something special was happening at 706 Union Avenue, agreed that Sam could have the publishing rights for Hi-Lo.

There was just one problem: Elvis didn't like the song.

Won over by Sam's enthusiasm, Elvis decided to try it in a variety of styles, almost ignoring the writers' demo completely. Finally, he found an approach that worked for him, changing it from a C&W ditty into a slow, grinding blues. Scotty hit a striking opening phrase before slipping into the Delmores' hypnotic riff from "Blues Stay Away From Me", and Elvis turned in his most blatant and outrageous performance to date. And then they packed up and called it a day.

Sam, who was always open to new ideas, liked the slower take but had lingering doubts about its commercial viability. He cut a couple of acetates intending to play them for trusted acquaintances to test the water.

Everything was riding on this next single and he could afford to take no chances.

Last Train to Memphis: The Rise of Elvis Presley, Peter Guralnick
Restless Giant: The Life and Times of Jean Aberbach & Hill and Range Songs, Bar Biszick-Lockwood

East of Eden

WEDNESDAY 9TH MARCH 1955
NEW YORK CITY, NEW YORK

JOHN STEINBECK had been unusually lucky in the way in which his best work was successfully transferred to the screen. The adaptations of *The Grapes of Wrath* and *Of Mice and Men* were both superlatively realised as films, and Elia Kazan's interpretation of his epic novel *East of Eden* now added to that list.

Upon its release in March 1955, what surprised everyone, however, was not the quality of the script or the excellence of the direction, but the riveting performance of newcomer James Dean, as the disaffected son. Dean, twenty-four years-old, had appeared in numerous TV dramas, including the popular Kraft Televison Theatre, but this was his debut starring cinematic role. With swept-back hair and chiselled good looks, he was charismatic on screen, and young viewers instantly related to him — Elvis Presley being one such typical audience member.

He was transfixed, recognising himself within the actor, physically and emotionally. He loved the sensitivity, the frustration, and the need for acceptance that Dean expressed within his portrayal. For the first time, Elvis Presley — and millions more across America — had a hero and idol from his own generation.

And there was a line of dialogue from early in the movie that must have resonated so strongly with the young singer ... "Why is he so alone all the time ... nobody wants to be alone all the time."

John Steinbeck: A Biography, Jay Parini

Renegotiated contracts

TUESDAY 15TH MARCH 1955
MEMPHIS, TENNESSEE

HAVING SEARCHED THROUGH the paperwork looking for the catch for some considerable time, Steve Sholes finally looked up at Tom Parker and agreed to all of his demands for Hank Snow's new RCA contract. But Steve just couldn't work out what Parker was up to. All of the Colonel's requests were reasonable.

In later years, Hank would bemoan Parker's bargaining skills, declaring he'd have done better himself. The truth was that Tom Parker had no intention of upsetting Steve Sholes, a man who might prove very useful over the coming months. And Steve was probably going through the contract in his head for days afterwards, trying to work out how he'd been shafted.

But not all was going according to plan for the Colonel. Word had reached him about Bob Neal's interest in the *Arthur Godfrey Talent Show*, and once again he was obliged to take a gamble. Through his contacts in the William Morris Agency — who seemed to be dragging their heels somewhat — Parker set up an audition for that very TV show on 23rd March in an attempt to steal the initiative from Neal. The only problem was ... what if Elvis' audition was successful? Parker would be left for dust.

To get around this, the Colonel generously offered to finance the entire trip on the understanding that he would take a share in any business that subsequently arose from the audition. This was yet another expense incurred in his pursuit of Presley, and he issued explicit instructions to Tom Diskin that they needed to keep a careful eye on the budget from now on. Parker had no intention of paying out only to find that others were reaping the benefit. If only Bob Neal would stop interfering. There was no doubt in Parker's mind that Bob would have to go, and the sooner the better.

Sadly for the Colonel, an updated contract between Elvis and Bob Neal was drawn up on Tuesday 15th March and, when Elvis eventually signed it, the two men were tied together for a further twelve months, which pleased both parties. Elvis liked Bob — he'd just acted as guarantor on Elvis' new pink Cadillac — and there was every reason to hope that by the spring of 1956 they'd both have done very well by each other.

The Hank Snow Story, Hank Snow with Jack Ownbey & Bob Burris
Last Train to Memphis: The Rise of Elvis Presley, Peter Guralnick

The Country Cats

PERHAPS SPRING 1955
WEATHERFORD, TEXAS

ELVIS, SCOTTY AND BILL weren't the only hillbilly boys playing with R&B music. There may have been dozens — perhaps hundreds — of Southern boys hammering away at their guitars, most of whom lacked even a fraction of Presley's ambition, drive and talent. But one high school boy who knew there was something worth searching for was fifteen year-old Mac Curtis, from Weatherford, Texas.

He sang and strummed with his friends, Jimmie and Ken Galbraith (electric guitar and bass respectively), and Dick Powell (drums), and they called themselves The Country Cats. The four guys were a band and, even though Mac was the front man and handled the vocals, they thought of themselves as a unit, all parts equal.

Living out in the sticks — and because Sun had such poor distribution — they'd never heard of Elvis Presley, or Sun Records. Nevertheless, they'd devised their own approximation of a country-blues hybrid, following the R&B tunes they'd heard on the black radio stations, and added them to their repertoire. They registered Marty Robbins' hit record, "That's All Right", and soon worked up their own more exciting version, because Marty's single seemed awfully polite.

Then, one day in the spring of 1955, a friend called them over to the jukebox at a local joint, and played the Sun 209 version of "That's All Right" and suddenly, The Country Cats knew they were not alone in the universe: there was intelligent life outside of Weatherford. Here was what they'd been striving for. Mac focused on Elvis, and his bandmates absorbed every lick The Blue Moon Boys played. They pursued the Elvis sound with the zeal of religious converts.

The Mac Curtis rockabilly blog

The city that never sleeps

WEDNESDAY 23RD MARCH 1955
MADISON AVENUE, NEW YORK CITY, NEW YORK

TOUCHING DOWN IN NEW YORK, Elvis said a little prayer of thanks and prepared to meet the Big Apple. They'd flown in on the Tuesday to be fresh for the *Arthur Godfrey* audition on the Wednesday. Bob and the excited trio booked into a tiny but respectable hotel and headed off to see the sights. They played tourist until late then retired, to ready themselves for what could be a life-changing ten minutes. The Blackwood Brothers gospel quartet had previously appeared on the celebrated TV show and their career subsequently kicked into a much higher gear.

Elvis, dressed in an eye-popping pink suit, was too nervous to eat breakfast. His fingers drummed relentlessly on the table and his leg trembled as he glanced again at the hotel clock. A cab drove them the short distance to the studio and they sat in line for almost an hour before their moment.

Microphones and cameras were adjusted as singer, guitarist and bass player stood in the harsh spotlight. The New York crew gave no indication of emotion as they signalled for the closed audition (there was no audience) to begin. Elvis, Scotty and Bill blazed through both sides of Sun 209 and then unleashed the as yet unreleased "Baby, Let's Play House", Elvis already sensing its potential as a crowd pleaser.

Perspiring heavily, Elvis brought this third and final song to a close. Bob had observed the crew swaying and tapping their feet, and felt sure this was a good sign. They journeyed home to prepare themselves for a small gig in Arkansas on the Thursday. They were confident they'd done well for the *Arthur Godfrey* people and wondered how long it would be before the phone call came?

It didn't.

A Boy from Tupelo, Ernst Mikael Jørgensen
Last Train to Memphis: The Rise of Elvis Presley, Peter Guralnick

The gospel according to Alvin Krolik

PERHAPS SPRING 1955
TOPAWA, ARIZONA

Russ Davis had taken young Alvin Krolik, who was half his age, under his wing. They had formed a meaningful friendship during late '54 and early '55, both men mourning the loss of their wives, and also having a shared sense of creative passion.

Perhaps it was in the early spring that Davis came up with a suggestion for his talented buddy: a religious commission. Davis would pay the Jewish artist to travel to Arizona and visit a number of Roman Catholic monasteries, with the express intention of painting Christian murals on the walls.

And so it was that Alvin and a fellow student of the arts — no one remembers his name — travelled to the remote San Solano Franciscan monastery, about seventy miles south-west of Tucson. It was the first of several such buildings they would visit together before the summer.

San Solano was a beautiful, small, white-painted brick-built construction, looking more like a Mexican chapel than a monastery. It was framed perfectly against the bright blue desert sky, and Alvin must have been moved to see it for the first time.

He well remembered the wonderful and uplifting paintings on the wall of his boyhood school, and took inspiration from them. He was greatly encouraged to receive this commission — to be seen as an artist who had something to say.

To this day, there are small religious paintings and murals on the wall at San Solano. They portray primitive but dynamic images of Christ crucified and the Stations of the Cross. The curator recalls them as being painted by a local man, or perhaps it was a church member … no one really remembers … they were probably painted a long time ago, I guess …

Anniston Star, Alabama, 25th August 1955
Chicago Daily Tribune, Illinois, 25th August 1955

When Glenn met Tommy

PERHAPS APRIL 1955
RADIO WPDQ, JACKSONVILLE, FLORIDA

Opportunities occasionally came along for hard-pressed local deejays to indulge in side deals and publicity work. Glenn Reeves would often welcome guests onto his radio show to plug their upcoming gigs, and this is how he first met Tommy Durden, who had dropped in with his mellifluous speaking voice to advertise a forthcoming performance by Smilin' Jack Herring and his Swingbillys.

Tommy hung around after the interview and talked to Glenn about music and the ups and downs of the business. Tommy mentioned that he sometimes composed his own songs and Glenn remarked that he also wrote a little himself and, what's more, he had a close acquaintance who had a real talent for getting her tunes published and recorded. In fact, they'd just written a number together called "That's What I Like" for one of Glenn's friends.

Tommy was interested in meeting this lady. Maybe all three of them — Glenn, Mae and Tommy — could try writing something together sometime?

Country Singers As I Know 'Em, Mae Boren Axton
Glenn Reeves / *Johnny on the Spot* CD Sleeve Notes, Martin Hawkins & Richard Weize

A different drum

PERHAPS MID-APRIL 1955
706 UNION AVENUE, MEMPHIS, TENNESSEE

REPORTS HAD COME BACK TO Sam Phillips that the test pressing slow bluesy version of "I'm Left, You're Right, She's Gone" had not proven popular among deejays, so he had the boys revisit the studio, finding a brief respite between their almost constant touring.

Sam played the slow acetate back to the band who, in the cold light of day, agreed it lacked that vital commercial punch as a possible B-side of "Baby, Let's Play House". Elvis had warmed to the song itself but didn't see what else he could bring to it. Which is when Sam produced his master stroke, and local drummer Jimmie Lott stepped into the studio.

This was one of those days when everything just clicked at 706 Union. They returned to the original mid-tempo approach, and Jimmie's simple percussive beat took the pressure off Elvis' guitar, allowing him to focus more on the singing, which he did to great effect. Bill locked in with Jimmie's kick-drum and Scotty came through with his sparsest and cleanest licks yet — Sam was pleased.

There was still time enough at the end of the session to fool around with Jimmie Snow's recent release, "How Do You Think I Feel?", to which they applied an unlikely rhumba-style rhythm. They were just blowing off steam, and had energy and creativity to spare.

Sam packaged up the master tapes and prepared the paperwork for an end of month release date (Sun 217).

So the boy would get nowhere on Sun Records, eh?

He'd show that fat bastard, Tom Parker.

A Boy from Tupelo, Ernst Mikael Jørgensen

Welcome to Texas, I

SATURDAY 16TH APRIL 1955
DALLAS, TEXAS

Every weekend, Elvis was obliged to travel to Louisiana from wherever he happened to be playing in order to appear on the *Hayride*. To miss the radio show meant incurring a fine from the producers, but sometimes it was worth paying that penalty in order to build bridges elsewhere. Bob Neal booked Elvis in for four non-consecutive Saturdays on the *Big D Jamboree* in Texas, and his debut show on 16th April would also feature Charline Arthur.

It lacked the impact of the *Opry*, or even the *Hayride*, but it was an exciting stage to play and a definite step up for the band. It was also a step up for Bob Neal who was struggling to obtain bigger bookings, which meant Elvis, Scotty and Bill continued hitting smaller venues, night after night, still clocking up thousands of driving miles each week.

Bob had heard from Tom Parker, though, about a fantastic deal coming along in May. Through Hank Snow Attractions, the Colonel had set up a three-week tour covering new territory for Elvis and also for Bob, taking in New Orleans, North Carolina and a series of dates in Florida. Bob had no knowledge of that state, so Tom suggested he should ring Hank Snow's PR agent, Mae Boren Axton, and she would gladly offer advice pertaining to accommodation and travel arrangements. Bob, who had already met Mae professionally, said he would ring her at his earliest convenience.

It was no coincidence that the next move forward in Parker's pursuit of Elvis was to bring him on a tour of Florida. There was nowhere on the continent that Parker knew better, and nowhere he had more contacts.

And there was no doubt that Mae would be happy to advise and serve Elvis upon his arrival in Florida, because she had already been instructed to do this by the Colonel. Her remit was simple: she was to look after the boy and, whenever the opportunity arose, remind him that what he really needed in order to hit the big time was a record contract with a major label (like RCA) and an experienced, top-of-the-range manager (like Tom Parker).

Bob Neal's contract was due to run until March 1956, but in Parker's mind, the countdown had already begun.

A Boy from Tupelo, Ernst Mikael Jørgensen

When Tommy met Mae

PERHAPS APRIL 1955
JACKSONVILLE, FLORIDA

As promised, Glenn Reeves spoke to Mae Boren Axton about Tommy Durden, the songwriter he'd met at radio station WPDQ. Mae, keen to talk to anyone and everyone about songwriting, arranged to have Tommy visit her when next he was in Jacksonville, and they hit it off famously. Tommy was impressed as Mae name-dropped all through the conversation, and she fell for the sheer niceness of the tall, deep-voiced gentleman perched on her sofa. He told her about his life as a travelling musician, playing gigs here and there with the Swingbillys throughout Florida and parts of Texas.

They set themselves a challenge of writing together for Glenn Reeves' next TNT single, and came up with "Wasted Time, Wasted Tears", a mid-tempo country bop-type number.

Tommy brought his bright clean rhymes to the task, and the result was a strong, lively song — it was immediately obvious that it was an artistic leap forward for Mae. Neither of them had much confidence in their tune writing, but the track held together well. And this was a proper song, not a novelty number — a well-disguised piece of angry prose in which the writers berate an ex-lover for years of mistaken affection: mild-mannered Tommy was using it as a vehicle for expressing the frustration he felt over his failed marriage. But, dressed up as it was with an upbeat melody, chances are, no one thought too much about the lyric.

The first verse, "I woke one day to find you gone", was a simple variation on the classic blues opener, "I woke up this morning", but the finished song was hillbilly through and through, and Mae had little hesitation in offering it to Murray Nash Asociates. Tommy didn't care who took the publishing, to be honest. He just wanted to get his stuff out there.

Mae felt good about writing with Tommy. He lived in Gainesville — which was over an hour's drive away — but he promised to visit whenever possible. Maybe they could work out a regular slot to meet up? Mae said she was already booked for the next month or so, but after that she was sure she could find some time.

Country Singers As I Know 'Em, Mae Boren Axton
Glenn Reeves / *Johnny on the Spot* CD Sleeve Notes, Martin Hawkins & Richard Weize

The Platters: "Only You"

TUESDAY 26TH APRIL 1955
CAPITOL RECORDING STUDIO, HOLLYWOOD, CALIFORNIA

THE PLATTERS were a five-piece vocal group who couldn't quite get their act together. But a fluctuating line-up had finally settled by mid-1954 and, more importantly, they also brought in songwriter and entrepreneur Buck Ram as their manager and creative director.

On 20th May 1954, they recorded four sides for Federal, including a song Ram had originally composed and intended for The Ink Spots, "Only You". The Platters struggled, painfully showing their lack of coherence, and the label ran out of patience. By the end of the year they had moved on to Mercury and, under Ram's guidance, they started to gel. Lead tenor, Tony Williams, had a spectacular voice and Ram blended the other four singers around him, determined to shift the group outside of the strict R&B category and into the more lucrative pop market.

On 26th April 1955, at their first Mercury session, they re-recorded "Only You" and this time they absolutely nailed it, with Williams playing fast and loose with the sound of the words. Released a month later (Mercury 70633X45), it simply became one of *the* records of 1955 and sat perfectly, as Ram had planned, at the top of the R&B listing and also crossed over to reach number five in the *Billboard* pop chart.

In November, hoping to cash in, Federal released the earlier and inferior version of the song. Ram, unsuccessfully, sued. It didn't matter though: the public were astute enough to know the real deal when they heard it, and they ignored the Federal disk.

The Platters became the dominant vocal group of the era, and lovers everywhere danced and romanced to their timeless masterpiece.

Marv Goldberg's R&B Notebooks, 2008 (online)

The TNT tour

LATE APRIL 1955
TEXAS

DURING THE WEEK leading up to the forthcoming Hank Snow Attractions tour in May, Elvis headlined a short series of dates in Texas sponsored, interestingly enough, by Mae Boren Axton's friend, Bill Tanner of TNT Records. The only other real "name" on the bill was Dub Dickerson, still grinning and probably featuring an Axton song in his set list.

Also among the cast was twenty-four year-old pianist, Floyd Cramer, who regularly played the *Hayride*, and had made a record or two for Fabor Robison's Abbot label. Floyd was giving considerable thought as to whether he should give up the life of a touring musician and maybe look for permanent work as a session pianist in Nashville. The city was beginning to attract attention as a centre of country music, although the local authorities — who felt hillbilly music was too lowbrow — were doing their best to dampen enthusiasm.

Earlier in the month, a fan sitting in the front row had, for the first time, captured a few fleeting moments of silent colour film of Elvis performing at the Breckenridge High School Auditorium. The flickering frames reveal a ravishingly handsome young man exploding with talent and energy. The colours are vivid and eye-catching, and the singer seems poised to take on the world.

Although he would still play the occasional smaller gig, as from Saturday 1st May 1955, when he arrived in New Orleans — with his latest record just hitting the shops — Elvis began a new and bigger chapter in his career.

It was less than ten months since his first professional recording session, and things were about to go crazy.

A Boy from Tupelo, Ernst Mikael Jørgensen

Snow in New Orleans

SUNDAY 1ST MAY 1955
NEW ORLEANS, LOUISIANA

THE THREE-WEEK TOUR was intended to be a big money spinner for Hank Snow and Tom Parker. The cast would change every few days as they picked up and dropped off various artists en route. Hank was top of the bill, and his son, Jimmie, was also listed; The Wilburn Brothers, Mother Maybelle and The Carter Sisters, Slim Whitman, Martha Carson, and Faron Young would also feature. Whichever way you sliced it, this was a substantial hillbilly tour and fledgling stars would have an opportunity to earn their spurs alongside the established hit-makers.

The first week of gigs involved two or sometimes three shows a day throughout Louisiana and Alabama, but it was clear from day one that there was a problem no one could possibly have foreseen. In the few weeks since Snow and Parker had last seen Elvis on stage, his skills as a performer had increased exponentially. He had worked, studied and experimented night after night to the point where his control of the assembly — be it ten or ten thousand — was almost absolute.

It became impossible for other players to follow Elvis because the crowd kept screaming for more. Although he stayed mid-bill in terms of advertising, he moved nearer and nearer to the headline act until only Hank Snow himself remained above him in performance order. But Snow would not be moved. Faron Young advised Hank to reconsider and to think the unthinkable: allow Elvis to close the show, but still Hank would not shift. Until, that is, the moment when the crowd shouted for Elvis throughout Hank's first two songs.

A meeting was swiftly called and a resolution was hammered out. The younger performers would play the early part of each show and Elvis would close the first act, allowing the audience time to calm down during the intermission. Then the real stars would take their turn.

Snow was livid. Parker was quietly ecstatic.

A Boy from Tupelo, Ernst Mikael Jørgensen
The Faron Young Story: Live Fast Love Hard, Diane Diekman

The long goodbye

FRIDAY 6TH MAY 1955
MEMPHIS, TENNESSEE

A PROMISE IS A PROMISE. Elvis had assured his sweetheart, Dixie, that he would escort her to the Junior Prom, and so, having cleared it with the Colonel, he drove mid-tour almost four hundred miles from Mobile to Memphis (missing the Friday night tour performance) in order to keep his word.

They made a handsome couple; she in a strapless white gown; he in a baby-blue tuxedo jacket, black trousers and white buck shoes. They enjoyed a beautiful fleeting evening together, putting aside their worries and silly arguments, and wallowed in the warmth of their friendship.

She loved him beyond measure, but becoming the wife of a travelling musician was not for her. She suspected — heck, she knew — he was not short of female company on the road, and this was reflected in his mild obsession in knowing what *she* was up to while *he* was away. Dixie had already accepted that their time was over. She would tell him this. When the moment was right.

Gladys and Vernon were similarly torn. They wanted the best for their son, but didn't fully understand what his career choice meant for his life, or indeed for theirs. Gladys fretted about his safety, and she still hoped he would give it all up, marry Dixie (such a nice girl) and settle down nearby.

But everyone put on their best smiles before dawn on Saturday morning, as Elvis hugged and kissed his goodbyes, pointing the car towards Birmingham, Alabama, where he would pick up Scotty and Bill, and then head on to Daytona Beach, which was eight hundred miles south-east of Memphis.

They had to be there in time to re-join the tour as it broke into Florida. Bob Neal had told him to park near the city limits where they would meet a lady who would show them to a good motel before the Saturday gig.

The lady's name was Mae — Mae Boren Axton.

A Boy from Tupelo, Ernst Mikael Jørgensen
Last Train to Memphis: The Rise of Elvis Presley, Peter Guralnick

When Mae met Elvis

SATURDAY 7TH MAY 1955
DAYTONA BEACH, FLORIDA

As suggested by the Colonel, Bob Neal had phoned Mae the previous week, and she was glad to hear Bob's voice again. He asked if Mae wouldn't mind keeping an eye out for Elvis and the boys while they were in Florida. She told him it would be a pleasure, and she was sure the Colonel wouldn't mind — which she knew for certain since it had been Tom Parker's idea in the first place and she was following his lead.

She'd never heard Elvis sing, nor had she seen a picture of him, but there was no doubt in her mind that the devastatingly beautiful young man who stepped out of the car at the city limits on Saturday afternoon was her designated target for the week. It took her just a moment to recover her composure, as he gave his best lopsided grin, and politely shook her hand.

She suggested Elvis climb into her car and they'd lead Scotty and Bill to a nearby motel where she had already reserved rooms, including one for herself, as she'd be travelling with the tour throughout the state. She told them she'd already paid their bill — pretending it was all part of the Hank Snow Attractions deal — and spent an hour getting to know Elvis a little better.

He talked about his parents, about how he wanted to earn enough money so they could retire. Glancing out of the window at the ocean, he told Mae how much they would love to come to Daytona Beach. He spoke respectfully about Sam and Bob, and also about how grateful he was that Mr Snow and the Colonel had been so generous to him — Mae concurred that the Colonel was a wonderful man and also an excellent manager.

And all at once, Mae fell for him, head over heels, in a maternal fashion. He was irresistible. He was funny. He was shy. He was intelligent. But at no time did she see anything — other than his classic features and outrageous clothes — that would indicate a performer in whom the Colonel would take such an interest.

She escorted the boys to the Peabody Auditorium that night and stood in the wings while the younger performers ran through the first act. And then Elvis took to the stage, with Scotty and Bill in tow.

And from the first note, she understood everything.

A Boy from Tupelo, Ernst Mikael Jørgensen
Last Train to Memphis: The Rise of Elvis Presley, Peter Guralnick
Country Singers As I Know 'Em, Mae Boren Axton

Deadman's Curve

SATURDAY 7TH MAY 1955 (LATE NIGHT)
ON THE ROAD FROM TERRELL TO DALLAS, TEXAS

HELEN HALL'S FIRST RELEASE on Coral had been out for two months and she had thrown herself into its promotion, knowing that an unsupported single would make little progress. "Wasted Life" and "Honky Tonk Husband" required Helen's full-time attention.

Driving home after yet another gig, with her neighbour and twenty-six year-old fan club president, Mrs Martha McCullars, in the passenger seat, Helen lost control of the car and it turned over several times on a sharp curve. Sadly, Mrs McCullars was killed outright and Helen suffered severe facial lacerations, multiple head injuries and a leg fracture.

She was taken to Methodist Hospital, Dallas, for several weeks of treatment and recuperation. Her record's chances of success were taken directly to the morgue.

Billboard, 21st May 1955
The Galveston Daily News, Texas, 8th May 1955

Terry Fell: "That's What I Like"

WEDNESDAY 11TH MAY 1955
RCA VICTOR STUDIO, 1525 McGAVOCK STREET, NASHVILLE, TENNESSEE

TERRY FELL WAS A PLAYER in the ad hoc band that Mae Boren Axton had assembled in Jacksonville around Glenn Reeves. He'd recorded a few songs for several labels since the end of the war, eventually signing for RCA Victor in the spring of 1955, and was ushered in for a session on 11th May.

RCA, like most big labels, didn't have a permanent studio in Nashville so, since the beginning of the year, they'd been hiring the recording facility belonging to the Methodist Television, Radio & Film Commission, located at 1525 McGavock Street. Whenever the Methodists weren't taping services or Sunday School lessons, RCA would move in and lay down four songs in a three-hour session, often produced by Chet Atkins and Steve Sholes.

The union was very strict about temporary studios of this nature. RCA engineers could only use their own equipment, so between sessions it was put in storage, ready to be installed again — by union-approved technicians — every time Steve Sholes scheduled a session.

Though professional, the studio was not ideal and had a high, rounded ceiling which caused problems for bass players, as their sound tended to roll around the room. Sitting at the control desk was engineer Bob Ferris, a precise man, who came across as somewhat terse — which didn't always make for an easy atmosphere. He also had a tendency to rub Atkins the wrong way.

Of the four songs Fell recorded that day, one was called "That's What I Like", an uptempo hillbilly novelty number written earlier in the spring by Mae Boren Axton and Glenn Reeves. Being so very country-esque, the publishing rights went straight to Murray Nash, and the song was chosen by Sholes as the first single from the date.

Sholes was a meticulous worker and would have noted the names of the songwriters and also the publishers. He liked to keep abreast of who was hot and who was not.

Released in the autumn as RCA 6526, and well reviewed in *Billboard*, the song sank without trace.

Country Singers As I Know 'Em, Mae Boren Axton
Glenn Reeves / *Johnny on the Spot* CD Sleeve Notes, Martin Hawkins & Richard Weize
Billboard, 24th September 1955

The Jacksonville riot

FRIDAY 13TH MAY 1955
THE NEW BASEBALL PARK, JACKSONVILLE, FLORIDA

By the time the tour reached her home town of Jacksonville for two days of shows at the end of the week, Mae was a total convert. There had been near riots at some concerts, and she had observed one young woman completely lose control, babbling, "Oh, Ms Axton, he's just a great big beautiful hunk of forbidden fruit." But none of this prepared Mae, or indeed any of them, for the Friday show.

During the day, Mae suggested the cast should all sit down to lunch together and, as they relaxed and ate, the conversation turned to Elvis' lacy pink shirt — an astonishingly bold choice of clothing. The females at the table, including Mae, laughed and each demanded Elvis should give it to them because it was such a pretty and feminine item. He blushed, joining in the laughter when someone pointed out that the girls in the audience were likely to tear it from his back anyway.

Their venue that night was the new Jacksonville baseball park. It seated fourteen thousand customers, and Elvis worked until there was barely a breath left in his body. The patrons responded loudly and enthusiastically, scarcely able to restrain themselves in their seats. Drenched with sweat, Elvis closed the act and thanked the audience. Then, with a grin, he added, "Girls, I'll see you backstage."

That was it. The dam burst, as perhaps half of the crowd leapt forward and sprinted towards the stage. The musicians grabbed whatever instruments and amplifiers they could and ran for their lives. Below the stage, in the box office room, Tom Parker and Mae Boren Axton were counting the night's proceeds when they became aware of the ominous rumble above their heads.

When the mob hit the stage, they spilled over onto the boards and continued their pursuit, hundreds of them squeezing down the passageway which led backstage. Elvis sought refuge in the shower cubicle of his dressing room, while his fellow performers attempted to barricade the door. Dozens poured into the room, clutching and grabbing at the singer. By the time Mae and the police established order, not just his pink shirt, but his boots, his coat and most of his clothing had been torn off, and his body bore the marks of a hundred desperate fingernails.

This was beyond anything even Tom Parker had hoped for, but he had severely underestimated one crucial factor. This was all happening at a much, much faster rate than anticipated, and he would need to work with equal speed in order to capture his quarry.

Elvis was already booked to play the third Jimmie Rodgers Memorial later in the month, and after that Parker knew he must get him back to Florida as soon as possible. Hank Snow (pushing for a management deal) and Bob Neal (pushing for an RCA contract) were already crooning the right tune to the boy as far as Parker was concerned, but no one could sing as sweetly as Mae.

A Boy from Tupelo, Ernst Mikael Jørgensen
Country Singers As I Know 'Em, Mae Boren Axton
Last Train to Memphis: The Rise of Elvis Presley, Peter Guralnick

Man of the Year, 1955

SATURDAY 21ST MAY 1955
NASHVILLE, TENNESSEE

COUNTRY AND WESTERN MUSIC had grown so popular since the turn of the decade that in May 1955 *Billboard* decided to honour its most prestigious personalities, But rather than focus on the singing stars, the poll celebrated the men — not women, note — behind the scenes, the men who made the singing stars shine.

Taking the award for 1955 was the late Fred Rose, who had died on 1st December 1954 of a sudden heart attack, aged just fifty-seven: as has often been pointed out, death can be a good career move.

In second place was Steve Sholes, and behind him, Jim Denny, who was hailed as a figure of influence and importance.

Alongside the list of winners, *Billboard* published an editorial which spoke in glowing terms of the assured continued success of c&w music. Referencing Roosevelt, it declared, “We have nothing to fear but fear itself.”

Billboard, 21st May 1955

The 1955 Jimmie Rodgers Memorial

WEDNESDAY 25TH MAY 1955
MERIDIAN, MISSISSIPPI

THE TWO RCA MEN had first caught Elvis' act in Richmond the previous week, just a few days after the Jacksonville incident, and had been impressed. So much so, they'd purchased two copies of all four Sun singles, and sent them to Steve Sholes back at HQ. Brad McCuen and Chick Crumpacker knew there'd be a chance to watch Elvis again at the Jimmy Rodgers Memorial event and, as they were already booked in there to support RCA superstar Hank Snow in his big annual tribute, they knew they could kill two birds with one stone. They introduced themselves to Elvis in Meridian and made sure he knew they represented RCA.

Elvis had arrived in time for the festivities on the Tuesday, and he and Jimmie Snow sat on the wings of his pink Cadillac as they were driven through the streets of the city on the Wednesday parade. Elvis bumped into Mae ("Hi, Elvis, gee what a coincidence.") and they had their picture taken together. She dropped Parker's name into the conversation, while still tending diligently to Hank's PR.

And Elvis' performance at the Wednesday gala show was wild. Capturing the sexiness, the fun and the sheer entertainment value of Jimmie Rodgers himself, he laid waste to the crowd with a devastating set, which included both sides of his new — and very popular — single.

At the end of the show, Elvis gathered on stage with the other performers and, led by esteemed ex-Governor Jimmie Davis, they chorused together on "You Are My Sunshine", as if it were a hymn. Hank Snow and Ernest Tubb were delighted that the two-day festival had gone so well.

Interestingly, also present, and also supporting its client Hank Snow, was Hill & Range Publishers, in the person of Mr Grelun Landon from the California office.

Landon also intended to kill two birds and, having first paid court to Hank, made a point of speaking to Elvis and Bob Neal about a proposal from the Aberbachs. Jean and Julian felt it was time Elvis had his very own songbook to sell on the road. Hill & Range had no publishing contract with

Elvis but they would be delighted to assemble the sheet music for his Sun singles and add a few photographs and an attractive picture cover.

They would take care of the legal niceties, renting songs they didn't own, and Elvis, Bob and Sam would all end up taking a cut. Scotty and Bill would also earn a few extra bucks by selling the books at each gig. Hill & Range would ensure they themselves were well recompensed, obviously, but more importantly, they would have quietly and politely established official contact with a young singer in whom they had considerable interest.

In fact, the only person who was not party to, or indeed aware of, this sweet little side deal was Tom Parker. As far as the Aberbachs were concerned, Tom Parker had no contractual connection with Elvis Presley at all at this point in time; hence his non-involvement.

But sweet little side deals were very much Tom Parker's favourite snack, and he had a way of sniffing them out.

A Boy from Tupelo, Ernst Mikael Jørgensen
Restless Giant: The Life and Times of Jean Aberbach & Hill and Range Songs, Bar Biszick-Lockwood

Yonder comes Jim Reeves

TUESDAY 31ST MAY 1955

RCA VICTOR STUDIO, 1525 MCGAVOCK STREET, NASHVILLE, TENNESSEE

THE FOUR SUN SINGLES had arrived on Steve Sholes' desk and he'd listened to them because he had the utmost respect for McCuen and Crumpacker. This was the second time McCuen had recommended Elvis Presley to his boss, but right now Steve had other things on his mind.

He had recently signed Jim Reeves to RCA Victor from Fabor Robison's Abbot. It was a big step forward for Reeves and he'd turned up at the RCA studio on McGavock Street on the last day of May 1955, ready to tape his first singles for his new label. He'd brought a song he'd composed himself, "Yonder Comes a Sucker", basing the melody on an old folk tune.

Bea Terry, knowing that Reeves was chasing a permanent contract with the *Grand Ole Opry*, had advised her lover to place the uptempo song with Jack Stapp's Tree Publishing in the hope it might have a positive influence.

Therefore, Buddy Killen sat as an observer during the session, and then approached the temperamental singer, introducing himself and expressing his gratitude that Reeves had decided to entrust his song to Tree. Having previously had nothing but trouble regarding contracts and finance, Reeves replied sharply, "I might as well place it with you as anybody else; you're not going to pay me anyway."

Buddy stood silently, nonplussed by this. Reeves, realising he'd misjudged the situation, offered to come to Buddy's tiny office the next day to sign the paperwork. Subsequently, Reeves and Killen became great friends and confidants and, more importantly for Tree, after four long years of plugging and selling, Jim's song would go on to become their first substantial hillbilly hit when issued a few weeks later as RCA 47-6200.

But Buddy Killen's joy proved to be Steve Sholes' nightmare: when Reeves' single peaked in the late summer, Fabor Robison gathered together a dozen old Jim Reeves tracks and released an LP, competing directly with Reeves' new RCA product. Sholes learnt a valuable lesson: when you gamble on an artist's future, be sure you've purchased his past.

By the Seat of my Pants, Buddy Killen with Tom Carter
Jim Reeves: His Untold Story, Larry Jordan
Billboard, 25th May 1953

Mae and Glenn: just like Elvis

PERHAPS JUNE 1955
JACKSONVILLE, FLORIDA

Mae Boren Axton was now obsessed with all things Elvis. Glenn Reeves had also seen the boy perform first-hand — as a local deejay, he must certainly have seen the Jacksonville shows — and he could fully understand her fascination.

Mae told Glenn about "Wasted Time, Wasted Tears", the song she and Tommy Durden had written for one side of Glenn's next TNT single. The smiling Mrs Axton then suggested she and Glenn should write something for the flip side — something based very firmly on Elvis' new style of music, and the deejay heartily agreed.

They brought in friend and guitarist Harold Meeks to help with the tune, and for reference they played a copy of Sun 210 "Good Rockin' Tonight". They plundered the lyrics and stole "rocking shoes" and the "rock rock rock" refrain and had a ball while composing "I Ain't Got Room to Rock". As they finished each verse, Glenn cracked up his co-writers by singing the rough-hewn number in a mock-Elvis voice — complete with deep slurs — and they all dissolved in laughter.

Once again, Mae attributed her part of the song to her husband and offered it as another Axton original to Bill Tanner's publishing company to sweeten the deal. The two new songs were recorded and released in July as TNT 129.

Over the course of the past five months, Mae had co-composed eight songs, four of which had been published by TNT. Bill Tanner had invested time and money in Mae and Glenn, and was hoping for some measure of return on his investment.

But it was not to be.

Country Singers As I Know 'Em, Mae Boren Axton
Glenn Reeves / *Johnny on the Spot* CD Sleeve Notes, Martin Hawkins & Richard Weize

Dinner with Jean

SUNDAY 5TH JUNE 1955
NEW YORK CITY, NEW YORK

THE COLONEL just happened to be in New York to attend a Hank Snow concert, or at least that's what he told Jean Aberbach when he suggested they meet for dinner. There's no question, however, that the topic of mealtime conversation would have been Presley's future.

Parker was no closer to achieving his goal. He had nothing to take to RCA, nor was he any nearer to removing Sam Phillips and Bob Neal from the picture. Jean, who could be as discreet as a priest when required, said nothing about the songbook deal, but listened with interest when Tom pitched a proposition.

The Colonel wasn't yet convinced that RCA would make a move for Elvis' recording contract and, even if Sam Phillips decided to let Elvis go, it would surely be for a figure in excess of what Steve Sholes would be willing to pay. And Parker dearly wanted Elvis at RCA because that was still the company where he had strong contacts and, assuming his management bid for the boy came through, he would have almost unlimited influence.

And so, he invited Aberbach to opt in to a buyout deal from Sun Records. In effect, he was asking Hill & Range to supply serious money and to invest in Elvis. Aberbach was surprised at this move, and reminded Parker that he was in the business of investing in songs and not singers. Besides, there were legal issues pertaining to conflict of interests.

Parker quietly seethed: he'd seen Jean as a friend and co-conspirator in the mission to capture the Presley boy, but he was now running out of options. He smiled at his dinner guest — although Jean would certainly be paying for the meal — and picked up the dessert menu. Perhaps the time had come to gamble again. Maybe he needed to stir the waters in order to get things moving.

And, by strange coincidence, just three days later, Sam Phillips received an unsolicited enquiry from Frank Walker at MGM Records asking if it was true that Presley's contract was up for sale. Soon after, there was a call from Mitch Miller at Columbia, and then Sam heard from Dot, and Capitol, and Mercury, and …

Restless Giant: The Life and Times of Jean Aberbach & Hill and Range Songs, Bar Biszick-Lockwood
Sam Phillips: The Man Who Invented Rock 'n' Roll, Peter Guralnick

The $64,000 Question

TUESDAY 7TH JUNE 1955
CBS-TV STUDIOS, NEW YORK CITY, NEW YORK

THERE WERE SEVERAL REASONS why Lou Cowan remained a silent partner in Tree Publishing, but the most important was that he was so very busy in his full-time job as a radio and TV producer. All through the spring of 1955, the industry had been buzzing with talk of his forthcoming CBS-TV game show, to be called the *The $64,000 Question.*

During its development, Cowan had some trouble locating a sponsor, and several big companies passed on the opportunity before cosmetics giant Revlon reluctantly signed up.

There had been quiz shows before, but this was to be something special. The premise was simple but brilliant — do I keep what I've already won or should I gamble it all on the next question? And, when first broadcast in June 1955, it became a TV phenomenon and Lou Cowan became the number one guy in media production.

Revlon doubled its sales within twelve months, and Cowan — a well-respected, honest and intelligent man — quickly moved up the ladder at CBS. His future and his fortune were assured.

Exploring Media Culture: A Guide, Michael R. Real
Billboard, 19th March & 28th May 1955
www.cosmeticsandskin.com

Welcome to Texas, II

SATURDAY 18TH JUNE 1955
DALLAS, TEXAS

THE AUDIENCE OF SIX THOUSAND seated at the *Big D Jamboree* just looked silently at Joe Poovey as he stood before them. Joe was the third act to take to the stage since Elvis had vacated with the sound of screams and applause ringing in his ears, but as performers all over the South were beginning to discover, you just couldn't follow Presley.

Saturday 18th June saw Elvis' third appearance in as many months at the *Jamboree* and he'd now become a serious headliner. That night marked a turning point for Joe Poovey: from this time forward, everything Joe sang, wrote and wore would be influenced by this encounter. Joe was just one of many who saw Elvis and changed their entire approach to music. The old adage "Women wanted to be near him and men wanted to be him" was entirely fulfilled as Elvis relentlessly toured the South, night after night.

Meanwhile, the news concerning "Baby, Let's Play House" was all good, and sales reports were very encouraging for Sam Phillips. And Sam needed all the encouragement he could get. His creditors continued to press and the unexpected calls, letters and telegrams concerning Elvis' contract were just an annoying distraction.

Mitch Miller, the A&R man at Columbia, had even gone so far as to enquire how much Sam was asking for the contract. Sam, who wasn't asking anything because the contract wasn't for sale, plucked a random figure out of the air and suggested $20,000 (that's twice the price of the house Sam had recently bought, for a singer who hadn't yet even bothered the hillbilly top twenty, let alone the pop chart). When Mitch picked himself off the floor he said to forget he'd even called, because no singer was worth that kind of money.

What Steve Sholes thought of it, no one knew, because at this point RCA Victor wasn't making any kind of an offer at all.

Sam Phillips: The Man Who Invented Rock 'n' Roll, Peter Guralnick
We Wanna Boogie, unknown author

Bob and Tom reach an agreement

TUESDAY 21ST JUNE 1955
MADISON, TENNESSEE

THERE HAD BEEN SOME CONFLICT, there's no doubt about that. Bob Neal and Tom Parker were both trying to find the best possible gigs for Elvis, but with two people doing the same job, inevitably, problems arose.

So Tom invited Bob over to his home office for a little chat on Tuesday 14th June, just like he had previously done with Hank Snow. Cigars were lit, compliments were paid, stories were exchanged, coffee was drunk and, in a surprisingly short space of time, the men came to an amicable agreement.

Bob would carry on as Elvis' personal manager but Tom would now handle all bookings. It seemed a sensible proposal and Bob was pleased. Parker, though, was elated. He was now on the inside. Tom was also able to update Bob on a new tour he'd arranged: following on from the very successful visit to Florida in May, they were going back to the Sunshine State at the end of July.

They firmly shook hands and Bob bid his goodbyes, feeling positive about the future. But Parker was a distrustful man and, even though he now knew that Bob was a pushover, he instructed Tom Diskin to watch him like a hawk.

On the Monday, the Colonel received a call from Tommy Sands, who had played once again alongside Elvis the previous day. Tommy had, as instructed, engaged Elvis in a conversation regarding record labels and, after weeks of similar pep talks from Hank and Bob, Elvis had finally conceded that there might be some merit in the idea of moving to a company like RCA Victor.

This was the news Parker had been waiting to hear, and on Tuesday 21st June he dictated a letter to Steve Sholes, informing him of his new position within the Presley organisation, and suggesting that if Steve had some interest in the boy's contract then he should let him know.

But Sam Phillips still wasn't selling.

A Boy from Tupelo, Ernst Mikael Jørgensen
Restless Giant: The Life and Times of Jean Aberbach & Hill and Range Songs, Bar Biszick-Lockwood

The lonely death of Barbara Reed

SATURDAY 2ND JULY 1955
DELRAY BEACH, FORT PIERCE, FLORIDA

CONSTABLE BRUCE WHEELER found the body. Barbara Reed, just twenty, was slumped over the wheel of her car on a lonely street in Delray Beach. A water hose had been connected to the exhaust pipe and it ran through the left front door. Cause of death was given as suicide.

Four notes were found, one of which was addressed to her parents in San Antonio, asking that no one be blamed for her death. Married and divorced, she considered herself a "failure".

Local newspapers printed the story modestly over the next couple of days. Articles of this nature were considered tasteless, but did occasionally appear. A handful were reported in Florida throughout the year of 1955 and it's possible that someone like Mae Boren Axton, a professional wordsmith, would have mentally noted such tales and filed them away in her memory in the unlikely event she might need to draw upon them.

For most writers, life itself is the greatest topic but, failing that, death will often act as a good stand in.

Fort Pierce News, Florida, 3rd July 1955

Buddy's invitation

EARLY JULY 1955
NASHVILLE, TENNESSEE

EVERY NOW AND THEN, Buddy Killen would see a little glimmer of light in his publishing efforts: a novelty weeper called "Daddy, You Know What" by small-timer Jim Wilson looked like it might scrape into the c&w top ten which would be Tree's first hit of any type; he also had hopes for Jim Reeves' "Yonder Comes a Sucker", which was issued on RCA in early July, but there really wasn't much else to be excited about.

It was around about this time that Buddy received a phone call from an old friend in Florida. Buddy's pal ran a joint called the Mello Club in Daytona Beach, and had an unusual offer for the amiable bass player. Money was tight but the club owner needed a small band to fill in for a few weeks from the end of July, playing two shows a night so the patrons could dance before and after dinner. There would be no pay, but the owner was willing to offer bed and board at the club for Buddy and two other musicians and all three wives. For a couple of hours every evening they would perform, but for the rest of the time they could enjoy a free holiday in sunny Florida.

Well, Buddy thought it was a great idea and, once he'd talked it over with his wife and fellow players, the Robinson brothers, it was all agreed. They'd head out at the end of the month and Buddy could forget about the publishing game for a while. He would sunbathe, spend some time with his wife, see the sights, and maybe look up one or two old acquaintances.

It might be just the break he needed.

By the Seat of my Pants, Buddy Killen with Tom Carter
Billboard, 25th June & 9th July 1955

A short intermission

TUESDAY 5TH JULY 1955
MEMPHIS, TENNESSEE

VACATIONS ARE INDEED IMPORTANT, and Elvis and the boys took a well-earned three-week breather starting on Tuesday 5th July 1955, exactly one year to the day since they had recorded "That's All Right". To the three of them, it felt as though they'd been playing two shows a night, every night for twelve months.

The free time was welcomed but there was still business to attend to. Elvis, for instance, was ushered in to local photographer William Speer who took a series of publicity pictures that captured the remarkable way in which his features had matured into something irresistibly beautiful.

Many have commented over the years about how the young Elvis was constantly looking in a mirror. But this misses the point, which is that there is a magnetic attraction to great natural beauty — one is compelled to look. Elvis wasn't just combing his hair each time he stopped by a mirror: he was looking at himself. This is not to imply narcissism; rather it is simply to understand the vital importance of Presley's appearance with regard to his rapid success.

When combined with his immaculately styled hair, his height, his fashion sense, his natural ability as a dancer, his knowledge of music, his willingness to ignore the rules of segregation, and, most importantly, his remarkable voice, it would seem as if he was pre-destined for fame.

One young lady who certainly fell for him was Wanda Jackson, daughter of Mae Boren Axton's old school friend. They shared a bill together later in the month, as Elvis and The Blue Moon Boys warmed up with a gig or two prior to the Florida tour. Wanda was bowled over by his looks and his performance and, taking inspiration from what she'd seen, re-invented herself in his image, just as countless young men had already done.

Elvis, Scotty and Bill had come so far in just one year, changing lives wherever they played. Who could imagine where they'd be and what they might have achieved in another twelve months' time?

A Boy from Tupelo, Ernst Mikael Jørgensen
Last Train to Memphis: The Rise of Elvis Presley, Peter Guralnick

From Tom to Jean, from Jean to Steve

WEDNESDAY 6TH & THURSDAY 7TH JULY 1955
NEW YORK CITY, NEW YORK

ONCE AGAIN, "just by chance", Tom Parker happened to be in New York for a couple of days, and he spent Wednesday and Thursday with Jean Aberbach, and the topic of conversation was, undoubtedly, Elvis Presley.

Parker was a great student of the game, and he knew his chances of moving Elvis to RCA Victor were greatly increased if Hill & Range was part of the package. So, although he was still hurting over Jean's refusal of his proposed buyout offer, Tom continued to make nice to the Aberbachs, and suggested to Jean perhaps their position might be stronger if Steve Sholes was assured of the publisher's intentions.

Jean nodded his agreement — but still made no mention to the Colonel of the songbook deal because, in his eyes, Tom still had no guarantee of being involved in any of Elvis' publishing or recording processes. And maddeningly for Parker, Steve Sholes still made no bid for the contract that still wasn't for sale.

Tom boarded the train back home to Madison on the Thursday evening, and Jean caught a cab to Steve Sholes' home to attend a party celebrating Mrs Sholes' birthday. As the guests mingled and civilised conversation buzzed gently around the spacious rooms, Jean and Steve found time for a quiet word. Jean wanted the RCA man to know that Hill & Range would always be on hand to help an exciting young talent like Elvis Presley. Steve pondered that thought, and made a mental note to investigate further.

A few days later, Jean wrote to Sam Phillips asking for printing rights for the Elvis Presley Hi-Lo tunes so they could proceed with the songbook. Sam was happy to comply because he rightly figured it would be a good deal for all involved and he needed whatever cash he could get.

Jean was very keen to slip aboard the good ship Presley, because as any fool could see, a change was imminent in the pop chart. And maybe Elvis Presley was the man who could turn that change into dollars.

Restless Giant: The Life and Times of Jean Aberbach & Hill and Range Songs, Bar Biszick-Lockwood

The A-side

SATURDAY 9TH JULY 1955
AT THE TOP OF THE *BILLBOARD* CHART

Hollywood producers could likewise sense the mood of public uncertainty. They had been surprised and delighted by the success of James Dean and his appeal to the younger audience, and many were already developing projects of their own that focused on the well-discussed topical problem of "juvenile delinquency".

Pandro Berman, for example, was producing *Blackboard Jungle* starring Glen Ford, exploiting the supposed violent unpredictability in schools. When casting around for suitable music, the film-makers spoke to Peter Ford, the young son of the film's star.

They borrowed some of his record collection, and chose the B-side of Bill Haley's "Thirteen Women" as the ideal song to act as their anthem to teenage unrest. Haley was already in the ascendancy following his very popular cover of Big Joe Turner's R&B hit, "Shake, Rattle and Roll", but when the movie was released in the spring, with "Rock Around the Clock" playing over the opening credits, fame and fortune washed over the singer like a tidal wave.

"Rock Around the Clock" was re-released as an A-side and purchased by over a million young people. It hit number one in the pop chart on 9th July 1955 and stayed there for two months. It was the first significant hit of a musical genre that was now being called rock 'n' roll (a phrase coined by deejay Alan Freed), and it marked the beginning of mass public awareness of the cultural changes that were taking place.

Juvenile delinquency now had a soundtrack: rock 'n' roll. And record producers fell over each other in their search for the best way to capitalise on this development. Haley was soon proclaimed the King of Rock 'n' Roll but, in truth, his was but the voice of one crying in the wilderness and preparing the way.

Home in Tucson, Arizona

JULY 1955
THE OZARKS, ARIZONA

At the completion of his religious painting commission, Alvin Krolik returned from his own wilderness, and reported back to his benefactor, Russ Davis, who suggested they celebrate with a two-week vacation in the Ozarks, a highland plateau region of the central United States, and a popular holiday destination. Chances are the pair did some fishing, maybe some climbing and hunting. For Davis, it was a time to escape from the rat race. For Krolik, it was an opportunity to re-evaluate his life, and decide on his future.

Indeed, he did make a decision of sorts. He'd enjoyed his time in Arizona and opted to make his home there, choosing to rent a place in Tucson. It was a place where he thought he could put down roots and maybe re-establish regular contact with his family.

He'd been pretty much cut off from the outside world since the turn of the year — moving from monastery to monastery, travelling through the desert, camping in the Ozarks — so he hadn't caught up with the news from Chicago: Agnes Sampson, whom Alvin had wed in June 1952 and divorced shortly afterwards, had remarried in February.

Anniston Star, Alabama, 25th August 1955
Chicago Daily Tribune, Illinois, 25th August 1955

The fifth single

THURSDAY 21ST JULY 1955
706 UNION AVENUE, MEMPHIS, TENNESSEE

SOME DAYS ARE PERFECT: Thursday 21st July 1955 was one of those days. It had been a little over a year since Elvis recorded his first Sun single with Scotty and Bill, and they had subsequently visited the studio dozens of times. Usually, the songs came slowly and the boys sweated blood in order to achieve those beautifully-crafted records. But on this day, it all came so easily.

Perhaps it was because they had become one of the tightest bands in the business after twelve months of constant touring. Or maybe it was that they'd just taken a few weeks off, giving them a chance to recharge their batteries. Or it could have been the news that "Baby, Let's Play House" had finally crashed in at number fifteen on the *Billboard* c&w chart.

Whatever alchemy was responsible for the mood of creativity in the studio that day, Sam didn't care. He just kept the tape rolling.

"Tryin' To Get To You" was a song they'd previously struggled with back in February. A mid-tempo, gutsy belter of a number, this time Elvis grabbed it by the scruff of the neck and delivered a strikingly confident vocal. He sang while seated at the keyboard — he was a competent and self-taught pianist — and the boys were joined by drummer Johnny Bernero, who laid down a simple but solid beat.

Bernero also featured on the second selection which was another c&w pop track from the pen of Stan Kesler. Sam liked the wordplay of the title, "I Forgot to Remember to Forget", but once again, Elvis was not instantly taken with the demo. It was similar to Kesler's previous submission and Elvis felt it needed a little something extra. So Sam came up with the idea of switching the drum pattern during the guitar solo which made the song seem faster, encouraging Elvis to deliver a strong clean performance. There was a beautiful sense of elegance and economy about the finished take, and Sam Phillips was convinced he could smell a hit record.

Two songs completed, the drummer went home, but the room was still buzzing and no one wanted to quit. They jammed, they laughed, and they whooped it up, until Sam threw the title "Mystery Train" into the melee. He'd talked about the boys recording this before: Little Junior Parker's non-hit from 1954 was one of Sam's personal favourites.

Soon, either Sam or Elvis — it didn't matter which, they had become like one person in the studio by now — came up with the idea of marrying the lyrics and tune of "Mystery Train" to the uptempo rhythm of Parker's B-side, "Love My Baby". And this was when things got really funky. They tried a simple run through, and Sam noticed Elvis had subtly changed the lyrics. The original singer complained that the Mystery Train had stolen his lover, but Elvis — bursting with youthful confidence — insisted "it never would again."

The musicians took their places at the mikes, and Sam cued the Ampex and the slapback. Scotty hit the riff, Bill leapt in, and Elvis drove the song forward with acoustic guitar, his vocal soaring above the clickety-clack bass rhythm that captured the feel of the train so well. At one point, Elvis added an extra beat but no one flinched, that's how synched they were on that day.

As the song approached its natural conclusion, Elvis let out a laughing train whistle "whooo-hoooo", sounding for all the world like Howlin' Wolf or a reborn Jimmie Rodgers, the singing brakeman himself, yodelling off into the setting sun.

To the casual bystander it would all have appeared so easy and so effortless. But it had taken twelve months of graft and dedication to reach this point. Years later, Sam recalled this session and declared "Mystery Train" to be "a fucking masterpiece."

He was not wrong.

A Boy from Tupelo, Ernst Mikael Jørgensen
Last Train to Memphis: The Rise of Elvis Presley, Peter Guralnick
Sam Phillips: The Man Who Invented Rock 'n' Roll, Peter Guralnick

The first RCA offer

FRIDAY 22ND JULY 1955
MEMPHIS, TENNESSEE

THE THRILL OF YESTERDAY'S SESSION was still fresh in Sam's mind and he'd already chosen "Mystery Train" and "I Forgot to Remember to Forget" as the next single. He owned the publishing on both, and was listed as co-writer on the first: if Elvis could maintain his trajectory, maybe there was some light at the end of Sun's long dark tunnel of debt.

Whilst it was generally good news that "Baby, Let's Play House" had hit the national hillbilly chart, Sam was having to pay upfront to have these records pressed, but the dealers and shops were not quick to send in their cheques. As such, Elvis' increased success was actually making Sam's life even more difficult and stressful.

Added to which, he was still being bothered by folks wanting to buy Elvis' contract, which was still very definitely not for sale. Hank Snow and Tom Parker (who was now more desperate than he'd ever been) had tabled an offer themselves, suggesting a straight buyout for $10,000. How serious this was is anyone's guess. Perhaps Parker was simply trying to goad Steve Sholes into action.

If this was the case, then it proved successful because later that day RCA (now comforted by Jean Aberbach's assurances) came up with a couple of ideas based around the idea of a bid of $20,000. But it wasn't quite that simple. RCA weren't actually intending to pay anything at all for Elvis' contract. Yes, they would give Sam the cheque, but they would then deduct the money from Elvis' royalty payments for as long as it took to clear the books.

In effect, Elvis would be buying his own contract: RCA would just be forwarding the money on his behalf. Not that it mattered, of course, because Sam Phillips still wasn't selling the damn contract.

Tom Parker resolved to give Jean Aberbach another call soon. He felt he was getting nowhere and the growing sense of frustration was suffocating. The best chance of a step forward now rested with the boy himself. Tomorrow, Elvis would be playing again at the *Big D Jamboree*, and then on Monday he'd be back in Florida, Parker's home territory. And if anyone could persuade the boy to make a move it would be Mae Boren Axton.

A Boy from Tupelo, Ernst Mikael Jørgensen
Restless Giant: The Life and Times of Jean Aberbach & Hill and Range Songs, Bar Biszick-Lockwood

"Ain't That a Shame"

JULY & AUGUST 1955
THE POP CHART

INSTANT COVER VERSIONS were still the record producer's best friend. For every hit record released you could bet your boots there'd be half-a-dozen carbon copies or other-genred versions in the shops within a week. Generally, this was done in the fair name of capitalism and competition, but there were times when labels could certainly be perceived as exploiting the racial situation.

The most notorious example of this concerned the song "Ain't That a Shame", recorded and co-written by the ever-reliable Fats Domino, and issued on the Imperial label (5348) in the early summer of 1955. It was sexy, catchy and commercial and started selling heavily in the black markets, hitting the peak of the R&B chart and number ten on the pop listing.

Dot Records realised that neither Imperial nor Domino had the profile to top the national pop chart, so they rushed out a cover version (45-15377) by a new fellow they'd signed from Murray Nash's Republic Records. His name was Pat Boone, and he just happened to be white.

So the story goes, Pat objected to the grammatically incorrect title and wanted to rename his version "Isn't That a Shame", and that kind of clapping-on-the-beat sensibility can be heard throughout every second of his misconceived cover version. Fats was always perfectly behind the rhythm of the song, especially the gloriously staggered opening, giving it a lazy and sassy feel, whereas Pat's seemed more like a military march.

It was a sad indictment of the American pop industry when Pat Boone replaced Bill Haley at the top of the pop chart in the summer of '55, leaving Domino's original for dust saleswise (although Fats was very grateful for his writer's royalties, that's for sure). Thankfully, history and posterity chose Fats' single as the classic and Boone's cover was consigned to the bargain bins and second-hand shops.

Over at Republic — where they were kicking themselves for letting Boone go — they quickly repackaged a couple of his earlier recordings and rushed them out as a single, hoping to cash in on the nation's new favourite singer. The record flopped. Ain't *that* a shame.

A change of plan, I

LATE JULY 1955
NASHVILLE, TENNESSEE

Rumours had been flying around for a while, but towards the end of July it was officially confirmed: the proposed dates for the fourth c&w deejay convention and WSM weekend in Nashville had been changed. The original plan had been for the gathering to take place as usual in mid-November but, to guarantee better media coverage, the entire package had been brought forward by a week.

This caused some upset in the hillbilly community as many performers had already made bookings for shows during this period. Red Foley and Wanda Jackson, for instance, were among those who were now faced with the choice of missing the convention or cancelling a fee-paying gig.

Mae Boren Axton noted the change but didn't make too much fuss about it. Unbeknownst to anyone, she was already quietly planning to scale back her activities starting in the autumn. It was possible she might not even attend the convention, hoping to stay closer to home and certainly intending to avoid time away from Jacksonville. In an ideal world it would have been easier if she had a house in Florida (her home) and another in Tennessee (the home of country music), but the world was currently not ideal, nor was the state of her bank account.

But there was something about the new dates that registered in the back of her mind … Thursday 10th until Saturday 12th November? Oh, yes. It would be her dad's birthday on the Saturday.

Billboard, 30th July & 12th November 1955

Back in Florida

MONDAY 25TH JULY 1955
FORT MYERS, FLORIDA

THE SECOND FLORIDA TOUR was due to run for one week and, although this was a Hank Snow Attractions production, Hank himself would not appear as he would be spearheading a separate set of gigs elsewhere. But as co-promoter, with Tom Parker, he'd still be picking up a hefty pay cheque from this series of concerts.

Actually, he *assumed* he'd be receiving a hefty pay cheque because he'd let the Colonel take care of all the money from this new venture. When he'd recently asked for a set of accounts for the previous visit to Florida, he was presented with a crude hand-written page, and Hank wasn't entirely convinced about some of the surprisingly low receipts, but he hadn't had time to look into it properly.

Popular comedian, Andy Griffith, headlined this new Florida tour, but he knew he'd be the butt of the joke if he attempted to follow the Presley boy on stage. He'd already been given the heads up on this, so insisted Elvis should close the show. Other performers who had signed on included the Colonel's friend, Marty Robbins, Mae's pal, Glenn Reeves, and Hank's son, Jimmie. It really was a family affair.

The reaction to Elvis at every show was overwhelming and the audience threatened to spill over with every manic and driven performance. Mae was unable to follow the tour this time — perhaps she was focusing more attention on her employer, Hank Snow, after he complained to Tom Parker about her recent travelling expenses — but she still oversaw all publicity with her customary finesse and attention to detail. And she had her lines perfectly rehearsed ready for Thursday and Friday when Elvis was due to play three shows in her home town.

Meanwhile, over in Daytona Beach, about a ninety-minute drive south of Jacksonville, Mr and Mrs Buddy Killen and their four companions were checking in at the Mello Club, ready to enjoy a few weeks of fun in the sun.

A Boy from Tupelo, Ernst Mikael Jørgensen

The interview, II

THURSDAY 28TH JULY 1955
JACKSONVILLE, FLORIDA

JUBILANT WITH THE KNOWLEDGE that "Baby, Let's Play House" was about to hit *Billboard*'s c&w top ten, Elvis blew into Jacksonville on the last Thursday in July for what would turn out to be another riot-inducing set of shows. Mae greeted him like a long-lost son and they caught up with each other's news, she bringing the conversation back again and again to the Colonel's suitability as a manager and Sun's inadequacy as a record label.

Always wearing her PR hat, she requested a recorded interview for local radio and Elvis, who really didn't care too much for the whole interrogation process, agreed because he knew it would make her happy.

Tape machine running, she rattled on in her best let's-not-stop-for-breath style and drilled question after question at her reluctant participant, who answered politely and without fault until, that is, the conversation turned to the various parts of the country in which he was well known.

Elvis complained this wasn't straightforward because "I'm with a small company, and my records don't have the distribution they should have," at which point Mae leapt in and dragged the chat in a different and more diplomatic direction.

But Elvis' faux pas was an interesting glimpse into what was going through his head at this time. He had always stood firmly by Mr Phillips and by Sun Records. But having been told so many times by the likes of Hank Snow, Bob Neal and Tommy Sands that Sun was holding him back, perhaps Elvis was now beginning to believe it.

Indeed, one might even say that Elvis' very words were those offered by Mae herself during their pre-interview catch-up. Was that why she jumped in so speedily? Had he proven too quick a study?

Okay, so let's tick the box marked "Get the boy thinking about leaving Sun Records". Now, Mae, what else was on the checklist? Oh, yes, the thing about finding a big-time manager.

A Boy from Tupelo, Ernst Mikael Jørgensen

Friday (mid-afternoon)

FRIDAY 29TH JULY 1955
JACKSONVILLE, FLORIDA

KEEPING A DISCREET DISTANCE, Tom Parker followed the Florida tour when Mae couldn't. Not wanting to appear to be on Elvis' trail too much, he popped up from time to time, having his picture taken with Andy Griffith, or perhaps slipping Elvis a $50 note to congratulate him on a dynamic performance.

The tour was due to hit Daytona Beach on Saturday and would conclude on Sunday in Tampa. After that, Elvis would immediately start another run of gigs in Texas.

The week was running like clockwork and Parker's attentions turned once again to the bigger picture. He'd had no word from Jean Aberbach since early July, so decided to place a call to New York and suggest meeting up with the publisher to devise a way to break the RCA deadlock.

It was perhaps mid-afternoon on the Friday when Parker rang Jean from his hotel room. They exchanged pleasantries and Parker requested a dinner appointment for Tuesday. But Jean replied he would be unavailable until Thursday because he was flying out to their California office on Sunday to check over the details for the forthcoming Elvis Presley songbook.

There was an ominous silence from the Florida end of the conversation. Parker struggled to maintain his composure as he repeated the words back: "Elvis Presley songbook?"

"Yes, we're running it through Bob Neal and Sam Phillips," replied Aberbach, sensing Parker's silent fury.

Parker cleared his throat and continued, "Yes, let's meet on Thursday; that will be fine."

The Colonel replaced the receiver and sat quite still for several moments. It wasn't even the thought of the lost money-making opportunity that offended him. It was the absolute lack of respect on the part of Aberbach in not even *informing* him about a songbook, let alone inviting him to the deal-making table, that truly stuck in his throat.

How were decisions of this importance being made without his inclusion? This would have been an ideal opportunity for the Aberbachs to have brought him into the inner circle — to have declared that in their opinion Tom Parker was a player in the Elvis situation — but they'd left him out in the cold.

Part of him wanted to cut off the brothers immediately, but the Colonel was canny enough to know he couldn't proceed without Hill & Range. Steve Sholes valued them highly and there'd be no RCA deal without the Aberbachs. There was little point in him losing his temper. There were better ways to express his displeasure with Jean, whom Tom felt was beginning to take certain things a little too much for granted. He wanted to hit Hill & Range where it hurt. And there was nothing the brothers cared more about than songs.

Knowing Mae would already be in attendance, Parker felt able to skip Elvis' final Jacksonville concert and instead lit a cigar and paced the floor for an hour. By the time the show was over and Elvis was en route to Daytona Beach, the Colonel had devised his plan of revenge on the Aberbachs. It was a slow strategy — one that might take several weeks or even months to bear fruit — but, if it worked out, that was so much the better.

Firstly, he had to get the boy's signature — and also those of his parents — on a proper contract that would give him some influence over future events. This would remove the danger of his being ignored during any further negotiations.

Secondly, he would need a reliable songwriter; one who would trust his word implicitly. He required a songwriter with whom he could share some — but not all — of his plan. Someone who could write a hit record for Elvis Presley and ensure *Hill & Range would never take the publishing*, while Tom himself still received his cut.

And he knew just who to ring.

Friday (late evening)

FRIDAY 29TH JULY 1955
3239 DELLWOOD AVENUE, JACKSONVILLE, FLORIDA

SHE'D ONLY JUST FLOPPED DOWN on the sofa when the phone rang. The Colonel's voice came firmly through the receiver: he hoped all had gone well with the show tonight, and he was sure Mae had done a great job looking after the boy. He'd like to visit tomorrow morning, perhaps about 10:00 AM. He didn't ask if it was convenient, nor did he apologise that he'd be interrupting her weekend. That wasn't how the Colonel did things. She said that would be fine, but she did probably wonder if something was wrong. The Colonel didn't visit: he usually summoned.

Mae hung up. The three men in her life were already in bed and she was keen to turn in too. Then the phone rang again.

A familiar voice spoke, "Hi, Mae, guess who this is?"

She guessed correctly. It was Buddy Killen, whom she hadn't seen in months, calling from Daytona Beach of all places. He was sorry to ring so late, but explained why he was in Florida, and said he'd love to drive over to have lunch with her tomorrow.

Well, Mae always enjoyed Buddy's company and it had been so long since they'd had a chance to catch up, so she readily agreed. Buddy would arrive at about noon — presumably the Colonel would be gone by then — and they'd have time to enjoy a leisurely lunch before he needed to drive back over for his duties at the Mello Club.

She had planned on a quiet family weekend but, thankfully, husband John would be at home so he could look after the boys.

Mae was exhausted and felt she needed a break. And that's exactly what she was about to receive.

Country Singers As I Know 'Em, Mae Boren Axton

Saturday (morning)

SATURDAY 30TH JULY 1955
3239 DELLWOOD AVENUE, JACKSONVILLE, FLORIDA

HE WAS PROMPT, NATURALLY. Mae opened the door at 10:00 AM and there stood the Colonel. He seemed unusually happy, asking after her family and graciously accepting a steaming cup of strong coffee. Eventually, he sat down and cut to the chase.

He complimented Mae on her handling of the Presley boy, and she responded honestly that it had been a pleasure, which indeed it had — she genuinely liked Elvis and truly did believe he'd be better off with RCA and with the Colonel. Indeed, she had told nothing but the truth in all her dealings with Elvis.

Tom confessed he had his worries about the future because the boy was naive and could be so easily led astray. Just imagine, he hypothesised, if we do get him all the way to RCA (having invested so heavily in him) and he bumps into some random songwriter before we've had a chance to sign him up with Hill & Range.

Just think about it — he's such a good-hearted kid he might record that guy's song for RCA and not even think about the publishing. And what would we get out of it? Nothing. We'd have put in all the hard work and someone else would reap the rewards. The important thing was to protect the boy and keep everything "in the family", so to speak.

Mae agreed that Elvis was indeed an innocent soul and Tom's scenario was not too far-fetched. Parker said it was crucial the boy did not feel he was being managed "creatively", as it were: he shouldn't feel restrained or that he was being manipulated in terms of choosing songs.

What they really needed, continued Tom, was a good songwriter who knew the value of loyalty, someone who was already part of the team. They needed someone who could write a song for Elvis: someone, in fact, like Mae. Not to put too fine a point on it, Tom wanted Mae to write a song specifically for Elvis. And not just any song — it had to be his *first* record for RCA Victor.

Well, Mae almost slipped off the sofa at that point, and checked that she'd heard Tom correctly. He calmly clarified: if all goes according to plan, Elvis will sign with RCA and we want to ensure he has the right song to record in case Hill & Range isn't ready at that time. Let's not allow anyone to take from us what is rightfully ours. Mae had already written several songs, Tom knew that.

Mae raised three obvious concerns: What sort of song should I write for Elvis? How will I make sure he accepts it? How do I ensure he chooses it as his first record when he gets to RCA?

Parker brusquely noted that the first two problems were hers to solve, but as for the third, she should simply do what songwriters had done for decades: offer him a writer's credit if he chooses it as his first RCA single. She understood the implication that if the Colonel was installed as manager by this time he would also take a slice of Elvis' share of this deal.

She repeated her first concern, and he suggested in an offhand fashion that she should write something like his other stuff. Or maybe the type of thing the kids go for. Neither suggestion was of much help to her.

Still bemused, her mind turned to the business end of the situation. She began to understand that this could be a very good deal for her. Even sharing the writers' credit with Elvis, she stood to make a tidy sum if the song entered the pop chart. She voiced her assumption that the song would be going to Hill & Range for publishing but, to her surprise, Parker was adamant that the Aberbachs were not to be involved in the process at any time. Indeed, they shouldn't even know about the song.

In fact, Tom continued, he would welcome her thoughts on a small publishing house which might be hungry for just such a potential hit and would be willing to be … *flexible* … regarding arrangements. Mae — who grasped the subtle insinuation — said she'd give the matter some thought, privately wondering if Murray Nash might go for an under-the-table deal.

Tom brought the meeting to a close with a short speech about how much he liked Mae and how he appreciated all she was doing. She had earned his respect and admiration. She was part of the family. He then told her about the Snowmen's League, his own private little club, into which only his most trusted associates were invited. She was genuinely moved as he spoke, and he made clear to her that she was henceforth to consider herself part of this exclusive and elite League, indeed she was the first ever female member.

He stood by the opened front door, and made ready to leave. With a wink and a nudge, he shook her hand.

"*Welcome to the club.*"

Saturday (lunchtime)

SATURDAY 30TH JULY 1955
3239 DELLWOOD AVENUE, JACKSONVILLE, FLORIDA

WHEN THE DOORBELL RANG AGAIN, just before noon, Mae couldn't think who it might be. And as she opened the door to the grinning figure of Buddy Killen, she realised she'd totally forgotten about his visit, so bemused was she by the Colonel's commission.

They chatted while she prepared lunch and indulged in a little gossip about some of the stars that had crossed their paths. Buddy asked if Mae had worked with Jim Reeves; she hadn't, but had heard he was a fine gentleman with a good voice. Buddy was awfully excited about Jim's latest single release which was published by Tree. Then he talked some about Jack Stapp and about how life in the publishing game was so difficult. He joked with Mae, begging the sometime songwriter to give him a hit record.

She spoke a little about being on the road with Hank Snow, but at no time did she mention the Colonel or Elvis Presley. A thousand thoughts ran through her head, as she tried to maintain a conversation with Buddy while still digesting her meeting with Parker. But as Buddy spoke, a possibility blossomed in Mae's mind.

All too soon, their time together came to an end, and Buddy hugged Mae goodbye, then began his journey back to Daytona Beach in time for his first show. Without hesitation, Mae closed the front door, picked up the telephone and dialled a local number. Tom Parker answered and Mae spoke five words that brought a wide smile to his pudgy face:

"Buddy Killen at Tree Publishing."

Saturday (early evening)

SATURDAY 30TH JULY 1955
THE MELLO CLUB, DAYTONA BEACH, FLORIDA

THE BOYS BROKE INTO A WALTZ as they neared the end of their first set. Dinner would soon be served and Buddy and the Robinson brothers could step down for a couple of hours. The club was more than half full, but even so Buddy recognised Mae Boren Axton the minute she came in through the door. He mouthed a silent "Hello", and she sat at a nearby table and ordered a couple of drinks.

When finished, he moseyed on over, expressing his surprise and delight at seeing her again so soon, just hours after they'd parted. She explained she was here on a job for the Colonel and couldn't resist popping in to see Buddy play. When pressed further about her business, she confessed she was looking after the latest Elvis Presley tour, and he was singing just down the road in Daytona Beach right now. Hey, would Buddy like to go and see Elvis perform? There'd surely be enough time before Buddy's second set. Buddy, who'd heard reports of Elvis' stagecraft, thought this was a great idea, so they jumped into Mae's car and snuck backstage at the Peabody just in time to watch him close the first show.

And Buddy was astonished. He'd not seen Elvis since his one-off appearance at the *Grand Ole Opry* and could hardly believe this was the same guy who was now tearing them up with his wild presentation. With Presley's awe-inspiring show fixed firmly in his mind, Buddy was driven back to the Mello Club by Mae, who explained that the Colonel was trying to fix up a move to RCA Victor for Elvis. He was surely going to be a big star. Buddy, who was still in shock, could do nothing but agree with that assessment.

Mae stayed all through Buddy's second set so they could talk again at the end of the evening. As the club emptied, Mae asked Buddy to tell her more about his publishing company, and he poured out his frustrations while he drained another glass. When his monologue finally lulled she casually mentioned she might have a song for him. She asked whether Tree would be interested in publishing Elvis' first record for RCA? Buddy raised his eyebrows as if to say: Hell, yes — who do I have to murder?

But Mae simply suggested he'd be doing the Colonel a favour by agreeing to this deal. They might speak again about this. Perhaps she could talk to Jack Stapp at some point to … finalise the details?

And Mae took her leave, driving ninety minutes back to Jacksonville, knowing she'd be making an unscheduled two hundred mile journey to Tampa tomorrow morning, to catch up with the last date of the tour. She needed to see Elvis before he left the state, and she wanted to tell him something — she needed to sow a seed.

Most importantly, as ever, it was her intention to be honest with the boy. She would hold fast to the facts as far as was possible, but there were ways of using language which allowed one to project certain parts of the truth while leaving the less desirable elements in the shadows.

Country Singers As I Know 'Em, Mae Boren Axton

Sowing seeds, II

SUNDAY 31ST JULY 1955
THE ARMORY, TAMPA, FLORIDA

He was surprised to see Mae when she arrived backstage before the 2:15 PM show, but Elvis exclaimed how happy he was that she'd made the end of the tour. Elvis introduced Mae to a photographer sent by the Colonel to take pictures while he performed that day. Mae smothered him in charm as she did everyone, and said she was sure his photographs would turn out just fine. They did. In fact one picture subsequently became the definitive image of Elvis the young rebel: head tilted back, mouth open, guitar raised.

But it was not Elvis the rebel Mae had come to see that day: it was Elvis the quiet and respectable young man she sought, and that's who she sat down with between shows to talk about his family and his plans for the future. She reiterated her belief that Elvis should be at RCA, and what he truly required was a good manager like Tom Parker. And Elvis nodded: the Colonel was a fine man, and so too was Bob.

But Mae now added an extra item to her short list of recommendations. The other thing he really needed to make the big time was a song. Not just any song, mind you. He needed the right song: he needed a million-seller; a number one. And then she said the darndest thing that really made Elvis sit up and take notice —

"Now you may think I'm crazy, but I have the strangest feeling — call it a premonition if you like — that one day I'm going to be the person who brings that song to you."

Country Singers As I Know 'Em, Mae Boren Axton

The change in my pocket

MONDAY 1ST AUGUST 1955
TUPELO, MISSISSIPPI

THE FIRST POST-FLORIDA GIG was in, of all places, Tupelo. The crowds flocked to see the hometown boy make his return. Elvis wasn't yet what you'd call famous — he could still walk down the street unmolested — but he was already *someone*. He lunched with a few old school friends and played his first single on the jukebox. He was able to spend freely and order milkshakes without giving thought to the cost, a luxury he'd never known when he'd lived in the small town.

His financial situation was, in fact, definitely on the up. He'd moved his parents out of public housing and into their first proper Memphis home; a two-bedroomed rented house on Lamar. It was not ostentatious (there was no phone — they had to borrow a neighbour's) but in doing this, Elvis made a simple declaration that his parents would share in his good fortune.

Money in general was a hot topic during the summer. Scotty and Bill had been advocating adding a drummer to the band, an easy-going fellow named D.J. (Dominic Joseph) Fontana from the *Hayride*. Elvis agreed but said he couldn't afford to pay all of the expense himself, so his wages were split between the three of them.

It was also near this time that a certain unpleasantness was confronted and dealt with. Although Scotty and Bill were essential to his creativity, it was Elvis who was drawing the crowds and it was Elvis who was selling the records. The original split of 50/25/25 was no longer a reasonable expectation. The Blue Moon Boys would have to move from a percentage-based salary to a regular wage.

As manager, it was Bob's job to deliver the bad news. Scotty and Bill were furious but they bit the bullet and carried on.

This type of development was not unprecedented in the music business. Eddy Arnold's band had, of course, encountered exactly this situation when Tom Parker moved in. Odd then, isn't it, that as the Colonel started to seriously court Elvis — and offer advice to Bob Neal — that history should repeat itself in so ruthless a fashion.

Last Train to Memphis: The Rise of Elvis Presley, Peter Guralnick

The memo

TUESDAY 2ND AUGUST 1955
RYMAN AUDITORIUM, NASHVILLE, TENNESSEE

AT THE VERY TOP OF THE MOUNTAIN AT THE *Grand Ole Opry* was John DeWitt. It was his job to ensure the ship sailed smoothly — and profitably — and also to keep all and sundry in line. He had observed that various staff members were still placing themselves in compromising situations regarding their continued employment at the *Opry*.

And so, to clarify the company's position, DeWitt drafted and circulated a memo which said, in effect, if anyone had outside interests that conflicted with their standing at WSM then they should either leave the *Opry* or resign from said conflicting interest.

Several employees did indeed immediately cash in their chips and confine themselves to WSM exclusively. Jack Stapp — who had just received a very interesting phone call from Buddy Killen — read the memo carefully and considered. He knew he was operating generally in a grey area and, yes, there were moments when he had crossed the line. He had a discreet thing going on with several record labels: he would give their artists guest slots on the *Opry* if they would consider recording Tree songs. He often spoke to Don Law at Columbia, Paul Cohen at Decca; and up at RCA, Jack was on very friendly terms with Steve Sholes. Once again, he read DeWitt's words and weighed up his options.

Jim Denny, however, laughed and threw his copy of the memo directly into the waste paper basket.

Discovering Country Music, Don Cusic
CMA Oral History Project interview with Jack Stapp, 8th August 1972

Friendly persuasion

WEDNESDAY 3RD AUGUST 1955
LITTLE ROCK, ARKANSAS

THE DEBACLE OVER THE SONGBOOK had convinced Parker that he needed to up his game. He had to tie himself to the boy as an advisor in a proper contractual way. It was no longer just about booking gigs: Parker needed leverage.

By now, although Elvis wasn't *entirely* sold on the idea of leaving Sun, he was certain that signing to Jamboree Attractions — while keeping Bob as his manager — would be of great benefit to his career. Parker knew serious people and had real contacts. But the problem lay with his parents, who were required to co-sign because Elvis was still legally a minor.

So, Parker drew up a contract and invited Mr and Mrs Presley to Elvis' gig in Little Rock, intending to woo them backstage, and convince them of his value to their son's progress. Vernon was already sold on the Colonel, even before arriving at the auditorium. But Gladys was sceptical. She couldn't understand how Elvis could be advised by Bob Neal and by the Colonel (as he insisted on calling himself). She knew Bob and she understood Bob. Tom Parker was an unknown quantity and she just couldn't take to him on a personal level.

Realising he was his own worst enemy in this situation, Parker withdrew from the front line and called his reinforcements. The Duke of Paducah (a famous Little Rock local) spoke on behalf of his dear old friend, the Colonel; Hank Snow (a God-fearing genuine hillbilly superstar) offered counsel to the Presleys; Bob Neal himself may have pitched in. But Gladys would not be railroaded. She saw no need to rush.

Parker knew the moment had passed, and stepped in to say that Mrs Presley was quite right and there was no need to move too quickly. Much to Elvis' dismay, the contract remained unsigned. But Parker was nothing if not persistent. He arranged for Gladys and Vernon to receive telegrams, letters and phone calls (via a neighbour) every day from this point forward, reminding them of the Colonel's importance to their son's career.

And then he packed a suitcase and headed to the airport: he was New York-bound.

Last Train to Memphis: The Rise of Elvis Presley, Peter Guralnick

Mae Boren Axton: on my own

A SHORT DIVERSION ON
THE NATURE OF SONGWRITING

ALTHOUGH SHE WAS NO JENNY LOU CARSON, it cannot be denied that Mae Boren Axton was a reasonably prolific songwriter. Adding up all of her published compositions logged in the BMI database today — including those attributed to her husband, John — would give you a number close to one hundred.

Since completing her first proper published effort for Dub Dickerson on 17th March 1954, she'd turned out new songs quite regularly.

Actually, it would be more accurate to say that Mae was a reasonably prolific *co*-writer, because, as the story so far has confirmed, Mrs Axton much preferred writing with a partner, or failing that, she liked to have a title or a theme suggested for her.

If you wanted to take this thought a little further and you looked in greater detail at Mae's published compositions from the 1950s you would find that almost all of her works were written with someone else, be it the designated singer or a fellow songwriter.

There are, in fact, only three solo Mae Boren Axton songs hidden away in the long, long list of co-compositions. One of these is a simple religious narration, but the other two are proper songs and are much more intriguing. Both were copyrighted in the summer of 1956. But both have surprisingly strong connections to the summer of 1955.

That's curious, isn't it?

Tom has his say

THURSDAY 4TH AUGUST 1955
NEW YORK CITY, NEW YORK

IT WAS GOING TO BE AN UNPLEASANT MEETING, Jean Aberbach understood that. Technically, he knew he'd done nothing wrong, but Tom Parker was a man of many moods and he was clearly very upset about being left out of the songbook deal, as Jean had sensed in their telephone conversation the previous Friday.

When the Colonel arrived, he was shown into Jean's office and made his feelings known with great clarity. His voice was raised throughout the entire discussion, and he spat out words like "loyalty" and "integrity". He said he'd be writing to Hill & Range later that day, fully explaining his dissatisfaction at the way in which he'd been treated, and he wanted the letter to be filed in their official records so there'd be no doubt as to his feelings on the matter.

And Jean took it all without complaint. He was confident that Parker still needed him on board to seal any deal between Presley and RCA Victor, so there was little chance of the Colonel issuing any sort of wild ultimatum. It was just a question of letting Parker have his say and then getting on with business as usual.

Actually, Jean Aberbach was having serious doubts as to whether Parker would have any influence at all with regard to Elvis' recording contract, and had already made gentle enquiries along other lines. It was important that Aberbach kept his eye on the main prize, which was Elvis Presley, and not necessarily worry too much about Tom Parker.

But when Parker's ranting finally subsided and he haughtily took his leave from the Hill & Range office, Jean couldn't help but feel he'd gotten away with it quite lightly. He'd been expecting a much bigger scene.

Riding down in the elevator, Parker regained his composure, and smiled once again. Even amidst the hassle and pressure of the Presley situation, he so loved these little games.

Restless Giant: The Life and Times of Jean Aberbach & Hill and Range Songs, Bar Biszick-Lockwood

Seeking inspiration

EARLY AUGUST 1955
3239 DELLWOOD AVENUE, JACKSONVILLE, FLORIDA

THE COLONEL'S GREAT COMMISSION weighed heavily upon Mae's shoulders during early August. She felt sure the task would prove too great, even though she'd already taken the small but crucial step of planting a seed in Elvis' fertile mind. The whole conversation with Tom Parker kept playing over and over in her head. She could still feel his firm handshake, and still hear his closing words: "Welcome to the club."

Of one thing she was sure — if she got this right, she was liable to make a tidy sum. She'd have to share the money with Elvis (and the Colonel) of course, so her best plan of action, financially speaking, was to somehow try to write a song by herself. And this was a daunting challenge. What the heck kind of song was she going to write for Elvis on her own?

She remembered how she and Glenn had written "I Ain't Got Room To Rock" together in the early summer, which had been inspired by Elvis' "Good Rockin' Tonight". What was it the Colonel had said? "Write something like his other stuff. Or maybe the type of thing the kids go for."

Duly inspired, she left the house and headed for the record shop in downtown Jacksonville.

Country Frolics, I

SUMMER 1955
JACKSONVILLE, FLORIDA

TELEVISION WAS SWEEPING THE NATION. Jacksonville had launched its first stations at the beginning of the decade, broadcasting bought-in shows from New York on an evening-only schedule. Within a year or so, as the audience expanded, homegrown programmes were also televised and, inevitably, local media entrepreneur Toby Dowdy (who had invested in WMBR-TV) was involved. His thirty-minute pre-recorded music programme entitled *Country Frolics* was shown each Tuesday from 7:00 PM.

As a member of Smilin' Jack Herring and his Swingbillys, Tommy Durden had landed himself a regular spot as a player and occasional singer on the show. Tommy wasn't exactly a TV star, but it did supplement his income and, being pre-recorded — as were all of WMBR's transmissions — there was no big panic with regard to warm-ups and recordings.

But in the summer of 1955, WMBR readied itself for a significant step forward: live broadcast. And, as you might expect, Dowdy chose his own programme as the first candidate. The show time would shift from Tuesday to prime-time Saturday 6:30 PM, and the first airing was scheduled for 8th October 1955. This meant that Tommy would be required in Jacksonville for rehearsals and live broadcast every Saturday; and so, to avoid any risk of being late, he made advance plans to stay over with his brother, Sam, each Friday night. Samuel B. Durden, a motor mechanic, lived with his wife and son at 2955 Collier Avenue, Jacksonville, by coincidence just a five-minute drive from Mae's house at 3239 Dellwood.

Tommy Durden filmed interview with *Michigan Magazine*, 1991 (available on YouTube)
The Bradford County Telegraph, Florida, 14th September 1951
Fort Pierce News Tribune, Florida, 22nd September 1955

Finding inspiration

EARLY AUGUST 1955
3239 DELLWOOD AVENUE, JACKSONVILLE, FLORIDA

As REQUESTS GO it must have seemed a little odd to the young lady behind the counter. Mae had asked for Elvis Presley's latest record and also a copy of whatever was popular with the kids at the moment. Mae could have listened to her new purchases in one of the booths, but she took the two 45s home so she could study the songs at her leisure, and see where they took her creatively.

Seated at the table where she did much of her writing, near the piano and the record player, she spun both sides of Elvis' fourth Sun single, and recognised the songs from the Florida concerts. She liked "I'm Left, You're Right, She's Gone", but it was "Baby, Let's Play House" that leapt out at her, as it had done for thousands of listeners and purchasers all over the South: she loved that stumbling, half-stuttered opening; the "Come back, baby, come" refrain lodged itself at the front of her head; the descending bass line before each chorus was fascinating; and the giggle during the coda brought a wide smile to her face.

When she slipped on the other 7 inch single, however, she was stunned. She'd bought "Ain't That a Shame", the nation's current favourite song — but by good fortune, the record shop assistant had sold her Fats Domino's vastly superior version. In truth, Mae wasn't hip enough to understand there was a difference, but the opening phrase certainly grabbed her attention, especially when the band punctuated each line with an explosive *Boom Boom!* This was glorious. This was how a pop record should sound. This was how a song should be written.

The B-side — a mid-tempo R&B track called "La-La" — also fascinated her, although it was more about the groove than anything else. Again, it had a striking introduction, a series of seven stabbing piano notes before launching into two minutes of good time boogie woogie.

For the next couple of days, she played these four songs at home whenever she had the chance, absorbing the lyrics and, more importantly, absorbing the *feel.*

Why can't you be true?

SUMMER 1955
CHESS RECORDS, CHICAGO, ILLINOIS

WHILE ELVIS PRESLEY merged white and black music from his side of the racial fence, so too others tried the same trick from theirs. Chuck Berry was a black singer in his late twenties who'd recently signed to Chess Records. He had brought with him his clever rewrite of an old Bob Wills' country hit, "Ida Red", which he eventually dubbed "Maybellene".

The white owners of the label, brothers Phil and Leonard Chess, were smart enough to understand that some records needed a little assistance, so they offered a co-writer's credit to top deejay Alan Freed, knowing he'd then give the song a bigger plug on his popular radio show. The song was released in the summer of 1955 (Chess 1604), and hit number three on the R&B chart, also reaching top ten in the pop listing.

The ever-attentive Marty Robbins recorded his own hillbilly version by the end of August. All's fair in love, war, and the record business.

Writing the song

EARLY AUGUST 1955
3239 DELLWOOD AVENUE, JACKSONVILLE, FLORIDA

HAVING DRIVEN the other three residents of her home crazy by playing the same songs all week, Mae at last found time to sit at the table with her legal notepad and made a determined effort to write her song for Elvis.

She'd already decided on the title: it would be called "Welcome to the Club". That phrase had been dancing around in her head since the weekend and she took it for a good omen. But what did it mean? What was the song about? Well, there were two obvious directions in which she could go: she could follow the literal meaning of the phrase and write about a popular nightspot where folks could dance and have a good time; or, more dramatically, maybe she could focus on a place of gloom and sadness — the sort of venue you'd visit when you had the blues.

It was the second notion that appealed to her, especially as her primary "inspiration" songs tended to embrace the idea of fractured relationships. So she wrote her proposed song title at the top of the sheet, and made notes as she listened again to "Baby, Let's Play House" and "Ain't That A Shame". She copied down the phrase "Come back, baby, come"; she copied down the line "You're the one to blame"; she scribbled a few other lines too, and in the side margin she wrote about the descending bass line and that great *Boom Boom!* opening that had caught her attention.

She liked the structure of Fats' single, but she also liked the exciting rhythm of Elvis' Sun record too. How was she going to squeeze all of this into one song? There was just too much going on.

She tried and she tried, but the song wouldn't come.

Hot August night

FRIDAY 5TH AUGUST 1955
TUCSON, ARIZONA

WITH APPLAUSE RINGING IN HIS EARS, Hank Snow took to the Tucson stage on the first Friday evening in August as part of his latest tour. Tomorrow and Sunday he was booked in at the Hollywood Bowl. The shows would all be well attended and Hank would run through his biggest hits for his adoring audiences. He'd sing "I'm Movin' On" and also his latest RCA release, "I'm Glad I Got to See You Once Again". But even while performing, somewhere in the back of his mind he was mulling over the situation with this Presley kid, and wondering what was going to come of it.

Elvis himself had taken a day's respite from a Texas tour and was again playing Bob Neal's annual Overton Park gig in Memphis, with Wanda Jackson supporting and Johnny Cash sitting at the bottom of the bill. Marion Keisker attended the concert — it was the first time she'd seen Elvis perform since the *Grand Ole Opry* — and she was somewhat distracted by the sound of a woman screaming manically. And then realised it was her.

Hank meanwhile worried a little about Parker's tactics, but he was greatly encouraged by the thought of the money they'd be making if the boy really did hit the big time. And then the good people of Tucson clapped heartily as Hank took yet another bow.

Nearby, in an apartment in the same city, Alvin Krolik put pen to paper and wrote to his mother in Chicago. He told her how he was already feeling at home in Arizona, how he was much more settled within himself. Perhaps he was responding to a letter she'd sent. Maybe she'd written to bring him up to date on all that was happening among his friends and family back in Albany Park. Mothers tend to do that sort of thing. Perhaps she told him about Agnes' marriage.

She received Alvin's letter just a couple of days later, and felt reassured by his optimistic words.

Billboard, 20th August 1955
Chicago Daily Tribune, Illinois, 25th August 1955

Writing the songs

EARLY AUGUST 1955
3239 DELLWOOD AVENUE, JACKSONVILLE, FLORIDA

SUDDENLY, OUT OF NOWHERE, the answer to Mae's problem came to her. She was quite right when she'd thought there was too much going on to fit into one song. And that's because she wasn't writing just one song: she was writing *two*.

Sitting at the table, she tore off two sheets of paper and placed them side by side. At the top of one page she wrote: *"Welcome to the Club" — in the style of "Ain't That A Shame".* And holding her pen atop the other page she paused. The other song didn't even have a name yet.

Looking again at her notes, she sought inspiration. There was that one phrase she liked so much from Fats' song: "You're the one to blame". She kicked around a few ideas based on that line: "It's all your fault"; "I blame you"; "It's all because of you"; and then she hit upon the one she liked, and wrote *"You're The Cause of it All" — in the style of "Baby, Let's Play House".*

From this point on, the songs came fast, and both pages filled with words. "Welcome to the Club" was a slightly clumsy number which copied the arrangement of its template a little too closely, complete with the strident *Boom Boom!* punctuation. The lyrics were over-dramatic, with references to the club being crowded and patrons crying, although the only charge for entry was, apparently, a broken heart. It also couldn't make up its mind whether it was a male or female song; but Mae was pleased.

The real winner, in her eyes, though, was "You're The Cause of it All", which she heard as a barnstorming rock 'n' roll anthem, even though the tune was non-existent, and the words didn't always scan too well. The actual title line jumped randomly from "You *Were* The Cause of it All" to "You *Are* The Cause of it All", but Mae still managed to squeeze in the "Come back, baby" line of which she was so fond. It was this second song that she felt sure would be her ticket to the big time. "Welcome to the Club" had some promise, but it wasn't the sort of track that might interest Elvis.

The next step forward would be a little delicate. She needed a friend to record a couple of demos — one of which had to be done in a distinctive Elvis-type style.

Jean Aberbach's double date

TUESDAY 9TH AUGUST 1955 (AFTERNOON)
NEW YORK CITY, NEW YORK

WITH OR WITHOUT Tom Parker, Jean Aberbach knew that Elvis Presley was an artist worth pursuing and so, beginning on 9th August, he made moves to secure Hill & Range's position.

In his personal daybook for that date he wrote the words "Elvis Pressley" (*sic*) and, just above, he listed the names of Jerry Leiber and Mike Stoller, the renowned composers of "Hound Dog". If Jean was going to chase after a young hillbilly who could also sing the blues then he'd need suitable songs from talented writers, and this was the day he started to make long-term plans.

Jerry and Mike were no pushovers when it came to their own music and creativity, but by the end of September Jean had cajoled them into signing with Atlantic Records as independent producers and, crucially, they merged their publishing with Progressive, thus ensuring that, as fifty percent partners, the Aberbachs received fair recompense for their part in the deal. But more importantly, Jean had established a definite connection between Leiber and Stoller and Hill & Range.

One step at a time, the pieces were moving into place on the giant chessboard in Jean Aberbach's head. At some undetermined point in the future, he intended to link the singer and the songwriters to everyone's mutual benefit.

But especially his.

Restless Giant: The Life and Times of Jean Aberbach & Hill and Range Songs, Bar Biszick-Lockwood

Bob Luman: on the road to Damascus

TUESDAY 9TH AUGUST 1955 (EVENING)
KILGORE, TEXAS

Bob Luman was a tall good-looking boy who liked to sing country songs and loved to play baseball. He sang plain hillbilly music in a small band, and he felt sure that if he put his mind to it he could make it his career. But it was baseball that really held his heart and, now that he was out of school, he had secured a try-out with the Pittsburgh Pirates in the forthcoming spring trials, and news of this had made him a small-time local celebrity — he was the boy from Kilgore who was going to play ball for the Pirates!

Shooting the breeze with his best girl on a hot summer afternoon, they bumped into a friend who told them in a gabbled rush that she'd seen the most amazing singer last night over in Tyler. His name was Elvis Presley — or something like that — and he was on a week-long tour of these parts and was just the best thing she'd ever seen. She could hardly get the words out fast enough and Bob could see how excited she was: something deep down inside him knew he had to go see this Elvis Presley guy for himself.

So, that same evening, Bob and his girl drove over to the next scheduled show in nearby Henderson. They bought tickets and sat in the front row, determined to see what the fuss was all about. Tour promoter and local deejay, Tom Perryman, saw Bob and recognised him as that baseball kid, noting it was unusual to see a boy sitting in the female-only front row.

The lights dimmed and the show started. Elvis came out and changed Bob's life forever in the space of half-a-dozen songs. Bob followed Elvis all week, attending each gig, soaking up every nuance and move, ending up in his home town of Kilgore on the Friday. Bob got talking to Perryman after the show, and the deejay was surprised to learn the boy also played in a band.

"What sort of stuff do you play, son?" asked Perryman, always keen to keep up with local groups. Bob hesitated and looked back at the empty stage where the messiah had stood not twenty minutes previously.

"We're going to play just like Elvis."

Bright Lights and Country Music: The Nashville Sound, Paul Hemphill

Moving on up

MONDAY 15TH AUGUST 1955
MEMPHIS, TENNESSEE

THE BARRAGE OF PHONE CALLS and telegrams finally wore down Gladys Presley's resistance. As Elvis returned home on 15th August for a five-day break, a meeting was called and the contract was signed. Bob Neal continued as manager but Tom Parker was officially taken on as a "Special Advisor" for Elvis, and was given authority to negotiate renewals on existing contracts, a small but key step forward in his quest.

Parker wrote to Hill & Range almost immediately, telling them of his rise in status. He would not allow himself to be excluded from any further discussions regarding Elvis Presley's rapidly developing career.

The "Special Advisor" contract was somewhat vague in terms of Parker's duties, but it did contain a crucial phrase, listing the party of the second part as being "Col. Thomas A. Parker and/or Hank Snow Attractions". It's the "and/or" section you might wish to ponder and remember.

Also signing contracts was Lou Cowan who was given an open assignment to repair ailing programmes and come up with new ideas for CBS-TV. He was awarded carte blanche with regard to creativity and production. His triumph with *The $64,000 Dollar Question* had marked him as the man with the golden touch, and CBS was keen to exploit his talent to the fullest.

When reported in *Billboard*, it was noted that the very popular Mr Cowan had previously had ties to RCA, and one wonders if he had ever had cause to bump into our friend the Colonel who, for the previous decade, had been well known at that company? Either way, *Billboard* suggested Cowan stood to make $1,000,000 over the next five years at CBS.

And while all of this was going on, Elvis' fifth single "Mystery Train"/ "I Forgot to Remember to Forget" (Sun 223) was released. With his previous record still hanging around in the hillbilly top ten, this could be perceived as a rash move: there were still plenty of sales yet to be garnered from "Baby, Let's Play House". Sam Phillips understood this, of course, but he released the new pairing so quickly for one simple and beautiful reason: the songs were so damn good he couldn't wait another moment to share them with the rest of the world.

A Boy from Tupelo, Ernst Mikael Jørgensen
Sam Phillips: The Man Who Invented Rock 'n' Roll, Peter Guralnick
Billboard, 13th August 1955

East on Highway 10

MID-AUGUST 1955
TUCSON, ARIZONA

THERE ARE THINGS THAT PEOPLE DO that seem to make no sense, no matter how many times you look at the facts. Alvin Krolik, as far as is known, had been on the straight and narrow for over a year. He'd done honest work, and associated with good people. He was attempting to put down roots in Tucson, a city where he was totally anonymous, and which afforded him the chance to start afresh.

So why, having assured his mother that all was well in his life, did Alvin spend $55 on a holster and a .38 calibre snub-nosed revolver? To compound the mystery, a day or two later, he started a journey due east on Highway 10. In his hand luggage he was carrying the gun.

Geographically speaking, if there was a logical place to be travelling to, it was the next major city, El Paso, Texas, just over three hundred miles away.

When rain falls in El Paso it makes the front page news, that's how rare it is. In mid-August 1955, storm clouds were gathering along Highway 10.

El Paso Herald-Post, Texas, 25th August 1955
Time Magazine, 5th September 1955

Making demos, I

MID-AUGUST 1955
RADIO WPDQ, JACKSONVILLE, FLORIDA

THEIR FRIENDSHIP WENT BACK to the turn of the decade and that's why Mae felt a little anxious about approaching Glenn Reeves. In a more straightforward world she'd have invited Glenn into the writing process, but she'd taken the entirely understandable decision to work on her Elvis song alone. And now she was imposing upon the deejay by asking him to cut demos of her solo compositions.

When it came down to it, Mae just felt embarrassed by her selfish action. She confessed to Glenn she'd been writing solo for Elvis and, if he would oblige by singing a couple of Elvis-style demos, she would gladly add his name as a co-writer. But Glenn, a good friend and a very gracious person, wouldn't hear of it: he was happy for Mae to have her shot at the big time.

In fact, Glenn himself was feeling pretty optimistic about his own career. Just last week he'd been the guest of honour at a special luncheon for Jacksonville c&w deejays, hosted by Murray Nash Associates. Added to which, he'd also just signed to Murray's Republic Records (TNT could afford to invest no more time and money in Glenn). Did Mae — who was very close to Murray — have a hand in this? Who knows, but it likely added to Glenn's willingness to oblige.

He taped both songs at radio WPDQ with his own guitar accompaniment. Despite having a good sense of rhythm, he ended up singing "Welcome to the Club" like Pat Boone rather than Fats Domino. It definitely felt like a woman's song to Glenn, and he struggled a little to find a sense of direction.

But he had great fun with "You're The Cause of It All", bringing out his best Elvis voice, as per his writing session for "I Ain't Got Room to Rock" earlier in the summer. Mae explained about the descending bass run and Glenn added that to the opening, mimicking the instrument as best he could on his acoustic guitar.

As the taping finished, Glenn told Mae that Murray had scheduled his own first Republic recording session for October so he'd be looking for a new song for himself. Would Mae be interested in meeting up sometime soon so they could write it? Mae said that'd be fine and would book a date for September in her diary.

All in all, Mae was delighted. She had a song for Elvis and a song to spare. It was now a matter of dubbing them to acetate disks, waiting until the Colonel confirmed that the RCA deal was going ahead, and then determining the precise moment to speak to Elvis. Mae was convinced that Elvis would love "You're The Cause of It All", and felt sure he would choose it as his first RCA single, especially if she offered him a financial cut.

She slept well that night and, the following morning, placed two important phone calls — one to her father in Oklahoma and one to Hank Snow — that signalled the beginning of a whole new chapter in her life.

Billboard, 6th August 1955

Men with broken hearts

MID-AUGUST 1955
TEXAS

THE LONE STAR STATE was as good a place as any to head to when loneliness was your state of mind. During Elvis' August break, he and Dixie finally ended their eighteen-month romance. They'd already parted and reunited several times during the summer but it was Dixie who eventually called time and it broke both of their hearts. They wept and hugged, and resolved to remain friends.

Elvis, of course, was never short of female company, but the loss of Dixie hurt him deeply. In later years, he would suggest he'd only "thought" he was in love during this time. But how does one attain that level of emotional separation? The answer is that one doesn't. Dixie loved Elvis and he was equally smitten. With Scotty and Bill in tow, Elvis packed his case and headed for Texas via Shreveport for yet more shows, fully focused on his expanding career.

Tommy Durden, another broken-hearted lover, was also likely bound for the twenty-eighth state that week. His new TV show, *Country Frolics*, would start in October and his Saturday night opportunities for making money would then be curtailed. He had played Texas often over the years and, when not sitting in with the Swingbillys, he still hit various towns and cities looking for solo bookings. He preferred to be busy; it kept his mind off Boots. There had been no one for him since the divorce, and though he appeared to carry his pain lightly, those who knew him best sensed his hurt.

Alvin Krolik, who wore his grief like an overcoat, had already crossed the Arizona state line and was headed east into Texas. The dark clouds that had shadowed his journey, blackened and wept as he arrived in a town on the Mexican border.

Standing at the crossroads

SATURDAY 20TH AUGUST 1955
BUSY BEE LIQUOR STORE, 3728 ALAMEDA AVENUE, EL PASO, TEXAS

THE SHOP CLOCK TICKED ON TO 6:35 PM. It was raining in El Paso. Pinney didn't like the rain; it kept the customers away. He strolled over to the window and peered out as the drops raced down to the sill.

Sitting in the doorway to the living quarters was his daughter, Frances. It was one of her favourite places in the world. She was hidden from the shop but could hear her daddy's comforting voice whenever he served the locals. Her mother and brother were out back, and Frances was vaguely aware of their quiet conversation.

Standing out of sight just around the corner, at the crossroads of Alameda and North Latta, was a well-built six-footer who'd been in town for a day or so, and was doing his best to blend into the scenery. The young man wore a black T-shirt and khaki trousers. His red and green golfer's cap offered little protection against the drizzle. The rain-drenched pavement had soaked through the soles of his soft yellow moccasins. He was dressed for comfort and not the weather.

In one pocket he carried fifteen cents and a Marine Corps identity card bearing his name and index finger print. In the other pocket was a $55 pistol. He glanced up and down the avenue. There were no pedestrians and cars passed by infrequently. The liquor shop, an easy target, was empty.

Having robbed several such establishments before, he knew it would be quick and painless. He would quietly walk in, then produce the gun and start shouting. The startled shopkeeper would be flustered and would open the till. He would take the money and disappear.

Alvin Krolik looked at his watch. It was 6:37 PM. This would all be over and done by 6:40.

Pinney was standing behind the till when Alvin opened the shop door, instantly noting this was a man to be taken seriously — someone who carried himself well and had received military training. Placing his hands on the counter, Pinney enquired how he might be of help. Krolik pointed to the shelf behind the shopkeeper, saying he'd like a bottle of whiskey.

Pinney turned, took the bottle and as he swung back around he found himself looking at the wrong end of a .38 calibre snub-nosed revolver.

"Give me all the green money!" Krolik shouted and, secreted in the doorway, Frances Pinney stopped playing and froze. But she'd heard raised voices in the shop before and knew her daddy would deal with it.

Never shifting his gaze from the gunman, Delta Pinney calmly put down the bottle, and edged to his right towards the till. He slowly removed the money and deliberately laid the notes out on the counter. He took half a pace backwards and said, "Help yourself."

Krolik lowered the pistol, blinked and reached out with his left hand. This was the small opportunity for which Pinney had been waiting. He dropped low, and quickly grabbed a loaded revolver from under the till. Standing tall, he shot four times and Krolik fired back before going down hard, the pistol landing nearby.

As Krolik writhed on the floor, Pinney was convinced he was reaching for his dropped weapon and, knowing the robber was a man who could handle himself, he pulled out another revolver and fired a further five shots.

Frances Pinney, hidden from view, had been aware of two things that happened very quickly: a loud popping sound just above her head, and the arms of her mother pulling her away from the door, taking her into the living quarters. But Frances would not be kept apart from her daddy and ran back into the shop. As she passed through the doorway, she noticed an assailant's bullet lodged in the frame just above where she had been sitting.

She found her father standing in front of the counter, cradling one hand. A pool of blood was rapidly expanding around the body of the man lying face down on the floor. Krolik's pistol lay near his feet. It wasn't the sight of the dead body that struck Frances the most, but the smell of the blood which would remain in her memory forever.

Pinney hugged his daughter to him with his good hand, while his wife phoned the police and went to fetch the mop and bucket.

The shop clock ticked on to 6:40 PM.

El Paso Herald-Post, Texas, 25th August 1955
Time Magazine, 5th September 1955

The morning after the night before

SUNDAY 21ST AUGUST 1955
EL PASO, TEXAS

THE BODY WAS MOVED to nearby Martin Mortuary, and attempts were made to trace and contact Alvin Krolik's family — his identity was established via his Marine card — but no reply was forthcoming from Illinois. The police took a statement from Pinney, and quickly concluded this was another justifiable defence of life and property. Nevertheless, a report would have to be filed and presented to District Attorney William Clayton.

As newsworthy incidents go, this was no earth-shaking event. The *Ogden Standard-Examiner*, Utah, carried a small report inside their Sunday morning edition; five short paragraphs that named Krolik and Pinney. The article highlighted Pinney's long-standing protection of his store.

Looking for an interesting angle, the reporter chose the obvious one: Alvin was just another notch on Pinney's gun.

El Paso Herald-Post, Texas, 22nd August 1955
Ogden Standard-Examiner, Utah, 21st August 1955

Open for business as usual

MONDAY 22ND AUGUST 1955
BUSY BEE LIQUOR STORE, ALAMEDA AVENUE, EL PASO, TEXAS

THE PHONE CALL CAME early in the morning. Pinney answered as he was preparing to open the shop, and was slightly taken aback when the anonymous caller declared that he was nothing but a "bloodthirsty tough". Delta gave no answer but firmly replaced the receiver and carried on about his business.

As he unlocked the shop door a man from the *El Paso Herald-Post* slipped in and enquired if he could ask a few questions and maybe take a photograph. Pinney had no desire for publicity but realised this situation was inevitable. The *Herald-Post* had covered his previous incidents fairly and without hysteria, so he agreed to a short interview.

"I had to kill him, or he might have killed me. When a man comes in and 'throws' a gun on you, he's serious and he's going to get you if you make a wrong move — if you don't get him: I got him. I don't know why I kept shooting after he went down, except he kept wriggling, like he was going to get his gun. I wanted to make sure he didn't get it. I don't know what anyone would want a man to do when a guy comes in with a gun and attempts to stick him up."

Referring to the earlier phone call, Pinney said, "I'm not tough and I'm not bloodthirsty, but I'm going to protect my family, myself and my property. I know this: when a man comes into my store and pulls a gun on me — I'm going to get him if I can."

A photograph was taken with Pinney leaning against his till. The reporter spoke to the neighbouring businesses looking for a good quote, then returned to his office to file copy for that day's edition. It was no big story: it made page nine, headlined *'Had to Kill Him,' Says Slayer of Bandit.* But there was something about the name "Krolik" that stuck in the reporter's head, and he decided to make further enquiries.

Later that day in Chicago, police finally made contact with Harry and Edith Krolik, and broke the worst kind of news that any parent could hear. Distraught, they immediately made arrangements to bring their boy home.

El Paso Herald-Post, Texas, 21st August 1955

I read the news today

THURSDAY 25TH AUGUST 1955
EL PASO, TEXAS

THE KEEN-EYED NEWSPAPER REPORTER did a good job of back tracking through Alvin's life, and eventually uncovered the report of his previous brush with the law back in 1953. This now gave Saturday's incident a much greater human interest element, and the editor of the *El Paso Herald-Post* decided to run the follow-up article on the front page of the Friday edition, the day before Alvin's funeral. The piece was copied in various periodicals throughout the country and *Time* magazine also ran a short essay.

But none captured the story as well as the *El Paso Herald-Post*. The report filled the bottom left corner of the cover page and merited two columns, although there was no picture. The writer had clearly read a few too many cheap crime novels and opened with the line, "Funeral services for a young artist will be held in Chicago tomorrow. The artist was never very successful, but he showed promise. His promise ended Saturday night when he tried to hold up an El Paso liquor store and was shot to death."

Mention was made of Alvin's recent history: his failed marriage; his crime spree; and his unpublished autobiography, including the short speech he'd made to reporters in Chicago. And it was from this monologue that the editor fashioned his eye-catching headline:

Killing Ends Heartache — 'Story of Person Who Walked Lonely Street'

And Tommy Durden, no stranger to Texas and no stranger to heartache and loneliness, somehow, somewhere, picked up this newspaper and instantly empathised with the tragic story of Alvin Krolik.

El Paso Herald-Post, Texas, 25th August 1955

Showmen's Rest

FRIDAY 26TH AUGUST 1955
WOODLAWN CEMETERY, CHICAGO, ILLINOIS

ALVIN'S BODY had been transferred from El Paso to the Weinstein Chapel in Chicago, a fifteen minute drive from his parents' home. It was a quiet and dignified funeral home, favoured by the city's Jewish community.

At 3:00 PM on the Friday, Harry and Edith, bid a final goodbye to their troubled son. Without question, they'd have held themselves responsible for his death. Their minds would be filled with missed opportunities and unspoken words. The death of a child is an unimaginable trauma, and they would carry their grief all their days.

The mourners then drove thirty minutes to Woodlawn Cemetery where Alvin was laid to rest, a space also being reserved either side for his inconsolable parents. The tombstone carried a beautiful photographic portrait of Alvin, and the inscription in English and Hebrew was simple and heartfelt — *Alvin Bert Krolik: Beloved Son.*

Harry and Edith made their way out of the green and peaceful cemetery on that hot afternoon, and passed by five white statues of elephants with their trunks lowered in mourning. Alvin's final resting place was but a short distance from Showmen's Rest; the graveyard of the men with the painted faces.

Chicago Daily Tribune, Illinois, 26th August 1955

The yellow Cadillac

FRIDAY 2ND & SATURDAY 3RD SEPTEMBER 1955
TEXARKANA, ARKANSAS

THEY'D ALREADY SCRAPPED two cars during their non-stop touring, and at the beginning of September, Elvis, Scotty and Bill wrote-off their pink Cadillac on the way to Texarkana following a disagreement with a truck. Life on the road wasn't just tiring; it was also dangerous, as many performers could testify. The trio limped into town that night and performed in their travelling clothes. Elvis borrowed Charline Arthur's guitar but delivered yet another stunning performance.

Presley was picking up songs wherever he could find them, performing not only his own records but hits like "Rock Around The Clock", "Shake, Rattle and Roll", "Maybellene" and "Only You", which was a favourite. He loved the way Tony Williams played with the words, singing, "Only you can-*d*-make-*a*-this world seem right." On paper, the pronunciation made little sense, but to hear it sung thus was thrilling, and Elvis milked it for all it was worth, wishing he had a gospel group behind him.

Buying fresh transportation (a nearly-new yellow Cadillac) they headed on to Dallas for Elvis' fourth and final Saturday appearance on the *Big D Jamboree*. Preceding him on stage that night was Helen Hall, who until recently had been performing on crutches with her jaw wired together. She could verify the dangers of touring and her career had not recovered — nor would it — from her enforced absence.

She watched the Hillbilly Cat (as some had dubbed Elvis) and laughed a little at his overly-macho performing style as well as admiring his talent. And it's quite possible she went home that night humming the tune of "That's All Right" and wondering if she couldn't write herself an answer record by way of good-humouredly puncturing his growing ego.

Elvis and the boys, meanwhile, jumped into their yellow Cadillac and headed off to Arkansas, and then Missouri, and then Mississippi, and then Louisiana … and that was just over the next seven days.

A Boy from Tupelo, Ernst Mikael Jørgensen

When Bob met The Country Cats

PERHAPS SATURDAY 3RD SEPTEMBER 1955
HOUSTON, TEXAS

THE COUNTRY CATS, and also baseball hopeful Bob Luman, were among those who signed up for a talent competition in Houston to be held at the end of the summer. The Cats wanted to take another step towards the big time before school re-opened on Monday. They'd spent the summer playing small gigs and store openings. And Bob, now a solo artist — his band apparently did not share his enthusiasm for all things Elvis — wanted to test himself after a fortnight of intensive practice.

The five boys mingled with the other performers backstage, but gravitated towards one another when it became clear they were the only artists who'd come to play the new brand of uptempo country music. They instantly became friends, Bob expressing his admiration in particular of the group's rhythm section. Both acts performed well, but Luman was a charismatic entertainer and he took first place.

Bob returned to Kilgore with his trophy and with the intention of spending the next six months playing as many gigs as possible before his spring baseball trial. The Country Cats returned to Weatherford, impressed by the guy who'd beaten them, and ready to restart school now that summer was over, but looking forward to the demo session they'd booked for themselves in Fort Worth three weeks hence.

Bright Lights and Country Music: The Nashville Sound, Paul Hemphill
The Mac Curtis rockabilly blog

Doctor's orders

SUNDAY 4TH SEPTEMBER 1955
RCA VICTOR STUDIO, 1525 MCGAVOCK STREET, NASHVILLE, TENNESSEE

SUNDAY MARKED THE LAST DAY OF RECORDING for Hank Snow's new RCA album project, entitled *Old Doc Brown* (LPM 1156). It was to be a collection of narratives, partly spoken, partly sung, usually designed to tug at the heartstrings. The penultimate song to be taped was called "What Do I Know Today?", and was from the team of Mae Boren Axton and her faithful brother, Lyle. By chance, and perhaps influenced by current family circumstances, he'd written a religious poem and shown it to Mae, who took it and contributed a simple accompanying tune. It fitted well to the concept of Hank's LP — which was sort of a tribute to Luke the Drifter, you might say — so he was happy to add it to the list. The meticulous Steve Sholes once again noted the name of Axton on the lead sheet.

As a gesture of good faith (and maybe also as a dry run), Mae gave the publishing rights to Buddy over at Tree, knowing he'd have been delighted to get a song on a big-hitter like Hank Snow, even if it was just an album track and not a single. And it would have been a gentle but effective nod to Buddy's employers, demonstrating that Mae had contacts in high circles and wasn't just whistling "Dixie".

As far as her relationship with Hank Snow was concerned, this composition would in fact be Mae's swan song. She'd been on board for almost a year, earning the money she'd needed. Just a few days after the session, she planted a story in *Billboard* indicating she was leaving Snow due to "pressure of other business", as she so delicately worded it.

Her widowed father, Mark, who had perhaps been unwell since the summer of 1954, packed his belongings and moved from Oklahoma into the Axton home at 3239 Dellwood Avenue. There are several possible scenarios as to why an elderly parent would move from their own comfortable house into one of their children's, but there is only one likely reason.

The doctors remained vague about how much time he had left but, as the weeks crept by, Mae became increasingly aware that each time she straightened his tie, or bid him goodnight, or placed a kiss on his delicate cheek, it could well be for the last time.

Country Singers As I Know 'Em, Mae Boren Axton
The Ada Evening News, 5th April 1956
Billboard, 10th September 1955

Selling faith

THURSDAY 8TH SEPTEMBER 1955
RCA VICTOR STUDIO, WEBSTER HALL, MANHATTAN, NEW YORK

THERE WAS A LOT MORE going on in Steve Sholes' life than just worrying about the merits of Elvis Presley. On a day-to-day basis he was still supervising sessions, approving artwork, considering songs and signing new artists. When he bought Jim Reeves, he also welcomed Martha Carson to the RCA stable. Her transfer from Capitol was inexpensive, and Steve rightly felt he'd picked up a bargain.

Martha's chart success had faded since her 1951 blockbuster, "Satisfied", but Steve had faith in her continued sales potential. Indeed, after her first RCA session, he started making plans for an LP of inspirational material. But making an album was not necessarily a quick and easy process in the 1950s record business, and there were procedures to be followed.

One of the main challenges concerned the album cover: artwork had to be prepared well in advance, and proper 4-colour proofs had to be produced so the art department could check the balance. Allowing for tweaks, adjustments and errors, the entire preparation process might take four months, or possibly even longer.

Meanwhile, the singer and the producer would be choosing and arranging songs for the album. These would then be taped according to a strict schedule of four songs per three-hour session — no more and no less. Therefore, a typical twelve-track project would be recorded in three sessions, often spread over three days.

Martha's studio recordings for what would become her *Journey to the Sky* debut LP started on 8th September 1955, but the finished project didn't hit the shops until January 1956 (RCA Victor LPM 1145). It was a good album and the track list focused strongly on that ole-time-religion approach. Her strong voice was well presented, especially on a stirring version of "The Battle Hymn of the Republic" or, as it was listed on the cover, "Glory Hallelujah".

Coincidentally, RCA's previous catalogue entry (LPM 1144), was also a religious album, this one belonging to The Speer Family — mother, father, a daughter (Nina), and two sons (Ben and Brock) — another recent signing. One of the oldest established white gospel groups in the country, they had a substantial audience that Sholes hoped to exploit with a string of uplifting singles and LPs.

But, while RCA were waiting for salvation to take its course through their slow-moving album administration and printing process, there was no reason why they all couldn't make a buck on the side. So, Ben and Brock were contracted out as voices-for-hire to various RCA artists who required backing singers. Chet Atkins paired them briefly with (of all people) Charline Arthur, and was keen for RCA to get its money's worth by using them as often as possible, regardless of whether the singer was God-fearing or not.

Classic Country: Legends of Country Music, Charles K. Wolfe
Billboard, 13th August 1955

The end of the special relationship

FRIDAY 16TH SEPTEMBER 1955
NEW YORK CITY, NEW YORK

TROUBLE HAD BEEN BREWING between Tom Parker and Bob Neal for several weeks. Bob was insistent that Parker was selling Elvis too cheaply, but the Colonel countered with various arguments that amounted to his standard retort: "The Colonel is the boss."

In a bid to assert his position, Bob advised Elvis to sign a new contract with the *Louisiana Hayride* on Thursday 15th September. Parker was against the idea of tying an artist to long-term low-paid radio broadcasts — as he'd demonstrated with Eddy Arnold and the *Opry* — but Bob pushed the deal through with Vernon's help.

Indignant, and now determined to remove Bob from the picture as soon as possible, Parker visited Jean Aberbach the following day in New York. Again, they discussed Presley and, although the conversation was not noted or recorded, it seems that Jean offered Parker assurances he would give whatever support he could, because when Parker returned home after the meeting he did so with considerable confidence.

Indeed, he phoned Bob Neal and initiated — one might say provoked — an argument which so infuriated Bob, that the deejay insisted their special relationship be terminated (although the contract was still valid and legal, of course) and Parker go back to acting as a normal bookings agent.

Once again, the Colonel seemed to have vigorously stirred the waters hoping to instigate movement. Parker wrote to Elvis, explaining his side of the falling-out, and expressed his desire to keep working with the boy. He then started planning his next two big projects: a special Hank Snow tour planned for mid-October and, unbeknownst to Bob Neal, a concerted effort to get the Presley family's permission to proceed with negotiations for the move to a new record company.

Behind the scenes, Tom Diskin was having conversations with Elvis about how great the Colonel was and how there were big things ahead. And by now, Elvis — who had heard Tom Parker's love song a hundred times — was beginning to believe it too.

A Boy from Tupelo, Ernst Mikael Jørgensen
Restless Giant: The Life and Times of Jean Aberbach & Hill and Range Songs, Bar Biszick-Lockwood

At the crossroads of the lonely street

SEPTEMBER 1955
TEXAS AND FLORIDA

TOMMY DURDEN WAS NOT A PROLIFIC SONGWRITER. But his compositions were well crafted and carefully structured. There was an economy about his words and a sense of logic to his tunes. He wrote like a singer, ensuring a regular scan with sensible intervals between the notes.

When inspiration struck, as it had with "Hula Boogie" and "Crossroads", the songs came quickly to him. Which is why Tommy was becoming somewhat frustrated by the newspaper article from El Paso.

That headline had burned itself into his brain, and he knew there was a spark in there somewhere. Whenever he had a spare moment as he drove between gigs, he kept trying to find a way into the lyric. Sometimes it was just a question of discovering the right rhythm, or hitting upon the best word for a rhyme. From there, the song would just pour out.

It would be a blues-type composition, of that he was sure, and so, in order to make a start, he'd once again lifted a standard phrase to open the verse, and then added his own personal theme: "Now, since my baby left me … I walk a lonely street."

But then what? It was a good metre. The first two lines scanned properly, but what appropriate word rhymed with "street"? He was stuck. Lyrically, he needed something solid and dramatic for the end of the verse. And if he could establish that pattern then he knew the song would come easily.

How did he know this? Because Tommy was the man walking the lonely street, and this was his story. It would be the third and final part of his post-Boots exorcism; from "Crossroads" to "Wasted Time, Wasted Tears" to … the saga of what had happened since the breakup.

He just needed the words to tell his tale.

"The Last Time"

PROBABLY SEPTEMBER 1955
JACKSONVILLE, FLORIDA

SECURE IN THE KNOWLEDGE that their friendship remained strong, Mae met up with Glenn Reeves in September to see about writing a song he could use for his first Republic session scheduled for the following month. Murray Nash already had one track lined up — a jolly uptempo number called "That'll Be Love" — but a flip-side was required. Maybe, ventured Glenn, they should write something sad as a contrast.

Mae and Glenn exchanged a few ideas (she immediately remembered why she so preferred writing with a partner) but little inspiration was forthcoming. She found it hard to concentrate because her mind was fixed on two subjects: getting that song to Elvis and, obviously, Mark Boren's failing health.

As Glenn strummed a melancholy progression on his guitar, her thoughts wandered to the everyday things she shared with her dad — simple pleasures that would soon be denied her: sitting together; just talking; a fatherly hug.

She looked up at Glenn and told him she had a title to accompany his sad chords: "The Last Time".

The Country Cats make a demo

PERHAPS AUTUMN 1955
CLIFF HERRING STUDIO, FORT WORTH, TEXAS

THE COUNTRY CATS were excited but nervous as they tuned up. They were recording a double-sided demo for their own use, and were sure it would lead to something big.

The first number they cut was a Joe Poovey/Jim Shell composition they'd picked up from the ubiquitous producer himself — it seemed everyone in the Texas music world knew Jim Shell — called "What'll I Do", which owed a lot to the version of "I Got A Woman" that Elvis had been hammering out all over the South for the previous nine months.

The second track, however, was a Mac Curtis original called "Amarillo Blues", a slow sexy song which was punctuated with a guitar riff lifted directly from The Platters' opening to "Only You".

Job done and acetate demo carefully wrapped, they packed up their instruments and headed home, confident they had taken another step towards the big time. This new style of music was going to hit hard soon, and the Cats wanted desperately to be part of it. There was change in the air: you could almost taste it.

The Mac Curtis rockabilly blog

East on Highway 46

FRIDAY 30TH SEPTEMBER 1955
EAST OF CHOLAME, CALIFORNIA

THE 1950 FORD TUDOR was travelling east at 55mph along Highway 46. Behind the wheel was twenty-three year-old student, Donald Turnupseed, on his way home to Tulare from Carl Poly State University. Just after 5:00 PM, with the setting sun behind him, he looked ahead and there to his left was the familiar turnoff for Highway 41.

The road was quiet, but as Turnupseed made to turn, from out of nowhere on Highway 46, a silver Porsche Spyder appeared and ploughed into the side of the Ford which span around and came to rest in the middle of the road. Trembling, Turnupseed stepped onto the blacktop. Apart from a few cuts and bruises, he was unharmed.

The passenger from the Porsche, a mechanic named Rolf Wutherich, en route to a motor racing event in Salinas, had been thrown clear of car and had hit the ground hard. He was broken but breathing.

The Porsche itself lay several yards off the road, crumpled almost beyond recognition. In the driver's seat was the body of James Dean, just one year older than Turnupseed. He was pronounced dead about an hour later at Paso Robles War Memorial Hospital.

Later that night, on tour in Gladewater, a shocked Elvis Presley heard the news on the radio of the death of his hero. He sat alone in his gloomy hotel room and wept.

Live Fast, Die Young: Remembering the Short Life of James Dean, John Gilmore

Scheduling meetings

MONDAY 3RD OCTOBER 1955
GAINESVILLE, FLORIDA

HIS YEARS IN THE NAVY had instilled in him a certain discipline, and Tommy Durden liked to be prepared and organised. The first *Country Frolics* live TV show was scheduled for this coming Saturday, but Tommy pre-packed a small case on the Monday evening and looked through the songs he was due to play.

He then placed a call to his brother, Sam, checking that the plan for him to stay over on Friday night was still in place. Sam said he was really looking forward to seeing Tommy, and suggested they establish a regular time for him to arrive each week so they could all sit down to dinner together. It was agreed that Tommy would arrive in time for the 7 o'clock meal every Friday. Tommy insisted he would make a financial contribution but Sam wouldn't hear of it: family is family.

Tommy then placed a second call, this time to Mae Boren Axton: she'd been on his mind for the past few weeks. The "lonely street" newspaper article kept running through his brain, and he couldn't make any kind of progress in terms of lyric or structure. When he'd written with Mae a few months earlier, the words came easily and he wondered if she could help him make sense of it all.

Mae answered the phone, and Tommy explained he'd be in Jacksonville most Friday evenings from now on and — if Mae was still interested — perhaps they'd be able to meet up to work on some songs? In fact, Tommy had one song idea he'd love to share with her this week if possible? Mae, keen to keep one foot in the business, thought this would be a fine notion and she'd look forward to seeing him on Friday at 8:00.

Meanwhile, over at 706 Union Avenue in Memphis, Marion Keisker addressed an envelope to Hill & Range. Inside was the signed paperwork giving permission for Elvis' Hi-Lo published songs to be used in the forthcoming songbook. When Jean received the package, he scheduled a meeting for 15th October with his attorney to draft a provisional agreement for a publishing contract with Elvis Presley. It was time to step up the pursuit — regardless of who was managing the singer.

Restless Giant: The Life and Times of Jean Aberbach & Hill and Range Songs, Bar Biszick-Lockwood

The room where it happened

FRIDAY 7TH OCTOBER 1955
3239 DELLWOOD AVENUE, JACKSONVILLE, FLORIDA

IT HAD BEEN ANOTHER BUSY DAY FOR MAE: she was trying to finish an article to meet a deadline for *Life Today* magazine and, while she wrote, an intern in the next room was typing and filing.

The menfolk were out for the evening: maybe they'd all gone to a Friday night football game after dinner. Her dad was mobile but required some assistance, and Mae knew his situation would not improve. It would do him good to get out of the house for a while. And it was right that his grandsons should spend time with him. A year ago, money had been the most precious commodity in their lives: now it was time that was in short supply. All of Mae's considerable energies were focused on her family, and she tried to put the inevitable forthcoming sadness out of her mind.

Tommy took dinner with his brother and sister-in-law shortly after arriving in Jacksonville in the early evening. The men rounded off the meal with a whiskey before Tommy made the short stroll to Dellwood as the streetlights began to wake, and arrived promptly on the hour. Mae opened the door and welcomed her guest, inviting him to take a seat. They shared a little small talk before Tommy broached the subject of the song.

He produced the newspaper article from his jacket pocket, and Mae read the tragic story of Alvin Krolik.

"How awful," said Mae. "How awful for his family," she continued, her words betraying the thoughts uppermost in her own mind.

"But look at that headline," said Tommy, standing up and reciting:

Killing Ends Heartache — 'Story of Person Who Walked Lonely Street'

He wanted to tell Mae how he empathised with the boy — how he felt his own journey was along that very same lonely street. But he couldn't. Mae scanned the article over again. She noted the odd name of *Alvin* and made the obvious short jump to the other unusual but similar name in her life at the moment; that of *Elvis*.

"There's a song there, Mae, but I just can't get to it. It's a sad song — it's a blues. I have the first couple of lines but no more than that."

Now, since my baby left me, I walk a lonely street.

Tommy looked at Mae, expecting her to magically complete the verse, but Mae just looked blankly back at him. She had nothing to give. She was empty. The busy-ness and the raw emotion of the past year was catching up with her. Somewhere in the back of her mind, she registered she'd been here before; looking for a way into a song about sadness and heartache. The word "heartache" chimed loudly as it also featured in the newspaper headline.

She half-whispered: "It's a shame people don't have some place they can go when they're this sad."

"How do you mean?" queried Tommy.

"Well, like a … like a club, I suppose. Somewhere they can visit when they're feeling low."

She thought again of her own position. Sadness was no longer about visiting, as it had been in the summer. Sadness was now about staying with someone until the end.

"Actually, perhaps it's less like a club, and more like a place you can stay. Perhaps it's a home ... a hotel, or … something?" She glanced at the headline and saw again the word "heartache". She ran the phrase though her thoughts and liked the alliteration, but harked back for a better word to her earlier composition about broken hearts.

"It's a Heartbreak Hotel: that's what it is. There should be a Heartbreak Hotel on that lonely street."

Tommy stared at her, dumbstruck for a moment, and then spluttered, "That's it! That's the song! Let's write it."

He picked up a pencil and a used envelope from Mae's table, and the first verse arrived all by itself. "Street" was no longer the dominant word — and "Hotel" was a splendid sound for rhyming. Tommy sang and scribbled:

Now, since my baby left me, I've found a new place to dwell
Down at the end of Lonely Street at Heartbreak Hotel
I'm so lonely, I'm so lonely, I'm so lonely, that ...

There was a pause as Tommy cast around for an ending to the simple chorus. It was Mae who supplied the three words that defined the song:

I could die

That was heavy, and Tommy knew it. But it perfectly fit the tenor of what he'd written so far. He jotted it down on the envelope, and by now he was pacing back and forth across Mae's living room.

"It should be a crowded place," she suggested, once again pulling from "Welcome to the Club". Tommy loved that idea and the second verse came as effortlessly as the first:

And tho' it's always crowded you still can find some room
For broken-hearted lovers to cry there in the gloom
And be so lonely, oh so lonely, oh so lonely
They could die

Tommy took off on his own for the third verse, describing the staff at the hotel. Mae chipped in with a thought now and then, agreeing strongly with the idea of constant weeping and the desk-clerk dressed for the funeral mentioned in the very first line of the newspaper article:

The bell-hop's tears keep flowing; the desk clerk's dressed in black
They've been so long on Lonely Street they never will go back
And they're so lonely, oh they're so lonely, they're so lonely ...

And at this point, Tommy stepped away from the pattern and inserted a line so devastatingly sad he had his own doubts about it. Referencing Alvin's commission at the monastery, he ended the third verse:

They pray to die

Mae looked at him long and hard. This took it into a different place altogether, and Tommy wondered if perhaps the song should end on this dramatic line. But Mae, again mining her earlier work, wanted to invite the listener into the hotel — she wanted a sense of inclusivity.

Tommy had read the article a dozen times over the past month and he knew the story well. He knew it was the breakup of his marriage that had sent Alvin over the edge. And Alvin had told his tale in an autobiography which would never see the light of day.

The fourth verse came quickly because it was ripped straight out of Tommy's own life:

So if your baby leaves you and you have a tale to tell
Just take a walk down Lonely Street to Heartbreak Hotel
Where you'll be lonely, and I'll be lonely, we'll be so lonely
That we could die

There was no middle eight, no variation from the melody or the structure. It was four simple narrative verses of hard-hitting pure emotion that read and scanned beautifully.

Tommy said he already had the tune, and asked if Mae could tape him singing it while it was fresh in his mind. She brought out her reporter's tape recorder, and Tommy — knowing that Mae played a little piano — asked her to provide a simple accompaniment.

Mae shrugged, saying she knew nothing about playing a blues song other than a simple walking bass line, which she demonstrated in C, the simplest of keys, with her left hand. Tommy declared it perfect and stood near the piano holding the microphone.

Thinking back to the stabbing phrases at the beginning of Fats Domino's "La-La", Mae stumbled around the top end of the keyboard for a moment. She played the bass line then added six staccato notes with her right hand to punctuate the opening. She looked at Tommy who nodded his approval. He switched on the recorder and they taped a slow demo, right there in Mae's living room.

There was nothing dramatic about the performance. It wasn't a notable tune, musically speaking, but it stood up well lyrically and, without even realising, Mae and Tommy had continued that age-old folk tradition of singing the news. At the completion of the song, he clicked off the tape machine and glanced at the clock: it was 8:22 pm. The entire process had taken just twenty-two minutes.

Tommy was full of talk about what they'd done, but Mae was uncharacteristically quiet. Although most of the words had come from Tommy, she'd contributed substantially to the birth of the song and felt drained.

The similarity between the names of Alvin and Elvis played in her mind. Had providence taken a hand and delivered a song into her lap? This new composition was nothing at all like Elvis' previous recordings, nor was it like anything else on the pop chart. She still felt strongly "You're The Cause of It All" was the number that would make her fortune, but it wouldn't hurt to have a song in reserve, would it?

Mae explained to Tommy that she had been doing some work with the rising star, Elvis Presley, and was considering offering some material to the boy. Perhaps she could also give this new song to him? They might need to concede some of the writers' share to Elvis to make it viable, if that was okay with Tommy? Well, Tommy was indeed fine with that idea — he'd heard only a little about Elvis but felt sure he'd have more luck with the song than anyone else in his acquaintance.

Tommy left the tape and the envelope with Mae (he'd already memorised all four verses), then bid her goodbye, and strolled back to his brother's house, more than pleased with his evening's cathartic work and looking forward to the TV show the following day.

The intern was still pecking away at the typewriter in the next room. Mae sat back at her desk to complete the article she'd been working on all afternoon. She now had one small hurdle to overcome: the song was unlikely to attract Elvis' attention as it stood, and it would need to be re-recorded in a more obvious style.

She would need another favour from her talented deejay friend.

Who wrote "Heartbreak Hotel"?

A SHORT DIVERSION ON
THE NATURE OF POSSIBILITIES

THERE IS A SCHOOL OF THOUGHT that suggests Tommy Durden wrote "Heartbreak Hotel" literally by himself. Indeed, there are people I have contacted who personally knew Tommy Durden and insist that his sole authorship is an absolute fact. Therefore, for me to have written the previous chapter must seem to some like a slap in the face. Let me establish that it is not my intention to offend or be disrespectful.

Is it possible that Tommy wrote "Heartbreak Hotel" alone? Yes, it is absolutely possible, and if Tommy said privately, "Oh, I completely wrote the song in a room by myself," then that is a very clear statement. But if he said, "Well, Mae was there and threw in a word or two, but I remember writing the whole thing pretty much by myself," then that is a very different situation.

My research into Mae and Tommy's writing styles gives me every reason to suppose that Tommy was *at least* the main songwriter of "Heartbreak Hotel": of that I have no doubt whatsoever. But, having lived with this story for almost a decade, I find it impossible to discount Mae's creative presence, and it should be clarified that, for the most part, Mae was usually quite modest about her own specific contribution. She always suggested that the song title was hers, and that she was the catalyst, enabling Tommy to write the song and express his feelings in those remarkable words.

There are also some who remember Tommy playing "Heartbreak Hotel" on stage with the Swingbillys before Elvis Presley sang it, and that is quite possible as there were perhaps four months between writing and release. But some have suggested it was played years previously at the Cedar Key Arts Festival. This makes for an intriguing notion, bar the fact there was no Cedar Key Arts Festival in the 1950s. However, if the Swingbillys performed the song at a small gig in Cedar Key in October 1955 and Elvis' record became famous some six months later then one can see how that theory may have started.

But perhaps the most fascinating loose end here relates to the nature of the song's inspiration because, as you will have noted, there was not one potentially inspiring newspaper article, but two. The infamous and all-important "Walk a lonely street" phrase appeared in print in November 1953 and again in August 1955. On neither occasion did it appear in the suggested *Miami Herald* but, on the first occasion it did feature in, among other publications, the *Miami News* in a relatively detailed report.

Is it possible that Tommy read the 1953 article and wrote his song completely by himself at that time? Again, yes, it is possible. But what makes this unlikely is that there is nothing in the 1953 story that has the necessary gravitas to inspire a song like "Heartbreak Hotel". This is not the article that might lead to a lyric like, "They'll be so lonely they could die". Truly, and sadly, the song absolutely requires a tragic and dramatic death to properly and fully register — the 1953 article does not have that impact at all.

Which leaves one possible unexplored avenue: Tommy may have read the 1953 *Miami News* article and felt it was an interesting story. He may have noted the vital "Walk a lonely street" phrase. And then he may have done nothing about it at all, or indeed he may have felt there was poetry in the words but have gone no further. And, eighteen months later, when the story came to its awful conclusion, he may have remembered having seen the article first time around, and taken the story to his infrequent collaborator in Jacksonville. This "two newspaper" theory remains a possibility.

Having considered the various options for years, my thoughts on the probabilities and possibilities of this complex situation are as published in this book. But the essentials of the story are these: the song was inspired by the newspaper reports of the shooting of Alvin Krolik; Tommy empathised with the death of a man who was wounded in love; and Mae, wrestling with her own emotional trauma, acted as the conduit, allowing Tommy to express his grief lyrically.

And this is my truth.

Country Frolics, II

SATURDAY 8TH OCTOBER 1955
WMBR-TV STUDIOS, JACKSONVILLE, FLORIDA

REHEARSALS HAD GONE WELL, and the live thirty-minute *Country Frolics* TV broadcast went like a dream. Even so, it seemed to the Swingbillys that Tommy Durden was especially ebullient throughout the whole day. When transmission ceased at 7:00 PM, the band travelled downtown where they had a late Saturday gig planned for a small club (two paydays in one evening), and they hung around for a drink or two afterwards as the nightclub closed its doors.

They then piled into Tommy's car for the drive back to Gainesville and, en route, Tommy, who just couldn't stop smiling, asked the boys a peculiar question: How would they like to hear Elvis Presley's next record?

"Elvis who?" was the reply from most of his passengers, but Tommy would not be deterred, and launched into an unaccompanied rendition of his new co-composition, his passengers becoming the first unwitting audience of this song. The reaction was unanimous: they hated every miserable word and insisted Tommy turn on the radio instead.

Tommy obliged, but absolutely nothing they said could remove the smile from his face.

Fort Pierce News Tribune, Florida, 22nd September 1955

Making demos, II

MID-OCTOBER 1955
RADIO WPDQ, JACKSONVILLE, FLORIDA

It was a rare occurrence for Mae Boren Axton to be lost for words. But, standing in front of Glenn Reeves in his radio studio after hours, she struggled to explain her actions. Having already written a couple of songs for the fastest-rising star in hillbilly music, she'd now written another for the same guy — and this time she'd worked with Tommy Durden. Once again, to all intents and purposes, she'd left Glenn Reeves (her favourite writing partner) on the shelf. And to make matters worse, as before, she was asking for help to record an appropriate demo. She genuinely feared Glenn's reaction. But he just laughed. And he laughed louder still when she told him the name of the tune.

"Well, that's the silliest damn title I ever heard, Mae," he exclaimed, but said he'd be happy to put on his best Elvis voice for another demo tape.

"And this time you simply must accept a writer's credit: I know Tommy won't mind."

But Glenn would not be moved and motioned for Mae to play him the version they'd already made, while he scanned Tommy's handwritten lyrics on the back of the envelope. Mae explained that she wanted to hear the song in a much more dynamic format. Maybe it too should have an opening like "Ain't That a Shame". Each line should be acapella with a note or two on the guitar punctuating the breaks.

Glenn worked out the key as C major, and searched around for his Presley voice for a moment. Ignoring the existing tune, he let out a sort of dramatic bellow and struck the required chord at the end of the line. She encouraged him to ham it up yet further and he was happy to oblige.

Drawing heavily on "Baby, Let's Play House", Glenn slurred and swooped, exaggerating the song way beyond Tommy's crooning, and by the time Mae switched off the machine she had a 1:49 musical sketch that she felt not only stood a much better chance of catching Elvis' ear, but also now had a stronger structure as a song. Between them, Mae and Glenn had taken "Heartbreak Hotel" to a new place.

Reeves went to case his guitar but Mae wanted to push her luck just one more time. She explained to Glenn that she really didn't believe Elvis would go for "Heartbreak Hotel", but maybe someone else would. Could she impose on her friend and ask him to quickly put on tape a less Elvis-ized version of this new arrangement? And he did. Removing the Presley impression and toning down his mannerisms, he followed Mae's instructions to the letter.

Again, she offered a writer's credit: again he refused. She asked if she could at least buy him a beer? And this he accepted — but just the one. Tomorrow he'd be driving to Nashville for his first Republic session with Murray Nash. That was quite a coincidence, said Mae, because if Elvis opted for "You're The Cause of It All", she had every intention of offering "Heartbreak Hotel" to her pal, Murray — in the non-Elvis version, of course. They headed on down to the nearest bar, each feeling very optimistic about their respective futures.

The big time was surely just around the corner for both friends.

Glenn's big chance

MID-OCTOBER 1955
NASHVILLE, TENNESSEE

Murray Nash was a hands-on sort of guy, and liked to involve himself in all aspects of his businesses, including the recording sessions. He welcomed Glenn Reeves into the studio and, with precious little preamble, they got down to work. Glenn was due to tape two songs this day, the first being the uptempo "That'll Be Love", given to Murray Nash Associates by a little-known hillbilly writer named Al Horn. It rattled along at a fair pace and Glenn rode it well, his voice blending with the fiddle and steel guitar accompaniment.

After the previous day's successful demo session with Mae, however, Glenn was feeling more experimental, and suggested to Murray that they might try changing the song. "How so?" enquired Murray, raising a sceptical eyebrow. The singer felt they could try a different tempo and Murray nodded, agreeing the band might try playing yet faster. This new take had a breakneck feel to it but, although it was more exciting, Murray had no hesitation in choosing the original version.

Glenn then demonstrated "The Last Time" to the room with his acoustic guitar, clarifying the chords that he and Mae had written and the number of verses. He also made sure Murray knew he'd be taking the publishing rights. The finished performance was professional and slick, and arranged as a simple honky tonk dance hall song.

Murray was pleased with the session and scheduled the single to ship as Republic 7121 — just two catalogue numbers after the misconceived Pat Boone release — in mid-November.

Intriguingly, the paperwork for Glenn's session was never properly completed, and the notes suggest another song was tried and rejected between the two masters. Did Glenn give Murray a short taster of "Heartbreak Hotel", the track Mae said she'd be dropping on Nash's desk in the near future? In all probability, the answer is to that question is "No" — for the simple reason that Glenn really didn't think the song was worth a damn.

Glenn Reeves / *Johnny on the Spot* CD Sleeve Notes, Martin Hawkins & Richard Weize

The beginning of the Legend

MID-OCTOBER 1955
FLORIDA

THE CONSENSUS WITHIN THE BAND was that the song wasn't worth a damn. Tommy was determined to give "Heartbreak Hotel" some exposure, and had arranged the tune for the Swingbillys in its original slow format — he knew nothing about Mae and Glenn's reworking — and they'd tried it at a few shows over the past week.

But the audiences didn't like it and the band didn't like it, and Tommy couldn't deny they'd given it a fair crack of the whip. So they dropped it from their repertoire. But Tommy retained a great belief in his song — knowing that it perfectly expressed the sadness he'd felt since the end of his marriage.

Some of his bandmates had already asked him why on earth he'd written such a morbid dirge, and he hadn't been sure how to answer the question. It seemed a little macabre to say it was inspired by a guy called Alvin who'd been shot in an attempted robbery. So Tommy contented himself with one simple explanation: "It was just something I read in a newspaper."

Small screen: big audience

SATURDAY 15TH OCTOBER 1955
NASHVILLE, TENNESSEE

TELEVISION WAS TAKING OVER from radio and cinema as the most influential and powerful entertainment outlet. And there was no surer sign of this than when on Saturday 15th October 1955 the *Grand Ole Opry* broadcast its first TV show, starring America's favourite hillbilly singer, Hank Snow.

TV sales were growing at such an astonishing rate that one single nationwide performance could guarantee an artist a bigger audience than a whole year on the road. And the three networks — ABC, CBS and NBC — were falling over themselves to find bigger and more popular stars to attract more viewers and wealthier sponsors.

And with this in mind, as Tom Parker continued drawing up ambitious plans for Elvis Presley, he was convinced that television had to be worked into the schedule. With his movie star looks, the boy would be a natural on screen. The most prestigious programme on TV was *The Ed Sullivan Show*, a variety hour broadcast to millions every Sunday on CBS, but Ed booked only the best and Elvis was a nobody, so the Colonel ruled out that one.

Logically speaking then, NBC would be the obvious place to go as it was part of the same giant media conglomerate as RCA Victor — and RCA Victor was most definitely where Tom Parker wanted to be.

Billboard, 8th October 1955

The King of Rock 'n' Roll

SUNDAY 16TH OCTOBER 1955
OKLAHOMA CITY, OKLAHOMA

As well as pursuing Elvis Presley, Tom Parker was also still working at his day job of managing Hank Snow and running Hank Snow Attractions. During the autumn, the Colonel assembled a sweet deal that involved putting Snow on the same tour as Bill Haley, currently being referred to as the King of Rock 'n' Roll. It was a solid business arrangement featuring the number one hillbilly singer and the number one pop star, and tickets sold out as soon as they were released.

Parker offered Bob Neal a spot for Elvis on a few dates of the tour, beginning 16th October in Oklahoma City and, despite still being upset at the Colonel's shenanigans, Bob knew it was too good an opportunity to pass up. Before the show, Elvis ingratiated himself with Haley and then watched his performance closely. Elvis had energy and sex appeal on his side, but Haley was a pro who knew his job inside out, and Elvis learned plenty from observing the star's stagecraft.

During the planning for the short tour, Parker had requested that he and Snow both deposit $15,000 in their joint account to cover promotional expenses, which Hank duly did. Tom himself may have been a little remiss with his own contribution to the fund, but he was fully focused when the time came for sharing out the profits. To be fair to the Colonel, he may simply have forgotten about paying his half because he'd had so much on his mind, having spent much of the past month once again buttering up Vernon and Gladys Presley pertaining to his importance to Elvis' future.

And by the end of the week, Tom Parker finally achieved his reward in the form of a telegram from Elvis and his parents authorising him to sell Elvis' recording contract to whomsoever the Colonel felt was best suited. The Presleys had finally come around to Parker's way of thinking and believed he was the man who could progress their son's career and move him away from Sun to a bigger label.

The Presleys naturally assumed that the Colonel had cleared everything with Elvis' manager and record producer.

But Bob Neal and Sam Phillips knew not a cotton-picking thing about it.

A Boy from Tupelo, Ernst Mikael Jørgensen
The Hank Snow Story, Hank Snow with Jack Ownbey & Bob Burris

The missing movie, II

THURSDAY 20TH OCTOBER 1955
BROOKLYN HIGH SCHOOL, CLEVELAND, OHIO

After the Oklahoma gig, Elvis bounced on to Arkansas and then ended up in Cleveland, accompanied by some of the best hillbilly talent, including Roy Acuff, Hank Snow, Jimmie Rodgers Snow, Pat Boone, Kitty Wells, and Johnnie and Jack.

But it was the Thursday show at Brooklyn High School with, once again, Bill Haley that was deemed the centre-piece of the tour, because radio and music entrepreneur Bill Randle had arranged for Universal Pictures to film the concert, with a view to releasing a short movie entitled *A Day in the Life of a Famous Disk Jockey*.

Bill Haley and Pat Boone, technically speaking, were intended to be the star performers — not to mention Randle himself, of course — but as Elvis hit the boards it was instantly obvious he had not come to play second fiddle to anyone. His five-song set stole the show, and it was felt that Randle would edit the film around Elvis' breathtaking performance.

Indeed, it was expected that Randle and Universal would produce a popular and profitable feature: except they didn't. The reels were buried, lost or destroyed. No one explained why and no one saw one second of filmed material.

A Boy from Tupelo, Ernst Mikael Jørgensen

Name your price

MONDAY 24TH OCTOBER 1955
WARWICK HOTEL, NEW YORK CITY, NEW YORK

ARRIVING IN NEW YORK with the Presleys' telegram, Tom Parker booked himself a room at the Warwick Hotel. He'd come to the city because the two organisations he was chasing — RCA and Hill & Range — were both located there.

His first stop was the office of Jean Aberbach and, now that Tom had a guaranteed part to play in Presley's career, the publisher was very attentive. He showed Tom the contracts his lawyer had been drafting: they were the standard Hill & Range shared ownership deals. Jean reassured the Colonel he would be happy to support the boy no matter what record company he ended up at — and if it was with Steve Sholes at RCA, so much the better.

Seated back in his room at the Warwick, Parker took a deep breath and called Sam Phillips. Earlier that morning, he'd sent a telegram to 706 Union Avenue, passing on the news that he was in New York to negotiate a new recording contract with the Presleys' permission. As one might expect, the ensuing telephone conversation became somewhat animated, partly because Sam Phillips was emotionally torn between wanting to keep Elvis and knowing he desperately needed the cash infusion that the contract sale would bring.

Eventually, Parker posed a hypothetical question to Sam: Let's imagine you might consider selling — how much would you want for the contract? Phillips said he'd need a moment to think about that and hung up. About one minute later, Parker's hotel phone rang and Sam came back with his answer: $35,000 for the contract and $5,000 for the royalties he owed Elvis. Parker paused. That was an outrageous and unheard of figure for an unproven artist.

Clearing his throat, the Colonel checked if he'd heard Sam correctly and, taking this as a sign that he could proceed with tentative investigations, said he'd be in touch soon.

Sam Phillips was finally willing to sell the contract.

Restless Giant: The Life and Times of Jean Aberbach & Hill and Range Songs, Bar Biszick-Lockwood

Be careful what you wish for

THURSDAY 27TH OCTOBER 1955
NEW YORK CITY, NEW YORK

HAVING PUSHED SO HARD for Presley's recording contract to be put on the market, Tom Parker felt overwhelmed by the task that now rested on his shoulders. RCA was still Parker's preferred choice — and his remit was simply to find the best company. There was no contractual stipulation regarding best financial deal, nor did the Colonel have to reveal to anyone else (not even Elvis) who was bidding. His job was to move Elvis from Sun to a bigger label; one that could progress his career.

Proven hit-maker Frankie Laine had been sold to Columbia for $25,000 in 1951, but who would be willing to part with $40,000 for an unknown Southern singer? It would take all of Parker's bravado to pull this off; and if he failed he could kiss goodbye to any hopes of managing the boy.

But RCA was adamant: $25,000 was their limit, despite the Colonel's week-long overture. They did finally concede a rise in Presley's royalty rate, and agreed to consider assistance in obtaining national TV appearances, but they were very clear that the purchase price would be taken out of any future income Elvis might generate.

Other record companies, however, felt they were still in the picture. The most notable of these was Atlantic, which was essentially an R&B outfit, but recognised Elvis' huge crossover potential. Label owners, Ahmet Ertegun and Jerry Wexler indicated to Parker they would give every last dollar they had in the hope it would be enough.

Comforting though this was, Parker wanted to be at RCA. And certainly financially, if not necessarily artistically, RCA was probably a better bet for Elvis and for the Colonel. Feeling deflated, Parker made plans to return to Memphis on Saturday to talk to Sam man-to-man in the forlorn hope he might drop his price.

Meanwhile, back in Memphis, Bob Neal learned for the first time what was going on behind his back. He was livid, and wrote to Parker, but he finally recognised his protests were too little too late. Parker had his feet under the table and, if he came through with the new recording contract, Bob's professional relationship with Elvis Presley would be history.

A Boy from Tupelo, Ernst Mikael Jørgensen
Restless Giant: The Life and Times of Jean Aberbach & Hill and Range Songs, Bar Biszick-Lockwood

Yin and yang

SATURDAY 29TH OCTOBER 1955
MEMPHIS, TENNESSEE

He literally had not slept for three days when Parker and Diskin turned up to talk turkey about the price of Elvis' recording contract and so, understandably, Sam Phillips was somewhat on edge when the discussion began. He had been finalising the launch of his new female-only radio station (WHER) and was in no mood for any of the usual horseshit that surrounded the smooth-talking Jamboree men. This became abundantly clear when he threatened to punch Tom Diskin in the mouth early in the conversation, leaving Parker to handle the negotiations from thereon in.

Phillips and Parker were poles apart personality-wise: Sam was all passion, art and a vision of community; the Colonel was a man of trickery, artifice and the rights of the individual. But their mismatched ideals came together in this one question: *How much was Presley's contract worth*? And Sam would not be moved from his figure. If Tom Parker wanted to make progress, he'd have to take the deal and make it work.

The final agreement was this: Parker had until midnight on Tuesday 15th November to finalise a sale for $40,000, and Sam's price for even agreeing to this stressful process was a non-refundable deposit of $5,000, to be paid at any time between now and the deadline day. This would at least allow him to clear his back royalties debt to Elvis.

Parker had a personal maxim he applied to all business dealings: if you can't negotiate from a position of strength then don't negotiate at all. On Saturday 29th October 1955 he broke that rule and accepted Sam Phillips' terms unconditionally.

Travelling back to Madison, the Colonel rifled through his diary, looking for any and all opportunities to resolve the deadlock over the next two weeks. He needed some luck — a chance to try and bring the interested parties together in the hope that something might just turn in his favour. Because as things stood, he didn't have a buyer with $40,000 and he didn't want to lose Elvis, nor $5,000 of his own money.

The clock was ticking.

A Boy from Tupelo, Ernst Mikael Jørgensen

Rebel Without a Cause

EARLY NOVEMBER 1955
1414 GETWELL ROAD, MEMPHIS, TENNESSEE

JAMES DEAN'S FIRST POSTHUMOUS FILM, *Rebel Without a Cause*, was released less than a month after his death. It was instantly acclaimed by the younger generation as being a movie that expressed the frustration and alienation of life as a 1950s teenage American.

Dean-disciple, Elvis Presley, had a few spare days at the beginning of November — and returned to a new and bigger rented family home on Getwell Road in Memphis — and it's possible he saw the film in a local cinema at this time.

He became obsessed with the movie, and legend has it that he memorised the entire script by heart. Thousands of grieving Dean aficionados went out and purchased a red jacket like the one their hero wore during the latter part of the film. Presley was way cooler, and picked up a copy of the brown sports coat favoured by his idol through the opening scenes.

Had Elvis thought about it all, he'd have realised that Dean's death left a definite cultural vacancy for the role of sensitive young hero. But, as Presley sat in the dark movie theatre, mouthing Dean's words, he just marvelled at the actor's ability to express his own confusion and loneliness.

The price of success

EARLY NOVEMBER 1955
706 UNION AVENUE, MEMPHIS, TENNESSEE

THE STUDIO AT 706 UNION AVENUE had always been a place of comfort and inspiration to Elvis. But as he met with Scotty, Bill and Sam for a session in early November, he could sense something had changed. Their previous date had scaled the peaks of creativity, but now there was a subtle atmosphere of unease.

Johnny Bernero was again present behind the drum kit, and the foursome worked on a fine R&B song owned by Sam entitled "When It Rains, It Pours", which had been a minor hit on Sun for Bill Emerson in January. The plan was to find a suitable B-side for Elvis' proposed sixth Sun single, the already-recorded "Trying To Get To You".

Sam was still developing Johnny Cash and Carl Perkins, but his cashflow situation was crippling any thoughts of pushing those artists forward. Word had come through that "I Forgot to Remember to Forget" would be appearing on the *Billboard* C&W chart on Saturday, and sales of "Baby, Let's Play House" were still strong — but the money was not coming back to Sam fast enough. He was staring collapse in the face. Today, with the boy present in the studio, Sam finally accepted the inevitable.

He called a break and asked Elvis to step into the control booth. The two men talked privately. They discussed the future — Sam's future and Elvis' too. At this point in time, Sam was juggling a dozen different balls in the air. Every day seemed to bring new opportunities, but every single one of those opportunities was another drain on his time and his non-existent monetary resources. For Elvis, his dreams were on the verge of coming true: Bob had suggested he would possibly receive the prestigious "Best Newcomer" award at next week's deejay convention and Sam assured him his contract would soon be bought by a big label.

Elvis returned to the studio floor and gave $50 to Johnny and thanked him for his time: they wouldn't be finishing the session. This would be Elvis' final professional visit to the Memphis Recording Service. It had cost him $4 to get in — and it would cost him $40,000 to get out.

That's the price of success.

A Boy from Tupelo, Ernst Mikael Jørgensen

A change of plan, II

TUESDAY 8TH NOVEMBER 1955
NAVAL AIR STATION, JACKSONVILLE, FLORIDA

SHE'D KEPT HERSELF BUSY since leaving Hank Snow's employ. Already Mae Boren Axton was involved in local radio production (*Country Music Musings* on WFBF and WOBS) and was handling PR for Jacksonville advertising agency Seitner Associates. And in her spare time she still dabbled in promotion for regional concerts and good causes.

On Tuesday 8th November she produced a show at the naval air station in Jacksonville, which featured hillbilly singer Jimmy Newman, and likely used Glenn Reeves and the pick-up band too.

Her days were full and she tended not to stray too far from home, which was how she liked it. Mark Boren was becoming frailer as the weeks passed by, and his eighty-sixth birthday this coming Saturday would be marked privately. There would be an unspoken significance about the occasion.

Mae had taken a call from the Colonel the previous weekend when he arrived back in Madison after his trip to see Sam Phillips. He wanted to know if she had her song ready for Elvis. She replied in the affirmative, but he didn't enquire about a title or a musical style. Rather, he informed Mae that the moment had now come. She should pack her bags on the Wednesday and join him in Nashville, ready for the deejay convention starting on the Thursday.

Elvis would be there; Hill & Range would be there; Steve Sholes and RCA would be there; Hank Snow would be there — it was the perfect opportunity to stir the pot and mix everyone together. And it would be the ideal moment to present the unsuspecting Elvis with his new song.

But it was now likely that the one tune Mae would not be singing that weekend was "Happy Birthday".

Country Singers As I Know 'Em, Mae Boren Axton
Billboard, 12th November 1955

Last minute preparations

WEDNESDAY 9TH NOVEMBER 1955
804 CHURCH STREET, NASHVILLE, TENNESSEE

In all, there would be three days of festivities. The deejay convention would run on the Thursday and the Friday, blending in with the WSM celebration on the Friday and the Saturday. Mae arrived late Wednesday having made a booking at the Andrew Jackson Hotel, ahead of Elvis' arrival the following morning. She'd brought a few changes of clothing, a small record player and two copies of both acetate demos in case of accidents.

Having settled in, she walked the short distance to Buddy's tiny office at 804 Church Street, where she'd agreed to meet Tree's sole employee. She played both songs for him (using the plainer version of "Heartbreak Hotel"), but suggested that Elvis would certainly choose the uptempo "You're The Cause of It All", and she therefore intended to give the publishing on the Tommy Durden co-write to Murray Nash (again, it would be the plainer side she intended to offer).

She asked Buddy for three Tree record labels, then sat at his typewriter and picked out the title and songwriting credits for all three sides, editing her own name to Mae Axton so it fitted tidily in the small space. She pasted the paper circles onto the disks to ensure Elvis would be clear that Tree owned the publishing on whichever song or version he chose. She was confident which one he would select, but wanted to leave nothing to chance.

It was a typical Mae Boren Axton attention-to-detail touch. She made a note of a small discrepancy on one side of the "Heartbreak Hotel" disk so she could recognise which was the Elvis-ized version: there was an over-type on the second "D" in Durden — invisible to the casual observer.

She slipped the disks into her bag and asked Buddy when she might have a chance to speak to Jack Stapp. Disappointingly, Jack was booked until Saturday night, so if Mae wanted to complete the Colonel's mission, she'd have to see the WSM man backstage during the *Opry* broadcast — which meant she'd definitely miss her father's birthday.

But Mae nodded at Buddy and enquired as to whether his employer was ... prepared for the Colonel's terms? Buddy assured Mae that Jack would indeed be carrying his wallet.

Country Singers As I Know 'Em, Mae Boren Axton
Billboard, 12th November 1955

The c&w deejay convention, IV

THURSDAY 10TH NOVEMBER 1955 (EARLY MORNING)
RYMAN AUDITORIUM, NASHVILLE, TENNESSEE

She rose early on the Thursday and phoned home to check on the health of her father. Reassured, Mae breakfasted and then, knowing that Elvis wouldn't arrive for an hour or so, strolled down to the Ryman, taking both labelled disks with her. The *Opry* building was already a hive of activity, as singers and stagehands prepared for the gala concert on the Saturday night.

To her delight, she found Teddy and Doyle Wilburn sitting quietly and waiting for a chance to practise their repertoire. It had been almost exactly a year since the brothers had given Mae that most precious of gifts — extra time with her father — and she did not easily forget that type of generosity. And it suddenly struck Mae that she now had a chance to balance accounts with the brothers. Their recent releases hadn't troubled the hillbilly top ten: perhaps she could help put them back on the charts.

She told the Wilburns she had a song she felt sure could be a big hit. A portable record player was located, and the boys hovered while Mae cued up the plainer version of "Heartbreak Hotel". Convinced that Elvis would go for her solo composition, this seemed like a perfect opportunity to line up an act to sing her spare song — and also to repay her dear friends.

The brothers listened and a feeling of awkwardness filled the room. Teddy and Doyle eyed each other and glanced at Mae who, for the first time, was hearing the track not as a co-writer but as a detached listener. Damn, but this was a weird song. It was Teddy, the more diplomatic sibling, who spoke first, saying it was a great number and if Mae found the right singer it would surely be a hit. Doyle noted that the disk carried a Tree label but asked if the publishing rights were up for grabs.

Mae replaced the acetate into its sleeve and assured Doyle that the rights were already taken care of. She understood the brothers' unvoiced disdain for the song but loved them all the more for their gentle rebuff. Suddenly feeling somewhat less confident about her forthcoming meeting with Elvis, she kissed the Wilburns goodbye and made her way back to the Andrew Jackson, and as she walked through the door she felt that unmistakeable charisma: Elvis was in the building.

Country Singers As I Know 'Em, Mae Boren Axton

The most promising c&w artist

THURSDAY 10TH NOVEMBER 1955 (LATE MORNING)
ANDREW JACKSON HOTEL, NASHVILLE, TENNESSEE

THE CONVENTION OPENED with a membership meeting at 9 o'clock sharp, and Mae slipped in to hear the to-ing and fro-ing of the deejays' conversations and motions. Although she was currently only on the very fringes of country music she retained a great interest in all that was going on.

As the formal business drew to a close, the room began to fill with singers, celebrities and managers in anticipation of the awards ceremony. Elvis and Bob Neal sat together, and Mae caught the singer's eye and waved. He nodded, sitting resplendent in an open-necked check shirt and a pale four-button jacket with gathered cuffs.

Elvis had scored well in the "Favorite Artists" and "Most-Played Artists" polls but had finished a clear winner in the "Most Promising C&W Artists" chart. In addition to which, *Cashbox* magazine had voted him "Up-and-Coming Star of the Year", and Murray Nash's *Country & Western Jamboree* had declared him to be the "New Star of the Year". Clearly, his moment was coming.

At 11:48 AM, his name was called and applause thundered. He moved elegantly around tables and chairs and approached the podium to receive a handshake and the framed certificate which confirmed that everyone in the industry expected great things of him in 1956.

How very prescient was that suggestion.

Country Singers As I Know 'Em, Mae Boren Axton

"Hot dog, Mae, play it again."

THURSDAY 10TH NOVEMBER 1955 (EARLY AFTERNOON)
ANDREW JACKSON HOTEL, NASHVILLE, TENNESSEE

IT SEEMED AS IF EVERYONE IN NASHVILLE wanted to congratulate him after the ceremony. Well-wishers, including many folk he'd never even met, crowded around and patted him on the back, telling Elvis how they'd always liked his music.

Eventually, Mae found her way to the front of the queue and hugged him, saying how proud she was and how proud she knew his parents must be, and invited him over to the corner of the room for a moment of privacy. Once there, she quietly spoke the words she'd been practising for a month or more.

"Do you remember how I promised I'd bring you your first big hit?"

Elvis nodded, looking curiously at her.

"Well … I've got it. I know you have important meetings all day but if you and Bob can spare just a few minutes to come upstairs I'll play it."

And so, they headed up to Mae's cramped room and Elvis listened expectantly as she placed a single-sided acetate disk on her portable player.

Elvis sat on the one small chair, Bob stood in the corner and Mae perched on the edge of the bed. Glenn's simple run down the bass scale opened the demo, and Elvis cocked one ear as the lyrics of "You're The Cause of it All" tumbled out in a hectic fashion without ever really going anywhere. Elvis tapped his foot a little, but he was feigning interest and was beginning to wonder what he should say to Mae as the record drew to a close.

Bob seemed to like it (and said so), but Elvis was completely unmoved: the song had not one shred of authenticity or originality and he was unable to connect with it on any level. Glossing over the obvious discomfort, Mae widened her smile and pulled the acetate off the player, replacing it almost immediately with the double-sided disk, removing the need for Elvis to comment at all.

"And of course, I also have this one as well. I wrote it with a friend called Tommy Durden," she said, professionally breezing over the disappointment of the first song by not even mentioning it. Elvis cleared his throat and adjusted himself slightly on the chair. Again, the sound of Glenn Reeves' guitar burst out of the primitive speaker, and Elvis sat transfixed for one minute and forty-nine seconds. His foot tapped of its own accord; his fingers kept time on the arm of the chair; his head nodded with each guitar stroke; and as the demo ended, he leapt to his feet exclaiming, "Hot dog, Mae, play it again!"

Mae — stunned — did indeed play it again, and again, as Elvis absorbed and memorised the words. It had been exactly what he was looking for without even knowing he was looking for something. All his deepest emotions of the past few months were contained in this one song: the loss of Dixie; the death of James Dean; the end of his childhood; and the loneliness of the road.

Mae excitedly explained how she thought the song might sound better with a double beat at the end of each line (as per "Ain't That a Shame") and she also did a little singing part based around the stabbing piano notes she'd keyed on Tommy's demo. And Elvis liked all of it. He loved it.

"Well, that's just fine, Elvis. And if you make it your first RCA record, Tommy and I will give you a writer's share."

He looked at her, somewhat shocked, his expression asking "Why?"

"I remembered how you said you wanted to bring your parents for a holiday in Florida. Well, if this song is a hit and you have a writer's credit then you'll be able to afford to do that much sooner."

Overcome, he hugged Mae close to him then asked if he could take the demo, and she, of course, agreed. Bob ushered his young charge downstairs back to the crowds, and Elvis affirmed to his manager that "Heartbreak Hotel" would definitely be his first RCA record.

Mae stood quite still in the empty room for a minute or even longer. Then, closing her eyes, she fell backwards onto the bed and laughed until she cried.

Country Singers As I Know 'Em, Mae Boren Axton

The elephant in the room

FRIDAY 11TH NOVEMBER 1955 (EARLY AFTERNOON)
ANDREW JACKSON HOTEL, NASHVILLE, TENNESSEE

THE BIG GUNS HAD ARRIVED ready for the main event which began at 8:00 AM on Friday: the WSM anniversary celebration. The RCA top brass were there, including Steve Sholes and his boss, Bill Bullock. Hill & Range was present in the persons of Grelun Landon from the California office, and Freddy Bienstock, the Aberbachs' ambitious and trusted young cousin. Many others were also represented, of course, but it was these two particular companies around which Tom Parker hovered.

At noon, RCA hosted a lunch at the Andrew Jackson, and the Colonel did everything in his power to mix Elvis in with the RCA executives, thus re-inforcing the impression that Elvis' transfer was a done deal: except it wasn't, and nobody seemed willing to address this. And after today, Tom had just four days to complete the pact or lose face and $5,000 to Sam Phillips.

But to all not directly involved, it seemed as if Elvis was an RCA artist already. When Chick Crumpacker bumped into the rising star, he said, "Hey, I hear you're with us now," to which Elvis replied, "Yeah, I guess I am." Indeed, other record labels assumed Steve Sholes had agreed to Sun's outrageous figure. In fact, everyone pretty much went along with this idea. Everyone except RCA, that is, who still stuck with their $25,000 offer.

Oblivious to the backroom dealings (or lack thereof), Elvis met up with Hank Snow, and they had their picture taken together in front of a huge promotional (live) elephant as organised by Colonel Tom. Elvis did everything asked of him by Parker, and impressed everyone before taking his leave, with his certificate and his acetate, so he could make a paying gig the following day in Carthage.

And every time Steve Sholes turned around that Friday, there was Tom Parker, suggesting Sam Phillips was bound to release another successful Sun single soon, and that would surely put the price up even higher. Of course, Tom told Steve, he already felt the price was too high but, hey, he was just trying to get the best deal for everyone.

And that obviously included himself.

Last Train to Memphis: The Rise of Elvis Presley, Peter Guralnick

Good things come to those who wait

FRIDAY 11TH NOVEMBER 1955 (AFTERNOON)
CAPITOL STUDIOS, NEW YORK

ALMOST EVERYONE PRESENT at the Andrew Jackson on Friday 11th November had assumed Elvis Presley was already an RCA Victor recording artist. Which meant several companies believed they had lost the opportunity to sign the most exciting new C&W singing star in the business. Sadly, the less attractive side of human nature came to the fore, and many began a campaign of sniggering, declaring that RCA was wasting its money and Steve Sholes was losing his touch.

Two guys who were most definitely not part of the mockery were Ahmet Ertegun and Jerry Wexler over at Atlantic Records. They had offered Tom Parker every cent they owned because they recognised Elvis' worth not only as a potential money-making machine but also as an artist, and it must have been a great frustration for them to have evidently been trumped by RCA. But it now seemed clear that Elvis would not be contracted to Atlantic, so Ahmet and Jerry returned to the business of running their own record label, as well as watching over the promotion of their new subsidiary company, Atco Records

And on that very afternoon, at Capitol Studios in New York, Atlantic's number one group gathered for a session. The Clovers were one of the most popular vocal ensembles of the early 1950s, placing eleven hits on the R&B chart — Elvis was a devoted fan, incorporating "Fool, Fool, Fool" and "Little Mama" into his concert repertoire.

The quintet recorded three songs that day, one of which was released as a single in January 1956, and became a number three R&B smash hit (Atlantic 1083). It was called "Devil or Angel", a cute doo-wop ballad, which was the only unsolicited composition that ever became a big-seller for the Atlantic label. The song had recently arrived by mail with a Florida postmark on the envelope.

Blanche Carter had finally written her hit record.

Marv Goldberg's R&B Notebook (online)

Happy birthday, Mark Boren

SATURDAY 12TH NOVEMBER 1955 (MORNING)
ANDREW JACKSON HOTEL, NASHVILLE, TENNESSEE

MAE WOKE AT DAWN on what was very likely going to be her father's last birthday. She'd spent most of Friday networking and pressing-the-flesh. She'd devoted some time to Hank Snow (old habits die hard) and several other major players, happily building up egos and making sure everyone knew she was still available for writing duties, even if she couldn't travel around the country at the moment.

Mid-Saturday morning, she phoned home to speak to her dad. She was full of good cheer throughout the conversation, but there were eight hundred miles between them and it weighed heavily upon her mind. With a catch in her voice, she told him she loved him and then gently hung up.

The rest of her day was already mapped out: she would attend the various receptions and presentations throughout the afternoon, and then in the evening, during the final gala concert, she would meet up with Jack Stapp backstage and complete the Colonel's mission.

But there was also a little personal business she wanted to take care of first.

Ray Scrivener tells it like it is

SATURDAY 12TH NOVEMBER 1955 (AFTERNOON)
CUMBERLAND LODGE BUILDING, NASHVILLE, TENNESSEE

THE CUMBERLAND LODGE BUILDING was located almost adjacent to WSM. Murray Nash Associates had set up office there, and Mae had been a frequent visitor over the months. She considered Murray a friend: he had supported her work as a writer and as a composer and she wanted to repay him by giving him the publishing rights on "You're The Cause of it All", the song Elvis had rejected. Mae still believed it was a fine track and, if Murray could adapt it into more of a country style, she felt sure it could be a hillbilly hit.

Unlabelled acetate disk carefully wrapped, she made her way to the familiar office and tapped on the door. Entering, she was met by the stern face of Murray's partner, Ray Scrivener, who declared without a hint of emotion that Murray was out for the afternoon. Mae held up the packaged demo and explained she had something she wanted him to hear.

This was the moment Scrivener had been waiting for. He loaded both barrels and opened fire. He told Mae that Murray Nash Associates already had too many non-selling Axton songs on its books. He told her he was tired of seeing her hanging around and he'd personally be very happy if she'd take her damn acetate somewhere else and stop bothering Murray.

Mae, aghast, just stared at him. On this day especially, to be unexpectedly berated in this fashion was more than she could cope with. With tears of anger brimming in her eyes, she bit her lower lip and leant fully on her inherent good manners.

"Thank you, Ray. Please tell Murray I stopped by, won't you."

And with that, she turned and left the office, being sure not to slam the door on her way out.

Douglas Green's interview with Murray Nash, 15th May 1974,
Country Music Oral History Project

Mae twists the knife

SATURDAY 12TH NOVEMBER 1955 (LATE AFTERNOON)
ANDREW JACKSON HOTEL, NASHVILLE, TENNESSEE

When Murray Nash returned to the office that afternoon, he was horrified as Ray Scrivener gleefully updated him on how he'd put Mae Boren Axton straight. Murray was convinced Mae had a hit in her and Ray's actions were an absolute betrayal of trust. He bawled out Scrivener, and then rang Mae at the Andrew Jackson. She was surprised to hear his voice but graciously agreed to his request that he come to her room and try to resolve this embarrassing situation.

And while she waited for Murray's arrival, Mae ran through exactly what she would say. She liked Murray, but she was damned if she was going to be treated in this way. Therefore, when Murray arrived full of apologies, Mae drew upon all of her well-honed debating skills to ensure Murray Nash Associates felt the full weight of Scrivener's error.

Murray wanted to know if Mae had intended to give him a song to publish, and Mae said she had indeed been planning to give him the rights to a certain song for several weeks, but she was now giving it to Jack Stapp at Tree. Murray was crushed but asked if he might at least hear the song. Mae picked up an acetate and slipped it onto the portable player. But what she played was not the song she'd taken to Murray Nash Associates ("You're The Cause of it All") — instead she chose the less intense side of the spare "Heartbreak Hotel" acetate. And as it played, she clarified that rising star Elvis Presley had already claimed the song as his first RCA Victor single.

Murray was too much of a gentleman to try to change Mae's mind. He apologised again and took his leave, determined to have it out once and for all with Ray Scrivener. Mae wrapped the disk and put it back in her suitcase: it was almost time for her appointment with Stapp, and it might be deemed inappropriate if she was seen passing acetates to the WSM man.

Twisting the knife in Murray's guts had brought her no pleasure, and she was well aware she'd told a very selective version of the truth to her friend in order to hurt Murray Nash Associates and Ray Scrivener in particular. But Mark Boren's daughter was not going to be fucked with by some half-wit of an office boy on this day of all days.

Douglas Green's interview with Murray Nash, 15th May 1974,
Country Music Oral History Project

Mae and Jack at the *Opry*

SATURDAY 12TH NOVEMBER 1955 (EVENING)
RYMAN AUDITORIUM, NASHVILLE, TENNESSEE

CALM AND COMPOSED, Mae fixed her make-up and headed on down to the Ryman during the gala concert and sought out Jack Stapp backstage. He greeted her with a modest hug. She knew Buddy had prepared the ground, and when Jack showed her to a quiet spot, she realised this was the make or break moment.

"So, Mae," said Jack, "when are you going to give me a song I can publish?"

"I just happen to have Elvis Presley's first million-seller, and you can have it."

Jack understood how the game worked: he knew WSM President John DeWitt would soon be cracking down on *Opry* employees to give up their lucrative outside activities, and Stapp also knew there was far more money to be made outside the *Opry* than inside.

He needed to give his publishing concern the very best possible chance of success. He remembered the feeling he'd had last year when drinking Jim Denny's cocktails. It was likely Tree might just scrape into the list of best-selling publishers this year, but that wouldn't be enough to justify walking away from his *Opry* position. Whatever Tom Parker was asking for the song would be cheap in the long run.

"What's the name of the song?"

"It's called 'Heartbreak Hotel'," said Mae, "and I'll throw in another as a bonus."

"Good. I'll take them both. What's the price?"

"Why, Jack, what kind of a question is that? Perhaps it's a free gift to you from the Colonel."

"A gift from the Colonel?" smiled Jack. "So, how much does it cost if it's free?"

Country Singers As I Know 'Em, Mae Boren Axton

How much does it cost if it's free?

A SHORT DIVERSION ON
THE NATURE OF DEALS

FIVE THOUSAND DOLLARS was a lot of money in 1955. Fifty years later it was worth almost ten times that amount. But it's certain Tom Parker had access to that kind of cash, so when he promised Sam Phillips a non-refundable deposit for that amount, he knew he could afford it if required. Naturally, he didn't want to pay out of his own pocket at all, so if he could arrange for someone else to come up with the necessary cash then he most certainly would have done so.

There is no question that Jack Stapp was an honourable man but, as the situation with "Chattanoogie Shoe Shine Boy" demonstrated, he was savvy to backroom deals. And Stapp definitely needed a big hit record to give Tree Publishing the boost which would allow him to move away from WSM and start making the kind of money he knew was out there.

So, is it possible to prove that Jack Stapp paid $5,000 for the rights to "Heartbreak Hotel"? No, of course not: but there are a number of coincidences regarding dates and contracts that point in that direction. And the thought of Parker forwarding $5,000 of his own money to Phillips is so unlikely one fears it would have brought on a heart attack. The simple symmetry of taking the cash from Stapp, sending it to Sam and then having it refunded by RCA would have appealed to every bone in the Colonel's body.

And when Presley did eventually sign with RCA Victor (keep reading), rumours immediately spread that a publisher had paid a substantial fee to ensure they were also part of the deal. And for over forty years it was assumed the publisher in question was obviously Hill & Range, thus guaranteeing themselves a share in the potential future Presley fortune. But the Aberbachs paid no part of the requested $40,000, and their bank accounts reveal not a single cent was unaccounted for during this period.

The insistent rumours, though, were correct. A publishing company did indeed part with thousands of dollars in connection with Elvis' move to RCA. It's just that everyone missed the obvious truth of the situation because it was hidden in plain sight.

And that, dear reader, is the genius of the Snowman.

Restless Giant: The Life and Times of Jean Aberbach & Hill and Range Songs, Bar Biszick-Lockwood

How things stood

SUNDAY 13TH NOVEMBER 1955
ELLIS AUDITORIUM, MEMPHIS, TENNESSEE

TOP OF THE BILL and on top of the world, Elvis played two shows at Ellis Auditorium on the Sunday. He wore a red suit and whipped up a storm, marking the beginning of a six-day tour which also featured Hank Thompson, Carl Perkins, Charline Arthur and Johnny Cash.

Tom Parker, who had received confirmation from Mae regarding the Jack Stapp situation on Sunday morning, spent much of this and the following day on the phone to Bill Bullock at RCA. Although it was Steve Sholes' decision as to Presley's potential, Bullock held the purse strings, and he was not going to be shoe-horned into any kind of ridiculous deal. With the clock ticking down to the Tuesday midnight deadline, this is what was being negotiated:

1. Sun wanted RCA to pay $35,000 for Elvis' recording contract. And Sam was guaranteed $5,000 of that from the Colonel just for even thinking about making a deal.
2. If the deal went ahead, Elvis would repay the $35,000 to RCA from whatever royalties he might earn in the months ahead. Essentially, he'd be working for free until the books balanced.
3. Sun also wanted RCA to give Presley $5,000 in unpaid back royalties.
4. In return, Sun would also give RCA all of the tapes they had on Elvis, including songs they hadn't yet released, thus avoiding a repetition of the unpleasant Jim Reeves *v* Abbot Records situation.

As such, Bullock and Sholes felt they stood a reasonable chance of recouping the money. In fact, it was possible that they might even make the money back just by re-issuing the five Sun singles. With their better distribution and stronger marketing muscle it was probable they'd at least break even within a few months.

If Elvis also happened to record a hit single or two for RCA then they'd be making a profit. Of course, the entire industry would be aware of the extraordinary price of the contract and should the whole thing descend into farce, then heads would roll.

It was reassuring for RCA that Hill & Range would be behind the boy, and if Sholes could be confident of the Aberbachs' support and also have his trusted lieutenant Chet Atkins on hand in the studio then maybe it would all work out.

The Aberbachs themselves already had their publishing contracts for Elvis drafted and, as usual, they were one step ahead of the other players: they were talking to Sam Phillips about purchasing a piece of Hi-Lo music. In this way, the Aberbachs felt sure they had all bases covered. And being on the cusp of sewing up a share in Elvis' Sun songs and his RCA music too, Jean and Julian felt confident they'd be guaranteed of a cut of every important record Elvis Presley released from here on in.

How wrong they were.

Last Train to Memphis: The Rise of Elvis Presley, Peter Guralnick

Down to the wire

TUESDAY 15TH NOVEMBER 1955
MADISON, TENNESSEE

THE TELEGRAM WAS INTENDED as a friendly reminder but it came across in more desperate terms. As soon as the Western Union office had opened, Tom Parker dictated the wire to Bill Bullock in New York, pointing out that although they had until midnight to seal the deal, the banks in Madison closed at 2:00 PM sharp, and Tom needed to organise that $5,000 deposit on RCA's behalf.

Finally, Bill Bullock gave the go ahead at $40,000, and also indicated that RCA would help organise three TV appearances for the boy to assist with promotion. It was decided that all parties would meet in Memphis the following Monday to sign contracts and seal the deal.

Relieved and overjoyed, Parker phoned Sam and passed on the news. He asked if Sam wanted the deposit transferred immediately, as per their agreement. Phillips, who sat oddly still and emotionless throughout the conversation, absent-mindedly suggested it would be fine if Parker just mailed the cheque. He gently hung up. It was a key moment in Sam's life. For the first time since opening the Memphis Recording Service, he was debt-free and had cash spare to promote Carl Perkins' and Johnny Cash's forthcoming singles. But he felt the loss of Elvis keenly.

Tom Parker, meanwhile, drove down to the bank and drew a $5,000 cashier's cheque, very likely matching the $5,000 that Jack Stapp had paid for two acetates on Saturday evening. Playing his part to perfection, he then wrote a letter to RCA confirming this action, instructing them to reimburse him as soon as possible. He noted that the cheque to him should be marked as a refund to clarify that he personally was not making a single cent out of this deal. As an RCA shareholder, he was just glad to have been of service.

Last Train to Memphis: The Rise of Elvis Presley, Peter Guralnick

One more for the road

TUESDAY 15TH NOVEMBER 1955 (MIDNIGHT)
BUSY BEE LIQUOR STORE, 3728 ALAMEDA AVENUE, EL PASO, TEXAS

PINNEY HEARD NOISES in the store around midnight. Sure that he was being burgled, he dressed and crept to the front of the premises. Two young men were hanging around outside the shop. When Pinney appeared, they slowly sauntered across the avenue. But Pinney was convinced they were trying to break in, and called the police who soon arrived and took the boys to the station for questioning.

A day or so later, they were released without charge, although the police made a point of noting that the pair had twice been recently stopped for suspicious behaviour.

Pinney was being extra cautious. His wife was due to deliver twins in a month (and another son would follow in years to come). Soon enough, he would make a decision to get out of the alcohol trade and focus instead on the sale of fishing tackle. The lit sign above his store said "LIQUOR" but it might as well have said "TROUBLE" because that's what it attracted.

With his family near complete, and his change in profession imminent, perhaps he finally found the peace he'd sought. Gus Chitwood's last cigarette had long since crumbled and gone. It was time to raise a final glass to the patrolman's memory.

Adios, Gus, *salud.*

El Paso Herald-Post, Texas, 17th & 18th November & 9th December 1955

The unsigned contract

WEDNESDAY 16TH NOVEMBER 1955
NASHVILLE, TENNESSEE

THE DEAL WITH RCA having now been given the green light, the very next day Tree typed up a publishing contract between themselves and the three composers of "Heartbreak Hotel": Mae Boren Axton, Tommy Durden and Elvis Presley. But the contract would remain unsigned until a crucial condition had been met in full: Elvis' legal recognition as a co-writer hinged entirely on the song being chosen as his first single release for his new record label.

Mae's offer to Elvis has, over the years, been viewed as a kind and generous gesture (that's certainly how she told the story), but once one removes the rose-tinted glasses, the truth is this: it was RCA who now called the shots and if they chose a different song as his debut single, then Elvis would receive not a penny from Tree Publishing for "Heartbreak Hotel", and his name would not appear as a co-writer on the record label or sheet music.

Had Mae been feeling truly soft-hearted, she'd have given him the writer's credit regardless of how and when the song was to be released. But Tom Parker wanted the Aberbachs to know he was not a man to be messed with. If the song was a hit — and if it launched Elvis into the big time — then Hill & Range would miss out on a substantial pay day and Tree would be laughing all the way to the bank. And only one person would know the full glorious detail of this Machiavellian plan: Tom Parker himself.

And the snow kept falling in Tennessee.

A measure of success

SATURDAY 19TH NOVEMBER 1955
MADISON, TENNESSEE

HOT OFF THE PRESS, the latest issue of *Billboard* arrived on Tom Parker's desk, and within its pages was printed a chart of the most successful BMI C&W publishing companies of 1955 and, bringing a smile to the Colonel's lips, he noted that Tree had finally scraped itself onto the list. He read too that Arthur Crudup had polled as one of the year's most popular composers, on the back of Marty Robbins' cover of "That's All Right".

It all bode well for the future, but Parker was a cautious man and placed a call to his neighbour, client and partner, Hank Snow. He reminded Hank that the Presley boy would be signing his RCA contract in Memphis on Monday. He'd also be signing a deal with Hill & Range so they could guarantee a regular supply of good Presley-owned songs for recording (although Parker would still make no mention of "Heartbreak Hotel" to Snow or the Aberbach brothers).

Tom wanted Hank to be there in Memphis with his reassuring superstar presence in case of any last minute hitches, and also to advance their plan to eventually take over the management of the boy. Together they would both represent the interests of Hank Snow Enterprises-Jamboree Attractions — the very successful promotions company that didn't actually exist.

The Hank Snow Story, Hank Snow with Jack Ownbey & Bob Burris
Billboard, 19th November 1955

A done deal

MONDAY 21ST NOVEMBER 1955
706 UNION AVENUE, MEMPHIS, TENNESSEE

THE PARTIES GATHERED at the tiny premises of the Memphis Recording Service to sign the paperwork that would move Elvis from Sun to RCA. A handful of RCA and Hill & Range people, also Hank Snow, Sam Phillips, Tom Parker, Tom Diskin, Bob Neal, Elvis and his parents all posed for a selection of photographs as the signatures were affixed to the four-page document. Marion was unable to attend (she was fronting Sam's female-only radio station), so, feeling much more confident financially, Sam hired in a new permanent employee to mind the office — eighteen-year old Sally Wilbourn.

Tom Parker also brought with him a contract which established that Parker and Neal would each take a management share of Presley's income until the end of March 1956 when, as was already clear, Bob would bow out of the relationship. And Hank Snow obviously assumed that when Tom Parker signed he was doing so as "party of the second part" on behalf of their joint company ("and/or").

The key players gave a live interview with Marion on WHER, and she delighted in teasing the somewhat pompous Snow, before spinning one side of Presley's fifth Sun single, currently sitting in the top three of the *Billboard* C&W chart.

Sam, who was now $35,000 to the good, immediately made plans to release and promote two new records: one by Johnny Cash, "Folsom Prison Blues" (Sun 232), the song he'd cobbled together during his air force days; the other by Carl Perkins called "Blue Suede Shoes" (Sun 234). Before leaving the studio, Sam took Elvis aside and gave him sincere words of advice to the effect of "Whatever happens next, stay true to yourself."

Sam then also completed his deal with the Aberbachs as they bought into Hi-Lo, which gave Hill & Range part-ownership of another three Presley songs. The brothers now had a stake in a quarter of all the tracks Elvis had released thus far.

Elvis signed his own contract with Hill & Range, and they agreed to present suitable songs for the emerging star to record. They would open two shared-ownership companies for Elvis, named Elvis Presley Music (BMI) and Gladys Music (ASCAP), which meant, basically, Elvis would receive a much bigger pay cheque when he recorded and released songs from those two Hill & Range affiliated companies.

The Aberbachs' lawyers were probably waiting for the Colonel's twist in the tale. With Tom Parker there was often a little extra demand and Jean Aberbach knew full well that Parker still held a bitter grudge over the songbook deal. So when Parker suddenly demanded Hill & Range print an extra three thousand songbooks for free, the lawyers calmly accepted the terms.

Jean Aberbach then figured the Colonel had finally exacted his revenge and all debts were now settled ...

Restless Giant: The Life and Times of Jean Aberbach & Hill and Range Songs, Bar Biszick-Lockwood
Sam Phillips: the Man who Invented Rock 'n' Roll, Peter Guralnick

Sitting down with the Lord

LATE NOVEMBER 1955
3239 DELLWOOD AVENUE, JACKSONVILLE, FLORIDA

UPON HER RETURN HOME from the convention in Nashville, Mae had two things on her mind: checking on her dad, and placing a call to Tommy Durden. For a dying man, Mark Boren remained in encouragingly robust health, but his daughter knew that time was short.

Tommy Durden was pleased to hear that Elvis had accepted their song (and the one-third writer's credit), and he looked forward to a measure of moderate financial success come the New Year. Mae made no mention of her and Glenn's re-imagining of the feel and structure — there seemed no need to bring it up. Tommy had long since dropped the number from the Swingbillys' act — by popular demand, so to speak — but he retained great faith in his composition.

The subject of faith in itself was understandably high in Mae's mind at this time and, a week or so after her homecoming, she sat and wrote a few verses of religious poetry. Almost always requiring some form of creative inspiration or assistance, perhaps Mae took her cues from brother Lyle's recent effort as she wrote "When I Sit Down With God", her third and final solo song of the decade.

The opening line, "I'm sort of sick and sort of weary", encapsulated her own emotional exhaustion, a condition she hid well from those around her. There was no tune because Mae composed it as a poem or, more accurately, as a narration to be placed over a simple organ accompaniment. Feeling guilty about her behaviour towards Murray Nash, she placed the manuscript in an envelope and addressed it to Murray in Nashville, offering him the publishing rights, and marking it as private lest Ray Scrivener should open it first.

Mae couldn't have known it but following Nash's fierce argument with Scrivener, Murray Nash Associates in part and Republic Records in particular were careering towards closure. Mae's Christian gesture would be too little and too late.

Back in the Big Apple

THURSDAY 1ST DECEMBER 1955
RCA STUDIOS, NEW YORK, NEW YORK

IT WAS THE FIRST TIME Steve Sholes had properly met and spoken to Elvis. The Colonel and his boy had flown to New York for further photographs and a chance to impress the brass before heading off on a concert tour with Hank Snow, Roy Acuff and Kitty Wells. By chance, Parker's former client Eddy Arnold was also present at RCA HQ that day, and he posed with the new signing. Sholes figured that any and all publicity was welcome because, in truth, he was becoming a little worried.

Elvis' first recording session had been pencilled in for 10th and 11th January, and Steve had little idea what material should be considered, but had started to assemble a list anyway (a list that Elvis would politely mainly ignore). RCA's pressing of "Mystery Train"/"I Forgot to Remember to Forget" would hit the shops before the weekend, and they would soon re-release the other four Sun singles to improve chances of recouping their cash. It wasn't expected that these other four disks would chart, but Sholes had high expectations of "I Forgot to Remember to Forget" continuing its strong showing in the c&w ranking.

Steve had already listened through most of the tapes he'd received from Sam Phillips, and there were a few unreleased songs like "Blue Moon" and "I Love You Because" that could possibly feature on a Presley LP — Steve was determined to get his money's worth. He also took a liking to Elvis' halting version of "Harbor Lights", but knew it had zero commercial potential, so he slipped the tape into his desk drawer as a personal keepsake.

The Sun tapes contained a wide variety of music and the RCA man began to ponder very carefully his position. An artist with this creative range and repertoire needed to be developed with great care. Although Elvis would be promoted as a country & western act, it was hoped he could also appeal to the bigger and more lucrative pop audience.

Usually, when Sholes planned a session he felt prepared and in control. But, as far as Elvis' forthcoming dates were concerned, he was uncomfortably nervous. And with $40,000 on the line, a nervous producer was not a good sign.

Last Train to Memphis: The Rise of Elvis Presley, Peter Guralnick
Sam Phillips: the Man who Invented Rock 'n' Roll, Peter Guralnick

"A Mail Order from Heaven"

PERHAPS EARLY DECEMBER 1955
NASHVILLE, TENNESSEE

IT WAS PROBABLY ONE OF Murray Nash's last recording sessions as head of Republic Records. The company was already struggling and, following his argument with Ray Scrivener, its days were numbered. Murray had arranged for deejay and radio personality Marshall Pack to record a couple of novelty gospel narrations, hoping they might catch on within the niche religious market.

Firstly, they taped Mae's contemplative poem, "When I Sit Down with God", which Nash had recently received in the post. He'd been worried Mae might have permanently severed all connections, so it had been good to hear from her again so quickly. Pack recorded the song with a nondescript church organ chording in the background, and Murray knew it would make a good B-side.

Then Pack taped a self-composed number called "A Mail Order from Heaven", in a style very similar to Mae's song. It was a sincere parody of a commercial radio pitch for the latest miracle product, the punchline being that there was no charge and the product on offer was salvation.

Murray readied the single for rush-release at the beginning of the New Year, and posted a double-sided advance demo to Mae by way of thanks. The single (Republic 7124) sold in negligible quantities which added to Nash's troubles, but Mae loved the 45 and continued pushing the record for weeks afterwards.

The lyrics on the A-side were designed to catch the listener's attention, and Mae's heightened emotions latched on to Pack's quietly insistent voice as he asked:

Have you lost someone near to you?
Are you thinking, possibly, of self-destruction?

A mail order from Mae

PERHAPS EARLY DECEMBER 1955
804 CHURCH STREET, NASHVILLE, TENNESSEE

THE PACKAGE WAS WAITING FOR Buddy when he arrived at his Church Street office one December morning. Inside the carefully-wrapped parcel were two tapes as agreed with Mae and Jack Stapp. There was Glenn Reeves' Elvis-ized version of "You're The Cause of It All" along with a note from Mae suggesting this song could be a real hit. He played it first, but was unimpressed, as he had been back in November.

He then carefully threaded the second tape onto his office machine and listened to what turned out to be a copy of Mae and Tommy's original "Heartbreak Hotel" piano-based demo. When offered a choice, Buddy had requested the keyboard rendition rather than Glenn's guitar-led take, because it would save time and money for the transfer to sheet music, which remained an essential part of the publishing game — it would be cheaper to simply transcribe Mae's basic playing.

But what was being overlooked was the fact that the song had already moved beyond its simple origins, and Elvis Presley's dynamically creative approach to music was very likely to move it on yet further. No one gave this too much thought because, although all parties hoped for a successful song, nobody expected anything that would gather too much attention.

Having read the above, the reader is now privy to the answers to two questions that have vexed music historians for decades:

Why does the sheet music for "Heartbreak Hotel" bear so little resemblance to the finished record? — Because it was based on the original demo and not Elvis' or even Glenn's recording; hence the different tune, structure and lyric;

What did Mae and Tommy's original demo sound like? — It sounded very similar to the sheet music that has been available since 1956.

As with so many parts of this story, the answers were hidden in plain sight all the time.

By the Seat of my Pants, Buddy Killen with Tom Carter

"This will be my first hit record."

FRIDAY 9TH DECEMBER 1955
SWIFTON, ARKANSAS

SWIFTON WAS A SMALL TOWN with a population that rarely rose above the thousand mark. Elvis played there twice on Friday 9th December: first at the high school gymnasium, and then at the B&I Club later that night, with Johnny Cash (whose single was heading steadily towards the C&W top twenty) also on the bill. And it was at the second performance that Elvis gave a preview of what he described to the two hundred strong audience as his forthcoming "first hit record."

Drummer D.J. Fontana, who had recently returned to Elvis' band after illness, wasn't overly impressed when Elvis played Glenn Reeves' demo for them, but was drawn into it when Elvis described how he wanted to give the song a greater dramatic edge. Elvis hinted to Scotty about a staccato style guitar solo and suggested D.J. and Bill add a double beat at the end of each line. He also asked the drummer to draw upon his earlier experiences of playing in strip clubs to give the slow song a strong sense of rhythm.

The four musicians played with the number in their rare moments of downtime: Elvis focused on honing not only his vocal delivery but also his physical response to the music. He had no other song remotely like it in his set list, and he was aware that the shoulder pops and hip thrusts he choreographed would drive the female part of his audience wild.

After the Swifton gig, in the early hours of Saturday morning, the boys started the long car journey to Shreveport for their regular weekly appearance on the *Hayride*. By the time they arrived, the Hill & Range *Elvis Presley Songbook* — the project that had, after a fashion, connected Elvis Presley to "Heartbreak Hotel" in the first place — would at last be printed and ready for retail. Sales initially would be slow but good times were just around the corner.

A Boy from Tupelo, Ernst Mikael Jørgensen

He was a friend of mine

DECEMBER 1955
UNIVERSAL RECORDING CORP., CHICAGO, ILLINOIS

AS RICHARD PENNIMAN celebrated his twenty-third birthday in December 1955, Pat Boone gave him an unexpected but welcome gift. "Little" Richard, as he was known, was a flamboyant pianist and singer who had played around the fringes of the gospel and R&B world, and had signed briefly and unsuccessfully with RCA in the early 1950s. But in the spring of 1955, his contract was picked up by Speciality Records, on the recommendation of Fats Domino's friend and rival, Lloyd Price, whose 1952 debut single, "Lawdy Miss Clawdy", was a classic of the genre.

So, in September 1955, Richard arrived in Chicago for his first Speciality session and laid down a devastating record called "Tutti Frutti" (Speciality 5610). The nonsense lyrics covered up the original coarse words, and the beat screamed "rock 'n' roll" as loudly as Little Richard spat out the opening line: *A-wop-bop-a-loo-bop-a-wop-bam-boom!*

The single was released the following month and began its steady climb to number two in the R&B chart and number seventeen on the pop chart. But Dot Records, ever-vigilant, ushered Pat Boone into its studio in December to sanitise the song, just as he'd done with "Ain't That a Shame".

Boone's version outsold Little Richard's, but Penniman was, like Domino, very happy for the extra writer's royalties, and he was convinced many of the white kids who bought Boone's record then went out and purchased his too but hid the disk under their beds lest their parents discover it.

Little Richard's "Tutti Frutti" was the rawest song ever to hit the *Billboard* top twenty up until that time, and was an indicator of the changing tastes of the record-buying public. Suitably encouraged, Penniman would go on to release a remarkable run of pure rock 'n' roll singles, until he decided to return to the church two years later.

Elvis loved Little Richard from the off, and, recognising a kinship with the extravagant performer, he would enigmatically introduce Richard's material on stage by declaring that he was about to sing a song recorded by "a friend of mine".

They had never met, but were clearly brothers from another mother.

The CBS connection

THURSDAY 15TH DECEMBER 1955
NEW YORK CITY, NEW YORK

One of the recurring themes of Tom Parker's wooing of Elvis Presley was the importance of getting the boy on television. There'd been talk of RCA helping to arrange this (with their sister company NBC-TV), and Parker had also encouraged the William Morris Agency to investigate further.

However, in mid-December, Parker completed a deal of his own which would give Elvis four appearances on a weekly variety programme called *Stage Show* in early 1956. The show was hosted by Tommy and Jimmy Dorsey, the band leaders who had fallen a long way since the glory days of million dollar radio deals almost a decade previously.

The Dorseys didn't really care either way about Elvis and had little time for the new rock 'n' roll music fad. *Stage Show* was not a bankable programme, but it was broadcast each week on CBS-TV prior to the hugely popular sitcom, *The Honeymooners*, which gave it an extra boost and improved its ratings slightly. Big show or not, it afforded Parker the opportunity to blow off about how he had stolen a march on all the other parties and put his client on national television.

The Colonel had arranged his TV deal privately through the Yates Artist Corp., a small-time agency on 5th Avenue. It's curious though, isn't it, that Parker should land a deal that did not include the obvious NBC (who were joined corporately to RCA), but should link up with CBS. That's the same CBS where wonder-boy Lou Cowan had been given carte blanche to do what he wanted with a whole selection of programmes.

Perhaps that list of programmes also included *Stage Show* which was co-hosted by Tommy Dorsey whose professional relationship with Cowan went back a long way. And that's the same Lou Cowan who now had a definite vested interest in the career of Elvis Presley.

I'm not drawing any conclusions, you understand. I'm just pointing out that it's curious.

The Colonel: The Extraordinary Story of Colonel Tom Parker and Elvis Presley, Alanna Nash

Steve Sholes' desk

THURSDAY 22ND DECEMBER 1955
RCA STUDIOS, NEW YORK CITY, NEW YORK

STEVE SHOLES was looking ahead to Elvis' two-day Nashville recording session booked for 10th and 11th January and, keen for the dates to be productive, he assembled and posted a selection of ten demos to the boy in the hope of being able to direct him creatively. Of the ten songs, at least four had been supplied by the Aberbachs, so it was clear that Sholes was intending to fit Elvis into his long-established and very successful pattern.

Sales of RCA's pressing of "I Forgot to Remember to Forget" were already impressive, and Steve had worked out it was likely they'd break even on the $40,000 just from this single alone. But the entire industry had read of the Presley deal with raised eyebrows and Steve needed to make a big splash with this forthcoming session. He hoped that among the pop songs and R&B demos he'd sent perhaps Elvis could find something to sing in his effervescent Sun style. Elvis, for his part, had made one simple request for the session: that The Jordanaires be present to offer vocal back up. Steve spoke to Chet about this and also ensured Atkins himself would be in attendance.

And there was another thing on Steve's mind: none of his engineers could figure out how Sam Phillips managed to get that special sound. It was something to do with echo and microphone placement, that much they knew, but whether they'd be able to recreate it in the McGavock Street studio was an unanswered question. There were nine hours of studio time booked over two days so the producer would have plenty of time to resolve any technical issues while recording twelve songs in the standard professional manner.

Steve toyed with the idea of inviting Sam Phillips to act as Elvis' producer under an RCA contract, but it was a thought that came to nothing. No, the buck stopped at the desk of Steve Sholes. And it was at that desk that an increasingly nervous Steve Sholes sat and stared with his head in his hands for much of the time in the days leading up to Christmas 1955.

Ring out the old

LATE DECEMBER 1955
FROM MEMPHIS TO CHICAGO

LATE ONE NIGHT, Elvis Presley sat anonymously in a quiet corner of the Variety Club, Memphis, watching the crowds drift out into the street. At his table were deejay Dewey Phillips and Dewey's protégé, George Klein, one of Elvis' Humes High classmates. They spoke about the possibilities of the months that lay ahead and, once the club had emptied, Elvis moved to the piano and gave the men a preview of the new song he was planning to cut at RCA. His guests were impressed and Klein, a natural born enthusiast, declared "Heartbreak Hotel" would be a smash hit.

Five hundred miles away, as the last seconds of 1955 counted down, Agnes Sampson led her musical trio at a New Year celebration gig at the Old Heidelberg Club in Chicago. Now remarried and already a mother, Agnes was fully focused on the future. She had little time to dwell on the past, and yet, still within her private belongings she kept a beautiful studio portrait photograph of Alvin Krolik.

And it would stay among her personal effects until the day she died.

Elvis, My Best Man, George Klein with Chuck Crisafulli
Chicago Daily Tribune, Illinois, 25th December 1955

Ring in the new

A SHORT DIVERSION ON
THE NATURE OF PERCEIVED CHANGE

There's a tendency for amateur historians to ascribe dramatic changes to the beginning of a new year or a new decade; the assumption being that people wake up on 1st January feeling somehow different, or believing that things have moved on. In truth, of course, this is rarely the case.

And when people today think of "the fifties", what they're referencing is the part of that decade from 1956 onwards, just as "the sixties" actually means 1963 – 1969, certainly apropos popular music.

But the early days of 1956 *did* mark a change, and it *was* the year that ushered in the modern cultural era — one that shook off the shackles of the Second World War and, for the first time ever, found teenagers and young adults coming to the fore in terms of media recognition and spending power.

In reality, change had been in the air since the early 1950s: beat poetry; the films of Brando and Dean; the writings of Kerouac; the Teddy Boy fashion prevalent across Britain — these were all indications of a new direction. But what the movement needed was a figurehead, an icon around whom the emerging youth could rally.

And as many have testified, especially those who had significant cultural impact of their own a decade later, the man who brought it all together was Elvis Presley when he sang "Heartbreak Hotel" — a record that perfectly captured the previously unheard voice of the post-war generation.

Business first

TUESDAY 3RD JANUARY 1956
NASHVILLE, TENNESSEE

THE PRESSURE OF trying to fulfil his father's wishes had taken Jimmie Snow into a dark place. The drink, the medication and the wild living all added up to what today would be described as a car crash lifestyle. Ironically, but not surprisingly, that's precisely how the situation played out.

On the first Tuesday of 1956, Jimmie sustained serious injuries as the vehicle he was driving collided with a stolen car which was being pursued by the Nashville police. He was taken to hospital with a broken leg, concussion and an assortment of cuts.

Father Hank made no reference to this event in his own autobiography written years later, but must have been concerned for his son's wellbeing. And he was probably also upset that schedules would have to be changed and show dates re-arranged. Blood may be thicker than water but with Hank, business always came first.

Indeed, on that note, Hank was beginning to have some concerns about his partnership with Tom Parker. The Colonel's interpretation of regular financial accounts seemed to consist of scribbled sheets of paper with figures roughly pencilled in, and these numbers didn't always make sense.

Afraid to confront his blustering overbearing manager, Hank passed on his worries to his solicitor. If the Presley boy was going places then Hank wanted to make sure the legal arrangements were watertight.

It wasn't so much that he didn't trust Tom Parker … it was more … actually, he just didn't trust Tom Parker.

Billboard, 14th January & 25th February 1956

Tom makes two phone calls

SUNDAY 8TH JANUARY 1956
MEMPHIS, TENNESSEE

ELVIS TOUCHED DOWN in Memphis in the early hours of Sunday and crawled into his own bed as soon as he arrived home. The five-day tour had been draining, and he needed to catch up on some shut eye before the all-important two-day Nashville recording sessions planned to begin on Tuesday. He slept through much of his twenty-first birthday, thus missing the Colonel's congratulatory phone call.

RCA had placed a half-page advertisement in the previous day's edition of *Billboard*, drawing attention to their quartet of "Country & Western Pace Setters for the New Year", to wit, Eddie Arnold, Chet Atkins, Hank Snow and Elvis Presley. Apart from Presley, they were all proven big-sellers and hit-makers.

Steve Sholes remained concerned about the sessions, especially when he heard Sun's latest release entitled "Blue Suede Shoes" by Carl Perkins. It was a bright, catchy original pop song (which would be ably supported by Sam's new $35,000 promotional budget), and the RCA man began to worry he'd maybe bought the wrong artist from Sam Phillips.

For his part, Elvis remained outwardly calm. He brought Scotty and Bill over to the house on Monday to run through the songs he was planning to tape for Mr Sholes. The rehearsals were loose and good-humoured, just like the sessions they'd done for Sam Phillips over the previous eighteen months. Neither Elvis nor The Blue Moon Boys had ever attended professional recording dates outside of 706 Union Avenue, and what Mr Sholes expected of them was a mystery.

Quietly observing all the pieces moving into place was Colonel Tom Parker. After his failed birthday call to Elvis, he phoned Mae Boren Axton in Jacksonville to let her know she should attend the Nashville session. His plan for the non-Hill & Range song was working out very nicely, but he wanted Mae in the studio to iron out any problems. Her father's health was worsening by the day but Mae, ever loyal, made the necessary travel arrangements and packed a case.

Elvis Presley: A Life in Music, Ernst Mikael Jørgensen
Billboard, 7th January 1956

Porter Wagoner: late in the evening

MONDAY 9TH JANUARY 1956
RCA VICTOR STUDIO, 1525 McGAVOCK STREET, NASHVILLE, TENNESSEE

IT WAS THE COLDEST Nashville day of the winter and the mercury bottomed out at minus 9 degrees. The RCA engineers had spent most of the afternoon installing and testing the equipment at McGavock Street in line with union regulations. Steve Sholes was present, naturally, and Chet Atkins was there to supervise the recordings as usual. It's possible the setting up may have taken longer owing to the weather: the session didn't begin until 7:00 PM and ended up running for four and a half hours, a most untypical length, perhaps compensating for a late start.

Porter Wagoner was the star due to lay down songs for a single release. He'd been at RCA since 1952, and had enjoyed an unspectacular career until he topped the c&w chart in 1955 with his recording of "A Satisfied Mind". As such, his career was on the rise and Steve was determined to capitalise on this, allowing the session to overrun to capture as much music as possible.

Midway through the evening, Porter started on a cover of Bill Monroe's popular bluegrass composition "Uncle Pen". Seated at the desk was the terse but professional figure of engineer Bob Ferris, who set the controls to capture the tight vocal harmonies, but then also came up with a clever trick during the instrumental passages: in order to create the impression of a fiddler playing high up on a hill (as per the lyrics) he brought an echo effect into the proceedings, using it only during the fiddling sections. It was a primitive device that involved running an extra microphone and speaker into the stairwell, which had an independent natural echo, and then running the signal back to the desk. By switching this device on and off, Ferris could create the required contrast.

At 11:30 PM, having taped six songs, Steve Sholes called time. Once the musicians had packed up and departed, he was last to leave that night. One can imagine him taking a final look at the silent half-lit cavernous room, knowing that his future career could well be decided by the events that would take place there over the next forty-eight hours.

Steve Sholes' worst day ever

TUESDAY 10TH JANUARY 1956
RCA VICTOR STUDIO, 1525 McGAVOCK STREET, NASHVILLE, TENNESSEE

IT WAS STILL COLD. The thermometer stayed below zero throughout Tuesday in Nashville. Elvis and his band had driven from Memphis that morning, well wrapped against the bitter chill, and arrived in good time for the scheduled 2:00 PM start at McGavock Street. Steve Sholes had set aside three sessions over two days, each lasting three hours and each expected to yield four songs — Porter Wagoner had taped six masters in four and a half hours on the Monday.

Elvis appeared calm and confident as handshakes were exchanged inside the relatively vast recording complex. Coats were removed and instruments uncased. Already the musicians could sense the difference as the RCA men kept one eye on the clock and refrained from too much casual chat.

On the studio floor stood Elvis, Scotty Moore, Bill Black and, on his first recording session for Elvis, drummer D.J. Fontana. Sholes' Nashville man, Chet Atkins, was also on hand, as was Floyd Cramer who had been invited to sit in on piano by Chet to fill out the sound. In the control room were Bob Ferris, Tom Parker, Mae Boren Axton, Jimmy Day (Cramer's musical partner) and Steve Sholes.

The plan was for Elvis to record uptempo songs on the Tuesday and ballads on the Wednesday. For the slower songs, Elvis had requested The Jordanaires' presence, so he was delighted to see Gordon Stoker slip into the booth. Elvis greeted The Jordanaire, expressing surprise that he'd arrived a day early. Stoker explained that Chet preferred to use the Speers on vocal duties and it was the brothers who would be present the following day, although Gordon had been temporarily bolted on to the duo to ensure a bigger (if somewhat unbalanced) sound.

Elvis absorbed this information without flinching, but remained discouraged that Chet had failed to follow his instructions. Gordon, who had turned up today purely out of curiosity, wished Elvis well and then hid himself discreetly in a corner to observe. Elvis glanced across the studio to see Chet engaged in a brief chat with his starstruck disciple, Scotty Moore, who was meeting his idol for the first time. Scotty enquired about Chet's particular brand of amplifier, but the conversation proved stilted. He then asked if Chet had any advice about how they might approach the session. Chet phlegmatically suggested they just carry on doing what they'd always done before.

Bob Ferris, meanwhile, had been tasked with recreating the sound of Elvis' Sun records, but his experimentations thus far had failed to produce even a flicker of the warmth and excitement that Sam had generated. Ferris knew it was a form of electronic echo — or slapback as Sam termed it — and he'd already applied this to the desk, but it just didn't sound the same. In a final effort to achieve something different, he ran Elvis' vocal mike through the same stairwell set-up he'd used sparingly for Porter Wagoner the previous day. Elvis' first RCA sessions, therefore, would be buried under two layers of echo, neither of which came anywhere near doing what Sam had achieved so elegantly.

In part, Steve was hoping to assemble songs for an album, and he planned to use some of the unreleased Sun recordings to bolster this LP. His main purpose, however, was to record a chart-topping crossover single — in the C&W field and also in the much more desirable pop market. This would silence his critics and the naysayers. The only problem with this plan was that Elvis had rejected almost all of Steve's suggested demos, and the sole original track he'd brought to the session — "Heartbreak Hotel" — was like nothing Steve had ever heard before, and he had grave doubts about its commercial potential.

In fact, this whole session was something of a frustrating mess in Steve's opinion. Normally, as A&R man and producer, Steve would have absolute say over what was and what wasn't recorded. He would call the master take, he would decide what songs would be released and which would stay on the shelf, he would set the schedule before even one note was recorded. But today, he felt out the loop and found himself looking to Elvis for clues and cues. Even the usually reliable Hill & Range had failed to come through in Steve's eyes.

As the clock reached the hour, Chet assembled the players, and Elvis confirmed they'd be starting with a new version of Ray Charles' "I Got A Woman", a song they'd previously taped but not used at 706 Union, and a proven crowd pleaser for the past twelve months. It wasn't hit single material but it was a good place to begin.

Had the boys followed Chet's instructions literally and done what they'd always done under Sam's direction, they'd have fooled around with this one song for several hours, changing tempo, changing key, adding lyrics, merging genres. In short, they would have played it to death before finally alighting on their own take of the song. Here at RCA, they were expected to supply a professional master suitable for release within a prescribed time. Having delivered this track hundreds of times on stage, however, they knew exactly what they wanted to do with it and stood by their microphones ready to get under way. Floyd Cramer, who had accompanied The Blue Moon Boys in concert several times — and had played this song with them previously — had his part already picked out.

The first definite sign of the change in circumstances came when Bob Ferris announced, "G2WB 0208 — take one", over the studio intercom. At Sun, Sam would generally just say, "Okay, here we go", or "Fine, let's try that one more time", but now they were working on company time and every song was given its own matrix number.

Elvis opened with his trademark "Well" and then they were off and running on a slightly over-fast rendition of the Ray Charles hit. Chet watched quietly from the sidelines, having decided to see what the band could do on their own before picking up his own instrument. The sound as captured on tape was muddy and distant, and it bore no resemblance at all to the clean acoustics of Porter Wagoner's efforts the previous day. But it was a strong performance and the excitement level went through the roof as Elvis peaked on each verse and D.J. (always tasteful and discreet behind the kit) lent on the ride cymbal to accentuate the vocal. The song came to a close and the studio stood silent for a few seconds until Ferris gave the thumbs up.

“Can we try that one again, Mr Sholes?” enquired the singer, and Sholes, who recognised the value of having a good spare take in the can in case of technical problems, was happy to agree. But Elvis asked the same question after take two. And after take three. And after take four.

“I think we’ve got it now, Elvis”, the producer suggested after take five, glancing again at his watch.

“I’d just like to do that one more time, Mr Sholes”, the singer insisted. And finally, as take eight was wrapped up, Elvis agreed they at last had the master they needed. Steve was mildly concerned at this turn of events. Half of the session was gone and only one song had been taped: a song which had no hit single potential whatsoever. What Sholes hadn’t cottoned on to was the simple but revolutionary fact that Elvis was using the studio as a place to experiment and develop songs, just as Sam had taught him. Not a songwriter in the conventional sense, Elvis looked to his studio time as a place to invent and interpret, and he would keep working until he felt he’d nailed it. But even if he fluffed a lyric or if he missed a note (a rare occurrence) he would still approve a song as long as it had the right feel.

Many stories have surfaced about Elvis’ first RCA session: some say he moved about so much while singing that two microphones were placed either side of him; others say he played his guitar so powerfully he was given a felt ukulele pick to dampen the sound; Chet remembered Elvis splitting his trousers because he was fully *performing* his songs while recording; Chet also recalled phoning his wife and inviting her down to watch Elvis singing because it was just so damned exciting. There’s little in the way of documentary evidence for these memories, but it’s clear that as early as his very first RCA recordings, those present were aware of something special happening. But the most remarkable thing was simply that Sholes, Atkins and Ferris, imperceptibly, were deferring to the artist at the microphone.

The band took a break as Elvis introduced Chet and Floyd to “Heartbreak Hotel”, a song that neither had heard before, and one on which Elvis wanted a piano part after Scotty’s guitar solo. Mae hovered.

At about 3:30 PM, the musicians again took their places. Elvis stood nearest the console window on the carpeted floor. To his right was Bill; behind Bill were D.J. and Floyd; furthest from Elvis was Scotty. Chet offered to fill in a little on acoustic guitar to augment the sparse arrangement and Elvis nodded his consent.

Bob Ferris announced, "G2WB 0209 — take one," and Mae held her breath. And what she heard over the next two minutes took her completely by surprise, because this was not the song she and Tommy had written, nor was it the song Glenn had demoed. Elvis had re-invented the composition and transfigured a roughly-sketched cartoon into a masterpiece, fully justifying his co-writer credit.

From the opening notes, sung acapella (he'd lifted the key from C to E), it was clear this was a song unlike any other on the charts, be it pop, country or blues; and although it was not rock 'n' roll music per se (you couldn't dance to it), it carried all of the rebelliousness and inherent sexiness of that new genre. It sounded savage, primal, and it came straight from the gut.

It was the most prepared he'd been with any recording since "That's All Right". He had worked out which syllables to stretch and which beats to accentuate. Taking his cues from "Only You", he'd established how to mangle words and add nonsensical sounds to the lyrics, transforming "I'll be so lonely, baby" into something like "I'll be-kuh so lonely, bay-beh", which added to the rhythm while making the narrative yet more mysterious. He had streamlined some of the chorus pronouns, removing the "we" from the final line, ensuring it was more radio-friendly. But the one lyric that still remained unfixed in his mind was "pray to die", and he wondered whether it was just too deep: but on take one it was present and correct.

For such a stark, unornamented song, he'd gone to great lengths to assemble the arrangement, but this was indicative of its importance to him. Even on the early takes, he spat out the first verse with absolute and shocking conviction, the band punctuating each line with a perfectly timed double strike (slightly behind the beat in best Fats Domino style), and as he slid into the chorus, Elvis was almost naked vocally, backed purely by the double-echo and Bill's descending bass. Aside from the "kuh" affectations, his diction was immaculate, especially on the title words.

The second verse was equally powerful, and on the chorus D.J. (on brushes) and Scotty crept in to fill out the sound. By the third chorus, Chet was strumming and Floyd had added pitter-patter keyboard figures to complete the picture. The fourth verse and chorus maintained the full band, but it was the unrehearsed pianist who came unstuck during the following instrumental passage. Scotty carried the first part of this section leaning heavily on the staccato notes Elvis had suggested (as per his conversation with Mae), but Floyd couldn't find his mojo, having literally just learned the song. For the fifth verse, Elvis had decided to repeat the second, but instructed the band to add a flourish, D.J. again using his cymbals to accentuate the finale.

The studio was hushed as the last note tailed off. Mae smiled. Steve raised his eyebrows. Elvis asked for a playback. The sound caught him unawares: the heavy echo wasn't necessarily what he'd heard in his head during the weeks of preparation, but he recognised that it brought something otherworldly to the recording.

"I'd like to try that again, Mr Sholes", he suggested, not surprisingly. Bob Ferris announced a second take, and a third, and a fourth. Mistakes came and went: Scotty hit a bum note in the solo on take four; Elvis' vocal slipped during the last verse on take five; Floyd struggled with the piano solo each time; after a good take six, Elvis finally decided to drop "pray to die" and also to simplify the chorus pronouns yet further.

As they prepared for take seven, Floyd steeled himself, aware that he wasn't pulling his weight. Elvis stood calmly and, after the count-in, again launched himself into the song, seeming now to be inside the microphone. On the tape he can be heard breathing between lines, lending intimacy to the performance. Floyd nailed the solo this time, his right hand capturing perfectly the falling raindrops suggested but not mentioned by the lyric.

The take ended and the studio held its collective breath. For Elvis, as for Sam Phillips, the recording process was about capturing the moment or, as the popular phrase has it, "catching lightning in a bottle". With take seven of "Heartbreak Hotel", the cliché was fulfilled.

"I think we got it that time, Mr Sholes", said Elvis from the floor, and the playback confirmed it, at least, it did for Elvis. Steve, concerned and frustrated, called for the union-regulated 5:00 PM dinner break and Elvis, who felt he was just hitting his stride, ruefully agreed. Sholes had never supervised a session like this, and was at a loss as to how he could re-establish control. Mae slipped away, safe in the knowledge her song had been taped and eager to return home. Before leaving, she rang Buddy Killen to pass on the good news, and also expressed to Steve how she was convinced the record would be a big hit, just like Elvis had said.

The producer took the boys to a nearby restaurant and, for the most part, he sat and ate and observed the easy-going relationships between the band members: Elvis talking a mile-a-minute throughout the conversations; D.J. dry and witty; Bill interjecting hilarious asides; Scotty quiet but always involved. If Steve was looking for clues as to how to handle the remaining session hours then none were forthcoming.

They reconvened at 7:00 and Elvis announced he wanted to tape The Drifters' 1953 R&B hit, "Money Honey". Like "I Got a Woman", it was a song The Blue Moon Boys had perfected on the road (and they'd played it with Floyd), but it too had little potential for single release.

Perfected or not, post-dinner break, it still took them some time to find their groove. On stage, they'd played it at a strong mid-tempo pace, allowing Elvis to milk every second. In the studio, Elvis lifted the beat a little to give the song an extra dose of excitement. The opening bars were striking: Scotty hit dynamic power chords, D.J. maintained a steady high-hat rhythm, and Floyd ran through super-fast glissandi at the top end of his keyboard. When Elvis launched into the lyric, Bill kicked off on a walking bass pattern that held the band together.

During the verses, Bob Ferris used only RCA's equivalent of slapback, but, as D.J.'s drum-fill pushed into each chorus, the engineer switched on the stairwell echo to create a vocal contrast. Three verses and a biting guitar solo later, the song came to a resonant end and the studio stood quiet. Breaking the silence, Elvis grinned and suggested, "I'd like to try that again, Mr Sholes".

And so they did. Again. And again. Even Chet seemed unable or unwilling to wrest control of the studio floor back from the singer. Take five sounded good to Steve, and so did take six, but there were parts of both that Elvis thought could be improved upon. So they hit take seven. And take eight. And in between each performance there'd be playbacks, prompting debate and suggestions from the band. Elvis was determined for the session to remain loose and easy. If there was a missed beat or a wrong chord, he would laugh it off, knowing the boys were at least as nervous as he was.

And Steve kept checking the studio clock against his wristwatch. It was over two hours since they'd returned from dinner and still this one song remained unfinished. In the time he had set aside for taping eight numbers it seemed that three (at best) might be completed.

And yet, Elvis remained unfazed. He called for take nine, which came and went. As take ten was announced, Steve felt himself tipping over the edge. Elvis counted off the song with four foot stamps and the band leapt in. But Steve reached breaking point when it became apparent that Bob Ferris had forgotten to switch off the stairwell echo from the previous take's final chorus, and the first verse was saturated in extra reverb. The song fell apart before the first refrain.

Steve stepped out onto the studio floor: Elvis and the band looked at him with curious expressions.

"Listen, boys," said Steve, "It's getting late. I'll tell what I think we should do here: Elvis, we got two pretty good takes in the can already. I can have Bob splice the best parts together to make one final master, and we can call it a day."

Elvis noted that it was almost 10 o'clock. They'd been working on this one song for almost three hours, which was no time at all by Sam Phillips' standards, but at RCA it was considered a wasteful extravagance. Elvis had no previous knowledge of the splicing procedure but trusted the producer.

"Sure, Mr Sholes, that'll be fine. Could I hear it when we come back tomorrow, do you think?"

Steve nodded his agreement and pointed out that the fingers of Elvis' right hand were cut and bleeding.

"Oh, I dropped my guitar pick on that last take, but the song sounded so good I didn't want to stop it," came the reply.

Sholes, who'd never met an artist willing to bleed for his music before, stiffly congratulated one and all as they packed their instruments and wrapped up against the freezing night air. Tom Parker, a silent presence throughout the evening, buttoned his coat and replaced his hat. He and the band set off into the bitter night to make the short walk to the Andrew Jackson hotel in good spirits.

Sholes, Atkins and Ferris stood silently in the control booth. The engineer boxed the tapes and shut down the desk, drawing on his cigarette as he did so. He switched off the studio lights and unplugged the monitors, while Steve and Chet reached for their heavy coats. All three men caught each other's gaze briefly as they moved towards the door. Chet raised his eyebrows; Steve pushed out a long breath through pursed lips; Bob dropped his cigarette butt on the floor and stubbed it out with the heel of his boot.

And as he closed the door behind him, Steve Sholes began to calculate in his head exactly how long it would take to pay off $40,000 to his unforgiving employers.

Elvis Presley: A Life in Music, Ernst Mikael Jørgensen

Back at the Andrew Jackson

TUESDAY 10TH JANUARY 1956 (LATE EVENING)
ANDREW JACKSON HOTEL, NASHVILLE, TENNESSEE

ELVIS REACHED OUT and picked up the ringing phone on his bedside table. It was gone eleven already. He shushed the girls standing near the dresser and placed the receiver to his ear. He smiled when he heard Buddy Killen's friendly drawl. Mae had mentioned to him that Buddy would be taking the publishing on "Heartbreak Hotel", but Elvis had little interest in the business side of his career.

"Hey, Elvis, did you do Mae's song?" Buddy asked, already knowing the answer.

"Yeah, it came off great," Elvis enthused, and then his guests burst into fits of giggles. Buddy guessed the conversation would quickly disintegrate from this point onwards, and simply wished the singer well, suggesting they might meet soon.

Elvis said that would be just fine, and quickly hung up. The singer had confirmed what Buddy had heard from Mae: the song had been recorded and the plugger could relax just a little.

By the Seat of my Pants, Buddy Killen with Tom Carter

Steve Sholes' worst day ever...continued

WEDNESDAY 11TH JANUARY 1956
RCA VICTOR STUDIO, 1525 McGAVOCK STREET, NASHVILLE, TENNESSEE

STEVE SHOLES had given the matter considerable thought overnight, and he now knew for sure who was to blame for the debacle of Elvis Presley's first RCA recording session: the guilty party was none other than Jean Aberbach. Having captured Presley's signature on a Hill *&* Range contract at the end of November, Aberbach had taken off for Europe on a two-month pre-planned business trip which removed him completely from the picture during this crucial period. It was an untypical error, but Jean had indeed misjudged the situation and underprepared for Presley's debut session.

Sholes had gone along with the Sun buyout on the assumption he'd be supported by the Aberbach brothers, but Elvis had rejected almost all the songs they had suggested. In fact, the only two that Elvis had consented to try were both ballads, and the Wednesday evening session had been set aside for their taping. What he might record after those were done was anyone's guess.

Elvis and the band arrived shortly before the designated 4:00 PM start, again well wrapped up against the bitter weather. Gordon Stoker and the Speer brothers were already in attendance and warming themselves near a radiator. The musicians were oblivious to Mr Sholes' anxiety and, to a man, felt that Tuesday's session had gone well. Elvis, in particular, was in high spirits because today marked a double first for him: he would be supported by gospel singers, and he was going to record ballads that stood a good chance of actually being released.

Elvis approved Bob Ferris' edited master of "Money Honey" and then asked Mr Sholes to spin the demo of the first song he wanted to tape; a plodding but gentle country track called "I'm Counting on You", which was published on ASCAP via the Ross Jungnickel (H*&*R) company. The demo was sung by sweet-voiced Lou Dinning, wife of pianist and composer, Don Robertson. Robertson was an up-and-coming writer who would within months have his moment in the sun with his self-written instrumental hit, "The Happy Whistler". A pleasant and friendly man, Robertson was nevertheless upset when he discovered his song had been forwarded not to a big star but to a relative nobody, and he distanced himself from the Aberbachs for some time afterwards.

But Elvis liked the song, and asked the band to stick to the arrangement on the acetate. Floyd Cramer was most taken with Robertson's style of piano playing in which he seemed to slip effortlessly from one note to the next, and he added it to his own box of tricks. Chet busied himself, suggesting how the band might structure the song, and Elvis talked through the vocals with Stoker and the Speers: he was still upset that Chet hadn't booked The Jordanaires as requested, but saw no reason to take out his frustration on the three gospel singers. Gordon Stoker, for his part, was rooting for the boy — he'd taken a liking to the youngster, although he really couldn't see how he was worth $40,000.

Bob Ferris set the controls as he had the previous day, with the double-echo to give depth to what he felt was a frugal arrangement. With one eye already on the clock, Steve Sholes agreed there was time for a rehearsal before recording began. The practice take passed by without incident and, still playing through the chord changes, the band took their places. Scotty fidgeted as the engineer announced the first take. The guitarist played the plaintive introduction but came unstuck on the last note. Ferris nodded for him to try again, but still the song halted before the vocal. Sholes glanced nervously around the studio. Elvis cleared his throat. Ferris re-announced take one, but again the song stalled. They tried yet again but yet again it died. Sholes bit his lower lip.

Finally, on the next attempt, they cleared the introduction, and Elvis began singing in the same clear tenor voice he'd used for his earliest ballads at 706 Union. But still the performance fell apart less than a minute in. Elvis spoke to the band about leaving a break at the end of each verse, just like the demo. They nodded and turned back towards the console window.

Take two was announced and it also quit during the introduction. They tried again and still they were unable to complete the song. They started on take three, and then take four, and then take five. Some takes were complete, others weren't. Elvis chatted with the singers, asking them to accentuate the second bridge. The takes came and went. A casual listener could have left the studio and returned thirty minutes later to hear no discernible difference. The multiple takes didn't change tempo or key, and Steve Sholes really couldn't figure out what the boy was doing.

But Elvis was simply following Sam Phillips' instructions: to keep playing the song until you knew it inside out, and then maybe — when you could stop worrying about the chords and the lyrics — you'd find that magic moment and hit the groove you'd been searching for. Sometimes, of course, that moment came on take one — "Mystery Train", for example — and then you'd give thanks to the gods of spontaneity and run smiling to the pressing plant. But mostly, it was about graft and sweat.

Finally, well over an hour into the session, the last note faded on take seventeen, and Elvis nodded at a relieved Mr Sholes who stood behind the glass. Bob Ferris changed tapes, and the band milled about on the floor. Elvis grinned and drummed an excited tattoo on his thighs. He had taken a simple country ballad and invested it with a passion that far exceeded its merit. It wasn't a chart-topping classic by any means, but as a statement of intent Presley had raised the bar several notches. And he intended to raise it several higher on the next track.

"I Was the One", like "Heartbreak Hotel", was a song that defied classification. It was a ballad with a beat which probably owed more to the doo-wop genre than any other, and it was composed for Hill & Range by three white men (Hal Blair, Bill Peppers and Aaron Schroeder) and also a black songwriter named Claude Demetrius. It was packed with the sort of vocal tricks and tics that Elvis adored, and, backed by three gospel singers, Elvis was determined to deliver a top drawer performance.

The band listened to the demo and sped through a rehearsal or two. As the clock moved nearer to 6:00 PM, Bob Ferris called for take one. A nervous Scotty Moore fluffed the first note, and the engineer announced take two. Again, the introduction stalled and Steve Sholes sighed quietly and deeply. But his fears were eased when the next take ran flawlessly, and the young singer devoured the song like a starving man. He was all over the lyric; slurring, diving, swooping and pleading. The last note faded, and Presley, without hesitation, spoke to D.J. on drums, requesting what he called a "country shuffle" rhythm in the middle eight, and asked the vocalists to sing up because what he really wanted was that gospel quartet sound.

And then he was back at the microphone with wide eyes looking at the console window, ready for take three. And then take four. And five. And six. With each performance he invested more of himself, which spurred on his fellow players, and even the professionals behind the glass found themselves caught up in the moment.

When take seven — or was it eight? Ferris had lost count — was captured, Elvis grinned at Mr Sholes saying, "That's the one, sir", and indeed it was. The singer was exhilarated when he heard the playback, and it instantly clicked as his own favourite song from the two days of recording. It was a confident and huge vocal from the young Presley, certainly his finest non-rhythm performance to date.

Elvis asked for acetates of all five songs to take away with him. As the band packed up, Steve spoke briefly to the Colonel, telling him flatly that more sessions would be required — and soon. Tom Parker shrugged and said he'd need to check the boy's schedule. They were very busy, you know.

Steve really couldn't make sense of the two days he'd spent with Elvis, but the singer himself was very clear that it had been a total success, and he strongly suggested a pairing of "Heartbreak Hotel" and "I Was the One" as his first proper RCA release. Steve nodded in a non-committal fashion, hinting he'd need to speak to the folks in New York about that.

At 7:00 PM, the RCA technical crew arrived to remove their recording kit under Bob Ferris' supervision, leaving the studio free for the Methodists on the Thursday morning. Elvis and the band had no professional commitments until Saturday night at the *Hayride*, and began the journey home for some welcome rest and relaxation.

For Steve Sholes, there would be no opportunity to relax: he was due in New York on Friday to present the fruits of his labours to his peers and superiors. And in the cut-throat corporate world there was no room for sentiment. Steve knew the knives were out and were being sharpened. How long, he wondered, before they were plunged into his back?

Elvis Presley: A Life in Music, Ernst Mikael Jørgensen
TV Radio Mirror, January 1960

Steve Sholes faces the music, I

PERHAPS FRIDAY 13TH JANUARY 1956
RCA STUDIOS, NEW YORK CITY, NEW YORK

WEEK AFTER WEEK, year after year, the men at the table had drifted off or ignored Steve Sholes as he presented his new hillbilly and race records at the weekly meeting. Some would listen politely if he introduced Eddy Arnold's new single, knowing it would sell well, but for the most part, Steve was an invisible man. Not so today.

He sat listening to the guys from the Pop and Classical departments previewing their forthcoming releases around the boardroom table and craved his usual anonymity. On the afternoon of Friday 13th January — an unlucky day if ever there was one — there was a single thought in the minds of the suited executives as they bided their time.

Eventually, all eyes fell upon the plump perspiring man as he strode up to the record player, acetates in hand. He began by pointing out that RCA's re-release of "I Forgot to Remember to Forget" currently stood at number three in *Billboard*'s c&w chart, and RCA stood to recoup most if not all of their investment from this one record. Steve paused and smiled, but the grey men sat unmoved by his jollity. He explained that he had recorded five masters in Nashville — which instantly raised eyebrows around the room — and Elvis had expressed great confidence in two of the songs in particular. Sholes spoke for a while, in fact, which worried the executives who really just wanted to hear what the boy had taped.

Steve talked about a new sound, which again caused concern as it was surely Presley's existing style which had inspired the finance department to part with $40,000. Steve eventually played "I Was the One", recognising that it represented less of a slap in the face to the expectant listeners. The acetate finished to silence, and Steve hurriedly placed "Heartbreak Hotel" on the turntable, nervously and noisily dropping the needle. Presley's voice again cut through the room and glances were exchanged around the table.

In the quiet that followed, Steve re-sleeved the disks and waited, feeling more alone professionally than at any time since his first arrival at the back door as a part-time messenger boy.

The first comment wounded him like a blade: "Have you heard the new record from Sun by that Carl Perkins fellow? Are you sure you've bought the right boy from Phillips?"

Other barbed opinions followed quickly: "It sounds nothing at all like his other stuff"; "You'll need to go back and try again, surely"; "I can't make out what he's singing." There was not one voice of support, and Steve Sholes stood there and took it all without complaint.

When the clamour had ended, he said simply, "We plan to release on 45 and 78 in all territories by the end of the month. The boy has some TV slots booked to support the single."

And with that, he sat down, and began to rue the day he'd ever heard the name of Elvis Presley.

Last Train to Memphis: The Rise of Elvis Presley, Peter Guralnick

A done deal

PERHAPS SUNDAY 15TH JANUARY 1956
804 CHURCH STREET, NASHVILLE, TENNESSEE

Maybe he made the call on Friday afternoon, or perhaps at some point on the Saturday, but Steve Sholes certainly phoned Tom Parker before the end of the weekend to let him know that, in the absence of a better option, he was going to put his neck on the line and go with Elvis' own choice of single release. The Colonel was pleased to hear from Steve and he passed on the good news to Mae Boren Axton in Jacksonville who, in turn, relayed the message to Tommy Durden in Gainesville, and Buddy Killen in Nashville.

Buddy then rang Jack Stapp and, once Stapp had signed all copies of the paperwork, the completed publishing contracts were sent to the three named songwriters. Had Steve Sholes not heeded Elvis' instruction to release "Heartbreak Hotel" as a single then Elvis would have received no writer's share, and Tree Publishing would have invested in a song with much less potential value. That was the risk inherent in a deal of this nature.

As it was, the Colonel had already personally pocketed a sizeable "deposit" from Jack Stapp and, if his plans for sole management came off, he'd also be taking twenty-five percent of Presley's writer's cut too. If the song did well then Parker could be looking at a big fat pay day — and Jean Aberbach would collect not one cent from this song.

In years to come, questions would be raised regarding Elvis' legal standing as a songwriter affiliated to BMI. It would be suggested that Tom Parker had neglected to fully and properly sign him up with the royalty-collecting company. As such, it would further be suggested that Presley — and Parker — would be unable to collect any BMI monies owed to him as a songwriter.

Having looked briefly into the legalities of this situation, but more thoroughly into the character of Tom Parker, I believe it would be fair to assume that if anyone was going to be financially short-changed in any aspect of the career of Elvis Presley then it most categorically would not have been the Colonel.

If there was money to be claimed then, rest assured, one way or another, Tom Parker would get his share.

I'd better get right down to the job

TUESDAY 17TH JANUARY 1956
RCA STUDIOS, NEW YORK CITY, NEW YORK

MONDAY HAD BEEN FILLED with other business — Elvis Presley wasn't the only artist on Steve Sholes' agenda — but Tuesday was the day Steve had allocated to try and get a grip on the situation. He wrote to Parker and Presley confirming the single would be released near the end of the month. He also suggested a number of songs that Elvis might consider recording at the next session. And Steve knew there absolutely had to be another session and it had to be soon. He was taking no more chances, and had booked Elvis into RCA's flagship New York studio in late January to ensure maximum fidelity and complete control. The sessions would coincide with Elvis' visit to the city for his first appearance on the Dorsey brothers' TV show.

Steve then carefully re-sifted through all the tapes he'd received from Sam Phillips, preparing a Plan B in case the wheels came off the wagon. Including the songs Elvis had just taped, Steve reckoned he had enough material to cobble together a four-track 7 inch extended play (EP) disk, and perhaps even a 12 inch LP to release when — as many expected — "Heartbreak Hotel" bombed, in the vague hope of balancing the books.

Of the unreleased Sun songs, Steve felt five were usable: "Trying To Get To You"; "Just Because"; "I'll Never Let You Go"; "Blue Moon"; and also "I Love You Because", which he edited and ran slightly slower to give Elvis a more mature sound.

Elvis himself was half way through a Hank Snow tour of Texas — his last as a non-headliner — and was confidently performing his forthcoming single each night, and proclaiming for the crowds that it was going to be his first hit record.

Whether he was a fool or a genius remained to be seen.

Elvis Presley / *Young Man with the Big Beat* CD Sleeve Notes, Ernst Mikael Jørgensen

Placing a call to Memphis

FRIDAY 27TH JANUARY 1956
NEW YORK CITY, NEW YORK

PARKER AND PRESLEY touched down in New York on Wednesday in plenty of time for the Saturday TV appearance. The band started their one-day journey to the Big Apple by road on the Thursday. "Heartbreak Hotel" (RCA Victor 47- 6420) was shipped and released to the public on the Friday.

RCA was, of course, pushing the record, and their salespeople were telling all and sundry that Elvis Presley was sure to bring them a good return on their investment. But the consensus at the weekly meeting at RCA HQ was not positive, and the executives watched with envious eyes as Carl Perkins' "Blue Suede Shoes" on the Sun label gathered impressive early pop sales.

Steve Sholes came out of the meeting looking tense and harassed. He returned to his office and busied himself, preparing for Elvis' run of New York recording sessions which were due to begin on Monday. He rang Sam Phillips in Memphis on some flimsy pretext, but soon came around to the burning question: "Sam, did I buy the wrong guy?"

Sam laughed off Steve's query, telling him to be patient with the boy and he'd come good. What Sam didn't say was that he'd just bought his own copy of "Heartbreak Hotel" and hated every last second of it.

"He'll be fine, Steve. Just don't try to make him into something he's not." There was a pause on the line, then Sholes stuttered, "What if I have Elvis record his own version of 'Blue Suede Shoes'?"

"Now, we both know RCA has the muscle to blow Carl's record out of the water, Steve. But you wouldn't do that to me, would you?"

Steve mumbled something about taping the song and maybe not using it as a single — but the very idea of a gentleman like Steve Sholes threatening to cover and kill a song from lowly Sun Records showed the sort of pressure he was under.

The conversation ended with pleasantries, and Steve replaced the receiver. The chips were down, and the one ace he held at the moment was that Elvis was sure to plug his new record on the Dorsey show tomorrow in front of a sizeable TV audience.

Last Train to Memphis: The Rise of Elvis Presley, Peter Guralnick

The revolution will be televised, I

SATURDAY 28TH JANUARY 1956
CBS-TV STUDIOS, NEW YORK CITY, NEW YORK

THE DORSEY BROTHERS would both be dead within eighteen months. When Elvis debuted on their show they were in their early fifties but looked years older.

Stage Show was not a particularly popular programme, and the pouring New York rain kept many studio audience members away on that Saturday night. Presley paced backstage. Not one person seated out front had come specifically to see him, but that was not important: the millions watching at home were the real audience.

A month previously, he'd received two communications regarding the Dorsey shows: one from Tom Parker (via Bob Neal) warning him to avoid any of his off-colour stage gags; and the other from CBS asking for a list of his potential repertoire so that appropriate songs could be chosen. Elvis supplied the list but, as he had no national hits of his own, it was agreed (unbeknownst to Steve Sholes) he would sing two songs that the viewers might recognise, albeit by other artists: "Shake, Rattle and Roll" (Bill Haley) and "I Got a Woman" (Ray Charles or Jo Stafford).

The Dorseys genuinely had no idea who the boy was, so celebrity deejay Bill Randle was invited to introduce the singer on air and — luckily or presciently — in his preamble he suggested Elvis might be about to make "television history". And then, to lively applause, Presley bounded on stage, dressed in his James Dean sports coat, to join his waiting band of Scotty, Bill and D.J. as the closing act on that night's show.

His hair was dirty blond, his eyes were made-up, his shirt was dark, his tie was light, and he looked like he'd run all the way from Memphis and still had energy to spare. He blasted his way through "Shake, Rattle and Roll", blending the suggestive lyrics between those of Joe Turner and Bill Haley, and threw in a verse of the former's "Flip, Flop and Fly" for good measure.

Elvis thanked the audience, and launched wildly into Ray Charles' signature hit — his hair fell out of place, sweat poured down his forehead, and the crowd applauded and cheered spontaneously as each verse peaked.

Elvis bowed, the show closed, and Steve Sholes sat perfectly still having watched the performance at home. He then switched off the set and stared for quite some time at the blank screen. Elvis had not sung "Heartbreak Hotel". Steve dreaded arriving at work on Monday morning.

Meanwhile, elsewhere on the continent, Mae Boren Axton, seated backstage at an *Opry* gig in the Jacksonville Armory, unplugged her portable TV set and started composing a short congratulatory telegram to the Colonel and Elvis (in that order).

And in Hollywood, top movie producer Hal Wallis returned to his dinner table. Five minutes earlier he'd been enjoying a meal with his family when he'd received a call from a trusted associate who demanded, "Stop whatever you're doing and switch on to CBS right now." Having done so, Wallis considered carefully what he'd just seen on the Dorsey show, and walked back to his waiting family. He resolved to track down whoever was managing this Elvis Presley fellow first thing in the morning.

Last Train to Memphis: The Rise of Elvis Presley, Peter Guralnick

A surprise for Charlie Fachs

MONDAY 30TH JANUARY 1956
RCA STUDIOS, NEW YORK CITY, NEW YORK

LOGISTICS WERE CHARLIE FACHS' speciality. He'd been promoted to RCA head office when his talent had become too obvious to ignore, and he had redesigned their order forms, improved the LP cover printing process, and now oversaw various areas which were key to the smooth running of the media giant.

His first task each morning was to check the daily orders so he could advise the three country-wide vinyl pressing plants of any rise or drop in demand for a particular single. "Heartbreak Hotel", for example, had pressed a standard 35,000 copies in time for its release last Friday. But when Charlie checked the early morning teletype and added up the tally, he saw the projected demand for Presley's single had almost doubled.

Charlie was a careful man, so he sat on the information for an hour or so, rechecking his figures, before knocking on his supervisor's door and passing on the news. The supervisor was curt and to the point in his reply: "Call those simple sonsofbitches back and get a confirmation on those numbers!"

So that's what Charlie did and, when he returned an hour later, he clarified the situation: "You were right. The order hasn't doubled. Since we last spoke, it's trebled."

Despite Steve Sholes' fears, word about Elvis Presley was spreading — and it was spreading fast. His strong fan base in the South (who could now actually find his records in shops) were buying. And families all over the country had turned to CBS to watch the *The Honeymooners* on Saturday night which followed the Dorsey show. Keen not to miss a second of the hit sitcom, they had switched on five minutes early and caught the last part of Presley's dynamic performance. Parents shrugged their shoulders. Teenagers stared in open-mouthed wonder.

And, by curious coincidence, the particular episode of *The Honeymooners* broadcast that night was entitled "The $99,000 Answer" — a parody of the obvious Lou Cowan quiz show production. And what was the chosen question category of Ralph, the central character?

Popular songs.

How Nashville Became Music City U.S.A.: 50 Years of Music Row, Michael Kosser

The sound of the city

MONDAY 30TH & TUESDAY 31ST JANUARY 1956
RCA STUDIOS, NEW YORK CITY, NEW YORK

AT THE EXACT TIME Charlie Fachs was reporting the unprecedented figures to his supervisor, Elvis, Scotty, Bill and D.J. walked in the front door of the same building, ready for their recording session with Steve Sholes, hoping to capture more songs for LP or single release.

Sitting at the sound desk was talented engineer Ernie Oelrich, a ruggedly handsome man from the Bronx in his early forties who always carried a pen in his shirt pocket. Ernie had one simple brief: whatever the boy sings, capture it cleanly, which was indeed the trademark clinical sound of the studio. There would be no stairwell echo on Oelrich's watch.

Steve, working without Nashville-based Atkins, had received no input from Hill & Range on this hastily-arranged date, and had given Elvis little in the way of direction, other than to request strong, tough, uptempo material. And Elvis obliged in spades.

Shortly after 11:00 AM, the quartet tuned up as Oelrich set the levels. Steve requested that Elvis begin with a cover of Carl Perkins' "Blue Suede Shoes", which was doing very nicely for itself saleswise. Elvis assumed the songs recorded today would be earmarked for a possible album — he'd not been made aware of the discussion between Sholes and Sam — but he'd have vetoed a direct cover single anyway.

Elvis had already sussed he couldn't beat Perkins at his own game, so he dropped the laid back hillbilly approach and grabbed the song by the throat, increasing the tempo and the temperature. The finished master — take ten — was his first true exploration into rock 'n' *roll* (rather than what we now call rocka*billy*), and it stood alongside several of his finest Sun performances. Steve Sholes didn't blink an eye at the ninety-minute run it took to finish the song. He was becoming genuinely intrigued about Presley's approach because it had nothing to do with technical perfection and everything to do with the *feel* of the record.

After the playback and a Coke, Elvis drew the band together and talked his way through the second number of the session. Once again, he dipped into the Arthur Crudup songbook — "My Baby Left Me" — and, once again, he'd taken the basic structure of the 1951 song and written his own version. His four verses are undeniably similar to the original, but much of the poetry in the Presley version comes directly from the singer himself. Look through Crudup's recording for any mention of "stand at my window" or "one I love is gone" and you'll seek in vain. Elvis also sourced four lines from Crudup's 1950 B-side, "You Know That I Love You". All in all, he was doing what he'd done in the early summer of 1954 — writing his own song in the style of Arthur Crudup.

The performance as released was a direct continuation of the fluid and supple Sun sound, with the addition of a kick-ass percussion part, rather than the pedestrian beat-keeping Sam Phillips favoured. It opened with a drum riff (a nod to Crudup's original) and Bill's bass descended the scale in a style not dissimilar to "Baby, Let's Play House". From this point on, it was Elvis' and Scotty's show all the way, as the two men traded vocal lines and guitar riffs with an ease and confidence that would have thrilled Sam Phillips. By the time Elvis had the finished master in the bag (take eight), Steve Sholes was a convert.

When the group reconvened at 3:00 PM after a one-hour lunch break, they were joined by classically-trained hillbilly pianist and singer Shorty Long, currently enjoying Broadway success in Frank Loesser's *Most Happy Fella*. Now signed to RCA, Chet used him as a gun for hire on various sessions, and later in the year he'd have a minor hit record of his own with "Hey, Doll Baby". A diminutive but-larger-than-life character, Shorty immediately made his presence felt as he contributed a rollicking barrel-house piano to the first post-lunch song, a newly-written R&B stomper entitled "One-Side Love Affair".

This was the only one of Steve's suggested list of compositions that Elvis had agreed to record, and had been written by Bill Campbell, whose "Play it Fair" sung by Lavern Baker, was doing great business on the R&B chart. The new song was taken at a good pace and Elvis blustered his way through the lyrics, calling encouragement to the pianist during the boogie-woogie instrumental section. It took eight takes and eighty minutes to nail the master, and Steve, who by now had stopped clock watching, accepted that he had again become an observer on the session he was meant to be producing.

For the final song of the day, Elvis yet again referred back to Crudup, this time the 1946 single "So Glad You're Mine", a slower, sexy number, cut from a very different cloth to "That's All Right" and "My Baby Left Me". And, yet again, Elvis re-wrote Crudup's original, re-inventing the second, third and fourth verses. He also beefed-up the sound, giving it a bluesy honky-tonk feel, with Shorty taking the lead and D.J. hitting every burlesque stroke in the book. There was a feeling of boundless freedom to the master (take ten) that absolutely captured the spirit of freewheeling artistry in the studio that day.

The session resumed at noon on Tuesday, and the boys picked up exactly where they'd left off, launching into eighteen takes of a bouncy pop song called "I'm Gonna Sit Right Down and Cry", a 1954 B-side by big-voiced Roy Hamilton. There were many singers that Elvis truly adored, but if you were to back him into a corner and demand just one name, chances are he would point you in the direction of Hamilton. For the previous two years, Roy had been scoring on the R&B chart and also doing well on the pop listings, and, of the sixteen songs he had released on single by the end of 1955, Elvis would perform at least seven of them throughout his career. A measure of the love Elvis had for the singer is that he would listen to show tunes only if they were performed by Hamilton ("You'll Never Walk Alone", "Without a Song", "If I Loved You"): indeed, he might have been tempted to try one of those songs at this session had Steve not requested only uptempo numbers.

Shorty Long's piano was again high in the mix and, as with all songs from this week in New York, the tempo was just a little too fast, but the finished master was irresistible and, this being a song Elvis and the boys had used previously on the road, Presley knew exactly what he wanted to do with it and swallowed it whole.

To close the proceedings — Steve had booked just three hours today and also a session on Friday morning — Elvis chose "Tutti Frutti", another number they'd already christened on stage. In ten takes, the song was in the can. It lacked the drive and sexiness of Little Richard's original, but it could not be faulted on attack and enthusiasm. Scotty and D.J. delivered a slightly chaotic instrumental passage, and Shorty dropped low volume-wise. But Elvis just loved the sheer excitement of it all, and the band held on for dear life as he pushed them ever-faster towards the breathless climax of the song and of the session.

Elvis approved the playback, and at 3:00 PM the band packed up their instruments. Between now and the coming Friday morning's studio visit, Elvis was due to attend press interviews to give his single the promotion Steve felt it needed. He was also scheduled for a photoshoot, intended to produce a suitable portrait for his first album cover, tentatively scheduled for release late summer.

Steve Sholes bid goodbye to the players and closed the door behind them. He now had only one thing on his mind: he'd just received word that Jean Aberbach was at last back in town.

Elvis Presley: A Life in Music, Ernst Mikael Jørgensen

A quiet lunch

WEDNESDAY 1ST FEBRUARY 1956
NEW YORK CITY, NEW YORK

JEAN ABERBACH had touched down in New York on the Monday and, having been in Europe for almost two months, his desk was filled with paperwork regarding hundreds of different artists and songs. But the biggest pile of messages came from Steve Sholes, all of which said the same thing: *We urgently need to talk about songs for Elvis Presley.*

A lunch date was fixed for Wednesday, and Jean, Steve and Tom Parker sat down in a quiet restaurant to review the situation and make plans. As they placed their orders, Steve listed for Jean the songs that Elvis had thus far recorded, and reported that, much to everyone's surprise, early sales of "Heartbreak Hotel" were remarkably high. But Steve was quick to express his main concern: what he needed was a regular supply of new songs for Elvis, and not an endless collection of R&B covers.

Jean considered Steve's words. Hill & Range held copyright or part-copyright on six of the songs Elvis had taped for RCA (and there'd be a seventh on Friday). This was good news for Jean but it wasn't necessarily of much help to Steve. So, as he picked up his fork, Jean offered two thoughts, both intended to placate and reassure his companions.

Firstly, as a gesture of good faith, he would transfer the copyright for both Crudup-composed songs into Elvis' own publishing company, giving Elvis (and the Colonel) a bigger slice of the cake. This was by way of an apology for not coming up with enough suitable songs for the first RCA sessions.

Secondly, he would soon appoint a younger man to source appropriate material for Elvis. Freddy Bienstock, the Aberbach's cousin, was closer in age to Elvis and had been at H&R since November. Bienstock would willingly sign up for the challenge of sifting material for Gladys Music and Elvis Presley Music. At present, however, Jean had no songs to offer Steve for the session on Friday.

Eventually, Aberbach brought the conversation around to Elvis' current single. He thanked Steve for choosing a Ross Jungnickel song as one side of the record (whatever "Heartbreak Hotel" sold, "I Was the One" would take half of the sales money, but not much in the way of radio plays, jukebox dimes and sheet music). Jean was most interested to know where the A-side song had come from. He didn't recognise two of the composers' names and assumed Elvis' credit was a token gesture.

Parker had been untypically quiet throughout the meal, and remained so in the face of this question. Steve didn't have much of an answer either, mumbling something about one of the writers being known to Tom, at which point Jean raised an eyebrow.

"Oh," said the publisher passively, dabbing his mouth with his napkin and looking Parker in the eye, "How interesting."

Restless Giant: The Life and Times of Jean Aberbach & Hill and Range Songs, Bar Biszick-Lockwood

A second bite of the apple

FRIDAY 3RD FEBRUARY 1956
RCA STUDIOS, NEW YORK CITY, NEW YORK

ELVIS, SCOTTY, BILL AND D.J. returned to RCA on Friday at the ungodly hour of 10:30 AM for a final three-hour session. Parker had flown back to Nashville. Steve and Jean had spent much of Thursday working out what kind of songs Elvis might be interested in taping at future recording dates — but which of them really knew what Elvis had in mind?

On this day, though, Elvis knew exactly what he wanted to do. He'd been impressed by Shorty Long's playing earlier in the week, and came up with the inspired notion of covering Lloyd Price's "Lawdy Miss Clawdy", leaning on the pianist's exemplary skills. Right from take one, the song shone like a diamond and Presley was in glorious voice. Time and again they ran through it, and it swung beautifully on every take: it was only Scotty's hesitancy on the guitar solo (he loved the track but had never played it before) that stopped each one being designated as the master. Elvis took the song as far as take twelve, but stepped back and nominated take ten as the finished article — an indication of the fun he was having.

To close the session and the week, Elvis pulled out a song he'd performed dozens of times over the past year and at CBS the previous Saturday: "Shake, Rattle and Roll". But the one area of the song that wasn't settled was the lyric. Elvis started by singing a version that leaned towards Bill Haley's sanitised single, but by take seven, Big Joe Turner's bawdier original was firmly installed as the template.

During the first hour of practice and recording, the song's two instrumental solos were split between guitar and piano, until Mr Sholes — or Steve, as the producer insisted Elvis now call him — suggested D.J. try a drum break instead. He did, causing the song to collapse, and Elvis voiced his thoughts, giving both solo spots to Scotty instead.

After a barnstorming take twelve they called it quits, and then overdubbed the band members shouting the title line on each chorus. By this time they'd excised at least one lyrically suggestive verse, but Elvis still smuggled through the line about "the one-eyed cat" which presumably was a little too clever for Sholes to pick up on.

The musicians cased their instruments, and Steve found a private moment to speak with Elvis about his performance on tomorrow's Dorsey show. There was good news and bad news for the producer in that Elvis had heard talk of his contract being extended from four appearances to six but, once again, he wouldn't be plugging "Heartbreak Hotel", as the set list for the first two broadcasts had been decided weeks earlier. And with that, Elvis politely bid his goodbyes, shaking hands with the engineer, and thanking Shorty Long in particular.

Steve Sholes remained genuinely puzzled by the overall state of play. The New York sessions had, for the most part, gone well, and early sales of "Heartbreak Hotel" were indeed very encouraging, but he knew *Billboard* based its chart positions on a combination of sales, radio play and jukebox counts. It could take weeks or even months before Elvis made any kind of showing.

Still, it was with a cheerier disposition than of late that Steve Sholes made his way up several floors to attend the weekly boardroom meeting.

Elvis Presley: A Life in Music, Ernst Mikael Jørgensen

Steve Sholes faces the music, II

FRIDAY 3RD FEBRUARY 1956 (AFTERNOON)
RCA STUDIOS, NEW YORK CITY, NEW YORK

THE ROOM LISTENED ATTENTIVELY as Joe Carlton played the two songs he'd recorded on Perry Como at Webster Hall the previous day. "Hot Diggity" and "Juke Box Baby" were both novelty pop numbers, and everyone at the table agreed the single would be a smash hit, especially as Perry would be plugging it on his own successful NBC-TV show that ran opposite the Dorseys each Saturday night.

Eventually, all eyes fell upon Steve Sholes and he calmly reported that receipts for "I Forgot to Remember to Forget" remained strong and RCA had, indeed, already recouped their $40,000. He then read the figures for "Heartbreak Hotel" and the room fell silent. Steve spoke about the projections and how — if sales continued at the current rate — they could have a million-seller on their hands.

His fellow executives seemed unsure how to react until one voice, from the guy in charge of distribution, asked the most unexpected question: "How quickly can you get me an album on the Presley kid?" Steve was taken aback. He cleared his throat and said, "Well, we already have enough songs." He glanced across the table at Charlie Fachs' supervisor, who also cleared his throat and shuffled the papers in front of him. "The photoshoot went well on Thursday, but we're still in the very early stages of planning. If Steve gets me a track listing we could rush it through for release in perhaps June."

"June? The kid is selling records like there's no tomorrow. Who knows how long he'll last. If you can't get me a cover printed quickly enough then stick the vinyl in plain white sleeves and I'll sell them like that."

"When do you want the album?" asked Steve.

"By the end of the month."

One hour later, Charlie Fachs was called to his supervisor's office and apprised of the new situation regarding a Presley LP.

"Three weeks?" said Charlie. "Forget it. We'll need six months to print."

"Well, what can I tell them at the next Friday meeting?" came the reply.

Charlie considered for a moment. "If you give me six weeks we could maybe do a black and white cover with a couple of bright spot colours."

How Nashville Became Music City U.S.A.: 50 Years of Music Row, Michael Kosser

The worst record I ever heard

PERHAPS FRIDAY 3RD FEBRUARY 1956 (EVENING)
3239 DELLWOOD AVENUE, JACKSONVILLE, FLORIDA

TOMMY DURDEN first heard the record over his car radio on the Monday, then purchased a copy and rushed home to listen to it properly. Four days later, he drove to Jacksonville and ate with his brother's family. Then, without making a phone call, he strode purposefully over to 3239 Dellwood and rang the bell.

When Mae opened the door she was surprised to see Tommy standing there, holding a 45rpm copy of "Heartbreak Hotel". She welcomed him in with a smile, asked after his wellbeing and offered coffee, but Tommy wasn't in the mood for coffee or small talk. Tommy wanted to know what on earth she and Elvis Presley had done to his song? He'd listened to it over and over again, but could not comprehend how they'd turned his heartfelt bluesy lament into this savage and shocking travesty of a record.

Mae asked Tommy to sit down, and she talked him through the process of going from their original manuscript to Glenn's demo and then on again to Elvis' recording. She played her copy of Glenn's disk so Tommy could better understand the process, and it was at this moment she realised quite how far the song had come in four months.

Tommy listened to Mae's story and could make the link between Glenn's demo and Elvis' record — it was like they were even breathing in the same places — but he was not happy, and said he felt disappointed at how things had turned out. Politely, he stood and walked towards the door.

"It is," he declared with calm sincerity, "the worst record I ever heard."

The revolution will be televised, II

SATURDAY 4TH FEBRUARY 1956
CBS-TV STUDIOS, NEW YORK CITY, NEW YORK

He was, again, the show closer. At 8:20 PM, Presley took his place in front of the live broadcast cameras, having received a warm introduction from Tommy Dorsey — the brothers may not have cared for his music but he'd charmed them personally — and launched into "Baby, Let's Play House".

He delivered a no-holds barred full-on performance of his mother's favourite Sun single, with the lens so close to his face it was almost behind him. The audience clapped enthusiastically during the first guitar solo as per the cue card, but it was during the second instrumental break that a subtle change took place. Rather than clap, the female contingent began screaming. They screamed again at the end of the following verse, and applauded as though their lives depended on it when the song finished.

And when Elvis hit into "Tutti Frutti", a palpable sense of excitement could be heard running through the studio, as the audience, unable to contain themselves, turned and shared their feelings with their neighbours, and began shouting and squealing. Bill and Scotty exchanged sly smiles as the reaction grew. Elvis, sweating, dishevelled and breathless, brought the song to an end and the response bordered on the ecstatic.

Steve Sholes watched the performance very carefully. After the show, he accompanied Elvis to the press party, and observed how effortlessly he mixed with the guests. The Dorsey brothers had exclaimed at the end of the broadcast that "Elvis Presley is a fine performer", and the audience had roared their approval. Steve began to understand: Elvis Presley was a salesman. And as every successful salesman could testify, you don't sell the product — you sell yourself.

Unless, of course, slowly but surely, you yourself are becoming the product.

One for the money

A SHORT DIVERSION ON
THE NATURE OF INTEGRITY

STEVE SPENT MOST OF MONDAY drawing up the track listing for Presley's debut LP. Elvis had so far recorded thirteen songs for RCA, twelve of which were straight rock 'n' roll, R&B or doo-wop based and, if assembled as an album, would have made a definitive creative statement. But Steve was more concerned with dollars and cents than presenting an artistically cohesive release, and he just wanted to get product into the shops as soon as possible.

As such, he took five unreleased songs he'd bought from Sam Phillips, three songs from Nashville and four songs from New York, and compiled an album which was presumably intended to demonstrate Elvis' versatility. It still made for an enjoyable listen, and certainly the majority of the material was of the highest order.

A decision was made not to include "Heartbreak Hotel" or its B-side on the LP. Elvis was not the only artist who followed this approach: Frank Sinatra, for example, tended to release singles *and* albums, rather than singles *from* albums, and it arguably increased the saleability of the single, which was viewed as the real money maker and might sell as many as a million copies — a hit LP might shift less than quarter of that number.

Having had the weekend to better establish his plans, Steve also wanted to push for a second album to be issued before Christmas, which would need to be recorded and completed by mid-April in order to be properly processed and not rush-released. He would use one of the colour photos intended for the first album on the proposed second LP.

Steve dictated a letter to Tom Parker on Monday 6th February, bringing him up to date with these proposals, and listing the twelve songs to be used on the first album (it would appear Elvis had no input on the selection or programming). But most interestingly, Steve finished by naming the two Crudup-composed New York recordings as the best possibilities for a follow-up single after "Heartbreak Hotel".

And whilst one could wholeheartedly agree that "My Baby Left Me" was a cracking slice of rock 'n' roll with definite commercial possibilities,

"So Glad You're Mine" (a vulgar but beautiful blues) had very little going for it as an obvious single. Surely the uptempo "I'm Gonna Sit Right Down and Cry" or the bouncy "One-Sided Love Affair" would have been more logical suggestions?

What was it then that drew Sholes to the two Crudup songs? The obvious — and not altogether comfortable — point to note is that both were completely owned by Hill & Range, which brings forth a question that has been voiced but not answered many times over the past half-century: Was Steve Sholes receiving under-the-counter commission payments from the Aberbachs?

There were some, certainly within RCA, who felt sure he was supplementing his income by favouring Hill & Range songs for recording and single release. Sholes was on a good basic wage, that's for sure, but as he sat through endless sessions, producing artists who sang songs from writers and publishers who all stood to make much more money that he could ever dream of, might he not have succumbed to temptation.

And, in all honesty, which of us might not have done the same?

Last Train to Memphis: The Rise of Elvis Presley, Peter Guralnick

Do anything that you want to do

TUESDAY 7TH FEBRUARY 1956
RCA STUDIO, CHICAGO, ILLINOIS

HE HAD PROMISED Sam Phillips he would not release "Blue Suede Shoes" as a single by Elvis Presley. But Steve Sholes had said nothing about covering it by somebody else.

And so, once he was done with Elvis' album, he flew out to Chicago for a Pee Wee King session, and had him tape his own hillbilly version of the Perkins number, and released it within a week as RCA 47-6450. It should be remembered that the Aberbachs had a part-share in the song, and they flat-out owned King's B-side, "Tennessee Dancin' Doll", via Ross Jungnickel.

Pee Wee's pleasant but insipid take did not hit the C&W chart because Perkins' own superior record was doing nicely there already, thank you very much and, fascinatingly, it was also climbing the pop chart and the R&B chart too — the first record so to do. And the second such record was coming up fast just behind it.

The colour and genre barriers were slowly being dismantled and removed by two young men who'd learned their craft well at the feet of the master at 706 Union.

The revolution will be televised, III

SATURDAY 11TH FEBRUARY 1956
CBS-TV STUDIOS, NEW YORK CITY, NEW YORK

ELVIS HAD BEEN ON THE ROAD SINCE SUNDAY. He'd delivered four shows a day almost every day, and would be playing at least three a day for the next week, before heading back to Florida for a series of gigs beginning on 19th February. He was, to say the least, a very busy man, so it's no wonder he and the boys appeared slightly jaded for their third appearance on *Stage Show*. Elvis had been further moved out of his comfort zone by the Dorseys' insistence on supplying a big band arrangement for his much anticipated debut TV performance of "Heartbreak Hotel".

Elvis had refined his look and seemed less cluttered, wearing a paler coloured sports jacket, and a dark tie. He opened with a strong take on "Blue Suede Shoes", which drew applause but no screams: the looseness and fun of the previous shows was muted this evening. The clapping ended and the moment for which Steve Sholes had been praying finally arrived.

Elvis, picked out in a lone spotlight (hence the lighter coat), introduced his current RCA single. Scotty, Bill and D.J. disappeared into the shadows, and Elvis waited for the Dorsey orchestra to hit its newly-arranged opening phrase. Accompanied by the horns, Elvis appeared stiff but gave his all, then hammed it up during what was now the *trumpet* instrumental solo. Bemused and under-prepared, Elvis missed his cue for the final verse, coming in a beat after the orchestra and, although not a disaster, it justified his feelings of unease. He bowed politely to the audience, and made a mental note to avoid orchestras from this point onwards.

But Steve Sholes, watching at home, was pleased with the performance. He'd received word yesterday from Charlie Fachs that it would be more reasonable to schedule the LP for release in late March but, as the latest sales projections for "Heartbreak Hotel" were so encouraging, Steve was sure this wouldn't be a problem. Best of all, the c&w page of that day's *Billboard* gave "Heartbreak Hotel" a glowing review, suggesting potential success in the hillbilly and pop markets.

And with that comforting thought, Steve poured himself a glass of wine and settled down to watch *The Honeymooners* with his wife.

Billboard, 11th February 1956

One more for Dub

MID-FEBRUARY 1956
3239 DELLWOOD AVENUE, JACKSONVILLE, FLORIDA

Capitol Records had let Dub Dickerson's contract expire, and he'd received no offers from any other major label. And so it was with a discouraged but grateful heart that he had signed with the tiny Sims Records. Opened in 1955 and owned by Russell Sims, the company had released just five singles so far, and would issue only two in 1956, one of which would be Dub's.

Dub came a-calling at Mae's house — she didn't get out much these days — hoping she and he might write something together for his first Sims single. He had already composed one side, a dramatic gypsy ballad called "Each Time", and was looking to put together something a little more light-hearted and grin-able for the flip.

Mae was always happy to write with Dub: his composing sessions were fun and easy-going with no emotional lyrical undertones. They came up with a mid-tempo novelty number entitled "Shotgun Wedding", about a footloose young man from Tennessee (yes, really). The finished recording had a pleasant laid back beat, and Cedarwood took the publishing while Sims himself took a one-third writing credit. Dub signed the rights of "Each Time" over to Murray Nash, and the 45 (Sims 106) was released in early spring.

Dickerson had recently become a father again for the second time, so he was hoping for a hit to boost his flagging income. Sadly, it was not to be: the single flopped and the label cancelled his contract. It was a pattern Dub Dickerson would go on to repeat for years to come.

The revolution will be televised, IV

SATURDAY 18TH FEBRUARY 1956
CBS-TV STUDIOS, NEW YORK CITY, NEW YORK

DURING THIS WEEK, Elvis finally hit number one in the C&W rankings with RCA's "I Forgot to Remember to Forget", although this would be a temporary secret because *Billboard* always published the charts one week later to allow for printing schedules. It would remain in the hillbilly top ten until the end of May, but, even with this level of success, at no time did the song ever trouble the pop chart. *Billboard* — which was a trade publication — did however list "Heartbreak Hotel" in the Best Buys category, and the reviewer pointed out that sales had "snowballed rapidly in the past two weeks."

Greatly encouraged by the positive reports, and freed from the burden of the orchestra, Elvis paced backstage at CBS before his fourth Dorsey show. On cue, he sprinted onstage and launched into "Tutti Frutti" before Scotty even had time to plug in, and he was animated, wild and irresistible. After the guitar solo, the audience began to clap along but they were hopelessly out of time. Bill and Scotty exchanged a humorous glance — Southern audiences always clapped perfectly in time and on the off-beat.

The song ended to loud applause: Elvis removed his guitar, and introduced a song they "have on record." Scotty played the opening to "I Was the One", the B-side of "Heartbreak Hotel", and Elvis delivered a delicious performance, full of vocal leaps and hiccoughs. It was a daring rendition and the singer was unable to hide his delight, smiling broadly during the closing lines.

This was Elvis' last *Stage Show* appearance under his original agreement, but he would return for two extra dates in March. The most fascinating aspect of the four shows was the opportunity afforded viewers to watch the ongoing development and re-invention of Elvis Presley. He seemed to be changing on a day-by-day or even an hour-by-hour basis. He refined his clothes, his hair, his stance, his moves, his voice and his public face, as he hurtled towards the stardom he had manically pursued for eighteen months.

As more than one observer noted, he was smart: he watched, he learned. And he never made the same mistake twice.

Billboard, 18th February 1956

On the edge

THURSDAY 23RD FEBRUARY 1956
JACKSONVILLE, FLORIDA

He'd arrived in Florida on Sunday with the Carters in tow, and had moved around the state like a tropical storm, blowing in and out of towns, leaving post-concert carnage in his wake. He hit Jacksonville on Thursday, ready to play two days of sell-out gigs in the ball park, and he made it his business to seek out Mae before the evening show, and she insisted on bringing a photographer along.

Perhaps Elvis was taken aback by her appearance. Since their last meeting in January, Mae had retreated from the world to tend to her father almost full time. She looked thinner, and presented a more austere face, wrapping a fur stole around her shoulders. They posed for the camera, perched on the edge of a desk, both glancing down at the 45 of "Heartbreak Hotel" held between them.

Word would soon reach the Presley organisation that "Heartbreak Hotel" would debut at number sixty-eight on the pop chart to be published in the 3rd March edition of *Billboard*. This was no insignificant moment, for Elvis or indeed for Mae. He kissed her goodbye, and headed off to the gig with the Carters — his fourteenth in six days. After the concert, standing next to Bill Black in the parking lot, Elvis collapsed and was rushed to hospital where he was diagnosed with exhaustion. The doctors warned him he was doing more in a twenty minute show than a labourer might in eight hours.

Assuring his companions it had all been a stunt to get Anita Carter's attention, he checked himself out and hit the Jacksonville stage again the following night without missing a single performance.

The wall of sound

SATURDAY 25TH FEBRUARY 1956
MUNICIPAL AUDITORIUM, SHREVEPORT, LOUISIANA

LIVING IN A GOLDFISH BOWL, there was little opportunity for Elvis and the band to gauge how things were changing. They were travelling, sleeping or performing all day every day. Yet, despite the surge in his career, Presley was still tied to the weekly Saturday night performances on Shreveport's *Louisiana Hayride*. And whenever he missed a show (as he had the previous four weeks) he incurred a hefty fine from the producers.

Parker, of course, had never wanted to renew the *Hayride* contract (that had been a Bob Neal decision in September 1955), and his feelings on this had proven justified, because Elvis was tethered to a $200 a week radio show when he should have been earning ten times that amount on the road or on TV. The Colonel, therefore, negotiated a buy-out clause and, for the sum of $10,000 and a charity concert in December, it was agreed that Elvis' *Hayride* obligations would cease on the last day of March 1956.

There was little doubt now that Elvis Presley was moving ahead at breakneck speed. Parker planted a story in *Billboard* that claimed "Hank Snow Enterprises and Jamboree Attractions, headed by Col. Tom Parker, are enlarging their offices and augmenting their staff at their headquarters in Madison, Tenn. Booming business is given as the reason for the spread."

On Saturday 25th February, Elvis stood on the *Hayride* stage for the first time in a month and introduced "Heartbreak Hotel": without warning, he was hit by an explosion of screams from the audience which was so powerful and unrelenting that it drowned out all other noise.

Scotty remembered this as the moment when he thought to himself, "What is going on?" Unable to figure out what Elvis was singing over the wall of sound, the guitarist instead tried to take his cues from the singer's physical movements. "We were the only band in the business directed by an ass," he liked to joke.

And from this point forwards, that's how things were. Apart from a couple of quiet spring weeks in Nevada, Scotty Moore would never again be able to hear himself playing on a concert stage behind Elvis Presley.

Billboard, 25th February 1956

Man of the Year, 1956

SATURDAY 3RD MARCH 1956
NASHVILLE, TENNESSEE

JIM DENNY could not hide his pride at being the *Billboard* Country & Western Man of the Year for 1956, the first breathing recipient, and it added to his feeling of invincibility. The award was made based on his work at the *Opry*, as it continued to go from strength to strength. Denny and his radio show truly seemed unassailable. Country music had never been so popular.

There were a number of other familiar names within the Man of the Year list: Tom Parker was mentioned in dispatches, and Steve Sholes maintained his position as runner-up. Indeed, Steve was currently revelling in the *Billboard* trade press reports that described Presley as "A Winnah!" and trumpeted that all six of Elvis' singles (including the five Sun re-releases) featured in RCA's top twenty-five best-sellers.

This article appeared on the same page as a Paul Ackerman editorial which pointed to Presley as the spearhead of a new cultural movement which was bringing together all strands of popular music. "It's getting harder to tell 'em apart," he concluded.

One fellow who was not mentioned in the Man of the Year poll, however, was Bob Neal who had, to all intents and purposes, now withdrawn from Elvis Presley's career. Oh, technically he was still Elvis' personal manager until 14th March, but he knew the writing was on the wall and the Colonel was waiting in the wings.

Bob opened his own eponymous record store on Main Street in Memphis on Thursday 1st March, and Elvis popped in as a favour on the Friday to sign autographs and drum up publicity. On Saturday 3rd, as forecast, "Heartbreak Hotel" entered the *Billboard* chart at number sixty-eight: this was something he and Elvis had planned and worked towards for over a year. If Bob bore any ill will he kept it well hidden.

He exited the story as he'd entered: with class and with his dignity intact.

Elvis Presley / *Young Man with the Big Beat* CD Sleeve Notes, Ernst Mikael Jørgensen
Billboard, 3rd March 1956

It don't matter if you're black or white

EARLY MARCH 1956
IN RECORD SHOPS

THE PRACTICE OF ISSUING instant cover versions of successful records was not restricted to white singers and labels: The Cadets (or The Jacks as they were sometimes called), a West Coast R&B vocal group who signed to Modern Records in 1955, seemed almost to exist for this sole purpose. They covered a whole list of R&B hits, big and small, including a song called "Rollin' Stone" by Johnny Bragg's Prisonaires, who, although still imprisoned, were now singing as The Marigolds.

As such, The Cadets were always on the lookout for suitable records to add to their own pool. When they gathered in the recording studio in February 1956, they brought with them two new songs to cover: "Church Bells May Ring" a recent release by The Willows (which had also already been very successfully covered by white group The Diamonds), and — of all things — Presley's "Heartbreak Hotel".

They copied Elvis' general arrangement but toned down the drama somewhat, and added a saxophone solo. Their single was released in early March (Modern 985), and Elvis outsold it not only on the pop chart, as one might expect, but also on the R&B chart, which was indicative of the changing times.

The Cadets were a well-organised outfit and, although their version of "Heartbreak Hotel" was only a minor hit, it did bring them to the attention of some useful and powerful people: by the end of the month, they were snapped up by Buck Ram, manager of The Platters, the number one vocal group of the 1950s.

Perhaps more pertinently, popular comedian and radio personality, Stan Freberg, also added Elvis' hit to his own long list of satirical pop covers (Capitol 45-15601) and it scraped into the *Billboard* top 100. Some may have viewed it as insulting, but Mae, Tommy, Elvis and Buddy just added the revenue to their ever-growing pile of expected royalties.

Billboard, 17th March 1956
Marv Goldberg's R&B Notebook (online)

Lou Cowan on top

EARLY MARCH 1956
BILLBOARD

SKIES WERE BRIGHT BLUE and sunny for Lou Cowan. CBS couldn't do enough for him, and the corporate ladder was wide open. He may have also noted that there was excitement at Tree, his other vested interest, as Presley's single continued to sell in huge quantities.

Bringing together the various strands of his life, RCA Victor released a brand new single by Tony Travis in early March called "Love is the $64,000 Question" (47-6476), adding lyrics to the theme tune of his popular quiz show. The song was, of course, published by Tree, and Dot Records brought out a cover version the following week — yes sir, things were certainly looking good for Lou Cowan.

Meanwhile, the top brass over at show sponsors Revlon, started talking to the production team at CBS about perhaps giving a little assistance to some of the more appealing and photogenic contestants on their hit quiz show.

No one mentioned this to Lou.

The Powers That Be, Dave Halberstam
Billboard, 10th March 1956

The revolution will be televised, V

SATURDAY 17TH MARCH 1956
CBS-TV STUDIOS, NEW YORK CITY, NEW YORK

THE ELVIS PRESLEY who stepped in front of the CBS cameras on Saturday 17th March was a vastly different man to the one last seen by viewers just twenty-eight days previously. There was an assurance about him that came from a month of continued success: he was met by relentless screams at every concert; Colonel Tom had arranged a screen test with movie producer, Hall Wallis; he had topped the hillbilly chart with "I Forgot to Remember to Forget" and also with "Heartbreak Hotel", but it was the pop chart he currently had his eye on, and his RCA single was indeed hovering just outside the *Billboard* top twenty. And sitting at number eight was Carl Perkins' "Blue Suede Shoes", the song that continued to haunt Steve Sholes.

Steve had purposely chosen it as the lead track on Elvis' soon-to-be-released 12 inch album. There was some concern that teenagers would not be able to afford to buy an LP ($3.98), so RCA planned to issue a 7 inch EP ($1.49) and a 7 inch double-EP ($2.98) at the same time, all highlighting the Perkins' composition. Steve would hold true to his gentleman's agreement with Sam Phillips, but he wanted to gain as much mileage as possible from Elvis' driving cover version of the Sun hit.

And Elvis' set list at CBS on 17th March was chosen to advertise the two songs that Steve felt were vital to the singer's success: "Blue Suede Shoes" and "Heartbreak Hotel". The former was presented very well, in more of a Perkins rockabilly style, and punctuated by regular screams. The latter, though, might best be described as definitive. Every carefully choreographed shoulder pop and corkscrew leg motion brought forth a reaction from the audience. It was the work of a young master.

Photographing Elvis that night, and over the next four months, was twenty-six year old Alfred Wertheimer, assigned by RCA publicist Anne Fulchino, who felt strongly that Elvis had the artistic creativity that would bring out the best in her own work. Elvis welcomed Wertheimer into the most intimate areas of his life — he was happy, indeed keen, to be photographed because it meant, at last, he was on the brink of being *someone*.

Glenn Reeves: a friend indeed

PERHAPS MID-MARCH 1956
3239 DELLWOOD AVENUE, JACKSONVILLE, FLORIDA

AS MARK BOREN'S HEALTH slid rapidly downhill, Mae cut herself off from the outside world, allowing access only to her closest friends and family. Having kept her father's condition so private, few understood the sad irony of her situation — that of success and tragedy delivered at the same time. The family planned to mark Hoyt's eighteenth birthday quietly on 25th March, and his graduation celebration would follow in June, but the calendar remained otherwise closed for the duration.

She took a call from a trade magazine reporter who was interested in her involvement in this rapidly-selling record. "What inspired the writing of such an unusual song?" was the question he asked. "It came from a newspaper article," she said, and then politely ended the conversation.

Glenn Reeves visited Mae in mid-March. They spoke about Elvis and about "Heartbreak Hotel", naturally, but also found time to chat about other great stars. In particular, Mae talked about Faron Young, who was enjoying a tremendous run of hits on the C&W chart. He was, after Elvis, the most thrilling performer on the hillbilly circuit, and was well known to both Mae and Glenn.

And that's when Mae just said it: "Glenn, let's write a song for him." And Glenn smiled and said, "Yeah, let's do one for Faron". Young specialised in songs that celebrated the wild and exciting side of existence — "Live Fast, Love Hard, Die Young", "It's a Great Life" — so the composers plunged straight in and aimed for an uptempo hellraiser of a number.

There was something about writing with Glenn that allowed Mae to get in touch with her deepest emotions, no matter how well she was able to hide them from the rest of the world, and the words arrived very quickly.

Having now repaired her writing relationship with Glenn, she decided to offer the publishing to Murray Nash by way of redressing that balance too. Faron loved the finished song and released it as a B-side later that year. Its title gave every indication that Mark Boren's daughter would not be broken by current events, but would seize every day that lay before her: "I'm Gonna Live Some Before I Die".

Duet for one

TUESDAY 20TH MARCH 1956
RCA VICTOR STUDIO, 1525 McGAVOCK STREET, NASHVILLE, TENNESSEE

HANK SNOW was feeling pretty good about himself: three weeks earlier he'd finished one of the most successful concert tours ever given by a hillbilly star; he'd also headlined the *Opry* TV show broadcast from Nashville on St Patrick's Day; and he was booked from mid-April through until the 1956 Jimmie Rodgers Memorial in May.

Three days after Elvis' latest TV broadcast, Hank found himself sitting opposite Chet Atkins in the McGavock Street studio with a smile on his face as he and the talented guitarist laid down two instrumental duets — "New Spanish Two-Step" and "Reminiscin'" — which would be released as an RCA single (47-6558) in June. Playing with Chet was a joy for Hank, who was no mean picker himself, and the session simply added to his sense of satisfaction.

In fact, apart from son Jimmie's wayward lifestyle, there was only one dark cloud on Hank's horizon: Tom Parker (he shied away from using the "Colonel" affectation). After the recording session, Snow's attorney reported back to his eager client concerning the accounts for Hank Snow Enterprises-Jamboree Attractions. He had investigated the finances of the first Florida tour, and had definite concerns about Parker's bookkeeping skills.

More worrying by far, though, was the legal status of the company. In effect, it didn't *have* a legal status and, when Snow was unable to produce papers in accordance with statutory requirements, his attorney sighed and declared, "Parker is a dangerous man — you're a fifty percent partner of this agency, and you could be heading for serious trouble with the IRS. I advise you to speak to him and resolve this. Sooner rather than later."

The Hank Snow Story, Hank Snow with Jack Ownbey & Bob Burris
Billboard, 25th February & 31st March 1956

The dark blue Cadillac

THURSDAY 22ND MARCH 1956 (EARLY MORNING)
DOVER, DELAWARE

EVERYONE AT SUN RECORDS was tickled pink about Carl Perkins' climb up the pop chart with "Blue Suede Shoes", and it seemed sure this would be Sun's first million-seller.

Carl was booked on the successful Perry Como NBC-TV show for 24th March and, by fascinating coincidence, he'd be playing opposite Elvis, making his sixth and final appearance on the Dorseys' CBS-TV show at the exact same time. It would be a battle of the Sun superstars and, with Carl's record slightly ahead of Elvis' in the pop chart — and Perry Como's vastly bigger viewing audience — this could be just the push Carl needed to make the number one spot.

By way of celebrating Sun's imminent gold record, Sam ordered a brand new dark blue Cadillac for Carl (but quietly took payment for it out of his royalties) so he could drive to New York in style. The vehicle wasn't ready in time so Carl and his band borrowed a less sexy but much sturdier 1953 Chrysler Imperial for the long trip instead.

Three hours outside of New York, as they drove through Dover, Delaware, at dawn, Carl's manager fell asleep at the wheel and ran into a farm truck, killing the other driver. The Chrysler rolled four times before falling off a bridge, seriously injuring and hospitalising the passengers. Had they been driving the Cadillac, it could well have been yet more serious.

Scotty, Bill and D.J. visited — Elvis was unable due to his 24/7 schedule, but sent flowers and a sincere telegram — and Carl took comfort from this, especially as he was forced to miss his planned TV debut.

"Blue Suede Shoes" never made it to the top of the *Billboard* pop chart but it did sell a million; Carl collected his Cadillac and subsequently discovered Sam's royalty subtraction; and he did eventually play *The Perry Como Show* on 26th May, by which time his hit record had lost its impetus.

He remained hugely popular among c&w and rock 'n' roll devotees and recorded dozens of wonderful songs, but at no future time did he ever trouble the pop top forty again.

Sam Phillips: the Man who Invented Rock 'n' Roll, Peter Guralnick

Half of nothing

PERHAPS THURSDAY 22ND MARCH 1956
MADISON, TENNESSEE

TOM PARKER was not a man to shy away from confrontation. Bob Neal's tenure had ended on 15th March and the Colonel had already typed his own new management contract for Elvis to sign. But the Hank Snow situation had to be resolved, and this came down to a question of timing. Right now Elvis was on yet another tour under Diskin's care, and next week they'd be heading out to the Pacific coast for the screen test and an NBC-TV appearance courtesy of television superstar Milton Berle. Parker had spent several days at home, planning Elvis' and his own future: he would soon affix Presley's signature on the contract naming the Colonel — and *only* the Colonel — as his manager, and then he would break the bad news to Snow.

As it transpired, the timing was taken out of Parker's hands when Snow arrived on his doorstep looking terrified but determined, carrying a briefcase full of papers. They stepped into Tom's makeshift office and Hank came straight to the point, explaining what his lawyer had discovered about the accounting malpractices.

Parker — who grasped that his desired moment had been thrust upon him — drew himself up to his full height and, towering over his diminutive client/partner, launched into a raging tirade. "*How dare you accuse me of such things!*" was the gist of his argument, which ran for several minutes, culminating in a single demand: "*We should dissolve this partnership at once!*"

Snow considered, before countering, "If we split, what happens to my share of Presley?"

Parker lit a cigar and dramatically exhaled.

"You don't have a share. Elvis Presley is signed exclusively to the Colonel."

"*No! No! No!* I demand fifty percent of everything this company owns."

Parker reached into his desk drawer and pulled out a ream of "Hank Snow Enterprises–Jamboree Attractions" letterheads. He emptied the box and divided the contents into two piles, then pushed one towards Snow.

"There you go, Hank. That's your half."

The Party of the Second Part picked up the paper and stormed out.

The Hank Snow Story, Hank Snow with Jack Ownbey *&* Bob Burris

LPM 1254

FRIDAY 23RD MARCH 1956
RECORD SHOPS

For many consumers, LP records were still considered a newfangled expensive novelty, but the major labels continued to push the product and sales continued to grow. It's quite possible, in fact, that Elvis Presley — a quintessential young record buyer of the mid-1950s — didn't actually own an album until RCA gave him a gratis copy of his own debut LP, released 23rd March 1956 as catalogue number LPM 1254.

It was titled simply *Elvis Presley*, and featured the same black and white image of Elvis taken onstage in Tampa (31st July 1955) that was used on the cover of his songbook. The hand-drawn lettering, printed in pink and green to give it greater presence, formed a half frame around the portrait.

The back cover included four photographs taken on Elvis' visit to the New York studios on 1st December, and the twelve songs were listed:

1	"Blue Suede Shoes"	7	"Tutti Frutti"
2	"I'm Counting on You"	8	"Trying to Get to You"
3	"I Got A Woman"	9	"I'm Gonna Sit Right Down and Cry"
4	"One-Sided Love Affair"	10	"I'll Never Let You Go"
5	"I Love You Because"	11	"Blue Moon"
6	"Just Because"	12	"Money Honey"

Also released simultaneously were the EP and double-EP, which carried the same front cover imagery. *Billboard*'s review the following day suggested possible "healthy sales", meaning they expected it to reach 200,000 copies, matching RCA's current highest-selling LP. But from day one, each product shifted an unprecedented 50,000 units per week.

And by the end of March, Elvis accounted for half of RCA's pop single sales, and Steve Sholes was begging Parker to schedule more sessions. To keep pace with demand, Steve drew up plans for a new compilation EP, focusing on "Heartbreak Hotel", with a Wertheimer picture on the cover.

Sholes had been under incredible pressure to justify his purchase of Presley: having done so, he was now under even greater pressure to fully capitalise on that success. But the Colonel wasn't listening: he was already planning against the greatest enemy of every big star — overexposure.

Billboard, 24th March *&* 21st April 1956

The revolution will be televised, VI

SATURDAY 24TH MARCH 1956
CBS-TV STUDIOS, NEW YORK CITY, NEW YORK

ELVIS WAS ADAMANT he wouldn't be seen to take advantage of his friend's misfortune, and dropped "Blue Suede Shoes" for his final appearance on *Stage Show*. Ironically, Presley's gesture of solidarity meant the song would receive no airplay on either channel that night, and Carl Perkins would miss out on two royalty paydays.

Elvis' original intention had been to repeat the previous week's set list, thus plugging his single, his LP and both EPs all in one evening. Instead, as Perkins recovered in hospital, he opened with a song that featured on neither EP, but did close the album: "Money Honey".

Elvis was first on the bill and he strode commandingly to centre stage and delivered two strong performances. His guitar was miked a little too highly and "Heartbreak Hotel" was trimmed to just three verses — he'd sung four on the previous show — but this was still the work of a young man overflowing with confidence.

During the forthcoming week, sales of Presley's "Heartbreak Hotel" would overtake Carl Perkins' "Blue Suede Shoes" and this would be reflected in the *Billboard* pop chart by mid-April, by which time demand for Elvis' 7 inch EP (featuring "Blue Suede Shoes") would be so high, it would actually appear on the pop singles chart, peaking at twenty-four.

This success was also reflected in Elvis' sharply rising income, and he made a statement of intent when he purchased a $29,500 house in Memphis for cash. But the new home was not just for him — it was for him and his parents. They would, as he had always maintained, share in his success.

After the show he called his mother to make sure all was going well with the move, but Elvis — the man at the centre of this growing whirlwind — had thoughts for only one thing: tomorrow, Palm Sunday, he would fly to Los Angeles for an appearance on *The Milton Berle Show* and, more importantly, his screen test.

Movie stardom beckoned, even though the adult population of America still had no idea who he was.

Last Train to Memphis: The Rise of Elvis Presley, Peter Guralnick

The sky all full of stars

MONDAY 26TH MARCH 1956
LOS ANGELES, HOLLYWOOD

IT WAS, PERHAPS, the first time in five years that Elvis had worn normal clothes. No pink jacket, no white stripe down the leg of his trousers, no two-tone shoes. Instead he was clad in a farmer's shirt, denim jeans and cowboy boots. And he stood off-camera, with three pages of script immaculately memorised in his head, ready for his cue. The call came and he entered through the back door of a modest ranch-house kitchen, delivering the part of a headstrong young Southerner with sincere conviction.

This was the first of three screen tests he would take for Hal Wallis during his stay on the West Coast. He was reading the part of Jim Curry, a supporting character in *The Rainmaker*, a dramatic movie starring Burt Lancaster and Katherine Hepburn, due to start filming soon at Paramount. Whether Wallis was seriously considering Elvis for the part isn't clear but Elvis certainly felt he was a contender.

Soon after, dressed in his James Dean coat (for luck), he read a page or two from *Girls of Summer*, a Broadway play, and then lip-synced through a playback of "Blue Suede Shoes", although he felt strongly he didn't want to be singing in the movies — *real* actors (Marlon Brando, Humphrey Bogart, Gary Cooper) didn't sing on screen.

It was the happiest adventure of Elvis' life and it seemingly placed him in a position to perhaps emulate Dean and fill the cinematic void left by his hero. Tom Parker wisely chose this precise golden moment to sit Elvis down and have him sign the Colonel as his sole and official manager. The fee was twenty-five percent and no exclusivity.

Hal Wallis was pleased with the two acting tests, but was much more impressed when Elvis delivered "Blue Suede Shoes", his natural charisma bouncing off the ceiling and captivating the viewer. Wallis was a canny man intent on employing a new star who could very likely be this generation's musical hero. He signed Elvis to a seven-picture deal all of which would revolve around his musical gifts.

Like Bing Crosby before him, or perhaps more accurately, like Tex Ritter, Elvis would play the part of a singing cowboy; and also a singing bus boy; a singing lifeguard; a singing racing driver; a singing soldier ...

Elvis Presley / *Young Man with The Big Beat* CD Sleeve Notes, Ernst Mikael Jørgensen

All Fools' Day, I

EASTER SUNDAY 1ST APRIL 1956
JIM BECK STUDIO, DALLAS, TEXAS

THE COUNTRY CATS had wangled themselves an audition with Ralph Bass, owner of independent label King Records. They played a couple of numbers for Mr Bass and he seemed impressed, although the boys noticed he always spoke to lead singer Mac Curtis and not to them. Nevertheless, Bass booked the quartet in for a professional recording session on 1st April at the Jim Beck Studio.

The Cats arrived at Jim Beck's with four songs and a bellyful of nerves, but they rattled through all four numbers — three of which came from the pen of Jim Shell and Joe Price — in a three-hour session. After each master was taped, they carefully compared it to the sound of the *Elvis Presley* LP, a copy of which was on the turntable in the control room. King Records was seeking to find its own Elvis.

The Galbraith brothers had felt side-lined throughout the session, but Mac was sure there was nothing to worry about. A month later, the first single from the session was released — "If I Had Me a Woman" (King 4927) — but the label credited not The Country Cats, nor even Mac Curtis & The Country Cats: this was a Mac Curtis record pure and simple.

As the record hit the stores, and three-quarters of the group raged, producer Jim Beck died tragically while cleaning his recording equipment with carbon tetrachloride in a non-ventilated room.

Discovering Country Music, Don Cusic
The Mac Curtis rockabilly blog (online)

No reply

MONDAY 2ND APRIL 1956
MADISON, TENNESSEE

INCANDESCENT WAS PROBABLY THE BEST WORD to describe Hank Snow's mood over the Easter season. Since his meeting with Parker, he'd been pacing the floor, alternating between fury and incredulity.

Upon his return from the Colonel's office (with two hundred sheets of stationery tucked under his arm) he'd typed up his version of events while they were still fresh in his mind. He'd then booked another appointment with his lawyer, who was loving the extra business, and to whom Hank declared he was going to sue Tom Parker for every last penny he owned.

The lawyer read through the four-page statement, took off his glasses, rubbed his eyes and levelled with his client.

"You have very little on paper which would implicate Parker in any wrongdoing. In fact, as you went along with this whole scenario from the beginning, it could be argued that you were negligent in the running of the company. I'd be very happy to receive your instructions and start proceedings and take your money but I don't think you'll win."

Hank Snow digested this advice and said not a word.

"There is also another point to consider, if I may speak openly, Mr Snow. This whole episode reflects rather badly on you as a businessman: do you really want that to be discussed in court and printed in the newspapers?"

Hank took back his statement (resolving to find new legal representation in the near future) and returned home to place a call to Jean Aberbach. Snow was determined to cut all ties with existing contracts lest Parker had wormed his way into those deals too. He couldn't do anything about his RCA deal but he could darn well open a new publishing company with Hill & Range to give him peace of mind about that part of his career at least.

Over Easter he fumed at home. Eventually, he alighted on the name of someone he could talk to about this mess: someone who had been part of his set-up almost since the day Parker descended: Mae Boren Axton.

So Hank rang Mae's number in Jacksonville. No reply. So he rang again. And again. But Mae wasn't answering the phone at all today.

The Hank Snow Story, Hank Snow with Jack Ownbey & Bob Burris
Billboard, 31st March 1956

The death of Mark Boren

TUESDAY 3RD APRIL 1956
3239 DELLWOOD AVENUE, JACKSONVILLE, FLORIDA

MARK LATIMER BOREN finally succumbed as Easter ended. The festival of new life closed with the death of Mae's beloved father at the age of eighty-seven. The one-time rancher had valued two qualities above all others: family loyalty and the importance of education. Mae had held steadfastly to those ideals, and cherished her final hours with the man who had been her guide and inspiration.

They'd talked about her eight brothers; about husband John's new prestigious posting in another Jacksonville school; about her sons, both of whom were following in Mae's footsteps as fledgling songwriters. They talked too about Hoyt's rebellious streak — "Remember the time he stole a car in the eleventh grade and ran away from home for a week!" — about her work as a teacher and now also in the music business, and about the success that would soon be coming her way as a famous songwriter — Mae would at last be in the spotlight.

It was late in the evening when the room fell silent and Mark Boren's last breath faded away. Mae said a quiet prayer and sat quietly for a long time. Then she steeled herself and walked into the living room. She pulled out her address book and made eight sad phone calls.

Two thousand miles away, in a moment of Homeric perfection, Elvis Presley stepped in front of the NBC-TV cameras on *The Milton Berle Show* and sang Mae and Tommy's broken-hearted lament to eighteen million viewers.

Ada Evening News, Oklahoma, 5th April 1956

The revolution will be televised, VII

TUESDAY 3RD APRIL 1956
U.S.S. *HANCOCK*, SAN DIEGO, CALIFORNIA

He looked magnificent. Like an extra from *Guys and Dolls*, resplendent in solid black with white tie, belt and bucks, he stood on the deck of the U.S.S. *Hancock* before an audience of enthusiastic navy sailors and their girls, and belted out his hit record, which currently stood at number nine in the *Billboard* pop chart, neck-and-neck with Carl Perkins' song, which was his second number that night.

As a novelty, the show was being broadcast live from the aircraft carrier (while it was being refitted) on a breezy Tuesday evening in San Diego harbour. The host, Milton Berle, was a popular TV star — although many critics regarded him as low-brow and tasteless — and his off-beat humour came across loud and clear in millions of homes around the country. This was a definite step up for Elvis, and there's no doubt Gladys and Vernon were proudly watching on their top-of-the-range RCA television in the comfort of their new home.

As Elvis brought his act to a rapturous close, with a broken guitar string dangling due to his enthusiastic strumming, Milton appeared wearing a less cool copy of Elvis' outfit for a two-minute good-natured comedy skit with "America's new singing sensation". And Elvis, following his script to the letter, introduced this character as the man who "taught me everything I know: Melvin Presley — my twin brother."

Berle, playing the part of a country hick, had no idea of the potential for offence this posed for the Presley family, pertaining to Elvis' stillborn sibling, but so skilled was the presenter (the audience was laughing at *him* and not at Elvis) that Gladys, Vernon, Scotty, Bill, D.J. and even the singer himself just brushed it off.

Having just received $3,000 for performing two songs, Elvis could afford to be gracious.

Elvis Presley / *Young Man with The Big Beat* CD Sleeve Notes, Ernst Mikael Jørgensen

Technical Advisor, II

FRIDAY 6TH APRIL 1956
SAN DIEGO, CALIFORNIA

NEGOTIATING WITH THE COLONEL had been a nightmare, but eventually Hal Wallis finalised the non-exclusive film contract and Elvis signed before he left the Pacific coast, ready to begin another concert tour. Wallis had rarely met such a hard bargainer and every time the producer felt they had it sorted, Parker would come up with a new suggestion or a different angle.

Elvis would receive $15,000 for the first film, rising incrementally to $100,000 for the seventh. And there'd be all sorts of provisos to do with music (Elvis must own the publishing on every song used in his movies), clothing (Elvis would be paid extra if he wore even one item from his own wardrobe) and favoured nations (Parker had the option to renegotiate if other studios subsequently upped the ante).

But the clause that Wallis could never quite figure out was the one thrown in at the very end of the meeting. Colonel Tom Parker was to receive a screen credit in each Elvis Presley film citing him as the "Technical Advisor".

And indeed he did. Not only at Paramount, but also at Fox and MGM and every other studio in town. And it wouldn't surprise me one jot to discover that it was a paid position.

The dogcatcher of Tampa was avenged.

Last Train to Memphis: The Rise of Elvis Presley, Peter Guralnick

The funeral of Mark Boren

FRIDAY 6TH APRIL 1956
WEWOKA, OKLAHOMA

THERE WERE PRECIOUS FEW OCCASIONS when all nine Boren siblings gathered together. Their lives were disparate and busy and they lived in a variety of states. But at 3 o'clock on Friday 6th April, they assembled at the modest Church of Christ on South Mekusukey Avenue in Wewoka, the city of six thousand that had been Mark Boren's home from 1930 until 1955.

They sat in the row of pews nearest the casket, and honoured their father. There was William, almost sixty, eldest son and chief mourner, who still lived nearby; there was J.D., about to move to a new church in Texas; there was Dale, who also lived locally; there was James, a doctor practising in Wichita Falls; there was Lyle, now retired from the senate and working in industry; and there was Preston and there was Henry and there was Dallas. Grandchildren and great-grandchildren were also scattered throughout the large congregation.

And Mae sat peacefully with her own thoughts, giving encouragement to her kin, as was her way. After the service, while friends and family exchanged memories of happier times, Mae's mind kept slipping back to Jacksonville. There were a dozen or more professional associates who had left messages over the past four weeks, including Tommy Durden and Murray Nash, and she needed to return their calls. But top of her list was the very persistent and very desperate Hank Snow.

Like many before her and many since, Mae would bury her grief in work.

Ada Evening News, Oklahoma, 5th April 1956

Hank gives Mae the third degree

EARLY APRIL 1956
MADISON, TENNESSEE

SHE GENUINELY HAD NO IDEA what Hank Snow wanted to talk about and he wouldn't discuss it over the phone, so she offered to drop in at his Madison home on her way to Nashville, where she was planning to spend a couple of days catching up with business. When she parked in his drive, Hank escorted her into the den and relayed the whole sorry tale of how he'd been hoodwinked and swindled out of his share of Elvis Presley by Tom Parker. And Hank required one vital piece of information: "Did you know anything about this plot?"

And Mae could answer in the negative with absolute sincerity because the Colonel had shared nothing of his plans with her at all, although, knowing Snow as she did, she was fairly certain he wasn't telling her the whole story and, unpleasant though the tale was, she couldn't help but wonder if Hank hadn't blundered into the alleged trap with his eyes wide open.

Reassured by Mae's reply, he poured out his heart and asked her opinion, because he didn't like the advice he was receiving from his lawyer. But Mae said she was sure there had been some mistake because she couldn't imagine the Colonel would do such a thing, then launched into one of her charm offensives and salved his wounded ego for the next couple of hours. Hank insisted she stay over with himself and his wife instead of renting a Nashville hotel room, so they could talk more. Mae said that'd be fine but she did still need to visit the city that afternoon.

As he walked her to the car, Hank silently reflected that Ms Axton was a mighty fine woman who had a good head for PR and business. Mae, drove away, Nashville-bound. As she turned the corner into Donna Drive, she glimpsed a billboard sign advertising a new housing development and made a mental note to follow up on this. She journeyed on a further half a mile and neatly parked outside the home of her mentor and confidant — the esteemed Thomas Andrew Parker. There were now a few things she needed to go over with the Colonel before she did anything else at all.

Billboard, 14th April 1956

Bringing it all back home

WEDNESDAY 11TH APRIL 1956
EL PASO, TEXAS

ELVIS ARRIVED READY for his gig in El Paso on Wednesday 11th April, having played Lubbock the previous day, where a young Buddy Holly opened the show. Tomorrow, the tour would continue on to Albuquerque and then Amarillo, and then he was flying to Nashville for a shoehorned Saturday morning recording session at Steve Sholes' insistence.

Before his El Paso show, Elvis dined with deejay J.P. Richardson who was now serving his country at Fort Bliss in the border town: like Mae, Elvis knew the value of these men and went out of his way to be accommodating — and J.P. was always good company. Richardson pulled out a copy of that day's edition of *Variety*, the show business periodical, which proclaimed that, as of today, "Heartbreak Hotel" was now a million-seller. Elvis scanned the story and called for the bill, which he insisted on paying. He then took a taxi over to the Coliseum, the venue for yet another sold-out show, and hit the stage accompanied by a thousand screams.

And Elvis opened his El Paso concert with "Heartbreak Hotel" — on the very day it went gold — at a venue just five hundred yards due south of The Busy Bee liquor store on Alameda Avenue, the exact place where Alvin Krolik had been felled on a sad and rainy summer's evening almost eight months previously.

"I Want You, I Need You, I Love You"

SATURDAY 14TH APRIL 1956
RCA VICTOR STUDIO, 1525 McGAVOCK STREET, NASHVILLE, TENNESSEE

As journeys go it was one of the worst. The overnight flight from Amarillo had been fraught with drama — the engines cut in mid-air — and when Elvis arrived at McGavock Street for the 10:00 AM session on Saturday he was exhausted and in no mood to record.

Steve Sholes had been desperate to get Elvis back in the studio because the boy was selling records like they were going out of fashion and RCA had almost nothing in the can ready for release. Steve wanted a new album and a new single: in the cold light of day he'd re-assessed "So Glad You're Mine" and realised it wasn't commercially suitable.

But the Colonel, who enjoyed keeping Steve on a tight leash, said Elvis could spare only one morning in his manic schedule, and this would involve flying him in and out of Nashville in order to meet his touring obligations. A three-hour session would be enough for most c&w singers to lay down four songs, but Sholes knew it was more likely he'd capture just two with Elvis' relentless (im)perfectionism.

Steve caught the singer off guard as he stepped into the studio, presenting him with a wrapped package. When opened, he discovered a gold record from RCA to mark the millionth sale of "Heartbreak Hotel" and the room filled with chatter and laughter as the musicians uncased.

But Elvis noted the same three-man makeshift vocal group was standing in the corner and this brought him down to earth with a thud. The usual tension between Chet Atkins and Bob Ferris was also present, added to which Chet had brought in a new pianist, a session musician and long-time WSM staffer named Marvin Hughes. The short, stocky keyboard player was experienced and gifted but, like Ferris, had a reputation for brusqueness.

Hughes had played on an RCA Jim Reeves session on Friday when Jim had taped three songs, one of which (from Tree) would be left on the shelf but the other two (Hill & Range) would be issued as a single later that month. Jim had struggled chart-wise since "Yonder Comes a Sucker", but this studio visit would mark a watershed in his career and he would remain a c&w top tenner for the rest of his life from this moment on.

Elvis removed his jacket and shoes and started work in a room packed with conflicting personalities and opposing priorities. The main purpose, in Steve Sholes' opinion, was to capture at least one side of the next single: "My Baby Left Me" would serve as an acceptable flip should circumstances demand it.

Elvis had chosen a song submitted by Hill & Range, a doo-wop beat ballad taken from the files. "I Want You, I Need You, I You Love" was written by Maurice Mysels and Ira Kosloff, two nondescript composers who had agreed to sign over their rights to the newly established Elvis Presley Music, hoping the song would sell like "Heartbreak Hotel" and they would then be more than compensated for the loss of publishing revenue. It hadn't been written for Presley but Freddy Bienstock was still working out what would appeal to Elvis' musical tastes, and had presented the acetate to the singer who heard an opportunity to deliver another passionate performance like "I Was the One".

Steve played the demo disk for the band, then Elvis strapped on his guitar and ran through the song with Scotty and Chet who sat in front of him, while Hughes hovered. He sang it again, this time with the vocalists, as Steve Sholes joined the huddle and announced, "Let's try one," when the rehearsal ended.

Taking his place at the microphone, Elvis did his best to inject a little humour into the room, cracking a joke and flashing his smile. Bob Ferris, who had already set up the stairwell echo, announced the matrix number. Scotty's striking guitar introduction filled the studio, and Elvis, swamped with double echo, held nothing back as he crooned the opening lines: "Hold me close, hold me tight, make me thrill with delight."

It was melodramatic, heavy and just sounded *big* — bigger than anything he'd attempted before. Maybe he had The Platters' hit "The Great Pretender" in the back of his mind as he swooped and danced his way through the tune, living out the lyric as it was captured on tape.

The take ended and the boys sat quietly through the playback. Elvis was joined on the studio floor by RCA publicist Anne Fulchino and he casually draped an arm over her shoulder while they listened. This would be one of her final Elvis-related duties: the Colonel would soon assume complete responsibility for any and all future Presley PR, much to her anger.

"Let's try it just a little faster, fellas," came the singer's direction, and he laid aside his guitar and concentrated purely on the vocals from now on. The takes came and went, as they had done with "I'm Counting on You", and the changes were minimal: a slight emphasis on a certain lyric from the three-man gospel group; a less pedantic bass line in parts; a more dramatic edge to the percussion; but always the focus was on Elvis finding the heart of the song. And after almost three hours and seventeen takes, his frustration began to show, and this was when Steve stepped in once again with his "let's splice together a couple of good takes" solution, and Elvis, exhausted, ruefully agreed.

Steve now had a song to accompany "My Baby Left Me", but he'd sorely wanted more. Any other RCA artist would have delivered a further three masters — but Elvis seemed driven in his quest for the right sound and, bearing in mind the incredible level of profit this had brought about with "Heartbreak Hotel", Sholes did not feel able to query his approach.

If Steve was disgruntled, it was as nothing compared to Elvis' own feelings. The session had none of the easy-going atmosphere he preferred, and the pressure of working with Ferris, Hughes, Atkins and the Speer brothers had convinced him that a change was required. He'd make sure RCA knew, via the Colonel, that he wouldn't be coming back to Nashville in a hurry. If they wanted more music then he and they would need to find somewhere more conducive to his way of working.

And if Chet wasn't going to follow his specific instructions and hire The Jordanaires then Elvis would damn well do it himself.

Elvis Presley: A Life in Music, Ernst Mikael Jørgensen

Returning Murray's call

MID-APRIL 1956
3239 DELLWOOD AVENUE, JACKSONVILLE, FLORIDA

NOW THAT MAE HAD EMERGED from her cocoon, the phone calls, telegrams and letters began to arrive with increasing regularity. She'd relentlessly courted songwriters, producers, publishers, deejays, editors and singers over the past six years and now she was reaping what she'd sown: everyone wanted to talk to the co-writer of what looked like being the hottest record of the year, be it on the C&W, the R&B, or the pop charts.

One of the first calls she returned was that of Murray Nash. They'd long since put last November's unpleasantness behind them but he was silently struggling. Republic Records was all but finished and his publishing house was fading. The supposed loss of "Heartbreak Hotel" played often on his mind but it never passed his lips.

The specific reason for Murray's call was that he'd signed Jean Chapel, sister of Martha Carson (of "Satisfied" fame), to a recording deal — even though technically he no longer owned a record company — and he was looking for suitable material, preferably a song that he could also publish via Murray Nash Associates. Still feeling a tinge of guilt about the way she'd dealt with Murray last year, Mae remembered she had "Welcome to the Club" on her shelf, the song she had mined and cannibalised for Elvis' hit record. She promised she'd do her best to get something to him over the next couple of weeks.

And with an irony that he would never comprehend for as long as he lived, Murray joked: "I don't suppose you've got something like another 'Heartbreak Hotel' lying around somewhere, have you?"

The offer

PERHAPS MID-APRIL 1956
804 CHURCH STREET, NASHVILLE, TENNESSEE

ALTHOUGH HE NEVER QUITE FIGURED OUT exactly how Tom Parker had shafted him over the publishing rights to "Heartbreak Hotel", it's likely that, as it neared the top of the pop chart, Jean Aberbach developed a definite understanding that he had been deliberately passed over by the Colonel. Furthermore, he was missing out on a substantial payday which might easily run into tens (hundreds?) of thousands of dollars. But the publisher was philosophical and practical about such matters. Rather than rue his lost opportunity, he decided to take action and continued doing that which had occupied him for the past thirteen months — pursuing and buying the rights to any Elvis Presley recordings not yet owned by Hill & Range.

As such, Jack Stapp received a telephone call from Jean Aberbach and the old master poured on the charm and suggested a not-inconsiderable figure for the immediate purchase of the rights to "Heartbreak Hotel". Jack said he'd need to think about the offer, hung up and then summoned Buddy to his office. The plugger listened with interest but quickly confirmed his thoughts: "If the song goes, so do I."

He then gave a heartfelt speech about how Tree needed good resources so they could grow. If they started selling off every successful song then they might as well quit. Jack Stapp, impressed by Buddy's stance, nodded and returned Jean's call. He politely but firmly rejected the offer.

There was also the possibility, of course, that certain parties had privately made it very plain to Buddy that under no circumstances was Hill & Range to be allowed one single cent from this particular song.

Buddy went back to his desk and continued sifting through the ever-growing pile of paperwork relating to their incredible hit record. And life would be busier yet in the coming weeks as RCA had just released a 7 inch EP using "Heartbreak Hotel" as the title track.

Chances are, Tom Parker got to hear about the Hill & Range offer and, when told about the figure that Aberbach had suggested, would have almost swallowed his cigar with laughter.

It was the perfectly ironic amount of $40,000.

By the Seat of my Pants, Buddy Killen with Tom Carter

Tommy comes around

PERHAPS FRIDAY 20TH APRIL 1956
3239 DELLWOOD AVENUE, JACKSONVILLE, FLORIDA

MUCH TO HIS DELIGHT and embarrassment, Tommy Durden watched disbelievingly as "Heartbreak Hotel" continued its steady climb up the chart. Having made his feelings over the record very clear to Mae in February, he was now obliged to eat humble pie: even if he didn't care for the transformation of his song it seemed many other people did. In fact, it seemed that over a million people liked it.

He'd tried several times to contact Mae earlier in the spring but she'd been incommunicado. He was in town for *Country Frolics* one Friday in mid-April and rang Mae one more time and, to his relief, she answered. He tried to stutter through an apology but Mae was having none of it and insisted he walk round to her home on Dellwood so they could toast the triumph of their song together.

An hour or so later, after much good-natured chat and speculation about what they might do with the money that was headed their way, Mae eventually broached the obvious subject: they'd written one hit record together — why shouldn't they do it again? She told Tommy about her conversation with Murray Nash and confessed she already had a song to give to Jean Chapel, but suggested they might write the B-side right there and then.

And that's exactly what they did, only this time, still feeling sheepish, Tommy allowed Mae to take the lead throughout the process. She again took inspiration from Elvis' second Sun single for the title, coming up with "I Won't Be Rockin' Tonight", a mid-tempo and slightly awkward number written from a female perspective, which literally referenced the current buzz-phrase "rock 'n' roll". In their ebullient mood they were both convinced it would be their next hit, and Mae decided she wouldn't need a demo record because she'd be delivering it in person to Jean and Murray. And once again, Mae and Tommy would surely be heading for the top ten.

Which was all very nice: but where did this leave Glenn Reeves?

"Hound Dog": Freddie Bell

MONDAY 23RD APRIL 1956
NEW FRONTIER HOTEL, LAS VEGAS, NEVADA

FOR THE ASTUTE OBSERVER it would already have been made clear that Tom Parker's career plan for the most creative and ambitious pop musician of the post-war generation was marked simply as "EDDY ARNOLD PART 2". The Colonel had guided Eddy and Elvis away from weekly radio shows to Hill & Range, William Morris, RCA Victor, television, Hollywood movies and, as such, the next stop on Elvis' journey was to play a stint in Las Vegas. But whereas with Eddy it had taken years to achieve those goals, with Elvis it had taken mere months.

The Colonel had booked Elvis in for a fortnight at the New Frontier Hotel, sharing the spotlight with the Freddy Martin Orchestra, and it soon became apparent that the Vegas crowd were not Elvis' audience, being at least twice as old as his regular customers. But still, he persisted and, ably backed by Scotty, Bill and D.J., he achieved a modicum of respect and recognition as he battled his way through twenty-eight performances.

For the insomniac Elvis though, the main attraction — apart from the $30,000 fee — was the opportunity to wander Las Vegas at any time, day or night, and check out the cabaret acts. And it was at the Sands Hotel that he caught the fabulous Freddie Bell and The Bellboys, a well-drilled six-piece outfit which specialised in covering R&B hits in a rock 'n' roll swing style.

The previous year they'd put together their own record of Leiber and Stoller's "Hound Dog" (Teen 101), adding to the lyrics — "They said you were high class, that was just a line" — and doubling the speed. The single had not thrived, but its live performance in Vegas was a tour-de-force, as the singer rattled his legs in machine-gun fashion. Elvis found it fascinating and hilarious: it was the perfect send-up of the modern trend for updating old blues songs, and Elvis got the gag.

He also loved Thornton's original (which blues fan didn't?) and the well-played original 78 was safely stored in his personal record collection. But he memorised Freddie's adapted lyric on the spot and took careful note of the visual presentation, deciding to use it as a spectacular tongue-in-cheek show-closer on the road when his Vegas experience was over.

Elvis Presley: The King of Rock 'n' Roll, Jean-Pierre Hombach

"Welcome to the Club", I

PERHAPS APRIL 1956
MUSIC CITY RECORDING, NASHVILLE, TENNESSEE

MURRAY HAD BEEN THRILLED that the woman of the moment had delivered not one but *two* songs to him personally, and had then helped Jean Chapel familiarise herself with both numbers which would be registered as Murray Nash-published compositions.

Mae was in town to finalise the deposit on a brand new home in Madison which would allow her to more conveniently manage her personal and professional time. She and husband John had speculated about the royalty figure she'd be receiving in July, and they estimated the new house would be a sensible and worthwhile investment.

Jean Chapel was a gifted multi-instrumentalist, displaying competency in guitar, banjo, fiddle and bass, and had a more than passable singing voice. She was a hillbilly singer in a hillbilly studio with a hillbilly producer looking to record some hillbilly songs that would put her back on the hillbilly chart — a place she'd not troubled in over a year.

However, despite all of the obvious country *&* western intentions, the two finished masters leaned perilously close to faux pop-blues and both sounded heavy-handed and overdone. But Murray and Mae felt sure that "Welcome to the Club"/"I Won't Be Rockin' Tonight" would continue in the big-selling tradition of "Heartbreak Hotel" ... bar the obvious and odd problem that Murray didn't actually own a record label anymore.

But somehow — by hook or by crook — a solution was achieved, and a deal was forged with a small independent Southern label which was currently enjoying great chart success of its own.

On 15th May 1956, Jean Chapel's new single was released as Sun 244.

Top of the Chart

SATURDAY 28TH APRIL 1956
AT THE TOP OF THE POP CHART

SO HERE'S HOW THE POP CHART worked in *Billboard* magazine. Throughout the week, statistics were gathered as to how a record performed in three key areas: jukebox requests, radio plays and, of course, actual sales. At midnight each Wednesday, *Billboard* closed the books and asked for all data to be forwarded to their head office the following day.

Throughout Thursday and Friday, the figures were collected, checked and counted and then, presumably, a panel collated the results from the three categories and came to a decision as to which was the most popular record in the country. Sales, obviously, played a significant part in the process, but the compilers were looking for the songs which had truly captured all parts of the nation's attention.

Early on Saturday morning, the results were finalised and made ready for the copy department to start typesetting. As such, on the morning of Saturday 28th April 1956, a small group of people were able to absolutely affirm that "Heartbreak Hotel" finally and definitely held the number one spot on the *Billboard* pop chart.

And on that very day, Elvis Presley was literally and exactly half way through his allotted lifespan.

Top of the world

A SHORT DIVERSION ON
THE NATURE OF SUCCESS

WITHIN DAYS OF PRESLEY'S SINGLE topping the pop listing, his debut LP repeated the achievement on the album chart. "Heartbreak Hotel" was also the number one hillbilly record, and was at number six in the R&B best sellers. Had there actually been an EP chart Elvis would undoubtedly have been at number one there too, but the only way of gauging his incredible selling power in that market was to note that the EP disk that contained "Blue Suede Shoes" was at number twenty-four in the pop singles chart — very likely an unprecedented event.

Billboard reminded readers that the industry had sniggered when Sholes authorised the purchase of Elvis' contract, but RCA were now having the last laugh as they turned over $75,000 *a day* on Presley product alone. And it was a pattern that was being repeated around the world, wherever RCA had a subsidiary office. "Heartbreak Hotel" was selling big and Elvis Presley was being acclaimed as the voice of a new generation — but the effect was much greater than simply selling records.

Presley's music appealed to youth of both genders and all colours: Sam Phillips had been correct in his prediction that in order for black music to cross over to the mainstream it would need an authentic and talented white singer to make the breakthrough. As radio accepted and played Elvis' integrated songs, there seemed no reason not to welcome the records of Chuck Berry, Bo Diddley, Ray Charles and dozens of others.

Let's allow no less a witness than Little Richard to give testimony: "When I came out they wasn't playing no black artists on no Top 40 stations. I was the first to get played on the Top 40 stations — but it took people like Elvis to open the door for this kind of music, and I thank God for Elvis Presley. I thank the Lord for sending Elvis to open that door so I could walk down the road, you understand? He was God given, an integrator, a blessing, they would not let black music through."

Amen, brother Richard, Amen.

Top of the bill

TUESDAY 15TH MAY 1956
ELLIS AUDITORIUM, MEMPHIS, TENNESSEE

THE MONTH OF MAY had signalled a gear change for Elvis Presley's career in 1955, and so too it was in 1956. RCA confirmed its faith in their new star by releasing his second single while the first was still doing huge business. "I Want You, I Need You, I Love You"/ "My Baby Left Me" (47-6540) had gathered 300,000 advance sales before it was even issued and was soon declared another million-selling gold record.

Time and *Newsweek* both ran articles on the new singing star, and the FBI began to receive complaints about Presley's lewd on-stage behaviour, prompted by wild performances of his closing number, "Hound Dog".

As instructed, Tom Parker started negotiations with The Jordanaires to join Elvis on stage and in the studio, which would subsequently make them the most famous and successful vocal backing group of all time.

The Colonel also made significant changes to Elvis' live touring show at this point. He removed all other stars from the bill (why pay top dollar to hire an *Opry* artist when it was Elvis the crowd had come to see?), and he replaced them with a host of minor acts straight from the books of Al Dvorin's agency in Chicago, courtesy of Tom Diskin. And whenever they toured he now ensured Elvis stayed in a separate hotel to Scotty, Bill and D.J., confirming Elvis' position as the main man.

And on Tuesday 15th May, Elvis returned to Memphis as the headline act at the Cotton Carnival. On this special occasion he played above a host of other recognised stars, including the Carters, The Jordanaires and, most poignantly of all, Hank Snow himself, finally playing second fiddle to the boy from Memphis.

Hank no doubt shook hands with Presley and even with Parker. Snow put on a brave face: he had his Jimmie Rodgers Memorial planned for later in the month, and had already made plans for new management representation that he felt sure would propel him to even higher levels of success.

He'd show that fat bastard, Tom Parker.

"Welcome to the Club", II

FRIDAY 18TH MAY 1956

RCA VICTOR STUDIO, 1525 McGAVOCK STREET, NASHVILLE, TENNESSEE

JUST THREE DAYS AFTER Sun released Jean Chapel's "Welcome to the Club", Steve Sholes ushered Charline Arthur into the studio for her final throw of the dice at RCA. Two songs had already been allocated — "Later On" and "What About Tomorrow" — but when Steve caught wind of Mae's composition for Jean he added it to the list, now intending for it to be the A-side of Charline's next single.

Recognising the obvious link to Elvis' huge hit, Steve also had Bob Ferris, Chet Atkins and Floyd Cramer on hand in the Nashville studio, hoping some of that Presley magic would rub off on Ms Arthur. The finished record, although similar to the Chapel original, was a superior performance and sounded much more "with it" and less forced.

"What About Tomorrow", written by Charline's husband, was selected as the B-side and the publishing rights were signed over to Tree who suddenly found themselves in demand these days. Indeed, it was all Buddy Killen could do to keep up with the increased workflow, as he struggled to follow the income generated by "Heartbreak Hotel", while promoting other Tree songs and sending out demo disks to record producers and A&R men looking for their next hit.

Charline's pairing was released the following month as RCA 47-6520, in direct competition with Sun's recording. On paper, it looked as though all the elements for a smash hit were present and accounted for, and it would simply be a question of seeing which version ended up topping the chart — Sun or RCA Victor.

Axton, Durden & Reeves, I

PERHAPS FRIDAY 25TH MAY 1956
3239 DELLWOOD AVENUE, JACKSONVILLE, FLORIDA

SUCCESS HAD MANAGED TO AVOID Glenn Reeves with remarkable dexterity and conviction. He had failed as a recording artist and as a songwriter, certainly in terms of commercial accomplishment, and he'd now even been dropped from Murray Nash's non-existent record label following the "That'll Be Love"/"The Last Time" flop. Ironically, his one signficant contribution to the entertainment business — helping Mae re-interpret the demo of "Heartbreak Hotel" — had brought him no income or recognition because of his honesty in turning down a composer's credit.

With her first royalty cheque just weeks away, Mae felt embarrassed that the two parties to whom she'd been closest — Glenn and Murray — were the ones who would have no part in her prosperity. So when she heard Glenn had been signed to Atco, one of Atlantic's subsidiary labels, she called a summit of herself, Tommy and Glenn with the intention of writing at least one song to help him on his way, and they all agreed Murray Nash should take the publishing.

They gathered at Mae's on a Friday evening and set to work at once. It may have been the first time they'd all been in the same room since October 1955, and although the meeting was convivial it was not inspired. Tommy, the most gifted of the trio, was strangely mute: it was as if, having finally excised the ghost of Boots, he had no poetry left inside.

Within a couple of hours, though, they had cobbled together "Rockin' Country Style". It was a makeshift uptempo commentary on the current trend for hillbilly singers to move across to rock 'n' roll, and which sounded for all the world like a hybrid of "Blue Suede Shoes" and "Tutti Frutti", bearing the unforgettable punchline *A-wop-bop-a-lee-bop-a-bop-gee-haw!*

The boys bid their goodbyes before 10 o'clock and Mae closed the door feeling oddly deflated. Just as she sat at her desk to look over the final contract for their new house in Tennessee, the telephone rang and she answered to the voice of Hank Snow asking her the darndest question: *Mae, how would you like to be my new manager?*

"The Party of the Second Part"

THURSDAY 31ST MAY 1956
RCA VICTOR STUDIO, 1525 McGAVOCK STREET, NASHVILLE, TENNESSEE

It had been two months since Hank Snow had received the bad news about his split from Elvis, and although he was keen to move on (hence the phoned offer to Mae) he still bore the emotional scars of his tussle with Parker.

So when Steve Sholes invited Snow into McGavock Street on the last evening in May 1956 to lay down tracks for his next two singles, Hank wanted to use the session cathartically in the hope of putting the past behind him. He turned up at 7:00 PM with three songs from a variety of sources and, sure enough, he taped them in four hours.

As 11 o'clock approached, Hank asked if he might let the session run for an extra few minutes and try something he'd recently co-written with up-and-coming hillbilly writer, Harlan Howard. Steve nodded and listened as Hank demoed the number for the band on his acoustic guitar.

The song was called "The Party of the Second Part", and concerned itself with a legal split between Hank ("The Party of the Second Part") and the unnamed Party of the First Part who Hank believed must surely be feeling "lonely". You may draw your own conclusion about the inspiration, but on the surface it was disguised as a simple c&w weeper ballad.

The taped song had an unfinished feel to it and Steve vetoed its release, but seventeen months later, Hank recorded a slicker remake which was issued as the B-side of "The Last Ride" (47-7586).

The first version featured an instrumental passage which sounded like a gap for a guitar solo. Or, listening to it closely, one might say it could be the sort of space which might have featured one of those old corny dramatic narratives that were popular on hillbilly records.

That being the case, and thinking carefully about the likely subject matter — and remembering Hank's undoubted fury — I'd part with serious money to know what Hank's original draft contained in the way of words for this spoken section.

Your Hit Parade

SATURDAY 2ND JUNE 1956
NBC-TV STUDIO, LOS ANGELES, CALIFORNIA

ELVIS PRESLEY wasn't the only singer from Memphis who sang "Heartbreak Hotel" on national television during mid-1956. Snooky Lanson was the unlikely stage name of Roy Landman, one of the featured vocalists on the long-running NBC-TV show *Your Hit Parade*. The concept was simple: the producers gathered a list of the best-selling pop records each week and had their own singers perform the hits live on air.

This had worked fine throughout the golden age of American popular song but, as the new rock 'n' roll music made greater inroads into the top ten, the contracted vocalists failed to match the intensity of the original recordingss — and this is probably why the show was cancelled by the end of the decade.

But in June 1956, NBC struggled on manfully and broadcast "Heartbreak Hotel" as sung by Lanson because, as the number one national hit, they really couldn't ignore it. The song was portrayed as a dramatic vignette set on the subway, as three heartbroken lovers lit cigarettes and waited for the next train.

But the most intriguing aspect was the arrangement of the number, for it was presented as a fascinating hybrid of the printed sheet music and Presley's master recording. If Tommy Durden was viewing, chances are he'd have leaned in a little closer to the screen, no doubt delighted to finally hear something like the song he'd originally written at last being presented to the public.

The revolution will be televised, VIII

TUESDAY 5TH JUNE 1956
NBC-TV STUDIO, LOS ANGELES, CALIFORNIA

By all conventional show business logic, when Presley made his second appearance on *The Milton Berle Show* he should have plugged two obvious songs: his current number one hit and his brand new RCA single release. The latter, "I Want You, I Need You, I Love You", was indeed present and accounted for (accompanied by The Jordanaires), but Elvis replaced "Heartbreak Hotel" with a song that had become an absolute showstopper for him over the previous four weeks.

Although he clearly understood that his uptempo version of "Hound Dog" was a clever musical joke, Elvis had taken to performing it at the end of each gig with blistering intensity, driving the audience into a frenzy. And if that wasn't enough, he'd then added a coda in a half-tempo burlesque nod to Big Mama's original which always brought the crowd (and Elvis) to its knees.

As such, there would seem no doubt that his decision to perform the Leiber and Stoller R&B hit on live TV (albeit toned down for the cameras) was intended to provoke a reaction. And indeed it did: bringing forth screams, squeals, applause and giggles. Berle lauded Elvis' act. The show continued. There was no undue fuss.

But seated in an office in New York, Jean Aberbach stared incredulously at the small screen in the corner of the room, almost unable to believe his eyes and ears. All of his Christmases and birthdays had come at once: unbidden and unheralded, Elvis Presley was singing a Leiber and Stoller original on national television.

The following day, however, all hell broke loose as reveiwers and social commentators — many of whom had no love for low-brow Berle — decided Presley and his host were an affront to all decent Americans: Elvis and his pelvis (cue the inevitable pun) ought not to be allowed on television at all. Ed Sullivan let it be known he wouldn't have Elvis on his show at any price.

This was Elvis' first broadcast since topping the chart with "Heartbreak Hotel" and, in the opinion of the horrified establishment, Presley and his provocative rock 'n' roll music were entirely and solely responsible for juvenile delinquency and all that was wrong with American youth in 1956.

Last Train to Memphis: The Rise of Elvis Presley, Peter Guralnick

The juvenile delinquent

SPRING 1956
JACKSONVILLE, FLORIDA

HOYT AXTON had been raised in a decent God-fearing home but he had a mile-wide rebellious streak. And with immaculate timing, he chose to launch his own revolution in the spring of 1956 shortly after his eighteenth birthday. With the memory of his beloved late grandfather still weighing heavily on his mind, and his mother sitting at the top of the pop chart with a song by the coolest guy on the planet, Hoyt decided to finish high school in style.

The all-state lineman and a bunch of his friends left the graduation party early and, probably fueled by a bottle or two, borrowed a lit roadwork flambeau and randomly launched it through the window of Knauer's Hardware Store on Myrtle Avenue, razing it to the ground.

The police were called. Hoyt was arrested but refused to give the names of his accomplices. As such, the $23,000 judgement was handed down to him alone. But by that time, the accused was long gone. He fled town and eventually signed for a stint aboard the U.S.S. *Princeton* and was bound for the Persian Gulf.

But Mae held herself steady throughout this latest test. She fixed her smile, opened her address book and placed an important call to Hank Snow. She had pondered Hank's invitation for several weeks and, having discussed it with husband John and also with the Colonel, Mae finally decided to shatter the glass ceiling and accept the offer of becoming the latest manager of the feisty c&w superstar.

Bob Luman & The Country Cats

PERHAPS EARLY JUNE 1956
WEATHERFORD, TEXAS

THE COUNTRY CATS had not taken well to being cast as Mac Curtis' sidemen by King Records, and forged a new plan that did not involve their soon-to-be former lead singer.

Remembering the charismatic Bob Luman who'd beaten them soundly in the talent show the previous autumn, they called the tall singer to see what had become of his baseball trial, and enquired if he might still be looking for a band of like-minded musicians. Bob was non-committal in his answer to the baseball query — which, they suspected, meant he'd been rejected — but he was excited to hear from the Cats and was very interested in joining the group.

They met up in Weatherford with the intention of heading out to see Bill Haley play the Mosque in Pittsburgh on 14th June, hoping to learn something from such a seasoned veteran. En route to the gig, they fooled around with new names for their group, because they weren't going to continue as The Country Cats. Maybe it was a sly reference to Bob's recent disappointment over his baseball failure, but they decided upon The Four Diamonds as their new moniker.

All seemed rosy as they sped up the highway towards Pennsylvania. Of course, if you're intending to create a group in which all four corners are equal it would probably not be a good idea to invite a guy who was an even more spectacular showman than the fellow you've left behind.

The Mac Curtis rockabilly blog (online)

Glenn Reeves records for Atco

FRIDAY 8TH JUNE 1956
MUSIC CITY RECORDING STUDIO, NASHVILLE, TENNESSEE

SIX MONTHS PREVIOUSLY, Atlantic Records had been prepared to give Tom Parker every dollar they owned to capture Elvis' signature, but it wasn't enough. Little did they know it, but they now had the team behind Presley's first big hit ready to record: Glenn Reeves stood at the microphone with an Axton/Durden/Reeves composition on the music stand, and a tight band behind him.

Producer, Herb Abramson, had a sterling reputation. He'd co-founded Atlantic, although he currently found himself out of step with Ertegun and Wexler, and confined himself to their unspectacular off-shoot Atco. The label's one shining light, R&B combo The Coasters, were laying down some good tunes, but their production duties were in the safe hands of uber-cool duo Leiber and Stoller, so there was little for Abramson to do there.

Under Herb's guidance, however, Glenn taped a cover of popular blues stomper "Drinkin' Wine Spo-Dee-O-Dee", and then moved on to the recently-composed "Rockin' Country Style". Both tracks were played professionally, but betrayed a slight awkwardness.

Mission accomplished, Glenn was escorted out of the studio and his place at the microphone was immediately taken by a Canadian named Hank Willis who was also scheduled to record that day. With the same house band, he laid down a couple of self-composed rockabilly tracks. Like Glenn, he was a country singer who felt obliged to move with the times.

Willis was known to both Murray Nash and Tom Parker, which was probably coincidental, but the fact that Atco shared the session between two unknown singers did not demonstrate a great confidence in either performer. Nevertheless, all four songs were packaged and presented to Atlantic to prepare for summer release.

The simple truth was that Atco — and every other record label throughout the western world — was now looking for its own Elvis Presley, and they were willing to tape anything and anyone in the hope that they might strike it lucky and replicate RCA's success.

Under new management

MID-JUNE 1956
JACKSONVILLE, FLORIDA & MADISON, TENNESSEE

IT'S INEVITABLE that she'd talked over her Hank Snow management decision with the Colonel, and he could think of nothing better than having a friendly figure in Snow's camp, especially as the threat of litigation still hung in the air. Once she'd passed on the good news to Hank, she dropped a line to *Billboard* who printed a short update a week later, describing Mae as "the song writing school marm out of Jacksonville."

All in all, family issues aside, life looked pretty good for Mae as the first half of 1956 drew to a close: "Heartbreak Hotel" was shaping up to be the record of the year; "Welcome to the Club" stood two good chances of following it into the top ten; Glenn's new record would be released in the summer; and Buddy Killen was now sending out Tree demos of "You're The Cause of it All" to producers and A&R men. So confident of further success was she, that Mae finally registered and copyrighted that song and also "Welcome to the Club".

And it was in late June that she received a call from Ben Green, of the *Nashville Banner*, the city's evening newspaper. The show business reporter was keen to interview Mae about her part in the song that had captivated the nation's youth and Mae, relishing her moment in the spotlight, readily agreed to a meeting backstage at the *Opry* on Saturday 30th June.

Putting down the phone, she quickly realised she had some thinking to do. She'd need to tidy up the story of her involvement in the song. She would hold fast to the facts as far as was possible, but there were ways of using language which allowed one to project certain parts of the truth while leaving the less desirable elements in the shadows.

Billboard, 23rd June 1956
Letter from Mae Boren Axton to Slick Norris, 14th June 1956

Juneteenth

TUESDAY 19TH JUNE 1956
MEMPHIS FAIRGROUND, TENNESSEE

He was home for a few precious days inbetween tours. Calling on casual girlfriend, Barbara Hearn, Elvis invited her to attend the Memphis fairground with him that night. A local reporter and photographer came along for the ride and watched with fascination as the couple mingled with the almost entirely black crowd.

Elvis had intentionally chosen to attend the Juneteenth celebration, the unofficial but widely recognised annual day of celebration — June nineteenth — adopted by Afro-American communities to mark the anniversary of country-wide emancipation in 1865.

He and Barbara wandered freely among the crowds, most of whom recognised the hometown star and were surprised but glad to see him. He rode the rides and played the stalls, probably buying Pepsi and popcorn for his date along the way, like any other young American couple, black or white.

Photos were taken and one was published along with a modest write-up in the local press. Was it illegal for Elvis and Barbara to attend? No, of course not. Did it represent a statement of intent from the rising star? Without question.

Like Sam and Dewey before him, Elvis was a race-man — someone who acted as a friend and brother to the black community but who just happened to be white; or perhaps, more accurately, someone who was neither black nor white, but moved freely and respectfully between both worlds, ignoring boundaries and conventions.

And this is partly why devoted disciple Bruce Springsteen would, many years later, describe his hero as "the first modern 20th century man."

www.elvis-collectors.com

Panic

MID-JUNE 1956
NEW YORK CITY, NEW YORK

THERE WAS A SENSE OF barely controlled panic in the respective offices of Steve Sholes and Jean Aberbach. At every recent RCA Friday meeting, the first item on the agenda was "Elvis Presley" but, apart from astronomical sales figures, Steve had zero to report.

The Colonel had adopted a policy of keeping Elvis out of the studio (a hungry record company is an attentive record company) and Sholes had nothing prepared for Elvis' next single let alone a second album. He knew the boy would not return to McGavock Street but hoped he might consent to a day of sessions on 2nd July when he hit New York for another television appearance. Maybe, just maybe, they might be able to capture songs for a summer 45 release. And the key to the success of this plan rested squarely on the broad shoulders of Jean Aberbach.

Jean, as it happened, hoped he was ahead of the game. Cousin Freddy Bienstock had assembled a crackerjack collection of songs from talented writers, and had gone to the trouble of preparing top quality demo disks so Elvis could listen and then select the tracks that caught his fancy.

But the real point of interest as far as Aberbach was concerned, was the possibility that Elvis might consider recording the song he'd sung on live TV on 5th June: "Hound Dog", as written by Leiber and Stoller.

There were just three problems with Jean's scenario: (*i*) Elvis considered his own version to be a witty musical joke and not necessarily something he wanted to add to his recorded catalogue; (*ii*) neither Elvis nor the Aberbachs owned any of the publishing rights on the song; (*iii*) Mike Stoller was on vacation in Europe and Jean himself would leave the country at the end of June, rendering any pre-emptive discussion about the publishing impossible.

But Jean Aberbach was supremely confident in his own powers and gambled he could persuade the songwriters to renegotiate the copyright after the fact. There can be little doubt he lobbied the Colonel for the song to be chosen as Elvis' next single. Aberbach, without question, stood to gain more than almost anyone else from such a development.

Follow the money, friends, just follow the money.

The comedian

SUNDAY 24TH JUNE 1956
THE NBC-TV HUDSON THEATRE, NEW YORK CITY, NEW

STEVE ALLEN WAS NBC-TV'S new weapon in the Sunday night ratings war against the invincible *Ed Sullivan Show* over on CBS. A slick, quick-talking host, Allen had first come to national prominence four years previously when he'd guest-hosted *The Arthur Godfrey Talent Scouts* and more or less ad-libbed his way through the whole programme.

The first episode of *The Steve Allen Show* aired on Sunday 24th June and featured occasional good-natured digs at their rival's deadpan presentation style. There were gags, sketches and several numbers by chief guest, Sammy Davis Jr. Indeed, Allen, a reasonable musician himself, performed with Davis to great effect.

The debut show was well advertised, well hyped and well put together, yet failed in its main goal, which was to topple Sullivan from the top of the TV chart.

But a golden gift had dropped in Steve Allen's lap. Back in early June, before the Milton Berle incident, Allen's producers had booked Presley as a novelty guest for their second show, scheduled to air live on Sunday 1st July. The singer had since become the most discussed figure in America, and Allen figured, rightly, the potential audience would be enormous, as teenagers and parents tuned in to see what all the fuss was about.

NBC enquired as to Elvis' intended repertoire, and, one way or another, perhaps as the result of many suggestions from many parties with various vested interests — RCA, Steve Sholes, Hill & Range, Tom Parker, Steve Allen, Elvis himself — it was decided Elvis would repeat the songs from 5th June: "I Want You, I Need You, I Love You", his *current* single, and what was now apparently to be his *next* single, "Hound Dog".

Steve Allen's challenge was to simultaneously stoke the fires and defuse the controversy. If ever there would be a chance for Steve to overtake Ed Sullivan in the ratings, then this was it.

Mae's finest hour

LATE JUNE 1956
3239 DELLWOOD AVENUE, JACKSONVILLE, FLORIDA

BEING SO WELL VERSED in the art of the show business interview, Mae prepared for her meeting with Ben Green by sitting down and cross examining herself. She sat at her desk, legal pad and pencil at the ready and began the process.

Mae felt strongly she should stick as closely as possible to the truth, but there were elements of the story that didn't necessarily need to be broadcast. She still wasn't entirely sure of the Colonel's intentions regarding the non-involvement of Hill & Range but felt it best to avoid that part of the narrative. She was also convinced she should focus on the simple point that "Heartbreak Hotel" was the intended song for Elvis, and there was no need to speak of the one he'd rejected; and there should be a discreet separation of the date of her meetings with Elvis and with Jack Stapp.

This interview would give her an opportunity to get Glenn's name in print, so a mention of his recording the demo was crucial. She would avoid embarrassing Murray by name if the topic of the publishing arose. She could also talk about Jean Chapel's forthcoming record, and also let slip her new position managing Hank.

But the real challenge surely came with regard to the original inspiration for the lyrics. It seemed tasteless to admit to drawing from Alvin Krolik's tragedy — "He's still got people living" — so she cast around for a suitable alternative. That phrase, "I walk a lonely street", was essential, as was the notion of it coming from a newspaper article, although she would alter the title to the *Miami Herald* for safety. Having scribbled down several thoughts, she remained certain of the need for a dramatic demise to give her story the necessary gravitas and depth. But how could she conjure up an appropriate fatality without naming the deceased or the perpetrator?

And it was then that inspiration struck her like a lightning bolt, and she wrote the answer to her conundrum in capital letters on her pad.

THE PERFECT TRAGIC DEATH — NO KILLER AND NO VICTIM.

AN ANONYMOUS SUICIDE.

The green Cadillac

LATE JUNE 1956
GAINESVILLE, FLORIDA

At some point in late June 1956, an envelope landed on Tommy Durden's doormat, containing a cheque from Tree Publishing. This was to cover his royalty payments on Elvis Presley's "Heartbreak Hotel", the song he'd co-written in no time at all back in autumn 1955.

Tommy looked carefully at the figure on the cheque then sat down. He reached over to the phone and dialled Mae who quickly picked up and calmly confirmed that she too had received an identical envelope that very morning. She also told Tommy of her plans for the *Nashville Banner* interview on the last day of June, and he agreed her approach was sensible.

Neither of them had much more in the way of conversation, so they hung up and quietly went about their daily business. But on the way into town, Tommy stopped off at the Cadillac dealership and placed a very specific order for a pea-green model that he intended to purchase and drive up to his daddy's front door — not as an act of spite against his father, but as a demonstration that he'd at last fulfilled his dream.

Tommy and Mae rarely spoke about the financial side of their success, but one long term Durden family friend has suggested the first royalty cheque was made out to a total of $180,000, including record and sheet music sales, radio and jukebox plays, and TV performances.

And if that's how much Tommy received as a one-third songwriter, just imagine how many zeroes were on the paying-in slip over at Tree Publishing. And that's the exact same amount that Hill & Range lost out on by having disrespected the Colonel.

Revenge is a dish best served cold, so it is said. This particular plate had been sitting for almost a year and was most definitely chilled.

The interview, III

SATURDAY 30TH JUNE 1956
RYMAN AUDITORIUM, NASHVILLE, TENNESSEE

THE RYMAN AUDIENCE applauded when Hank took to the stage as host of the "Jamison Bedding" half-hour segment of the *Opry* on the last Saturday in June. He opened with a song from his 1955 LP, *Just Keep A-Movin'*, introduced a guest or two, reminded the audience of just how fine a Jamison mattress was, and called on Mother Maybelle and The Carter Sisters to come out and sing a number for the folks. Hank was in fine form, but couldn't help notice that for the first time in his five years as a WSM headliner, there were a few empty seats at the back of the auditorium.

Backstage, Hank's manager, Mae Boren Axton, sat down with Ben Green from the *Nashville Banner* and gave her first interview as a bona fide celebrity. She plugged Jean Chapel and Hank Snow. She also spoke of her husband's talent as a coach, and of her hopes for her sons.

But what Ben really wanted to know about was "Heartbreak Hotel", and Mae was only too happy to fill him in on the amazing details of this giant of a hit record. When Ben wrapped up the interview he said it would be published on Saturday 7th July and reprinted later in the week too.

Hank thanked the audience and made ready to leave the stage, and Mae thought over her answers to Ben's questions: she realised she'd made a couple of errors: she'd mentioned Glenn's contribution as the singer of the demo, but felt sure he could feature in the story again, perhaps stressing how he was almost part of the songwriting team; and she noted she'd foolishly suggested the method by which the anonymous suicide victim had taken his own life — it sounded clumsy to her now and she'd make sure neither she nor Tommy ever referred to it again.

But overall she was pleased with how it had gone and she had every right to be. Her part in writing the song had been small but crucial. Her most significant contribution to the whole process, however, would be in the tale she had just rattled off for Ben Green: the legend of "Heartbreak Hotel" would grow from this point onwards.

Just as Elvis had adopted the ways of his mentor, Sam Phillips, so too Mae had followed the Colonel: stories had become her stock in trade.

Country Music Hall of Fame archives
Nashville Banner, Tennessee, 7th & 13th July 1956

The revolution will be televised, IX

SUNDAY 1 JULY 1956
THE NBC-TV HUDSON THEATRE, NEW YORK CITY, NEW YORK

HE FELT MORE THAN A LITTLE RIDICULOUS as he stood backstage dressed in wing-collar shirt, white bow-tie, black tails and blue suede shoes. Elvis was scheduled to appear as the main guest during the last quarter of Steve Allen's second show on the first day of July.

Allen's big idea for the nation's number one singer was to present low art in the guise of high culture: Elvis would sing "I Want You, I Need You, I Love You" outfitted like a maître d', surrounded by Greek columns and chandeliers, accompanied by The Blue Moon Boys and The Jordanaires.

Then, for Allen's masterstroke, Elvis would sing the potentially offensive "Hound Dog" to a docile basset hound, raised on a plinth to waist height, which indeed he did, appearing to take it all in good humour. For the finale, Elvis joined with the assembled cast, dressed as a cowboy, to offer a parody of western musical shows, not dissimilar, in fact, to the *Louisiana Hayride*.

One could view the show today and not see anything particularly untoward, but one could also easily recognise an attempt by a middle-class, middle-aged pseudo-intellectual Yankee to denigrate Presley and all that he represented — the South, the new wave of integrated rock 'n' roll musicians, and the younger generation in general.

When the viewing figures came in, Steve Allen had overtaken Ed Sullivan, for the first and, as it transpired, the only time. It wasn't too long before CBS agreed a figure of $50,000 with the Colonel for three Elvis appearances on Ed's programme.

Being such a private person, it's difficult to know precisely how Presley felt about the show, but he seemed tired and downcast when he appeared live on the TV chat show *Hy Gardner Calling*, later that evening.

Milton Berle had laughed *with* Elvis but Steve Allen was laughing *at* him. And if that's what was running through Elvis' mind, it's little wonder he slept fitfully in a New York hotel bed that night, with the prospect of a whole afternoon in the RCA studio ahead of him tomorrow.

"Hound Dog": Elvis Presley

MONDAY 2ND JULY 1956
RCA STUDIOS, NEW YORK CITY, NEW YORK

STEVE SHOLES had allocated six hours studio time plus a sixty-minute break, and Elvis arrived promptly, ready to begin work at 2:00 PM. He greeted all in the studio with a grace and confidence that put everyone at their ease. Engineer Ernie Oelrich was once again behind the glass; The Jordanaires were in attendance for the first time; pianist Shorty Long was due to arrive soon; Scotty, Bill and D.J. were setting up; Steve was sifting through the pile of demo disks he'd played for Elvis before yesterday's TV show; H&R representative Freddy Bienstock stood behind Steve with a box full of further acetates if required; photographer Alfred Wertheimer had been on Elvis' trail for the previous two days and he discreetly worked as Elvis ran through a gospel song seated at the piano by way of a warm up with The Jordanaires.

Steve had zero preconceptions about how the session would play out. In fact, more than ever before, he was aware that it was Elvis, and only Elvis, who was in control of proceedings. Previously, the singer had hinted at being in charge: as from today he became his own de facto producer, a role he would fulfil for the rest of his life, allowing only those for whom he had the utmost professional respect to occasionally alter the sound and direction of his art.

Elvis had conceded that "Hound Dog" would indeed be a logical song choice given the free publicity it had received on TV. The problem, as he saw it, was working out how he might transform satire into something that was (*a*) artistically acceptable to his own ears, and (*b*) different to Thornton's original, but (*c*) good enough not to be an embarrassment.

And so they started work: Jordanaire Gordon Stoker sat at the piano while they waited for Shorty to arrive; Elvis and Scotty talked through how best to structure a two-verse song so it lasted more than thirty seconds; Bill and D.J. discussed the finer points of the burlesque coda; The Jordanaires worked up a simple vocal harmony section for the instrumental passage, as instructed by the man now standing at the microphone.

Elvis requested a run through before rolling tape and Steve nodded his agreement. They more or less busked their way through it but, without the deafening cover of a live audience, it came off sounding a little awkward. The guitar solo was clumsy and Scotty's accompaniment throughout had the odd effect of dragging the song down. The half-time ending had to go, of that Elvis was already sure.

"Let's try one," suggested Steve, and Elvis shrugged. The first few takes came and went in a blur, but Elvis remained unhappy with the overall feel. There was more discussion on the floor as Elvis offered direction from the centre of the carpet. Like Sam Phillips before him, Elvis asked Scotty to simplify his part and focus more on a sense of sheer noise which, as each take progressed, sounded harsher and spikier. For his own contribution, he removed the last two repeated words of the opening line, "You ain't nothin' but a hound dog, *hound dog*", keeping it shorter and to the point.

The take count crept up to ten. Bill and D.J. locked closer together, now carrying the beat completely between them as Elvis had not even uncased his guitar and Scotty had moved into a place between rhythm and lead. Gordon Stoker provided basic piano chords, strengthening the core of the song, and engineer Ernie Oelrich kept a careful eye on the sound levels.

In order to edge the song past the two minute mark, Scotty was asked to provide two instrumental solos while Elvis alternated between the written verses. The guitarist was rarely comfortable improvising in the RCA studio and was suddenly put on the spot as Elvis encouraged him to look for clean melodic lines played in a rough edgy fashion.

They reached the mid-teens in take numbers and Elvis spoke with The Jordanaires: their harmonies were working just fine and Elvis gave them a clever hand-clap pattern which worked against the beat while propelling it forward. The tempo crept up a little and Oelrich announced take eighteen, the highest of any song Elvis had recorded for RCA. The group gelled, the take was complete, the room fell silent.

Steve butted in over the intercom: "Sounds good to me, Elvis."

Elvis stood still for a moment, then raised his eyebrows, and replied, "Yeah." Steve grinned and turned towards Ernie Oelrich, preparing to tell him to cut take eighteen from the tape as the master. But Elvis' voice came through from the studio floor: "I'd like to try another one, Steve."

In Elvis' opinion, the song was coming together but lacked two elements: groove and purpose. The *groove* would come with more takes — the band just required more playing time to click. But *purpose* was a different ball game altogether and needed to be worked out. His first single had told a tale; his second was a descriptive narrative; but this? This had nothing to say at all. Lyrically it meant zip but Elvis wanted it to mean *something.* Maybe this was a song that would express itself musically rather than in prose? Perhaps he just had to keep pushing.

And push he did: take after take; some complete and some not. But as the band dragged the song forward, Elvis began to feel a quiet rage building inside. Perhaps no one had yet noticed the lyric change between Freddie Bell's version and Elvis'. Freddie had clearly sung, "They said you were high classed, but that was just a *line.*" Elvis was now declaring, "But that was just a *lie*", a subtle but crucial change in the appraoch to the song, making it far more accusatory.

And as the takes pushed into the mid-twenties, it was this sense of anger on which Elvis chose to focus. He brought to the front of his mind the sense of frustration and humiliation he'd felt throughout the Steve Allen gig and channelled his pent-up fury not just at Allen but at everyone who'd tried to remind him of exactly who he was and where he'd come from and where he belonged. Consciously or not, Steve Allen had triggered the insecurities Elvis felt when faced with those who acted superior not just to him but to all he represented — poor Southerners, black and white.

The band finally found their place; Elvis attacked the lyrics like a man possessed, reaching a part of his voice he'd not previously discovered, a rasping, biting, vocal sound — his most committed performance since "Heartbreak Hotel" — turning the word "crying" into something more like "cracking". Scotty hit two astonishingly good guitar solos, Bill drove the group forward with a bouncy, steady bass line, D.J. hammered out the machine-gun snare breaks, and The Jordanaires did everything Elvis had ever dreamed of them doing. Wertheimer would normally never shoot during a take but the noise from the band was so loud, he risked it, capturing the intensity of Presley standing at the mike and giving his all.

The performance finished. Steve spoke through the intercom: "Sounded great. I think we got it now, Elvis."

Elvis ran his hands through his hair and exhaled. "Thanks, Steve. Let's try just one more."

And they did, and another, and then another.

Oelrich announced take thirty-one. It was almost 4:30 PM. The song had taken on a life and identity of its own. Lyrically, it no longer had anything to do with Thornton's version; musically, it was now far removed from Bell's parody. And Elvis knew if he faltered even once then the song would sink. For it to ring true, every syllable had to be delivered as if his life depended on it. Fixing his eyes on the men behind the glass, he nodded then signalled to the musicians they were going yet again.

And go they did. And what came out over the next two minutes and seventeen seconds was the aural equivalent of a vicious sneer, that facial expression that Elvis was so easily able to effect with a twist of his upper lip.

Spent, the singer called for takes eighteen, twenty-eight and thirty-one to be played through the huge standing speaker, and he crouched down so better to hear. He remained motionless throughout, sweat beads breaking out on his forehead.

As the last take ended, he stood, turned to the glass and confirmed, "That's the one." Quiet chatter erupted in the studio and the air conditioning was switched on. Steve breathed a sigh of relief and called for a coffee break. Freddy Bienstock tapped Steve on the shoulder and pointed at his watch. Steve shook his head and gave a brief snort.

Freddy stepped down onto the studio floor and introduced himself to Elvis for the first time, and they chatted briefly about songs and writers. Bienstock, like his cousins the Aberbachs, was always working the angle and listened carefully to Elvis' casual comments and filed every word away for future reference. Freddy, twelve years Elvis' senior, said he had brought along a few demos and wondered if Elvis might like to hear them?

Elvis nodded his consent, and sat in the studio with a Pepsi and a paper cup while the publisher returned to the booth and placed an acetate on the record player. He dropped the arm onto the disk and the studio filled with music. Elvis listened all the way through and looked at Freddy with a neutral expression.

Bienstock then started working Elvis like a deejay would a dance floor: Okay, don't like that one, how about this? He played a second disk and Elvis gave a non-commital nod. Freddy felt he was zeroing-in on what Elvis might be looking for and slipped a third onto the player. Within seconds of the needle dropping, Elvis sat up straight in his chair.

"Hey, I like that. Play it again," said Elvis as the disk ended, and he stood and draped an arm over the studio speaker. His foot tapped and his fingers fluttered as the song repeated.

"You guys come and hear this," he said to the band as Freddy cued it up again. The group listened to what was a simple piano-and-percussion demo of a mid-tempo pop-shuffle called "Don't Be Cruel", sung by its composer, a struggling R&B artist called Otis Blackwell. He'd demoed the song for Shalimar Music on Christmas Eve 1955 and Freddy Bienstock had subsequently acquired a share in the composition figuring, correctly, it might be the sort of thing Elvis would like.

After several hungry years, Blackwell was about to have his moment in the sun: "Fever", written under the pseudonym John Davenport, was climbing the R&B chart in a recording by Little Willie John, and was starting to sell in big numbers.

Elvis sat at the piano and gathered the musicians and vocalists around him, as he held chords and showed exactly how he wanted the number to be played. On "Hound Dog" it was about filling the space; for this new recording it would be about *leaving* space. Scotty would play only during the opening and closing sections; Bill and Shorty would carry the performance; The Jordanaires would weave in and out of the lead vocal; Elvis would mimic the slapping sound of the demo using the back of his leather-covered guitar, a trick he'd not employed since "I Don't Care if the Sun Don't Shine"; D.J. would add light percussion.

The energy from "Hound Dog" still filled the studio and the band took their places with a feeling of absolute confidence. And from the earliest takes the song sounded just wonderful. Elvis borrowed some of Otis Blackwell's vocal tics and slurs from the demo, and absolutely *owned* the song. Steve Sholes relaxed a little behind the glass, and convinced himself this one would be in the bag within thirty minutes.

Two hours and twenty-eight takes later, Elvis gave the thumbs-up and asked for a playback. And what came through the speaker was a masterpiece of playful, sexy, easy rock 'n' roll which hung entirely on rhythm and vocal. From the opening notes played on Scotty's bass E string detuned to a D, via the suggestive stops and starts, through to the "That's all, folks" final chord, the song was and remains one of the great pop performances of the twentieth century, and a measure of Presley's ability as a singer and music producer. But on Monday 2nd July 1956, Steve Sholes was happy just to have it in the can.

The air conditioning was switched back on — this was New York in July and the temperature was in the early nineties — and the band stood close to the vents. But Elvis still seemed fresh as a daisy while he conferred with Steve and Freddy about another song he wanted to tape in the remaining hour, one of the demos he'd previously heard, which had also come from Bienstock by way of the Ross Jungnickel publishing company.

"Any Way You Want Me" had been co-written by black composer Otis Clyde (under the name of Cliff Owens) and Aaron Schroeder who had previously — and very profitably — supplied "I Was The One", the B-side of "Heartbreak Hotel", which was still currently selling vast quantities and sitting at number eleven in the pop chart, with "I Want You, I Need You, I Love You" rising at five.

A doo-wop flavoured ballad, as per Schroeder's first offering, "Any Way You Want Me" just sounded epic. Elvis loved the passion of the song and, wary of the ticking clock, pulled the band to him to work out the arrangement. They ran through two rehearsals during which Elvis mumbled and hummed the lyrics, more intent on directing the players through the peaks and troughs of what he had in his head, than practising his own part.

The musicians waited for the count-in. On cue, guitar, bass, piano and drums pushed through the steady introduction and Elvis and The Jordanaires launched into the song with absolute conviction, but when Elvis hit the high note at the beginning of the third line, his back-up vocalists took a step back from their spot in shock, causing a breakdown and requiring a new take.

For The Jordanaires, this moment was a revelation. They'd been impressed with Elvis' talent and mastery of the two previous songs and of the studio environment, but this was the first time when, to a man, they'd all come to the same blindingly obvious conclusion: "Woah — this guy can sing."

They tried take two, and three, each time bonding closer together as a recording unit, taking the song deeper and deeper until it sounded more like a spiritual than a ballad. Elvis called it a day at take twelve, having wrung every last ounce of emotion from this soulful tour-de-force.

In some fantasy world, Steve Sholes had imagined Elvis taping his next single and a whole album at this session, but felt sure he'd be able to hold his head high at the Friday meeting when presenting Presley's next 45 which had already been advance-scheduled for shipping on 13th July. Of course, had Elvis failed to deliver the required tracks for the next single, then Steve would have been in an awkward spot, to say the least, and he never became comfortable with Elvis' or the Colonel's working practices.

The session had been an absolute triumph for Freddy Bienstock and Hill & Range. They and Elvis held, or would soon hold, shares in all three songs mastered that day, and Freddy had already more than justified his appointment. Many years hence, RCA would release a compilation disk of Presley's eventual thirty-one transatlantic number one hit singles, and eleven of these would carry the names of Leiber, Stoller, Blackwell or Schroeder. By the autumn of '56, Bienstock would, as gatekeeper to Presley's songs, become the most important behind-the-scenes figure in popular music for the next seven years.

Elvis himself was satisfied with his day's work and felt in a much better place emotionally than twenty-hours previously. He asked Steve to deliver acetates of the three tracks to his room at the Warwick Hotel. Tomorrow, he would shake the big city dust from his feet and begin the long train journey back to Memphis, ready for his homecoming gig on Wednesday. It would be sixteen years until he chose to return professionally to New York.

Without realising it, on this day in July 1956, Elvis Presley had invented the modern recording format: that in which the artist at the microphone takes precedence over the suits in the booth; and the studio subsequently changed from being a place of clinical procedure into a home for experimentation and creativity.

"Hound Dog"/"Don't Be Cruel" was rush-released as RCA 47-6604 with a black & white picture sleeve featuring a Wertheimer photograph from *The Steve Allen Show*, and was so unprecedentedly successful that both sides took turns at the top of the *Billboard* chart for a total of eleven weeks, and would enjoy a run of over half a year in the pop listings.

It achieved an eventual sales tally in excess of seven million copies and cemented Elvis Presley's position as the most popular, important, transformative and influential musician of modern times.

Independence Day

WEDNESDAY 4TH JULY 1956
CHATTANOOGA RAILWAY STATION, CHATTANOOGA, TENNESSEE

ELVIS HAD BOARDED THE 11:30 AM train at Pennsylvania Station in New York on the Tuesday, accompanied by photographer Alfred Wertheimer, and was headed to Memphis for his spectacular and integrated homecoming concert on Wednesday, in direct competition with the Ku Klux Klan rally held across town on the very same evening. It would be almost two years to the day since he'd recorded "That's All Right".

The twenty-seven hour journey broke in Chattanooga in time for breakfast. Elvis washed, dressed immaculately, stepped onto the platform and headed for the nearby station restaurant. Tom Parker carefully folded a one dollar bill in half and held it aloft so it looked like two dollars and called for porters to transfer the instruments and luggage to the next train. When the chore was complete, he pocketed the bill and passed over two quarters to the uniformed suckers.

Elvis sat unmolested at the counter, watched and photographed by Wertheimer. He ordered a simple cooked breakfast and a glass of cold milk. Standing behind him was a middle-aged black woman elegantly dressed for travelling. Not permitted to sit, she collected her food and moved on. It was but one small example of the inequalities and injustices faced by Southern Afro-Americans every single day of their lives.

Elvis made no fuss or public protest. This is how things had always been in the South. Yet, had his fellow traveller sat alongside him Elvis would have given no objection. Indeed, chances are he would have paid for her meal, as he was often wont to do for friends and strangers alike. But what neither of them yet knew was that his openly anti-racist stance on music and entertainment was already removing fences between black and white, and his continued promotion of and devotion to black artists and black culture would continue to dismantle imposed and perceived barriers.

He was still just twenty-one. This was one of the last days of his life he would be free to travel, walk and eat like a normal human being. When "Hound Dog"/"Don't Be Cruel" was released in mid-July, his stardom would catapult him to a lonely place occupied by very few and, for his own protection and with the encouragement of his manager, he would begin to cut himself off from the rest of the world.

Later that same month, Sam Phillips was driving his family back from a Daytona Beach vacation, but almost veered off the road when he first heard "Don't Be Cruel" playing on the car radio. Listening to that glorious, infectious and natural rhythm, he was totally reassured that Elvis Presley had now taken charge of his own music, and exuberantly declared to his bewildered passengers —

"Now *there* is a groove! *Glory Hallelujah!*"

ILLUSTRATIONS, II

STATE OF ILLINOIS } SS
COUNTY OF COOK }

IN THE CIRCUIT COURT OF COOK COUNTY
IN CHANCERY

AGNES KROLIK
-vs-
ALVIN B. KROLIK
a/k/as
ALLAN B. KROLIK et al

NO. 52C 11515

DECREE FOR DIVORCE

This cause coming on to be heard upon the plaintiff's Complaint, the Answer thereto of the defendant, and by Stipulation of the parties hereto, through their respective attorneys to have this matter come on for an immediate hearing as a default, the plaintiff appearing in her own proper person and by ALBERT A. BROWN, her attorney, and the defendant appearing by HARRY X. COLE, his attorney, and the Court having heard the testimony of witnesses duly sworn and examined in open Court, and upon other evidence offered by plaintiff in support of her Complaint (a certificate of which evidence having been duly signed and sealed is filed herein and made a part hereof), and the Court having heard the arguments of counsel for the respective parties, and being fully advised in the prmises, DOTH FIND:

That it has jurisdiction of the parties hereto and the subject matter hereof; that the plaintiff is an actual resident of the County of Cook, and has been a resident of the State of Illinois for over one whole year next before the filing of the Complaint herein; that the parties hereto were lawfully joined in marriage onto-wit: the 22nd day of June A. D. 1952, at Chicago, Illinois; that no children were born to the parties hereto as a result of the said marriage; that subsequent to their intermarriage the defendant had been guilty of extreme and repeated cruelty toward plaintiff, on to-wit: the 26th day of June

The first page of the document of divorce between Agnes and Alvin Krolik, courtesy of Mitchell Pomper.

A 1961 publicity photograph of Agnes Sampson.
Author's collection.

The San Solano Mission today,
courtesy of Kate Convissor.

Killing Ends Heartache

'Story of Person Who Walked Lonely Street'

Funeral services for a young artist will be held in Chicago tomorrow.

The artist was never very successful, but he showed promise. His promise ended Saturday night when he tried to hold up an El Paso liquor store and was shot to death.

The artist was Alvin Bert Krolik and he lived 27 years. Once, in an unpublished autobiography, he wrote "This is the story of a person who walks a lonely street."

Krolik's "lonely street" took him through a series of Chicago stick-ups, to Franciscan monasteries where he painted murals, and finally to the Busy Bee Liquor Store in East El Paso.

'Just a Neglected Boy'

He saw service as a judo instructor in the Marine Corps and in 1953 he married a nightclub accordionist. The marriage lasted five weeks and his wife said later, "he's just a neglected boy who never really matured and needs help."

Shortly after the breakup of his marriage, Krolik walked into a police station and confessed that he had taken part in 10 holdups.

"I have to get it off my mind—I'm tired of the panderers and streetwalkers I've been living with," he said.

Judge Charles S. Daugherty put the artist on five years' probation, saying, "This is the first man to appear before me who apparently showed sincere contrition."

Krolik also found a friend in Russell W. Davis, chairman of Imperial World Films, Inc. Davis took an interest in the young artist and sent him to the Franciscan monastery at Topawa, Ariz.

Krolik and another artist painted 14 murals at the monastery. He later painted murals at other Arizona monasteries and last month accompanied Davis on a vacation in the Ozarks.

Something Went Wrong

Then something went wrong in Krolik's tangled brain. Last week he went to a Tucson store and bought a holster and a .38-caliber revolver. From there he went to El Paso.

D. R. Pinney, proprietor of the Busy Bee Liquor Store, told police Krolik came in and asked for a bottle of whiskey. Pinney turned to fill the order and swung back to find Krolik's revolver pointed at him.

"Give me all the green money," Krolik said.

Pinney laid all his money on the counter. Krolik reached for it and Pinney, who had previously killed another stickup man, came up with a pair of revolvers.

He fired nine shots into Krolik and the young monastery artist was dead.

From the front page of the El Paso Herald-Post, *25th August 1955, very likely the newspaper that Tommy Durden brought to Mae Boren Axton.*

D.R. Pinney as pictured in the El Paso Herald-Post, *25th August 1955.*

The body of Alvin Krolik lies on the floor of The Busy Bee after his failed robbery attempt, 20th August 1955, courtesy of Frances Pinney Erickson.

E9810 50

TEXAS DEPARTMENT OF HEALTH
BUREAU OF VITAL STATISTICS
STATE OF TEXAS — CERTIFICATE OF DEATH — STATE FILE NO. 38779

1. PLACE OF DEATH a. COUNTY: El Paso
b. CITY OR TOWN: El Paso — c. LENGTH OF STAY (in this place): Unknown
d. FULL NAME OF HOSPITAL OR INSTITUTION: 3728 Alameda Ave.

2. USUAL RESIDENCE a. STATE: Illinois — b. COUNTY: Cook
c. CITY OR TOWN: Chicago
d. STREET ADDRESS: 5748 No. Talman

3. NAME OF DECEASED (Type or Print) a. (First): Alvin — b. (Middle): Bert — c. (Last): Krolik
4. DATE OF DEATH: Aug. 20, 1955
5. SEX: Male — 6. COLOR OR RACE: White — 7. MARRIED, NEVER MARRIED, WIDOWED, DIVORCED (Specify): Married
8. DATE OF BIRTH: June 27, 1928 — 9. AGE: 27 Years, 1 Months, 23 Days
10a. USUAL OCCUPATION: Artist — 10b. KIND OF BUSINESS OR INDUSTRY: Art
11. BIRTHPLACE (State or foreign country): Illinois
12. FATHER'S NAME: Jack Krolik — BIRTHPLACE: Illinois
13. MOTHER'S MAIDEN NAME: Edith Borin — BIRTHPLACE: Illinois
14. WAS DECEASED EVER IN U.S. ARMED FORCES?: Yes 8-17-48 to 9-11-50
15. SOCIAL SECURITY NO.: 328-24-2306
16. INFORMANT'S SIGNATURE: Fam. Rec. C. W. Lynch

17. CAUSE OF DEATH — MEDICAL CERTIFICATION
I. DISEASE OR CONDITION DIRECTLY LEADING TO DEATH (a): Multiple bullet wounds
ANTECEDENT CAUSES — DUE TO (b): through chest and head
DUE TO (c):
II. OTHER SIGNIFICANT CONDITIONS

TEXAS DEPARTMENT OF HEALTH — REC'D SEP 1 1955 — BUREAU OF VITAL STATISTICS

18a. DATE OF OPERATION — 18b. MAJOR FINDINGS OF OPERATION: HELD INQUEST
19. AUTOPSY?: YES [X] NO [ ]

20a. ACCIDENT / SUICIDE / HOMICIDE (Specify): Homicide
20b. PLACE OF INJURY: Liquor Store
20c. (CITY, TOWN, OR PRECINCT NO.): El Paso, (COUNTY): El Paso, (STATE): Texas
20d. TIME OF INJURY: 8-20-55 6:40PM
20e. INJURY OCCURRED: WHILE AT WORK [ ] NOT WHILE AT WORK [X]
20f. HOW DID INJURY OCCUR?: Gun Shot Wounds

21. I hereby certify that I attended the deceased from ____, 19__, to ____, 19__, that I last saw the deceased alive on ____, 19__, and that death occurred at 7:05PM, from the causes and on the date stated above.
22a. SIGNATURE: [illegible] — (Degree or title): M. D. — 22b. ADDRESS: El Paso, Texas — 22c. DATE SIGNED: 8-21-55

23a. BURIAL, CREMATION, REMOVAL (Specify): Removal — 23b. DATE: Aug. 23, 1955
23c. NAME OF CEMETERY OR CREMATORY: Jewish Waldheim Cemetery
23d. LOCATION (City, town, or county) (State): Forest Park, Illinois
24. FUNERAL DIRECTOR'S SIGNATURE: MARTIN MORTUARY - RichardE. Martin

25a. REGISTRAR'S FILE NO.: 950
25b. DATE REC'D BY LOCAL REGISTRAR: August 23-1955
25c. REGISTRAR'S SIGNATURE: W. D. HORNEDO, M. D. By Z. Gonzales, Deputy Registrar

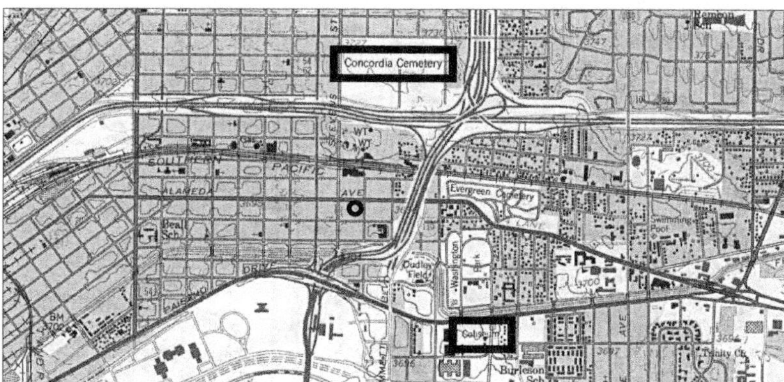

Alvin Krolik's death certificate.

Map of El Paso, 1955, showing The Busy Bee (circled), Concordia Cemetery & the Coliseum.

It Happened At Grand Ole Opry

Inspired By Suicide Note Written In 22 Minutes;

By BEN A. GREEN

"I walk a lonely street" he wrote—and the police reported "suicide."

But a song-writing schoolteacher put a "heartbreak hotel" at the end of that street—and it became America's No. 1 hit song of 1956 to date, composed in a fabulous 22 minutes flat by this teacher who cannot sing and a radio-tv vocalist who can.

That's the untold story behind "Heartbreak Hotel," the song that led all polls for weeks, has sold over 3,000,000 records and hundreds of thousands in sheet music, and is sweeping England, Germany and other countries. (One Nashville music publisher turned it down, but another took it without even looking.)

This schoolteacher, Texas-born Mrs. Mae Boren Axton, has just moved to Nashville from Jacksonville, Fla., occupying a home nearing completion in the Madison community.

First Of A Series

Editor's Note—This "behind the scenes" story of Grand Ole Opry was printed in The Banner latest edition Saturday, July 7. It did not appear in The Banner city edition the following Monday. It is reprinted herewith, because it starts for The Banner a new feature that will run each Saturday in the latest edition, and the following Monday in regular editions.)

Second Woman Manager

She has become exclusive manager for Grand Ole Opry star Hank Snow, being the second woman in America to take over management of a country music star. (The other is Bobbie Bennett, manager of Spade Cooley, Hollywood, Calif.)

"But how could you compose that hit song in less than half an hour?" we asked Mrs. Axton behind-stage last Saturday night at Grand Ole Opry, where 8,000 persons attended a double-show bill.

"It started with a newspaper story," she replied.

"Tommy Durden, steel guitar player-vocalist from Station WMBR-TV, Jacksonville, called me at home. He said he had read in the paper about a man gassing himself to death in a car.

"He couldn't put out of his mind the suicide note 'I walk a lonely street.' So he came over to my house and started walking the floor, repeating 'lonely, lonely . . . but why did he do it?'

"But think of the heartbreak he left behind," I commented. "Let's put a heartbreak hotel at the end of that lonely street."

'Of course,' Tommy came back. 'Let's get on with it.'

"Turning to my piano, with typewriter and tape recorder nearby, we started working—picking out music and words alternately.

"Usually I would throw in a line, and Tommy would add the next. In 22 minutes we had the complete song dubbed in on the recorder . . . We have made no changes since. There are two minor errors in the sheet music but the recordings are like the original.

"That was last September. I thought we had a good song that would fit Elvis Presley, who had become quite popular," added Mrs. Axton.

"I had met Elvis when he came to Florida with Hank Snow about 18 months ago, and remembered how the teenagers went wild over him. He was not well known then to Florida people, but I handled publicity for the Snow tour and saw how pleased the show sponsors were when they saw the reaction to Presley.

JEAN CHAPEL

New Personality—New Song—"Welcom

Glenn Reeves of Atlantic Records happened to come by my house and I asked him to sing 'Heartbreak Hotel' onto my tape recorder in Presley style.

"He did it well, and armed with my tape recorder I came to Nashville in October, 1955, to see publishers.

"I went to one well known publisher here and said 'I've got a song that will sell a million.'

Turned Down, With A Laugh

"One of his associates laughed and said 'all we have now are Axton songs.'

"I didn't like this but said nothing. That night at Grand Ole Opry I saw Jack Stapp, program manager for the Opry and WSM.

"He said to me, 'Mae, you never have offered me a song. Why?'

" 'I've got one for you right now. It's Heartbreak Hotel,' I replied."

" 'I'll take it,' Jack answered, without another word. He's a busy man at Grand Ole Opry, as you know.

"And that's how Tree Publishing Co. got the song." (Stapp is co-owner of Tree with Lou Cowan of New York, who is producer of the $64,000 Question, $64,000 Challenge, Big Surprise and other network quiz shows. Stapp and Cowan were wartime buddies in the Army.)

Mrs. Axton went back to Jacksonville after placing the song with Tree, but returned here for the disc jockey convention in November with her tape recorder.

"I happened to see Elvis Presley in the Andrew Jackson Hotel lobby," she continued. "I told him

—Elvis, I'v
going to lis
"He said
got to go
"But I in
of Memphis
time, also
song which
heard. Th
and played

10 Ti

" 'Hot d
again,' Pre
played it 10
I turned to
"If you
next releas
third of it.
"He agre
He sang it
that RCA-V
release for
his contract
Memphis f
A rhythm
cording als
The Cadets
it has sol
Presley rec
all the pol
"Stan Fr
takeoff, 'H
by Mammo
Records a
"That en
Hotel" con
ton began
boys, John
and her hu

15 Y

After 15
teaching, s
teach spec
high school
ferent coll
a doctor's
sought one

MRS. MAE BOREN AXTON

"Let's put a heartbreak hotel on that lonely street"

The first full interview given by Mae Boren Axton on the origins of "Heartbreak Hotel" from The Nashville Banner *7th July 1956 and reprinted as seen here 13th July 1956 © USA Today Network*

Note, 'Heartbreak Hotel'
utes; First Heard Here

JEAN CHAPEL

y—New Song—"Welcome To The Club"

Atlantic Rec-
ome by my
him to sing
nto my tape
style.
armed with
me to Nash-
to see pub-

known pub-
'I've got a
million.'

A Laugh

ates laughed
now are Ax-

ut said noth-
Grand Ole
pp, program
y and WSM.
ae, you never
ng. Why?'
ou right now.
' I replied."
k answered,
He's a busy
Opry, as you

Tree Publish-
" (Stapp is
Lou Cowan
producer of
$64,000 Chal-
d other net-
and Cowan
lies in the

ack to Jack-
he song with
here for the
n in Novem-
corder,
Elvis Pres-
ackson Hotel
"I told him

—Elvis, I've got a song you are going to listen to right now."

"He said, 'I can't do it. I've got to go to a meeting.'

"But I insisted, and Bob Neal of Memphis, his manager at the time, also urged him to hear the song which Neal had already heard. They went to my room and played the song.

10 Times for Presley

"'Hot dog, Mae. Play that again,' Presley shouted. And we played it 10 times, over and over. I turned to Elvis and said:

"If you make this song your next release—you can have one-third of it.

"He agreed, and that's the story. He sang it wonderfully well for that RCA-Victor record, his first release for them after they bought his contract from Sun Records of Memphis for a reported $40,000. A rhythm and blues Modern recording also has been made by The Cadets, a Negro quartet, and it has sold well, although the Presley record is the one that led all the polls.

"Stan Freberg has also sung a takeoff, 'Heartbreak Hotel (Echo by Mammoth Cave)' for Capitol Records and it is selling rapidly.

That ended our "Heartbreak Hotel" conversation, and Mrs. Axton began to talk about her two boys, Johnny 14, and Hoyt, 18, and her husband, John.

15 Years A Teacher

After 15 years she has given up teaching, although she loved to teach speech and journalism in high school. She attended six different colleges, and qualified for a doctor's degree — but never sought one because she thought it

(Editor's Note — This untold story behind "Heartbreak Hotel" has not before appeared in any newspaper. One reference to it came out in a trade magazine several months ago. But at the time the song was released, in February, Mrs. Axton was nursing her father, M. L. Boren, fatally ill at her home. She could not subject herself to interviews, declining to see a representative of Life Magazine and others. Mr. Boren died in April. He and Mrs. Boren, who died several years ago, sent to college their eight sons and one daughter, and also seven other children.)

might build a barrier between her and the teenage students. She taught in Texas, Oklahoma and Florida.

Her husband, Coach John Axton, has been athletic director at Paxon High School and formerly coach at Robert E. Lee High in Jacksonville. Hoyt was all-state tackle and has a football scholarship at Oklahoma A&M.

Coach Axton has a fine baritone singing voice but "plays only the radio or record player." Hoyt and Johnny both sing, and play the piano and cornet. Hoyt has two songs, "My Tree of Life" and "Strongest of Oak" now in publisher's hands.

But young Johnny is the leading man of the house in music—he already has a recording — "Cat Man Boogie" by TNT Records of San Antonio, Texas.

Soon all the Axtons will be at the home in Madison, songwriting, teaching, coaching and contributing their efforts to make the community and the world a better place. Meanwhile "Heartbreak Hotel" enters German in translation, and who can tell, maybe it will pierce the Iron Curtain with its message understood the world over.

HANK SNOW

Grand Ole Opry star, has become second in America with a woman manager, Mrs. Mae Boren Axton. Last Saturday Snow sang at the Opry "Conscience, I'm Guilty," which this week was chosen by Billboard Magazine as the "week's best buy" in the country and western music field.

Jean Chapel Sings 'Welcome To The Club'

Mae Boren Axton's first song released since "Heartbreak Hotel" is "Welcome to the Club" (of broken hearts), recorded by a new Nashville personality, platinum-blonde Jean Chapel. Mrs. Axton wrote this song and music alone, but on the reverse side is "No Rockin' Tonight," composed by Mrs. Axton and Durden as a team. Waxing was done by Sun Records of Memphis.

Charlene Arthur of Dallas also has sung it for RCA-Victor Records.

Miss Chapel is being introduced as the latest discovery of Manager Murray Nash of Nashville. He has challenged disc jockies throughout the nation to identify Miss Chapel, although most of them have seen her previously in other roles and different type songs.

She has been engaged for a 10-day run at the Palace Theater in New York, starting Aug. 14.

"Experienced show people tell me Jean Chapel has wonderful stage talent—and is one of the best," said Mrs. Axton. "I am highly pleased with her recordings and will not be at all surprised if they score hits over the nation."

JACK STAPP

He said "I'll take it" (the song)

Mae and Tommy pictured at the height of their songwriting success, courtesy of the estate of Mae Boren Axton.

Mae at the piano,
3239 Dellwood Avenue,
Jacksonville, 1957,
courtesy of the estate
of Mae Boren Axton.

Tommy Durden, performer, early 1960s,
courtesy of Art Kenney.

Mae and Elvis pictured with their single release,
23rd February 1956, Jacksonville, Florida,
courtesy of the estate of Mae Boren Axton.

D.R. Pinney at the shop counter in the 1970s, courtesy of Frances Pinney Erickson.

Mae's Snowmen's card, the Colonel's ultimate sign of professional respect, courtesy of the estate of Mae Boren Axton.

One side of Glenn Reeves' demo disk of "Heartbreak Hotel", courtesy of Anthony Stuchbury.

Elvis Presley's RCA Victor single release of "Heartbreak Hotel", courtesy of Paul Combs.

Part 3: Trials

If the myth gets bigger than the man,
print the myth.
Dorothy M. Johnson
The Man Who Shot Liberty Valance

Lincoln: Trials

1956
MEMPHIS, TENNESSEE

The Lincoln swung into the Gulf forecourt to fill up, and the most famous person on the planet was directly swamped by friendly locals requiring autographs. The station manager pushed his way through the mob and insisted the $10,000 Continental Mark II move on. Unable to comply due to the sheer number of people, the young driver politely offered assurances he would do so soon. After the third request, a fracas ensued and arrests were made. At the subsequent trial, the driver was acquitted but advised that his celebrity status demanded he take greater care when in public. Within six months, Elvis purchased Graceland, a gated house in Memphis, and his withdrawl would be complete.

Music had changed Elvis Presley's life just as surely as Elvis' songs were changing the world — and music itself had long been recognised as a vehicle for social and cultural transition. While the *Opry* stars sang of love and broken hearts, several of their contemporaries took folk songs in a different direction, protesting against inequality and injustice.

When Elvis had his day in court, Riverside Records released an album called *Offbeat Folksongs* (RLP 12-802) by little-known singer Bob Gibson. A collection of eighteen tracks, some self-written, others traditional, it sold poorly, but was heard by key people who knew that the civil rights movement needed its own soundtrack. The keeper on this LP was "Bahamian Lullabye", which opened with the line, "Hush, little baby, don't you cry; you know your mama's bound to die", and contained the haunting refrain, "All my trials, Lord, will soon be over".

As Sam Phillips had always known, it was not enough to challenge politically and intellectually: one must also appeal to hearts and souls. Which is why an emerging figure in the struggle, Dr Martin Luther King Jr, chose to lead not with speeches but with sermons.

For the previous ninety years, the movement had been contained by repression and Jim Crow laws. Elvis Presley, Bob Gibson, Chuck Berry and many others were now kicking in doors and leaping over barricades. But, as in any war, that's when hand-to-hand fighting and hostilities commence.

Inspired By Suicide Note, "Heartbreak Hotel", Written In 22 Minutes; First Heard Here

SATURDAY 7TH & FRIDAY 13TH JULY 1956
THE NASHVILLE BANNER, NASHVILLE, TENNESSEE

"I walk a lonely street" he wrote — and the police reported "suicide." But a song-writing schoolteacher put a "heartbreak hotel" at the end of that street — and it became America's number one hit song of 1956 to date, composed in a fabulous twenty-two minutes flat by this teacher who cannot sing and a radio-tv vocalist who can.

That's the untold story behind "Heartbreak Hotel", the song that led all polls for weeks, has sold over 3,000,000 records and hundreds of thousands in sheet music, and is sweeping England, Germany and other countries. (One Nashville music publisher turned it down, but another took it without even looking.)

This schoolteacher, Texas-born Mrs Mae Boren Axton, has just moved to Nashville from Jacksonville, Florida, occupying a home nearing completion in the Madison community.

SECOND WOMAN MANAGER

She has become exclusive manager for *Grand Ole Opry* star Hank Snow, being the second woman in America to take over management of a country music star. (The other is Bobbie Bennett, manager of Spade Cooley, Hollywood, California.)

"But how could you compose that hit song in less than half an hour?" we asked Mrs Axton behind-stage last Saturday night at *Grand Ole Opry*, where 8,000 persons attended a double-show bill.

"It started with a newspaper story," she replied.

"Tommy Durden, steel guitar player-vocalist from station WMBR-TV, Jacksonville, called me at home. He said he had read in the paper about a man gassing himself to death in a car. He couldn't put out of his mind the suicide note 'I walk a lonely street.' So he came over to my house and started walking the floor, repeating 'lonely, lonely ... but why did he do it?'

"But think of the heartbreak he left behind," I commented. "Let's put a heartbreak hotel at the end of that lonely street."

'Of course,' Tommy came back. 'Let's get on with it.'

"Turning to my piano, with typewriter and tape recorder nearby, we started working — picking out music and words alternately. Usually I would throw in a line, and Tommy would add the next. In twenty-two minutes we had the complete song dubbed in on the recorder. We have made no changes since. There are two minor errors in the sheet music but the recordings are like the original. That was last September. I thought we had a good song that would fit Elvis Presley, who had become quite popular," added Mrs Axton.

"I had met Elvis when he came to Florida with Hank Snow about eighteen months ago, and remembered how the teenagers went wild over him. He was not well known then to Florida people, but I handled publicity for the Snow tour and saw how pleased the show sponsors were when they saw the reaction to Presley. Glenn Reeves of Atlantic Records happened to come by my house and I asked him to sing 'Heartbreak Hotel' onto my tape recorder in Presley style. He did it well, and armed with my tape recorder I came to Nashville in October 1955 to see publishers. I went to one well known publisher here and said, 'I've got a song that will sell a million.'

TURNED DOWN, WITH A LAUGH

"One of his associates laughed and said, 'All we have now are Axton songs.' I didn't like this but said nothing. That night at *Grand Ole Opry* I saw Jack Stapp, program manager for the *Opry* and WSM. He said to me, 'Mae, you never have offered me a song. Why?'

"'I've got one for you right now. It's Heartbreak Hotel,' I replied."

"'I'll take it,' Jack answered, without another word. He's a busy man at *Grand Ole Opry*, as you know. And that's how Tree Publishing Co. got the song." (Stapp is co-owner of Tree with Lou Cowan of New York, who is producer of the *$64,000 Question*, *$64,000 Challenge*, *Big Surprise* and other network quiz shows. Stapp and Cowan were wartime buddies in the Army.)

Mrs Axton went back to Jacksonville after placing the song with Tree, but returned here for the disk jockey convention in November with her tape recorder.

"I happened to see Elvis Presley in the Andrew Jackson Hotel lobby," she continued. "I told him — Elvis, I've got a song you are going to listen to right now."

"He said, 'I can't do it. I've got to go to a meeting.'"

"But I insisted, and Bob Neal of Memphis, his manager at the time, also urged him to hear the song which Neal had already heard. They went to my room and played the song."

10 TIMES FOR PRESLEY

"'Hot dog, Mae. Play that again,' Presley shouted. And we played it ten times, over and over. I turned to Elvis and said, 'If you make this song your next release you can have one third of it.' He agreed, and that's the story. He sang it wonderfully well for that RCA-Victor record, his first release for them after they bought his contract from Sun Records of Memphis for a reported $40,000. A rhythm and blues Modern recording also has been made by The Cadets, a Negro quartet, and it has sold well, although the Presley record is the one that led all the polls."

"Stan Freberg has also sung a takeoff, 'Heartbreak Hotel (Echo by Mammoth Cave)' for Capitol Records and it is selling rapidly."

That ended our "Heartbreak Hotel" conversation, and Mrs Axton began to talk about her two boys, Johnny, 14, and Hoyt, 18, and her husband, John.

15 YEARS A TEACHER

After 15 years she has given up teaching, although she loved to teach speech and journalism in high school. She attended six different colleges, and qualified for a doctor's degree — but never sought one because she thought it might build a barrier between her and the teenage students. She taught in Texas, Oklahoma and Florida. Her husband, Coach John Axton, has been athletic director at Paxon High School and formerly coach at Robert E. Lee High in Jacksonville. Hoyt was all-state tackle and has a football scholarship at Oklahoma A&M.

Coach Axton has a fine baritone singing voice but "plays only the radio or record player." Hoyt and Johnny both sing, and play the piano and cornet. Hoyt has two songs, "My Tree of Life" and "Strongest of Oak" now in publisher's hands. But young Johnny is the leading man of the house in music — he already has a recording — "Cat Man Boogie" by TNT Records of San Antonio, Texas.

Soon all the Axtons will be at the home in Madison, songwriting, teaching, coaching and contributing their efforts to make the community and the world a better place. Meanwhile "Heartbreak Hotel" enters German in translation, and who can tell, maybe it will pierce the Iron Curtian with its message understood the world over.

Editor's Note — This untold story behind "Heartbreak Hotel" has not before appeared in any newspaper. One reference to it came out in a trade magazine several months ago. But at the time the song was released, in February, Mrs Axton was nursing her father, M.L. Boren, fatally ill at her home. She could not subject herself to interviews, declining to see a representative of LIFE MAGAZINE *and others. Mr Boren died in April. He and Mrs Boren, who died several years ago, sent to college their eight sons and one daughter, and also seven other children.*

Transcript from *The Nashville Banner*, 13th July 1956

Jack and Lou come clean

SATURDAY 7TH JULY 1956
NASHVILLE, TENNESSEE

IN A SMALL BUT SIGNIFICANT MOVE, *Billboard* and *The Nashville Banner* casually confirmed on 7th July that Jack Stapp was the co-owner of Tree Publishing. To many within the industry it was common knowledge, but it was now in the public domain. Stapp's coming-out may have been related to Lou Cowan's decision to remove himself from the company. CBS were wooing the talented producer with talk of a vice-presidency and he wanted to ensure no conflict of interests.

So Stapp bought him out, and gave almost a third share to hard-working — and very grateful — employee, Buddy Killen. Thanks to "Heartbreak Hotel", Tree was growing fast, and was now seen as a serious place for songwriters to bring their wares, and this was largely down to Killen's networking and persistence. In a short space of time, Tree became one of the world's most prominent publishing houses, and Jack Stapp's $5,000 investment became one of the smartest moves in entertainment history.

Meanwhile, as a high flyer at CBS, Lou had enough media pull to get his two teenage sons a lunch date with Elvis Presley in August on the set of his first movie, *The Reno Brothers*, a non-musical western over at 20th Century-Fox (canny old Hal Wallis had wisely let another film company test the waters).

And if Lou Cowan had any regrets about quitting Tree, then they disappeared when the offer of a CBS vice-presidency was improved upon.

The Encyclopaedia of Country Music (Second Edition),
Edited by Paul Kingsbury, Michael McCall & John W. Rumble
The Powers That Be, Dave Halberstam
Billboard, 7th July 1956

The Four Diamonds

PERHAPS JULY 1956
DALLAS, TEXAS

JIM SHELL, Dallas' most industrious music entrepreneur, looked out at the four keen young men gathered in the cramped studio. They probably gave Jim the name of their new group, The Four Diamonds, but he just thought of them as Bob Luman and the boys from Mac Curtis' band. He was always searching for original talent and they were looking for a break, so the five of them were going to spend a day putting songs on tape to see if anything clicked. Shell had assembled a bunch of demos, mainly from the *Big D* songwriters he knew well. Bob and the guys were nervous, but determined to rock up a storm.

Firstly, they tried two songs by Helen Hall, now fully recovered from her car crash but struggling to re-assert herself in the business. Titled "Hello Baby" and "Alright", the former sounded like a conversation Helen might have had with her husband while she recuperated in hospital, and the latter came across for all the world like an answer song to Presley's own "That's All Right". The Four Diamonds followed Helen's demos closely, but the finished product was raw and raucous, too much so for a commercial record.

For the next pairing, the boys leaned heavily on the sound and styling of Johnny Cash's and Elvis Presley's recent Sun singles: "Stranger than Fiction" was penned by Jim Shell and Joe Poovey, and "In the Deep Dark Jungle" was a Shell solo, and both carried a clickety-clack uptempo rhythm which brought the Diamonds together as a strong and convincing unit, even though the songs themselves lacked quality and definition.

Jim pushed swiftly onto two ballads, "Let It Happen" and "Let Her Go", each probably written by country singer, Joe Price, who had a nice deal going with Shell as a songwriter-for-hire. Both awkwardly borrowed the same "Only You" riff The Country Cats had used on "Amarillo Blues" when they demoed with Mac Curtis.

Six songs done, time was running short, and Jim cued-up a final acetate for The Four Diamonds to learn. Jim felt the demo disk he'd received in the post from Buddy Killen at Tree Publishing might have something special to offer. It was called "You're the Cause of it All" and everyone in the studio could hear the obvious connection, not just to "Baby, Let's Play House", but also to one side of Presley's current single, "My Baby Left Me". As such, the group stole the drum intro and the descending bass run from Elvis' latest hit, and laid down their last track of the day with a rowdy romp.

Although all seven performances lacked polish, they were overflowing with energy and attitude, and the players were upbeat as they packed away their instruments. Jim shook hands and thanked everybody as they left the studio. He'd liked what they'd done but he didn't hear the magic he'd been hoping for. He took the finished demo tape and placed it at the back of a tall wooden locker. He switched off the lights, turned the key in the door, and wandered home to his waiting wife.

And as far as can be ascertained, this was the one and only time that Mae Boren Axton's original song for Elvis Presley was ever properly recorded. It quietly died, and was unceremoniously buried without a marker in the darkest corner of a dusty cupboard.*

*The Shell tapes were finally discovered in 1974 by Ronny Weiser of Rolling Rock Records, and were released to an enthusiastic response from the faithful. There was little background information available on the songs, least of all writing credits. To this day, to the best of my knowledge, Mrs Boren Axton's name has never appeared on any vinyl or CD in connection with "You're The Cause of it All". It's almost as if Mae wanted the song to disappear ...

"Welcome to the Club", III

SUMMER 1956
NEW YORK CITY, NEW YORK

IT SEEMS UNDENIABLE THAT SOMEONE AT RCA — probably Steve Sholes — had fallen for the charms of Mae Boren Axton's "Welcome to the Club". Perhaps it was the producer's hope that the song would emulate the success of Presley's game-changing debut hit, and he could then trumpet that he'd also landed the *female* Elvis. But it was clear by the summer of 1956 that neither Sun's Jean Chapel release nor RCA's Charline Arthur single were going to make any impact at all on any chart — be it C&W, R&B, or pop.

But, remarkably, having watched the song already flop twice, Steve phoned Sam Phillips and asked if could buy Jean Chapel's contract and also the rights to re-issue "Welcome to the Club" as her first single on RCA Victor. Sam, with a bemused shrug of his shoulders, handed over the tape and the paperwork in exchange for another RCA cheque, and Steve prepared 47-6681 for release in late September, the third official but separate issue of Mae's song in three months.

It launched. It failed again. Steve finally got the message. The song was no damn good. And the simple fact is that Mae Boren Axton never again enjoyed even a brief flirtation with hit parade success. Not when writing alone, not when writing with Glenn Reeves, and not when writing with Tommy Durden ...

A Rocket in My Pocket: The Hipster's Guide to Rockabilly, Max Décharné
Billboard, 13th October 1956

Tommy's holiday

SUMMER 1956
NO PARTICULAR PLACE TO GO

According to popular legend, when his royalty cheque cleared, Tommy Durden took his newly-bought pea-green Cadillac and hit off into the sunset until the money ran out. The truth may be a little less romantic than that. Like Mae, Tommy had every reason to believe his luck had changed and he was now playing in the big leagues. But Mae had struggled (or indeed failed) with "Welcome to the Club" and Tommy would soon face similar disillusionment.

In the early summer, he was invited to make a disk by the notorious Dave Miller of Holiday Records who had released Bill Haley's version of "Rocket 88". Oddly, Tommy was not asked to sing one of his own compositions, but was given two nondescript and dated pop numbers, "A-Weepin' and A-Wailin' Song"/"Only When". The A-side became mildly interesting when Tommy belted out the awkwardly highlighted lyric, "*My baby left me*", followed by a *Boom Boom!* from the band, but, needless to say, the single (Holiday 777) did no business and Tommy was not beckoned back.

He continued working on TV in Florida with Johnny Tillotson, a Mae Boren Axton protégé, but also tried a sideline hawking his reputation as a killer songwriter, inviting the public to forward lyrics to him that he might tranform them into hits. But hits were not forthcoming.

He met up with a very respectful and grateful Elvis ("A pleasure to meet you, sir," said the singer) on a couple of occasions and they went on to exchange a Christmas card or two, but the Colonel was never keen on his client mixing with creative types lest they circumnavigate his strict publishing policy.

Long-term friends and family have suggested that Tommy did try to get further songs to Elvis but was placed on a Parker blacklist. Whether there's any mileage in this story or not it's impossible to determine, but what *is* known is that Tommy Durden never again enjoyed even a brief flirtation with hit parade success. Not when writing alone, not when writing with Mae Boren Axton, and not when writing with Glenn Reeves ...

Axton, Durden & Reeves, II

SUMMER 1956
3239 DELLWOOD AVENUE, JACKSONVILLE, FLORIDA

THE FABLED TRIO OF MAE, TOMMY AND GLENN gathered together again in Jacksonville one summer Friday night with the intention of composing a single for Wanda Jackson, daughter of Axton's schoolfriend, Nellie Whittaker.

Having just signed for Capitol, Jackson was looking for material and, sure enough, the team came up trumps with a number she went on to lay down during her second session in California on 20th September 1956.

"Honey Bop", an almost successful spoonerism, borrowed liberally from "Ain't Got Room to Rock" and "Hula Boogie" lyrically, and owed something to the structure of "Rockin' Country Style" musically. Murray Nash again took the publishing.

Wanda did a sterling job at the microphone but, when released in early 1958 (Capitol F3941), the single failed and Glenn, the only one of the composing trio not to be in receipt of a Tree royalty cheque, chalked it up as another missed opportunity.

Mae had taken to dropping his name whenever she was interviewed about "Heartbreak Hotel", suggesting that Glenn was almost present at the writing session but was called away on an errand, as well as contributing his essential Presleyesque demo. In time, he became the most infamous bit-part player in pop history after Pete Best.

And Glenn kept plugging away as a singer, songwriter and deejay, and handled his notoriety with typical humility and good grace. But Glenn Reeves never again enjoyed even a brief flirtation with hit parade success. Not when writing alone, not when writing with Tommy Durden, and not when writing with Mae Boren Axton ...

Glenn Reeves / *Johnny on the Spot* CD Sleeve Notes, Martin Hawkins & Richard Weize

Monday 10th April 1865 revisited

FRIDAY 24TH AUGUST 1956
20TH CENTURY FOX STAGE 1, HOLLYWOOD, CALIFORNIA

NEVER WAS AN ACTOR BETTER PREPARED than Elvis Presley as he approached the filming of *The Reno Brothers* for 20th Century-Fox. He had memorised the entire script, and was thrilled to be playing the part of a young Southerner in a post-civil war drama. Act 1 Scene 1 was set in Greenwood Railway Station, Louisiana, on the very day that Lincoln requested "Dixie" be played outside the White House.

The brass at Fox had now decided it would be absurd to have America's number one singing star in a movie without music, so a phone call was made telling Elvis there'd be a song in the film. And then came another call and another song. And then another. And then another.

Elvis arrived in Hollywood mid-August, and was introduced to composer Ken Darby of Bing Crosby/"White Christmas" backing-vocal fame, who had come up with a selection of authentic civil war tunes. Elvis chose those he liked, in particular the melody "Aura Lee" (which he undoubtedly already knew) and, working together with Darby's wife, Vera Matson, over the next week they translated the out-of-copyright ballad into the gentle and unassuming "Love Me Tender". The songs were assigned to Elvis Presley Music (BMI), and allocated to Elvis and Vera as writers.

Scotty, Bill and D.J. flew in for the recording but, despite Elvis' protests, were rejected because the producers apparently required *proper hillbilly musicians* to ensure an authentic Southern sound. The sessions themselves were held in the cavernous Fox studio, which was soon added to Elvis' ever-growing list of non-acceptable venues.

The movie was obviously re-named *Love Me Tender*, and did tremendous business when released in November. The single containing the title track (47-6643) sold over two million copies and dislodged "Hound Dog"/"Don't Be Cruel" from the top of the pop chart — the first time a singer had ever replaced himself.

Tom Parker, Hal Wallis, Steve Sholes and Jean Aberbach all watched the finished movie, of course, but their attention was focused on the most important part of the story: the bottom line.

Love Me Tender Recording Sessions, David English, 2010 (online)

When Elvis met Thorne

SATURDAY 1ST SEPTEMBER 1956
RADIO RECORDERS STUDIO, HOLLYWOOD, CALIFORNIA

STEVE SHOLES WAS RUNNING OUT OF OPTIONS. Elvis had made it known that, despite hit after hit, he wouldn't be returning to McGavock Street (too much conflict), New York (too Northern), or Fox (too officious). But Steve was desperate to tape the second album that he'd been advocating since February.

And so it was to Steve's great good fortune that his premier money-maker was temporarily located on the West Coast for the making of *Love Me Tender*, and also for his debut broadcast on *The Ed Sullivan Show*, and the best studio in town just happened to be free.

Elvis was ushered into Radio Recorders at the beginning of the Labor Day weekend, and was introduced to the genial figure of Thorne Nogar, and the singer recognised at once that he'd finally found his ideal studio and engineer. Over the course of three days, Elvis, his band, and The Jordanaires laid down thirteen songs that resulted in yet another number one single and LP.

And this session set the template for Elvis' entire subsequent recording career. There was little in the way of specific planning — Elvis just taped whatever he felt like singing. As per the music in his head, the genres were mixed and matched at random: rock 'n' roll, ballads, country & western, rhythm & blues, it made no difference — it was all just American music to him. And Steve Sholes was happy to sit behind the glass and tick the boxes and complete the paperwork while the workhorse at the mike ensured a very strong financial end to a very profitable year for the record company. Elvis accounted for an astonishing two-thirds of RCA's fifteen million single sales in 1956.

Hill & Range's Freddy Bienstock had brought to the sessions a song from Otis Blackwell and a song from Aaron Schroeder, and Elvis assembled a selection of other tracks, both ancient and modern, including his childhood favourite, "Old Shep", which he recorded at the piano, delivering every ounce of emotion from the song he'd been singing for over half of his life.

Most interesting of all, though, was a number supplied by Leiber and Stoller, via H&R. They had been fascinated and appalled by Elvis' chart-topping re-invention of "Hound Dog", and when the first writers' cheque arrived they declined to bank it, fearing the publishers had mistakenly added an extra zero to the figure.

They couldn't work out Elvis at all so, when asked to supply a song for his second album, they threw in "Love Me", originally written as a c&w parody (and covered by Jimmie Rodgers Snow), to see what he made of it. And Elvis nailed it, singing it straight, along with a doo-wop backing from The Jordanaires, and it swiftly became one of his signature songs even though it was never issued as a single.

When Jerry and Mike were then invited to contribute music for Elvis' forthcoming second movie (for Hal Wallis at Paramount), they felt it wise to start paying a little more attention to the man who was generating more royalties than all of their other artists combined.

A dumbfounded observer at these September sessions was the studio's tape boy, Dayton "Bones" Howe, a jazz fan who loathed rock 'n' roll. Until he watched Elvis, that is, and at once recognised the genius on display.*

Elvis fell in love with Radio Recorders, and it became his West Coast studio of choice, taping some excellent singles and most of his future film soundtracks there over the next decade.

And at some point in the autumn of 1956, RCA Victor, in a moment of underplayed generosity, decided that the man who had caused their profits to mulitply many times over need not actually pay for his own contract after all, and they negated his original $35,000 fee. But, as Elvis' second LP was rush-released in mid-October (*Elvis* LPM 1382) and sold in even higher and more astonishing numbers than his first, they could surely afford to be magnanimous.

Parker, meanwhile, had signed a big bucks deal with a marketing firm, placing his client's name or image on scores of assorted items: Elvis Presley had finally become the product.

---

*In 1959, RCA made the insane decision to destroy most of Elvis' 1950s session tapes, keeping only the master takes, in order to save storage space. A handful survived, most notably those that Bones Howe took home for posterity, knowing that the record company would be a-knocking on his door in years to come, desperately searching for those historic reels. Sure enough, in the early 1980s ...

From the waist up

SUNDAY 9TH SEPTEMBER 1956
CBS-TV STUDIOS, LOS ANGELES & NEW YORK

When it at last came time for Elvis to headline Ed Sullivan's New York-based weekly TV show, the host himself was not able to appear on screen owing to a serious car accident. Veteran actor Charles Laughton stood in for Sullivan, and Presley's performance was beamed in from Hollywood in between filming for Fox.

Elvis sang both sides of his current number one hit, and a Little Richard number he'd just taped for the second album. He also debuted "Love Me Tender" to the enraptured studio audience, and to the record-breaking eighty percent home-viewing figure.

And, as with all of his previous television appearances, Elvis presented himself as a new man — somehow more confident and more assured, someone who knew how to absolutely control this vital medium. This was also true of his second Sullivan gig at the end of the month, and even more so for his finalé in January 1957. It was then that Elvis was filmed only from the waist up, lest his movements inflame passions within the viewers.

The Sullivan appearances were, in essence, the coronation of the new king of popular music, and Elvis accepted the crown with modesty and a sly grin. On the final show, Ed proclaimed his guest "a real decent fine boy", as Elvis departed again for Hollywood to make his first Hal Wallis movie (*Loving You*). The Colonel, having achieved everything he wanted from the world of television, removed Elvis from the small screen for the rest of the decade. Why give away for free what people will pay to see at the cinema, where Parker could exert complete control over the presentation of his client.

And control was at the heart of Parker's entire gameplan. In a bid to keep everything within his grasp, he hired all three Dickens/Diskin sisters to act as his personal secretaries under the guidance of their brother (and the Colonel's right hand man), Tom Diskin. And when Mae stepped away from managing Hank Snow just before Christmas 1956*, can there be any doubt she did so only after seeking the Colonel's permission, and only after Parker was finally convinced there was no longer any possibilty of litigation from his ex-partner. The Snowman had played his hand to perfection.

Billboard, 15th December 1956

*In September 1957, Mae also severed connections with Tree and signed with Denny's Cedarwood.

The Showdown

MONDAY 24TH SEPTEMBER 1956
RADIO WSM, NASHVILLE, TENNESSEE

THE MEETING THAT EVERYONE IN C&W music knew was coming actually happened on 24th September 1956. Jim Denny arrived at WSM late that morning and was summoned to the office of President DeWitt who bluntly laid out his final terms: Denny was to quit all outside interests and focus entirely on his WSM duties in exchange for a substantial pay increase.

Denny, having already been warned several times, but still supremely confident of his position, turned down DeWitt, and was therefore fired on the spot. He exited the building, but returned a short while later. Striding past his secretary, he picked up his Man of the Year Award, turned on his heels and left, never to return.

He started his own very lucrative talent and bookings agency nearby. Several country stars went with him — including Minnie Pearl — and Denny's departure was a blow WSM could ill afford. The truth was that the *Opry* was now struggling in a way it had never done before. The arrival of Elvis Presley and rock 'n' roll had caused the *Opry* to rapidly lose audience members, as the younger listeners pursued the new and more exciting stars. Sometimes, the hallowed Ryman auditorium was only half full, or even less. Traditional country music was suddenly dying on its feet.

And Jack Stapp, the very man who had ushered in the Trojan horse of "Heartbreak Hotel", was kept at his post in an attempt to save the city.

Discovering Country Music, Don Cusic
The Grand Ole Opry: The Making of an American Icon, Colin Escott

The Four Diamonds disband

SATURDAY 3RD NOVEMBER 1956
MUNICIPAL AUDITORIUM, SHREVEPORT, LOUISIANA

EVENTS HAD HAPPENED VERY QUICKLY for The Four Diamonds throughout the summer of 1956. The recording session for Jim Shell had been exciting (even though nothing had come of it), and they'd gone on to win a place on the *Louisiana Hayride*. Horace Logan of KWKH was mightily impressed with the boys, especially young Bob Luman, and on 3rd November the group signed with the radio show.

Logan had been looking for a long-term replacement for Elvis and he was sure he'd found him in the group's lead singer. Other regular members of the *Hayride* took a liking to Bob too, including James Burton, a talented seventeen year-old local guitarist, who had joined the cast as a house musician, and was already making a name for himself.

Mr Logan then set up a recording session for the Diamonds with Fabor Robison of Abbot Records. The boys taped half-a-dozen songs, including — to reinforce the fact that they were an all-parts-equal band — three instrumental numbers. All six tracks were gutsy and well performed but, like Jim Shell before him, Fabor Robison chose not to release a single.

By Valentine's Day 1957, disillusioned with their stop-start careers, three-quarters of The Four Diamonds decided to call it a day and disbanded. Horace Logan, however, was adamant that he wanted to keep Bob Luman, and so he built a new group around him, using James Burton to drive them along musically.

They taped a small session in Dallas for Imperial Records before the month was out, and were then invited to appear in a rock 'n' roll B-movie entitled *Carnival Rock*. Bob moved from Imperial to Capitol, and then from Capitol to Warner. He joined the *Grand Ole Opry* and continued to be very popular in the world of country and rockabilly music. He remained a great talent, but his rightful day in the worldwide spotlight never came.

And he never knew he was the first person to professionally record the song intended to take his life-changing idol into the big time.*

---

*The opening title sequence of Elvis' hugely popular movie *Viva Las Vegas* shows random clips of the strip filmed in the summer of 1963, and many of the neon-lit signs advertise the celebrated performers at the various casinos. And who should be headlining at The Golden Nugget? None other than Mr Bob Luman.

The Million Dollar Quartet

TUESDAY 4TH DECEMBER 1956
706 UNION AVENUE, MEMPHIS, TENNESSEE

JOHNNY CASH PICKED UP THE INSISTENT PHONE and heard the voice of Sam Phillips telling him to get his ass on down to 706 on the double. Cash, who had no session booked that day, clarified that he was taking his wife Christmas shopping, and asked what could be so all-darned important anyway? Sam's answer curtailed any further debate: Elvis had dropped in at Sun, and Sam smelled a publicity photo opportunity,

When Johnny arrived, Elvis was holding court on the studio floor. Carl Perkins was mid-session and cradling his acoustic guitar, laughing politely, slightly in awe of his former label-mate. Sitting in the corner, but edging closer to centre stage every second, was Jerry Lee Lewis, the latest of Sun's fledgling stars and a man not lacking in self-confidence. To everyone bar Lewis, it was clear that Presley was the alpha in the room, but Jerry Lee wasn't about to play second fiddle to anyone.

The foursome soon hit a groove when Elvis picked up a guitar and Jerry Lee settled on the piano stool, and they off-handedly ran through dozens of c&w, pop and gospel songs, Presley and the blond newcomer trading lines, while Sam pressed the record button to get it all on tape for posterity.*

Jerry Lee was still singing long after the photographs were taken and everyone else was bidding farewell to Elvis as he left. Sam Phillips believed the occasion to be his moment of validation. Marion watched quietly and with mixed emotions. She'd recently discovered Sam was having an extra-extra-marital affair with Sally Wilbourn, the girl taken on to cope with the deluge of work after Elvis' sale to RCA the previous November.

In 1957, the woman who had first discovered Elvis Presley decided to quit Sun and signed up as a Captain in the air force. She was assigned to Germany and served in Armed Forces Television at the Ramstein air base. Marion had made no great fortune from her involvment with Elvis Presley, nor was she indeed looking for a material reward. That which she desired was less easy to quantify but infinitely more valuable: love and recognition.

Leaving 706 Union for the last time, she took with her the acetate demo of "Without You", a poignant keepsake of her time with Sun and with Sam.

*Sam sent a copy of the tape to Elvis, and another found its way onto the bootleg vinyl market in the 1980s. It's now available as an official CD and it is quite glorious.

The Singin' Idol

WEDNESDAY 30TH JANUARY 1957
KRAFT TELEVISION THEATRE, NBC-TV

As with his totem animal, the elephant, Tom Parker had a long and retentive memory. If there was a perceived slight from a business associate or an acquaintance, Parker would make a mental note and, at some future point, sweet revenge would be exacted.

If, however, the Colonel took a liking to you, then there would be no end to his support and generosity. Parker had taken Tommy Sands to his heart, and he regretted not having been able to steer him to fame. So when Kraft Television Theatre at NBC-TV approached the Colonel in late 1956 about Elvis appearing in a semi-autobiographical drama entitled *The Singin' Idol,* Parker rejected their advances on his boy but pointed the producers in the direction of his ex-protégé, Tommy Sands.

Sands was to play the part of a singer firmly based on Elvis Presley (his first spoken line being, "Hey, wait a minute, Arnie, yeah, *that's all right*"), and the script took a misanthropic look at an artist/manager relationship which mirrored the Presley/Parker/Diskin/Axton scenario.*

The Singin' Idol broadcast on TV at the end of January 1957, and proved so popular that it was remade a year later as the cinematic movie *Sing, Boy, Sing,* but it lacked all of the grit, charm and nous of the original. Still, it allowed Tommy Sands to move rapidly up the ladder to the point where he mixed with and married Nancy Sinatra in 1960.

Presumably, the provisional script from Kraft had landed on Parker's desk in December 1956 and he may have glanced through it before recommending his one-time client to NBC. Had he indeed leafed through the pages, he'd have registered that the main tension for Sands' character came from a pull between faith and fame — and it was suggested within the screenplay that the Singin' Idol might even record an album of hymns.

On 12th January 1957, Elvis Presley stepped into Radio Recorders to tape his next single ("All Shook Up", via Otis Blackwell), a new soundtrack LP (*Loving You*) — and, believe it or not, a four-track EP of gospel songs.

Life imitates art as art imitates life as life imitates art as art imitates life as life imitates art ...

---

*The character of Glenda Markle, Elvis' celluloid manager in *Loving You,* is a note-perfect amalgamation of Parker, Diskin and Axton — and Walter "Tex" Warner is clearly Clarence "Hank" Snow, including the fake hillbilly name. The whole movie is steeped in Elvis lore, right down to Hill & Range squeezing in an instrumental version of "Candy Kisses". When you've finished reading this book, watch the movie again with fresh eyes.

Man of the Year, 1957

SATURDAY 23RD MARCH 1957
NASHVILLE, TENNESSEE

At the third time of asking, Steve Sholes finally vacated the runner-up spot and was named country music's Man of the Year in March 1957. Having revolutionised c&w and pop via Elvis Presley it would surely have seemed churlish to not recognise his accomplishments. Jim Denny took second place, and Jack Stapp was listed in the top ten.

But many within the world of folk music did not consider Presley's arrival worthy of celebration. By what rationale, they wondered, did a song like "Don't Be Cruel" have a right to sit on top of the hillbilly chart, the r&b chart, and the pop chart simultaneously?

Traditional country music continued to nose-dive in popularity and, as the lines between black and white culture merged and blurred, the wider implications and "dangers" of a prominent figure such as Elvis Presley promoting racial equality became clear to many who preferred (and had a vested interest in) the unjust status quo.

And conversely, there were some on the other side of the fence who presumed, without knowing anything of the facts, that Presley had come by his success at the expense of black artists*, the selfsame artists, performers and writers that Elvis admired, befriended and relentlessly promoted.

But when did truth ever get in the way of a good story?

Billboard, 23rd March 1957

*That this appalling falsehood was still being peddled in a film as recent as *Cadillac Records* (Tri-Star 2008) is a cultural disgrace. The two most respected celebrity advocates for racial equality during Elvis' lifetime, Muhammad Ali and James Brown, both regarded him as a brother and a humanitarian. Every year, Elvis would quietly donate vast sums to Memphis charities, supporting local projects for citizens of all races and backgrounds. He remembered all too well how it felt to be poor and disadvantaged.

All Fools' Day, II

APRIL 1957
FORT WORTH, TEXAS

GEORGE LEVITAN was the white owner of *Sepia*, a popular monthly magazine aimed at a black audience. He was a tough businessman who knew the value of a dollar, but was also respected as someone who was fair to employees of all colours. *Sepia* ran some outstanding pieces on civil rights and the plight of Afro-Americans but, in a bid to boost circulation, it was also known to play fast and loose with celebrity interviews and profiles, and would easily stray into overt sensationalism.*

It was to Elvis Presley's great misfortune then that the periodical ran an unwarranted and malicious feature on him in their April 1957 edition, which focused on untrue quotations that he had apparently made while performing in Boston — a city he'd never actually visited.

In a bid to balance the coverage and establish the truth, rival *Jet* magazine questioned Presley on the unfounded allegations and he was, understandably, aghast. They quoted notable black figures — most prominently songwriter Otis Blackwell, and Elvis' new pianist at Radio Recorders, Dudley Brooks — both of whom spoke defiantly in Elvis' defence.

The irony of the greatest cultural integrator of the twentieth century being tarred with the racist brush was so appallingly perfect that one could only suspect an ill motive from a higher source: the most obvious way to counter Presley's musical inter-racial revolution was to deviously suggest that he himself held impure motives. Simple, effective and horrifying. As previously noted, when a man of Elvis' influence started mixing with the "wrong" colour then he most certainly would and did make enemies.

But anyone, be they black or white, truly listening to the records would know where his heart was at. As *Jet* hit the newsstands, refuting the lies, thousands of music-loving fans of all races purchased tickets for Presley's forthcoming stadium gig in Seattle, among them the fifteen year-old James Marshal Hendrix, who spent his school days doodling pictures of guitars and his beloved rock 'n' roll hero on the back of his textbooks. No fool he.

Race, Rock and Elvis, Michael T. Bertrand
Seeking a Place in the Sun: Sepia Magazine's endeavour for quality journalism and place in the negro market, 1951-1982, Mia Chandra Long
Jet, 1st August 1957 and *Texas Monthly*, October 1983

*Respected editor Ben Burns acknowledged as much after resigning the following year.

Jailhouse Rock

TUESDAY 30TH APRIL 1957
RADIO RECORDERS STUDIO, HOLLYWOOD, CALIFORNIA

IN EARLY 1957, Elvis had taped the soundtrack for *Loving You*, his first Hal Wallis movie, partly at the Paramount studio but then, more successfully, at Radio Recorders with Thorne Nogar at the helm. Leiber and Stoller wrote two of the songs, including the title tune.

As plans were made for his third film (*Jailhouse Rock*, a Pandro Berman production at MGM), the Aberbachs offered the entire score to Leiber and Stoller, who were still unsure what to make of the man solely responsible for such a serious chunk of their income.

They wrote four of the six required songs (Aaron Schroeder took the other two), and accepted the Aberbachs' invitation to meet the singer at Radio Recorders on the first day of taping. The composers sized up Elvis as he arrived with his small entourage, but he completely disarmed them with his obsessive knowledge of their own back catalogue, and then invited Mike to sit at the piano as they traded blues riffs.

The duo, like everyone else who met him, were taken with Elvis' charm, humour and sincerity. And when he started recording the soundtrack, they were stunned by his work ethic and dedication to getting it right. He was no cultural thief: he was the real deal, and he knew at least as much as did Leiber and Stoller about the history of the blues.

The title-song single* and the soundtrack EP sold in absurd quantities, and Leiber and Stoller (regardless of Steve Sholes' presence) became Elvis' accepted producers at Radio Recorders for the next twelve months. And everything they taped together was soaked in sweat, sex, humour, quality and profit.

The Aberbach brothers slept well that year, but Tom Parker was restless, as he always was when creative people were allowed access to his boy.

Let them step out of line once ... just once ...

---

*In the UK, "Jailhouse Rock" became the first single in history to enter the pop chart at the number one position. Between 1957 and 1962 inclusive, Elvis owned the top two places in the British chart. When The Beatles dreamed of being "bigger than Elvis", this was the sort of success they had in mind.

Jack steps down

EARLY JUNE 1957
RADIO WSM, NASHVILLE, TENNESSEE

THE TENSION HAD BEEN PRESENT AT WSM for some time. When Jim Denny departed there had been a temporary easing of the pressure — Denny had been confrontational and aggressive regarding his outside business dealings, whereas Jack Stapp, of course, had been passive and discreet. But John DeWitt, head of WSM, was still unhappy with Stapp's continued polite defiance, and so a compromise of sorts was reached.

In the summer of 1957, Stapp stepped down from his day-to-day position at the top level of *Opry* management, and worked instead on Jim Reeves' new show at radio ABN. But, he also continued to produce the *Opry* on a part-time basis. It was a stop-gap solution and everyone knew it.

Sure enough, one year later he left WSM altogether, and joined pop station WKDA, which had no problem with his ownership of Tree Publishing.

Tree itself continued to thrive and, during this time, Buddy Killen signed up a writer named Roger Miller, who would go on to compose and record a number of very profitable country songs ("King of the Road", "England Swings") over the next decade.

Roger had been directed towards Buddy Killen by old friend, Mae Boren Axton, who had never forgotten the awful fiddler who had helped record her first demo disks with Glenn Reeves back in Childress, Texas.

Mae, like her mentor, had a long memory.

Air Castle of the South: WSM and the Making of Music City, Craig Havighurst
Country Singers As I Know 'Em, Mae Boren Axton
Discovering Country Music, Don Cusic
Jim Reeves: His Untold Story, Larry Jordan
Billboard, 2nd September 1957
Nashville Banner, Tennessee, 11th June 1957

Irving Berlin *vs* Elvis Presley

FRIDAY 6TH SEPTEMBER 1957
RADIO RECORDERS STUDIO, HOLLYWOOD, CALIFORNIA

STEVE SHOLES had rarely felt so frustrated. He'd arranged a series of sessions starting on the Thursday with the sole intention of Elvis laying down an album of Christmas songs. But Elvis had begun by spending hours re-recording "Treat Me Nice" for the *Jailhouse Rock* soundtrack. After that, and before calling it a day, he recorded just one festive song, a slow and gutsy take of Ernest Tubb's 1949 hit, "Blue Christmas".

Sitting near Elvis was Millie Kirkham, Jack Stapp's one-time secretary, who had broken into the world of C&W back-up singing earlier that year, on Ferlin Huskey's single, "Gone". Elvis adored her high voice and now insisted on her studio presence whenever possible.

When they reconvened on the Friday, Sholes felt his blood boil as the singer laid down twenty-eight takes of a ballad, "My Wish Came True", a song given personally to Elvis by the great R&B star, Ivory Joe Hunter.

Finally getting back on track, Elvis announced he'd like to tackle Irving Berlin's "White Christmas". Elvis was no stranger to Bing Crosby's material, and here he was going up against the most popular and famous number in the history of the music business. But what Elvis wasn't doing was going up against Bing's version of the song.

He conferred with Jerry and Mike, and reminded them of The Drifters' ultra-cool 1954 doo-wop version — which in itself was based on The Ravens' 1950 cover. Following a consultation with The Jordanaires and session pianist, Dudley Brooks, Presley laid down his cute 'n' sexy master in nine takes. The rest of the LP followed quickly thereafter.

Elvis' Christmas Album was rush-released on 15th October and was an instant smash. With everybody except Irving Berlin, that is, so the unverified story goes. He was a big man in show business and had been at the forefront of popular music for almost half a century. Irving decided to stand Canute-like and halt the incoming tide of sleaze masquerading as music. Upon hearing the Presley version of his most beloved composition he called radio stations demanding they not play the LP.

It became the biggest selling album of the 1950s.

As Thousands Cheer: The Life of Irving Berlin, Laurence Bergreen
Elvis Presley: A Life in Music, Ernst Mikael Jørgensen

The beat goes on

WEDNESDAY 27TH NOVEMBER 1957
GALLATIN ROAD, MADISON, TENNESSEE

HE STUMBLED OUT OF BED AT 3:00 AM on a cool November night and, without switching on lights or disturbing his mother, managed to retrieve the pistol from the den and made his way into the yard. He knelt, cocked the gun, and put the barrel in his mouth.

It had been two weeks since Jimmie Snow had last stepped off stage in Bangor, Maine. As an extra added attraction on his dad's tour, he had received polite applause, but it was a long way short of the assurance and acceptance he needed deep inside. He'd since done a lot of thinking and a lot of drinking.

Tears rolled down his cheeks as he gently applied pressure to the trigger. In that moment, he had every intention of ending the misery of his existence. But he stopped. He felt an overwhelming presence all around him in the yard, and dropped the gun to the ground shouting, "*You are real!*" into the night air. The guilt and the bitterness left him, and he sobbed tears of relief and gave thanks to God.

He woke his mother, Minnie, and told her simply that he'd had a spiritual experience, and was giving up show business to train in the ministry. She told him sleepily that he was having a nervous breakdown and should return to bed.

Hank, needless to say, did not take the news well. But Jimmie was as good as his word, and he became Pastor of the Evangel Temple on Dickerson Road, sometimes called "The Church of Country Music Stars".*

Revd Jimmie preached against the evils of popular music, and a news crew famously filmed him denouncing "the beat, the beat, the beat." Look for it on YouTube; you won't have to search for long. The glorious irony of this, however, came decades later when society had largely accepted the musical revolution of the 1950s and a museum dedicated to it was opened in Cleveland. Vintage film was used to enhance the exhibits, and in pride of place is the Reverend's glorious berating of "the beat."

Yup, Jimmie Rodgers Snow is in the official Rock 'n' Roll Hall of Fame.

Hank & Jimmy: A Story of Country (documentary film)
Billboard, 4th November 1957

---

*Johnny Cash answered the call there in 1971, some three years after marrying June Carter.

Johnny Bragg: "Jailhouse Rock"

SATURDAY 21ST DECEMBER 1957
GOVERNOR FRANK CLEMENT'S MANSION, NASHVILLE, TENNESSEE

JORDANAIRE GORDON STOKER opened the door and there was Elvis Presley. The star was in Nashville dropping off Christmas presents and bonus cheques to his musicians. He'd just received his own festive gift from the Memphis Draft Board and was looking to cheer himself up. Stoker persuaded Presley to accompany The Jordanaires to the *Grand Ole Opry* that night, just for old times' sake.

Fully aware of his contractual restrictions, Elvis contented himself to play the part of enthusiastic supporter at the Ryman, but old acquaintances flocked to him backstage, all eager to be photographed with the star: Faron Young, Johnny Cash, Ray Price, a very young Brenda Lee, The Wilburns and, most curiously of all, a beaming Hank Snow.

Meanwhile, on the other side of town, Johnny Bragg and his fellow inmate vocalists were at Governor Clement's mansion for one of their regular performances. It had been one hell of a year for Bragg: celebrated singer, Johnnie Ray, had recorded his own version of "Just Walkin' in the Rain" in the summer of 1956, and it became a colossal pop hit.

Johnny and his guys sang throughout the early evening for a selection of faceless politicians but were astonished when, at around 10:00 PM, a fleet of vehicles arrived and in came the Governor's special guest, direct from his visit to the *Opry*, none other than Elvis Presley.

Bragg whispered to his comrades, "Let's do that new Elvis thing." They kicked into Presley's latest disk, "Jailhouse Rock", and the man himself was soon on his feet and supplementing the group. Presley and Bragg made eye contact and nodded to each other as the star slid onto the piano stool and returned the compliment by launching into "one of my favourite songs", and led the boys through an impromptu take of "Just Walkin' in the Rain".

Presley, Bragg and the group kept on singing through until the early hours, and Elvis left at 3:00 AM.

Just over two years later, in one of his last acts as Governor, Clement at last freed Johnny Bragg, and introduced him to Jack Stapp who signed him as a staff writer for Tree Publishing.

Just Walkin' in the Rain, Jay Warner

The death of Love

THURSDAY 14TH AUGUST 1958
MEMPHIS, TENNESSEE

ELVIS ENTERED THE ARMY ON 24th March 1958, his enrolment having been delayed to allow for the completion of *King Creole*, his fourth movie (Michael Curtiz directed, Hal Wallis produced, Leiber and Stoller oversaw the soundtrack). His last act as a civilian was to watch Tommy Sands playing in *Sing, Boy, Sing* on the big drive-in screen.

Amidst a blizzard of publicity, Presley was sent to Texas for basic training where he acquited himself well. His parents rented living space nearby, and began making plans to follow him to Germany for his posting in the summer.

In June, in response to Steve Sholes' pleading, Elvis spent a day's leave in RCA's new state-of-the-art studio in Nashville (which he loved) and laid down a handful of blistering singles to see him through the next two years.

By early August, however, it had become obvious that his mother was struggling healthwise, and Elvis sent her home from Texas for hospital tests, but still she continued in her downward spiral. By the second week, she was bed-ridden and Elvis threatened to go AWOL should the army brass defer his compassionate leave any longer. Permission granted, he touched down in Memphis on 12th August. Two days later, Gladys Love Presley passed in the early hours. Father and son were inconsolable.

Weeks later, Elvis boarded the U.S.S. *Randall*, bound for Germany, leaving New York in the shadow of Lady Liberty. Photographer Alfred Wertheimer was there to capture the end of Elvis' rock 'n' roll years, just as he had the beginning. A sympathetic peer handed Elvis a copy of *Poems That Touch The Heart*, the volume of verse that had so inspired Hank Williams, and the grieving soldier took solace in the words.

He would be gone for eighteen months — a lifetime in the pop music business, and pretty much the exact duration of time he had spent under the tutelage of Sam Phillips. During this period, Elvis would be visited in Germany by many of his professional advisors: Hal Wallis travelled over, as too did Jean Aberbach and Freddy Bienstock. But not the Colonel. Not once did Tom Parker get on a plane and visit his boy.

It's tricky to travel abroad without a passport.

Careless Love: The Unmaking of Elvis Presley, Peter Guralnick

The Bad Nauheim tapes, II

PERHAPS APRIL 1959
BAD NAUHEIM, GERMANY

EVEN THOUGH PRESLEY was out of the country and serving Uncle Sam, still his very name seemed to court controversial headlines. Illinois Circuit Court Judge Charles Dougherty had made a ruling pertaining to the village of Park Forest, the only location in all of America which banned jukeboxes. A local pizzeria had decided to test that ban, and Dougherty fined them $25, declaring, "I, for one, wouldn't want to be forced to listen to Elvis Presley play whatever he plays."

Presley, meanwhile, had settled into army life in Bad Nauheim, Germany. Every evening, when duties were done, he drove to his rented home, off-barracks, where his father, grandmother, and a few trusted friends, were living.

They would eat and chat, and often Elvis would retreat to his room to listen to the latest 45s sent to him by his publishing company. Sitting at the piano or strumming his Isana Jazz Gibson guitar, he would practise and plan for his return to the recording business.

Like Bing Crosby, Presley was blessed — and yet cursed — with the gift of making it all look too easy, and few listeners gave any thought to the countless hours of research and rehearsal that the singer invested in his art. He would croon into his new Grundig TK32 tape recorder, trying take after take of songs he was considering for his first post-army sessions. He listened back to the tapes critically, and then tried again.

He was fascinated by The Drifters' "There's No Tomorrow", a modern setting of the Italian aria "O Sole Mio". He was aiming high, but was convinced there was another hit in there, and commissioned Hill & Range to write new lyrics. He was serious about this. He worked. He planned. Soldier by day: record producer by night.

Into the wee small hours he would play through the tunes he knew and loved and had stored in his encyclopaedic memory. Every now and then he hit upon a gem that brought out the best in his maturing voice; and when he sang something like Hank Williams' "I Can't Help It" or the Jim Reeves' hit "I'm Beginning to Forget You", it seemed so natural and beautiful that he almost wept the tears of Roy Acuff.*

Billboard, 8th June 1959

*Elvis struck up a lifelong friendship with fellow soldier and professional gospel singer Charlie Hodge sailing to Germany in 1958, and he encouraged Presley to expand his vocal range.

The west Texas town of El Paso, II

TUESDAY 7TH APRIL 1959
BRADLEY FILM & RECORDING STUDIO, NASHVILLE, TENNESSEE

THE COLONEL'S UNSIGNED CLIENT AND FRIEND, Marty Robbins, continued his run of successful country & western hits late into the decade. In April 1959 he began recording a themed album based around the stories, heroes and villains of the old west, and the standout track was titled "El Paso", the narrative unknowingly combining the tales of John Wesley Hardin and Alvin Krolik, as young men fell in the west Texas town amid bullets, blood, love, alcohol and death.

Released as a single in October 1959 (Columbia 4-41511), it took the Grammy Award for Best Country & Western Recording, and hit the top spot in the hillbilly and pop charts. The song (and its attendant album) contained enough grit to be counted as genuine c&w product, but it also featured blander elements typical of the new so-called Nashville Sound, the latest attempt to fight back against the devil of rock 'n' roll that had so destabilised authentic country music.

The Nashville Sound involved a smoothing out of the old style and the replacement of steel guitars and fiddles with string sections and vocal accompaniment — The Jordanaires had never been so in demand. Steve Sholes and Chet Atkins* were among the pioneers of this new template, and many performers benefited enormously — Ferlin Huskey's "Gone" was the forerunner of the style — and Jim Reeves in particular absolutely found his oeuvre, his 1960 ballad "He'll Have To Go" almost topping both charts, pop and country.

The *Opry* also began to claw its way back, and re-established itself as the primrary icon of all things hillbilly. But for long-term fans of real country music, there could be no denying that the glory years were indeed just as Ferlin had suggested.

Gone.

*Chet Atkins was announced as *Billboard*'s Man of the Year in 1960 for saving country music.

The slaughter of the innocents

JUNE 1959
CBS-TV, NEW YORK CITY, NEW YORK

LOU COWAN may have seemed like the golden child to some at CBS, but he was not a universally popular president. His close friendship with controversial broadcasters Ed Murrow and Fred Friendly, together with his insistence on quality news and documentary shows at the expense of more obvious commercial ventures, ruffled feathers.

So when, in 1958, rumours began to spread that there had been fixing and rule-breaking behind the scenes of numerous quiz shows, Cowan seemed like the perfect scapegoat to placate the offended millions. He kept his own counsel in the face of the accusations, though many felt it would have been completely out of character for him to have known about, much less condoned, media fraud of this nature.

Television was not the only casualty of establishment ire. Alan Freed, dee-jay and rock 'n' roll entrepreneur, was singled out in what was known as the "payola" scandal. It was revealed that key people in the music business had taken cash payments and writing credits to ensure certain songs were given extra exposure.

By the end of 1959, like Freed, Lou Cowan was gone, not only from CBS, but from the world of entertainment in general. He spent most of his subsequent life quietly teaching until he and his beloved wife Polly — who had first thought of the name Tree Publishing — perished together in a house fire in their Manhattan apartment in 1976.

But did Cowan really know nothing at all about the rigged quiz shows?

That's the $64,000 question …

The Powers That Be, Dave Halberstam
Television Fraud: The History and Implications of the Quiz Show Scandals, Kent Anderson

Restless farewell

TUESDAY 1ST & WEDNESDAY 2ND MARCH 1959
GERMANY

DESPITE SERGEANT PRESLEY'S WISHES to be accorded no special treatment during his stint, the army requested his presence at a 9:00 AM press conference the day before he was due to return home. He fielded all questions with his usual humour and deference, but was dumbfounded when approched by a female air force Captain who flashed him a smile. With raised eyebrows, Sgt Presley grinned back and exclaimed, "Marion!?"

And it was indeed the very same Marion Keisker, now uniformed, who had first recognised his innate talent almost seven years earlier when he'd walked through the door at 706 Union.

"I don't know whether to kiss you or salute," he exclaimed.

"Both. In that order," she replied.

And when an army Captain stepped in to reprimand Marion for over-familiarity, Elvis was quick to clarify that they wouldn't even be having this press conference had it not been for her significant contribution to his life and career. That recognition meant more to Marion than she could say.

The following day, Elvis headed for the Rhine-Main air base to begin the flight home. During the last few months of his European stay, he had quietly become acquainted with Priscilla Beaulieu, the daughter of an air force Colonel, and she accompanied him to the airstrip. In a scene bizarrely reminiscent of the closing act of *Sing, Boy, Sing*, Elvis bid farewell to her as hundreds of reporters and photographers watched on. One could almost hear Parker (had he actually been there) saying the same words to Priscilla that Sands' manager used in the film: *Well, take a look around you, kid: this is his life. You wanna be part of it?*

And then, in an instant, he was gone. In his heart were myriad worries about resuming civilian life in the wake of his mother's death. In his head were dozens of songs he had rehearsed and honed, ready for his return to the music business.

Careless Love: The Unmaking of Elvis Presley, Peter Guralnick

Jim Reeves is back!

SUNDAY 20TH MARCH 1960
RCA STUDIO B, NASHVILLE, TENNESSEE

According to the studio log, Jim Reeves was booked in for a 7:00 PM session at RCA's new Studio B in Nashville, but when the crack group of local musicians (known as the Nashville A Team) began to arrive and noticed the additional presence of The Jordanaires, Scotty Moore and D.J. Fontana — Bill had departed in 1958 to form his own combo — they quickly understood that the Reeves tag (used with Jim's permission) was a ruse to fool the press and the fans.*

Sure enough, Elvis arrived and a bunch of suits filled the booth. At the desk was Bill Porter, an amiable and talented engineer, who had moved in when Bob Ferris and Atkins finally came to blows in early 1959.

Tom Parker had the whole year mapped out: there would be three singles; the astonishing *Elvis Is Back!* album; a TV appearance with Frank Sinatra; a gospel album at Elvis' insistence, in tribute to his mother, highlighting The Blackwoods' "His Hand in Mine"; two dramatic movies with Fox; a glossy musical, *G.I. Blues,* for Hal Wallis at Paramount, and a supporting soundtrack album. But everything hinged on the new recordings and Elvis' ability to continue doing what he'd done pre-army; to wit, delivering a string of ground-breaking, commercially strong hits. He did not disappoint.

On Sunday 20th March 1960, aged twenty-five, he re-launched his career with a Nashville recording session, and confirmed his position as the world's most celebrated singer. Over the course of the next twelve months, Elvis laid down seven huge transatlantic number one singles ("It's Now or Never" was the multi-million selling apex), all of which ushered in a mellower sound, marking a brave new artistic direction.

Records, occasional live performances, television and, in particular, movies, all fell within his remit. He appealed to listeners of every genre, and recorded songs that registered with every type of customer.

There had never been an entertainer like him and, it was widely agreed, there never would be again.

Careless Love: The Unmaking of Elvis Presley, Peter Guralnick
Elvis Presley: A Life In Music, Ernst Mikael Jørgensen

*Elvis wrote a letter of thanks to Reeves for permitting the subterfuge. Jim died on 31st July 1964 when the private plane he was piloting crashed. He was still very much at the top of his game and hugely popular in country music.

"Let the word go forth ..."

FRIDAY 20TH JANUARY 1961
WASHINGTON D.C.

THE YOUTH REVOLUTION that Presley had helped push into life continued apace as the youngest American president was sworn into office on Friday 20th January 1961.

It was some indication of how far Elvis had come in five short years to note that he received, and politely declined, an official gilt-edged invitation to the inauguration, and also a letter of thanks from runner-up Richard Nixon. On Parker's advice, he stayed well clear of politics and displayed no favouritism towards any party or movement.

However, as Kennedy established Camelot (with the Colonel's Texan friend and fellow Snowman LBJ at his side), Presley's second post-army film, *Flaming Star*, a western drama, was playing at cinemas worldwide.* In this movie, Elvis portrayed a troubled young man of mixed race and the musical numbers were kept to a minimum. It was almost exactly the direction in which Elvis wanted to go professionally.

The movie and its dramatic follow-up, *Wild In The Country*, both made money, but when they failed to reach the dizzying financial success of his first post-army film, *G.I. Blues*, the Colonel was able to demonstrate to his charge that what the public obviously wanted to see was Elvis singing lots of songs to lots of girls in lots of beautiful locations.

Two years later, infamous pop artist Andy Warhol produced a series of screenprinted images based on a publicity still of Elvis from the modestly-received *Flaming Star*. To date, the artworks have grossed $345,000,000. Even amidst apparent and relative failure, the Elvis Presley money-making machine rolled on.

The Archives of Graceland: The Official Auction Catalogue, 1999

---

*But not in apartheid South Africa, until 20th Century-Fox appealed, and even then it played in whites-only cinemas.

Leiber, Stoller and Spector

PERHAPS EARLY 1961
LOS ANGELES

SONGWRITERS Jerry Leiber and Mike Stoller had gone from strength to strength during the late 1950s and early 1960s. Their association with Elvis Presley had been of huge benefit to both parties, but there'd been a serious falling out between them and Presley's management.

They adored working with the young artist (and loved the cheques almost as much), but when they wanted to realise Elvis' full potential and started pitching ideas for more challenging avenues, Tom Parker warned them off in the strongest possible terms. Not needing the hassle, they walked away from the Presley camp.*

Instead, they focused some of their time on a gifted young man named Phil Spector. He had little talent as a singer, but they took him under their wing and guided him in the art of songwriting and production. Their faith was rewarded when he began to pick up a few hits and, never shy about his own achievements, Spector began to hawk his name around town.

So much so, in fact, that he received a call from Hill & Range asking if he'd be willing to submit songs for Presley's forthcoming Hal Wallis Paramount movie musical, *Blue Hawaii*. Spector, a devoted Elvis fan, was thrilled, and enthusiastically agreed.

His plans came to an abrupt halt, however, when Leiber and Stoller uncovered the situation, and the Aberbachs were quick to back off upon receipt of a curt letter from Jerry and Mike's attorney, the quick-witted, no-nonsense Lee Eastman. On this particular occasion, H&R were not looking for trouble.

Leiber and Stoller had been key to Presley's early success and to maintaining the quality of his musical vision, and Elvis loved working with them, but the Colonel objected to their interfering. An astute manager might have kept songwriters and producers of this calibre onside to ensure his client was enthused and driven. With rare exception, Leiber and Stoller never worked with Elvis Presley again.

He's a Rebel: Phil Spector — Rock and Roll's Legendary Producer, Mark Ribowsky

---

*Quality-wise, during the early 1960s, Leiber and Stoller's place was taken by pop-rock maestros Doc Pomus and Mort Shuman ("A Mess of Blues", "His Latest Flame", "Viva Las Vegas"), and also by Don Robertson, who returned to the fold and delivered a series of mature and introspective country ballads that allowed Elvis to express his increasing world-weariness.

Johnny Bragg meets the Colonel

WEDNESDAY 8TH MARCH 1961
STATE PRISON, NASHVILLE, TENNESSEE

LIFE HAD NOT BEEN KIND to Johnny Bragg since his release from prison on 28th January 1959. Fate would seemingly not allow any kind of peace for the singer. Two years later, he was locked away on another suspiciously flimsy pretext, and this time he shut up like a clam. He had no further interest in singing or songwriting, and simply kept himself to himself. Imagine then Johnny's surprise when, in March 1961, he received word that a visitor was waiting for him in the courtyard: none other than Elvis Presley.

Physically and vocally, Elvis was in perfect condition. A forthnight earlier, he had performed two electrifying charity concerts in Memphis — his first live gigs since playing Hawaii in November 1957. But on this particular day, Elvis was on his way home from a meeting with the joint convention of the Tennessee legislature. He had accepted an award and been named, just like Tom Parker, as an honorary Colonel on the Governor's staff.

Bragg greeted "Colonel" Presley in a cool but friendly fashion, and the two exchanged small talk. The star offered to intervene on Bragg's behalf, suggesting legal assistance or money, both of which Bragg politely refused. There was an understanding between the men based on mutual respect. Bragg joked that Elvis surely had everything that any man could want, but Presley deflected the question, indicating stardom was not always what it was cracked up to be.

Less than fifteen minutes later, they shook hands firmly and Presley disappeared out of the gate.

Perhaps encouraged by Elvis' visit, Johnny returned to singing, and played the game once again. He was back on the street before the end of 1967 but life was no easier. Bragg later insisted that he ran into Elvis one more time shortly after his re-release. Presley's career had taken a downturn by then and Bragg could sense that the star was in a darker place.

Both men had long since realised that not all prisons came with bars.

Just Walkin' in the Rain, Jay Warner

Hula Boogie, IV

MARCH 1961
HAWAII & HOLLYWOOD

THE COLONEL'S SENTIMENTAL ATTACHMENT to old times did not extend just to people but also to places. He retained a great fondness for Hawaii, happily remembering his time there as a soldier, so when Hal Wallis had suggested making *Blue Hawaii* on location the Colonel graciously permitted Elvis' presence. In fact, Parker, looking to kill two birds with one stone, also organised a charity concert on the island (Presley's third in a month) in aid of a proposed Pearl Harbor monument.

Elvis flew out with Minnie Pearl, whom the Colonel had added to the bill. She was horrified at the attention Elvis received upon his arrival at the airport, fearing for his safety and his sanity, and wondered how he appeared so level-headed amidst the chaos that ensued whenever he showed his face in public.

The show was glorious, and even from a low-fi source (the only existing private recording) one can hear the extent to which Presley was at the top of his game. The money was secured, the monument built, and Elvis continued his rise as the all-American hero, and as an entertainer now accepted as being part of the establishment.

Wallis then produced his fourth big-budget Elvis musical and Presley lip-synched along to the dozen-plus songs he'd recorded earlier in the month at Radio Recorders in Hollywood. Among them was a track destined to become an anthem, "Can't Help Falling In Love", his finest moment as a balladeer, and a performance so good it almost justifies the entire movie.*

The most pertinent soundtrack song, however, was an odd pop-polynesian hybrid named "Rock-a-Hula Baby", issued as a number one single with the above-named ballad (47-7968). Elvis and the band cut loose on the rehearsal take but toned it down a little for the released master.

And sitting there in the Radio Recorders studio, just yards from Presley, invited to play on the session by virtue of his skill on the Hawaiian ukelele, was none other than Bernie Kaii Lewis — Mr Hula Boogie himself.

Elvis Presley: A Life in Music, Ernst Mikael Jørgensen

---

*It is sometimes forgotten that Elvis Presley recorded large quantities of superb music between 1960 and 1963 at RCA Nashville (singles and albums) and Radio Recorders Hollywood (film soundtracks). Vocally and commercially, this was an undoubted peak, and the highlights from this period match his best work from any other part of his career.

Talking to himself

AUGUST 1962
THE ROAD TO NOWHERE

In the period leading up to the summer of 1962, the Colonel presided over a series of decisions that took Elvis further away from who he was and what he wanted to do. RCA allowed negotiations for a multi-city American tour to fall through, and Parker took no remedial action, ultimately removing his client from the stage for the next seven years. He also issued an instruction that Elvis should only record new songs that came directly from Hill & Range, cutting him off from the vast library of roots material that he'd always found inspirational.

Elvis was further dismayed to find that the scripts that followed the release of *Blue Hawaii* leaned again towards romantic musical territory, and knew he was being denied the more challenging roles he'd tasted from 1956 to 1960. The dollars kept rolling in, but Presley could sense the growing emptiness at the heart of these projects.

Let's eavesdrop on a private conversation between the Colonel and his client on an MGM movie set in August 1962, as Elvis tried once again to express his frustration:

"I wouldn't like to stay in the same vein, Colonel. I wouldn't like to be at a standstill, you know what I mean. I'd like to progress. I'd like to do a lot of things. But I — "

— *You realise that it takes time, son? You can't bite off more than you can chew in this racket. You can't go out of your limitations. You have to know your capabilities, you know. Like —*

"I have people say to me all the time, 'Why don't you do an artistic picture? Why don't you do this picture and that picture? Why don't you do something —'"

— *Well, that's fine, son. But —*

"I would like to. I'd like to do something someday where I feel that I've really done a good job, you know, as an actor in a certain type role. But —"

— *I feel that it comes with time and a little living and a few years behind you.*

"I actually, I think that, really —"

— *And I think that it will come eventually, you know?*

"That's my goal, sir. You have to have some —"

— *But in the meantime* —

"In the meantine?"

— *If you can entertain people with the things you're doing, well, you'd be a fool to tamper with it, to try to change it.*

"I can't, err —"

— *It's ridiculous to take it on your own and say, "Well, I'm, I'm gonna change, I'm gonna apply, I'm gonna try to appeal to a different type of audience. I'm gonna ... Because you might not. You might not. And if you goof a few times you don't get many more chances in this business, that's the sad part about it. So you're better off, if what you're doing is doing okay, you're better off sticking with that until, you know, until time itself changes things. I mean, that's the way I believe, really.*

And with that, the Colonel ended the conversation and promptly forgot all about it. But Elvis Presley remembered every word and every syllable.

Elvis Presley and Tom Parker had been a team for six years. At this point in the relationship between the Colonel and Eddy Arnold, Eddy had called it quits while he was still ahead, feeling that their visions of the future were no longer compatible. Sadly, Elvis Presley did not follow the Plowboy's example.

The enormous success of the Hawaii project (the ensuing LP hit number one and sold five million copies) demanded that he was now faced with a challenge: to change direction and try something new and difficult, or to carry on peddling the same product with ever-diminishing emotional and artistic rewards.

For Tom Parker, money equalled success. Creative satisfaction played no part in his mathematics. Soon, Hollywood producers would realise that Presley movies did not require huge investment and budgets were slashed, ensuring a bigger profit for themselves and also for Parker and his boy. Elvis still trusted the Colonel who had, after all, steered him to fame and fortune and, being at heart a non-confrontational person, he swallowed his pride, kept learning his lines, and stuck to the script.

Tape recorded interview with Lloyd Shearer, 17th August 1962

Mae and the President

SATURDAY 3RD NOVEMBER 1962
NASHVILLE, TENNESSEE

MAE BOREN AXTON had risen through the ranks in the world of country & western music via "Heartbreak Hotel" and, thanks to her talents as a speaker, writer and networker, her influence spread far and wide.*

But the achievement of which she was most proud was the establishment of the Country Music Association, which she helped found in 1958 when the profile of c&w was at its lowest ebb. Since then, she and the Association had been relentlessly promoting folk music and, by 1962, along with the success of the Nashville Sound, they felt they were making some headway.

On the first Saturday of November 1962, Mae sat in on a last minute committee meeting just before the CMA annual convention, double-checking that everything would run smoothly. One member suggested they should have organised a telegram from a dignitary to be read out during the opening speeches that afternoon.

"Like who?" Mae queried.

"Oh, I don't know ... President Kennedy, maybe?" came the sarcastic reply, followed by a roomful of laughter.

Mae sat thoughtfully and picked up the phone, placing a call to her good friend Governor Jimmie Davis, asking if it would be appropiate to read such a telegram. He replied in the affirmative.

The committee sat in silence as she asked the operator to connect her to the White House. She then explained her request to the first respondent and again to the second and the third, as she was passed ever closer to the centre of power. And when a distictive Boston drawl asked how he might help the CMA, Mae calmly bluffed her request, placing great emphasis on the nature of "public service and international friendships" that the convention would promote. A few hours later, President Kennedy's fifty-eight word greeting was read out to the disbelieving crowd.

Within the year, Mae received a printed Snowmen's League of America membership card from the Colonel confirming her official status. Having snowed the President himself, she was now playing with the big boys.

Country Singers As I Know 'Em, Mae Boren Axton

---

*Mae accepted an invitation to Elvis' appearance on the Frank Sinatra show in Miami in 1960, and she also met up with Parker and Elvis when they made a Florida-based movie in 1961.

Welcome to Texas, III

FRIDAY 22ND NOVEMBER 1963
DALLAS, TEXAS

WHEN THE NEWS FROM DEALEY PLAZA exploded around the world, Elvis Presley was at his beautiful West Coast home in Los Angeles between movies, almost two thousand miles from Graceland, where his permanent girlfriend Priscilla was now housed.

He embraced recent *Viva Las Vegas* co-star Ann-Margret, as they sat transfixed in front of the TV, watching, crying, and trying to make sense of the assassination of John Fitzgerald Kennedy, as he was driven in his Lincoln through Dallas.

Elvis remained outwardly apolitical, but had great respect for the office of the President, and applauded Kennedy's steps towards racial equality.

On the Sunday after the murder, in a moment watched by millions, the alleged assailant, Lee Harvey Oswald, was shot dead at 11:21 AM on live television outside the Dallas Police Department headquarters, despite being surrounded by dozens of officers. His killer was nightclub owner Jack Ruby, nemesis of Hank Snow and Dub Dickerson. The weapon of choice was a .38 calibre revolver, the same model favoured by Alvin Krolik.

And so it was that on Friday 22nd November 1963, Lyndon Baines Johnson became the first person in history to attain Presidency of the United States whilst already holding full membership of the Snowmen's League of America.

Careless Love: The Unmaking of Elvis Presley, Peter Guralnick
The Colonel: The Extraordinary Story of Colonel Tom Parker and Elvis Presley, Alanna Nash

The pursuit of happiness

THURSDAY 2ND JULY 1964
WASHINGTON D.C.

FORTY-EIGHT HOURS PRIOR to Independence Day 1964, President Johnson signed into being the Civil Rights Act, confirming the sacred privilege of all adult Americans to vote, regardless of colour. The war was a long way from being over, but this was a crucial victory.

It was almost exactly ten years since Elvis Presley had made his unacknowledged but key contribution, as he merged black and white music in the heart of a racist state and opened the ears of white listeners nationwide to the beauty and depth of black culture.

But the man who had once sung so eloquently of passion, love, joy and loneliness, and who had changed the world with "Heartbreak Hotel", seemed no longer to have anything of relevance to say as his record label released song after song from film after film. The suddenly out-of-date staff writers at Hill & Range were not submitting revolutionary anthems or soul-tinged ballads.*

So, when Presley-devotees The Beatles and Bob Dylan hit like a sledgehammer in the wake of Kennedy's death, Elvis had no counter: supremely confident of his position, he had left Nashville and the South to advance his career in Hollywood. But, in the spring, he read a humiliating article in which Hal Wallis essentially described Elvis the movie star as a cash cow, allowing the producer to reap money which he would use on more aesthetically viable non-Presley projects.

Elvis remained a giant in the entertainment industry, but his position had slipped from unassailable to that of merely very popular. Presley made three musical films a year and he was often paid a million dollars a picture. His manager and his Hollywood advisors determined that Elvis should keep remaking *Blue Hawaii* and he should retain the same boy-like character he had portrayed in his early movies.

He wore different hats and costumes, but the movies were essentially the same. And they all made a profit. They didn't need a title; they could've just

*Interestingly, Mae Boren Axton's firstborn, Hoyt, had developed a career as a singer-songwriter by this time, and featured an aggressive, almost proto-punk version of his mother's biggest hit on his new album released during this month. What that says about their relationship is open for discussion.

had a number and they still would've sold. Customers all over the world happily paid a dollar to watch Elvis sing to the bad guys he'd just beaten up.

For a man like Elvis, who understood the genius and beauty of music, it must have hurt to sell even just a little of his soul in this way. His acting career had started promisingly, but any dreams of art had been drowned in the river of commerce. He no longer performed on stage; he no longer appeared on TV; and, most damagingly of all, he abandoned the studio as a place of creativity.

At one film music recording session, in an attempt to improve the dire quality of one song, he leaned over and suggested The Jordanaires might sing along. The musical director disagreed, pointing out that, when filmed, Elvis would be riding on a motor cycle in the scene.

"Where would the backing vocalists be, Elvis?"

"The same damn place the band is," deadpanned the singer.

Apart from a brief oasis in the spring of 1966, Elvis Presley made not one professional recording of any artistic value whatsoever between 13th January 1964 and 9th September 1967. That's over three and a half years of mumbling his way through half-baked soundtracks for cheap movies.*

His ability to sing had brought him everything, but now it plagued his Hollywood ambitions like an albatross around his neck. So, in retaliation, he turned off his talent and stopped singing. Throughout 1964 and 1965 Elvis Presley spent less than one week earning his living as a singer.

He was lost.

---

*Of course, several of Elvis' movies are very enjoyable, but he's rarely engaged at all from 1964 onwards. From a historical perspective, however, they remain a fascinating resource for observing the changes of that decade from a consistent viewpoint. Witness: the U.S. army still appearing relatively cool and friendly (*G.I. Blues* 1960); pleas for racial tolerance (*Flaming Star* 1960); acceptance of psychoanalysis (*Wild In The Country* 1960); recognition of organised crime (*Follow That Dream* and *Kid Galahad* 1961); the beginning of the space race (*It Happened At The World's Fair* 1962); the arrival of the new fashions (*Viva Las Vegas* 1963); references to student life (*Roustabout* and *Girl Happy* 1964); the arrival of The Beatles (*Girl Happy* 1964); et al, through to the brutality of ghetto life (*Change Of Habit* 1969). Fabulous locations, great songs, lots of girls ... and also an education.

The oasis

25TH MAY – 12TH JUNE 1966
RCA STUDIO B, NASHVILLE, TENNESSEE

WHEN HE BEGAN HIS ARTISTIC HIBERNATION in the spring of 1964, Elvis Presley replaced his passion for music with a quest for revelation and salvation. A chance conversation with a well-read and charismatic young man named Larry Geller inspired Elvis to embark upon a journey to understand his divine purpose and mission.

While learning his mundane film scripts, he devoured books on religion and faith of all types, breaking away from his Christian upbringing in a bid to widen his appreciation of the very nature of God as revealed to the peoples of the world. Unsurprisingly, when his hunger for music rekindled in early 1966, it was with a leaning towards gospel. He planned a recording session weeks in advance, adding extra backing vocalists to supplement The Jordanaires, and provide the bigger sound he was looking for.

Steve Sholes and Chet Atkins had long since dropped out of Elvis' studio circle, and their places were taken by an enthusiastic cheerleader of a producer named Felton Jarvis who, by the end of the decade, would establish himself as the singer's full-time recording man.

Throughout May and June 1966, Elvis taped a handful of secular songs and a dozen gospel favourites in Nashville. For the most part he ignored publishing concerns and just sang what he wanted, even dipping magnificently into the Bob Dylan songbook.*

The resultant album, *How Great Thou Art*, was not released until February 1967 due to the number of banal movie LPs blocking the schedule, but it was warmly received and generated Elvis' first ever Grammy Award — Best Sacred Performance.

The Grammy was announced at the annual ceremony in February 1968 and Presley's achievement was calmly noted. The big hit of the evening (four awards), however, was "Up, Up and Away", an ebullient slice of modern music recorded and engineered at Radio Recorders by Bones Howe, the man who had first been turned on to the beauty of pop and rock a decade earlier by Elvis Presley, and had, along with his creative partner, Steve Binder, subsequently become the hottest property on the West Coast.

---

*Elvis taped "Tomorrow is a Long Time", a five-minute odyssey into his mid-'60s depression. Listen carefully to Dylan's lyric and understand that "she" is Presley's muse, abandoned and betrayed: hear the guilt and desolation in Elvis' faultless and haunting performance. Understand too why the sharp-as-a-razor Dylan called it his own favourite cover version.

I am a man

SEPTEMBER 1967 - JANUARY 1968
RCA STUDIO B, NASHVILLE, TENNESSEE

ELVIS PRESLEY MARRIED his long-term girlfriend, Priscilla Beaulieu, on 1st May 1967: Colonel Tom knew how to draw in the punters, and weddings always made for an easy headline. It garnered good publicity around the world for his client. Presley records still hit the charts and his movies still made a profit but, post-oasis, he was again no longer doing anything of creative value.

In the summer of that year, however, when he discovered he was to become a father, a switch clicked inside and he began to makes changes. He lost weight, grew his sideburns, and worked on a tougher vocal sound. Starting in September 1967, he attended a series of Nashville sessions and revisited his roots, choosing to ignore the then current pyschedelic revolution and embracing an acoustic country-blues sound.*

Rebel guitarist and gifted songwriter Jerry Reed was personally requested by Elvis to join him, and the two men sparked off each other, Reed opening with the disarming line, "Damn, but you're the best-looking thing I've ever seen!"

Jerry Reed brought a sense of life and excitement to these recordings, and Elvis loved working with him, but the Colonel objected to his pitching songs from outside the Hill & Range catalogue. An astute manager might have kept a songwriter and guitarist of this calibre onside to ensure his client was enthused and driven. Jerry Reed never worked with Elvis Presley again.

The singles they taped together were excellent, though not big hits, but their titles — "Guitar Man", "Big Boss Man", "U.S. Male" — revealed a singer determined to clarify his identity not as the boy his manager continued to promote, but as a man — which was the self-same message that the striking sanitation workers proclaimed at the end of March 1968 when Dr King arrived in Memphis and backed their cause to the hilt.

---

*Interestingly, Bob Dylan did exactly the same thing at almost exactly the same time with his *John Wesley Harding* LP, an album (mis)named for the notorious outlaw buried in El Paso. Works of this nature brought about a welcome rennaissance in country music, as Elvis acknowledged in a filmed interview in February 1970, confirming, "*Grand Ole Opry* was the first thing I ever heard as a child, probably."

The death of an honest man

THURSDAY 4TH APRIL 1968
LORRAINE MOTEL, MEMPHIS, TENNESSEE

THE CLOSING WORDS OF DR KING'S SERMON rang out around Mason Temple in Memphis: "I've seen the promised land. I may not get there with you. But I want you to know tonight, that we, as a people, will get to the promised land. So I'm happy, tonight. I'm not worried about anything. I'm not fearing any man. *Mine eyes have seen the glory of the coming of the Lord.*"

Elvis was out of town, making yet another movie in Los Angeles, while his current flick, *Stay Away, Joe*, played at Loew's State Theatre on Main Street in Memphis. On 4th April, about twenty-four hours after making his prophetic address, King was gunned down on the second-floor balcony of the Lorraine Motel, a dozen miles from Graceland.

Presley was appalled and embarrassed that such a tragedy should have ocurred, and that it should have happened in his home town reinforced the worst racist stereotypes of the South. He'd had the utmost respect for the slain preacher — an album of King's speeches held a favoured place in his home. Elvis wept in the arms of current co-star Celeste Yarnall. They spent the night seated together at a piano, singing through song after song, mainly gospel, but also The Beatles' recent hit "All You Need Is Love".

Elvis considered attending the funeral but knew the Colonel would not even entertain a discussion on the matter.* Instead, he and Celeste watched the live TV coverage the following Tuesday. He reverently stood mid-service and sang "Amazing Grace" acapella, his own private tribute to a fellow Southerner who had always spoken the truth.

There was much he wanted and needed to share publicly about the state of the nation, but frustratingly felt he had no obvious avenue of expression.

www.elvis.com.au

*No one had expected Elvis to attend, of course, nor was he missed, but Andrew Young, who wept over his friend's dying body on the motel balcony, had recently written in *Scope* magazine of Elvis as a "bridge" between the black and white worlds, and emphasised the importance of Presley's contribution to the cause: *Rock 'n' roll did more for integration than the church and if I was going to choose who I was going to let into the Kingdom ... I might have to choose Elvis.*

The death of a quiet man

MONDAY 22ND APRIL 1968
NASHVILLE, TENNESSEE

THE RENTED CAR CRASHED into the guard rails on both sides of the bridge. By the time police arrived at the scene they found Steve Sholes dead at the wheel, felled by a heart attack as he was driving to a concert by country music stars, Homer and Jethro.

Paul Ackerman penned a moving tribute in *Billboard*, pointing to his friend's honesty, gentleness and warmth. Behind the scenes there was a perception that, although Sholes had done well for himself, he had never risen to the heights he might have achieved had he been a more ruthless and cut-throat figure.

Sholes' death coincided with a sense of closure in Elvis Presley's career. There was an unspoken acknowledgement that the movies were no longer working, financially or artistically, and Tom Parker drew up a deal with NBC-TV to film a one-hour special television show to be produced in the summer and broadcast in December.

No one at NBC had any idea what to do with the suggested programme, so it was dumped at the door of the then current wunderkind of TV pop music, twenty-three year-old Steve Binder. Steve took the call from the brass and turned them down flat, having no interest in working with a yesterday man.

Later that day, Binder spoke with his creative partner Bones Howe, and casually mentioned that he'd given the Presley people the thumbs down. Bones insisted he get back on the phone and take the job.

"Forget what you've seen in his movies. I've worked with this guy in the studio. You and he are gonna hit it off perfectly."

Careless Love: The Unmaking of Elvis Presley, Peter Guralnick
Billboard, 4th May 1968

The death of a good man

THURSDAY 6TH JUNE 1968
BURBANK STUDIOS, LOS ANGELES, CALIFORNIA

On the first Monday in June, Elvis arrived at NBC-TV studios, rolled up his metaphorical sleeves, and threw himself into the production of his first television special with a passion that shocked Steve Binder, the crew, the writers, the musicians and everyone except Bones Howe, who quietly revelled in the accuracy of his prophecy.

After every day-long rehearsal, Elvis would sit for hours in his dressing room with his closest friends and the core team, talking, singing and playing, and the deep intimacy of these gatherings had a profound effect on Steve Binder, who had never witnessed anything like this before. But in the very early hours of Thursday morning, the freewheeling informal sessions were interrupted by the news that Robert F. Kennedy, presidential hopeful, had been assassinated at the Ambassador Hotel, just ten miles away from the TV studios.

Caught up in the history of the moment, Elvis talked non-stop through the night, picking randomly on his guitar, telling his small captive audience about his early career, about the racism he had seen and faced, about his hopes, fears and dreams for his country. Binder and the writers were transfixed by his stream-of-consciousness rap and, in the following days, they passed on parts of Elvis' conversation to songwriter Earl Brown, asking him to turn the words into an anthem with which they might close the show and end America's troubled year.

Elvis worked like a man possessed from that point on, and hours of video were edited down to an explosive programme which reminded everyone — including Elvis himself — of the depth of his talent.*

When Steve presented Elvis with "If I Can Dream", the song Earl Brown had fashioned from King's speeches and Elvis' monologue, the singer embraced it despite the Colonel's protests, and performed a live vocal on camera for the taping of the show's finale.

But it was the version that Elvis captured in the studio for the accompanying soundtrack album that was the revelation for Steve Binder and even

*The filming marked Scotty and D.J.'s final professional engagement with Elvis, and it was the perfect exit.

for Bones Howe, who had seen the younger Elvis at his most glorious. He recorded his vocals in the isolation booth, completely cut off from the rest of the world and entirely involved in the lyrics. As the song drew towards its heart-stopping climax, paying tribute to King and the Kennedys, Presley dropped to his knees and rolled into a foetal position on the concrete floor, wringing every ounce of emotion from the closing words.*

Everything he'd ever wanted to say about the events of the past five years was captured in three minutes and ten seconds. And the Colonel, resigned to Elvis' decision, approved the release but made damn sure Hill & Range owned every part of the song.

Binder and Howe revitalised Presley by involving him in the creative process, and Elvis loved working with them, but the Colonel objected to their royalty request on the soundtrack album. An astute manager might have kept directors and engineers of this calibre onside to ensure his client was enthused and driven. Binder and Howe never worked with Elvis Presley again.

Careless Love: The Unmaking of Elvis Presley, Peter Guralnick

*The now iconic white suit that Elvis wore during the "If I Can Dream" sequence was designed by Bill Belew. The striking red neckerchief was added to mark the blood spilled in Vietnam, a sentiment that moved Elvis to tears when the costumer confided in the singer. Belew also came up with the black leather ensemble for that show, and was subsequently given the job of providing Presley's stage outfits for life.

Harmony in Hollywood, II

PERHAPS LATE 1968
HARMONY RECORDERS, 1479 VINE STREET, HOLLYWOOD, CALIFORNIA

BOB ROSS CONTINUED WORKING out of the limelight and had done very well for himself. He'd opened his own publicity agency in late December 1966 and, thanks to his stepfather's influence, much of Elvis' PR work would be handled by Robert Ross Advertising, Inc.

Harmony, his recording studio on Vine Street, still welcomed all comers, and in late 1968, a little-known singer named Bobby Jameson booked himself in to tape the *Working* LP, a last ditch effort to save his fitful career.

Jameson had assembled a superb group of session musicians, led by James Burton, Bob Luman's guitarist from the 1950s who had since helmed Ricky Nelson's band, and was now offering his considerable talents as a gun for hire. It was during these sessions at Harmony that Burton first met bass player Jerry Scheff, a jobbing blues and jazz musician, who was also contracted for the Jameson album. The reserved Burton was impressed with Scheff, a melodic and busy player with a down to earth approach to work and life.

Jameson laid down the LP using his own piano accompaniment and the players then overdubbed their parts. The album flopped (GRT-10004) and Bobby Jameson added his name to the long list of talented artists who just didn't get their moment in the sun.

Burton and Scheff packed up their guitars, bid each other "Adios", and moved on to another session. And you never knew who might be on the phone next, in demand of their talents.

http://bobjameson.blogspot.co.uk/

Elvis Presley's first American recordings

JANUARY & FEBRUARY 1969
AMERICAN SOUND STUDIOS, MEMPHIS, TENNESSEE

ELVIS' NBC-TV SPECIAL WAS BROADCAST ON 3rd December and drew huge audience figures. Full of enthusiasm for his career again, Presley chose to make his next album not in Nashville but remained in Memphis, booking American Sound, the beaten-up studio run by local boy Chips Moman, and the hottest venue in the country. Chips was a feisty figure, not unlike Sam Phillips, and worked according to his own rules and with his own house band. But, as with his recent creative collaborations, Elvis relished the challenge and threw himself into the weeks of taping with absolute committment: he needed hits.

The resultant singles, "In The Ghetto" and "Suspicious Minds", and the LP *From Elvis In Memphis*, revealed a mature artist, completely at ease with himself and his material. He taped a song from Hank Snow, a song from Eddy Arnold, a song from Johnny Tillotson (the Axton/Durden protégé), a song for his father, a song for his mother, and a glorious mixture of tracks old and new, black and white, as Chips flouted the usual "Elvis-Presley-must-own-the-publishing" restrictions.*

Most importantly, Chips Moman ushered his client through the door marked CONTEMPORARY MUSIC, and Elvis learned to embrace modern sounds and a new generation of songwriters, as he prepared to leave the sixties behind and move into a new decade.

The highlight of the sessions for Elvis, though, was a chance meeting with his all-time vocal hero, Roy Hamilton, which added to the good feeling in the studio. Giddy with excitement, Elvis gave Hamilton a song from his own list of intended recordings and Roy gladly took it, taped it, and prepared it for single release.

Chips Moman pushed Presley to his considerable creative limits, and Elvis loved working with him, but the Colonel objected to his request for a printed credit on the singles and album. An astute manager might have kept a producer of this calibre onside to ensure his client was enthused and driven. Chips Moman never worked with Elvis Presley again.

---

*Bearing in mind Elvis rarely wrote his own songs, his choice of cover material was sometimes profoundly personal: his first recording for Chips was "Long Black Limousine", the lyric berating a country girl for betraying her roots and running off to the big city, and Elvis' performance is staggering. Know thyself indeed.

From Memphis to Vegas

JULY & AUGUST 1969
INTERNATIONAL HOTEL, LAS VEGAS, NEVADA

With his latest single, "In The Ghetto", climbing up the top ten and "Suspicious Minds" already tagged for smash summer release, Presley prepared for the third and most challenging part of his triple-whammy comeback: live performances. To raise the stakes yet higher, Tom Parker booked Elvis in at the only place he'd ever previously flopped: Las Vegas. To fully succeed, he'd need to re-invent himself again.

The Colonel's idea was that Elvis would play the showroom at the city's biggest hotel, the International, twice nightly for a month, backed by a small band and a gospel quartet — but Elvis had a much greater vision.

None of his original group were available for a month long booking (nor were Chips' boys), so he placed a personal call to the country's number-one session guitarist, James Burton, inviting him to act as his new band leader. Burton, much to his own surprise, agreed and started assembling the musicians, beginning with bassist, Jerry Scheff, and between them they gathered the kernel of what would later be dubbed the TCB Band (*Taking Care of Business* being Elvis' personal motto).*

To this ensemble, Elvis added two gospel vocal groups, the white all-male Imperials Quartet and the black all-female Sweet Inspirations, to give his show the soulful edge he'd always wanted. This was topped by the Bobby Morris Orchestra, and all of it came out of his own pay cheque. It didn't matter: artistic success was paramount.

Mid-rehearsals, Elvis received news that Roy Hamilton had collapsed with a cerebral haemorrhage. He died a week later, without having regained consciousness, aged forty. Just as The Blackwoods' tragedy had inspired him fifteen years earlier, so too the passing of his idol pushed Elvis forward.

On 31st July, a new Elvis Presley stepped onstage in front of two thousand paying customers and reclaimed his crown. Delighted with the financial returns, the Colonel signed the contract that tied Elvis to the showroom for years to come, playing twice a year, a month at a time, two shows a day, every day.

In time, the venue would become Elvis' own personal Heartbreak Hotel.

---

*Elvis and his band all wore a bespoke TCB necklace, which contained a lightning bolt logo. Presley eventually became the epitome of Captain Marvel, Jr, his favourite superhero, with immaculately quiffed black hair, a lightning bolt on his chest, and a short cape draped around his shoulders.

The photograph, II & III

LATE 1970
GRACELAND & THE WHITE HOUSE

IT TOOK A MOMENT for his eyes to adjust to the darkness. He ran his hand along the wall: the attic woke as he flicked the switch. He hadn't been up here in years and couldn't quite remember where the photograph albums were kept. He slowly moved past the boxes which lovingly stored his mother's clothes and possessions. His boyhood bike was in the eaves and in need of a good clean. His army uniform hung in the corner. On the shelves were a few demo tapes he'd recorded years ago with Charlie and old friend, Red West.

He found the albums in the bottom of a trunk and picked one at random. Sure enough, the picture he'd been looking for was there: Gladys, Elvis and Vernon, as snapped in 1937, just as Vernon was about to be dragged off to Parchman.

During the summer of 1970, Elvis had recorded an LP of country songs in Nashville, some old, some new, some slow, some wild: it was a concise history of American roots music and he wanted to use the cover to illustrate how personal this collection was to him. And this was the image he gave to the RCA art department with strict instructions to take good care of it.

He picked up another album from the trunk and browsed. It contained clippings his mother had cut from newspapers and carefully glued on each page, telling the story of his developing career. He smiled when he read a review of an early gig in Houston.

He'd recently started touring again, outside of Vegas, and had gone back there with his new band and blown out the Astrodome just a few months previously, but had been amazed at how little things had changed in some respects. When he'd arrived at the Texan hotel, the manager looked at his back-up vocalists, The Sweet Inspirations, and said, "We have no rooms for the black girls." Elvis fixed him with a steely stare and made it quite clear that if they didn't take the ladies then they didn't take him either. Apologies were proferred, but Elvis went further and insisted the manager's daughter act as personal chauffeur for the singers during their stay.

The new roots-themed album was subtitled "I'M 10,000 YEARS OLD" (*Elvis Country* LSP 4460)* to reflect how deeply Elvis felt connected to the history of the land itself. The loose-limbed sessions had been held at Studio B in Nashville with Felton Jarvis now on permanent duty behind the desk. During breaks, Elvis would retreat to a corner of the studio and perch on a speaker, chatting softly and amiably to one of his young band members. They'd maybe talk for fifteen minutes, then he would stand up and stretch and say, "Well, time to go back to being Elvis Presley."

Being "Elvis Presley" was clearly becoming a burden for him by this time, but it also gave him vast privileges, never more so than when he slipped out of Graceland alone while the album was being readied for release and flew incognito(ish) to the White House to request a private off-the-cuff meeting with then President Richard Nixon.

Nixon's staff were unsure of how to deal with the icon at their door dressed in a crushed-velvet purple jacket replete with gold belt and monogrammed sunglasses, but they were won over by his sincerity and charisma, and the King was granted an audience with the President.

Presley confided he was all for Nixon's stance against the drug culture and, as a collector of police ephemera, requested and received a personalised badge indicating that he was granted powers as a Special Assistant to the Bureau of Narcotics, so to enable him to join the crusade. In return, the President's people politely insisted on a photograph of the two men together, even though it had been agreed that the very existence of the meeting should be kept under wraps.

When the picture eventually came to light, it was rightly identified as one of the most bizarre summits of modern times, and printed copies of the photograph of Presley and Nixon became the single most requested souvenir in presidential history.

*The album was highly rated by critics, and modern country music became Elvis' default musical style during the 1970s. Even in Vegas during the August 1970 season, he played at being Luke the Drifter, holding his audience spellbound as he narrated his way through Hank Williams' "Men With Broken Hearts".

You're getting to be a habit with me

A SHORT DIVERSION ON
THE NATURE OF ADDICTION

THE IRONY OF ELVIS PRESLEY holding an honorary rank within the Bureau of Narcotics and Dangerous Drugs has been noted many, many times as, since his term in Germany and possibly even from his time at Sun Records, Elvis had most likely been using and abusing prescription medication.

Uppers and downers were common currency in country music during the 1950s and, as a life-long insomniac, Elvis would have welcomed any pill that could help him grab even a few hours sleep. When combined with the hectic pace of his early career and the prevailing culture that suggested science, pills and potions would cure everything, it's not surprising that Elvis (and millions more) may have embraced this very modern way of dealing with life's challenges.

During the mid-1960s, Presley's life ran along well-ordered if unspectacular lines, and his intake of amphetamines and barbituates had little impact on his health, other than stifling his natural creativity. When Elvis opened in Las Vegas in 1969, however, and then took that gig out on a never-ending tour the following year, he required ever-increasing amounts of medicinal support to help him rest after each show. Eventually, he required ever-increasing amounts of medicinal support to wake him up before a show too.

So what drove his decision to visit Nixon and obtain the federal badge that he felt sure would grant him immunity from official interference? Most probably, the drug-related deaths of rock stars Jimi Hendrix and Janis Joplin on 18th September and 3rd October 1970 respectively, followed by the President's signing of the Controlled Substances Act on 27th October. Elvis believed the badge would protect him, which indeed it did to some extent — but not from himself.*

In an ideal world, a good manager would have intervened. Sadly, Tom Parker, the master manipulator, was busy digging a hole of his own. In Vegas, he was merrily and obsessively dropping serious gambling money to the very hotels with whom he was negotiating contracts on behalf of his trusting client.

Tom Parker had finally become Oscar Davis. But without the class.

---

*The drugs Elvis was taking were not illegal, but the prescribed quantities became absurd by the mid-1970s, and they wreaked havoc with his body, mind, emotions and spirit.

Without a song

SATURDAY 16TH JANUARY 1971
HOLIDAY INN RIVERMONT, MEMPHIS, TENNESSEE

IN THE MIDST OF ALL THIS BUSY-NESS, on 16th January 1971, Elvis attended a very special ceremony in Memphis. He had decided to accept an award as one of the Ten Outstanding Young Men of 1970, made by the prestigious Jaycee's organisation. He'd been selected before but had turned down the honour, not wanting to draw further attention to himself. A friend persuaded him to accept the invitation, this being the last year he could be shortlisted because of his age.

The other nine nominees were men of great prestige and accomplishment, and Presley joined a long list of presidents, scientists and diplomats who had been similarly commended since the 1930s.

His self-written speech was brief, and he occasionally stumbled over his words (he was, ironically, very nervous), but he delivered a simple precis on life, taking an old Roy Hamilton hit, "Without a Song", as his theme.

He held the room in the palm of his hand* as he spoke of his childhood, and explained his guiding philosophy.

> *When I was a child, ladies and gentlemen, I was a dreamer. I read comic books, and I was the hero of the comic book. I saw movies, and I was the hero in the movie. So every dream that I ever dreamed has come true a hundred times. These gentlemen over here, these are the type who care, who are dedicated. You realise it's not impossible that they might be building the kingdom of heaven, it's not too far-fetched from reality.*
>
> *I'd like to say that I learned very early in life that*
> *Without a song, the day would never end;*
> *Without a song, a man ain't got a friend;*
> *Without a song, the road would never bend,*
> *Without a song.*
> *So I keep singing the song.*

It was the most beautiful and poignant sixty seconds of his entire career.

---

*Most perfectly of all, Marion Keisker was in the audience that day.

The Garden and "An American Trilogy"

JUNE 1972
MADISON SQUARE GARDEN, NEW YORK CITY, NEW YORK

BY 1972, PRESLEY'S TOURING CONCERT SHOW had become a finely-tuned machine. He visited city after city throughout America, beset by doubts before stepping out, and then wallowing in the roar of the crowd as he arrived centre stage. His life became that of a wandering troubadour. His home, such as it was, was in Memphis, but the road — particularly the South itself and Las Vegas — was where he found comfort. But it was in June 1972 that he hit New York to lay to rest the demons of racial and social judgement that had bludgeoned him as he'd reached the apex of his early fame.

He sold out four gigs at Madison Square Garden, and the stars were in attendance among the throng. George Harrison of the now-defunct Beatles was ushered backstage, and he stood in awe of this tanned, razor-thin, godlike, white-suited figure, recognising (as did the very self-aware Elvis) that he had exchanged spontaneous genius for unparalleled showmanship. The Beatles had separated two years previously in a legal battle over who would manage their business affairs. Canny Paul McCartney had nominated his new father-in-law, the ubiquitous Lee Eastman, but this — sadly for The Beatles, financially — was not to be.

Presley was involved in a separation of his own, as Priscilla had taken their daughter, Lisa-Marie, and moved out of Graceland, unable to deal with life as the wife of a deity. As Elvis candidly confessed to the New York press, "It's very hard to live up to an image."

He poured his conflicting emotions into the nightly performances, choosing his repertoire as a way of communicating that which he was not capable of expressing elsewhere. He'd added "Never Been to Spain" to his act, as written by Mae's son, Hoyt Axton, and it would feature in the same generation-spanning set list as "Heartbreak Hotel". Even more profoundly, he brought in an anthem entitled "An American Trilogy", an arrangement of "Dixie", "The Battle Hymn of the Republic" and "All My Trials", as recently assembled and recorded by folk artist Mickey Newbury.

Elvis loved the song, and it became the high spot of his show for the next three years, his singing reaching new levels of interpretative prowess throughout. He would tell acquaintances the story of how one stetsoned fellow in the front row resolutely refused to applaud or even move during an entire concert. But when Elvis sang the "Dixie" segment, the man stood, removed his hat and placed it over his heart. He then sat down again for the remainder of the gig. The divisions in the country were real, but Elvis maintained his belief that resolution was possible, and insisted on including the song every night wherever he was in the country, North or South.

He recorded it in February 1972, live in Las Vegas, and had RCA release it as a single over Easter (74-0672), even though it stood zero chance of being a hit as Newbury's single had already peaked over Christmas 1971. Clearly, though, Elvis wanted to say *something* and, by adding a full orchestra and drafting in one of his teenage gospel idols, J.D. Sumner, to sing a verse with his new quartet, The Stamps, Elvis ensured it was said clearly and defiantly.

Professionally, at least, Elvis seemed to be on top of the world at this time: "Burning Love", his imminent single (74-0769), would top charts in the summer; he'd recently joined the elite club of Frank Sinatra, Duke Ellington, Ella Fitzgerald and Irving Berlin as a recipient of the prestigious Bing Crosby Award from the National Academy of Recording Arts and Sciences; and the New York crowds and critics finally bowed down before him as he blew the roof off in June 1972.

Even the mighty *New York Times* finally surrendered, ecstatically reviewing his first show at the Garden, and describing him as being like a Prince from Another Planet, noting: *he stood there at the end, his arms stretched out in the spotlight, the audience applauding rapturously.*

He was a true son of the South who had conquered the North.

Hula Boogie, V

SUNDAY 14TH JANUARY 1973
HONOLULU INTERNATIONAL CENTER, HONOLULU, HAWAII

"ALOHA", screamed the neon lights as Presley took to the stage for his *non plus ultra* concert: Honolulu said "Hello" to Elvis, and also to the majority of the world, as the most celebrated singer of all time took to the stage for his second TV special, beamed live around the planet.

Unable to tour globally because of his manager's covert passport issues, Elvis agreed to a Parker-organised charity satellite broadcast in the long-favoured Hawaii, which would not be matched in conceit until *Live Aid* some thirteen years later.

Presley had honed his physical appearance, his hair, his costume and his repertoire to present a defining image that would live on far beyond his lifetime. As a posthumous producer astutely noted, it was Elvis viewed through stained glass.

The expanded set list included five selections from the *Blue Hawaii* album, including "Can't Help Falling In Love", his regular closer. "An American Trilogy" was the centrepiece of the concert, but there was room for songs by many of his favourite c&w artists, including Marty Robbins and Jim Reeves, and as Elvis crooned Hank Williams' "I'm So Lonesome I Could Cry", a bead of sweat trickled from his forehead and nestled on his chisled cheekbones as if he were crying to order, like the great Roy Acuff.

The enormous success of the Hawaii project (the ensuing double LP hit number one and sold two million copies) demanded that he was now faced with a challenge: to change direction and try something new and difficult, or to carry on peddling the same product with ever-diminishing emotional and artistic rewards.

He'd done a pretty good job of holding it all together since his creative rebirth at NBC-TV in 1968, but Elvis' slow descent would begin on Monday 15th January 1973. Who do you sing to when you've already serenaded the entire world?

Aloha also means goodbye.*

*Punchline courtesy Dr Robin Markowitz, Independent Scholar, Orange, California

Nixon at the *Opry*

SATURDAY 16TH MARCH 1974
GRAND OLE OPRY HOUSE, PENNINGTON BEND, NASHVILLE, TENNESSEE

OF ALL THE MANY THOUSANDS of performers to appear on the *Grand Ole Opry*, the most intriguing and obtuse must surely have been President Richard Nixon. On 16th March 1974, as the radio show moved from its iconic home at the Ryman Auditorium into the purpose-built Grand Ole Opry House, Nixon was invited to open the new building, and did so with his customary awkward humour. A six-feet circle was cut from the Ryman centre stage and inlaid at the new venue: the words HANK WILLIAMS STOOD HERE were engraved into the wood.

The President, an accomplished pianist and lover of classical music, was encouraged to play, and he sat at the keyboard and offered a rendition of Irving Berlin's "God Bless America". The audience clapped enthusiastically. They, and the listeners at home, were middle-Americans: they loved their nation, worshipped country music, and respected the President.

It was a demographic, young and old, that Nixon shared with Presley, who that very night was knocking them dead down the road apiece at the Mid-South Coliseum in Memphis. The two men had formed an unlikely bond since Elvis had dropped in at the White House, and they kept in touch infrequently, even after Nixon resigned in disgrace six months after his *Opry* debut.

But on this day, with the Southern crowds cheering and applauding the President and the King, who could possibly have forseen the events to come for them both?

---

*Vegas '69, Vegas '70, the Garden, Aloha and Memphis were all released as live concert albums and sold well, but there was a sneaking suspicion that they were becoming the movie LPs of the seventies, so to speak. His annual studio projects did contain many strong performances, yet there was a sense in which Elvis was not always fully engaging himself or his talent. Creative ambition had driven him during the peaks of his career, but creative stagnation was responsible for (or a symptom of) many of his physical and emotional problems during the mid-1960s and mid-1970s.

John Sousa finally joins the circus

PROBABLY LATE 1974
PERHAPS LAS VEGAS, NEVADA

ELVIS LOVED THE APPLAUSE of the crowds night after night, be it in Vegas or out on the road. He was still delivering the goods and packing them in, and the adulation helped lift the falling veil of depression. Occasionally, after a show, or during his month in Nevada, he would welcome VIP guests back to his suite and they'd sing together or just talk into the wee small hours. It was a safe way for him to unwind and come down, before reaching for the pills.

He was rarely, if ever, without company. The dread of loneliness that had haunted his first hit record pursued Elvis from hotel room to hotel room — his touring schedule demanded he become virtually nocturnal, hiding in the shadows and emerging only after sunset.

But in 1974, he discovered a TV programme that brought a smile to his face, and seemed to make sense of the insanity he'd endured for the previous twenty years. Carefully positioning himself in front of the screen in his Vegas suite, his new girlfriend, Linda Thompson, at his side, he would break into a grin as the familiar music of John Philip Sousa's 1893 composition "Liberty Bell" filled the room, and the screen flashed with seemingly random, bizarre images. And for the next thirty minutes, the King of Rock 'n' Roll laughed his ass off.*

After two decades of living in his own goldfish bowl, Elvis Presley had developed a keen sense of the absurd and the surreal, and those Monty Python boys were damn funny.

Know what I mean. Nudge nudge. Wink wink. Say no more.

Tuscaloosa News, Alabama, 7th October 1974
paleycenter.org

---

*It seems that almost everyone who was anyone in the 1970s has their own "When I met Elvis" story, but the best is the night Led Zeppelin dropped by in 1974: find it on YouTube. Linda Thompson was on the scene from 1972, and was one of the best things that happened to Elvis during his gradual decline. She has spoken of a poignant conversation they had in which he acknowledged an awareness of his own self-destructive tendencies. She could no longer bear to watch him slipping away and they parted on good terms before Christmas 1976.

Elvis Presley: the show must go on

NEW YEAR'S EVE, 31ST DECEMBER 1976
CIVIC CENTER ARENA, PITTSBURGH, PENNSYLVANIA

TO HIS ADORING PUBLIC it seemed as though he was on top of the world; but Elvis Presley was struggling. Between his abdominal pain, the pills, the hassle with his over-zealous bodyguards, the separation from his daughter, and the ever-growing list of expenses caused by his extreme generosity, there was little comfort he could take. Yes, he remained the single biggest touring star of the moment, but it was tougher than anyone knew for Elvis to cope with the pressures in his life.

Yet every now and then, when he absolutely had to be at his best, he could reach inside and pull the rabbit out of the hat with a grace that looked effortless. On New Year's Eve 1976, he was booked into Pittsburgh to bid goodbye to the bicentennial year.

Elvis positively radiated confidence as he sang his current hit "Hurt"; and when he sat at the piano to accompany himself on "Rags to Riches" and "Unchained Melody", it seemed as if time stood still, so riveting was the performance.

Just six weeks later, a less robust Elvis offered a spontaneous gospel song from his *How Great Thou Art* album to an audience in Hank Williams' home town of Montgomery, Alabama,* and the words of that hymn told the bitterest truth:

Like a king I may live ...
but I don't know a thing ...
that's worse than being alone ...

Back in the day, it was said that Elvis never made the same mistake twice. But here he now was in the mid-1970s, repeating the same error of the mid-1960s, locked into a soul-destroying routine, again and again, night after night after night.

*These two concerts have both been released as posthumous official bootlegs, and one can hear the change in Elvis' demeanour. The December tour was surprisingly enjoyable and he looked pretty good, but as he entered January it was like he'd finally tipped over the edge and could no longer claw his way back. Had the New Year's Eve gig been professionally recorded and filmed for his third TV Special rather than the June 1977 tour, the legacy of his final year would be far less painful.

Elvis Presley: it's all dark

SATURDAY 21ST MAY 1977
THE EXECUTIVE INN, LOUISVILLE, KENTUCKY

LARRY GELLER, Elvis' spritual advisor of the 1960s, had recently returned to the touring party, and was far from comfortable with Presley's failing health, nor with the carnival-like state of affairs that surrounded the entertainer.

One evening in May 1977, he was charged with guarding the door while Elvis' doctor urgently ministered to him in his private hotel suite, an hour before yet another show. The pills were taking their toll on this troubled, gifted man, and Larry feared for the life of his friend.

Colonel Parker burst into view, marched past Geller and entered his client's bedroom. Larry stared through the opened door to see the doctor dunking Elvis' head into an ice bucket in an effort to instill some life into the singer. Parker conferred with the physician and then left, bellowing that Presley had to be ready at curtain up whatever the circumstances.

Elvis eventually took to the Freedom Hall stage that night and gave a good-natured, if uninspired concert to a faithful nineteen-thousand strong audience. He grinned and acknowledged the applause. Now aged forty-two, his glory days were behind him, but his charisma and the magic of his name still lingered.

Thirty-seven minutes into the show, just before launching into "Heartbreak Hotel", Elvis calmed the crowd and began singing "My Way". A hush fell over the hall and thousands of fans held lighters aloft as Elvis steadied himself and intoned the infamous opening words.

At the completion of the show, Al Dvorin once again uttered his inevitable closing line, "Elvis has left the building." There was another set of concerts planned for June, two of which would be filmed for his third TV special, and he could then take a break for a few weeks in the summer, before the next tour in mid-August.

It had cost Elvis $4 to enter show business, and $40,000 to move into the big leagues. The cost to exit would be much, much higher.

With thanks to Rob/elvis-collectors.com

The white Cadillac

TUESDAY 16TH AUGUST 1977
GRACELAND, MEMPHIS, TENNESSEE

The end came on 16th August 1977, but there were several other occasions over the previous four years when death could easily have claimed Elvis Presley. Of those who knew him best, few doubted that his addiction to prescription medication had contributed to his cause of death, which was officially given as heart attack. He was forty-two. He died at Graceland. He died alone. Two days later, he took his final ride in a pristine white traditional Cadillac hearse.

His band were told as they gathered at the airport, ready to begin the next tour. Many wept openly. There would be no final encore for them as there had been for Buddy Killen.

News spread quickly and it dominated worldwide bulletins for the rest of the week. It was the most significant American death since that of Robert Kennedy nine years previously. Millions — literally millions — around the world considered their own mortality in the wake of his death. The personification of their youth was gone.

President Jimmy Carter issued this statement the following day:

> *Elvis Presley's death deprives our country of a part of itself. He was unique and irreplaceable. More than twenty years ago, he burst upon the scene with an impact that was unprecedented and will probably never be equaled. His music and his personality, fusing the styles of white country and black rhythm and blues, permanently changed the face of American popular culture. His following was immense, and he was a symbol to people the world over of the vitality, rebelliousness, and good humor of this country.*

The Colonel, meanwhile, was signing contracts for Elvis' image to be used on hundreds of promotional products, and RCA were re-opening recently-closed vinyl pressing plants to cope with the extreme demand for the music.

It was like 1956 all over again.

The final curtain

A SHORT DIVERSION ON
THE NATURE OF PASSING GRACEFULLY

IN THE MONTHS AND YEARS that followed Presley's death, many of the other players in this story made their own exits: some dignified and some not.

Bing Crosby, Presley's pre-war counterpart, having heard of his peer's demise, paid tribute from the stage on 16th August, and then passed away himself on 14th October, aged seventy-four.

Parker's stepson, Bob Ross, died on 25th July 1978, just fifty-three years-old. He'd struggled with multiple sclerosis, and there had been a financial falling out when the Colonel suddenly and without warning withdrew the Elvis account from Ross Advertising. Marie knew nothing of her son's death, her mind having long since crumbled with dementia, and she slipped away in 1986.

Vernon Presley died of a heart attack on 26th June 1979 (Parker's seventieth birthday and two years to the day since Elvis' final performance). His mother, Minnie Mae, who had lived at Graceland since its purchase, and had witnessed the deaths of Jesse Garon, Gladys, Jessie (her ex-husband), Elvis, and Vernon, passed a year after her son.

Jack Stapp died just before Christmas 1980, leaving Buddy Killen as the sole owner of Tree. Nine years later Buddy sold out to CBS Records for a figure believed to be in excess of $30,000,000.

One cast member who resolutely refused to leave the stage, however, was Irving Berlin, who turned ninety the year after Presley's passing, and would carry on for another eleven years. The real tragedy of his longevity, though, was made clear to him as that which he cherished above all, copyright control of his songs, began to eke away with each succeeding year. One by one, his early compositions fell into the public domain, including "Alexander's Ragtime Band", his first hit. He still called the office to check on the receipts until his dying day.

There really is no business like show buisness.

The New York Times, 8th December 2002

The final party

SATURDAY 4TH JUNE 1983
HILLCREST COUNTRY CLUB, BEVERLEY HILLS, LOS ANGELES

TOM PARKER was the only gentile in the room, and — just a few weeks short of his seventy-fourth birthday — he was also the only non-employee of the William Morris Agency invited to attend its eighty-fifth anniversary party. The Colonel was family as far as the agency was concerned, even since the death of his client, especially as he'd made it very clear it was business as usual, and requested their continued services to advise on Presley's hugely profitable posthumous legacy. Parker had been retained as manager by Elvis' estate, continuing to take fifty percent of all income for himself.

The guest of honour that night was Abe Lastfogel, a shadow of his former self since his stroke. He addressed the room haltingly, and spoke fondly of the old days. Younger members of the firm looked at the two elderly men and wondered what all the fuss had been about. But they hadn't known them back in the day, when they were both giants of show business negotiation. The world, however, was moving on and leaving them behind.

By the summer of 1984, Lastfogel would be dead and his empire would begin to fall. Parker would be exposed through the courts as an illegal immigrant, and as a manager who had not always acted in the best interests of his client. He would be forced to surrender all claims, rights and contracts with regard to Presley. He was paid handsomely for this concession, naturally, and would live out the remaining thirteen years of his life in financial comfort but failing health.

But as Tom and Abe journeyed to their respective homes from the Hillcrest Club in the early summer of 1983, they both knew the party was over.

The Agency: William Morris and the Hidden History of Show Business, Frank Rose

The final spin of the wheel

FRIDAY 5TH OCTOBER 1990
RECORD RELEASE

TOMMY DURDEN HAD LONG ACCEPTED his place in music history with typical good grace. He was the guy who had co-written Elvis Presley's first hit record, and that was more than enough for Tommy. As he ofttimes pointed out, you needed to pen a half-a-dozen of those in order to retire and live off the proceeds, but the royalty cheques still helped pay the rent and put food on the table. He eventually recorded his own low-key version of his signature composition with little fanfare or celebration. But he was a happy man, marrying again, and remaining on cordial terms with Boots' family.

It therefore seemed very odd when, in the early 1980s, he was rumoured to have given interviews declaring he was the main or even sole author of "Heartbreak Hotel". What might have caused him to behave in such an unusual fashion? A possible answer to this lies in two camps: firstly, the plethora of books and magazine articles that followed Presley's death often described Mae as the solitary writer of the song and this must have raised Tommy's hackles somewhat, as the lyrics were so very personal to him.

Secondly, at this general point in time, the copyrights on Mae's mid-1950s compositions were running out and she instructed a lawyer to renew her hold on the songs for a further period of twenty-eight years. Judging by the now current credits, it is probable that many of her co-writers chose not to pick up their option, and Mae became the exclusive owner. But, if Mae's counsel blithely assumed that Tommy would also dismiss his rights to their joint hit and then proceeded without consulting him, then Tommy's anger may have surfaced and he chose to hit back in print. The interviews, if they existed at all, have proven impossible to find, so this may be a moot point. Either way, Mae and Tommy resolved their differences, and carried on singing the same old song to anyone who wanted to listen.

Mae herself revelled in her position as the Queen Mother of Nashville, always present at galas and conventions, always keen to shepherd new talent towards green pastures, and always at her best when networking and writing puff pieces for magazines and newspapers.

Her husband, John, died in 1987, and their younger son, Johnny, was taken by cancer eight years later. Hoyt finally seemed to come to terms with being his mother's son: his 1964 recording of "Heartbreak Hotel", as previously mentioned, could be called interesting at best and disrespectful at worst, but twenty-five years later, it seemed that he had made peace with the song, and taped a more sedate interpretation (in a style not dissimilar to that in which it was originally written), and a cute video was made to coincide with its release on his 1990 album *Spin of the Wheel* (DPICD-1000), his last collection of adult-oriented country material.

The film is notable for a brief cameo at the end by Mae, and Hoyt's on-camera admission, "That's a good song you wrote there, Mom, thanks." One wonders if Mae ever shared the true story of "Heartbreak Hotel" with her troubled but talented son. By the end of the millennium, Mae and Tommy, and indeed Hoyt too, would reach the end of their own lonely streets and the secrets they kept would be buried with them.

Fame came late to Mae Boren Axton. Aged forty-one, the daughter of an industrious Texas rancher had come to public attention when she was challenged to write Elvis Presley's first hit single for RCA Victor. Using a newspaper article as their inspiration, she and Tommy Durden composed "Heartbreak Hotel", which opened doors for black and white music to integrate on a national and international scale.

The song was published by Tree in 1956, and soon became the unofficial anthem of the rock 'n' roll youth revolution, setting in motion the tumultuous events of the subsequent decade, and increasing the pace of the march for racial equality.

Mae Boren Axton died in 1997, aged eighty-two. She was survived by one son and also by her two great co-creations, a song for the lonely and an enigmatic riddle that remained unsolved for over fifty years.

Independence Day

WEDNESDAY 3RD JUNE 1992
STAGE 29, PARAMOUNT STUDIOS, LOS ANGELES, CALIFORNIA

THE SECRET SERVICE had already codenamed him ELVIS after his favourite singer. Just twenty-hours after securing the California primary, Democratic presidential hopeful Bill Clinton popped up on *The Arsenio Hall Show* in a bid to win over the younger demographic. The charismatic Southerner brought with him a tenor sax and a pair of borrowed Ray-Bans as he stepped in front of the TV cameras.

Accompanied by the house band, he ripped through Billie Holliday's "God Bless the Child" and Elvis Presley's "Heartbreak Hotel" to loud applause and then sat with the host, sharing his thoughts on race and the recent horrifying Los Angeles riots. One hundred and twenty-seven years after Colonel Parker had transcribed the document that reunited North and South, Americans were still casually slaughtering each other: almost fifty-thousand had died at the hands of their fellow citizens during Bush's then current administration.

Clinton carried the election in November and kept his pledge to Arsenio's band of having them play at the inauguration ball. Elvis was President, and the White House was Graceland. Clinton delivered on his feel-good promise to the country, but was soon inevitably mired in scandal, and struggled through his own lurid Watergate.

And this is because life is complicated — and presidents, like men, women, artists, kings and nations will ultimately fail, unless love, compassion, and a selfless quest for the common good are at the heart of their being.

In 1977, critic Lester Bangs memorably declared, "We will never agree on anything as we agreed on Elvis." But perhaps we can agree on this: that America must always aspire to fulfil its promises to all its citizens and to the world. And when the shackles of old times can finally be forgotten, and when all lives are deemed of equal worth, then that will be a day of true independence and freedom. It is a dream worth dreaming, and a tale worth telling, and a song worth singing.

One nation, under God, indivisible, with liberty and justice *for all.*

The original sheet music for "Heartbreak Hotel".

AN ENCORE

London calling

FRIDAY 2ND SEPTEMBER 2011
WEST LONDON, ENGLAND

THE PHONE RINGS TEN, MAYBE FIFTEEN TIMES TO NO REPLY. My mind overloads with the many possible outcomes of the potential subsequent conversation. It's not every day I ring Chicago and I'm absurdly nervous. On the twentieth ring someone picks up.

"Hello," says a fiesty female American voice.

"Hello," I reply. "May I please speak to Agnes Sampson?"

A pause. "Who's calling?"

"Oh, she doesn't know me. I am a writer calling from London, England. I'm working on a book and her name appeared a couple of times in my research. Are you perhaps her daughter?"

Another pause and I swear I hear a brief chuckle.

"No. This is she. Who are you?"

"Oh, wow." I'm genuinely surprised that the vibrant voice is that of a ninety year-old.

"My name is Tony. Might I ask you a few quick questions for my book?"

"Yes, I guess that would be okay?"

"Are you the Agnes Sampson who was married to an Alvin Krolik back in the 1950s?"

A further pause. "Yes, that's me."

"I'm writing a book about Elvis Presley's hit record, 'Heartbreak Hotel', and I think the song may have been inspired by a newspaper report about Mr Krolik's death."

"Oh?" Yet another pause. "I didn't know that."

"You were only married for a short while?"

"Yes, that's correct."

"The newspapers said he was an artist and that he was also perhaps writing an autobiography."

"I don't think I read the newspaper reports, to be honest."

"It must have been a difficult time?"

"Yes. But it was a long time ago."

We chat pleasantly for a few minutes, but I'm unable to properly explain to her how extraordinary it is for me to be speaking to someone who has played such a pivotal role in modern popular culture, and she certainly doesn't grasp why I might be remotely interested in something that happened decades earlier.

I begin to wrap up the conversation. I'm not even sure at this point why I rang, but I just needed to make contact with her, to let her in on the secret.

"I really don't think he did write an autobiography," she offers unbidden in closing.

"Thank you, Ms Sampson, it was lovely to speak to you."

In my head I am already thinking of her as "Baby" ("Well, since my *baby* left me ...").

At one point she absolutely loved Alvin Krolik, and he went to his grave still loving her.

But that's the terrible power love wields.

And it's still the only answer.

Agnes Sampson Lee passed away peacefully on 21st March 2013.

DRAMATIS PERSONAE

Unless otherwise noted, all singers, songwriters, musicians and managers functioned within the world of country & western music. Also listed is their creative work most relevant to this book.

Aberbach, Jean & Julian
sibling publishers Hill & Range
Ackerman, Paul *editor* Billboard *magazine*
Acuff, Roy *singer; songwriter; publisher Acuff-Rose; "Great Speckled Bird"*
Allen, Steve *comedian; musician; TV host*
Arnold, Eddy *singer; "I'll Hold You In My Heart"*
Arnold, Kokomo *blues singer; songwriter; "Milk Cow Blues"*
Arthur, Charline *singer; songwriter; "Welcome to the Club"*
Atkins, Chet *guitarist; producer; songwriter*
Ausborn, James *brother of Mississippi Slim; Elvis' boyhood friend*
Austin, Gene *pop singer; songwriter; "My Blue Heaven"*
Autry, Gene *songwriter; yodelling singer; "The Death of Jimmie Rodgers"*
Axton, Hoyt *elder son of John & Mae; singer; songwriter; "Never Been to Spain"*
Axton, John *husband of Mae; sports coach*
Axton, Johnny *younger son of John & Mae; attorney*
Bays, Coy *Sara Carter's second husband*
Bean, Orville *land owner Tupelo*
Beatles *defining pop group of the 1960s*
Beck, Jim *engineer; producer; owner recording studio*
Bell, Freddie *lead singer of The Bell Boys; "Hound Dog"*
Berle, Milton *comedian; TV host*
Berlin, Irving *pop songwriter; publisher; "Alexander's Ragtime Band"; "White Christmas"*
Berman, Pandro *movie producer;* Blackboard Jungle; Jailhouse Rock
Bernero, Johnny *drummer Memphis Recording Service; "Trying To Get To You"; "I Forgot to Remember to Forget"*
Berry, Chuck *R&B guitarist; singer; songwriter; "Maybellene"*
Bienstock, Freddie
Hill & Range rep for Elvis
Binder, Steve *director Elvis' 1968 TV Special*
Black, Bill *Elvis' bass player 1954-1958*
Blackwell, Otis *R&B songwriter; "Don't Be Cruel"*
Blackwood Brothers *gospel vocal quartet; "His Hand in Mine"*
Boone, Pat *singer; songwriter; "Ain't That a Shame"; "Tutti Frutti"*
Boren, Lyle *brother of Mae; politician*
Boren, Mark & Nannie Mae *parents of Mae*
Boren Axton, Mae *manager; PR agent; radio host; songwriter; teacher; "Heartbreak Hotel"*
Bragg, Johnny *singer; songwriter; leader The Prisonaires; "Just Walkin' in the Rain"*
Bulleit, Jim *music entrepreneur*
Bullock, Bill *Steve Sholes' boss RCA Victor*
Burnett, Howlin' Wolf *blues singer; songwriter; "Smokestack Lightning"*
Burton, James *guitarist Bob Luman, Ricky Nelson & Elvis*
Byrd, Jerry *musician; song-plugger Tree*
Cadets *R&B vocal group; "Heartbreak Hotel"*
Carson, Jenny Lou *songwriter; "You Two-Timed Me One Time Too Often"*
Carson, Martha *sister of Jean Chapel; singer; songwriter; "Satisfied"*
Carter, Blanche *songwriter; "Devil or Angel"*
Carter, Eck *manager Mother Maybelle & The Carter Sisters*
Carter Family *(A.P., Sara & Maybelle), musical group; songwriters; "I'm Thinking Tonight of My Blue Eyes"*
Carter Sisters *(Helen, June & Anita), performing daughters of Eck & Maybelle*
Cash, Johnny *singer; songwriter; "Folsom Prison Blues"*
Chapel, Jean *sister of Martha Carson; singer; songwriter; "Welcome to the Club"; "I Won't Be Rockin' Tonight"*
Charles, Ray *R&B singer; songwriter; "I Got a Woman"*
Chess, Phil & Leonard
sibling owners Chess Records
Chitwood, Gus *police officer El Paso*
Clement, Frank *governor of Tennessee*
Como, Perry *pop singer; TV host*
Country Cats *rockabilly group featuring Mac Curtis; "What'll I Do";*
Cowan, Lou *radio & TV producer; publisher Tree;* The $64,000 Question

Cramer, Floyd *pianist Nashville*
Crosby, Bing *actor; pop singer; "White Christmas"; "Harbor Lights"*
Crudup, Arthur *blues singer; songwriter; "That's All Right"; "If I Get Lucky"; "Dirt Road Blues"; "I Want My Loving"; "Mean Old 'Frisco Blues"; "My Baby Left Me"; "So Glad You're Mine"*
Crumpacker, Chick *C&W promotion RCA*
Curtiz, Michael *movie director;* Casablanca; King Creole
Darby, Ken *composer; leader The Ken Darby Singers; "White Christmas"*
Darrow, Clarence *lawyer*
Davis, Jimmie *politician; singer; "You Are My Sunshine"*
Davis, Oscar *manager Hank Williams; PR*
Davis, Russ *media entrepreneur Chicago*
Dean, James *actor;* East of Eden; Rebel Without a Cause
Delmore Brothers (*Alton & Rabon*), *sibling singers; songwriters; co-owners King Records; "Blues Stay Away From Me"*
Denny, Jim *publisher Cedarwood; manager artists service bureau* Grand Ole Opry
DeWitt, John *president WSM radio*
Dickens Sisters (*Patty, Nancy & Marge Diskin*), *sisters of Tom Diskin; sibling singing trio*
Dickerson, Dub *singer; songwriter; "Count Me In"*
Diskin, Tom *manager The Dickens Sisters; factotum for Tom Parker; co-owner Jamboree Attractions*
Domino, Fats *R&B pianist; singer; songwriter; "Ain't That a Shame"*
Dorsey, Jimmy & Tommy *sibling swing band leaders; TV hosts*
Dougherty, Charles *circuit judge Illinois*
Dowdy, Toby *musician; media entrepreneur*
Drifters *R&B vocal group; "Money Honey"; "White Christmas"*
Durden, Samuel *brother of Tommy*
Durden, Tommy *musician; singer; songwriter; "Crossroads"; "Hula Boogie"; "Heartbreak Hotel"*
Dvorin, Al *talent agent Chicago*
Dylan, Bob *folk singer; songwriter; "Tomororrw is a Long Time"; "John Wesley Harding"*
Eastman, Lee *show business attorney*
Emmett, Daniel *composer; "Dixie"*
Ertegun, Ahmet *R&B songwriter; owner, producer Atlantic Records; publisher Progressive Music*
Fachs, Charlie *logistics RCA New York*
Fell, Terry *singer; songwriter; "That's What I Like"*
Ferris, Bob *engineer RCA Nashville*
Fitzgerald, Ella *jazz singer; "My Happiness"*
Foley, Red *singer; songwriter; "Old Shep"; "Chattanoogie Shoe Shine Boy"*
Fontana, D.J. *Elvis' drummer 1955-1968*
Ford, Whitey (*The Duke of Paducah*), *comedian*
Four Diamonds *rockabilly group featuring Bob Luman; "You're The Cause of it All"*
Frank, Joe L. *manager Pee Wee King*
Franks, Tillman *bass player; songwriter; "Poison Love"*
Freed, Alan *celebrity deejay*
Fulchino, Anne *publicist RCA Victor*
Geller, Larry *Elvis' confidant & spriritual advisor*
Gilbert, Boots *first wife of Tommy Durden; musician The Westernaires*
Griffith, Andy *actor; comedian*
Haley, Bill *leader The Comets; singer; songwriter; "Rock Around the Clock"*
Hall, Helen *singer; songwriter; "Honky Tonk Husband"; "Alright"*
Hamilton, Roy *r&b singer; "I'm Gonna Sit Right Down and Cry"; "Without a Song"*
Hardin, John Wesley *outlaw of the old west*
Hendrix, Jimi *rock guitarist; singer; songwriter*
Hodge, Charlie *gospel singer & Elvis' friend*
Howe, Bones *engineer Radio Recorders studio & Elvis' 1968 TV special*
Howe, Julia *lyricist; "The Battle Hymn of the Republic"*
Huskey, Ferlin *singer; songwriter; "Gone"*
Imperials Quartet *gospel vocal quartet*
Jackson, Wanda *singer; songwriter; "Honey Bop"*
Jarvis, Felton *Elvis' producer 1966-1977*
Jenkins, Gordon *pop arranger; composer; "Crescent City Blues"*
Johnnie & Jack (*Johnnie Wright & Jack Anglin*), *singing duo; "Poison Love"*
Johnson, Lonnie *blues singer; songwriter; "Tomorrow Night"*
Johnson, Lyndon *American president 1963-1969*
Jordanaires *gospel vocal quartet*
Kaii Lewis, Bernie *Hawaiian musician; songwriter; "Steel Guitar Boogie"; "Hula Boogie"*
Keisker, Marion *radio personality; factotum Memphis Recording Service & Sun Records*

Kennedy, John *American president 1961-1963*
Killen, Buddy *bass player; singer; songwriter; song-plugger & co-owner Tree*
King, B.B. *blues deejay; guitarist; singer; songwriter*
King, Dr Martin Luther (Jr), *Baptist minister; perceived leader of 1960s civil rights movement*
Kings of Rhythm *R&B musical group featuring Ike Turner; "Rocket 88"*
King, Pee Wee *band leader The Golden West Cowboys; songwriter*
Kirkham, Millie *Jack Stapp's secretary; backing singer*
Krolik, Alvin *artist; U.S. Marine*
Krolik, Edith & Harry *parents of Alvin*
Laird, Elmer *auto dealer; songwriter; "Poison Love"*
Landon, Grelun *Hill & Range California*
Lansky, Bernard & Guy *sibling men's outfitters*
Lastfogel, Abe *manager William Morris Agency*
Leiber & Stoller (*Jerry & Mike*), *blues producers; songwriters; "Hound Dog"*
Lincoln, Abraham *American president 1861-1865*
Locke, Dixie *Elvis' girlfriend 1954-1955*
Long, Shorty *actor; pianist; singer*
Lott, Jimmie *drummer Memphis Recording Service; "I'm Left, You're Right, She's Gone"*
Luman, Bob *singer; songwriter; member The Four Diamonds; "You're The Cause of it All"*
Martin, Dean *actor; pop singer; "I Don't Care if the Sun Don't Shine"*
McCuen, Brad *RCA Victor Tennessee*
McCullars, Martha *fan club president Helen Hall*
McNatt, Speedy *fiddler for Eddy Arnold*
Miller, Roger *musician; singer; songwriter*
Moman, Chips *producer; songwriter; owner American Sound studio*
Monroe, Bill *singer; songwriter; "Blue Moon of Kentucky"*
Montgomery, Little Brother *blues pianist; singer; songwriter; "Crescent City Blues"; "Something Keeps A-Worrying Me"*
Morgan, George *singer; songwriter; "Candy Kisses"*
Moore, Scotty *Elvis' manager 1954 & guitarist 1954-1968*
Nash, Murray *producer; owner Republic Records; publisher Murray Nash Associates; editor* Country & Western Jamboree
Neal, Bob *deejay; Elvis' manager 1955-56*
Nixon, Richard *American president 1969-1974*
Nogar, Thorne *engineer Radio Recorders*
Oelrich, Ernie *engineer RCA New York*
Parker, Colonel Ely *Union officer civil war*
Parker, Little Junior *R&B singer; songwriter; "Mystery Train"*
Parker, Marie, *wife (?) of Tom Parker; mother of Bobby Ross*
Parker, Colonel Tom *manager Gene Austin, Eddy Arnold, Tommy Sands, Hank Snow & Elvis; co-owner Jamboree Attractions*
Payne, Tee-Tot *blues singer*
Pearl, Minne *C&W comedienne*
Peer, Ralph *producer; publisher*
Penniman, Little Richard *R&B pianist; singer; songwriter; "Tutti Frutti"*
Perkins, Carl *singer; songwriter; "Blue Suede Shoes"*
Petrillo, James *president American Federation of Musicians*
Phillips, Dewey *blues deejay WHBQ*
Phillips, Jud *brother of Sam*
Phillips, Sam *owner, producer Memphis Recording Service & Sun Records; publisher Hi-Lo*
Pierce, Webb *singer; songwriter; publisher Cedarwood*
Pine Ridge Boys (*Doug Spivey & Marvin Taylor*), *singers; "You Are My Sunshine"; "Old Shep"*
Pinney, Delta Richard (D.R.) *police officer; shop owner El Paso*
Pinney, Edna *Delta's third wife*
Pinney, Frances *Delta & Francisca's firstborn*
Pinney, Francisca *Delta's fourth wife*
Platters *R&B vocal group featuring Tony Williams; "Only You"; "The Great Pretender"*
Poovey, Joe *singer; songwriter* Big D Jamboree
Presley, Gladys & Vernon *parents of Elvis*
Presley, Lisa-Marie *daughter of Elvis & Priscilla*
Presley, Priscilla Beaulieu *Elvis' wife 1967-1973*
Price, Lloyd *R&B pianist; singer; songwriter; "Lawdy Miss Clawdy"*
Prisonaires *R&B vocal group featuring Johnny Bragg; "Just Walkin' in the Rain"*
Ram, Buck *R&B entrepreneur; songwriter; manager The Platters & The Cadets*
Reeves, Glenn *deejay; singer; songwriter; "Heartbreak Hotel" demo*

Reeves, Jim *singer; songwriter; "Yonder Comes a Sucker"*
Rice Brothers (*Hoke & Paul*) *sibling singers; "You Are My Sunshine"*
Riddle, Esley *guitarist The Carter Family*
Ritter, Tex *actor; singing cowboy; "You Two-Timed Me One Time Too Often"*
Robbins, Marty *singer; songwriter; "That's All Right"; "El Paso"*
Robinson Brothers *musicians with Buddy Killen*
Robison, Fabor *owner Abbot Records*
Rose, Fred *publisher Acuff-Rose; songwriter*
Rose, Wesley *son of Fred*
Ross, Bobby *stepson of Tom Parker; deejay; manager Slim Whitman, George Morgan & Hank Snow; employee RCA & Hill & Range*
Ruby, Jack *nightclub owner Dallas*
Sampson, Agnes *pop accordionist*
Sands, Tommy *actor; singer*
Scheff, Jerry *bass player*
Schroeder, Aaron *pop songwriter; "I Was the One"; "Any Way You Want Me"*
Scrivener, Ray *owner Republic Records; publisher Murray Nash Associates*
Shell, Jim *music entrepreneur Dallas*
Shelton Brothers (*Bob & Joe*), *sibling singers; songwriters; "Just Because"*
Sholes, Steve *producer RCA Victor*
Sinatra, Frank *actor; pop singer; "My Way"*
Skaggs, Jack *singer The Golden West Cowboys*
Slim, Mississippi *singer*
Snow, Hank *singer; songwriter; "I'm Movin' On"; "The Party of the Second Part"*
Snow, Jimmie *son of Hank; singer; pastor; "Love Me"*
Sons of the Pioneers *vocal group; songwriters; "Tumblin' Tumbleweeds"*
Sousa, John *composer of military marches; "Semper Fidelus"; "The Liberty Bell"*
Speer Family *gospel vocal group featuring siblings Ben & Brock*
Stapp, Jack *programme director & head of recruiting new talent* Grand Ole Opry; *publisher Tree*
Starlite Wranglers *musical group featuring Bill Black, Scotty Moore & Doug Poindexter*
Steinbeck, John *author;* East of Eden; Grapes of Wrath
Stone, Harry *station manager* Grand Ole Opry
Sullivan, Ed *TV host*
Sumner, J.D. *gospel bass singer*
Sweet Inspirations *gospel vocal group*
Swingbillys *musical group led by Smilin' Jack Herring & featuring Tommy Durden*
Tanner, Bob *owner & publisher TNT*
Tennessee Plowboys *Eddy Arnold's band*
Terry, Bea *PR agent Hank Snow & Jim Reeves*
Thompson, Hank *singer; songwriter; "The Wild Side of Life"; "Honky Tonk Girl"*
Thornton, Big Mama *blues singer; songwriter; "Hound Dog"*
Tubb, Ernest *singer; songwriter; "Blue Christmas"*
Tucker, Gabe *factotum for Tom Parker; musician for Eddy Arnold*
Turner, Big Joe *R&B singer; songwriter; "Shake, Rattle and Roll"*
Upson, Dean *manager Eddy Arnold & artists service bureau* Grand Old Opry
van Kuijk, Andreas *birth name of Tom Parker*
Wagoner, Porter *singer; songwriter; "Uncle Pen"*
Wakely, Jimmy *actor; singer; songwriter; "I'll Never Let You Go"*
Walker, Frank *producer Columbia Records, RCA, MGM*
Wallis, Hal *movie producer;* Casablanca; Air Force; Loving You; King Creole; G.I. Blues; Blue Hawaii
Wells, Kitty *singer; "It Wasn't God Who Made Honky Tonk Angels"*
Wertheimer, Alfred *photographer*
West, Red *songwriter; Elvis' schoolmate & bodyguard*
Westernaires *musical group featuring Tommy Durden & Boots Gilbert*
Wexler Jerry *R&B songwriter; owner, producer Atlantic Records; publisher Progressive Music*
Whitman, Slim *yodelling singer; "Indian Love Call"*
Whittaker, Nellie *mother of Wanda Jackson; schoolfriend of Mae Boren*
Wilburn Brothers (*Alton & Rabon*) *sibling singers; songwriters; publishers*
Williams, Hank *singer; songwriter; "Lovesick Blues"; "I'm So Lonesome I Could Cry"; "I Saw the Light"*
Wills, Bob *singer; songwriter; "Brain Cloudy Blues"*
Wills, Johnny Lee *singer; songwriter; "Milk Cow Blues"*
Young, Faron *singer; songwriter; "I'm Gonna Live Some Before I Die"*

P100 020515 DT83QE GS

Printed in Great Britain
by Amazon

64346628R00407